T0413794

'All My Books in Foreign Tongues'

Library of the Written Word

VOLUME 132

The Handpress World

Editors-in-Chief

Andrew Pettegree (*University of St Andrews*)
Arthur der Weduwen (*University of St Andrews*)

Editorial Board

Trude Dijkstra (*University of Amsterdam*)
Falk Eisermann (*Staatsbibliothek zu Berlin – Preußischer Kulturbesitz*)
Shanti Graheli (*University of Glasgow*)
Katherine Halsey (*Stirling University*)
Earle Havens (*Johns Hopkins University*)
Ian Maclean (*All Souls College, Oxford*)
Angela Nuovo (*University of Milan*)
Malcolm Walsby (*ENSSIB, Lyon*)
Alexander Wilkinson (*University College Dublin*)

VOLUME 108

The titles published in this series are listed at *brill.com/lww*

Portrait of Josephus Justus Scaliger, studying an Arabic manuscript, probably some leaves of a Qur'an. *Icones Leidenses* 31. Attributed to Johannes Cornelisz van 't Woudt, ca. 1608–1609. Senate room, Academy building, Leiden University

'All My Books in Foreign Tongues'

The Oriental Bequest of Joseph Scaliger and the University Library of Leiden

By

Kasper van Ommen

Translated by

Arthur der Weduwen

BRILL

LEIDEN | BOSTON

This publication was made possible by the generous support of the Octavie Siegenbeek van Heukelom Stichting and the Scaliger Institute.

Cover Illustration: Portrait of Josephus Justus Scaliger, studying an Arabic manuscript, probably some leaves of a Qur'an. Icones Leidenses 31. Attributed to Johannes Cornelisz van 't Woudt, ca. 1608–1609. Senate room, Academy building, Leiden University

Library of Congress Cataloging-in-Publication Data

Names: Ommen, Kasper van, author. | Weduwen, Arthur der, translator.
Title: All my books in foreign tongues : the Oriental bequest of Joseph
    Scaliger and the University Library of Leiden / by Kasper van Ommen ;
    translated by Arthur der Weduwen.
Description: Leiden ; Boston : Brill, 2025. | Series: Library of the
    written word, 1874–4834 ; volume 132 | Includes bibliographical
    references and index.
Identifiers: LCCN 2024024375 (print) | LCCN 2024024376 (ebook) | ISBN
    9789004701519 (hardback) | ISBN 9789004701526 (ebook)
Subjects: LCSH: Scaliger, Joseph Juste, 1540–1609—Library. | Scaliger,
    Joseph Juste, 1540–1609—Knowledge and learning. | Rijksuniversiteit te
    Leiden. Bibliotheek—Catalogs. | Libraries—Netherlands—Leiden—Gifts,
    legacies—Catalogs.
Classification: LCC Z997.S28 O46 2025 (print) | LCC Z997.S28 (ebook) |
    DDC 012—dc23/eng/20240711
LC record available at https://lccn.loc.gov/2024024375
LC ebook record available at https://lccn.loc.gov/2024024376

Typeface for the Latin, Greek, and Cyrillic scripts: "Brill". See and download: brill.com/brill-typeface.

ISSN 1874-4834
ISBN 978-90-04-70151-9 (hardback)
ISBN 978-90-04-70152-6 (e-book)
DOI 10.1163/9789004701526

Copyright 2025 by Koninklijke Brill BV, Leiden, The Netherlands.
Koninklijke Brill BV incorporates the imprints Brill, Brill Nijhoff, Brill Schöningh, Brill Fink, Brill mentis, Brill Wageningen Academic, Vandenhoeck & Ruprecht, Böhlau and V&R unipress.
All rights reserved. No part of this publication may be reproduced, translated, stored in a retrieval system, or transmitted in any form or by any means, electronic, mechanical, photocopying, recording or otherwise, without prior written permission from the publisher. Requests for re-use and/or translations must be addressed to Koninklijke Brill BV via brill.com or copyright.com.

This book is printed on acid-free paper and produced in a sustainable manner.

*In memoriam Harm Beukers, Jeanine De Landtsheer
and Henk Jan de Jonge*

Contents

Acknowledgements XIII
Translator's Note XIV
List of Figures and Tables XV

The Oriental Bequest of Joseph Scaliger and the University Library of Leiden

Introduction 3
1 New Research on Scaliger's Bequest 5
2 The Importance of Oriental Books in Early Modern Europe 8
3 The First Contemporary Description of the Bequest 9
4 The Project 12

1 A Life in Two Parts: Scaliger and His Collection before and after 1593 15
1 Scaliger's Move to Leiden 20
2 Push and Pull Factors 21
3 Leiden University and the Study of Hebrew 26
4 Correspondence and the Republic of Letters 28
5 The Printing House of Plantin and Raphelengius in Leiden 30
6 The Importance of Good Books and Good Libraries 36

2 Scaliger as Scholar and Collector in France, 1552–1593 39
1 Scaliger the Philologist: Learning Greek and Oriental Languages 43
2 Postel's Influence on Scaliger 49
3 Paris: Scaliger's First Hebrew Books 56
4 The Production and Sale of Oriental Books 57
5 Scaliger's Journey to Italy with Chasteigner de la Roche-Posay 60
6 The Influence of Cujas on Scaliger 63
7 Refuge in Geneva 66
8 Touraine: Exile without a Library 68
9 A Fragmented Library 75
10 Mastering Arabic 78
11 Multilingual Ambitions 82

3 **Supplying Scaliger with Books** 89
  1   The Context of Scaliger's French Network 91
  2   De Thou and the *Bibliothèque Royale* 93
  3   Claude Dupuy as Supplier of Oriental Books 98
  4   Dupuy and Pinelli 105
  5   A Fellow Protestant in Paris: Pierre Pithou 113
  6   Guy Lefèvre de la Boderie and Other Suppliers of Books 119
  7   Nicolas-Claude Fabri de Peiresc and the Samaritan Language 122
  8   Scaliger and Mitalerius 126
  9   Books from Jean Hurault de Boistaillé's Library in
       Scaliger's Bequest 128

4 **Scaliger in Leiden, 1593–1609** 135
  1   Transporting Scaliger's Books to Leiden 136
  2   Scaliger's 'Oriental Catalogue' of ca. 1600 140
  3   Books Left Behind in France 141
  4   Scaliger's Network in Leiden 146
  5   New Contacts in the Leiden Network: Casaubon, Bongars
       and Commelin 151
  6   The Operation of a Trade Network in Practice 153
  7   Scaliger and Daniël van der Meulen 156
  8   Supplying Arabic Books: Chasteigner in Rome and the *Tipographia
       Medicea Orientale* 164
  9   Gifts from around Europe 171
  10   The Brothers Labbaeus, Fellow Bibliophiles 174
  11   Scaliger's Books in Rare Exotic Languages, from Slavic
       to Chinese 176

5 **Expanding the University Library: a Will, a Bequest and
an Auction Catalogue** 181
  1   The University Library of Leiden before Scaliger's Arrival 182
  2   The Oriental Books of the Court of Holland 185
  3   Scaliger's Death 187
  4   Scaliger's Will 191
  5   The Auction Catalogue of 1609 194
  6   Scaliger's Oriental Bequest 201
  7   Heinsius and the *Arca Scaligerana* 204
  8   The Placement of the *Arca Scaligerana* in Leiden
       University Library 208
  9   The Legacy of Scaliger's Bequest 210

CONTENTS   XI

6 Scaliger's Bequest in the Leiden University Library Catalogues 214
   1   The Catalogue of Vulcanius 215
   2   Library Catalogues before 1612 220
   3   Cataloguing Scaliger's Bequest: the Printed Library Catalogue
        of 1612 224
   4   The Catalogue of 1623 238
   5   The Catalogue of 1640 241
   6   The Catalogue of 1674 246
   7   The Catalogue of 1716 252
   8   Conclusion 259

7 Oriental Collecting in Context 262
   1   Private Collecting in the Early Dutch Republic and
        Its Neighbours 262
   2   Oriental Books in Sixteenth-Century Scholarly Libraries 265
   3   Oriental Collections outside the Dutch Republic 267
   4   Burnett's Canon 271
   5   The Auction Catalogue of Johannes Drusius Senior (1616) 276
   6   The Auction Catalogue of Franciscus (I) Raphelengius (1626) 277
   7   Isaac Casaubon's Oriental Books 278
   8   Portaleone's Library 280
   9   Thomas Bodley's Oriental Collection 281
   10   Conclusion 287

Conclusion 290
   1   A Properly Functioning Network 291
   2   From France to Leiden 292
   3   Comparison with Other Collections 294
   4   The Fate of the Bequest and the *Arca Scaligerana* 296
   5   The Reconstruction of Scaliger's Bequest 297

Appendix 1: List of Books in Scaliger's Library, 1600 or later 301
**Appendix 2: List Compiled by Janus Dousa in August 1594 Containing
the *Libri Haebraici, Chaldaici et Arabici* from the Library of the Court
of Holland** 306
**Appendix 3: The list of Oriental Books and Manuscripts from Scaliger's
library Compiled by Bonaventura Vulcanius** 309

Appendix 4: Section of Scaliger's bequest in Daniel Heinsius, *Catalogus librorum Bibliothecæ Lugdunensis* (Leiden: s.n., 1612), with the current shelf marks of the printed books and manuscripts in Leiden University Libraries 312

Appendix 5: List of Arabic sources in Scaliger's library in 1608 322

Bibliography 325

Index 358

Acknowledgements

Writing a thesis is an exercise in humility. The quantity of research required sometimes overwhelms the PhD student, whose grasp of the necessary knowledge regularly feels inadequate. This was a sentiment that often crept up on me during the past ten years.

The idea to write a thesis about the Oriental bequest of Josephus Justus Scaliger emerged in 2008, thanks to the encouragement of Hélène Cazes, who was one of the fellows of the Scaliger Institute that year. A firm research plan was developed after stimulating conversations with Anthony Grafton and Henk Jan de Jonge.

A Humfrey Wanley Fellowship at the Bodleian Library and The Oxford Centre for Hebrew and Jewish Studies in Oxford in 2013 allowed me to engage in comparative research into the Oriental collections of Scaliger and Thomas Bodley. The assistance that I received on this trip from Alexandra Franklin, César Merchán-Hamann and Richard Ovenden made the research not only efficient but also very enjoyable.

Colleagues in Leiden and elsewhere provided me with many useful suggestions and references. I am grateful to François Déroche, Ingrid De Smet, Dirk van Miert, Corrie van Maris, Koos Kuiper, Jan Just Witkam, Karin Scheper, Jef Schaeps, Jos Damen, Albert van der Heide, Martin Baasten, John Lane, Theodor Dunkelgrün, Kees van Strien, Korrie Korevaart, Frederik de Wolff and Ernst Jan Munnik. I thank especially Anton van der Lem, who spent a Christmas vacation reading my thesis and provided me with much helpful commentary and Arnoud Vrolijk, who co-supervised my thesis and also has been a great help after my PhD defense. I frequently asked my colleagues in Special Collections at Leiden for favours, but my many requests never troubled them. I am also especially grateful to Cornelis van Tilburg, who revised and corrected the footnotes and bibliography of the thesis with such care.

I am grateful to Arthur der Weduwen for his translation of my thesis from Dutch to English, and to Andrew Pettegree for his encouragement to publish a translation of my work in the *Library of the Written Word*.

I could always rely on my study friend and former housemate Fred Hermsen, and on my partner Maureen Land. They shared their extensive historical and journalistic knowledge and insights with me. I am also extremely grateful for their linguistic assistance and for their help with the editing of this book.

Leiden, 18 September 2024

Translator's Note

When Joseph Scaliger wrote of 'foreign' books, or 'books in foreign tongues' ('livres des langues estrangeres'), he referred to books in languages that originated from beyond Europe. The major vernacular languages of Europe, whether they were French, Italian, Dutch or German, stemmed, to Scaliger, from the same world as Latin and ancient Greek. The Hebrew language Scaliger considered to be 'foreign', similar to Arabic, Syriac, Amharic, or the languages of south and east Asia. When Scaliger bequeathed his 'books in foreign tongues' to the university library of Leiden, he included Hebrew in this selection, but not Greek. The biblical languages were thus divided into the 'foreign languages' of the Old Testament and the 'common' language (Greek) of the New Testament.

It seems likely (but it is uncertain) that Scaliger counted the lesser-known vernacular languages of Europe, such as Russian and Gaelic, into the camp of the European languages, rather than 'foreign' languages, but this was not a sentiment necessarily shared by his contemporaries. Given the relative rarity and exotic nature of books in Church Slavonic, Icelandic or Welsh, such items were often treated in the same category as books in Chinese or Amharic by many European collectors.

In this work I have used the term 'Oriental' when referring to the languages considered by Scaliger to be 'foreign'. This is in part to remain true to the Dutch original (*Oosters*) in the text, but also to avoid potential confusion for the modern reader of English by referring to 'foreign languages' throughout. While 'Oriental' as a catch-all term for all Middle Eastern, North African and Asiatic languages is no longer fashionable, it does reflect the fact that for centuries after Scaliger's death, his bequest was considered 'Oriental', the first of a distinguished series of bequests and acquisitions that turned Leiden's library into one of the foremost centres of the study of Middle Eastern and Asian languages and cultures in Europe. Scaliger's contemporaries (and the generations that came afterwards) saw his bequest as consisting of 'libros Hebraicos, Syriacos, Arabicos & aliarum linguarum orientalium': books in Hebrew, Syriac, Arabic and other Oriental languages. The use of 'Oriental' in this sense serves also to underscore the historical reality of the early modern period and the contemporary perceptions of European scholars.

Figures and Tables

Figures

1 The university library in 1610, with the *Arca Scaligerana* in the right foreground, as engraved by Willem van Swanenburgh after Johannes Cornelisz. Woudanus; reproduced in *Stedeboeck der Nederlanden* (1649). Nederlands Scheepvaartmuseum Amsterdam   10

2 Jan Jansz. Orlers, *Beschrijvinge der stad Leyden* (1614). Orlers included an extensive description of Scaliger's Oriental bequest. UBL 1122 A 17   11

3 The portrait of the printer-scholar Franciscus Raphelengius, aged 58. *Icones Leidenses* 26   35

4 In the galleries of the Palais du Parlement and the Palais de Justice in Paris, one could find more than 200 shops, including those of many booksellers. Rijksprentenkabinet Amsterdam RP-P-OB-42.103   59

5 Louis Chasteigner de la Roche-Posay, seigneur d'Abain, the protector of Scaliger. Amsterdam, Rijksmuseum   62

6 The jurist Jacques Cujas. Portrait collection of the University of Amsterdam   64

7 The title page of Levita's *Lexicon Chaldaicum*, of which Scaliger received a copy in 1572 from Johannes Pappus as a token of their friendship. UBL 839 A 6   67

8 The title page of the *Pentateuch* from the library of Charles Macrin, gifted to Scaliger by Chasteigner. UBL 515A 12   70

9 The title page of a copy of Scaliger's *Opus Novum de emendatione temporum* (Paris: Sébastien Nivelle, 1583). The title page contains the inscriptions of two previous owners of this copy, Nicolai Massonis and Johann Jacobi. UBL 759 A 50   73

10 Title page of Giovanni Battista Castrodardo, *L'Alcorano di Macometto* (Venice: Andrea Arrivabene, 1547). Koninklijke Bibliotheek Brussel VH2482   80

11 Title page of the Icelandic Bible that Scaliger was able to acquire (Holum, Jon Jonsson, 1584). Lincoln College Oxford L.4.11 SR K 4   83

12 Title page of the *Y Beibl Cyssegr-Lan. Sef Yr Hen Destament, A'r Newydd* (London: Christopher Barker, 1588), the first complete Welsh translation of the Bible, including the Apocrypha   85

13 Jacques-Auguste de Thou, librarian of the Royal Library in Paris. Rijksprentenkabinet Amsterdam RP-P-OB-55.710   94

14 The Italian scholar, collector and bibliophile Gian Vincenzo Pinelli. Rijksprentenkabinet Amsterdam RP-P-1908-2636   106

15	*Saghmosaran* [Psalterium] curante Abgario Tokatensi (Venice: Yakob Meghapart, 1565–1566). UBL 876 G 31 111
16	The heart-shaped *Mappamondi* or world map of Hajji Ahmed (Venice: Marco Antonio Giustiniani, 1559–1560) 112
17	Portrait of Pierre Pithou (1539–1596). Rijksprentenkabinet Amsterdam RP-P-1882.-A 629 115
18	A creed of confession (*Doctrina Christam*) in Tamil, printed in Quilon (Kollam) in 1578. Houghton Library, Harvard University, Cambridge, MA 118
19	Nicolas-Claude Fabri de Pereisc (1580–1637). Rijksprentenkabinet Amsterdam RP-P-OB-33.164 124
20	The title page of Scaliger's copy of Abraham ben David ha-Levi, *Sefer Yeẓirah* (Mantua: Jacob ben Naphtali ha-Kohen of Gazzuolo, 1562). UBL 875 E 24 127
21	David [Ben Solomon] ibn Jachja, *Sefer l'shon limmudim* (Constantinople: Dav[id] et Sam[uel] Ibn Nachmias, 1506). UBL 871 F 6 129
22	Painted portrait of Isaac Casaubon (1559–1614). *Icones Leidenses* 44 149
23	Painted portrait of Daniël van der Meulen by Bernaert der Rijckere, 1583. Collection and © The Phoebus Foundation; photography: Museum De Lakenhal, Leiden 157
24	The brothers Pierre and Jacques Dupuy, the sons of Claude Dupuy. Rijksprentenkabinet Amsterdam RP-P-OB-5659 170
25	Arabic typeface sample, produced by Le Bé. Collection Museum Plantin-Moretus Antwerpen 173
26	Title page of Petrus Bertius's *Nomenclator* (Leiden: Franciscus Raphelengius, 1595), UBL 1408 I 57 184
27	Title page of Daniel Heinsius, *In obitum v. Illustr. Iosephi Scaligeri* (Leiden: Ex officina Plantiniana Raphelengii, 1609), UBL 1011 C 14: 1 190
28	One of the first pages from Scaliger's will, written in French, according to a transcript in the collection of the Leiden professor of history, Greek and rhetoric, Jacobus Perizonius, UBL PER Q5, f4^r 192
29	Title page of the *Catalogus librorum Bibliothecae Illustr. Viri Iosephi Scaligeri*. Leiden 1609. University library of Copenhagen, Collection Older, Cat. 79: 2, 39, vol. I (4) 196
30	Title page of *Cleomedis Meteora Graece et Latine* (Bordeaux: Simon Millanges, 1605). According to an inscription by Rudolph Snellius on this copy, the auction of Scaliger's books lasted at least until 12 March 1609. UBL 758 C 26 197
31	Depictions of Scaliger's epitaph and of one of the tombs of the Della Scalas in Verona. UBL 116 B 15 and UBL 1011 C 14 207
32	Proof of the engraving of the university library (1610), with in the right foreground the Arca Scaligerana The texts that adorned the front of the

FIGURES AND TABLES

XVII

Arca had not yet been cut into the plate. Rijksprentenkabinet Amsterdam RP-P-1895-A-18679   209

33   Bonaventura Vulcanius, *Catalogus Librorum omnium qui hodie conservantur a Josepho Scaligero*. UBL VUL 108 pars 5   216

34   Paullus Merula, *Catalogus rariorum Biblioth[ecae] Acad[emiae] Lugdun[ensis]*, 1607. UBL BA C N 3   222

35   Daniel Heinsius, *Catalogus librorum Bibliothecae Lugdunensis* (Leiden: 1612), UBL BA C N 2c   226

36   Alongside 'All my books in Oriental languages', Scaliger also bequeathed his Latin and Greek manuscripts to the university of Leiden. He also donated to the library a selection of his own works, some of which were published posthumously. UBL 540 D 19   230

37   In his funeral oration of 1609, Daniel Heinsius was the first to announce the news of Scaliger's momentous bequest to the University of Leiden. Remarkably, he did not mention any of Scaliger's Russian books in the process. UBL 1011 C 14   232

38   Title page of Thomas Erpenius, *Novum Testamentum Arabice* (Leiden: In typographia Erpeniana, 1616), UBL 842 D 36   235

39   Title page of Daniel Heinsius, *Catalogus Bibliothecae Publicae Lugduno-Batavae* (Leiden: Abraham and Bonaventura Elsevier, 1640), UBL BA C n 4   242

40   Title page of Frederik Spanheim junior, *Catalogus Bibliothecae Publicae Lugduno-Batavae* (Leiden: The widow and heirs of Johannes Elzevier, 1674), UBL BA C N 6   247

41   *Racuyoxu i.e. Lexicon Sinico-Japonicum et Japonico-Sinicum*. While this page indicates that this work used to belong to Franco Duyck [ens], the following page had a slip of paper applied that reads *Ex Legato Illustris Viri JOSEPHI SCALIGERI*. UBL SER 36   250

42   Title page of *Catalogus Librorum [...] Bibliothecae Publicae Universitatis Lugduno-Batavae* (Leiden: Petri van der Aa, 1716). UBL 1418 A 5   253

43   The university library as depicted in the *Les délices de Leide* of 1712, with the *Arca Scaligerana* and Vulcanius's *Arca* in the left background, underneath the staircase. UBL 403 G 15   258

Tables

1   Scaliger's most important correspondents during his period in France, 1561–1593   89

2   Overview of the auction of Scaliger's books by discipline, as categorised by H.J. de Jonge   199

3 Overview of Scaliger's bequest as reflected in the catalogues of the Leiden University Library, 1612–1716   215

4 Hebrew and Arabic books, partially selected from Burnett's canon, owned by Scaliger in comparison with those owned by Raphelengius, Drusius, Bodley and Bullioud   273

The Oriental Bequest of Joseph Scaliger
and the University Library of Leiden

∴

Introduction

> In this house, one man commanded more languages than any man in Europe. The house in this city was a centre of study for the entire world. Maronites and Arabs, Syrians and Ethiopians, Persians and Indians: in this city, there was one man who could understand their thoughts in their native languages.

With these words, Daniel Heinsius (1580–1655) described the home of his mentor, Josephus Justus Scaliger (1540–1609).[*,1] It was claimed that Scaliger mastered thirteen classical and modern languages. He was especially interested in the languages of the Levant, initially concentrating on Hebrew, and later in his life on the study of Arabic.[2]

In 1593, Scaliger was appointed as professor of Latin, Roman classics and history at the University of Leiden. Scaliger's international renown as scholar was meant to attract students to Leiden, yet ironically Scaliger was not required to undertake any teaching, a concession that the curators of the university offered him to induce him to move to Leiden from France. Scaliger also brought with him to Leiden a substantial part of his library, which included many rare Oriental works.[3] He had assembled such a fine personal library because he required many source texts for his study of chronology, and Scaliger knew that many of these sources were not available in established institutional libraries, or even the libraries of his fellow scholars.

Scaliger's arrival in Leiden and his accompanying collection of *Orientalia* would provide an important contribution to the development of the University of Leiden. Thanks to Scaliger, it would become the centre for the study of the languages and cultures of the Middle East in the Low Countries, and one of the foremost institutions in the wider world – a position it retains today. Scaliger's

---

* The references in the footnotes to the books from Scaliger's bequest beginning with 'see Bibliographic Survey', followed by a city and a number, refer to *Joseph Scaliger's Oriental Printed Books: A Bibliographic Survey* compiled by Frederik A. de Wolff and Kasper van Ommen, forthcoming in the Brill series Library of the Written Word.

1 Daniel Heinsius, *Danielis Heinsii in obitum V[iri] illustr[issimi] Iosephi Scaligeri Iul. Cæs. a Burden F. eruditorum principis Orationes duæ. Accedunt Epicedia eiusdem & aliorum: effigies item ac monumentum Scaligeri & principum Veronensium aeri incisa* (Leiden, ex officina Plantiniana apud Franciscus II Raphelengius and Andries Clouck, 1609; USTC 102909), f. D1ᵛ.

2 To avoid confusion with Josephus Justus Scaliger's father, Julius Caesar Scaliger, I will always refer to his father with his full name, meaning that when I write of 'Scaliger' I always mean Josephus Justus.

3 Philipp Christiaan Molhuysen, *De komst van Scaliger in Leiden* (Leiden: A.W. Sijthoff, 1913).

© KONINKLIJKE BRILL BV, LEIDEN, 2025 | DOI:10.1163/9789004701526_002

appointment also marked the beginning of the rise of the Dutch Republic as a centre of scholarship and printing in the seventeenth century.

When Scaliger, after sixteen years of life as a professor at Leiden, died on 21 January 1609, he possessed a library of some 2,250 books. A portion of this he bequeathed to the university library. This bequest concerned an unspecified quantity of Oriental printed books and manuscripts, a collection of forty-eight Greek and Latin manuscript, some of his own works and those of his father, the humanist physician Julius Caesar Scaliger (Giulio Cesare della Scala, 1484–1558). The remainder of Scaliger's library, printed in Latin, Greek and Western vernacular languages, was auctioned the same year of his death.[4] In his will, signed on 18 November 1608, Scaliger described his bequest to Leiden as follows:

> Concerning the library, which I leave ordered to the best of my limited abilities, I bequeath to the Academy of this city of Leiden all my books in foreign languages, in Hebrew, Syriac, Arabic and Ethiopian, which books are listed in the catalogue that I have added to the Latin copy of this will, and which I intend to be a part or appendix of my will, or to be used as a supplement in the form of a codicil.[5]

Scaliger's contemporaries regarded his Oriental bequest as a remarkable gift. The collection would be housed in the university library in a monumental, specially constructed bookcase, the *Arca Scaligerana*. Scaliger's bequest can in this sense be regarded as the foundation of the special collections of the university library of Leiden.

---

4 Henk Jan de Jonge (ed.), *The Auction Catalogue of the Library of J.J. Scaliger. A Facsimile Edition* (Utrecht: HES, 1977).

5 'Touchant la bibliotheque, laquelle selon mes petites facultez ie laisse bien fornie, ie legue a l'Academi de cette ville de Leyden tous mes livres de langues estrangeres, Hebraics, Syriens, Arabics, Aethiopiens, lesquels livres sont contenus dans le Catalogue que i'ay adiousté a la copie latine de ce mien testament, et que i'entens estre une partie ou appendence de mon dict testament, ou servir de supplement en façon de codicile'. The citation is from the transcript of the original will held at the University Library of Leiden (UBL), Codex Perizonii Q° N. 5, ff. 39–44. Scaliger's French will was published by W.N. du Rieu, 'De portretten en het testament van Josephus Justus Scaliger', *Handelingen en Medeedelingen van de Maatschappij der Nederlandsche Letterkunde te Leiden 1880–1881*, pp. 89–137 (the will is printed at pp. 131–137); it was also reprinted in the *Jaarboek van de Maatschappij der Nederlandsche Letterkunde 1881*, pp. 45–51. In his correspondence, Scaliger frequently used the term 'livres des langues estrangeres [étrangères]', by which he meant books in Hebrew, Arabic and other Oriental languages. He did not consider western languages, including Greek, to be 'foreign', but it is uncertain how Scaliger regarded his books in European vernacular languages, including Icelandic, Gaelic and Polish, that were relatively rare.

INTRODUCTION

1   New Research on Scaliger's Bequest

Scholars have thus far paid much more attention to Scaliger's legacy as scholar of classical philology, Biblical philology and chronology, than to his library. Anthony Grafton is undeniably the leading authority on Scaliger.[6] His works have provided us with a comprehensive overview of Scaliger's importance to sixteenth-century scholarship. This present work is not intended to repeat any of Grafton's findings; rather, it is a study of one aspect of Scaliger's life that has thus far received little attention: Scaliger's book collecting. Various studies have explored some of the Oriental and western manuscripts held in Scaliger's bequest, but virtually nothing has been written about Scaliger's printed books. A complete overview of Scaliger as book collector, and the contextual importance of Scaliger's library, is entirely absent.

To fill this vacuum, this present study offers a thorough investigation of Scaliger's library, with special importance attached to his collection of printed books. Researching Scaliger's collecting habits is a profitable exercise, because many of Scaliger's letters have survived, and his extant correspondence has been published in an exemplary edition by Paul Botley and Dirk van Miert. These letters are an important source for this research, because the acquisition and discussion of books is a perennial theme in Scaliger's correspondence. Furthermore, reconstructing Scaliger's book buying and collecting habits is an interesting exercise because he was one of the few scholars of his day who bequeathed a near-complete Oriental library to an institutional library.

This book charts in a chronological fashion the growth of Scaliger's library and his scholarly development – when did he require certain books for his research? The role of his network of correspondents and the many friends and colleagues who assisted him in his quest for books is treated thematically rather than chronologically. Some contacts of Scaliger were tied to a specific moment in his life, such as friends he made whilst studying in Valence under Jacques Cujas; other contacts remained a ubiquitous presence throughout

---

6   The standard work on Scaliger's life and work is: Anthony T. Grafton, *Joseph Scaliger. A Study in the History of Classical Scholarship*. Vol. I: *Textual Criticism and Exegesis* (Oxford: Clarendon Press, 1983); idem, Vol. II: *Historical Chronology* (Oxford: Clarendon Press, 1993), complemented by the various articles written by Grafton on Scaliger. Various articles by H.J. de Jonge discuss Scaliger's reading of the New Testament, his students and his relationship with the city of Leiden. Older, but still useful sources on Scaliger include: Jakob Bernays, *Joseph Justus Scaliger* (Berlin: Wilhelm Hertz, 1855); Charles Nisard, *Le triumvirat littéraire au XVIe siècle. Juste Lipse, Joseph Scaliger et Isaac Casaubon* (Paris: Amyot, 1852); C.M. Bruehl, 'Josef Justus Scaliger. Ein Beitrag zur geistesgeschichtlichen Bedeutung der Altertumswissenschaft', *Zeitschrift für Religions- und Geistesgeschichte*, 12 (1960), pp. 201–218 and *Zeitschrift für Religions- und Geistesgeschichte*, 13 (1961), pp. 45–65.

his life. These are therefore introduced when they are first mentioned, but their role is analysed comprehensively when they had the greatest impact on Scaliger's life and collecting.

An exhibition held at the University Library of Leiden in 2009 and the accompanying catalogue to commemorate the 400th anniversary of Scaliger's death provided me with the first stimulus to study Scaliger's bequest. The exhibition, entitled *'All my Books in Foreign Tongues'. Scaliger's Oriental Legacy in Leiden*, displayed a selection of Scaliger's books, which were described in extensive detail in the catalogue.[7] The exhibition also discussed the background to Scaliger's bequest, and the basic contours of Scaliger's network that allowed him to gather together so many rare books and manuscripts. In the preparatory work for the exhibition, a provisional list of Oriental printed books that belonged to Scaliger was also drawn up.

As the basis for this list, the title descriptions of the various seventeenth and eighteenth-century catalogues of Leiden university library were consulted. For this present work, these descriptions have been used to identify all copies from Scaliger's bequest in the university library. This was not a straightforward endeavour. The university library of Leiden contains several million printed books, and the early published catalogues of the library were by no means perfect.[8] Bert van Selm emphasised in his research on seventeenth-century Dutch catalogues that they 'rarely if ever contain a complete description of all the books in a particular library'.[9] This is certainly the case for the manuscript lists and printed catalogues that describe Scaliger's bequest. A variety of early inventories provide us with different totals, while the title descriptions of some of the books also changed over time. This meant that it was not always clear which book was referred to in the early catalogues. The confusion did not end there: with each new catalogue, some information was left out, and new information was added. Errors were sometimes corrected, or introduced anew. Some books went missing from the university collection, were replaced by new

---

7 Arnoud Vrolijk & Kasper van Ommen, *"All my Books in Foreign Tongues". Scaliger's Oriental Legacy in Leiden 1609–2009. Catalogue of An Exhibition on the Quatercentenary of Scaliger's Death, 21 January 2009* [Kleine publicaties van de Leidse universiteitsbibliotheek 79] (Leiden: Leiden University Library, 2009).

8 Kasper van Ommen, 'The Legacy of Scaliger in Leiden University Library Catalogues 1609–1716' in M. Walsby & N. Constantinidou (eds.), *Documenting the Early Modern Book World. Inventories and Catalogues in Manuscript and Print* (Leiden, Boston: Brill, 2013), pp. 51–82.

9 Bert van Selm, *Een menighte treffelijcke Boecken. Nederlandse boekhandelscatalogi in het begin van de zeventiende eeuw* (Utrecht: HES, 1987), p. 110.

INTRODUCTION   7

copies in better condition, or were sold as duplicates. Librarians also attributed new Oriental books that he never possessed to Scaliger's bequest.[10]

Initially, Scaliger's Oriental bequest was kept together, but over the course of time the collection was gradually dismembered and then dispersed entirely amongst the broader university collections.[11] This was largely the result of the reorganisation of the university library by format instead of subject classification – a reform implemented by librarian W.G. Pluygers (1812–1880) in the middle of the nineteenth century. Since then, Scaliger's books are spread out amongst the five million volumes held by Leiden (as of 2020). Happily, with steely detective work through the stacks and the careful inspection of all the lists of Scaliger's books compiled throughout history, it has been possible to trace the vast majority of Scaliger's original bequest from 1609.

---

10   Kasper van Ommen, "'Je suis pauvre en tout, mesmement en livres". Reconstructing the Legatum Scaligeri in Leiden University Library' in R. Kerr (et al., eds.), *Writing and Writings from another World and Era. Investigations in Islamic Text and Script in honour of Januarius Justus Witkam* (Cambridge: Archetype 2011), pp. 293–329.

11   The Oriental and western manuscripts from Scaliger's bequest have been described extensively by several researchers. For the Hebrew manuscripts, see: Albert van der Heide, *Hebrew Manuscripts of Leiden University Library* (Leiden: Leiden University Press, 1977), pp. 3–10; Moritz Steinschneider, *Catalogus codicum hebraeorum bibliothecae academiae Lugduno-Batavae* (Leiden: Brill, 1858), pp. 310–279. The old call numbers of Scaliger's Hebrew manuscripts at Leiden are SCA 1–21; the current call numbers are MS Or. 4718–4738 and MS Or. 6882. Work by A. Hamilton has demonstrated that MS Or. 4719, 4725 and 4733 never belonged to Scaliger's bequest, but belonged to Franciscus Raphelengius. This means that the total number of Hebrew manuscripts owned by Scaliger was eighteen. See Alastair Hamilton, "'Nam tirones sumus". Franciscus Raphelengius' *Lexicon Arabico-Latinum* (Leiden 1613)' in M. De Schepper & F. De Nave (eds.), *Ex officina Plantiniana. Studia in memoriam Christophori Plantini (ca. 1520–1589)*, *De Gulden Passer* 66–67 (1988–1989), 1989, pp. 557–591 and Alastair Hamilton, 'Franciscus Raphelengius: The Hebraist and his Manuscripts,' *De Gulden Passer* 68 (1990), pp. 105–117. The other Oriental manuscripts owned by Scaliger have recently been catalogued by Jan Just Witkam in the online *Inventory of the Oriental manuscripts in Leiden University Library*, Vol. 1 (Or 1–MS Or. 1000) (Leiden: Ter Lugt Pers, 2007). See: www.islamicmanu scripts.info. The Arabic manuscripts can be found in the UBL under call numbers MS Or. 212–268. The western manuscripts owned by Scaliger were described by Philipp Christiaan Molhuysen in his *Bibliotheca Universitatis Leidensis, Codices manuscripti II: Codices Scaligerani (praeter Orientales)* (Leiden: Brill, 1910). Antonius Henricus van den van den Baar also referred in his thesis, *A Russian Church Slavonic Kanonnik (1331–1332). A comparative textual and structural study including an analysis of the Russian computus (Scaliger 38B, Leyden University Library)* (Den Haag: Mouton, 1968), p. 15, note 13, to an otherwise untraceable list of western manuscripts in Scaliger's collection, based on a list attached to his Latin will of 1607, entitled *Manuscripta Graeca et Latina J. Scaligeri legata anno 1607*.

2   The Importance of Oriental Books in Early Modern Europe

We need to remember that Scaliger's interest in Oriental languages and cultures was no unique phenomenon. There were other scholars who preceded Scaliger in building collections of Oriental books. Johannes Reuchlin (1455–1522) became an enthusiastic collector of Hebrew, Arabic and other Oriental manuscripts. Yet because during Reuchlin's life there was limited production of printed books in Oriental languages, the number of Oriental books in his library were similarly circumscribed.[12] The introduction of printing, European global expansion, and an increase in trade with the Middle East and the Far East ensured that over time there was a steady increase in the number of printed Oriental books. We thus need to place Scaliger's collecting frenzy in this context. The good relationship between the Catholic Church and Christian churches in the Levant also provided a stimulus for the production of printed books in Oriental languages.[13] Contemporaries of Scaliger who also collected Oriental books were mostly based in France. They included the Protestant jurist Claude Mittalier in Vienne and the Catholic jurist Pierre Bullioud in Lyon.[14] In Spain, the theologian Benito Arias Montano possessed an extensive collection of Oriental works, while in the Dutch Republic, Johannes Drusius owned a library with a substantial number of Oriental books as well.

Patronage played an important role in the accumulation of Oriental books in early modern Europe. In France, Scaliger profited greatly from the financial support of his patron and protector, Louis Chasteigner de la Roche-Posay, seigneur d'Abain (1535–1595).[15] Chasteigner acquired various Oriental items for Scaliger, including an expensive four-volume Rabbinic Bible printed by

---

12   The first book printed in Arabic during Reuchlin's life was the *Kitab Salat al-Sawaʿi bi-Hasab Taqs Kanisat al-Iskandariyah*, a prayer book following the liturgy of the church of Alexandria. It was printed in Fano in 1514. The next book that included Arabic was a book of psalms with texts in Hebrew, Greek, Arabic and Syriac, with an accompanying Latin translation, printed in Genoa in 1516. The Qurʾan was first printed in Arabic in 1530 by Gregorio de Gregorii in Venice – only a single copy of the book has survived.

13   A. Hamilton, 'The English Interest in the Arabic-Speaking Christians' in: G.A. Russell (ed.), *The 'Arabick' Interest of the Natural Philosophers in Seventeenth-Century England* (Leiden: Brill, 1994). pp. 30–53.

14   Some of the Hebrew books owned by Bullioud are found in the Bibliothèque Municipale of Lyon: see http://www.bm-lyon.fr/decouvrir/collections/hebraica_bullioud.htm.

15   André Du Chesne, *Histoire généalogique de la maison des Chasteigners* (Paris: Sébastien Cramoisy, 1634; USTC 6003654). Louis Chasteigner de la Roche-Posay was Count of Abain, a renowned military commander and diplomat. He was also ambassador for the French king in Rome in the years 1576–1581.

INTRODUCTION 9

Bomberg in Venice in 1546–1548.[16] In Leiden, Scaliger enjoyed the support of the university, which granted him an exceptional position due to his renown as scholar. He received an extraordinarily high salary, which allowed him to purchase books that remained out of reach to many of his colleagues. Scaliger also received many books as gifts, mostly from scholars who wished to request a favour from him. Scaliger's move to Leiden in 1593 can be regarded as an important moment in his collecting: did he find better or alternative sources for the acquisition of Oriental books, or did he remain loyal to his old networks from France? And indeed, were there any channels that were closed to him after moving to the Protestant Dutch Republic?

3 The First Contemporary Description of the Bequest

The *Arca Scaligerana* – the monumental bookcase that contained Scaliger's bequest – was first depicted on an engraving of the Leiden university library of 1610, cut by Willem van Swanenburgh after a drawing by Jan Cornelisz van 't Woudt (Jan Cornelis Woudanus, ca. 1570–1615).[17]

Five years after the death of Scaliger, Jan Jansz Orlers (1570–1646), a nephew of the secretary of the city and university of Leiden, Jan van Hout (1542–1609), published a description of Leiden. In this he recorded the earliest account of the *Arca* in the library (described as the *Boeck-kamer*) and added a description of Scaliger's will and bequest.[18]

Orlers also included in his work a mirrored version of the engraving of the library by Van Swanenburgh.[19] These sources provide us with useful indications how Scaliger's bequest was interpreted and represented in the early seventeenth century.

Despite the fact that Scaliger stipulated in his will what he wished to happen to his books, there are many uncertainties about the bequest. In his will, Scaliger specified that he wished to bequeath 'all his books in foreign languages' to the university, without providing an indication of the total number of books, or which languages were included in the description of 'foreign

---

16   *Sha'ar bet Yadwah ha-qadmoni* (Venezia, Daniel Bomberg, 1546–1548; USTC 1792527). UBL 515 A 12–15; see Bibliographic Survey Venice 1546–1548.

17   Rudi Erik Otto Ekkart, *De Leidse Universiteit in 1610* (Leiden: s.n. 1975).

18   Jan Jansz Orlers, *Beschrijvinge der Stad Leyden* (Leiden: Henrick Lodewijcxsoon van Haestens and Jan Jansz Orlers and Jean Maire, 1614), pp. 151–153 (USTC 1028432).

19   This version of the engraving, which is smaller and mirrored compared to the original (and therefore has the *Arca* in the left foreground), has as caption the phrase 'Bibliotheca Publica'. Orlers, *Beschrijvinge der Stad Leyden*, p. 150.

FIGURE 1 The university library in 1610, with the *Arca Scaligerana* in the right foreground, as engraved by Willem van Swanenburgh after Johannes Cornelisz. Woudanus; reproduced in *Stedeboeck der Nederlanden* (1649). Nederlands Scheepvaartmuseum Amsterdam

languages'.[20] The will was accompanied by a codicil which included the titles of the books to be gifted to the university. Yet because this list was lost during the course of the seventeenth century, we cannot identify exactly which titles it concerned. Orlers's account of Scaliger's library, as well as other contemporary sources, all raise questions about the precise nature of the bequest. Were Scaliger's instructions actually followed? Was the number of books identified by contemporaries correct? At a certain moment, the books were removed from Scaliger's home to the library, transported in chests. Who decided which

---

20 In a letter dated 13 October 1607 to Isaac Casaubon, Scaliger described 'foreign languages' as *exoticis linguis*.

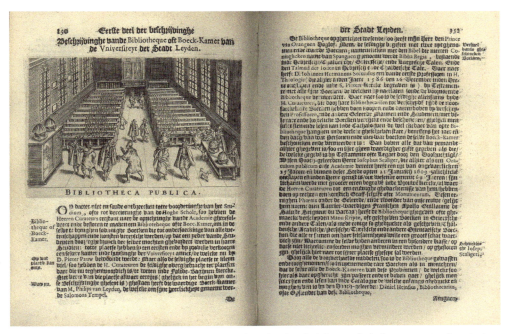

FIGURE 2 Jan Jansz. Orlers, *Beschrijvinge der stad Leyden* (1614). Orlers included an extensive description of Scaliger's Oriental bequest. UBL 1122 A 17

books were involved in this transportation, and how were they organised when they arrived in the library?

We can reconstruct Scaliger's library through a variety of critical sources. They include Scaliger's French and Latin wills and a variety of manuscript inventories compiled by Scaliger and his contemporaries. The printed auction catalogue of the remainder of Scaliger's library from 1609 also provides important information about Oriental books that for some reason were not included in the bequest.[21] The printed catalogues of the university library of Leiden, beginning with the 1612 catalogue (in which the bequest is described for the first time) until the catalogue of 1716 (in which the bequest is described as a separate collection for the last time), are also crucial sources. Each of the university catalogues provides a different overview of the bequest.[22]

---

21 *Catalogus librorum bibliothecae Illust. Viri Iosephi Scaligeri Iul. Caes. F. Quorum auctio habebitur in aedibus Ludovici Elzevirii, bibliopol. Lugd. Bat. Ad diem 11. Martij* (Leiden: Thomas Basson, 1609; USTC 1506505) – hereafter: Auction Catalogue 1609. This is incidentally the earliest auction catalogue that contains Hebrew books.

22 For the development of these catalogues, and their respective shortcomings, see chapters 5 and 6.

Another important source for this study is the correspondence of Scaliger, published in 2012 by Paul Botley and Dirk van Miert.[23] This edition, in eight parts, offers vivid insights into Scaliger's network, and has rendered the previous editions of Scaliger's correspondence, published by Revius (1624), Heinsius (1627) and Tamizey de Larroque (1879) functionally redundant.[24] An in-depth reading of Scaliger's letters demonstrates why Scaliger wished to acquire certain Oriental books, and how he was able to accumulate his desired titles, often through cunning means. The correspondence also portrays the breadth of Scaliger's personal network. Charting this network of friends and colleagues spread throughout Europe, we can learn more about Scaliger's bequest, and his impact on the contemporary library world. This present work also makes helpful use of the *Prima* and *Secunda Scaligerana*, two books published after Scaliger's death that contained extracts from his letters from 1574–1593, as well as attributed sayings and annotations on his life by the brothers De Vassan from 1603–1606. The two volumes contain important information on Scaliger's remarks on texts, manuscripts and libraries that provide further insights into his relationship with books.[25]

4   The Project

A single collection of books can only tell one so much. The character of a library can only be assessed for its contemporary importance when it is compared with other collections. This work will therefore also offer a comparative analysis of Scaliger's library and that of other sixteenth- and seventeenth-century Oriental book collections. Thanks to printed auction catalogues, we can compare the libraries of Johannes Drusius and Franciscus Raphelengius,

---

23   Paul Botley & Dirk van Miert (eds.), *The Correspondence of Joseph Justus Scaliger* Supervisory editors Anthony Grafton, Henk Jan de Jonge and Jill Kraye (*Travaux d'Humanisme et Renaissance* 507) (Genève: Droz, 2012). Hereafter: *Correspondence*, followed by the date and recipient or sender of the letter.

24   Jacques de Reves, *Epistres Françoises des Personnages Illustres & Doctes a Monsr. Ioseph Iuste de la Scala* (Harderwijk: Weduwe Thomas Hendricksz, Amsterdam: Hendrick Laurensz, 1624) USTC 1010292; Daniel Heinsius, *Illustriss. viri Iosephi Scaligeri, Iulii Caes. A Burden F. Epistolae omnes quæ reperiri potuerunt, nunc primum collectæ ac editæ* (Leiden: ex officina Bonaventura Elzevier and Abraham I Elzevier, 1627; USTC 1028641) and Philippe Tamizey de Larroque, *Lettres françaises inédites de Joseph Scaliger* (Agen, Paris: Alphonse Picard, 1879).

25   Pierre des Maizeaux, *Scaligerana, Thuana, Derroniana, Phitoeana et Colomesiana* (Amsterdam: Johannes Covens, 1740). This edition comprises the text of the previous editions of the *Prima Scaligerana* from 1669 and the *Secunda Scaligerana* from 1667.

INTRODUCTION

two prominent Dutch scholars and contemporaries of Scaliger, to Scaliger's collecting. Additional comparisons will be made with libraries outside the Netherlands: with the library of Isaac Casaubon in London, and the library of the Italian Jewish physician Abraham ben David Portaleone. Finally, Scaliger's Oriental collection will be compared in depth to the Oriental books collected by Thomas Bodley for the Bodleian Library in Oxford. Because Bodley's collection has remained together, it is possible to subject Bodley's books to a closer examination than those of Drusius or Raphelengius, whose libraries were dispersed in the seventeenth century. It is also a worthwhile comparison because Bodley and Scaliger were keen scholars of the Hebrew language, and passionate collectors of Oriental books. The comparison will reveal to what extent Bodley and Scaliger owned similar books, and whether the praise that was lavished upon Scaliger's collection by his contemporaries as a truly exceptional library was indeed deserved.[26]

This book seeks to trace in their present location all the items that formed part of Scaliger's original bequest. For each item I have tried to determine whether it can indeed be found in the collections of Leiden University Library, and to reconcile the frequently incomplete or erroneous information provide by various sources. In other words: how do we establish whether a book listed as part of Scaliger's bequest in a seventeenth-century catalogue is a book that now sits on a shelf of Leiden University Library? To aid the reader, I have offered a reconstruction of Scaliger's bequest in its entirety in a catalogue appended to this work. I received valuable assistance in preparing this catalogue from professor emeritus Frederik A. de Wolff, who described many of the Hebrew and Aramaic titles with great care. The title descriptions have been supplemented with information on donors, provenance and other details that refer to Scaliger's correspondence or network of contacts. The provenance information also provides insights into books that ended up in Scaliger's library from other dispersed collections.[27]

This present work seeks to provide the answers to a variety of critical questions concerning Scaliger's life and his books. How did Scaliger acquire his Oriental books? With whom did he exchange correspondence, who were the most important suppliers of books, and how did books reach Scaliger in

---

26   Kasper van Ommen, 'Ommen, Kasper van, "Early Modern Oriental Collections in Oxford and Leiden. Scaliger, Bodley and Anglo-Dutch Encounters and Exchanges"', Part I. *Bodleian Library Record*, 28/2 (2015), pp. 152–178 and 'Early Modern Oriental Collections in Oxford and Leiden. Scaliger, Bodley and Anglo-Dutch Encounters and Exchanges', Part II. *Bodleian Library Record* 29/1 (2016), pp. 47–72.

27   David Pearson, *Provenance Research in Book History. A Handbook* (London: The British Library, 1998), p. 171.

France and Leiden? What was the impact on his collection of Scaliger's move to the Netherlands?

This book will also establish what contribution Scaliger's bequest made to the development of the University of Leiden and its library. To what extent was the bequest regarded as an exceptional collection? How did the physical *Arca Scaligerana* showcase the status of Scaliger's collection, and that of the university library?[28] Did the accession of Scaliger's collection spur the development of Leiden's Oriental collections? How did the university exploit Scaliger's legacy? Was the bequest more important as a symbol of scholarly erudition and institutional prestige, or a practical resource to future generations of scholars and students? Who had access to the collection, and under what terms? What happened to Scaliger's bequest in the centuries after his death?

Chapter one of this book outlines the basic contours of Scaliger's book collecting before and after his arrival in Leiden in 1593. Chapters two and three discuss Scaliger's French period, focussing in particular on his scholarly networks and correspondents, and the means available to him to acquire a library. Chapter four concentrates on Scaliger's Leiden period as collector. Chapter five discusses the presence of Oriental books in the Netherlands before Scaliger's bequest, and the manner in which the bequest was documented, transferred and stored in Leiden after his death, as well as the auction of the remainder of Scaliger's library. Chapter six offers a comprehensive reconstruction of Scaliger's bequest by analysing the manner in which it was presented in the various published catalogues of the university library of Leiden, and charts the gradual loss of distinction of Scaliger's bequest within the growing institutional library. Chapter seven concludes with a contextualisation of Scaliger's library, by comparing it to other contemporary Oriental collections, especially that of Thomas Bodley.

---

28   E. Hulshoff Pol, 'The Library' in Th.H. Lunsingh Scheurleer & G.H.M. Posthumus Meijers (eds.), *Leiden University in the Seventeenth century. An Exchange of Learning* (Leiden: Universitaire Pers, E.J. Brill, 1975), p. 426.

CHAPTER 1

A Life in Two Parts: Scaliger and His Collection before and after 1593

Scaliger's life can be divided into two periods. In the first period, until his fifty-third birthday, he resided in France.[1] Towards the end of this first phase, Scaliger's contemporaries already regarded him as a distinguished scholar. Yet Scaliger was a Protestant scholar in a Catholic state: because of his faith he could not consider employment at court or at a university. He did not live or work permanently in the same location; often he was secluded and lonely. He was, for a long time, in the employ of the noble family of Chasteigner de la Roche-Possay, who offered him protection. In many letters from this period, Scaliger complained about the hardships that he had to endure, and his sense of isolation from the goings-on of the intellectual centres of France. His letters from this phase give us an indication of the wide range of cities and villages in which Scaliger resided: at the castles of his protector Chasteigner in Preuilly and La Roche-Possay, in his hometown of Agen; in Paris, Touffou, Poitiers, Chantemille, Valence and many other places. Scaliger's life was a wandering, uncertain one. It was only his correspondence with similarly minded scholars in France which kept up his spirits. Letter-writing and books provided the most important means to maintain close contact with scholarly developments throughout Europe. In Scaliger's case, however, access to books was not to be taken for granted. He was often forced to work without access to his books: sometimes he had to do without them for more than three months, as during his stay at Chantemille in 1576.[2]

Despite the great uncertainty that plagued Scaliger during this time, he was able to complete a remarkable number of scholarly projects and publish various influential works. Around his thirty-fifth birthday, Scaliger's scholarly interest shifted gradually from poetry to history. It is noteworthy that Scaliger's conception of the classical era, as a historical subject, did not only encompass the world of the Greeks and Romans, but also those of Eastern cultures.

---

1 This division of Scaliger's life is also present in Scaliger's autobiography, found in his *Epistola de vetustate et splendore gentis Scaligeri* (Leiden: Franciscus Raphelengius, 1594; USTC 423322). In this Scaliger reveals very little about his youth, time as student and his adult life in France (1563–1593).

2 *Correspondence* 5 November 1576 to Claude Dupuy.

© KONINKLIJKE BRILL BV, LEIDEN, 2025 | DOI:10.1163/9789004701526_003

In order to learn about their world, Scaliger began to master their tongues: Hebrew, Aramaic, Syriac, Arabic, Armenian and Persian. Language would only be a starting point. Scaliger was able to collate divergent historical facts and improve upon the great miscellany of knowledge of these ancient cultures by studying their chronology and astronomy, alongside philology, history, religion, literature, laws and institutions. To this end he relied not only on literary sources, but also on ancient inscriptions, coins and other historical objects.

The pinnacle of his research on the history of the classical and eastern ancients were his books *Opus novum de emendatione temporum in VIII libros tributum* (hereafter referred to as *De emendatione temporum*) of 1583 and the *Thesaurus Temporum*, a reconstruction of the chronicle of Eusebius of Caesarea, of 1606.[3] These two books would bring Scaliger everlasting fame. A richer representation of Scaliger's activities is derived from his correspondence. From his letters it becomes clear that his interest in Hebrew blossomed to its greatest heights and that his interest in Arabic grew considerably over time. The first signs of this philological scholarship are expressed in *De emendatione temporum*.

From various letters it also becomes clear that Scaliger did not only invest much energy and time to the study of Eastern and other languages, but also in the collecting of books on the same subjects. He requested correspondents of his to speak with their contacts in Italian print centres – including Venice, Rome and Mantua – to send him books that were on his wish list. Some correspondents reached out to Scaliger, and provided him with Eastern books as gifts, or in exchange for information or other favours. Others asked for his help with the study of Hebrew or Arabic. Scaliger was clearly well respected in his circle for his knowledge of these languages; and despite his relative isolation, French scholars and others further afield were aware of his exceptional talents and expertise in the Eastern languages thanks to Scaliger's publications. This international renown was cultivated by Scaliger, who may have exaggerated his knowledge of these languages in his correspondence.[4]

---

3 On Scaliger's publications about chronology from a historical context and his importance as founder of historical chronology as a discipline, see Anthony T. Grafton, 'Joseph Scaliger and Historical Chronology. The Rise and Fall of a Discipline', *History and Theory* 14 (1975), pp. 156–185; Paul Nothaft, *Dating the Passion. The Life of Jesus and the Emergence of Scientific Chronology (200–1600)* (Leiden: Brill, 2011) and Emile Walter van Wijk, 'Josephus Justus Scaliger, grondlegger der wetenschappelijke tijdrekenkunde', *De Natuur* 60 (1940), pp. 153–157; 192–195; 224–229.

4 Both Bernays and Grafton question the extent of Scaliger's expertise in Hebrew. Cf. Bernays, *Joseph Justus Scaliger*, p. 36 and A. Grafton, 'The Jewish Book in Christian Europe. Material Texts and Religious Encounters' in: A. Sterk (et al., eds.), *Faithful Narratives. Historians, Religion, and the Challenge of Objectivity* (Ithaca, London: Cornell University Press, 2014),

A LIFE IN TWO PARTS 17

In 1593, Scaliger moved to Leiden, and this can be considered decisively as the beginning of the second period of his life. In Leiden he would display an even greater scholarly productivity, as well as the ability to work co-operatively with other scholars. He urged his friends and colleagues at Leiden to undertake new research, and he evolved into a true mentor to his students, to whom he assigned specific classical texts, to study, annotate and publish.

In Leiden, Scaliger could rely on the library of the university, while he also had access to the personal book collections of Leiden's scholars and collectors. The distinguished position that he accepted at Leiden was accompanied by a lavish salary, which allowed him to expand his personal library. The growth of his collection was not reliant only on acquisitions: Scaliger regularly received books as gifts from friends and admirers throughout Europe. Such supplicants would hope to be received positively by Scaliger, and receive in a return a portrait of the scholar or other gifts.

His generous salary did not prevent Scaliger from complaining continually about the high prices of the French, German and English imprints found in the bookshops of Leiden. It cost him substantial sums to maintain his library:

> To set up a small, mean library I need three or even four times as much as I would do in Paris. And a foreigner needs to keep and save that little bit of money that he has, like me, who lacks much, in order to remain moderately, or even poorly accommodated.[5]

Scaliger's appointment as professor at the University of Leiden attracted the attention of many scholars throughout Europe. His correspondence expanded at a rapid pace, as did his exchange of scholarly information with his peers. At the same time, Scaliger would remain in close contact with his old French friends, like the jurist and bibliophile Claude Dupuy (Claudius Puteanus, 1545–1594), the historian Jacques-Auguste de Thou (1553–1617) and the jurist and classical scholar Pierre Pithou (1539–1596).[6] When one of his friends died,

---

p. 98: 'In fact, the one letter of his in Hebrew [UBL MS Or. 6882] suggests that his written Hebrew did not match his Latin and Greek for fluency.'

5 *Correspondence* 16 [October] 1600 to Gillot and: *Correspondence* 25 December 1600; 6 November 1601; 10 January 1602 to the brothers Dupuy; 6 February 1600 to Casaubon and 13 August 1601 to Pinelli. 'Pour bastir une petite meschante librairie je despens trois fois plus, voire quatre fois, que je ne ferois dans Paris. Et un estranger a besoin de garder et espargner ce peu de finances qu'il a, comme moy, à qui manque beaucoup, pour rester mediocrement, voire peniblement, accommodé'.

6 De Thou or Thuanus was one of the most important and influential historians during the reign of King Henry IV of France. His most important publication was the *Historia sui temporis* (1604). De Thou studied to become a jurist and subsequently travelled through Italy,

Scaliger regularly maintained contact with their descendants, as with Pierre Dupuy (1582–1651) and Jacques Dupuy (1586–1656), the sons of Claude Dupuy. Scaliger's arrival at Leiden thus heralds two important transformations in his life: the manner in which his contemporaries regarded him as scholar, and his development from an 'iconoclastic intellectual adventurer' to a 'collaborator and organiser of intellectual communities.'[7]

The consistent thread that runs through both periods of Scaliger's life is his desire for books. Scaliger always wrote passionately about the books that he hoped to acquire and the libraries that he wished to visit. Especially in his French period, books provided him with a certainty in a world which he otherwise experienced as a lonely and uncertain one. Scaliger not only suffered from the lack of a permanent residence, but he remained unmarried and childless.

Time and time again, Scaliger hoped to discover rare manuscripts, and he ensured that he remained informed of all the new titles that appeared from the printing presses throughout Europe. Various correspondents sent him books and manuscripts, and Scaliger always expressed himself as a grateful recipient of such gifts. He was less adept at sharing books from his own library with other scholars. He was fearful that the books would be damaged during their travels or that they might even be lost.[8] That this was the genuine fear of a bibliophile, rather than only the stinginess of a collector, can be deduced from the fact that Scaliger was very generous when sending copies of his own

---

Germany and the Dutch Republic. On his return to France he became one of the most loyal councilors of the king. Henry IV appointed De Thou in 1593 as his 'grand maître' of the royal library. De Thou was a true bibliophile and dedicated himself as librarian to the expansion of the royal book collection. The addition of the rich collection of Catherine de' Medici to the library was his greatest achievement. Pithou, the well-regarded and talented jurist from Troyes, was appointed as 'procureur général' by the king in 1594. He had instructions to defend royal privileges against noble and ecclesiastical attempts to infringe upon them. Pithou was also responsible for the royal archive. He was also the author of a variety of juridical and historical tracts.

7 Kristine Louise Haugen, 'Joseph Scaliger's Letters. Collaborator, Teacher, Impresario', *History of Humanities* 18 (2014) 1, p. 119.

8 One of the rare occasions on which Scaliger did do this, concerned an Arabic-Greek manuscript containing three liturgies of the Eastern Orthodox Chruch, which he loaned out to Marcus Welser. The Latin translation of the *Liturgiae S. Basilii Magni, S. Gregorii Theologi, S. Cyrilli Alexandrini. Ex Arabico conversae, a Victorio Scialach, Accurensi Maronita è monte Libano* by Victor Scialach was published in 1604 in Augsburg by Christoph Mang (USTC 2013179).

A LIFE IN TWO PARTS

publications to other scholars.[9] This generosity, of course, was also motivated by the desire to make his name and reputation as scholar.[10]

Upon his arrival in Leiden, Scaliger reflected in a long letter to Isaac Casaubon (1559–1614) on his life in France.[11] Scaliger was dissatisfied with his scholarly efforts. What he considered to be a mediocre achievement on his own part, he blamed on his accident-prone itinerant period in France. He characterised himself as a late bloomer, as a scholar who had to teach himself everything before he could embark on his work.[12]

In Leiden, an increasingly important centre of the book trade, Scaliger felt like a child in a sweetshop. He regularly visited all the local bookshops for new and antiquarian publications. Thanks to the extensive international network maintained by the Leiden booksellers with their colleagues in other publishing centres of Europe, like Paris and Venice, and with traders at the book fairs in Frankfurt, it was relatively straightforward for Scaliger to expand his library with his desiderata. This was a flourishing time for the book trade. Twice a year, European booksellers would ship their books in bales, vats and chests to the German fairs. As soon as the rivers were navigable, they made use of water-borne transport for their heavy and vulnerable book cargo.

In the sixteenth and seventeenth centuries, the Frankfurt Book Fair was the most important meeting place for European book dealers and printers. Initially, they could sell their most recent publications for cash; from the end of the sixteenth century onwards, books were mostly traded by the exchange of new, unbound books. Sheets were traded against sheets. At the fair, antiquarian books also changed hands, for which booksellers would take commissions from their customers at home and take care of the transport from the fair.

---

9   That Scaliger sent his publications, in bound or unbound form, to his friends, is evidenced by the auction catlaogue of Carolus Clusius (1609), in which a copy of the *De emendatione temporum* (Leiden: ex officina Plantiniana apud Christophorus Raphelengius, 1598; USTC 424143) in the unbound section is listed as 'Ex dono Auctoris'. See Sylvia van Zanen, *Planten op papier. Het pionierswerk van Carolus Clusius (1526–1609)* (Zutphen: Walburg Pers, 2019), p. 313.

10   In 1594, Scaliger sent a copy of his *Cyclometrica elementa duo* (Leiden: ex officina Plantiniana apud Franciscus I Raphelengius, 1594; USTC 429546) to Henry Savile. With this book, Scaliger tried to enhance his reputation as mathematician by attempting to solve the scientific paradox of the quadrature. Savile, however, would demonstrate that Scaliger had made many errors in his reasoning.

11   In 1604, Casaubon was appointed as deputy librarian of the royal library. After the death of Henry IV in 1610, he fled France and settled in England, where he would remain until his death. Simone Balayé, *La Bibliothèque nationale des origines à 1800* (Genève: Droz, 1998), p. 49.

12   *Correspondence* 7 May 1594 to Casaubon.

During the fairs, the acquisition and exchange of books was only one important aspect of the trade amongst printers: they also took the opportunity to make payments or settle accounts with one another.[13]

The print shops of Leiden, especially that of Franciscus I Raphelengius (1539–1597) and his sons, offered Scaliger the opportunity to bring his own new publications to the market. He availed himself of this opportunity gratefully and repeatedly. In a short time, there appeared a revised edition of the *De emendatione temporum* (1598) and the *Astronomicon* (1599), a complex didactic poem on astronomy by the Roman author Marcus Manilius. At the same time he published, shortly after his arrival at Leiden, various new titles, including the *Cyclometrica* (1594), the family history of the Della Scala's (also in 1594) and an edition of the *Canon Paschalis* of Hippolytus (1595). In this sense, Scaliger was not only an eager consumer of books (according to himself he suffered from a disease caused by a lack of books), but he was also an active supplier of texts to local printers.

1   Scaliger's Move to Leiden

On 19 August 1593, after a long journey through France and a crossing at sea, Scaliger first set foot on Dutch soil at Schiedam. The day after he arrived at Delft, where he was met by Janus Dousa, who accompanied him onwards to Leiden.[14] On 26 August, around 6 PM, he entered Leiden. Scaliger was appointed at the still relatively young university as the successor of Justus Lipsius (1547–1606): he was not appointed as an ordinary professor, but as *Decus Academiae*, the jewel of the Academy. The use of such a title reinforces the notion that Leiden wanted to establish itself as a renowned institution and attract students from far and wide.[15] Scaliger's journey to Leiden was preceded by a difficult series of negotiations. The jurist Gerardus Tuningius (1566–1613), who negotiated

---

13   Johannes Hermann Kernkamp, *Economisch-historische aspecten van de literatuurproductie* ('s-Gravenhage, Martinus Nijhoff, 1949), p. 16 and J.L. Flood, '"Omnium totius orbis emporiorum compendium". The Frankfurt Fair in the Early Modern Period' in: R. Myers (et al., eds.), *Fairs, Markets and the Itinerant Book Trade* (Newcastle & London: Oak Knoll Press 2007), p. 12.

14   *Iusti Lipsi Epistolae* (here after: *ILE*) XIX, 93 08 21, Cornelis Aerssens [The Hague] to Lipsius (Louvain): 'Monsieur Scaliger arriva hier a Delft en bonne sante, ayant veu le Roy avant son partement. Le S[ieu]r de Noirtwyck est allé devant luy pour le convoyer et mener à Leyden.'

15   In the early years of the University of Leiden, the curators tried to attract scholars of international renown, through substantial financial expenditure and other efforts. The first of the celebrity scholars attracted to Leiden in this manner was Justus Lipsius from Overijse.

A LIFE IN TWO PARTS

with Scaliger in the name of the university, even offered Scaliger two copies of Tacitus to sweeten the deal.[16]

What possessed Scaliger to leave his fatherland and travel to Leiden to attach his name to a university that was not yet two decades old, and that had just experienced a great blow in the sudden departure of Justus Lipsius, its great star? What did Scaliger expect of his life in a foreign country that was still at war with the King of Spain? The questions that he asked himself can easily be guessed. Could he further his scholarship without taking with him his own books, the sources he considered so vital for his research? The library of the University of Leiden was, at the end of the sixteenth century, limited in scope. Many of the sources that would have been essential to Scaliger would not be available to him there. Would he be offered the opportunity to take with him the most important books, and have the rest sent from France later? Would he receive a salary large enough to purchase new books in Leiden? Succinctly put, what was the foundation of Scaliger's trust that he could have a successful career, and continue his scholarly activities, in these new surroundings? It is understandable that, early on in the negotiations with Leiden, the transportation of his library became a critical condition to Scaliger.

2   Push and Pull Factors

Various factors instigated Scaliger's departure from France. As for many of his fellow Protestants, the conditions of life in sixteenth-century France were not ideal for a Huguenot like Scaliger. Since 1562, there raged in France a series of civil wars between Protestants and the Catholic League, sponsored by Spain. During the years 1591 and 1592, these conflicts developed gradually into

---

For an exhaustive report of the negotiations with Scaliger and his journey to Leiden, see Molhuysen, *De komst van Scaliger in Leiden.*

16   Philipp Christiaan Molhuysen, *Bronnen tot de geschiedenis der Leidsche Universiteit* (Den Haag: Martinus Nijhoff, 1913), p. 206*: 'alsdoen tot Leyden door raed van D. Baudius gecocht twe boucken van C. Tacitus, om in Vrancrijc aen eenige te schencken, die de zake mochten vorderen' (cost: 1 gulden and 16 stuivers). It probably concerned a publication by Tacitus, his *Opera quae extant* edited by Justus Lipsius and published in 1581, 1588 or 1589. Lipsius was responsible for introducing this historical text into the curriculum of Leiden University. These editions were regarded as one of the most eloquent expressions of Lipsius's scholarship. They were printed by Plantin in Antwerp and Raphelengius in Leiden. See V.A. Nordman, 'Justus Lipsius als Geschichtsforscher und Geschichtslehrer. Eine Untersuchung', *Annales Academiae Scientiarum Fennicae* 28 2 (1932), p. 12. One of these copies possibly found its way to Leiden at a later date: in the auction catalogue of 1609 there is listed on page 21: *Tacitus cum Notis Lipsii. Plantin 81. 2. Voll.*

pan-European warfare. At the end of the sixteenth century, the Huguenots were a clear minority in France. Scaliger was faced by two distinct Catholic factions that could cause serious trouble for him: the Gallicans and the Ultramontanes.[17] Scaliger's public status as a scholar ensured that both groups were actively trying to convert him to Catholicism.[18] The anarchy of the French Religious Wars did not pass Scaliger by. In January 1589, the conflict came closest to home when his friends François Vertunien and Claude Dupuy are arrested and imprisoned in Paris. On 1 August of the same year, King Henry III (1551–1589) was murdered.

After 1585, the French book trade also suffered greatly from the consequences of the wars. In 1588, the French economy as a whole came to a virtual standstill because of the latest outbreak of conflict; transport routes over land and water were no longer safe. The publishing centres of Paris and Lyon both fell in the hands of the Catholic League after 1588. The effect of this on the print shops and bookshops of Paris was, as one might expect, disastrous. The provincial and foreign trades were largely suspended.[19] Because of this situation, Scaliger's supply of books also dried up. He became especially depressed about the bleak future of his country, and he regularly feared for his own life. Due to the continued threat of war and the political uncertainty, Scaliger was repeatedly forced to move between various castles owned by his patron, Louis Chasteigner de la Roche-Posay (1535–1595).

Sudden departures ensured that Scaliger could not always take his books with him. The lack of access to his collection meant that it became largely impossible for Scaliger to devote himself to his scholarship. Given that he had no association with a university, he was also unable to make use of institutional

---

17   Gallicanism was a movement led by French nationalist Catholics who wished for a degree of autonomy from the Church of Rome. See Robert Jean Knecht, *French Renaissance Monarchy. Francis I & Henry II* (London, New York: Routledge, 1984), p. 79.

18   Dirk van Miert, 'The Limits of Transconfessional Contact in the Republic of Letters around 1600: Scaliger, Casaubon and their Catholic Correspondents', in J. De Landtsheer & H. Nellen, red., *Between Scylla and Charybdis. Learned Letter Writers Navigating the Reefs of Religious and Political Controversy in Early Modern Europe* (Leiden: Brill, 2010), p. 381. Especially after the arrival of Scaliger in Leiden, which had grown in less than fifteen years into an important international Protestant intellectual bulwark, attacks by these groups on Scaliger increased in ferocity.

19   M. Walsby, 'Printer Mobility in Sixteenth-Century France', in B. Rial Costas (ed.), *Print Culture and Peripheries in Early Modern Europe. A Contribution to the History of Printing and the Book Trade in Small European and Spanish Countries* (Leiden, Boston: Brill, 2013), pp. 249–268; I. Maclean, 'The Market for Scholarly Books and Conceptions of Genre in Northern Europe, 1570–1630', in Georg Kaufmann (ed.), *Die Renaissance im Blick der Nationen Europas* (Wiesbaden: Harrassowitz, 1991), p. 18.

libraries. His correspondence with his friends from this period is marked by a growing frustration: in 1581, Scaliger compared his intellectual isolation in the Limousin with life in a desert.[20]

Scaliger was largely dependent on the protection and funding of his patron. In return for this support he tutored Chasteigner's son, another call on Scaliger's time that restricted his time for study. Chasteigner occasionally provided Scaliger with necessary books, but most books Scaliger had to purchase himself using his salary as a private tutor. The physical protection offered by Chasteigner was much valued by Scaliger, but the services he had to provide in exchange he deemed to be below his station. Due to his presumed noble descent, Scaliger considered himself Chasteigner's equal. This sense was only strengthened by the great international renown that Scaliger was acquiring by the end of the sixteenth century. An appointment at a university would undoubtedly have befitted Scaliger's status. At least, this was the opinion of Dominicus Baudius and Janus Dousa, when they approached Scaliger to fill the void at Leiden left by Justus Lipsius.[21]

Scaliger's move to the Dutch Republic was also instigated because of the favourable conditions present in the young Dutch state. There was a certain degree of religious toleration, while scholars could, to an extent, speak, discuss and write freely without the threat of censorship. At Leiden, Scaliger could profit from the close connections that the university and its professors maintained with scholars in England and in the Protestant lands of the Holy Roman Empire. The young university of Leiden was undoubtedly in a phase of growth, but it had the ambition and the potential to grow into a successful institution. In direct contrast to France, a professorial appointment in the Republic granted a scholar complete freedom to devote himself to his scholarship.[22] The prospect of more time on his studies would thus have formed one of the principal attractions to Scaliger. The financial independence granted by his enormous salary – more than that received by any other professor at Leiden – was extremely attractive, and allowed Scaliger to expand his library substantially in the longer term.

The vision of the young university of Leiden was sketched out eloquently by Bonaventura Vulcanius (1538–1614), professor of Greek, in several orations held to mark the promotion of three students in 1591 and 1592, shortly

---

20   *Correspondence* 4 September 1581 to Chrestien: 'Car depuis que je suis en ces deserts de Limosin, je n'ai point receu lettre d'un ami de telle marque que vous, ni duquel je fais plus d'estime; addo etiam, lequel je desire plus voir' and he signed the letter with 'Chantemille in Arabia deserta'. See also *Correspondence* 14 April [1568–1569] to Pithou.

21   Molhuysen, *De komst van Scaliger in Leiden.*

22   Van Miert, 'Limits of Transconfessional Contact', p. 379.

before Scaliger's arrival at Leiden.[23] In these orations, Vulcanius described the foundation of Leiden University in 1575 and the development of its scholarship in the two following decades. He argued that Leiden could be compared favourably to every other European university, thanks in part to the quality of its students. According to Vulcanius, the curators of the university considered that the knowledge of *bonae litterae*, the study of letters, was the highest form of scholarship; the honour afforded to the arts at Leiden was influential in granting Leiden its unique character and attractive curriculum. Vulcanius maintained that scholars of the humanities had a profound impact on the prosperity of a community and its society. Students of jurisprudence and medicine certainly fulfilled an important role in society, in the case of jurists as the future regents who ruled the Dutch state; yet if these students were to neglect the liberal arts, it would spell the doom of the young nation. Vulcanius also pointed to the importance of acquiring copies of (Greek) manuscripts from Italian and other libraries for Leiden. He praised the university library, the *hortus medicus* and the anatomical theatre as assets of the university that were not only of importance to the students, but also contributed to the international renown of the university. The critical investigation of sources was, in the eyes of Vulcanius, of utmost importance to the study of texts. Above all, he lauded the freedom of conscience and expression at Leiden, so much less evident in other parts of Europe.

Scaliger was certainly aware of the plans of the university of Leiden thanks to the text written to celebrate its foundation in 1575. This was the work of his friend Janus Dousa (1545–1604), entitled *Carmen in gratiam novae Academiae conscriptum*. In this, Dousa outlined a similar picture as that of Vulcanius concerning the foundation, curriculum and vision of the university. The text was incorporated into an edition of Dousa's *Poemata*, printed at the costs of the secretary of the university, Jan van Hout, 'at our new academy'.[24] The tone of

---

23 VUL 9, ff. 56–72; the passages concerning the library are at f. 58; P.A.M. Geurts and J.A. van Dorsten, 'Drie redevoeringen van Bonaventura Vulcanius over de stichting van de Leidse universiteit', *Bijdragen en mededelingen van het Historisch Genootschap* 79 79 (Groningen: J.B. Wolters, 1965), pp. 387–413. Vulcanius regarded these three orations as the core of a piece of publicity that was supposed to be published under the title *Leidensia*. In 1595, he had finished the copy for this work in part. He wished to append to this publication, which would never appear, an overview of the books which had been published with financial support of the curators of the university, and lists of the names of Leiden's professors and students who had defended doctoral theses. The project was a forerunner of later works of publicity for the university, like *Athenae Batavae* (1625) of Joannes Meursius. See Molhuysen, *Bronnen* I, 1913, pp. 342*–343*.

24 'In nova academia nostra'. Janus Dousa, *Nova poemata. Carminum Lugdunensium sylva. In nova academia nostra Lugdunensi excusum* (Leiden: [Andries Verschout] Jan van Hout,

A LIFE IN TWO PARTS   25

the text would undoubtedly have appealed to Scaliger, as it was made clear that scholarship at Leiden was unimpeded by church or state. He could not have wished for better circumstances.

The arrival of Scaliger at Leiden in 1593 took place in the midst of the period that the historian R. Fruin fixed upon as the crucial decade of the Eighty Years war, from 1588 to 1598.[25] For the Republic of the Seven United Provinces this was a period of economic, intellectual and societal flourishing. It was also a time of political consolidation. Thanks to a series of military successes, the Republic was able to stabilise and strengthen its borders. Leiden had developed into one of the most important industrial centres of Holland, which in its turn had become the most powerful province of the Republic.[26] Crucially, Holland was throughout this time entirely unthreatened by Spanish troops.[27] The years preceding this relatively peaceful time had been of an entirely different nature, when the young Republic was in constant threat of being overwhelmed by the armies of King Philip II of Spain (1527–1598). War had been the business of everyday life. The first fifteen years of Leiden University's existence – roughly the years before the prosperous period identified by Fruin – were especially difficult. The arrival of Justus Lipsius had brought some alleviation of these troubles, but the future of the university was not guaranteed, and the destruction of the Republic was not unthinkable.

In the 1580s, Vulcanius was appointed as professor alongside Lipsius to bolster the image of the university and underpin its scholarly activities. The great blossoming of the university, however, remained elusive in these years, because many Reformed students continued to prefer Heidelberg and Geneva over Leiden. There was also domestic competition in the shape of the university

---

1575), sign. P3–Q4 (USTC 421704). Scaliger owned a copy of the second edition of Dousa's Novorum poematum secunda Lugdunensis editio, plus dimidia parte locupletata et aucta (Leiden: [Andries Verschout], 1576; USTC 421733). See Auction catalogue 1609, p. 36. This academic vision was also to be found in the privilege for the foundation and the first statutes of the university. From its inception, Leiden was to advance not only 'the knowledge of theology' but also 'various good and liberal arts and sciences.' See Molhuysen Bronnen I, 1913, bijlage 1 (pp. 1*–2*).

25   Robert Fruin, De Tachtigjarige Oorlog. Historische opstellen. Tien jaren uit den Tachtigjarigen Oorlog 1588–1598 ('s-Gravenhage: Martinus Nijhoff, 1941).

26   R.C.J. van Maanen, 'De vermogensopbouw van de Leidse bevolking in het laatste kwart van de zestiende eeuw', BMGN 93 (1978), p. 11. From 1580 onwards, and especially after the fall of Antwerp on 17 August 1585, a great influx of artisans from the Southern Netherlands was instrumental in changing the declining economic circumstances of Leiden. In 1581 the population of Leiden had increased to 13,000, and by 1600 had risen to around 26,000.

27   Friso Wielinga, Geschiedenis van Nederland. Van de Opstand tot heden (Amsterdam: Boom, 2012), pp. 54–61.

of Franeker, founded in 1585, and which had appointed Johannes I Drusius (1550–1616) as a rival star to Leiden's Lipsius. Despite an attempt by William of Orange to keep Drusius at Leiden through the offer of an increased salary, the talented professor of Greek, Hebrew and Syriac nevertheless departed to Frisian Franeker.[28]

In the early 1590s, the situation at Leiden improved drastically. The university developed a renowned international profile, which saw students from all over Europe flock to Leiden for their education.[29] These favourable developments granted Scaliger his necessary peace and protection at Leiden. Life in the Republic also granted him the support to acquire and maintain scholarly connections abroad, which guaranteed that a stream of books and information would flow into and out of Leiden.

3   Leiden University and the Study of Hebrew

The liberal structures of the Dutch Republic in the late sixteenth and early seventeenth centuries provided an ideal environment in which the study of the humanist arts could be undertaken. Philosophy and the classical languages were an essential part of the *Artes* all over Europe, but in Leiden much attention was also afforded to the study of the Hebrew language and culture as part of its humanistic discipline.[30] In the sixteenth century, Hebrew culture was considered to be the oldest in the world. Study of the Hebrew language was cultivated extensively in the Dutch Republic, and interactions between Jewish and gentile communities took place without major tensions, marked as they were in general by reciprocal respect. The mutually supporting functions of scholarship, culture and politics in the Republic was not unique, but the complementary relations between these three elements were beneficial for the

---

28   Molhuysen, *Bronnen* I 1913, p. 39.

29   Jonathan Israel, *The Dutch Republic. Its Rise, Greatness, and Fall 1477–1806* (Oxford: Clarendon Press, 1998), pp. 570–571: 'Matters improved dramatically, as with so much else, with the transformation of the military and economic situation, in the early 1590s. Suddenly the Republic was secure and money available for new professors, books, and facilities. [...] Academic printing and bookselling at Leiden suddenly flourished and during the 1590s the Leiden University Library became one of the most considerable in Protestant Europe'.

30   Cf. Frank E. Manuel, *The Broken Staff. Judaism through Christian Eyes* (Cambridge, Mass. & London: Cambridge University Press, 1992), p. 50; J.C.H. Lebram, 'Hebräische Studien zwischen Ideal und Wirklichkeit an der Universität Leiden in den Jahren 1575–1619', in M.J.M. de Haan (et al., eds.), *In navolging. Een bundel studies aangeboden aan C.C. de Bruin bij zijn afscheid als hoogleraar te Leiden* (Leiden: Brill, 1975), pp. 317–357.

A LIFE IN TWO PARTS   27

contacts maintained between Christians and Jews.[31] Leiden played a critical role in fostering this atmosphere.[32]

At Leiden, the faculty of liberal arts did not occupy a minor or preparatory role in the university curriculum, but enjoyed a mature and independent position in the academic hierarchy. 'It was ultimately not theology, but the classical and Eastern studies ... which would ensure the perpetual renown of our university.'[33] The intention that 'the principal motivation for the foundation of this university would be [the study of] theology', was made clear from the erection of Leiden's academy.[34] Although the influence of the Reformed religion on the education and governance of the university should not be underestimated, it concerned mostly the manner in which theology was taught. The liberal arts were entirely outwith the sphere of Calvinism and the Reformed creed.[35] The appointment of Scaliger, the botanist Carolus Clusius (1526–1609) and the polymath Claude Saumaise (1588–1653) as honorary professors, who could enjoy an unfettered role in teaching and scholarship, fits entirely within this notion.

The privilege that confirmed the foundation of Leiden University spoke of the ideal of *eruditio trilinguis*, of erudition in Latin, Greek and Hebrew. The Hebrew language was regarded not only as the original tongue of the Bible and therefore closely bound to the study of theology, but also as a formative part of the classical education of scholars.[36] The appointment of a professor in Hebrew was an integral part of the university's programme. The Leiden minister Caspar de Gendt was the first to occupy this chair, but he did so symbolically,

---

31   Aaron L. Katchen, *Christian Hebraists and Dutch Rabbis. Seventeenth Century Apologetics and the Study of Maimonides* Mishneh Torah (Cambridge: Harvard University Center for Jewish Studies, 1984), p. 15.

32   For the first years of Leiden University, see the concise overview by Johan Huizinga, 'Wat de jonge hoogeschool te bieden had' in *Verzamelde werken* VIII (Haarlem: Tjeenk Willink, 1951), pp. 351–354.

33   The privilege for the foundation of the university of 6 January 1575 emphasises a vision to include the liberal arts and sciences alongside the 'study of theology' in the curriculum. Molhuysen, *Bronnen* I, pp. 7*–9*: 'Privilege for the foundation of the university': 'To allow doctors and teachers to read and study freely and publicly in the same academy and university, the study of theology, jurisprudence and medicine, as well as the philosophies and the liberal arts, and in the languages Latin, Greek and Hebrew, and to employ the same doctors and teachers for this purpose'. See also Lebram, *Hebräische Studien*, pp. 317–357.

34   Jan Jansz Orlers, *Beschrijvinge der stadt Leyden, inhoudende den begin, voortganck ende oprechtinghe vande Academie* (Leiden: Abraham Commelinus and Delft, Andries Cloeting, 1641), p. 228 (USTC 1121993).

35   Johan Huizinga, *Nederlandse beschaving in de zeventiende eeuw. Een schets* (Amsterdam: Contact, 1998), p. 87.

36   Lebram, *Hebräische Studien*, p. 317.

and never taught at the university. The promise of Prince William of Orange to offer the possibility of Hebrew education at Leiden was finally fulfilled with the appointment of Hermannus Rennecherus (1550–after 1605); this appointment did not last long, as Rennecherus was fired after being involved in a tavern brawl. It was only on 20 June 1577, with the appointment of Johannes Drusius as professor of Hebrew, Chaldaic and Syriac that the study of Hebrew became a permanent fixture in Leiden's curriculum.[37] The strong foundation laid for the study of Eastern languages would later be of immense benefit to Scaliger.[38]

The study of philology at Leiden advanced rapidly alongside the study of Hebrew and the other Eastern languages. The foundation of the university in 1575 gave a powerful impulse to the development of philology in the Dutch Republic. It is true that the two stars of the discipline, Justus Lipsius and Scaliger, were from the Southern Netherlands and France, but they would be responsible for developing a Dutch philological school that would play a leading role in European scholarship. To Scaliger, philology was an all-encompassing field of study in which theology, jurisprudence, languages, history, poetry and medicine could be investigated alongside one another.

Leiden was long considered to be a humanist university. The university was liberal in its make-up and was a bulwark of tolerance.[39] This would change in 1618, when sterner Reformed elements of the Republic clashed with its liberal rulers. The conflict between the Arminians or Remonstrants (the supporters of Jacobus Arminius) and the Gomarists or Contra-Remonstrants (the supporters of Franciscus Gomarus) would lead during the Synod of Dordt to a decisive victory of the Contra-Remonstrants. After 1619, the university of Leiden would become more stringent and dogmatic in its outlook. This phase Scaliger would never witness; instead, he perceived Leiden as a political, religious and scholarly haven compared to the situation in his native France.

4   Correspondence and the Republic of Letters

Scaliger maintained good contacts with his old friends in France. These often gathered together in so-called 'cabinets' or 'salons'. In these gatherings in Paris

---

37   In the sixteenth and seventeenth centuries, Chaldaic was the common term for the language that today is often described as Aramaic. Both are used in the text.

38   Lebram, *Hebräische Studien*, pp. 336.

39   J.J. Woltjer, 'Introduction' in Th.H. & G.H.M. Posthumus Meyes (eds.), *Leiden University in the Seventeenth Century. An Exchange of Learning* (1975), pp. 16–18; Willem Otterspeer, *Het bolwerk van de vrijheid. De Leidse universiteit, 1575–1672* (Amsterdam: Bert Bakker, 2000), pp. 138–140.

A LIFE IN TWO PARTS

and other French cities, jurists and philologists would meet each other, read letters together and exchange books. The cabinets were inspired by the scholarly circles of the Pléiades and the Palace Academy of Henry III, in which Desportes, Dorat and Ronsard had played important roles.[40]

One of the most important cabinets was that of De Thou, founded in 1575. This gathering was maintained after De Thou's death by Pierre and Jacques Dupuy under the name of *Cabinet des frères*. After their death, Ismaël Boulliau (1605–1694) took charge of the cabinet until 1669. Scholars like De Thou, Dupuy and the brother Pithou would gather together every Sunday between 8 and 11 AM and on feast days at the Franciscan convent of the Cordeliers.

The Pithou brothers belonged to a group of *érudits du roi*, also known as the *Pléiades*. These scholar-poets fulfilled an important role in society, the arts and the sciences. Other influential members of this group included the jurist and writer Antoine Loisel (1536–1617), who, like Scaliger, had studied with Jacques Cujas, or Cuiacius (1522–1590), the historian and poet Étienne Pasquier (1529–1615), Claude Fauchet (1530–1602) and Louis le Carron (1534–1613).[41] The salons of the family Dupuy and De Thou were prominent centres where humanists met one another and exchanged information and books.[42] Both families belonged to the cultural and political elite of Paris; there were also familial ties between the two groups, thanks to the marriage in 1576 between Claude Dupuy and Claude Sanguin, a member of the De Thou family.[43]

During his time in France, Scaliger would never stay long in Paris, and was not a frequent participant in the cabinets and salons. He did join happily in meetings at the house of De Thou, but not in those at the Franciscan convent of the Cordeliers.[44] During these sessions he would make the acquaintance of various scholars with whom he would keep in contact later in life. This included the physician Jacques Houllier (1498/1504–1562), Claude Dupuy's

---

40 Harcourt Brown, *Scientific Organizations in Seventeenth Century France (1620–1680)* (Baltimore: Williams & Wikons, 1934), p. 6.

41 Other guests who took part frequently in these gatherings included Nicolas Levèfre, the French diplomat Jean Hotman, Isaac Casaubon and Jacques Houlier. Scaliger corresponded with most of these men and maintained cordial relations with them. D.R. Kelley, *Foundations of Modern Historical Scholarship. Language, Law, and History in the French Renaissance* (New York, London: Columbia University Press, 1970), p. 245.

42 Cf. Mark Pattison, *Isaac Casaubon 1559–1614* (London: Longmans Green and Co, 1875), pp. 128–131.

43 Claude Sanguin († 1631) was the daughter of Jacques Sanguin, seigneur de Livry, and niece of the premier président Christophe de Thou and aunt of Jacques-Auguste de Thou.

44 *Scaligerana* 1740, p. 595 below De Thou: 'Je n'ay point veu la bibliotheque de Monsieur [Jacques-Auguste] de Thou, car je n'ay point esté à Paris lorsqu'il estoit maistre de son bien'. Also: W. McCuaig, 'On Claude Dupuy (1545–1594)', pp. 51–52.

best friend and member of the *grand conseil* of Paris, Pierre Pithou and the councilor Louis Servin (1555–1626).[45]

The bond between Scaliger and Dupuy was close: Scaliger's dedication to Dupuy in his edition of Catullus, Tibullus and Propertius of 1576 is testimony of this. In 1584, Scaliger would also dedicate his *Stromateus versuum Graecorum proverbialium* to Dupuy. For his part, Dupuy kept Scaliger informed of all the latest titles that appeared that might have been of relevance to him. His two sons also continued to be loyal suppliers of books to Scaliger until his death. They even supplied him with a manuscript of Eusebius from their own library, which Scaliger made use of for his edition of the *Thesaurus temporum* of 1606.[46]

5   The Printing House of Plantin and Raphelengius in Leiden

Scaliger also maintained good relations with printers, including with the famous Christopher Plantin (1520–1589) of Antwerp, with whom he was in touch via his correspondents. One cannot speak of an extensive correspondence between the two, but Plantin was indirectly of critical importance for the contact between Scaliger and Lipsius. In 1583, Plantin fled from Antwerp and settled in April of that year in Leiden. There he continued his printing business.[47] On 1 May 1583, he was appointed printer to the University of Leiden. The university had become a significant source of business for print shops and the book trade.[48] With the arrival of Plantin at Leiden, the centre of gravity of the Netherlandish print trade moved gradually from Antwerp to the Northern Netherlands. The arrival of Plantin in effect marked the beginning of Hebrew printing in Leiden. Plantin, who would remain loyal to the Catholic faith, did not stay long in Leiden. His premises there he regarded as

---

45   *Perroniana Et Thuana. Ed. Secunda* (Coloniae Agrippinae, Scagen, s.n., 1669), pp. 345–346 (USTC 2662512). Houllier travelled, like Dupuy, to Italy and mainta. ined contacts with various scholars there. See the letter of Dupuy to Pinelli of 15 August 1579 in: Anna Maria Raugei (ed.), *Gian Vincenzo Pinelli et Claude Dupuy. Une correspondance entre deux humanistes* (Roma: Olschki, 2002).

46   The manuscript from the library of Dupuy used by Scaliger survives today as BnF MS. lat. 4884.

47   Colin Clair, *Christopher Plantin* (London: Cassell & Company LTD, 1960), pp. 150–160; Sandra Langereis, *De Woordenaar. Christoffel Plantijn, 's werelds grootste drukker en uitgever (1520–1589)* (Amsterdam: Balans, 2014), pp. 336–343.

48   J.G.C.A. Briels, *Zuidnederlandse boekdrukkers en boekverkopers in de Republiek der Verenigde Nederlanden omstreeks 1570–1630. Een bijdrage tot de kennis van de geschiedenis van het boek* (Nieuwkoop: De Graaf, 1974), p. 83.

A LIFE IN TWO PARTS

a temporary solution, 'to keep him above water while his business in Antwerp was in danger'.[49] After the conquest of Antwerp by the Duke of Parma on 27 August 1585, he returned to the city to take charge of the recovery of his print shop. The following year, on 3 March, he formally handed over the premises at Leiden to his Protestant son-in-law.

From 1589 onwards, the daily operation of the print shop in Leiden would be led by the sons of Raphelengius, Christopher and Franciscus II. Under their leadership, printing in Hebrew and other Eastern languages would become a specialty of the Leiden print trade. This was most necessary too, as apart from a few grammars, dictionaries and Bibles, there was little Hebrew printing, and demand far outstripped supply.[50] Especially after the fall of Antwerp, large numbers of highly skilled artisans migrated from the Southern Netherlands to the north, where they contributed much-needed expertise in the fields of printing, composition and typefounding. The growth of the print industry in Leiden received an enormous impulse from this wave of migration. In the period 1557–1605, twenty-six southern printers and booksellers arrived in Leiden, twenty-one of whom came from Antwerp.[51] In the final quarter of the sixteenth century, almost as many new print shops and bookshops were established in Leiden as there had been in the entire hundred years previously.[52]

The blossoming of the Leiden print industry was used as one of the principal means to entice Scaliger to come to the city. To persuade him, Scaliger's good friend Paul Choart de Buzanval (1551–1607), the first French ambassador in The Hague, sent him a letter on 2 January 1593. In this he urged him to take over the position left by Lipsius at the university.[53] De Buzanval described the

---

49   Briels, *Zuidnederlandse boekdrukkers en boekverkopers*, p. 89.

50   R.G. Fuks-Mansfeld, 'The Hebrew Book Trade in Amsterdam in the Seventeenth Century' in C. Berkvens-Stevelinck (et al., eds.), *Le magasin de l'univers. The Dutch Republic as the Centre of the European Book Trade* (Leiden: E.J. Brill, 1992), p. 156.

51   A large number of the active printers, some 150 between 1570 and 1619, came originally from the Southern Netherlands, 40% of whom settled in Amsterdam or Leiden. In the period 1600–1630, this share increased to 50%. In 1610, there were some 12 print shops in Leiden, which, together, printed some 1,650 titles. See Claartje Rasterhoff, *Painting and Publishing as Cultural Industries. The Fabric of Creativity in the Dutch Republic, 1580–1800* (Amsterdam: Amsterdam University Press, 2017), pp. 36–45. See also Briels, *Zuidnederlandse boekdrukkers en boekverkopers*, pp. 83–111, especially Table A (page 17) and Table B (page 24).

52   E. van Gulik, 'Drukkers en geleerden. De Leidse Officina Plantiniana (1583–1619)', in *Leiden University in the Seventeenth Century* (Leiden: E.J. Brill, 1975), pp. 367–393 and P.G. Hoftijzer, 'De "belabbering" van het boekbedrijf. De Leidse Officina Raphelengiana, 1586–1619', *De Boekenwereld* 7 (1990–1991), p. 8.

53   Paul Choart de Buzanval was chamberlain of King Henry IV and a good friend of Scaliger. In 1590, he was sent to The Hague as ambassador of France. There he stayed,

32 CHAPTER 1

city of Leiden and its academy in a positive but faithful light. The presence of the flourishing book trade and that of a number of talented printers was also noted by De Buzanval, highlighting especially the *Officina Plantiniana*.[54] It can safely be stated that the local book and print trade was one of the most important factors that persuaded Scaliger to undertake the move.

The printer Raphelengius was in his own right also a learned scholar of Greek, Hebrew and Arabic. He also maintained an extensive network of correspondents and possessed a famous library. These too were factors of importance to Scaliger. In 1586, the year in which Raphelengius took charge of the Plantin print shop in Leiden, he was appointed as extraordinary professor of Hebrew as the successor of Johannes Drusius. A year later this position was upgraded to that of ordinary professor.[55] Raphelengius taught Arabic alongside Hebrew, and can therefore be called the first professor of Arabic at Leiden University. Before the arrival of Scaliger, he was the foremost Orientalist and the pioneer of Arabic studies in the Northern Netherlands.[56] As soon as he was able to hand over the practical business of the print shop to his sons, he

---

except for a brief period in 1602, until his death in 1606. The friendship between the two men also becomes clear from the efforts that De Buzanval made to acquire a privilege for the second edition of Scaliger's *Manilius* (1599–1600) from N. de Neufville, seigneur de Villeroi (1542–1617), Henry IV's secretary of state. See Georg Willem Vreede, *Lettres et Négociations de Paul Choart, Seigneur de Buzanval [...] et de François d'Aerssen* (Leiden: S. & J. Luchtmans, 1846), letter XXV, pp. 153–158.

54 *Correspondence* 2 January 1593 of Choart de Buzanval: 'Ilz ont la plus belle imprimerie de ces pays et tout ce qui estoit de bon dans celle de feu Plantin et Raphalingius, docte personnage et professeur des langues hébraique, syriaque, qui y préside; tant de beaux labeurs que vous tenez soubz la clef et en ténèbres pourront par ce moyen veoir la clairté.' The letter is cited in Molhuysen, *Bronnen* I, pp. 242*–243*. See also Van Gulik, 'Drukkers en geleerden', p. 369; R. Breugelmans, 'Scaliger en de Officina Plantiniana Raphelengii', in: P.G. Hoftijzer (ed.), *Adelaar in de wolken. De Leidse jaren van Josephus Justus Scaliger 1593–1609* (Leiden: Scaliger Instituut, Universiteitsbibliotheek Leiden, 2005), pp. 93–100 especially p. 93.

55 Molhuysen, *Bronnen* I, pp. 46 and 50.

56 Molhuysen, *Bronnen* I, pp. 44, 50, 124*. Raphelengius had studied Arabic in Paris with Postel, just like Scaliger. From 1591 onwards, Raphelengius was studying Arabic on a daily basis. See the letter of Raphelengius to Justus Lipsius of 9 May 1591: 'Ego totos dies domi desideo, in meis studiis Arabicis, ut aliquid certe absolvam antequam Deus me vocet.' ('I dedicate myself at home these days to Arabic, so that I could offer up something worthwhile, before the Lord calls me to him.'). In a letter of Franciscus II Raphelengius to Jan Moretus of 17 January 1591 we read concerning Raphelengius senior that: 'Mon père est totus in studiis arabis et sommes en délibiration de faire des poinçons de la lettre arabesque.' [Museum Plantin-Moretus Antwerpen, Oud Archief, no. 92, pp. 89–90]. It should be noted that in Antwerp, Christopher Plantin already regarded Raphelengius more as a scholar than as a printer: 'un savant et non un homme de métier'.

A LIFE IN TWO PARTS

33

devoted his days to the study of Arabic. Raphelengius is known to have begun a translation of the Qur'an as he admired the poetical style in which the work was written.[57] He also studied the geographical work of Muhammad al-Idrisi, printed by the *Tipographia Medicea* in Florence and sent to him by Hans Dressel of Frankfurt.[58]

De Buzanval expressed the hope that Scaliger would benefit greatly from Raphelengius's knowledge of Eastern languages. The timid Raphelengius was rather more modest about his philological expertise, especially once he had come to know Scaliger after his move, as he later admitted to his friend Lipsius.[59] It is clear that this was humility on the part of Raphelengius. At his appointment as ordinary professor, the senate of the university described him as a man who

> has for a long time studied the ancient languages of Hebrew, Chaldaic, Syriac and Arabic, and is most experienced in these tongues, and is praised most highly by all learned men; so that he cannot only teach beginners in these languages, but can also advance the knowledge of scholars.[60]

Scaliger was also impressed by Raphelengius's knowledge. Never before had he met someone who had learned so much Arabic through self-study.[61] On 20 July 1597, after the death of Raphelengius, Scaliger characterised his friend as the best and most learned man of his time. His death was a great loss for the study of the Eastern languages.[62] Raphelengius had worked closely on the editing and production of the Antwerp Polyglot Bible, and he owned a large library with many rare Eastern manuscripts and books.[63] This library would be of immense value to Scaliger.

---

57   Johannes Henricus Hessels, *Abrahami Ortelii Epistulae* (Cambridge: Typis Academiae, 1887), no. 216: 'si essem liberior a curis typographicis, ego pergerem vertere, ut coepi'.

58   Hessels, *Abrahami Ortelii Epistulae*, no. 226.

59   *Iusti Lipsi Epistolae* (*ILE*) Pars. VI: 1593 ed. by Jeanine De Landtsheer (Brussel: Koninklijke Academie voor Wetenschappen Letteren en Schone Kunsten van België, 1994), no. 1478: Letter from Raphelengius to Lipsius, 31 August 1593: 'nosti me semper timidiorem esse, ac de viribus meis diffidentem.'

60   Molhuysen, *Bronnen* I, p. 127*.

61   H.F. Wijnman, 'The Origin of Arabic Typography in Leiden' in: *Books on the Orient, published by E.J. Brill, Leiden, Holland* (Leiden: E.J. Brill, 1957), p. xi.

62   *Correspondence* 18 August 1597 to Casaubon: 'Nam et his diebus amisimus optimum et doctissimum virum Franciscum Raphelengium.'

63   Van Gulik, *Drukkers en geleerden*, pp. 367–393.

In the publication of his books, Scaliger would profit greatly from Raphelengius's expertise as printer, but also as scholar. Indeed, almost immediately after Scaliger's arrival, there emerged a fruitful co-operation between the two men. Their interest in Arabic and Hebrew soon also encompassed the study of Persian. Scaliger considered Persian of importance for his study of chronology. Together, they collected a large number of Eastern manuscripts and books. The co-operation extended further too: Raphelengius printed several scholarly works by Scaliger in which he used his specialised Oriental typefaces. For the publication of the *De emendatione temporum*, Raphelengius ordered Arabic, Ethiopian and Samaritan type. These were cut and cast in Leiden by Thomas de Vechter, a former collaborator of Henri vander Keere of Ghent.[64] We can assume that the presence of Raphelengius's printing house and library not only contributed to the development of the study of Eastern languages at Leiden, but also contributed greatly to Scaliger's decision to settle there.

That Raphelengius was both curious and delighted about the arrival of Scaliger to Leiden is clear from a letter which he wrote to Lipsius on 31 August 1593, five days after Scaliger's entry in the city. In this he sketched an image of Scaliger as an extremely learned man, and underscored the importance of the fact that Scaliger's library would also come to Leiden.[65] Raphelengius expected that he and the broader university community would benefit greatly from the valuable sources held in Scaliger's collection. Almost immediately after his arrival, Scaliger offered Raphelengius access to a part of his collection of historical and cosmographical books, so that they could publish these works in translation together. Given Raphelengius's interests, we can presume that virtually all these items would have been books in Eastern languages. The project was ultimately not fulfilled, but the two men would work together, in a co-operative manner proposed by Scaliger, on the production of an Arabic dictionary.

---

64   Leo Fuks & Rena Fuks, 'The Hebrew Production of the Plantin-Raphelengius Presses in Leyden, 1585–1615', *Studia Rosenthaliana* 4/1 (1970), p. 3; H.F. Wijnman, 'De studie van het Ethiopisch en de ontwikkeling van de Ethiopische typografie in West-Europa in de 16de eeuw' II: 'De ontwikkeling van de Ethiopische typografie in West-Europa in de 16de eeuw', *Het boek* 32 (1955), pp. 237–239.

65   Letter from Franciscus Raphelengius to Lipsius of 31 August 1593. Cf. J. Lipsius, *ILE*. Pars VI: 1593, no. 1478; 'Habet libros historicos et cosmographicos, ad quos vertendos me hortatur, me extricaturus, ubi res obscurior moram iniicere possit.' Intially, the curators had considered housing Scaliger with Raphelengius, according to Molhuysen, *Bronnen* I, 1913, p. 76.

FIGURE 3   Portrait of the printer-scholar Franciscus Raphelengius, aged 58. *Icones Leidenses* 26

In Leiden, Raphelengius occupied a crucial place in Scaliger's network. As printer, he maintained good international connections, not only with the Plantin press in Antwerp but also with colleagues in other great European print centres. Thanks to Raphelengius, Scaliger was able to gain access to the annual book fairs at Frankfurt.[66] Frankfurt was an important centre of trade for Hebrew books, at this point mostly of Italian origin, as the city was home to the largest Jewish community in Germany.[67] The efficient trade links with Paris, where Plantin had an agent, was also to Scaliger's advantage when it came to the supply of books. Scaliger's relationship with Raphelengius was in this sense essential, especially for the acquisition of more items for his collection of Oriental books.

On 20 July 1597, after a short period of illness, Raphelengius died, aged 58.[68] After his passing, Scaliger remembered his friend as 'an upright and erudite man, a friend who I will miss with much pain in my heart.'[69] Printing activities at the Raphelengius firm continued the next month under the auspices of Raphelengius's sons, Christopher, Franciscus II and Joost. After the death of Christopher on 17 December 1600, Franciscus the younger remained active until 1619, when the printing house ceased operation.[70]

6   The Importance of Good Books and Good Libraries

When one investigates Scaliger's arrival at Leiden, it becomes clear that from the very beginning of the negotiations, there was abundant talk of books. Scaliger received books as gifts, and from the first letters from Tuningius it is

---

66   Plantin and Raphelengius were sometimes forced to travel to Frankfurt via Amsterdam and Hamburg, and thence over land. In *Correspondence* 2 September [1598] to Taubmannus in Wittenberg, Scaliger wrote that he considered the routes used for the book fairs in Frankfurt to be the only reliable routes to keep up his correspondence with scholars in Germany.

67   Stephen G. Burnett, *From Christian Hebraism to Jewish studies. Johannes Buxtorf (1564–1629) and Hebrew Learning in the Seventeenth Century* (Leiden, New York, Köln: Brill, 1996), p. 37.

68   Raphelengius discussed his illness in a letter to Justus Lipsius of 1 April 1595 in: ILE Pars VIII, 2004.

69   *Correspondence* 18 August 1597 to Hoeschelius. See also *Correspondence* 18 August 1597, note 8 to Casaubon.

70   For the activities of Plantin, Raphelengius and his sons as printers of the university in Leiden: P.C. Molhuysen, 'De Academie-drukkers' in *Pallas Leidensis MCMXXV* (Leiden: S.C. van Doesburg, 1925), pp. 305–322 and Hoftijzer, 'De "belabbering" van het boekbedrijf', pp. 8–17.

A LIFE IN TWO PARTS   37

obvious that Scaliger would not leave France without his books. This was an
absolute necessity for him.

At the end of the sixteenth century, the size of the university library of
Leiden was modest. The library contained all the standard editions and reference works one would expect, and a small collection of manuscripts. Scaliger
expected that he would find few relevant sources for his research. In the section of Oriental works: the library was indeed badly equipped. More attractive
to Scaliger was the notion that he might profit from the personal libraries of
Leiden's collectors and professors. These libraries, like that of the statesman
Philips van Marnix van Sint Aldegonde (1538–1598) included many Eastern
books of relevance to theology: Hebrew Bibles, psalters, concordances, grammars and dictionaries.[71] The library of the diplomat and merchant Daniël van
der Meulen (1554–1600) also contained useful sources that would come within
reach of Scaliger if he settled in Leiden.[72]

Scaliger expected that other book collections in Leiden would not prove
rich in works in Eastern languages, excepting some Hebrew books. This did
represent a problem to Scaliger, especially because both he and the curators of
the university initially supposed that he would not be employed at the university for a long time. The curators therefore thought that it was not advisable to
transport Scaliger's entire library to Leiden. Instead, Scaliger decided to select
that portion of his library that was absolutely vital to his research, and take
these books to Leiden. One can presume that Scaliger chose to leave behind in
France those books and manuscripts that he would expect to find in the university library of Leiden, or could purchase in Leiden without much trouble.
The choice was rather clear: Scaliger selected all his books and manuscripts
printed or written in Eastern languages.

In Leiden, Scaliger reveled in the opportunity to supplement his library with
many more rare Eastern printed books and valuable manuscripts. He relied on
the local booksellers for this purpose, but he also remained dependent on his
French network, built up before 1593 with much care. With the aid of innu-
merable letters, Scaliger requested books and manuscripts from his circle of
scholars, diplomats, printers, agents and students. These correspondents all

---

71   Marnix van Sint Aldegonde owned a library of some 1,600 volumes, which, excepting his
      juridical books, was sold at auction after his death in 1599. See *Catalogue of the Library
      of Philips van Marnix van Sint-Aldegonde sold by Auction (July 6th), Leiden, Christophorus
      Guyot, 1599* (Nieuwkoop: B. de Graaf, 1964).

72   Van der Meulen's library contained at auction in 1600–1601 some 1,200 items. *Catalo-
      gus librorum bibliothecae clarissimi doctissimique viri, piae memoriae Danielis Vander
      Meulen. Catalogue vande boecken* ([Leiden], ex officina Plantiniana apud Christophorus
      Raphelengius, 1600; USTC 429992) and Van Selm, *Menighte treffelijcke Boecken* no. 23.

tapped into their own networks, creating the vast European book network that Scaliger profited from so greatly. Scaliger's library in Leiden would ultimately grow to a collection of some 2,250 books. Until the final days of his life, Scaliger made use of books from his library. Daniel Heinsius remarked that 'the last books that Scaliger consulted before his death were an edition of Polybius and Lipsius's book on the art of war.'[73] Scaliger cared for all of his books, but his books in Eastern languages undeniably occupied an exceptional position in his library. This collection of Eastern books fulfilled an important role in the final decade of Scaliger's scholarly development. At his death in 1609, Scaliger bequeathed specifically this part of his library to the University of Leiden, supplemented by a number of his Greek and Latin manuscripts.

---

73   Cited in: George W. Robinson, *Autobiography of Joseph Scaliger. With Autobiographical Selections from His Letters, His Testament and the Funeral Orations by Daniel Heinsius and Dominicus Baudius* (Cambridge: Harvard University Press, 1927), p. 112, note 1. The annotated edition of Scaliger's Polybius came into the possession of Daniel Heinsius, who gave the copy to his cousin Janus Rutgersius (1589–1625), who had also been a student of Scaliger. The book by Lipsius concerns an edition of *De militia Romana libri quinque, commentarius ad Polybium* (Antverpiae: ex officina Plantiniana apud vid. Plantin & Joannem Moretum, 1596; USTC 402380). A copy of this edition, annotated by Scaliger, is found in the auction catalogue of the library of Nicolaas Heinsius (1682). Scaliger also owned a copy of *Ek ton Polubiou tou Megalopolitou eklogai peri presbeion* (Antwerpen: ex officina Christophe Plantin, 1582) edited by Fulvio Orsini (UTSC 401920, UBL 757 D 6).

CHAPTER 2

Scaliger as Scholar and Collector in France, 1552–1593

Julius Caesar Scaliger, Joseph's father, was Italian, hailing from Rocca di Riva on Lake Garda. Until the age of thirty-one he was a soldier, but then left the martial life behind to study philosophy, Greek and medicine at the University of Padua. Legend has it that Julius Scaliger developed an interest in medicine during his military adventures, and that on one of his campaigns he made a partial translation of the *Opera* of the classical physician Galen, the forefather of Renaissance medicine.[1] Around 1525, Julius Scaliger moved to Agen in France, where he was employed as the personal physician to the Bishop of Agen, Antonio della Rovere.[2]

As a classically trained humanist, Julius Scaliger maintained polymath interests. He wrote a treatise on Latin grammar, *De causis latinae linguae* (1540), and a treatise on *Poetica*, published posthumously in 1561. He produced commentaries on works of botany by Aristotle and Theophrastus. Julius Scaliger was also not afraid to enter in scholarly polemical disputes.[3] In his *Ciceronianus* (1531) he lashed out at Desiderius Erasmus of Rotterdam (1467–1536), whose interpretation of Latin grammar he deemed erroneous.

It is likely that Scaliger senior would not have been able to write his works without access to a decent library. The young Joseph Scaliger would therefore have been surrounded by books and manuscripts from a very young age. It is impossible to reconstruct what books Julius Scaliger would have kept in his library, but we can deduce, given his scholarly interests, that this must have included some works on philology, anatomy, and botany.

---

1 This is now manuscript UBL SCA 18. Two epigrams in this work, one by Julius Scaliger on himself, and one by Joseph Scaliger about his father, give the impression of the proud identity of the Scaliger family.

2 On the life of J.C. Scaliger, see: V. Hall, 'Life of Julius Caesar Scaliger (1484–1558)', in *Transactions of the American Philosophical Society*, New Series, Vol. 40, No. 2 (1950), pp. 85–170; M. Billanovich, 'Benedetto Bordon e Giulio Cesare Scaligero,' *Italia Medioevale e Umanistica* 11 (1968), pp. 187–256.

3 Julius Caesar Scaliger is often characterised as a vain and prickly individual. He had a great memory, a profound perspective on issues, and made many enemies. These qualities are sometimes also ascribed to his son. Cf. F. Galton, *Hereditary Genius. An Inquiry into its Law and Consequences* (London, New York: Macmillan & Co., 1892), pp. 181–182.

© KONINKLIJKE BRILL BV, LEIDEN, 2025 | DOI:10.1163/9789004701526_004

In June 1552, when Joseph Scaliger was twelve years old, he moved to Bordeaux together with his brothers Léonard and Jean Constant, to attend the Collège de Guyenne.[4] They enrolled in the school at an auspicious time, as it flourished thanks to the talents of skilled teachers and a growing number of students, including Michel de Montaigne (1533–1592). Grammar schools like the Collège de Guyenne provided an excellent education for young men from the upper strata of society, and offered essential preparatory instruction for university. The young Scaliger's lessons were mostly focussed on Latin grammar and classical literature, the core of the curriculum of all grammar schools; there was relatively little time for Greek.[5] Julius Scaliger bought books for each of his sons for use at school, and these Latin grammars and classics are highly likely to have laid the foundation for Joseph Scaliger's own future library.[6]

At Bordeaux, Scaliger showed himself to be an ambitious and intelligent student. He made rapid progress in mastering the Latin language.[7] The professor of Latin, Marcus Antonius Muret (1526–1585), an exceptionally learned philologist, was an important influence. Muret was an admirer of Julius Scaliger, and took the young Joseph under his wing. He would meet him again in Paris, when Joseph Scaliger studied there. It was Muret who taught Scaliger the principles of philology and emphasised the importance of source-based inquiry into the Latin and Greek languages. These lessons would be instrumental for Scaliger's development as a scholar, and he would adopt similar principles of comparative, source-based philology when studying Oriental languages.[8] Muret's advocacy for the use of original sources would be a lifelong inspiration

---

4 This period lasted from June 1552 until July 1555. Reports on Josephus Scaliger's progress as a student can be found in the letters of various tutors to Julius Caesar Scaliger in J. de Bourrousse de Laffore, 'Jules-César de Lescale', *Recueil de la Société d'agriculture, sciences et arts d'Agen* 2/1 (1860), pp. 33–42.

5 Scaliger senior spent little time teaching Josephus Greek, because, like many scholars of his age, he considered it an 'Oriental' language that was therefore inferior to Latin.

6 V. Hall, 'The Scaliger Family Papers', *Proceedings of the American Philosophical Society* 82/2 (1948), p. 121.

7 Joseph was taught Latin by his father at a young age. See for more reports on Scaliger's progress as a student the letters from his tutors Girard Roques, Simon Beaupé and Laurens de Lamarque to Julius Caesar Scaliger in UBL BPL 2623, some of which have been reprinted in: De Bourrouse de Laffore, 'Jules-César de Lescale', pp. 33–42.

8 Muret's philosophy of teaching, that strove towards a fusion between poetry and philosophy, also exercised considerable influence on his students Michel de Montaigne and Justus Lipsius. See on Muret: Charles Dejob, *Marc-Antoine Muret. Un professeur français en Italie dans la seconde moitié du XVIe siècle* (Paris: Ernest Thorin, 1881) and Sidney Lee, *The French Renaissance in England. An Account of the Literary relations of England and France in the Sixteenth Century* (New York: Charles Scribner's Sons, 1910), p. 382.

SCALIGER AS SCHOLAR AND COLLECTOR IN FRANCE

to Scaliger. The collecting of reliable historical sources, both handwritten and printed, to cast a new light on ancient texts, would dominate Scaliger's life.

Between June 1552 and July 1555, when Scaliger and his brothers returned to Agen to escape a plague epidemic in Bordeaux, another tutor, Laurens de Lamarque, bought a variety of classical works for Scaliger, money provided by father Julius. These included an edition of the letters of Ovid, the *Proverbs*, Cicero's *Epistolae ad Familiares* and *Epistolae ad Atticum*, two editions of Textor, and editions of Horace, Caesar, Valerius Maximus and Virgil.[9] Other purchases for Joseph Scaliger included a Greek grammar, the Latin grammar of Philip Melanchthon (1497–1560), a Portuguese grammar and an edition of the psalms of David.[10] These acquisitions demonstrate that the philological interests of the young Scaliger were already broadening beyond Latin. One can surmise that the editions that were bought for Scaliger were mostly school-books, published in small formats and available for relatively low prices. More expensive folio editions of these texts would have been intended for established scholars and book collectors.

The personal book collection that Scaliger possessed at school was probably of limited size, but he did enjoy access to other collections. He and his brothers shared books, and it is likely that his tutors would grant them access to their personal libraries and loan out books to students, a common practice at many schools. To the young Scaliger, maintaining relations with scholars and collectors was as important as the collecting of sources. At home he would have met various scholarly friends of his father, including the lexicographer Robert

---

9   In the Auction Catalogue of 1609 there is a Manutius edition of the *Epistolae ad Atticum* of 1544 listed on page 17. Given the scholarly nature of this edition it is unlikely to have been marketed towards a young student. The editions of Jean Tixier de Ravisi (1480–1524) are *Specimen epithetorum* (Paris: ex officina Henri Estienne (I) in aedibus Regnault Chaudière, 1518; USTC 181875): a work concerning classical mythology, and widely used for the study of Latin; and an edition of the *Officinae partim historicis, partim poeticis referta disciplinis* ([Paris]: typis Antoine Aussourd prostat vaenalis in taberna Regnault Chaudière, 1520; USTC 181968).

10   Possibly a copy of the *De prosodia de syntaxi grammatica Philippi Melanchthonis, Latina, iam denuo recognita, et plerisque in locis locupletata* (Nürnberg: apud Johann Petreius, 1548; USTC 660368) or Melanchton's Grammatica Latina, jam denuo recognita, et plerisque in locis locupletata (Paris: ex officina Robert Estienne, 1550; USTC 196286). Possibly a copy of the *Grammatica da lingoagem portuguesa* by Fernão de Oliveira (Lisboa: Germão Galharde, 1536; USTC 347221). See: Antonio Joaquim Anselmo, *Bibliografia das obras impressas em Portugal no século XVI* (Lisboa: Officinas Graficas da Bibliotheca Nacional, 1926) no. 607. The book cost 30 sol, and was the most expensive item in this selection. De Bourrousse de Laffore, *Jules-César de Lescale*, pp. 33–42. The list of purchased books and their prices is taken from a letter of De Lamarque to Julius Scaliger of 1555. A portion of this letter is printed in Robinson, *The Autobiography*, pp. 29–30.

Constantin (1530–1605), who stayed in Agen between 1555 and 1557. The bond between Constantin, Joseph Scaliger and Sylvius Scaliger (1530–1585), Joseph's older brother, was especially close.[11] Constantin garnered renown with the publication in 1555 of his *Nomenclator*, the first attempt to provide an overview of all the books printed in France.[12] For this work, Constantin gathered considerable information about the contents of English libraries, as well as the French Bibliothèque Royale.

After the death of Julius Scaliger in 1558, Constantin remained a close friend of the family. He offered Joseph Scaliger his first introduction to the book trade, to the world of printers and booksellers. Constantin also introduced Scaliger to his network of scholars and correspondents and urged Scaliger to offer his services to the botanist Jacques Daléchamps (1513–1588), a good friend of Constantin. Scaliger also took his first steps as editor of a scholarly text thanks to Constantin, who involved Scaliger in the publication of the posthumous edition of Julius Scaliger's *Poetices libri septem*, which appeared in 1561. It had been an explicit wish of Julius Scaliger that Constantin publish this work: a month before his death on 21 October 1558, he presented his son with the manuscript, and instructed him to hand it to Constantin. An earlier attempt to publish the same text, made by Jean de Maumont (1505–1584) and the Parisian printer Charles Estienne (1504–1564) had failed.[13] Joseph Scaliger promptly sent the manuscript to Constantin, who was then resident in Lyon.

Initially, Constantin approached Jean Crespin (1520–1572), a prominent Lyon printer and key figure in the Reformation, to publish the *Poetica*.[14] To Constantin and the Scaligers it was clearly important to maintain good relationships with co-religionists, and Crespin seemed a natural choice. Yet Crespin was not the first publisher of the *Poetica*: apparently he delayed the project, so the text was sent to the press in Geneva at the behest of Antoine Vincent (1536–1568), one of the most important *marchand-libraires* of Lyon

---

11   M. Magnien, 'Le *Nomenclator* de Robert Constantin (1555), première bibliographie française?', in H. Cazes (ed.), *Renaissance and Reformation* 34/3 (2011), p. 68.

12   Robert Constantin, *Nomenclator insignium scriptorum, quorum libri extant vel manuscripti, vel impressi: ex Bibliothecis Galliae & Angliae.* [...] (Paris: Apud André Wechel, 1555; USTC 151872). Concerning this *Nomenclator*, see Magnien, 'Le *Nomenclator* de Robert Constantin (1555)', pp. 65–89.

13   R. Magnien, 'Robert Constantin, éditeur de J.-C. Scaliger', in Franco Giacone and Jean Dupèbe (eds.), *Esculape et Dionysos. Mélanges en l'honneur de Jean Céard* (Genève: Droz, 2008), pp. 1045–1063.

14   Jean-François Gilmont, *Jean Crespin. Un éditeur réformé du XVIᵉ siècle* (Genève: Droz, 1981).

SCALIGER AS SCHOLAR AND COLLECTOR IN FRANCE

in the middle of the sixteenth century. Shortly afterwards, the book was also re-issued with a Lyon title page, also by Vincent.[15]

Thanks to his role as co-editor of his father's *Poetica*, Joseph Scaliger became well known to Antoine Vincent. This connection, and the broader introduction to the world of publishing, would be of great value to Scaliger later in life, when publishing his own works. His debut would be his *Conjectanea in Varronem*, a commentary on Varro's use of the Latin language, that appeared in Paris in 1564. In Lyon, Scaliger made contacts with printers, merchants, and scholars. Many of them were Calvinists; Scaliger himself had converted to Calvinism in 1562. Religious loyalties did not shape entirely Scaliger's scholarly network, and he corresponded intensively with Catholic scholars.[16] What is obvious, is that Scaliger was less trusting of Catholics. With the exception of his patron Chasteigner, Scaliger loaned out his books only to Protestant contacts, and it was Protestant friends who acted as his messengers or agents. These Calvinist contacts would be of immense use to Scaliger after his arrival at Leiden in 1593.

1   Scaliger the Philologist: Learning Greek and Oriental Languages

It is undeniable that, at the end of his life, Scaliger was regarded as one of the foremost philologists of his time. How Scaliger gained this expertise and learned so many languages, especially the Eastern tongues, remains somewhat of a mystery. Scaliger did not leave any coherent account of his early philological tutelage. It is certain that he first encountered Oriental languages during his time at the University of Paris. He matriculated at the University of Paris in 1559, at the age of nineteen, and from this moment onwards his life became ever more shaped by books. An enthusiastic autodidact, in Paris Scaliger taught himself Greek and Hebrew.[17]

---

15   Antoine Vincent received the privilege for the printing of the *Poetica* in September 1560. Constantin received the privileges for several other books by Julius Caesar Scaliger, including his edition of Theophrastus, seven months later, on 13 April 1561. The second, third and fourth printings of the *Poetica* appeared with Petrus Santandreanus in Geneva in 1581, 1586 and 1594.

16   According to Table 1 in Van Miert, *Limits of Transconfessional Contact*, 2010, p. 383, the religious affiliation of his 230 correspondents was broken down as 41.3% Protestants, 31.7% Catholics and 27% unknown.

17   Josephus Justus Scaliger, *Epistola de vetustate et splendore gentis Scaligerae, et Julii Caesari Scaligeri vita, Julii Caesari Scaligeri oratio in luctu filioli audecti, item testimonia de gente Scaligera et Julio Caesare Scaligero* (Leiden: ex officina Plantiniana apud Franciscus I Raphelengius, 1594; USTC 423322): 'Biennium continuum Graecis literis impenderat, cum

It was Scaliger's belief that whoever wishes to announce oneself in the Republic of Letters, must gain full knowledge of Greek.[18] This was an opinion that conformed entirely to that of most French humanists and jurists of the second half of the sixteenth century, who regarded the study of Greek as essential to the educational curriculum. The jurist Jean de Coras (or Corasius, 1515–1572) wrote in 1560 that fluency in Greek was indispensable for the intellectual development of a scholar, and for engagement in other scholarly faculties.[19]

Scaliger taught Greek to his friend, the physician François Vertunien (15??–1607), and together they read and commented upon various medical texts in the castle of Touffou.[20] During one of these sessions, Scaliger explained his preferred method of learning a new language: mastering a language lay in translating a text of that language into another. Vertunien later recalled that 'to practice the Greek language, he [Scaliger] told me that there was nothing better than to translate one language into another: and so he made me translate the book of Hippocrates.'[21]

---

ad Hebraeas ecce impetus animi rapit' ('For two years, I had been immersed In Greek literature, when suddenly a surge of enthusiasm carried me toward Hebrew studies').

18   Scaliger, *Epistola de vetustate*: 'Lutetiam post obitum patris petii literarum Graecarum amore, quas qui nescirent, omnia nescire putabam' ('after the death of my father I learned Greek in Paris. Who does not command Greek does not know anything'). Cited in Robinson, *Autobiography*, pp. 30–31. Heinsius mentioned the issue in his funeral oration as follows: 'When Scaliger realised that Greek is the mother of all languages and the source from which all disciplines develop, he temporarily abandoned all other ventures and in a short time commanded this language'.

19   Johannes de Coras, *De juris arte libellus quo instituuntur legum studiosi, universum jus populi Romani dispersum antea, diuulsum, et dissipatum, in artis rationem, formamque reducere* (Lyon: Symphorien Barbier apud Antoine Vincent, 1560; USTC 152944), p. 15. 'Unless the candidate for legal degrees has combined his Latin studies with Greek, it is only with the utmost difficulty that he will be able to penetrate the secrets of our science. In fact, it is impossible to say how great are the advantages of knowing Greek literature in respect to civil law, and, on the other hand, I, having tried it, can testify to the handicap involved in ignorance of Greek', cited in L.C. Stevens, 'The Contribution of French Jurists to the Humanism of the Renaissance' in: *Studies in the Renaissance*. Vol. 1 (1954), p. 94.

20   François de Saint-Vertunien, sieur de Lavau, was the physician of Louis Chasteigner de la Roche-Posay. Scaliger called him a 'héros d'un génie absolutement divin'. See: R.L. Hawkins, 'The Friendship of Joseph Scaliger and Vertunien', *Romanic Review* 8 (1917), pp. 117–144 and 307–327.

21   Vertunien reported on one of these lessons in a letter to P. Dupuy of 2 July 1602, cited in Hawkins, 'The friendship of Joseph Scaliger and François Vertunien', 1917, p. 130. In 1578, Mamert Patisson published an edition of Hippocrates's *De capitis vulneribus liber*, a tract on head wounds, with the joint annotations of Scaliger and Vertunien.

Already in 1559, his first year as student in Paris, Scaliger commenced the study of Greek literature and grammar. The young scholar worked at a frenzied pace. In his autobiography, Scaliger would later recall proudly that he had learned Greek on his own in three weeks. He also claimed to have composed his own Greek grammar in his first year of study.[22] Scaliger asserted that he read the entire corpus of Greek classical literature in this same year, without neglecting the study of Latin.[23] Scaliger's claims about his own philological precocity mirror those made by the Orientalist scholar Guillaume Postel, who asserted that he had learned Hebrew after having the alphabet explained to him by a local rabbi. This exaggeration was outdone by Postel's claim that he had mastered Arabic in a single year with the fluency of scholars who spent six years studying the language.[24] Scholarly boasts of this nature were common in the sixteenth century, as scholars liked to project a confident image of themselves in the Republic of Letters; for this reason we should not give too much credence to these claims.

It is more likely that Scaliger studied Greek under the close tutelage of Adrianus Turnebus (1512–1565), professor at the Collège Royal and the most gifted Greek scholar of his era.[25] Scaliger was attracted to the erudite Turnebus, and according to Anthony Grafton was influenced to a greater extent by Turnebus than is usually acknowledged.[26] After two months of listening to Turnebus's lectures, Scaliger came to the conclusion that his Greek was insufficient to follow them properly. He set to work with Homer's *Iliad* in the Greek original, with a parallel Latin translation; he probably made use of the 1551 Basel edition.[27] Thereafter he continued by reading the Greek poets, and in the two following years he mastered Greek prose.

---

22 Robinson, *Autobiography*, p. 31.

23 Grafton, *Joseph Scaliger* I, p. 103.

24 Manuel, *Broken Staff*, p. diii.

25 Adrien Turnèbe or Tournèbe was *Professeur Royal* in Greek at the Collège de France between 1547 and 1562 and between 1552 and 1565 also *Professeur Royal* in Greek philosophy. For some time he was also 'imprimeur du roi en grec'. See: John Lewis, *Adrien Turnèbe (1512–1565). A Humanist observed* (Genève: Droz, 1998), pp. 57–58. Scaliger held sincere admiration for Turnèbe and in his *Scaligerana* (1666), p. 143, called him: 'Turnebus vir maximus erat doctissimusque': Turnèbe was the greatest and most scholarly of men. Scaliger reported that books from Turnèbe's library were destroyed or went msising in his *Scaligerana* II, lemma Turnèbe: 'Turnebus n'a pas beaucoup de livres et quasi tous en blanc; ils se gastent ainsi ou se perdent.'

26 The *Coniectanea in Varronem*, Scaliger's first publication, appeared in the same year as the *Commentarius in Varronis opera* of Turnebus; according to Grafton there was a degree of cooperation between the two men in this regard. Grafton, *Joseph Scaliger* I, p. 109.

27 In the Auction Catalogue of 1609, there is a copy of the *Homerus graece, cum Scholijs Didymi & aliorum*. Basel 1535, although this edition does not include a Latin translation.

There is other source material that illuminates Scaliger's path towards fluency in Greek. On the flyleaf of a copy of the tragedies of Euripides (Basel, 1544), edited by Joannes Hervagius (1497–1558) and bought by Scaliger in 1560, he wrote his name and the date on which he purchased the book in Greek. From his marginal annotations, it is also clear that Scaliger read the text with some care. He provided his own commentary, corrected compositor's errors, and expanded upon the text. It is remarkable too that he noted his name in Hebrew, 'Yôsep Sulāq', alongside the Greek.[28] This can be interpreted as evidence that Scaliger was, by this date, already advanced in his study of Hebrew.[29] In the university library of Leiden there is a copy of Caninus's *Institutiones linguae syriacae, assyriacae atque thalmudicae, una cum aethiopicae atque arabicae collatione* (1554) from the collection of Scaliger.[30] It is likely that he bought this book around the same time as the copy of Euripides: in this copy too Scaliger practised writing his name in various languages, including Greek and Hebrew. In Scaliger's copy of the *Tade Enestin en tēi parousēi biblōI*, which he probably owned before the other two texts, the struggle to decide upon the preferred spelling of his name as well as the uncertainty of his familial descendance from the Della Scala's, is fully on display.[31] On the flyleaf he wrote his name as 'Josepho delascala F. de Meßer Julio Cesare'; this was later crossed out several times. On the title page, Scaliger used the printer's device of Zacharias Kallierges to fashion the coat of arms of his forefathers, and wrote under the image of the two-headed eagle the phrase: 'Scaligerorum Principum insignia'.

In sixteenth-century France, the study of Greek, Latin and Hebrew were irrevocably bound to one another. The languages were known as the *trias linguistica*, the three languages that each scholar should aspire to master. It was only towards the end of the 1530s that there emerged in Paris a scholarly environment that enabled the study of other exotic languages. That Hebrew

---

28 Auction Catalogue 1609, p. 34, *Libri Poetae et Poetici, In Octavo* no. 2. Scaliger took this copy with him from France to Leiden. The copy can now be found in Oxford, in the Bodleian Library (call number Auct. S.4.11). Cf. Grafton, *Joseph Scaliger* I. 1983, p. 103 and note 14.

29 It seems likely that Scaliger first called himself Sulaq because he could not distinguish the handwritten -*q* from the -*m* that has the same form at the end of a word as a -*q* [with thanks to Professor F.A. de Wolff for this reflection]. In a later phase of his life, Scaliger would write the name correctly as Yosep Sulam or Sulami. Sulam is the Hebrew word for ladder, just as Scala means ladder in Italian.

30 UBL 874 D 12-1; see Bibliographic Survey Paris 1554: 3.

31 *Theokritou Eidullia hex kai triakonta. Tou autou Epigrammata enneakaideka. Tou autou Pelekus kai Pterugion. Scholia ta eis auta heuriskomena ek diaforōn antigrafōn, ei en sullechthenta* (Roma: Zaccaria Callergi, Cornelio Benigno, 1516; USTC 858936, UBL 755 D 26).

was the language of the Old Testament, and, in the words of Isidore of Seville (560–636), 'the mother of all tongues', were principles that guided the development of interest in other Oriental languages.[32] Scaliger was also deeply interested in the Hebrew language, and considered the language essential for his broader development of philology and the study of grammar. In France, various printers produced Hebrew study books, such as the *Alphabeta hebraïca* (1528, and many later reprints) by Robert I Estienne (1503–1559) and various grammars.[33] Scaliger bought several of these books.

The scholars who studied Hebrew in Scaliger's day had liberated themselves from more traditional prejudices against the language. The study of the Torah, Talmud and Kabbala by Christian scholars were frequently denounced as dangerous and undesirable activity.[34] Guillaume Postel had battled this traditionalist perspective and paved the way for other Christians to study Hebrew and Jewish culture. Scaliger followed in Postel's footsteps by entering into direct dialogue with Jewish scholars. During his student days, he sought the council of the Jewish communities in Avignon on multiple occasions, and when he visited Rome, he also conversed with Jewish theologians.[35]

In the century after 1550, most humanist scholars in the northern Netherlands were only interested in Biblical Hebrew. Scaliger was different: he studied not only the Hebrew Old Testament, but also other ancient Jewish writings, including the Mishna and the Talmud.[36] To achieve this, Scaliger had to come into contact with Jewish scholars in the Republic, because their tutelage was essential to study these writings properly. Scaliger was delighted when he learned that a Jewish community would settle in Haarlem. Whether he actually found a suitable teacher in Haarlem to help him with his study of the Talmud is uncertain, but Scaliger did maintain good contacts with the Jewish

---

32   Cf. B. Gokkes, 'Fransch en Hebreeuwsch bij enkele XVIᵉ eeuwsche Fransche grammatici', *Neophilologus* 23/1 (1938), pp. 1–11.

33   Robert Estienne (Robertus Stephanus) published many Latin, Greek and Hebrew books. On 24 June 1539, he was appointed by King Francis I as 'Imprimeur & libraire ès lettres Hébraïques & Latines' and *Typographus regius* at the Collège des trois langues, which would later become the Collège de France. See: Elizabeth Armstrong, *Robert Estienne, Royal Printer* (Cambridge: Cambridge University Press, 1954), pp. 117–123.

34   The Kabbala is the key text of the Jewish mystical tradition that developed in Spain and southern France at the end of the twelfth century.

35   Bernays, *Joseph Justus Scaliger*, p. 123.

36   *Mishna* (literally 'repetition') is the written record of the Jewish legal coda in six parts; the *Talmoed* or Talmud is an extensive version of the same compilation of laws. The Talmud can be considered to be an encyclopedia of Jewish culture as codified by leading rabbis of the period. There is a Babylonian and Jerusalem Talmud.

48   CHAPTER 2

community at Amsterdam.[37] Various Amsterdam Jews complimented Scaliger
on his knowledge and pronunciation of the Hebrew language; citations in the
Scaligerana provide further supporting evidence for this.[38]

The ease of Scaliger's contact with the Jewish community and his work on
Hebrew books did troublesome Christians, especially because Scaliger spoke
with such admiration on rabbinical pronouncements concerning philological
questions.[39] Scaliger's interest in Eastern languages and cultures were motivated purely by his scientific interests; doctrinal issues or confessional rivalries
played little part role, and presented no obstacle to engage in dialogue with
those of a non-conformist faith.[40] In the realm of philology, Scaliger can be said
to have 'had a passion to learn languages *for their own sake*' [my emphasis].[41]

After studying Greek for two years in Paris, Scaliger realised that it was a
necessity to master Hebrew too. 'Biennium continuum Graecis literis impen-
deram, cum ad Hebraeas me impetus animi rapit', he would write later.[42] The
rapidity with which he taught himself Hebrew must have encouraged Scaliger
to try and study other languages too. Between 1558 and 1562 or 1563 he began to
teach himself Arabic and Syriac as well, but Hebrew would remain his favourite field of study.[43] Scaliger had developed into a *homo trilinguis*, a man in command of the three holy tongues, a noble ideal in the intellectual aura of the
sixteenth century. He taught himself Hebrew as he had taught himself Greek,
by textual comparison. We know that to study Hebrew he began by comparing

---

37   Portuguese Jews first settled in Amsterdam in 1595. From 1603 they were followed also by
      Spanish Jews. On the Maranos (Iberian Jews who were forced to convert to Catholicism
      or did so voluntarily, while maintaining their Jewish past), see H. de Ridder-Symoens,
      'Maranos and Universities in the Renaissance Netherlands', *History of Universities* 27 1
      (2013), pp. 20–43.

38   *Scaligerana* 1740, p. 407: 'J'ay disputé à Rome & ailleurs avec les Juifs: ils m'aymoient &
      estoient fort estonnez que je parlois fort bien l'Hebreu & me distoient que je parlois l'He-
      breu de la Bible.'

39   W. den Boer, 'Joseph Scaliger en de Joden' in S. Groenveld (et al., eds.), *Bestuurders en
      geleerden. Opstellen voor J.J. Woltjer* (Amsterdam, Dieren: De Bataafsche leeuw, 1985),
      p. 66.

40   Den Boer, *Joseph Scaliger en de Joden*, p. 70.

41   Manuel, *Broken Staff*, p. 51.

42   Scaliger, *Epistola de vetustate*, p. 56; reprinted in Scaligers *Epistolæ omnes quæ repe-
      riri potuerunt* (Leiden: ex officina Bonaventura Elzevier and Abraham 1 Elzevier, 1627;
      USTC 10128641).

43   Heinsius repeated a version of this narrative in his funeral oration for Scaliger: 'Tempted
      by the wondrous sweetness of Greek and Hebrew, a flame was lit in him, encouraging him
      to study other languages, and thus he learned Aramaic, Arabic, Phoenician, Ethiopian,
      Persian and, especially, Syriac.' See also: Robinson, *Autobiography*, p. 31 and p. 76.

the Hebrew Bible, the *Tanach* and the Vulgate.[44] For this purpose he probably used the copies of the *Hamishah humshe torah* and the *Sefer tehillim* that he had bought in Paris.[45]

In his autobiography, Scaliger claimed that when he commenced his studies, he did not know a single letter of the Hebrew alphabet.[46] Yet as we have seen, Scaliger received more support and instruction for his Greek studies than he wanted the readers of his life story to believe. It is therefore entirely reasonable to suggest that Scaliger's self-laudatory narrative is somewhat misleading when it comes to his study of Hebrew too. We can presume that Scaliger did much to teach himself, and that he relied on his own book collection, and those of his peers and tutors, to do so. Even when he had an elementary grasp of Hebrew, and could read and write in that language, he lacked the necessary education to devote himself to further study. Scaliger thus called for the help of a mentor, his friend and teacher Guillaume Postel.

2   Postel's Influence on Scaliger

Scaliger and Postel first met each other in Paris in 1561. There may not be solid evidence, but it seems likely that Scaliger's sudden urge to study Hebrew, which he mentions in his autobiography, was prompted by Postel.[47] Around this time, Postel was the only true authority in France in the field of Oriental languages. He inspired Scaliger to follow him down this path, and we can assume that he saw in Scaliger a gifted student and a talented philologist.

We can say with greater certainty that Scaliger's first tentative engagement with Arabic and Syriac was made with Postel's help. In 1562, Scaliger offered Postel a roof over his head for a few days, and they shared a room in Scaliger's accommodation. Scaliger's room was located above a print shop, most likely the printing house at the sign of 'The Pelican', belonging to Hierosme de

---

44   Scaliger wrote about his method of study: 'non diu viva voce, sed potius mutis magistris usus sum' ('I made use of silent rather than living masters'). The *Tanach* consists of three parts: the *Tora* (the five books of Moses), *Nevi'im* (Prophets) and *Ketuvim* (Chronicles, Psalms, Proverbs, etc.).

45   Scaliger owned an edition of the *Hamishah humshe torah* (Pentateuch) and *Sefer tehillim* (Psalms) (Paris: Robert I Estienne, 1540–1544) in two volumes [UBL 499 B 6–7; See: Bibliographic Survey Paris 1539: 1].

46   This claim by Scaliger was adopted by Bernays, *Scaliger* and Robinson, *Autobiography*, p. 31.

47   Cf. *Scaligerana* 1740, p. 515.

50   CHAPTER 2

Marnef and Guillaume Cavellat, in the Latin Quarter, 'Au Mont St Hilaire'.[48] In gratitude for his generosity, Postel taught Scaliger his first words of Arabic during this stay.[49] Shortly thereafter, Postel was arrested on suspicions of blasphemy, and Scaliger continued his study of Arabic, a language he was beginning "o love dearly, alon".[50] He might have made use of Postel's Arabic grammar, but no copy of this work can be found in Scaliger's collection.

François Vertunien, one of Scaliger's good friends, confirms that it was indeed in 1562 that Postel encouraged Scaliger to study Oriental languages. He also reveals that it was Postel who urged Scaliger to provide and publish translations of important Hebrew writings that had not yet been studied by Christian scholars, as these writings might contain a wealth of information unknown to the broader Republic of Letters.[51] Scaliger took this advice to heart: only a few months later, Scaliger sent Postel a letter from the castle of Touffou entirely in Hebrew.[52]

Surprisingly, Scaliger makes no mention of Postel in his autobiography. It is probable that Scaliger was somewhat embarrassed about his intellectual debt to Postel when it came to his study of Arabic.[53] When he mentioned Postel

---

48   Grafton, *Scaliger* I, p. 104; Secret 1998, pp. 99–108; Bruehl, *Josef Justus Scaliger*, pp. 201–218 and xiii (1961), pp. 45–65. Vertunien confirmed that Postel and Scaliger stayed with one another in Paris for three days. According to Vertunien, Postel encouraged Scaliger to study Oriental languages and Greek further, thereby being able to understand the mysteries ('miranda [...] mysteria') of Hebrew, and to delve into the writings of Jewish authors who had not yet been consulted deeply by others. Cf. *Scaligerana* I under *Lingua*, pp. 113–114.

49   *Correspondence* 15 October 1607 to Ubertus.

50   Josephus Justus Scaliger, *Opuscula varia antehac non edita. Omnium catalogum post præfationem lector inueniet* (Paris: apud Adrien Beys, 1610; USTC 6017215), p. 461; P. de L'Estoile, *Journal de Henri III, roy de France et de Pologne, ou mémoirs pour servir à l'histoire de France*. Vol. V (Den Haag: chez Pierre Gosse, 1744), p. 6. See also Grafton, *Joseph Scaliger* I, p. 104. In *Correspondence* 15 October 1607 to Ubertus, Scaliger wrote that he held a great love for the Arabic language ('incredibili amore huius linguae'), but that the more he studied the language, the less knowledgeable he felt.

51   *Scaligerana* 1740, pp. 113–114: 'Is igitur Postellus cum diligentiam Scaligeri in Graecis valde eamdem operam in Hebraïcâ, Chaldaïcâ, Syriacâque linguâ poneret: miranda quippe mysteria in his esse linguis lectuque dignissimos auctores apud Hebræos haberi, qui nondum in alienigenas linguas versati essent, quorum cognitione privaretur, si modo linguæ insudaret.'

52   If one is to believe the narrative of Saint-Vertunien in the *Prima Scaligerana*. See also: Nisard, *Le Triumvirat* 1852, p. 159. This letter to Postel has not survived.

53   See Hartmut Bobzin, *Der Koran im Zeitalter der Reformation. Studien zur Frühgeschichte der Arabistik und Islamkunde in Europa* (Würzburg: Ergon Verlag 1995), p. 367 and Bruehl, *Josef Justus Scaliger*, p. 209. Bobzin called Scaliger a 'Schüler' of Postel (p. 442). Johann W. Fück, *Die arabischen Studien in Europa bis in den Anfang des 20. Jahrhunderts* (Leipzig: Otto Harrassowitz, 1955), p. 47, wrote that Scaliger 'den eigentlichen Erben des

SCALIGER AS SCHOLAR AND COLLECTOR IN FRANCE

in his correspondence, Scaliger was scathing, describing his former mentor as a fool: 'Postellus erat stultus'.[54] This condescension extended to denigrating Postel's knowledge of Arabic.[55] It is only in the *Scaligerana* that Scaliger offered some praise of Postel's expertise, albeit as philosopher, cosmographer and mathematician, rather than philologist: 'he commands many languages, but is no expert in any of these languages'.[56] In Scaliger's mind, Postel thought that his grasp of Arabic was far better than it really was.

Scaliger would often damn with faint praise, and he would express similar ambivalence about the talents of his peers when discussing his future Leiden colleague Bonaventura Vulcanius. This was all a veil, shrouding Scaliger's own reliance on others, and promoting a self-image of independent genius. He was largely successful in this task: many of Scaliger's contemporaries were entirely unaware of Scaliger's meetings with Postel. Some must at least have been suspicious. In 1597, Isaac Casaubon asked Scaliger how he first learned so many Oriental languages. Casaubon supposed that Scaliger was taught Hebrew by Jewish scholars, but considered that he could never have learned Arabic from them.[57] Casaubon guessed that he might have picked up Arabic from Postel, and also asked whether Postel had taught him Persian, even, as Scaliger asserted, if Postel had no knowledge of his language.[58]

Despite Scaliger's criticisms of Postel, it is Postel who can be considered to be the true pioneer of Arabic philology in the western world, and the father of comparative philology. His grasp of the language, and his proposed

---

ausgedehnten Wissens bezeichnen, welche Postel sich in den verschiedensten Sprachen erworben hatte.'

54   *Scaligerana* 1740 p. 515: 'Postellus [...] fuit vere stultus, nam alioqui fuit combustus: il couroit les rues. Fecit librum debere foeminas per foeminam salvari, ut viros per Christum' in which the publication of *Les très merveilleuses victoires des femmes du nouveau monde* (Paris 1553) is referred to.

55   *Correspondence* 22 March 1608 to Ubertus; *Prima Scaligerana* I under lemma *Lingua*, pp. 113–114. Den Boer wrote in his article 'Joseph Scaliger en de Joden' that Scaliger honoured Postel as his tutor and refers thereby to Bruehl, *Josef Justus Scaliger*, pp. 201–218 and 13 (1961), pp. 45–65.

56   *Scaligerana* 1740, p. 515 under *Postellum*: 'Postellum Syrus docuit, neminem vidi qui Postello melius scriberet'; [...] en 'Postellus excellens philosophus, cosmographus, mathematicus, historicus, stultus, linguarum non ignarus, sed nullius ad unguem peritus. Invideo illi Arabicam linguam'.

57   This supposition of Casaubon is incorrect.

58   *Correspondence* 15 July 1597 from Casaubon. At the end of his life, Scaliger composed a Persian grammar and lexicon. The manuscript is written in Judaeo-Persian, on the basis of the Pentateuch of Rabbi Jacob ben Joseph Tawus (*Francisci Rafelengii Lexicon Persicum ex Rabbi Jacob filii R. Joseph Tawus Pentateucho. Accesserunt quaedam ex Baal Haruch*) from the collection of Raphelengius [UBL MS Or. 2019]. See: *Correspondence* 13 October 1607 to Casaubon.

methodology of studying and teaching Arabic, were truly revolutionary.[59] His *Grammatica Arabica*, first published in Paris by Petrus Gromorsus around 1540, was his most important contribution to the study of Oriental languages, thanks to the clear depiction of the Arabic alphabet, the translation of the *Lord's Prayer* into Arabic and the Latin translation of the first Sura by Theodorus Bibliander (ca. 1504–1564). In his *Grammatica*, Postel acknowledged the intellectual debt owed by Europeans to Arabic culture, while also committing himself fully to the belief that Europe could build upon Arabic achievements.[60] The *Grammatica* was one of the earliest publication that made use of moveable type in the Arabic language, and it would remain, despite its shortcomings, the only available grammar of its sort for seventy years. It would inspire all other Arabic grammars that appeared afterwards.[61] Postel was furthermore also one of the first western scholars to study Samaritan and Syriac seriously. It can never be proved decisively, but might all these pioneering achievements have inspired jealousy on the part of Scaliger?

Scaliger nevertheless did not consider Postel's contributions worthy of praise. There is no sign of a copy of the *Grammatica Arabica* in Scaliger's bequest to Leiden, but it is certain from his correspondence that Scaliger once possessed a copy in his library. He once even recommended the book as a helpful guide to study Arabic.[62] It seems that Scaliger wished to obliterate any evidence of his previous connection with Postel from his library. In his bequest, there is only a single publication by Postel: 'Postelli XII. Lingua cum Grammatica Arabica'.[63] This copy of Postel's *Linguarum duodecim characteribus differentium alphabetum* (1538) is last mentioned in the Leiden library

---

59   A. Hamilton, 'Guillaume Postel (1510–1581)', in: *Catalogue 1343 Bernard Quaritch* (London: Bernard Quaritch 2006).

60   According to J.J. Witkam, 'Verzamelingen van Arabische handschriften en boeken in Nederland', in N. van Dam (et al., eds.), *Nederland en de Arabische wereld. Van Middeleeuwen tot twintigste eeuw* (Lochem: De Tijdstroom, 1987), p. 19.

61   A. Hamilton, 'Guillaume Postel', p.2; Fück, *Die arabischen Studien*, p. 41: 'Diese recht mangelhafte, dazu von Druckfehlern wimmelnden Grammatica Arabica ist Postels letzter unmittelbarer Beitrag zu den arabischen Studien.'

62   *Correspondence* 23 October 1606 to Buxtorf.

63   *Linguarum duodecim characteribus differentium alphabetum, introductio, ac legendi modus longè facilimus. Linguarum nomina sequens proximè pagella offeret / Guilielmi Postelli Barentonii diligentia* (Paris: excudebat Pierre Vidoué apud Denis Lescuier, 1538; USTC 147464, UBL 873 C 1-1; see Bibliographic Survey Paris 1538). The book contains a description and examples of alphabets and grammars of eleven languages from the Middle East and the Balkans, and one language that he described as Indian (which is really the Semitic *Geez* language of Ethiopia). According to Postel, these twelve languages all originated from one language: Hebrew. Claude Postel, *Les écrits de Guillaume Postel. Publiés en France et leurs éditeurs 1538–1579* (Genève: Droz, 1992), no. 1538-1.

SCALIGER AS SCHOLAR AND COLLECTOR IN FRANCE   53

catalogue of 1674. Thereafter, Scaliger's copy was replaced by another copy, unrelated to his collection, bound together with copy of Postel's *De originibus seu de Hebraicae linguae* (1538).[64] Scaliger did own a copy of a comparative study between the Qur'an and the Bible, which includes Postel's translation of the Qur'an.[65] Lastly, in the auction catalogue of Scaliger's library there is mention of a copy of Postel's *Des histoires orientales et principalement des Turkes ou Turchikes et Schitiques ou Tartaresques et aultres qui en sont descendues* (Paris: 1575).[66]

In his *Scaligerana*, Scaliger wrote that he knew of more than a hundred authors who had written about the Turks, and that he owned more than fifty books on the subject. This was no exaggeration, because we can find many works of this sort in Scaliger's auction catalogue, including a copy of Paulus Crusius's *Turcograeciae libri octo* (Basel, 1584) and the *Musulmannica* of Johannes Leunclavius (1541–1594).[67] Some of these historical works on the Turks from Scaliger's collection, also annotated by Scaliger's hand, are listed in the auction catalogue of the library of "icolaas Heinsius.[68]

After receiving Postel's encouragement to delve into the study of Oriental languages, Scaliger encountered most problems with the study of Hebrew. He

---

64   *De originibus seu de Hebraicae linguae et gentis antiquitate deque variarum linguarum affinitate liber* (Paris: excudebat Pierre Vidoué apud Denis Lescuier, 1538; USTC 147381). Postel, *Les écrits de Guillaume Postel*, no. 1538-2.

65   Guillaume Postel. *Alcorani, seu legis Mohameti et Evangelistarum concordiae liber* (Paris: excudebat Pierre Gromors, 1543; USTC 153696). See: Postel, *Les écrits de Guillaume Postel*, no. 1543-2.

66   François Secret offers in the *Bibliographie des manuscrits de Guillaume Postel* (Genève: Droz, 1970), pp. 13–25 under the heading 'Catalogue des ouvrages imprimés' an overview of 66 titles of books by Postel.

67   *Scaligerana* 1740, p. 603–604. The copy of Martinus Crusius with copious annotations by Scaliger is UBL 766 A 11 and is listed in the Auction Catalogue of 1609 on p. 16; the copy of Johannes Leunclavius, *Historiae Musulmanae Turcorum, de monumentis ipsorum exscriptae, libri XVIII* (Frankfurt am Main: apud Andreas Wechel (heirs of), Claude de Marne et Johann Aubry, 1591; USTC 662570) can be found in the Auction Catalogue of 1609 on p. 18. This copy, with some marginal annotations by Scaliger in Arabic, is now found in the Bibliotheca Thysiana in Leiden under call number THYSIA 868:1. With thanks to Dr Nil Pektas (John Rylands Library, Manchester) who referred me to this copy. Scaliger held considerable admiration for Leunclavius and in his *Scaligerana* (p. 139) called him 'le meilleur qui ait escrit des Turcs'.

68   In the catalogue we find copies of Leunclavius's *Annales Turcici & Pandectes Historiae Turcica* (Frankfurt am Main: apud Andreas Wechel (heirs of), Claude de Marne et Johann Aubry, 1596; USTC 611616), the *Historia della guerra fra Turchi, et Persani* by Gio Thomaso Minadoi (Venezia, appresso Andrea Muschio & Barezzo Barezzi, 1594; USTC 842794) in part 2, p. 191 and the *Les navigations, pereginations et voyages faicts en la Turquie* by Nicolas de Nicolay (Antwerpen: Willem Silvius, 1577; USTC 11420) in part 2, p. 227.

54 CHAPTER 2

realised that learning the elementary principles of Hebrew was far simpler than mastering the language. This was in part another swipe at Postel's limitations: Scaliger argued later that the serious study of Hebrew required the support of a Jewish scholar who truly understood Hebrew.[69] At Leiden, Scaliger would later have the pleasure of studying the language alongside Philippus Ferdinandus (1556–1599), the first known Eastern European Jew in the Netherlands, and briefly professor of Arabic at Leiden.[70] Shortly before Ferdinandus's death, Scaliger described how they studied the Talmud and other Rabbinical literature together, 'with equal profit, and no less pleasure'.[71] Together they also provided commentary on various Hebrew texts.[72] Scaliger wrote that:

> In vain, we Christians make attempts at this work: one cannot understand such [Hebrew] literature properly without the aid of a Jew, who himself has been educated in these matters. I can confirm most sincerely that I have learned from Philippus [Ferdinandus] what no one but a Jew could have taught me.[73]

At the same time, Scaliger also noted that he frequently corrected Ferdinandus on grammatical errors and omissions in Hebrew texts. His interaction with Ferdinandus definitely deviated from the then acceptable norms of

---

69   *Scaligerena* 1740 under lemma *Lingua* en *Talmud* p. 110. 'Les commencements de la Hebraïque sont faciles, mais le progrès en est si difficile et fascheux, que je ne sçache homme vivant qui l'entende bien [...]. Mais c'est qu'il en sçaist quelques principes et s'estime par la fort sçavant. On ne sçauroit l'entendre sans la vive voix d'un Juif: le Juif qui lisoit icy, m'en appris quelque chose, nous y leusmes ensemble. Je fus auteur qu'on le mist Professeur en Arabe.' The Jewish scholar that Scaliger referred to here was Philippus Ferdinandus.

70   He was appointed professor of Arabic on 6 November 1599. Ferdinandus died before he could take up this post. See: A. Hamilton, 'Ferdinand, Philip (1556–1599)' in *Oxford Dictionary of National Biography* 2004, 26.

71   *Correspondence* 31 December 1599 to Drusius: 'Iam multa in Talmud magno cum fructus, neque minore voluptate, una legeramus.'

72   *Secunda Scaligerana* 1740, pp. 590–591 under *Thalmud*; H.F. Wijnman, 'Philippus Ferdinandus. Professor in het Arabisch aan de Leidse Universiteit, de eerste Oost-Europese Jood in Nederland (1599)', *Jaarbericht van het Voorolaziatisch-Egyptisch Genootschap "Ex Oriente Lux"* 19 (1967) pp. 558–580. Scaliger owned a manuscript copy of the Talmud (UBL SCA 3), as well as a printed edition. See on Ferdinandus's appointment also: Molhuysen, *Bronnen* I, pp. 120–121.

73   *Correspondence* 31 December 1599 to Drusius. In the early sixteenth century, it was still relatively uncommon for Jews to help gentiles with the reading of the Talmud, because this was explicitly forbidden by the text. See further on this: Reuchlin, cited in Katschen, *Christian Hebraists*, p. 10 note 19.

SCALIGER AS SCHOLAR AND COLLECTOR IN FRANCE

engagement between Christians and Jews.[74] They had evidently such a good relationship that Ferdinandus gave Scaliger a book, a rare copy of the *Sepher Ikkarim*, printed in Lublin in 1597.[75] Scaliger's desire to expand his knowledge of Hebrew was dealt a serious blow by Ferdinandus's unexpected death in 1599, which Scaliger later described as taking place at 'a most unfortunate moment in my studies'. The death of his colleague and friend affected Scaliger deeply, and, in an embittered mood, he reflected that 'a Christian like myself, who has not been raised surrounded by Jewish language and culture, is barely able to grasp the principles of this tongue'.[76] It fell to Scaliger to find a suitable replacement for Ferdinandus as professor of Arabic in Leiden. He approached Étienne Hubert (or Ubertus, 1567–1614), the scholar who had instructed Casaubon in Arabic at Paris, but Hubert showed no interest.

We can conclude that Guillaume Postel was a critical influence upon Scaliger as the man who first encouraged him to study Oriental languages, and taught him the basic principles of Arabic. Postel also influenced Scaliger in his love of collecting Oriental and especially Arabic manuscripts. It was only when Scaliger realised that he had reached a point from which Postel could no longer help him, that he distanced himself from his former mentor, and demolished Postel's reputation in his correspondence and publications.

---

74 Den Boer, *Scaliger en de Joden*, p. 66, 70, compares Scaliger's attitude towards Jewish culture and other cultures with those of modern anthropologists, as one 'that recognises that the characteristics of this society are alien to the researcher, but that all contact with them is separated from the demands of religious dogmas and premises.'

75 The copy from the bequest of Scaliger is now UBL 874 D 27; see Bibliographic Survey Lublin 1597. It is also possible that Scaliger acquired this book from the auction of the library of Ferdinandus in 1601.

76 *Correspondence* 31 December 1599 to Drusius senior: 'Mira tamen eius exercitatio erat in Talmudicis et quanta non potest cadere nisi in hominem edaeum eumque a puero informatum. Nam certe frustra haec conentur nostri Christiani, qui nihil illarum literarum perfecte tenere possunt sine praesidio hominis Iudaei, et Iudaice instituti. Hoc ego mihi semper persuasi, et verum esse reipsa expertus sum. Hoc serio affirmare possum, me ab eo didicisse quod praeter Iudaeos nemo me docere poterat.' In *Correspondence* 22 January 1602 to Casaubon, Scaliger repeats this once again. See also: *Secunda Scaligerana*, 1740 pp. 590–591 under *Thalmud*. Similar statements are made by Scaliger towards the end of his life, when describing his engagement with Arabic, a language he loved dearly: 'The more [Arabic] material I gather, the more I have the feeling that I am incompetent in this language.' Cf. *Correspondence* 22 January 1602 to Casaubon; Gerardus Willebrordus Johannes (et al.), *Levinus Warner and his Legacy. Three centuries Legatum Warnerianum in the Leiden University Library. Catalogue of the commemorative Exhibition held in the Bibliotheca Thysiana from April 27th till May 15th 1970* (Leiden: E.J. Brill, 1970), p. 27: 'quo plura congero, eo me huius linguae imperitiorem esse sentio'. Van Hal, *Moedertalen & taalmoeders* 2008, pp. 145–148.

3   Paris: Scaliger's First Hebrew Books

During his study in Paris, Scaliger probably acquired a large part of his book collection from local bookshops. It would not have been difficult for students at this time to buy copies of all elementary study books from the well-stocked Parisian establishments. Theological works were especially well-represented in the bookshops, including publications by Christian Hebraists.[77] Bookseller Frichon stocked Hebrew, Aramaic and Syriac books, including the *Nomenclatura Hebraica* (Isny: 1542), a Hebrew grammar by Levita and Fagius.[78] Grammars of this sort were marketed specifically at students like Scaliger. Despite their relatively small print runs, Hebrew books were not necessarily more expensive than other texts. Yet on a student budget, Scaliger could probably only afford cheaper student editions rather than scholarly reference works. His personal library was most likely of modest size during his student days.

Scaliger probably bought most of his books from the bookshops in the rue Saint-Jacques and its surroundings, an area where one could find dozens of bookshops in the sixteenth century. The stock available here came from all over Europe. Those booksellers who specialised in domestic French publications were mostly found on the Pont-Nôtre-Dame and the rue Neuve-Nôtre-Dame. Those looking for foreign books would instead head towards the Jewish quarter and the Galerie Marchande of the Palais de Justice.[79]

In the middle of the sixteenth century, many of the Protestant printers who played an important role in the production of Hebrew works moved away from Paris. As censorship increased and printers like Robert Estienne in Paris feared for their future, they settled in Geneva and other cities beyond the borders of France.[80] The production of Hebrew books in France was adversely affected as a result and suffered a downturn. When Paris became the centre of the Catholic League in 1585, the print trade was seriously impacted. Scaliger must have experienced this gradual decline, and this will have influenced his decision to move to Leiden.

---

77 Roger Doucet, *Les bibliothèques parisiennes au XVIe siècle* (Paris: A. et J. Picard, 1956), p. 68: The bookseller J. Janot sold copies of Münster's *Decalogus* (Basel: apud Johann Froben, 1527; USTC 661159) and the *Cantica Canticorum* of Schreckenfuchs and Petri (Basel: [per Heinrich aus Basel Petri, 1553]; USTC 161162).

78 Doucet, *Bibliothèques parisiennes*, p. 70.

79 Philippe Renouard (et al.), *Imprimeurs et libraires parisiens* (Paris: Droz, 1964–1982). Around 1500 there were 75 print shops in Paris; fifty years later this had increased to 102.

80 Lyse Schwarzfuchs, *Le livre hébreu à Paris au XVIe siècle. Inventaire chronologique* (Paris: BnF, 2004), p. 45.

Despite the political and religious uncertainties that plagued Parisian life, Paris would always play a crucial role in Scaliger's network, even when he had moved to the Dutch Republic. He corresponded with scholars, statesmen and booksellers, all men who adhered to the Protestant faith and who would always be trustworthy in Scaliger's eyes. The Huguenots formed a very tight community. They may have been dispersed around France, and represented only a minority, but they maintained strong bonds with one another, traded, loaned money and offered to provide mutual support in the realms of finance, commerce and news. The French Protestant community received protection during the reign of Henry of Navarre, most prominently through an informal system of patronage. The Huguenots were always bound to one another by 'sociabilité à distance', fraternity at a distance.[81] Protestant students at universities and academies became friends for life; families helped one another in all possible ways. Invisible bonds also existed between Protestants in France and those abroad. Scaliger relied heavily on this network and chose most of his contacts from the Huguenot community. The printed book and correspondence played important roles in the dissemination of ideas and ideals within this group.[82]

4 The Production and Sale of Oriental Books

Oriental manuscripts were naturally perceived as unique objects, but printed books in Oriental languages were also seen as desirable rarities, given that they were often produced in small print runs. It was not easy to acquire Oriental books. Most were printed and traded in the Italian city states, especially in Venice, home to a large Jewish community. A book destined for a buyer in northern Europe would have to be transported over a considerable distance.[83]

---

81   M. Greengrass, 'Informal networks in sixteenth-century French Protestantism', in R.A. Mentzer and A. Spicer, eds., *Society and Culture in the Huguenot World 1559–1685* (Cambridge: Cambridge University Press, 2002), p. 79.

82   Greengrass, 'Informal Networks', p. 95: 'Frameworks of friendship provided recurrent ideals and images, which were expressed in the epistolary traffic of the French Huguenot world.'

83   Around 1500, a print run of 1,200 copies was not unusual for Latin books. The average print run of the sixteenth century seems to have increased over time; many books in this period will have been printed in a run of 1,500–2,000 copies. Plantin's Polyglot Bible (1568–1573) was printed in 1,400 copies. Print runs for Hebrew books from the period are uncertain, but it is likely that they were lower than those of works in Latin. See A. Ruppel, 'Die Bücherwelt des 16. Jahrhunderts und die Frankfurter Büchermessen', *De Gulden Passer* 24 (Antwerpen: Vereeniging der Antwerpsche Bibliophielen, 1956), p. 26; Johannes Hermann

58   CHAPTER 2

Hebrew books were printed mostly for a Jewish audience, and circulated within closed Jewish communities. There were strict rules within the Jewish community concerning the supply of holy liturgical texts to Christians. Scaliger would, later in life, encounter such restrictions when assembling Hebrew books.[84]

Hebrew works edited and translated by Christian Hebraists made up a very different segment of the market. Some books in other Oriental languages were also printed specifically for western Christian scholars. What united the efforts of Christian Hebraists, was the selective use of Jewish sources to investigate and clarify the Christian Bible. Scaliger represented a deviation from this norm: his collecting of Oriental books was omnivorous. His scholarly contemporaries regarded his collection as remarkable for its diversity in content as in languages, and there were very few western scholars who could read all the books in Scaliger's library.

While printed books in Oriental languages were rare, there were various French printers in the sixteenth century outside Paris who produced a range of books, mostly reference or study books, in Hebrew. Scholarly printers played an important role in this production: one of them was Sébastien Gryphe (1492–1556), the 'prince of Lyonnais publishers.'[85] In Lyon, the most important print centre in France beyond Paris, he would produce 41 books with Hebrew content between 1528 and 1556.[86] His most famous publication in this field was his Hebrew-Latin dictionary, composed by Santes Pagninus in 1529. Scaliger owned a copy of this edition which he annotated extensively.[87] Other Hebrew alphabets, grammars and study books were produced for the French market by the printers Gilles de Gourmont (1499–1533), who produced

---

Kernkamp, *Economisch-historische aspecten van de literatuurproductie* ('s-Gravenhage, Martinus Nijhoff, 1949), p. 13.

84 Bruehl, 'Josef Justus Scaliger', note 27.

85 Lucien Febvre and Henri-Jean Martin, *L'apparition du livre* (Paris: Les Editions Albin Miche, 1971), p. 291.

86 L. Schwarzfuchs, 'Sébastien Gryphe éditeur en hébreu', in R. Mouren (ed.), *Quid novi? Sébastien Gryphe, à l'occasion du 450ᵉ anniversiare de sa mort.* (Villeurbanne, Presses de l'Enssib, 2006), p. 88. The texts of the 41 publications by Gryphius only included a few phrases or occasional words in Hebrew, not continuous text.

87 Santes Pagninus, *Osar leson haq-qodes, hoc est, Thesaurus lingvæ sanctæ. Sic enim inscribere placuit lexicon hoc hebraicum* […] (Lyon: excudebat Sébastien Gryphe, 1529; USTC 146079) [UBL 874 B 7]. This dictionary was inspired by the *Sefer ha-Shorashim*, the etymological work of the twelfth-century grammarian David Qimhi from Narbonne. Scaliger owned two copies of the edition of this work revised by Santes Pagninus: *Hebraicarum institutionum libri IIII* […], *ex R. David Kimhi priore parte Mikhlol, quam Heleq hadiqduq inscripsit, ferè transcripti* (Paris: ex officina Robert Estienne 1549; USTC 150280), that also included a revision of the *Institutiones linguae Hebraicae* (Lyon: Sébastien Gryphe, 1526) [UBL 873 D 15 and 873 D 17; see Bibliographic Survey Paris 1549:3].

FIGURE 4   In the galleries of the Palais du Parlement and the Palais de Justice in Paris, one could find more than 200 shops, including those of many booksellers. Rijksprentenkabinet, Amsterdam: RP-P-OB-42.103

various alphabets between 1514 and 1517, and Chrétien Wechel (1495–1554), publisher of Sebastian Münster's *Compendium Hebraicae grammatica* of 1537. Denys Lescuyer (fl. 1538–1551) and Jean Petit (?–1540) were other important publishers of Hebrew works, and both printed works by Guillaume Postel. The renowned Estienne family (Robert the elder and the younger and Charles) were also responsible for many Hebrew editions.[88]

In sixteenth-century France, printers in Paris and Lyon were responsible for the lion's share of Hebrew printing; it was only at the end of the century that several books with Hebrew typefaces were printed in La Rochelle. Hebrew book production in France was, in contrast to Hebrew books printed in Venice, targeted at Christian scholars, rather than Jews. In Parisian bookshops one could

---

88   See for an extensive overview of sixteenth-century Hebrew editions from Paris: Schwarzfuchs, *Le livre* 2004.

also find second-hand Hebrew books for sale. The bookseller Galliot du Pré (1512–1560), who had a shop in the neighbourhood of the Palais de Justice, had various titles in Hebrew in stock, including editions of Santes Pagninus and Agostino Giustiniani's polyglot psalter in Greek, Hebrew, Arabic and Syriac.[89] Hebrew study books could also easily be found in sixteenth-century Parisian bookshops, and Scaliger would have had no problems acquiring these texts.[90]

Outside France, Johann Froben (1460–1527) of Basel was an important producer of Hebrew books. Scaliger owned multiple Hebrew editions printed by Froben. It is certain that there would have been enough Hebrew books available in France when Scaliger was studying in Paris. The capital was home to various scholars who taught the language, and with whom Scaliger could have been in contact. Most Christian Hebraists worked at the Collège de France, which employed professors of Hebrew from its foundation in 1530. Some sources suggest that Scaliger contributed actively to the provision of Hebrew classes at the Collège, but this seems improbable.[91]

5   Scaliger's Journey to Italy with Chasteigner de la Roche-Posay

In Paris, Scaliger befriended several members of the *Pléiade*, a gathering of scholars, poets and writers who laboured to raise the prestige of the French language to the same heights as those of the classical languages. One of the prominent members was Jean Dorat (1508–1588), professor of Greek at the Collège de France. Scaliger attended his lectures and admired him greatly. Dorat was similarly impressed by Scaliger's talents, and in 1563 he introduced Scaliger to Louis Chasteigner, seigneur d'Abain de la Roche-Posay et de Touffon

---

89   This included copies of the Santes Pagninus, *Isagoge ad sacras literas liber unicus* [...] (Lyon: François Juste apud Hugues de La Porte [et] Thomas Guadagnus, 1536; USTC 147110) and *Institutionum hebraicarum abbreviation* (Lyon: excudebat Sébastien Gryphe, 1528; USTC 155796). See: Annie Parent, *Les métiers du livre à Paris au XVIe siècle (1535–1560)* (Genève: Droz, 1974), pp. 229–230.

90   Nicolas Rigault (1577–1654), jurist and *ancien garde* of the royal library in Paris, requested Scaliger's advice in 1601 which books were suitable to learn Hebrew without the aid of a tutor. Sadly, Scaliger's letter with his answer, which would have been most revealing, has not survived. *Correspondence* 9 September 1601 from Rigault.

91   The Scottish humanist Andrew Melville (1545–1622) recorded in his diary that Scaliger taught Hebrew at the Collège de France without having a formal appointment to do so. Cited in John Durkan and James Kirk, *The University of Glasgow 1451–1577* (Glasgow: University of Glasgow Press, 1977), p. 276; Abel Lefranc, *Histoire du Collège de France* (Paris: Hachette, 1893), pp. 381–382; Abel Lefranc, *Le Collège de France 1530–1930* (Paris: Hachette, 1932), pp. 15–16; 18–22.

SCALIGER AS SCHOLAR AND COLLECTOR IN FRANCE 61

(1535–1595).[92] This introduction would be of great consequence to the development of Scaliger's career. Chasteigner employed Scaliger as tutor for his son Henri Louis (1577–1651) and invited him to travel with him as his companion on his diplomatic travels to Rome, which he visited in 1565 and 1566 as French envoy. Together they travelled the length and breadth of Italy, going as far south as Naples. In Verona, Scaliger paid homage to the graves of his supposed ancestors, the Della Scala's, the erstwhile rulers of Verona in the thirteenth and fourteenth centuries. In Rome, Scaliger also made new connections to add to his growing network of scholarly contacts, including Carlo Sigonio (1523–1584) and Fulvio Orsini, the librarian of Cardinal Alexander Farnese (1520–1589).[93] Orsini's renowned collection would be donated to the Vatican at his death.[94]

In Italy, Scaliger also renewed his friendship with the Latinist Muret, who he had first encountered during his youth in Agen.[95] Thanks to Muret, Scaliger was able to meet the classical expert Onofrius Panvinius (1529–1568) in Rome. Muret had studied at Padua and Ferrara, and maintained good relations with the printer Paulus Manutius (1512–1574) in Venice. From 1563 onwards, Muret worked at the university La Sapienza in Rome in the service of Pope Gregory XIII (1502–1585); one of his duties was the integration of the library of the *Collegium Romanum* into the Vatican library. During his stay in Rome, Scaliger first understood how extensive Muret's network of scholars was, but he could only take full advantage of it in the spring of 1576, when Chasteigner

---

92 Scaliger and Louis Chasteigner de La Roche-Posay met each other in Paris during the years 1559–1562. Chasteigner also studied under Turnèbe and Dorat. Chasteigner married on 15 January 1567 with Claude Dupuy (1538–1632), the daughter of Georges Dupuy, Seigneur du Courdary. André du Chesne, *Histoire généalogique de la maison des Chasteigners*, Paris, chez Sébastien Cramoisy, 1634, p. 124 and Christine de Buzon and Jean-Eudes Girot (eds.), *Jean Dorat. Poète humaniste de la Renaissance* (Genève: Droz, 2001).

93 The historian, philologist and Christian Hebraist Sigonio published his *De republica Hebraeorum libri VII* in 1585. Scaliger would send him several of his own publications. See, for example, the books that Scaliger sent him and Pietro Vettori (1499–1585) via Chasteigner, according to the *Correspondence* 22 January 1574 to Monluc and 26 June 1576 to Dupuy.

94 Jeanne Bignamie Odier, *La Bibliothèque vaticane de Sixte IV à Pie XI. Recherches sur l'histoire des collections de manuscrits* (Città del Vaticano: Biblioteca Apostolica Vaticana, 1973), p. 92. *Secunda Scaligerana* 1740, p. 555: 'J'ay esté deux fois à Rome, ayant 25 et 26 ans, deux ans l'un après l'aultre.' En '[…] anno MDLXVI cum essem in Italia, et M. Antonio Mureto exposuissem me habere in animo Venetias proficisci […].' The second visit probably took place when Scaliger was twenty-six years old.

95 The friendship would deteriorate considerably when Muret tested Scaliger by sending him two 'authentic' ancient poems, that he had in fact written himself. Grafton, *Scaliger* I, pp. 161–162.

FIGURE 5　Louis Chasteigner de la Roche-Posay, seigneur d'Abain, the protector of Scaliger. Amsterdam, Rijksmuseum

was appointed as French ambassador in Rome. He would remain in this post until 1581, which provided Scaliger with five fruitful years.[96]

It is noteworthy that Scaliger made little use of the rich collections of classical manuscripts available in Roman libraries, but he did make many transcriptions from Roman antiquities. The annotations that he made during these years would later form the basis of the *Inscriptiones antiquae totius orbis Romani* of Janus Gruterus (1560–1627), published in 1603. In Venice, Scaliger visited the print shop of Paulus Manutius and his son Aldus (1547–1597), with both of whom Scaliger would keep in contact. The contacts that Scaliger made during his five years in Italy would provide the foundation for his European network, which would play an instrumental part in his collecting of Oriental

---

96　*Lettres inédites de Cujas et de Scaliger, publiées par S. de Ricci, annotées par P.-F. Girard* (Paris: L. Tenin, 1917), p. 422; *Correspondence* 12 February 1576 to Vertunien.

SCALIGER AS SCHOLAR AND COLLECTOR IN FRANCE

books and manuscripts. By this time, Scaliger was (according to his own claims) an expert in Hebrew: with some pride he wrote that he had amazed the Jewish community in Rome with his pronunciation of passages from the Old Testament.[97] This boastfulness masked Scaliger's shortcomings when it came to the practical use of Hebrew, which Bernays noted missed the 'finer nuances' of the language.[98]

6   The Influence of Cujas on Scaliger

In 1570, after a turbulent period of religious warfare in 1567–1568, calm was restored in France. As soon as he was able to, Scaliger travelled to the university town of Valence in the Dauphiné, in the south-east of France. He would study at Valence for two years, finding lodging with the professor and jurist Jacques Cujas.[99]

Cujas owned a substantial library, including a large quantity of annotated printed works, together with around one hundred Greek and Latin manuscripts. His collection was divided amongst seven or eight rooms, and Scaliger was free to make use of this library for the duration of his stay. This bountiful collection temporarily satiated Scaliger's craving for books, but at the same time also awakened in him a desire to build his own library, filled with manuscripts.[100] Cujas became Scaliger's mentor and tutor, and introduced him to the study of Roman law, and to the leading scholars in the field of jurisprudence.[101] Scaliger recognised in Cujas a fellow scholar devoted to the critical study of sources, and respected him greatly.[102]

---

97   *Secunda Scaligerana, Thuana, Perroniana, Pithoeana, et Colomesiana, ou remarques* 1740, pp. 407–408: 'J'ay disputé á Rome & ailleurs avec les Juifs; ils m'aymoient & estoient fort estonnez que je parlois fort bien Hebreu, & me disoient que je parlois l'Hebreu de la Bible, & que paucissimi ex illis ita loquebantur, sed lingua majorum Rabbinorum loquebantur, Rabbotenu Zicronam.'

98   Cf. Bernays, *Joseph Justus Scaliger*, p. 36.

99   Since 1567, Cujas had been professor at the University of Valence. He had also taught Roman law at the universities of Bourges en Orléans. In Valence, Scaliger also befriended the eminent jurist Enimundus Bonefidius (Ennemond Bonnefoy, 1535–1574), who also kept himself occupied with the study of Hebrew. He published an edition of the *Juris orientalis libri III* ([Genève]: Henri II Estienne, 1573; USTC 450635).

100   Heinsius, 'Funeral Oration' in: Robinson, *Autobiography of Joseph Scaliger* 1927, p. 76.

101   This prestigious faculty was also home to other noteworthy professors: the Italian jurist Philippus Decius (Filippo Decia 1454–ca. 1535), António de Gouveia (Antoine Gouvea) and François Hotman (1524–1590). These scholars attracted students from across France to study law at Valence. Cf. Henry Heller, *The Conquest of Poverty. The Calvinist Revolt in Sixteenth Century France* (Leiden: E.J. Brill, 1986), pp. 210–211.

102   Grafton, *Joseph Scaliger* I, p. 121.

FIGURE 6   The jurist Jacques Cujas. Portrait collection of the University of Amsterdam

Cujas was of immense influence on Scaliger and his fellow students at Valence. The methodology of textual criticism that Cujas taught demanded that students constantly criticised the content of ancient texts, and evaluated whether the arguments in Cujas's own lectures held up.[103] While scholastic

---

103   On Cujas's approach to Roman law, see: Randall Lesaffer, *Inleiding tot de Europese rechtsgeschiedenis* (Leuven: Leuven University Press, 2004), pp. 317–318.

SCALIGER AS SCHOLAR AND COLLECTOR IN FRANCE

scholars concentrated mostly on the study of Latin texts (or Latin translations from Greek and Arabic), Cujas broadened the horizons of his students by forcing them to engage with original Greek texts. The realisation that ancient texts, including the Bible and the canon of Patristic authors, were not necessarily reliable sources, would exercise profound influence on Scaliger's scholarly development. Cujas showed his students that the trustworthiness of texts could only be tested by a thorough examination of the original sources, which required expert knowledge of all classical languages (Latin, Greek, Hebrew, Aramaic and other languages from the Middle East) as well as a keen historical mind. Lacking these fundamental skills, no scholar could provide *emendationes*, or enhancements to classical texts.

All of Cujas's students enjoyed access to his library for their philological exercises and their research. It was this library that truly opened Scaliger's eyes, instilling in him the value of manuscript sources for the study of antiquity and the mediaeval era. Scaliger transcribed and studied manuscripts of Catullus, Petronius, Martial, Priscianus, Dositheus, Victorinus and Propertius from Cajus's library.[104] Cujas also introduced Scaliger to his network of correspondents and scholars.[105] His time in Valence strengthened Scaliger's belief that only through the collecting of an extensive library of sources, ranging from books and manuscripts to other physical artefacts, could one undertake original research. Initially, Scaliger concentrated on acquiring manuscripts of classical authors, but from the middle of the 1570s, he would focus on collecting sources for his research on chronology. Cujas, who died childless on 4 October 1590, seems to have considered nominating Scaliger as his heir, and granting him his entire library.[106] This never materialised, however, and only a single codex with two Latin and Greek manuscripts made its way from Cujas's library to that of Scaliger.[107]

---

104 Bernays, *Joseph Justus Scaliger*, p. 143. See, for example, the manuscript of Sextus Propertius in the British Library [Egerton 3027] from the library of Cujas that Scaliger consulted.

105 Grafton, *Joseph Scaliger* I, pp. 121–123.

106 *Scaligerana* 1740, vol. 2, p. 446; *Perroniana et Thuana. Ed. Secunda.* Keulen 1669, p. 335.

107 VUL 108, pars 5 verso: 'C. Marii Sacerdotis de versibus cum exemplis Graecis. Liber instar Hephaestionis, descriptus ex Bibliotheca Cuiacii'. It probably concerned a copy of the *Ars Grammatica* or *De Metris* by the classical grammarian Marius Plotius Sacerdos and a copy of the *Metris Enchiridion* of the Greek grammarian Hephaestion of Alexandria.

7 Refuge in Geneva

The St Bartholomew's Day Massacre of 23–24 August 1572 would see the slaughter of the Protestant community in Paris, and thereafter in many other French towns. When the massacre took place, Scaliger was in Strasbourg, preparing for a journey to Poland with the diplomat Jean de Monluc (1508–1579). When the terrible news reached him, he fled almost immediately to Geneva. There he stayed for several days at the house of the professor of Greek, Franciscus Portus (1511–1581). Calvin's city was evidently impressed with its new refugee: on 8 September 1572 Scaliger was registered as an inhabitant of the city, and only a month later he received the 'droit de cité'. This was followed by an invitation to become professor of philosophy.[108] On 21 October, Scaliger gave his first public lecture, and ten days later he was formally appointed professor.[109] News of Scaliger's appointment travelled fast, and a month and a half later, he received a letter from the jurist Obertus Giphanius (1534–1604) in Strasbourg, congratulating him with his success in Geneva.[110] Giphanius had been Scaliger's host on a previous visit to the city, when Scaliger also met the Lutheran professor of Hebrew, Johannes Pappus (1549–1610).

Scaliger would only teach in Geneva for a short period of time. He did not enjoy lecturing, and it was clearly not his forte; the experience was unpleasant enough that Scaliger would never lecture in Leiden.[111] His scholarly research, mostly focussed on commentaries and textual criticism of classical authors, did advance with leaps and bounds. In Geneva, Scaliger also began to busy himself with textual criticism of the Bible, which would stimulate his increasing interest in the study of chronology.

---

108 Paul Frédéric Geisendorf, *Livre des habitants de Genève*, Vol. II (1572–1574; 1585–1587) (Genève: Droz, 1963), p. 8.

109 Jean François Bergier (ed.), *Registres de la Compagnie des Pasteurs de Genève au temps de Calvin*, III, 1565–1574 (Genève: Droz, 1969), pp. 92–94.

110 *Correspondence* 14 December 1572 from Giphanius.

111 A remark by Scaliger was recorded as follows: 'Si vitam Josepho Scaligero deus longiorem concesserit, nullus auctor futurus est, primarios dico, quem non emendaturus sit, ad id enim aptus natus est, non à caqueter en chaire et pedanter' in: *Scaligerana primera* p. 18. Scaliger would write later to the curators of the University of Leiden that he had a poor experience teaching at Geneva. His former student Johannes Woverius (1574–1612), would note that: Scaliger '[...] publicitus non legit neque lecturus unquam, ne derogetur quid dignitati.' in: Franz Felix Blok, *Nicolaas Heinsius in dienst van Christina van Zweden* (Delft: Ursulapers, 1949), p. 273 (note 44, *sub* 1).

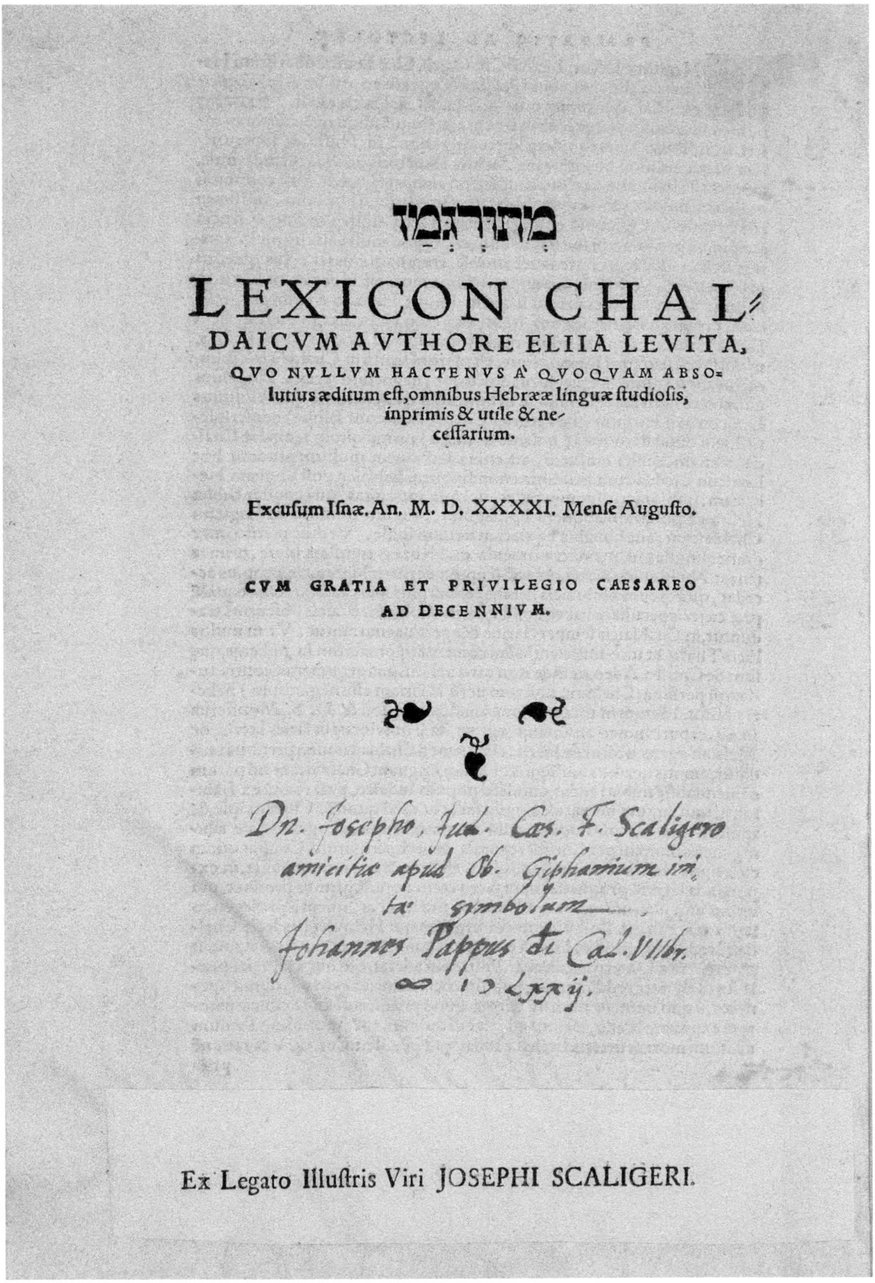

מְתוּרְגְּמָן

LEXICON CHAL⸗
DAICVM AVTHORE ELIIA LEVITA,
QVO NVLLVM HACTENVS A' QVOQVAM ABSO=
lutius æditum est,omnibus Hebrææ linguæ studiosis,
inprimis & utile & ne⸗
cessarium.

Excusum Isnæ.An. M. D. XXXXI. Mense Augusto.

CVM GRATIA ET PRIVILEGIO CAESAREO
AD DECENNIVM.

Dn. Josepho, Jud. Cæs. F. Scaligero amicitiæ apud Ob. Giphanium inita symbolum.
Johannes Pappus die Cal. VIIbr.
∞ I ɔ Lxxij.

Ex Legato Illustris Viri JOSEPHI SCALIGERI.

FIGURE 7   The title page of Levita's *Lexicon Chaldaicum*, of which Scaliger received a copy in 1572 from Johannes Pappus as a token of their friendship. UBL 839 A 6

During his time in Geneva, Pappus presented Scaliger with a copy of Levita's *Lexicon Chaldaicum*.[112] This lexicon provides an explanation of all words used in the *Targum*, the Aramaic paraphrase of the *Tenach*. This was a practical reference work, and one that Scaliger could use extensively in his studies. One can interpret this gift as an encouragement to Scaliger to pursue further the study of Aramaic. The dedication in the copy states: 'D[omi]n[o] Josepho Jul[ii] Caes[aris] F[ilio] Scaligero amicitiae apud Ob[ertum] Giphanium initae symbolum Johannes Pappus D[ed]it Cal[endis] VIIbr [= Septembribus]. MDLXXII' (Johannes Pappus donates this book to Joseph, son of Julius Caesar Scaliger, as a symbol of friendship that started at the house of Obertus Giphanius on the 7th day of September 1572). One can discern Scaliger's interest in Oriental languages throughout his time in Geneva; a highlight for Scaliger was a remarkable Greek text written in a Hebrew script that the theologian Theodorus Beza (1519–1605) showed him from his library.[113]

8   Touraine: Exile without a Library

On 19 September 1574, after a stay of more than two years, Scaliger left Geneva to return to France. There he was received once more in the bosom of the Chasteigner de la Roche-Posay family. Despite their confessional differences – Chasteigner remained Catholic, while Scaliger had been a Calvinist since 1562 – the relationship between Scaliger and his protector was close. In 1564, Scaliger had dedicated to Chasteigner his first publication, a commentary on the works of the classical author Varro.[114] Chasteigner's patronage granted Scaliger a certain social status. Chasteigner also offered Scaliger a salary that (to an extent) allowed him to purchase valuable books for his study. Scaliger was also supported in other ways: from an inscription in one of the books in his collection, it is clear that Chasteigner gave him the book.[115] It is possible that he made

---

112   Elia Levita, *Sefer meturgeman* [...] (Isny: Paul Fagius, 1541; USTC 661243; UBL 839 A 6; see Bibliographic Survey Isny 1541).

113   *Secunda Scaligerana* 1740, p. 515 under *Portus*.

114   Josephus Justus Scaliger, *Conjectanea in Marcum Terentium Varronem de lingua Latina* (Paris: ex off. Rob. Stephani, 1565; USTC 157958, UBL 569 E 30). See for the relationship between Scaliger and his Catholic contemporaries: Van Miert, *Limits of Transconfessional Contact*, pp. 367–408.

115   As indicated by an inscription in the copy of the *Pentateuchus quadrilinguis: Hebraice, Chaldaice e vers. Onkelosi, Arabice Saadiæ Gaon, Persice Jakob Tawus: cum comment. Rashi* (Constantinople: 1546), UBL 839 A 7; see Bibliographic Survey Constantinople 1546, in which Scaliger wrote: 'Hunc librum Constantinopoli mihi mittendum curauit delitiae humani generis, ac pater literarum Ludovicus Castaneus ex nobilissima Rupiposeorum

SCALIGER AS SCHOLAR AND COLLECTOR IN FRANCE

other gifts, but no further hard evidence can substantiate that. What is certain is that during this period, Scaliger's library expanded with some books that he could never have afforded himself: consider the four-volume Bible printed by Daniel Bomberg (1483–1553) in 1546–1548 that Chasteigner bought for Scaliger in 1578 in Touffou, from the widow of Charles Macrin (d. 1572), a poet and scholar of Greek who was killed in the St Bartholomew's Day Massacre.[116]

The fragile peace in France prevented Scaliger from devoting himself to his scholarship. The permanent threat of war forced him to move from chateau to chateau throughout the Touraine and Poitou. His intellectual isolation was greatest at the chateau of Preuilly, eighty kilometres south of Tours, where he stayed often.[117] In his correspondence from Preuilly, Scaliger regularly complained that the lived like a nomad, without access to his library.[118] With each departure, he could only take several books with him; others could only follow later in *tonneraux*, small barrels. He rarely knew when he would see his collection again.[119] Scaliger's frustration was apparent in at least one letter to De Thou: 'I am here without books. I cannot do anything on the New Testament

---

      gente, eques Tourquatus Regius, orator Christianiss[imi] Regis ad summum Pontif[icem]'. [Source: UBL BA C 42. Vol. X, Standcatalogus Tydeman]. Sadly, this annotation was lost during the rebinding and cropping of the copy in the nineteenth century.

116   Scaliger noted in the copy: 'Ego Iosephus Scaliger emi hos quatuor tomos Bibliorum ab vidua *Caroli Macrini*, quinquaginta florenis. Anno Christi MDLXXVIII, Tufolij in pictonibus'. The annotation on the title page is in the hand of Macrinus. An erroneous strip of paper was later added that indicated that the book was part of the bequest of Warner. Graecus Charilaus Salmonius Macrinus or Charles Macrin (?–1572) received this copy in March 1569 as a gift from Jeanne III (Jeanne d'Albret) of Navarra (1528–1572), the niece of King Francis I [UBL 515 A 12–15; see Bibliographic Survey Venice 1546–1548].

117   The fortified castle of Preuilly was located on an isolated hill, and was protected by strong walls and a moat.

118   See for example: *Correspondence* 3 December 1574 to Vertunien concerning the naming of a plant in the works of Dioscorides and Pliny, in which Scaliger indicated that he did not have access to his copies of Pliny, Theophrastus and Dioscorides at his current location. See also: *Correspondence* 2 February 1575 to Vertunien in which Scaliger named the books above in addition to an edition of Avicenna. See further: *Correspondence* 2 February 1575, written from Malval, one hundred kilometres north-east of Limoges, to Duguinas: 'Cum enim ex Pictonibus discederem, nihil librorum mecum forte attuli [...]' and *Correspondence* 11 May 1576 to Dupuy, in which Scaliger complains that he has had to be separated from his books for three months, as they are all left in the Poitou: 'Je vous donne à penser comment je puis estudier oultre ce que il y a plus de trois mois que je n'ay veu mes livres. Et pour vous dire la verité, il n'y a homme au monde plus desbauché que je suis.'

119   *Correspondence* 9 November 1590 to De Thou.

FIGURE 8 The title page of the *Pentateuch* from the library of Charles Macrin, gifted to Scaliger by Chasteigner. UBL 515A 12

SCALIGER AS SCHOLAR AND COLLECTOR IN FRANCE 71

for want of tools. And when I'll have some, I know well that to touch it, I shall be no more unpunished than to have touched profane book.'[120]

Even before his time as a student at Valence, Scaliger had experienced similar travails. In the chateau of Chantemille-sur-Creuse near Ahun, in the Limousin, where Scaliger stayed in 1568 and 1569, he was also bereft of his books. His work on the manuscript of the *Appendix* and *Catalecta* of Virgil was interrupted, because at that moment he could not access the right reference works. At that point, Scaliger expressed the wish to return to the civilised world, as he framed it: he longed for news from Paris and Italy, to be in touch again with the great centres of scholarship.[121] In Chantemille Scaliger felt especially bereft through lack of books, as one letter to Pierre Pithou attests: 'I do nothing because I took no books with me, thinking that I would not have to stay here long.'[122] A decade later, in 1579, when Scaliger was at La Roche Posay, he echoed similar sentiments in a letter to Claude Dupuy:

> Don't you know that it has been more than six weeks since I have seen my books? And the last time that I was at Touffou, I specifically put the book of Guilandinus aside to read it and provide it with annotations. It is a poor book. Since then I have been distracted by minor things, and cannot find the time for study. It is now exactly a year ago since I found the time for two hours of uninterrupted study.[123]

---

120   *Correspondence* 12 December 1590 to De Thou. In *Correspondence* 13 April 1591 to De Thou, Scaliger repeated his complaint from Preuilly: 'Les notes du Nouveau Testament ne se peuvent faire sans mes livres, car il fault avoir le Talmud et plusieurs aultres livres. Mais si nous estions ensemble, en discours familiers, je vous pourrois encores entretenir de beaucoup de choses sur ce, qui vous contenteroint à mon advis. À un aultre, je ne le vouldrois, ni oserois. Vous estes le seul de ce monde qui habes imperium in animum meum. Et parce que vous saves que je hai mortellement le mensonge, je m'asseure que vous me croies.'

121   *Correspondence* 14 April 1568/69 to Pierre Pithou: 'Nam sum hic in agro Lemovicensi, hoc est Σκυθῶν ἐρημία [Erasmus, *Adagia*, no. 2494: 'Scytharum solitudo'], longe a chartis meis, ubi nisi fortasse rabularum aliquot schedas, nullum praeterea libri nomen neque audio neque video.' *Correspondence* 6 May 1568/69 to Pithou: 'maxima penuria librorum laboro in hac solitudine'. See also: *Correspondence* 11 May 1576 to Claude Dupuy, 4 September 1581 to F. Chrestien and 5 June 1586 to Claude Dupuy, note 7. Scaliger used this expression also to characterise his residence at Malval in *Correspondence* 2 February [1575] to Irlandus. For the same statement about Touffou, see: *Correspondence* 12 February 1577 to Lipsius. See for his isolated stay in the Limousin also *Correspondence* 21 June 1582 to Claude Dupuy.

122   *Correspondence* 4 December 1586 to Pierre Pithou: 'Je ne fai rien, car je n'ai apporté ici aulcun livre, ne pensant poinct y faire le sejour que j'ay esté contrainct y faire. Parquoi je fai bien le poultron.'

123   Scaliger's books had remained at Touffou. The copy of Melchior Guilandinus was probably: *Papyrus. Hoc est commentarius in tria C Plinij Maioris de papyro capita. Accessit.*

During the 1580s, Scaliger's situation did not improve substantially. At the end of 1584, Scaliger wrote to Dupuy from Abain that all his books had been left at Touffou.[124] Six months later, Scaliger wrote again to Dupuy that: 'I find myself [in Abain] in a deserted corner of the world and I am in need of new books. Without new books, I know nothing.'[125] Scaliger's frustration was perhaps expressed most vividly in a letter to the printer Mamert Patisson (ca. 1530–ca. 1602), which he signed off with 'De Chantemille in Arabia deserta'.[126]

It is ironically during this period of sustained isolation that Scaliger received increasing praise from other scholars, impressed by his publications, especially his commentaries on classical texts. After the publication of his *De emendatione temporum* in 1583, Scaliger's renown was secured. His reputation did ensure that admirers sent him books as gifts, while he was also granted permission to study in certain libraries that were inaccessible to other scholars.[127] Scaliger expanded his own library by exchanging some of the books he received as gifts for other titles. He also disseminated copies of his own publications amongst his circle of correspondents, and in return received books from them too.

The collection of books that Scaliger had access to when he moved between chateaux in the Touraine was probably not that substantial. It is possible that one of the chateau belonging to the Chasteigner de La Roche-Posay family, like that of Abain, served as a central repository for a larger collection, but hard evidence for this is lacking. It is more likely that Scaliger kept with him a small core selection of books that he always took with him.

The situation in France did not improve as years went by. On 7 July 1585, King Henry III signed the treaty of Nemours with the Duke of Guise, the leader of the Catholic League. This was followed by a royal edict on 19 July

---

Hieronymi Mercurialis Repugnantia, qua pro Galeno strenuè pugnatur. Item Assertio sententiæ in Galenum â se pronunciatæ (Venezia: [Cristoforo Zanetti] apud Marcantonio Olmo, 1572; USTC 835555). See: Auction Catalogue 1609 p. 26, in which the word *mutilus* is included after the title. The copy can today be found at Cambridge University Library, call number M.16.49. *Correspondence* 14 April [1568–1569] to Pierre Pithou, note 6: 'Mais asseures-vous qu'il y a plus de six semaines que je n'ai veu mes livres. Et dès la premiere fois que j'arrivai à Touffou, je mis à part le livre du dict Guillandin pour le courir en lisant, et marquer ce qu'il me semble avoir mal prins. Mais depuis j'ai esté tracasser ça et là. Car je n'estudie qu'à boutée. Il y a justement un an que je n'ai estudié deux bonnes heures continuelles'. Guillandin was the German physician and botanist Melchior Wieland or Guillandinus (1519/1520–1589).

124   *Correspondence* 3 December 1584 to Claude Dupuy.

125   *Correspondence* 4 June 1585 to Claude Dupuy: 'Je suis ici confiné en un coing du monde où je n'ai nulles nouvelles de livres, comme je m'asseure que beaucoup on esté imprimés, dont je n'en sai rien.'

126   *Correspondence* 4 September 1581 to Patisson.

127   *Correspondence* 27 December 1584 from Friedrich Sylburg (1536–1596), editor in residence with the printer Johann Wechel in Frankfurt.

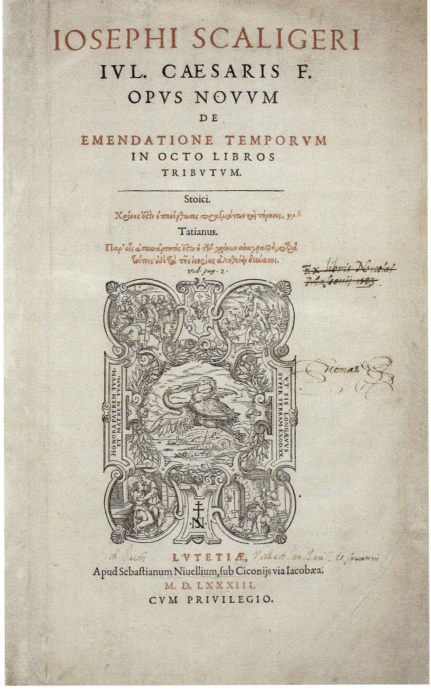

FIGURE 9　The title page of a copy of Scaliger's *Opus Novum de emendatione temporum* (Paris: Sébastien Nivelle, 1583). The title page contains the inscriptions of two previous owners of this copy, Nicolai Massonis and Johann Jacobi. UBL 759 A 50

which annulled most of the privileges granted to the Huguenots earlier in the religious wars. Scaliger feared that he would be forced to leave France once again.[128] The decade between 1585 and 1595 would be a low point in French economic activity. Scaliger himself was more isolated than ever during this period, which inevitably affected his access to books and manuscripts.[129] He was still able to make occasional trips from Abain to Paris; with each visit he tried to meet with as many friends as possible, especially Dupuy, Pithou and the writer Florent Chrestien (1541–1596). These journeys to Paris often coincided with the editorial or proof stages of one of his publications. The trips also allowed Scaliger to visit Parisian bookshops.

Until 1593, Scaliger's intellectual world rotated around Paris. He sought out many contacts amongst the jurists at the Parisian Parlement, and other scholars active in Paris. During the second phase in his life, which played out in Leiden, Scaliger's would devote himself to a broader European intellectual network. Yet he would never neglect his Parisian friends and correspondents. Some of his Parisian contacts would travel between Leiden and Paris. The fact that the Dutch Republic maintained good diplomatic relations with the French court during this time was also beneficial to Scaliger, because these formal political channels would provide secure lines of communication between the Netherlands and France.

It is remarkable that Scaliger's relative isolation and forced movements did not inhibit his scholarly productivity or his quest for sources. While Scaliger continued to acquire Hebrew titles for his library, his interest in Arabic and other Oriental languages expanded considerably during the 1580s. The number of requests that Scaliger made for Oriental books in his network of correspondents increased notably in this period. Here Scaliger's eyes were fixed firmly on Italy, and then specifically Venice, the most important market for the trade in books from the Levant and the Middle East. Many of Scaliger's requests were addressed to Pithou and Dupuy, who maintained good contacts with dealers and scholars in Italy. The correspondence with Italy travelled mainly via Lyon, where the printer Antoine Gryphe (1527–1599) acted as middleman for Pithou.[130] In Lyon, the *Superintendant de la Justice*, Meric de Vic,

---

128   *Correspondence* 22 October [1585] to Pithou and 4 November 1585 to Claude Dupuy.
129   *Correspondence* 13 December 1588 to Claude Dupuy: 'Mais je ne suis poinct à moi, et suis ici parmi les bergers et masons [maçons], n'aiant moien de recouvrer un pouvre livre quand j'en ai besoing.'
130   *Correspondence* 23 August 1573 to Pithou. Gryphius printed a number of works by Scaliger.

SCALIGER AS SCHOLAR AND COLLECTOR IN FRANCE 75

also played a critical role as correspondent with the French ambassadors in Rome and Venice.[131]

Since the sixteenth century, France had maintained diplomatic relations with the Levant, often via Venice, which had close connections with the principal cities of Istanbul and Aleppo. It is therefore no surprise that Scaliger and other scholars looked to these connections as a means to acquire books. By the second half of the sixteenth century, it was no secret that the Levant presented excellent opportunities to collect Oriental books; this is most obvious from the letters of Antoine de Petremol, seigneur de la Norroye (?–1604). Between 1561 and 1566, Petremol was the French ambassador at the Porte, the court of the Sultan in Istanbul. He spent much of his time, commissioned by the king, on the hunt for Oriental and Greek manuscripts. In a letter to Michel de Boistaillé, then French ambassador in Venice, he reported on the scarcity of Greek manuscripts in the local book trade. Oriental books were in abundance: 'Arabic works like the Qur'an and many other similar books, including those on the history of the Turks or their laws [...] are available to be bought for any price between 10 to 500 ducats.'[132]

9 A Fragmented Library

Scaliger would remain in the service of Chasteigner for almost twenty years. Between 1590 and 1593, when Scaliger was frequently on the move, most of his books were kept in the chateau at Abain, then the most secure location. Scaliger wrote once from Preuilly to Scévole de Sainte-Marthe (1536–1623), the *Trésorier de France* in Poitiers, that he had to leave his books behind in Abain and Agen.[133] In Agen, Scaliger would lose the library of his father, and some of his own books, after his father died.[134] Even in castles, Scaliger's safety (or that

---

131 *Correspondence* 1 August 1599 from Meric de Vic, the stepfather of Meric Casaubon (1599–1671), the son of Isaac Casaubon.

132 'Quant à l'Alcoran, si vous le désirez en langue et lettres turquesques, j'entends arabesques, il sera facile de le recouvrer et autres semblables livres tant des histoires de ces Turcs que de leur loy, [...] de tout prix, depuis dix jusques à cinq cents ducats.' Cited in: Clarence Dana Rouillard, *The Turk in French History, Thought, and Literature (1520–1660)* (Paris: Boivin & Co., 1940), p. 9, note 5.

133 *Correspondence* 22 July 1590 to Scévole de Sainte-Marthe.

134 When Scaliger left for Leiden in 1593, a part of the library of his father was left behind at Agen; this part was ultimately lost. It seems that his father's library was already incomplete in 1590, as Scaliger complained in his correspondence: *Correspondence* 9 November 1590 to De Thou: '[...] non plus que ceux qui sont dans Agen, les restes de la bibliotheque de mon pere; qui sera un grand dommage s'ils sont dissipés [...].' Scaliger only took a

of his books) was not guaranteed. In May 1591, the fort of Bellac near Preuilly was besieged by Catholic forces. Chasteigner's sons were successful in countering the assault, but Scaliger feared that his residence at Preuilly would also come under siege.[135] In July 1591, the danger had passed, and he took a chance to transport a portion of his library, including his collection of classical inscriptions, from Abain to Preuilly. In September, Scaliger finally received a small writing desk which held some of his Oriental books from Abain.[136] His joy did not last long: the next month, the fort near Touffou surrendered, and Preuilly also came under siege. This naturally brought all of Scaliger's communication with scholars, printers and agents to a halt.

When Scaliger left France in 1593, he claimed that large parts of his library were still in three French chateaux.[137] Chasteigner confirmed this, indicating that Scaliger had left a collection of books at the chateau at Preuilly. In a letter to Scaliger, he revealed that he had been reading books from this remainder, and that he assured Scaliger that he was safeguarding the books until Scaliger returned to France.[138] This correspondence proves that Scaliger had deliberately left a part of his library in France: it seems that he did not expect to stay long at Leiden, and would ultimately return to France.[139] This, of course, never occurred.

It is remarkable that Scaliger's itinerant period in France did not impede his scholarly productivity. During his stay with Chasteigner, he composed several

---

     select number of manuscripts from his father's collection with him to Leiden, where they are still kept today. See also: *Correspondence* 25 December 1600. note 2 and 14 August 1601 to the brothers Dupuy. 'Les Cordeliers m'ont desrobé mes meilleurs livres à Agen. Ils y ont remis de vieux volumes en droit'. *Secunda Scaligerana*, 1740, s.v. 'Joseph Scaliger', p. 555.

135   *Correspondence* 28 May 1591 to De Thou.

136   *Correspondence* 25 September 1591 to Claude Dupuy: 'Aiant receu ces jours un petit bahu où j'avois mis quelques livres es langues estrangeres. [...] Mais le plus beau de toutz c'est un testament en langage dorique que le Seigneur Pinelli donna à Monsieur d'Abain pour me le bailler, lequel vous pouves estimer les plus excellent de tout ce qui se trouve en pierre ou cuivre, soit pour la grandeur d'icelui, contenant huict grandes pagees, que pour la cognoissance des choses singulieres y continues. [...] C'est que tombant sur ce livre, je ne me suis peu contenir de regretter le malheur qui est cause qu'une si grande peine que j'ai prise s'est trouvée vaine, et laquelle peust-estre ne reuscira jamais. Mais et ce livre et quelques aultres seront mis à part pour vous les laisser, affin que si Dieu faict sa volunté de nous, ils ne se perdent. Mais il y a de la longueur à renger et mettre par ordre le tout.'

137   *Correspondence* 18 July 1594 to Casaubon. Scaliger wrote that his books had been left behind in the Touraine.

138   *Correspondence* 22 September 1592 from Chasteigner: 'J'employe le temps à regarder mes livres qu'avez prins la peine de me si bien choisir comme mes plus favorits et que m'aviez laissé sur la table de vostre estude.'

139   Molhuysen, *Bronnen* I, 1913, p. 259*.

important works, including his edition of the *Astronomicon* (1579) by Manilius and his own *De emendatione temporum* (1583). Around 1579, Scaliger also composed a short Ethiopian grammar, a considerable achievement given that he did not have sufficient access to relevant sources and other reference works on the Ethiopian language.[140] *De emendatione temporum* was published on 1 August 1583 in Paris, by Sébastien Nivelle. Already by the end of 1583 a second edition appeared with Robert Estienne.[141] In this monumental work, Scaliger provided a series of improvements on chronological calculations and existing historical calendars. It offered a ground-breaking model for the systematic study of ancient chronology, and with this work, Scaliger set a new standard for philological research on classical and Oriental sources. His knowledge on this subject was unrivalled.[142]

Scaliger's *De emendatione temporum* distinguished itself from similar publications on ancient chronology, because Scaliger demonstrated that the study of classical history was not restricted to the era of the Greeks and Romans, but should include the history of Babylonian, Persian, Egyptian and the Jewish people. Scaliger discussed the chronological traditions of various western Asian and north African cultures; in the seventh chapter, entitled *Quid est de computibus annalibus nationum*, he treated the calendars of the Jewish people, the Samaritans, Abyssinians, Copts, Arabs, Persian and Armenians. These calendars were all printed in the respective scripts of these cultures, accompanied by a Latin translation and a Hebrew transcription. Scaliger's accomplishment deciphering a variety of complex texts in a wide range of languages earned him his distinguished reputation.[143] Scaliger also incorporated into his work the new astronomical principles pioneered by Nicolaus Copernicus (1473–1543) and Tycho Brahe (1546–1601); that Scaliger studied their publications carefully is especially clear from the second edition of *De emendatione temporum*.

---

140 Wilhelmina Maria Cornelia Juynboll, *Zeventiende-eeuwsche beoefenaars van het Arabisch in Nederland* (Utrecht: Kemink en Zon N.V. – Over den Dom, 1931), p. 48.

141 A second edition was published in Leiden by Raphelengius in 1598, and a third posthumous edition appeared in Geneva in 1629. The second edition was remarkably different from the first, with considerable refinements in the dating of events in the life of Christ. Cf. Marijke Hélène de Lang, *De opkomst van de historische en literaire kritiek in de synoptische beschouwing van de evangeliën van Calvijn (1555) tot Griesbach (1774)* (Leiden: s.n., 1993), *Excurs III: Josephus Scaliger* p. 79.

142 C.S.M. Rademaker, 'Scriverius and Grotius', *Quaerendo*, 7 (1977), p. 47.

143 Scaliger and other scholars of the sixteenth and seventeenth centuries were often forced to create their own help-aides when learning uncommon languages, like Arabic. Juynboll, *Zeventiende-eeuwsche beoefenaars*, p. 47.

78   CHAPTER 2

10   Mastering Arabic

In the *Scaligerana*, Scaliger relates how he first learned Arabic from his father:
'my father was very competent in Arabic and other languages, except for
German'. A marginal annotation to this note reads: 'from this [young] age, I
learned both [languages]'.[144] It is improbable that Scaliger did actually learn
Arabic from his father; there is no other evidence for this beyond Scaliger's
own claim. It is more likely that Scaliger's father did know some Arabic words
or phrases because of his interest in medical texts, many of which were translated from Hebrew or Arabic. In the sixteenth century, various translations
of medical texts, like the works of Avicenna, circulated in Europe, and these
included some Arabic passages.[145] The assertion that Julius Caesar Scaliger
knew Arabic is otherwise difficult to support: in none of this publications is
there any indication that he knew the language.

The growing interest in Arabic that emerged in France around 1600 (after
Scaliger senior's lifetime), was a result of more frequent contacts between
French ambassadors and diplomats and the court of the Sultan in Istanbul.
This interest explains why there were many professors who taught Arabic at
the Collège Royal, alongside their official disciplines of mathematics or medicine, two fields that were heavily indebted to Arabic texts. Two prominent professors in Paris who fell into this category included the physician and diplomat
Arnoult de Lisle (1556–?) and Étienne Hubert (1567/68–1614).[146] Close study
of the Old Testament also convinced some scholars that knowledge of Arabic
might help solve some of the philological uncertainties in the original Hebrew
text. Arabic was also studied for missionary purposes.[147]

When, in 1573, Scaliger commenced his research on classical sources for his
edition of the astronomical poem of Manilius, his attention was also drawn

---

144   *Scaligerana* 1740, p. 112 under *Linguae sacrae*: 'Linguam Arabicam Pater Jul. Scaliger calle-
       bat, nec ejus omnino sum ignarus nec germanicae etiam' with a marginal note on the text
       of Vertunien, written by Scaliger: 'Ab eo tempore utramque didici'.
145   See for example the translation of Avicenna by Andrea Alpago, *Liber canonis, de medicinis
       cordialibus et Cantica* [...] (Venezia: apud haer. Lucantonio I Giunta, 1544; USTC 811600).
       Scaliger himself owned a translation of Avicenna, *Liber Canonis, De medicinis cordi-
       alibus, et Cantica*, with annotations by Andreas Bellunensis, printed in Basel in 1556.
       Scaliger annotated this copy extensively. See: Auction Catalogue 1609, p. 10: *Avicenna,
       Bellunensis. Basil [15]56.
146   The combination of these two disciplines can also be found in the work of professor
       Jacobus Golius of Leiden later in the seventeenth century.
147   Alastair Hamilton and Francis Richard, *André du Ryer and Oriental Studies in Seventeenth-
       Century France* (Oxford: Arcadian Library, 2004), p. 16.

SCALIGER AS SCHOLAR AND COLLECTOR IN FRANCE

to texts in Oriental languages.[148] By the middle of the 1570s, Scaliger had an elementary grasp of Arabic, and in these years he possessed at least one manuscript of the Qur'an.[149] He wanted to compare his manuscript with one in the possession of an acquaintance of Dupuy, to correct errors in his copy, which was apparently poorly written. A part of his manuscript was also difficult to read because the it had been bound too tightly.[150]

In 1576, Scaliger finished his edition of Catullus, Tibullus and Propertius, and cast his eye more firmly on the Orient.[151] He repeatedly asked Claude Dupuy for help in acquiring Oriental books and manuscripts; he trusted his friend greatly in these matters, because Dupuy had made himself valuable in the hunt for rare books on many previous occasions. Scaliger once wrote to him that 'I cannot find a man whom I can ask for rare books, except for yourself'.[152] In the same letter, Scaliger asked Dupuy to send him the Italian translation of the Qur'an, the *L'Alcorano di Macometto, nel qual si contiene la dottrina, la vita, i costumi, e le leggi sue. Tradotto novamento dall'arabo in lingua italiana*, translated by Giovanni Battista Castrodardo (1517–1587/88), and printed in Venice in 1547 by Andrea Arrivabene.[153] Scaliger was desperate to see a copy, because he presumed from the title page description that the work had been translated

---

148   In *Correspondence* 23 August 1573 to Pithou, the Manilius project is mentioned for the first time. The work first appeared in 1579.

149   Even at the end of his life, Scaliger seemed to have been fully satisfied with this copy of the complete text of the Qur'an (probably UBL MS Or. 258). He notified Johannes Lydius (1579–1643) that he would not have to look for another copy of the Qur'an for him at the auction of the library of the Frisian professor of Greek, Johannes Theodoretus Arcerius (1538–1604). Scaliger was, incidentally, saddened to know that the library was brought to sale so quickly after the death of Arcerius, and that none of his friends had brought it to his attention before the auction was already underway. See *Correspondence* 27 November 1604 to J. Lydius.

150   *Correspondence* 1 May 1578 to Claude Dupuy: 'Mais il est si mal relié que la lettre, oultre ce qu'elle est escrite d'une tres mauvaise main, est toute cachée dens la cousture [...]'.

151   The work was published in 1577, and Scaliger dedicated it to Dupuy.

152   *Correspondence* 25 September 1576 to Claude Dupuy.

153   USTC 803229. *Correspondence* 25 September 1576 to Claude Dupuy: '[...] et vous remercie tres humblement de ce qu'il vous a pleu me le prester, et vous vouldroys supplier de vous enquerir si vous pourries trouver un Alcoran tourney d'arabic en italien, imprimé à Venize il y a plus de cinquant'ans.' There is no copy of his book from the Scaliger collection in the UBL, but strictly speaking it does not concern a book in an Oriental language. The work is not mentioned in the Auction Catalogue of 1609. Scaliger repeated his request about this translation of the Qur'an in his *Correspondence* 18 December 1576 to Dupuy.

FIGURE 10   Title page of Giovanni Battista Castrodardo, *L'Alcorano di Macometto* (Venice: Andrea Arrivabene, 1547). Koninklijke Bibliotheek Brussel; VH2482

SCALIGER AS SCHOLAR AND COLLECTOR IN FRANCE

directly from the Arabic.[154] This made the book an invaluable point of departure to Scaliger for improving his own command of the language.[155]

On 18 December 1576, several months after enquiring after this edition, Scaliger wrote to Dupuy once more to request his assistance. He impressed on him that he required the work soon: 'how could it be possible that there is not a single copy [of the Qur'an] in all the libraries of Paris?'[156] Apparently the printer Patisson knew that there was a copy to be found in Sens, a town southeast of Paris. This, Scaliger argued, was evidence that the edition was not particularly rare, so why had it taken so long to source a copy? 'I beg you to find a way, if possible, to acquire it', he emphasised. In other letters, Scaliger also mentioned this edition, but it turned to be for naught, as the translation had not been made directly from Arabic, and was thus less useful for Scaliger's purposes.[157] After this futile search, Scaliger admitted that there were few reliable help-aids to improve his Arabic. He was obviously familiar with Postel's grammar, but claimed to be unaware of any others; it therefore became his ambition to compose one himself.[158]

In general, Scaliger did not trust Latin transliterations of Arabic texts. The dedication with which he studied the language stands out in his *Thesaurus Linguae arabicae*.[159] For this thesaurus, Scaliger relied on information from his

---

154   In the introduction of the book, Arrivabene claimed that he was responsible for the translation from the Arabic, and the editing of the work in the print shop: 'Questo è Sig. Illustr. l'Alcorano di Macometto, il quale come ho gia detto, ho fatto dal suo idioma tradurre e dar alla stampa'. The translation was in fact based on an earlier translation of the Qur'an into Latin, made by Robert van Ketton. See: Pier Mattia Tommasino, *L'Alcorano di Macometto. Stroai di un libro del Cinquecento europeo* (Bologna: Il Mulino, 2013) and A. Hamilton, 'The Quran in Early Modern Europe', in J. Schaeps (et al.), *Oostersche weelde. De Oriënt in westerse kunst en cultuur. Met een keuze uit de verzameling van de Leidse Universiteitsbibliotheek* (Leiden: Primavera Pers, 2005), pp. 133–135.

155   This was an established method to learn a new language amongst early modern scholars. Casaubon, for example, read the *Advancement of Learning* (1605) of Francis Bacon to learn English. Cf. William H. Sherman, *Used Books. Marking Readers in Renaissance England* (Philadelphia: University of Pennsylvania Press, 2007, pp. 13–15.

156   *Correspondence* 18 December 1576 to Claude Dupuy.

157   *Correspondence* 12 February 1577 to Claude Dupuy. Scaliger received a copy of this book in the early months of 1577. The book disappointed him greatly, and it cannot be identified in Scaliger's collection later.

158   *Correspondence* 22 January 1602 to Casaubon.

159   See UBL SCA 212. That Scaliger thought highly of his own collection of Arabic manuscripts also comes through when he compares it in quality to the lexicographical writings of Phrynichus Atticista (2nd c. AD), who was able to construct the purest Attic Greek: Scaliger claimed that his contemporaries were able to learn the purest Arabic thanks to his collection. Cf. *Correspondence* 23 January 1602 to Lindenbrogius.

82 CHAPTER 2

own collection of Arabic books and manuscripts. In 1608, he would provide an extensive overview of the Arabic sources that he consulted for this work in a letter to Étienne Hubert (Ubertus), a Parisian physician and Arabist.[160] To understand a language properly, Scaliger wished to engage with its original sources, a process we have now observed multiple times. When these sources were not easily available in institutional collections, or those of his friends, Scaliger did his very best to assemble a collection himself.

11   Multilingual Ambitions

In a letter of 1577 to Dupuy, Scaliger expressed his seemingly boundless desire for new books. He had not received any books recently that inspired him to begin new research.[161] The shortage of books drove him to despair. This emotion would remain a constant throughout Scaliger's life, and would stimulate him to write to his many correspondents with demands to locate rare books for him. Thus we find Scaliger searching for the New Testament in an Irish Gaelic translation (the *Novum Testamentum Hirlandicum*).[162] He also desired to acquire a copy of an Icelandic Bible (*Gudbrands Biblia* or *Biblia það er Øll Heilög Ritning vtlögð a Norraenu: með formalum Doct. Martini. Lutheri*, printed in Holum by Jon Jonsson, 1584), and for this he turned to Geverhard Elmenhorst, who, as he reported to Scaliger, thought he might be able to buy a copy in Copenhagen.[163]

The Icelandic Bible did indeed find its way to Scaliger, but it was not auctioned with his library in 1609, nor was it part of the bequest to Leiden University Library, as Daniel Heinsius picked this rarity for himself.[164] The Bible in Gaelic, as well as a Bible in Welsh made their way to Scaliger's library, but were similarly not included in the bequest of books in foreign tongues that

---

160   *Correspondence* 22 March 1608 to Ubertus.
161   *Correspondence* 18 December 1576 to Claude Dupuy.
162   *Testamentum Novum Domini nostri et Salvatoris Jesu Christi, ad verbum translatum e Graeco in Gaelicum* (sc. *Hibernicum*) or *Tiomna Nuadh ar dTighearna agus ar Slanaightheora Josa Criosd: ar na tarruing gu firinneach as gréigis gu gáoidheilg* translated into Irish Gaelic by Hulliam O. Domhnuill (William Daniel) (Dublin: William Ussher re [William Kearney and] John Franckton, 1602; USTC 3000895).
163   *Correspondence* 12 November 1602 from Elmenhorst and 5 December 1602 to Elmenhorst. The copy of the Icelandic Bible with the dedication 'Viro illustri incomperabili Iosepho Scaligero Iul. Caes. Fil. Generbrardus Elmenhorst D.D.' today belongs to the collection of Lincoln College Oxford [L.4.11 SR K 4]. Scaliger noted on the title page: 'Hallgrimůs Theodori F. Islandus. Kopenhagen. 1602. 24 o[cto]bris'.
164   *Correspondence* 16 January 1604 and 14 June 1604 from Woverius.

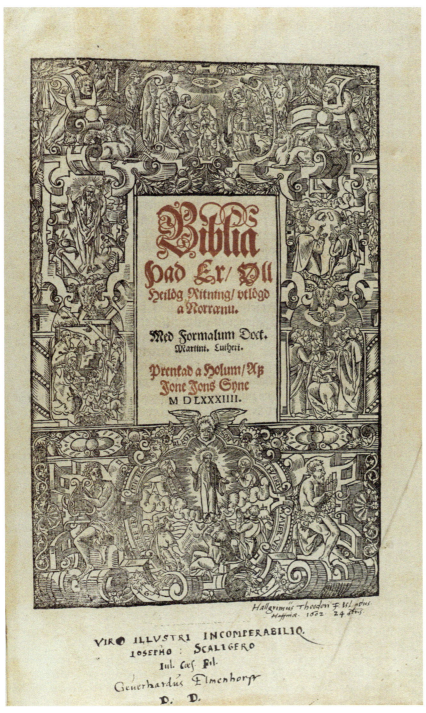

FIGURE 11 Title page of the Icelandic Bible that Scaliger was able to acquire (Holum: Jon Jonsson, 1584). Lincoln College Oxford L.4.11 SR K 4

84   CHAPTER 2

made their way into the university library.[165] From Scaliger's letters we also know that he searched for a *Biblia Danica* and a Bible in the Vandal tongue.[166] Neither of these works seems to have ended up in his collection.

Incidentally, Scaliger's determination to acquire rare books ensured that some very special items found their way to his house in Leiden. This included the Welsh Bible, sent from England to Scaliger by Richard 'Dutch' Thomson (ca. 1570–1613).[167] In 1590, Thomson had studied in Leiden under Vulcanius and Drusius senior, and three years later he would return to Leiden to meet Scaliger.[168] Thomson was an itinerant scholar, and during the 1590s travelled throughout most of Europe. He regularly criss-crossed Germany and travelled the length of his native England to visit its ancient institutional libraries in the hunt for manuscripts and rare books. In Geneva and Italy, Thomson was repeatedly fulfilling requests for books from his friends, including Scaliger, Vulcanius and Casaubon, who admired Thomson and respected him as a useful agent.

In 1599, Thomson settled definitively in Cambridge. Scaliger 'often consulted [him] on the availability of (oriental) books and manuscripts' in the British Isles, and he became Scaliger's most trusted mediator in Britain. In Cambridge, Thomson was able to acquire various rare Hebrew books for Scaliger, and he also offered to search for other rarities, including a Slavonic Bible (*Biblia Sclavonica*).[169] Scaliger sent Thomson lists of books that he

---

165   Scaliger's copy ultimately ended up in the library of Nicolaas Heinsius. See Heinsius' auction catalogue, p. 10, no. 195: *N.Testamentum Irlandicum, 1602* with the addition *Ex biblioth. Scaligeri*.

166   The Danish Bible possibly concerns the *Biblia, det er, den ganzske Hellige Scrifft, paa Danske, igen offuerseet oc prentet effter salige oc höylofflige ihukommelse, Kong Frederichs den II Befalning* (København: Mads Vingaardt, 1589; USTC 302815). *Correspondence* 20 November 1600 to Martinus Lydius (1539/1540–1601).

167   *Correspondence* 7 March 1603 to Thomson; 9 August 1604 and 3 September 1605 to Thomson; 28 February 1604 to De Laet and the letter of 30 June 1604 from Thomson to Petrus Scriverius (UBL BPL 748) in: P. Botley, *Richard 'Dutch' Thomson, c. 1569–1613 The Life and Letters of a Renaissance Scholar* (Leiden: Brill, 2015), pp. 285–287. *Y Beibl Cyssegr-Lan Sefyr Hen Destament. Ar Newydd* (London: Christopher Barker 1588; USTC 1791668) is the first translation of the complete Bible, including the Apocrypha, into Welsh. The Bible was printed by William Morgan (1545–1604). In the Auction Catalogue of 1609, there is listed on page 50 a copy of a *Biblia lingua Cambrica sive Wallica. fol. Londini 1588*. The UBL does own a copy of this Bible [UBL 1370 D 8], but this not Scaliger's former copy, the current location of which is unknown.

168   Pattison, *Casaubon*, pp. 62–63.

169   It is uncertain whether Thomson asked if Scaliger wished to acquire this Bible. It concerns a copy of the Old and New Testament printed in Cyrillic type, with the title *Biblija si rec Knigy Vetchago i Novago Zaveta po jazyku slovensku* (Ostróg: Iwan Fedorow, w Drukarni Konstantego Ostrogskiego, 1581; USTC 568885). See the letter of 30 June 1604 from

SCALIGER AS SCHOLAR AND COLLECTOR IN FRANCE 85

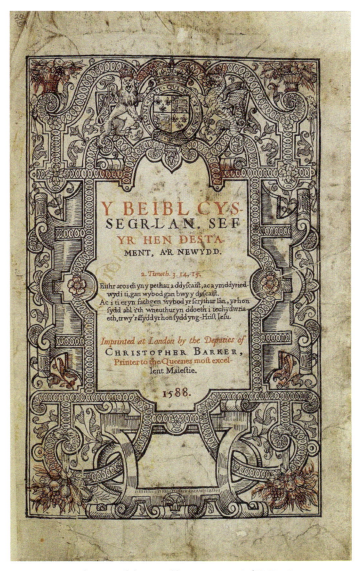

FIGURE 12 Title page of the *Y Beibl Cyssegr-Lan. Sef Yr Hen Destament, A'r Newydd* (London: Christopher Barker, 1588), the first complete Welsh translation of the Bible, including the Apocrypha

wanted to add to his library. We know that Scaliger received some of the items on his wish lists, including a copy of Maimonides' *Moreh nevukhim* (*The Guide of the Lost*), bought by Thomson in London, because he could not find a copy in Cambridge.[170] It is possible that this copy was acquired by Thomson in 1601 at a public sale, together with two other unidentified Hebrew books, that he then despatched to Scaliger via Denis Perrot.[171] Thomson also used the services of Raphelengius and other booksellers who attended the Frankfurt Fair to send books to the continent and made use of an alternative trade route from London to Middelburg.[172]

In London, the French ambassador Jean de Thuméry and the Italian bookdealer Ascanio de Renialme (or Renialmi) likewise played a role in disseminating books acquired by Thomson for continental scholars.[173] Payment for these books was handled by Raphelengius in Leiden, or via de *Officina Nortoniana*, the London firm of cousins Bonham (1565–1635) and John (d. 1612) Norton.[174] Another important figure was Johannes de Laet (1581–1649). De Laet studied at Leiden under Scaliger between 1597 and 1602, after which he moved to London, where he would remain until 1607. He was in regular contact with Thomson in Cambridge.[175] In 1604, he was searching for another copy of a

---

Thomson to Petrus Scriverius (UBL BPL 748) in: Botley, *Richard 'Dutch' Thomson* 2015, pp. 285–287.

170   *Correspondence* 23 August 1601 to Thomson and the letter from Thomson to Denis Perrot in London from the first half of 1601 in: Botley, *Richard 'Dutch' Thomson*, pp. 252–253.

171   Botley, *Richard 'Dutch' Thomson*. 2015, p. 111. The sale concerned that of an extensive library of a scholar which included many Hebrew books of interest to Scaliger. It is possible that it was the library of Richard Hooker (1554–1600), who spent much of his life as teacher of Hebrew at Oxford. See for the inventory of Hooker's possessions, including his library (although the books are not described individually): R. Keen, 'Inventory of Richard Hooker, 1601', *Archaeologia Cantiana being transactions of the Kent Archaeological Society* 70 (1956), pp. 231–237.

172   Botley, *Richard 'Dutch' Thomson*, p. 154.

173   Pier Paul Laffleur de Kermaingant, *L'Ambassade de France en Angleterre sous Henri IV. Mission de Jean de Thuméry, sieur de Boissise (1598–1602)* (Paris: Firmin Didot, 1886). Botley, *Richard 'Dutch' Thomson*, p. 188, See on Renialmi: Ronald Brunlees MacKerrow (ed.), *A Dictionary of Printers and Booksellers in England, Scotland and Ireland and of Foreign Printers of English Books, 1557–1640* (Oxford: The Bibliographical Society, 1968), pp. 225–228.

174   *Correspondence* 23 August 1601 to Thomson. In this fashion Scaliger received, amongst others, a copy of Maimonides, *Sefer Moreh nevukhim* [...] (Sabyonitah: Kornilyo AdilKind, 313 [1553]; USTC 1791668, UBL 877 B 12; see Bibliographic Survey Sabbioneta 1553).

175   R.H. Bremmer Jr and P.G. Hoftijzer (eds.), 'Johannes de Laet (1581–169): A Leiden Polymath', special issue of *Lias. Sources and Documents Relating to the Early Modern History of Ideas*, vol. 25/2 (1998), pp. 135–229, especially Bremmer, 'The correspondence of Johannes de Laet', at pp. 139–164.

SCALIGER AS SCHOLAR AND COLLECTOR IN FRANCE

Gaelic Bible for Scaliger, to replace the incomplete copy he had received from Thomson.[176] De Laet also received wish lists for Oriental books from Scaliger. He also brought to Scaliger's attention some Hebrew books that he found in London, not all of which led to a purchase.[177] After De Laet wrote to Scaliger about a copy of the Arabic grammar of Ibn al-Hajib, Scaliger responded that he already owned this edition: 'Caphiam Arabicam habeo, eandem quam designas.'[178] Thomson's efforts similarly did not necessarily lead to interest on Scaliger's part. One intriguing episode concerns a letter by Thomson of 1604 in which he notes that a dealer in London had a collection of Arabic books in his possession; Thomson promised Scaliger to provide him with a catalogue.[179] Scaliger was initially very interested in acquiring books from this collection, but ultimately did not make any purchases because he considered he already had a substantial number of printed Arabic books.

These Arabic books had come into Scaliger's collection early, at least by the later 1570s. In 1577, Scaliger was already labouring on a project in which Arabic played a prominent role. In a letter to Lipsius, Scaliger mentioned that he was working on a *Hexapla*, a psalter in six languages, composed of six columns of text, in Hebrew, Syriac, Ethiopian, Arabic, Greek and Latin.[180] This

---

176   *Correspondence* 28 February 1604; 22 May 1604 and 7 September 1604 to De Laet. Scaliger wrote in the first letter about the two Bibles: 'Nihil illis addo, nisi uno verbo, quod pluribus a te contendi, ut Biblia illa et Novum Testamentum Hibernicum, quod Thomson promiserat, mihi curentur.' The *Novum Testamentum Hibernicum* is the *Tiomna nuadh ar dTighearna agus ar Slanaightheora Iosa Criosd, ar na tarruing gu firinneach as Gréigis gu gáoioheilg, re hUilliam O Domhnuill* [...] (Dublin: William Ussher re [William Kearney and] John Franckton, 1602; USTC 568885). On this Bible, see: Botley, *Richard 'Dutch' Thomson*, p. 288, note 5.

177   *Correspondence* 12 July 1603 to De Laet. This list has not survived.

178   *Correspondence* 15 November 1605 to De Laet. Ibn al-Hajib, 'Uthman ibn 'Umar, *Grammatica arabica dicta Kaphia autore filio Alhagiabi Kāfiya* (Roma: In tipographia Medicea, 1592; USTC 836127, UBL 839 C 25; see Bibliographic Survey Rome 1592: 2). This is a short Arabic syntax, written in the thirteenth century. Some copies of this edition have the Latin title *Grammatica Arabica dicta Caphia auctore filio Alghagiabi*. Raimondi prepared a Latin translation of the work, that never appeared, see: Angelo De Gubernatis, *Matériaux pour servir à l'histoire des études orientales en Italie* (Paris etc.: Renest Leroux, 1876), p. 204 [UBL 839 C 25 and 839 C 26; see Bibliographic Survey Rome 1592:2 and Rome 1592:3].

179   *Correspondence* 7 September 1604 from De Laet. This collection of Arabic books was possibly acquir3ed from the continent after the Somerset House Conference, the peace treaty that was agreed to on 16 August 1604 in London between England and Spain.

180   *Correspondence* 12 February 1577 to Lipsius: 'Conabor tamen, si possum, editionem Psalterii mei quam molior, aut per me, aut per alium emitter. Hexaplun feci, Hebraice, Syriace, Aethiopice, Arabice, Graece, et Latine, una cum scholiis, et in eas aliquot linguas praeceptis'. Cf. De Landtsheer, 'Justus Lipsius en Josephus Justus Scaliger', Hoftijzer, *Adelaar in de wolken*, pp. 59–92 (especially pp. 61–62, 66). According to Origenes, *Hexapla*

psalter would be accompanied by Scaliger's annotations and a philological commentary, but also by a brief note on how one could learn these languages. He referred the reader to several titles that he owned himself, including the *Linguarum Duodecim Characteribus Differentium Alphabetum* by Postel of 1538 and the *Psalterium, Hebraeum, Graecum, Arabicum, & Chaldaeum* (Genoa, 1516) by Augustinus Justinianus and the *Introductio in Chaldaicam linguam* by Theseus Ambrosius Albonesius of 1539.[181]

The project never came to fruition. In 1595, De Thou urged Scaliger to publish the work, indicating that it was far advanced.[182] Although the psalter was never published, the letter to Lipsius of 1577 does give us the indication that Scaliger had some understanding of Oriental languages by this date, especially of Hebrew. He was clearly very interested in texts that provided comparative translations of classical and Oriental languages, and Scaliger had already acquired several printed Arabic books to support his work on the project while he was in France. His contemporaries were also aware of Scaliger's skill and his ambition, because as time progressed, they would send him more and more Arabic manuscripts and other documents.

---

     is the name given for a study version of the Old Testament with six columns. Origenes compared the Greek Septuagint word by word with the original Hebrew and other Greek translations. No manuscript *Hexapla* is known from Scaliger's bequest. It also goes unmentioned in Molhuysen, *Codices Scaligerani*, Van der Heide, *Hebrew Manuscripts* and in Witkam's *Inventory*.

181   UBL 873 C 1-1; 1368 C 2; 1497 D 23; see Bibliographic Survey Paris 1538; Genua 1516 and Pavia 1539. In various extant copies of Justinianus, *Psalterium Hebraeum, Graecum, Arabicum, & Chaldaeum*, the *Chaldaeum* has been corrected in manuscript to *Aethiopicum*.

182   *Correspondence* 31 October 1595 from De Thou: 'Cela vous donnera courage de nous donner vostre Psautier.'

CHAPTER 3

Supplying Scaliger with Books

Scaliger urged all his correspondents who travelled abroad, especially those who went to Italy, to look out for Hebrew and Arabic books and acquire them. When, in 1588, Pierre del Bene had plans to visit Italy, Scaliger immediately sent him a wish list. Del Bene would ultimately suspend his travel plans because of poor weather and reports of piracy in the Mediterranean; he had to disappoint Scaliger that no rare books would come his way on this occasion.[1] He did try to reassure Scaliger that Chasteigner, who was then in Florence, would probably not return home with empty hands. A different journey made by Del Bene, through the Languedoc and Provence, did result in a gift for Scaliger which was gratefully received: 'a paper written in Arabic that I have recovered, together with an idol that I was assured came from Egypt, but the characters [on it] seem to me to be Ethiopian'.[2] This is one example of the type of documents, written or printed in exotic languages, that circulated in sixteenth-century Europe. Most scholars struggled to make sense of their contents, but they were all convinced that Scaliger would be able to decipher them. This was another reason why Scaliger received so many books and manuscripts as presents.

TABLE 1   Scaliger's most important correspondents during his period in France, 1561–1593. Most of the correspondents were resident in Paris. To Scaliger, Claude Dupuy was the most prominent source for information on books

Correspondent	Extant letters
Claude Dupuy	76
Jacques-Auguste de Thou	36
Pierre Pithou	36
Justus Lipsius	15
Jacques Daléschamps	6
Pierre Daniel	4

---

1   He wrote: 'Les Corsaires, Turcs, et Ligueurs qui occupoyent la mer m'ont empesché le voyage d'Italie.'
2   *Correspondence* 23 October 1588 from Del Bene. The document has not been identified; it is possible that it concerns an ushabti.

© KONINKLIJKE BRILL BV, LEIDEN, 2025 | DOI:10.1163/9789004701526_005

Many of Scaliger's correspondents helped him search for, buy and despatch manuscripts and books. They included merchants, dealers, patrons, diplomats, scholars, printers and others. Yet Scaliger's personal friends Jacques-Auguste De Thou, Claude Dupuy and Pierre Pithou played a decisive role in Scaliger's network (see Table 1). Scaliger met the three men in 1571, during his student days at Valence. They would continue to write to each other, even when Scaliger moved to Leiden and the geographical distance between them grew. Scaliger admired Dupuy as scholar and book collector, and after Dupuy's death, Scaliger would correspond with Dupuy's sons as if he was their father. Pithou, with his great library in Paris, filled with classical manuscripts, was a natural point of call for Scaliger's quest for unknown texts and newly published books. Pithou regularly provided Scaliger with books and other documents. Scaliger's bond with De Thou blossomed into the most loyal friendship after they met each one again in Lyon in 1582.

Scaliger also made fortuitous use of the correspondents of his closest friends. This led to an extensive exchange of knowledge between Scaliger and many scholars and collectors whom he would never meet. This secondary network, most notably Gian Vincenzo Pinelli in Italy and Pereisc in the south of France, also played an important role in gathering books for Scaliger. Dupuy provided the connection through which Scaliger communicated with Pinelli, and although the two men would never encounter one another face to face (Pinelli rarely left Padua), the two great collectors happily exchanged information via letter. Until 1593, Scaliger relied heavily on his original Parisian network developed in his youth, but afterwards he made more use of the network of contemporaries who studied with him under Cujas at Valence in 1571.

The friendships that Scaliger made during his study days in Valence would last a lifetime. His three key correspondents – Dupuy, Pithou and De Thou – each resided for periods in Paris, undoubtedly the most important node in Scaliger's French network. Even when these three men were not present in the capital, they had their own agents there who they could recommend to Scaliger as a go-between. Beyond this, Scaliger could make use of his contacts among the bookselling community. What becomes clear from Scaliger's correspondence is that his network was often sustained by an expansive circle of trusted agents who carried letters, parcels and books. In 1584, De Thou sent Scaliger several letters via Jonathan Petit, sieur de Claux Hardy (?–1652) and 'Advocat au grand Conseil'. Fédéric Morel, another Parisian contact of Scaliger, also made use of Petit's services for the despatch of books to Scaliger.[3]

---

3 *Correspondence* 5 February 1585 from Fédéric Morel and *Correspondence* 28 May 1586 to Dupuy.

1 The Context of Scaliger's French Network

Scaliger's life was influenced greatly by the political and religious divisions of his age, but personal circumstances, tastes and prejudices also played their part. In his correspondence, Scaliger often reflected on the necessity of using trustworthy couriers for the exchange of letters and books. He trusted only a small group of individuals, especially when it concerned valuable books, manuscripts or objects. The political climate of the moment also concerned Scaliger a great deal, as this affected the reliability of his network. In the spring of 1588, he was separated from his Parisian contacts because the Protestant Henry IV of Navarre had been forced to leave the city after the Catholic League refused to recognise his claim to the French throne. Now that the Catholic League effectively ruled Paris, in February 1589 Henry moved his headquarters and parliament to Tours. Dupuy, Patisson, the *premier président* Achille de Harlay (1536–1616) and other leading members of the Parlement had all been imprisoned in the Parisian Bastille a month earlier.[4] This situation naturally did not expedite the efficiency of Scaliger's network of correspondents. When Lyon also fell into Catholic hands, it proved impossible for Scaliger to have this works printed there, or to communicate with Lyonnais printers and booksellers.

Even when the political situation stabilised, and Scaliger's principal contacts could safely return to Paris, it often still proved impossible for Scaliger to make a personal visit. Scaliger regularly complained of feeling isolated. Yet despite the political turbulence of 1588, he was able to advance his scholarly activities: in this year he published an edition of the *Opera* of Ausonius, while he also made significant progress in his study of Hebrew. In a letter from Abain, sent to Petrus Caierus (1525–1610), Scaliger discussed at great length the meaning of a Hebrew word in the Book of Jonah.[5] He also mentioned several of the sources that he had been able to consult for his research, including the reference works *Sefer Shorashim* by Kimchi and the *Baal Aruch* of Nathan ben Yechiel.[6]

To source books, Scaliger also continued to rely on a large network of printers and booksellers. The great hall of the Palais de Justice in Paris functioned as a key marketplace for the trade in textile and jewels, but also for the sale of

---

4 After a short stint in prison, Dupuy was released in January 1589.
5 *Correspondence* 28 June [1588?] to Petrus Caierus. It is possible that this is the Protestant minister and historian Pierre Victor Palma Cayer or Cayet (1525–1610), who, in 1595, was appointed professor of Hebrew in Paris.
6 UBL 874 B 4, and/or 875 B 5 and 838 A 14 and/or 838 A 15; see Bibliographic Survey Naples 1491, Venice 20, Pesaro 1517 and Venice 1531–1532.

art and books. Around eighty booksellers had a stall in the building. A second important location for the book trade was the Latin Quarter, home to the university buildings of the Sorbonne. At the heart of the Latin Quarter, around the rue Saint-Jacques, some two hundred printers and booksellers practiced their trade.[7] These traders possessed an extensive network of trusted agents and contacts spread across Europe. This was a practical trade and a financial network, but also one that advanced the exchange of scholarly information. Frankfurt was probably the most important node in this European network, because it was home to its great biannual fair. Frankfurt was easily accessible by water transport and also suitably located for the exchange between the east German and Baltic market, the important Italian trade centres and the commercial centres in the Low Countries and on the Atlantic seaboard.

One printer who loomed large in Scaliger's network was Charles Périer. In 1564 he sent Scaliger a copy of the *Vocabularium* of Papias that the scholar and bibliophile Pierre Daniël (1531–1604) had bought for him in Paris.[8] The familial bonds between printers were also helpful to Scaliger: Périer was able to function as an agent who could pass on letters, manuscripts and money to other printers in the trade, like his relation Mamert Patisson.[9] Thanks to his contacts with Périer, Scaliger was able to ask Patisson to acquire books for him at the Frankfurt book fair, where Patisson was a regular visitor.[10]

---

7 A. Parent, *Les métiers du livre à Paris au XVIe siècle (1535–1560)* (Genève: Droz, 1974), pp. 169–171.

8 Scaliger's copy of Papias's lexicon (Venice, 1496) is currently located in the University Library of Amsterdam (call number OTM inc. 211). Daniel wrote the following annotation on the title page: 'Ego, Petrus Daniel, hunc vocabulistam 8 assib[us] emi, Lutetiae, pro Ios. Scaligero I.F. 1564'.

9 Dupuy functioned as contact between the two men. Patisson was related to the Estienne family through marriage to the widow of Robert II Estienne. See William Parr Greswell, *A View of the Early Parisian Greek Press. Including the Lives of the Stephani* [...] (Oxford: S. Collingwood, 1833), Vol. 2, p. 101.

10 In 1577, Patisson supplied Scaliger with a copy of the edition of Ptolemy's *Quadripartitus* in Greek and the scholia in preparation for Scaliger's edition of Manilius. Scaliger complained in his *Correspondence* 13 July 1577 to Dupuy about a poor Arabic translation of Ptolemy that he owned, and that he wished to compare to the Greek. Thanks to Dupuy, Scaliger also received a copy of Ptolemy's *Tetrabiblos* (Nürnberg: [apud Johann Petreius], 1535; USTC 662928). The copy is listed in the Auction Catalogue 1609 on p. 15. On the same page there is also listed a copy of the λαυδίου Πτολεμαίου Ἀλεξανδρέως φιλοσόφου ἐν τοῖς μάλιστα πεπαιδευμένου [...] (Basel: Johann Froben, 1533). Cf. *Correspondence* 26 August 1577 and 8 March 1589 from Pierre Del Bene, abbé de Bellozane, the secretary of Queen Margaret of France and King Henry III.

2 De Thou and the *Bibliothèque Royale*

Jacques-Auguste de Thou, who possessed an extensive diplomatic network, was one of Scaliger's most important correspondents and suppliers of books. De Thou and Scaliger would remain good friends after they first met each other as students of Cujas in Valence. After finishing his studies, De Thou travelled in 1574 through Italy in the entourage of the diplomat Paul de Foix (1528–1589). In Italy, De Thou was introduced to Muret and Francesco I de' Medici (1541–1587), Grand Duke of Tuscany. His contact with the Grand Duke would later be of significant value to Scaliger for the purchase of Arabic books published by the *Tipographia Medicea*. Between 1582 and 1585, Scaliger and De Thou maintained correspondence on a regular basis. What is noticeable in their exchange is the large number of requests made by Scaliger to supply him with various Hebrew books.[11] In a letter of 14 August 1601, he wrote in an emotional tone to De Thou: 'I am poor in everything, especially in books, as the remainder of my late father's books have been looted from me in Agen since the time I was last here. The bone never falls in the mouth of the good dog. Such is my fate.'[12]

That the friendship between Scaliger and De Thou was heartfelt comes out clearly in their correspondence, but it can also be deducted from the close personal bond that they maintained after their student days. De Thou even took Scaliger on as a scholarly mentor. In 1583, Scaliger travelled to Paris to live with De Thou and to teach him Hebrew.[13] According to Scaliger, learning this beautiful and elegant language was not difficult. Indeed, after eight or ten days of his tutelage, De Thou was able to continue studying Hebrew on his own.

On 7 February 1593, after the death of Jacques d'Amyot (1513–1593), De Thou was appointed by King Henry IV as *Maître de la librairie du Roi*, a post he would hold until 1617. This position had been created in 1522 by King Francis I for Guillaume Budé: at that point it was the greatest literary honour that a scholar could aspire to in the kingdom. The officeholder had to reckon, however, with the *Garde de la librairie*, responsible for access to the library. Jean Gosselin (1510–1604), *Garde* between 1560 and 1604, was infamous for never granting access to anyone. De Thou ensured that his friend Casaubon would succeed

---

11 See for example *Correspondence* 24 February 1583 in which Scaliger asks De Thou for a copy of Avraham Bar-Hasdai's *Sepher ben hammelec vehannazir* (Mantua: 1557) [UBL 871 G 20; see Bibliographic Survey Mantua 1557: 2].

12 *Correspondence* 14 August 1601 to the brothers Dupuy. 'Je suis pauvre en tout, mesmement en livres, que le reste des livres de feu mon père m'ont esté pillés dans Agen depuis le temps que je suis ici. Jamais à bon chien ne tombe bon os en gueule. Hoc est meum fatum'.

13 *Correspondence* 21 March 1583 to De Thou. Scaliger also reflected on this in *Correspondence* 23 February 1587 to De Thou.

FIGURE 13   Jacques-Auguste de Thou, librarian of the Royal Library in Paris.
Rijksprentenkabinet Amsterdam RP-P-OB-55.710

Gosselin.[14] Before this, during the period of Gosselin's iron rule, De Thou was one of the few people who could access books – many of which were of interest to Scaliger – from the Royal Library. Almost immediately after De Thou's appointment, Henry IV ordered that the library was moved to Fontainebleau, to the south of Paris, to be held in the Collège de Clermont on the rue Saint-Jacques. After this move the library became known formally as the Bibliothèque Royale. The move was fully completed in 1595, while De Thou was also responsible for the incorporation, in 1594, of books from the library of Catherine de' Medici.[15]

Thanks to their friendship, Scaliger enjoyed access to De Thou's private library, but after De Thou's appointment as royal librarian, this magnificent collection also came within reach. On multiple occasions, Scaliger made requests to De Thou to borrow sources for his research. He wanted to see the manuscript of Aristarchus of Samos, on astrology and the *Hierakosophion*, as well as a thirteenth-century manuscript by Demetrius Pepagomenus on falconry, both from the collection of Catherine de' Medici.[16] Scaliger asked if

---

14   De Thou had a decisive influence on the appointment of Casaubon. Although he only took up the post in 1604, Casaubon was already named as successor in November 1601. According to Scaliger, in *Correspondence* 23 February 1605 to Casaubon, Gosseling was unable to judge the value of the manuscripts in the library accurately or to use them, and was therefore suspicious of anyone who was able to do so. See on Gosselin and De Thou: Pattison, *Casaubon*, pp. 173–175, 178.

15   E. Quentin-Bauchart, *La Bibliothèque de Fontainebleau et les livres des derniers Valois à la Bibliothèque nationale (1515–1589)* (Paris: E. Paul, Huard et Guillemin: 1891), p. 41. Cathérine de' Medici (1519–1589) was married to Henry II and was the mother of King Francis II, Charles IX and Henry III. Her son-in-law, the future King Henry IV, inherited her library. In her library of 776 volumes, only a small part (some 40 volumes) concerned theology or the Hebrew language. Ronsard wrote a poem on the library: 'Pour de dégénérer de ses propres ayeux / La reine a fait chercher les livres le plus vieux / Hébreux, grecs, latins, traduits et à traduire, / Et par noble despense elle en a fait reluire / Le haut palais du Louvre, a fin que sans danger, / Le François fut vaingueur du sçavoir estranger.'

16   De Thou published a poem on falconry: *Hieracosophioy, sive de re accipitraria libri très* (Paris: M. Patissonium, in officina R. Stephani, 1584; USTC 147110). This publication contained a dedication in verse by Sainte-Marthe and a separate dedication by De Thou: 'Ad. Philippum Huraltum Chevernium, Franciae cancellarium epistula'. On 26 July 1584, De Thou sent a copy of the book, via Sainte-Marthe, to Scaliger in Touffou. Scaliger confirmed receipt in a letter to De Thou on 27 August 1584 and announced in delight that it was a 'most precious pearl' of a book. On the scholarly work of De Thou, see: *Correspondence* 3 July 1583 and 27 August 1584, both to De Thou, 7 November [1584] from Du Faur and 30 April [1591] to Lipsius. After Scaliger's death, the works of Pepagomenus and De Thou were jointly published under the title *Hierakosophion. Rei accipitrariae scriptores nunc primum editi. Accessit Kynosophion. Liber de cura canum ex biblioth. Regia Medicea* (Paris: sumbtibus Jérôme Drouart, 1612; USTC 6116126). Ingrid De Smet recently published the text in a French translation and commentary as *La fauconnerie à*

De Thou could have copies made of both books.[17] In 1601, Scaliger asked if he could borrow from the Royal Library a manuscript of the *Chronicon* by Eusebius with a commentary by Georgius Monachus. It was agreed that Louise de Coligny (1555–1620), the fourth wife of Prince William of Orange, who was planning to travel to Leiden in October 1601, would carry the book for Scaliger; there were few professors who could rely on princesses to deliver books to them. De Buzanval would then return the book to Paris when Scaliger was finished with it.[18] Ultimately, De Thou did not give the book to Louise de Coligny, but to a former student of Scaliger, Johannes Westhovius or Johan Boreel (1577–1629).[19]

De Thou also played an important role as Scaliger's foremost supplier of books from Venice. Between 1582 and 1585, Scaliger sent repeated requests to De Thou to purchase Hebrew books in Venice.[20] He referred specifically to the *Siddur tephilloth*, printed in Venice in 1571 (the Jewish calendar year 5331). He added that he also wished to acquire an old edition, but that this was very

---

      la Renaissance. Le Hieracosophion (1582–1584) de Jacques Auguste de Thou. Édition critique, traduction et commentaire précédés d'une étude historique de la chasse au vol en France au XVIe siècle (Genève: Droz, 2013).

17   *Correspondence* 9 November 1582 to De Thou.

18   *Correspondence* 4 September 1601 to De Thou.

19   Johan Boreel, lord of Westhoven (1577–1629), had studied law at Heidelberg. Around 1600, he travelled through the Middle-East, Syria and Palestine and took back with him to Europe some important Oriental books and manuscripts. These included the so-called *Codex Boreelianus*, a ninth-century Biblical manuscript in Greek, written in Constantinople, which has been in the possession of the University Library of Utrecht since 1830 as Hs. 1 (Hs 1 a 7). Boreel stayed in Basel in 1598 with Reigerberch and in all likelihood also studied under Scaliger. He was a good friend of Hugo Grotius. Boreel later became pensionary of Middelburg and he was the Dutch ambassador at the court of King James I of England. His library was auctioned in 1632. His manuscripts probably came into the hands of his younger brother, the theologian Adam Boreel. See P.J. Meertens, *Letterkundig leven in Zeeland in de zesteinde en eerste helft van de zeventiende eeuw* (Amsterdam: Noord-Hollandsche Uitgeversmaatschappij, 1943) pp. 443, 469, note 223 and Jodocus Heringa, *Disputatio de Codice Boreeliano, nunc Rheno-Trajectino, ad iposo in lucem protacto* (Utrecht: Kemink et filium, 1843).

20   *Correspondence* 24 February 1583 to De Thou: 'Au reste, si vous aves quelque cognoissance avec quelcun qui aist prattiqué les juifs de Venize, je vous supplie tres humblement de recouvrer par son moyen un breviaire des juifz nommé par eux *Siddur tephilloth*, imprimé à Venize l'an 5331 sellon leur conte. Car j'en ai bien un de plus vieille impression, mais cestui-ci est plus ample, et a les explications des mots plus difficiles. Ledict livre est fort aisé à recouvrer. Item un livre nommé *Sepher ben hammelec vehannazir* un aultre nommé *Igghereth baale haiim* item un aultre nommé *Misle suhalim*. Ces trois sont trois petits livrets imprimés à Padoue. Vous avez bien le moyen de les recouvrer de Padoue ou de Venize. De quoi je vous supplie tres humblement, et feres beaucoup pour moi, s'il vous plaist d'en prendre la peine.'

SUPPLYING SCALIGER WITH BOOKS

rare, and difficult to find.[21] He also required the *Sepher ben hammelec vehannazir*, the *Iggeret ba'alei chayim* and the *Mislei shu'alim*.[22] Scaliger knew that editions of these works had been printed in Padua. This particular letter is of great importance, because Scaliger provides us with information about specific Hebrew books which were clearly not available in France. Did Scaliger receive this information from members of the Jewish community at Aix-en-Provence with whom he was staying at that point? In any case, he presumed that these books would still be available in their place of publication. Indeed, the request did not give De Thou much trouble. In July 1583, less than four months later, Scaliger thanked De Thou for the despatch of the books from Italy. They were delivered to Scaliger by André Hurault, sieur de Maisse (1539–1607), who would become French ambassador to England in 1597.[23]

Scaliger also regularly reminded De Thou to chase up contacts in his network to speed up the supply of books. On one occasion, De Thou was urged

---

21   According to a footnote in Tamizey de Larroque, *Lettres* this concerned an edition from 1571, published by Giovanni de Gara in Venice. A.M. Habermann, *Giovanni di Gara. Printer, Venice 1564–1610. List of Books Printed at his Press, completed and edited by Y. Yudlov* (Jeruzalem: Re'uven Mas, 1982) does not include this edition. This edition cannot be located in Scaliger's bequest either. It was only after 1600 that he could acquire a copy of the *Seder tefillot* ([Venezia]: Daniel Zanetti 5360 [1600]; UBL 854 D 20–1; see Bibliographic Survey Venice 1600).

22   The copy that Scaliger would come to own of the first of these items, a twelfth-century Hebrew translation by Abraham Bar Hasdai, from the original Greek narrative on Barlam and Josaphat, was printed in Mantua in 1557 [UBL 871 G 20; see Bibliographic Survey Mantua 1557: 2]. The second item was Kalonymus ben Kalonymus, *Iggeret ba'alei chayim* (Mantua: Joseph ben Jacob of Padua, [5]317 [= 1557]; USTC 1791940, UBL 854 F 5–2; see Bibliographic Survey Mantua 1557: 1). This book is a translation from the Arabic by Kalonymos ben Kalonymos, from the middle decades of the sixteenth century. See also: Julius Landsberger, *Iggereth Baale Chajjim. Abhandlung über die Thiere ... oder Rechtssstreit zwischen Mensch und Thier vor dem Gerichtshofe des Königs der Genien. Ein arabisches Märchen nach Vergleichung des arabischen Originals aus dem Hebräischen ins Deutsche übertragen und mit Textescorrecturen* (Darmstadt: G. Junghaus, 1882), p. xxix. The Berechiah ha-Nakdan, *Misle sualim* (Manṭōvah (= Mantua): Ȳōsef [ben] Ȳa'aqov miPadū'ah [Joseph ben Jacob of Padua], [5]319 [1558]; USTC 1791942; UBL 854 F 18; see Bibliographic Survey Mantua 1558) is a collection of 180 fables collected by Rabbi Berakhia (ca. 1400). See: H. Schwarzbaum, 'The Impact of the Mediaeval Beast Epics upon the *Mishlé Shu'alim* of Rabbi Berechiah Ha-Nakdan' in E. Rombauts and A. Welkenhuysen (eds.), *Aspects of the Medieval Animal Epic*, Leuven/Den Haag 1975, pp. 229–239 and Haim Schwarzbaum, *The* Mishlé Shu'alim *(Fox Fables) of Rabbi Berechiah Ha-Nakdah. A Study in Comparative Folklore and Fable Lore* (Kiron: Institute for Jewish and Arab Folklore Research, 1979).

23   *Correspondence* 3 July 1583 to De Thou: 'Je vous remercie tres humblement des livres hebraiques qu'il vous a pleu faire retenir pour moi à Venize par Monsieur de Maisse, et vous supplie aussi d'escrire au dict Sieur de retenir celui dont le juif lui a faict grand feste imprimé à Constantinople.'

98 CHAPTER 3

to write to Henri de Mesmes, seigneur de Malasisse et de Roissy (1532–1596), himself a fervent book collector who then resided in Italy, as he had forgotten to buy several Hebrew books in Padua and Venice for Scaliger.[24] If it took too long, Scaliger threatened petulantly, he would look for different avenues to acquire these books.[25]

3   Claude Dupuy as Supplier of Oriental Books

In the autumn of 1575, Scaliger renewed his friendships with Dupuy and with Pierre Pithou and his brother François (1543–1621), all former students of Cujas, at a meeting of the scholarly circle that gathered at the house of De Thou in the Grand Couvent des Cordeliers in Paris.[26] Dupuy took part in these meetings regularly, even before he was appointed a councillor at the Parisian Parlement in 1566. Scaliger admired the young jurist, and he would later dedicate two books to him: the *Élégiaques* (1577) and the *Stromateus versuum Graecorum proverbialium* (1600). The admiration was mutual, and Dupuy and Scaliger would exchange a lively correspondence.

From the point when they reignited their friendship, Claude Dupuy would play a critical role in Scaliger's network. Dupuy had begun his career as a talented jurist with a practice in the south-west of France, and even before he came to Paris he was renowned as a great bibliophile. In March 1570, he travelled to Italy. During this journey, which would last for more than a year, he made contacts with a large number of scholars and collectors in Venice, Bologna, Florence, Rome and Padua. In Venice he met Paulus Manutius (1512–1574), who in 1533 had taken over the printing firm established by his father. Dupuy also became acquainted with Paulus's son, Aldus Manutius the younger.[27] The following months, Dupuy made contact in Padua with the

---

24   De Mesmes owned one of the finest libraries in France, comparable in distinction to the library of Pinelli in Italy. Cf. Calude Jolly, *Histoire des Bibliothèques françaises: Les Bibliothèques sous l'Ancien Régime. 1530–1789.* vol. 2. *Les bibliothèques sous l'Ancien Régime 1530–1789* (Paris: Promodis – Éditons du Cercle de la Librairie, 1988), pp. 85–86 and the letter from Dupuy to Pinelli of 10 November 1571 in Raugei, *Gian Vincenzo Pinelli et Claude Dupuy* 2001.

25   *Correspondence* 3 July 1583 to De Thou: 'Je chercherai un aultre moien pour les recouvrer' and 2 November 1584 to De Thou.

26   Raugei, *Gian Vincenzo Pinelli et Claude Dupuy*, p. xxxiii. In Valence, Scaliger had resided for some time in the house of Sebastien Senneton, an old friend of Pithou.

27   Letter from Claude Dupuy to Pierre Daniel 19 May 1570. Paulus Manutius would later be asked by Pope Pius IV to set up the 'Typographia Romana' in Rome. The successor of Pius IV, Gregory XIII, made much use of the Roman Manutius press, while Aldus the

SUPPLYING SCALIGER WITH BOOKS

collector, scholar and antiquarian Gian Vincenzo Pinelli (1535–1601), while in Bologna he met Carlo Sigonio.[28] It was in Rome that Dupuy was able to develop his scholarly network in full. By the end of the year he had become acquainted with Fulvio Orsini, Orazio Amaduzzi, François Guillemer and Marc-Antoine Muret.

Claude Dupuy became one of Scaliger's most important suppliers of books. It was unsurprising that Dupuy, like De Thou and Scaliger, was also a fanatical book collector. He would gather some 8,000 books in his library, from which he generously lent works that Scaliger asked for.[29] In Paris, Dupuy was a critical node in a network of jurists and historians who assembled themselves around De Thou. This circle exercised considerable influence on the cultural climate of Paris. Scaliger's friendship with Dupuy was therefore of great value to gain access to sources found in private collections across the city. Scaliger called Dupuy his 'patron' and 'protector' in various letters. By supplying Scaliger with books, Dupuy allowed him to finish projects in the Dutch Republic that he had begun in France.[30] Scaliger shared Dupuy's yearning for the latest information on newly published books as well as antiquarian works.[31] In his letters, Dupuy sent Scaliger information about items in his own library, while the correspondence between the two men also reveals that Scaliger considered his own collection insufficient, and that he thought that he owned too few precious or

---

younger (1547–1597) would initially continue his father's firm in Venice, before leaving for Rome in 1590 to take over the Vatican printing house.

28   The 106 extant letters from Pinelli to Dupuy, written between 6 October 1570 and 2 June 1593, can be found in the BnF under call number Dupuy 663, f. 110 3n, Dupuy 704, f 2–113. The 61 extant letters from Dupuy to Pinelli can be found in the Bibliotheca Ambrosiana in Milan. On the relationship between the two men, see W. McCuaig, 'On Claude Dupuy (1545–1594)', *Studies in Medieval and Renaissance History* Vol. XII (old series vol. CXXII). New York (1991), pp. 45–104. Sigonio was a historian, philologist and Christian Hebraist, who, in 1585, published the *De republica Hebræorum libri VII*. On several occasions, using his network of agents, Scaliger sent copies of his published works to Sigonio. Cf. William McCuaig, *Carlo Sigonio. The Changing World of the Late Renaissance* (Princeton: Princeton University Press, 1989), pp. 71–72.

29   *Correspondence* 5 December 1588 from Claude Dupuy: 'Au contraire, je m'asseure tousjours que puisque les livres-là sont en vostre librairie, que j'en puis user comme miens, et les avoir toutes fois que je vous en requerrois'. The families Dupuy and Chasteignerwere bound to each other through the marriage of Louis Chasteigner and Claude Dupuy, the daughter of Georges Dupuy, in 1565.

30   Isaac Uri, *Un cercle savant au XVIIe siècle. François Guyet, 1575–1655, après des documents inédits* (Paris: Hachette, 1886), p. 10.

31   *Correspondence* 9 October 1585 to Dupuy: 'Je desire fort en savoir des nouvelles, si en aures apris quelque chose; item si on a faict imprimer en Allemagne je ne sai quoi sur le Talmud, comme l'on m'a donné entendre'.

100   CHAPTER 3

remarkable books.[32] We should interpret such expressions as false modesty, as on other occasions, Scaliger seemed to be very keenly aware of the distinction of his library, rich as it was in Oriental books.[33]

The contact between Scaliger and Dupuy was essential for the development of Scaliger's Oriental collections. From the late 1570s onwards, when Scaliger turned increasingly to the study of Oriental languages, he regularly required Dupuy's help in sourcing Oriental works; a process that, judging by Scaliger's correspondence, was often troublesome and frequently unsuccessful. In December 1577, Scaliger asked Dupuy, with the aid of a certain Monsier Mansoldo, to acquire a Pentateuch printed in Thessaloniki with text in Hebrew, Arabic, Chaldaic and Persian, entirely set in Hebrew type.[34] Scaliger also asked Chasteigner about this edition; although Chasteigner could not trace the work in Venice, he was able to ask the French ambassador at the Turkish court, Arnaud du Ferrier (1505/08–1585) to look out for it.[35] Chasteigner suggested that Du Ferrier try to acquire a copy through local Jewish merchants in Istanbul, but the Thessaloniki Pentateuch still proved elusive.

The books that Dupuy was able to acquire for Scaliger were sent alongside parcels destined for Chasteigner via the banker De la Voulpière in Lyon.[36] For other consignments from Italy, Scaliger also made much use of the services

---

32   *Correspondence* 5 December 1588 to Dupuy, in which Scaliger indicates that Friedrich Sylburgius overestimated the size of Scaliger's library considerably. 'Sylburgius, lequel pense que j'aie quelque opulente biblioteque pleine de livres rares. [...] Ceux qui savent mes moiens, savent qu'il s'en fault beaucoup que je soie si riche jusques-là; et ceux qui me cognoissent de plus pres, savent aussi que je n'ai ni le lieu, ni la commodité.'

33   See for example the *Correspondence* 29 June 1578 to Pithou, in which Scaliger boasts about the number of Ethiopian books in his collection.

34   This Mansoldo was probably the Bishop of Reggio, related to Dupuy. *Correspondence* 12 February 1577 to Dupuy. Scaliger begged for the book: 'Je suis en grande peine de ce livre'. An edition of the polyglot Bible edition from Thessaloniki has not been identified, if it ever existed. See: Marvin J. Heller, *The Sixteenth Century Hebrew Book. An Abridged Thesaurus*, vol. II (Leiden, Boston: Brill, 2004), pp. 294–295. Scaliger did own a copy of the *Pentateuchis Hebraicus cum commentario R. Schelomo Jarchi, & triplici versione, Chaldaica Onkeli, Arabica R. Saadiæ, Persica R. Jacobi Tawusi, filii R. Joseph Tawusi; omnia charactere Hebræo* (Constantinopoli: 1551 [= 1546]; UBL 839 A 7; see Bibliographic Survey Constantinople 1546). Scaliger may have been confused about the place of publication, as the title of this book is otherwise identical to his request for the Thessaloniki edition.

35   Arnaud du Ferrier was also the French ambassador to Venice during the reign of Charles IX and Henry III. See Edoard Frémy, *Un ambassadeur libéral sous Charles IX et Henri III. Ambassades à Venise d'Arnaud Du Ferrier (1563–1567, 1570–1582)* (Paris: Ernest Leroux, 1880).

36   Lyon was the banking capital of France. This sector was dominated by several Italian families. Jean de la Voulpière was, according to Tamizey, probably *Conseiller* of Lyon. Cf. Tamizey pp. 61–62, note 2.

of his friend François Vertunien, and other unidentified merchants in Lyon.[37] Poitiers was another important node in the communications network of Scaliger and Dupuy. Couriers delivered letters from Scaliger's various hideouts in the countryside to Poitiers, from where they were sent on to Dupuy in Paris. For this relay, Scaliger used local agents, probably Poitiers merchants: Albonetus and Bosellus are two such agents for whom we know their names.[38] They received correspondence and books destined for Scaliger.

Dupuy's extensive Italian network was especially useful to indulge Scaliger's need for Oriental books. This is confirmed again in a letter in which Scaliger thanks Dupuy for sending him a copy of the *De epochis*.[39] In the same correspondence, Scaliger asked Dupuy to send him a copy of the Gospels in Coptic. He revealed that he already owned a *Computus* (a calendar with which one can calculate the dates of the Coptic Easter), but he wanted the Gospels in Coptic to advance his study of the language.[40] Scaliger emphasised that Dupuy was of critical importance to his network: he called him a benefactor and a leader amongst his friends and acquaintances.[41] Indeed, Dupuy seems to have been one of Scaliger's most efficient suppliers of books. On 4 September 1581, Scaliger wrote from Chantemille to Dupuy with a request to ask Pinelli to source several books for him. On this occasion it concerned an Armenian New Testament, printed in Venice.[42] Scaliger also asked whether Pinelli's Jewish family from Istanbul could send him more information on the Samaritan calendar, as well as the Coptic calendar. Scaliger may have owned the coptic calendar already,

---

37 *Correspondence* 30 March 1584 to Daléchamps. See also: R.L. Hawkins, 'The Friendship of Joseph Scaliger and François Vertunien', *Romanic Review*, viii (1917), pp. 117–144 and 307–327.

38 Possibly a member of the printer's family of the same name, which had a firm in Venice.

39 *Correspondence* 4 September 1581 to Dupuy. Grafton, *Joseph Scaliger* II, 1993, p. 110 identified this book as Paulus Crusius, *Liber de epochis seu aeris temporum et imperiorum* [...] *editus opera Ioan. Thomae Freigii, una cum eiusdem praefatione* (Basel: per Sebastian Henricpetri, [1578]; USTC 672920). In the Auction Catalogue 1609, no copy of the book can be traced.

40 We do not know whether Scaliger received a copy of the Evangelists in Coptic.

41 *Correspondence* 4 September 1581 to Dupuy; 'Ne vous esbahisses poinct si je coquine ainsi les livres, car ceste caimanderie m'a servi beaucoup. Je confesserai tousjours mes bienfacteurs, et ceux qui m'ont aidé à ma picorée. Vous estes les chef et premier de toutz, et pouves encores m'aider d'avantage quand il vous plaira.'

42 Scaliger had tried earlier (with the help of Dupuy) to borrow a copy of the New Testament in Armenian from the library of Pierre Pithou; see *Correspondence* 15 February 1580 to Pithou, note 4. The book in Pithou's library probably concerns a manuscript, because the first printed edition of the Armenian New Testament appeared in Amsterdam in 1666.

but it was written in Arabic.[43] Scaliger's impatience to gain access to new sources is a recurring theme from his correspondence, and it is testament to his unceasing interest in learning new languages.

Almost five years later, in a letter of 5 June 1586, Scaliger was on the hunt for an Armenian psalter. He begged Dupuy to provide him with information whether a printed Armenian psalter existed, and, if so, where it had been printed. If it had been printed in Rome, Scaliger reflected, then it should not be too difficult to acquire a copy.[44] From a letter dated twenty-five days later, it is clear that Scaliger had received the psalter thanks to Dupuy. The book had been found in Italy by Pinelli and sent to Scaliger via Claude Vernelle.[45] In this case, it is clear how efficiently Dupuy's transport network between Rome and France operated.[46] Scaliger had now received his first edition of the Armenian psalter (the *Saghmosaran*), published by Akbar Dpir Tokhatetsi and printed by Jakob Meghapart in 1565. Scaliger would write in his copy: 'Donum eruditissimi atque amplissimi viri Claudij Puteani Consiliarij Regij in suprema Curia Parisiensi', as well as his own name in Armenian, as 'Josef Skaliger'.[47]

---

43   *Correspondence* 4 September 1581 to Dupuy: 'Je vouldrois aussi qu'il vous pleust à vostre loisir d'escrire au Signor Pinelli de recouvrer un Nouveau Testament armenien de ceux qui ont esté imprimés à Venise, ce qu'il peust avoir aisement. Puisqu'il a un ami juif (comme vous m'escrives) à Constantinople, il seroit bon qu'il lui escrivit de recouvrer des Samaritains leur computus et la maniere qu'ils usent en leurs mois lunaires, car ils ne sont pas du tout semblables aux juifz. J'en ai bien quelque chose, et vous asseure que par ce moien on descouvre merveilles. Aussi par le mesme juif on pourroit recouvrer quelque chose des chrestiens copti, qui sont chrestiens egyptiens fort anciens, usans de l'ancienne langue egyptienne; et il en y a un'eglise en Pera à Constantinople. J'ai bien leur computus et kalendier mais, il est en arabic. Je vouldrois quelque Evangile en leur langue, et si le Seigneur Pinelli veult, il ne peust estre qu'il ne le recouve par ledict medecin juif.'

44   *Correspondence* 5 June 1586 to Dupuy: 'Quant au Psaultier armenien, je vous supplie de m'escrire où il a esté imprimé, car j'en recouvrerai. Et si c'est à Romme, j'espere que je le pourrai avoir aisement. Il fauldra tousjours adresser vos lettres à Monsieur Vernelle, qui nous faict tousjours tenir les paquetz et nouvelles de Paris et de la Court.'

45   *Correspondence* 30 June 1586 to Dupuy. Dupuy regularly used the services of Claude Vernelle and Jonathan Petit for the dispatch of letters and books. See: *Correspondence* 8 July [1580?] to Vernelle; 28 May 1586 to Dupuy; 5 June 1586 to Dupuy.

46   *Correspondence* 30 June 1586 to Dupuy. In comparison, letters sent between two branches of the same merchant's firm between Genoa and Haarlem took an average of four weeks. The transport of goods between these two cities generally took two or three months. Transport over land could vary between two months (for example, between Naples and Frankfurt) to ten months (from Naples to Amsterdam). J.C. Vermeulen, 'De handelsbetrekkingen met het Middellandse Zeegebied in de jaren 1588–1592, naar gegevens uit het archief van Daniël van der Meulen' in: J.H. Kernkamp, *De handel van Daniël van der Meulen c.s. in het bijzonder rond de jaren 1588–1592* (Leiden: s.n., 1969), pp. 15–16.

47   Scaliger's copy is no longer in the University Library of Leiden. Since 1749, it is in the possession of the Royal Library of Copenhagen [call number 82,175 04922]. My thanks to Anna

SUPPLYING SCALIGER WITH BOOKS

Pinelli's efficiency in acquiring the Armenian psalter only encouraged Scaliger to send further requests for books. Only a month later, at the end of July 1586, Dupuy sent Pinelli a list with new books that Scaliger wished to acquire.[48] This list includes a *Psalterium, et Lunarium lingua Armenica*, a *Testamentum Novum lingua Slavonica, editum à Primo Trubero Carniolanoi* in octavo and a *Testamentum Novum, Epistula ad Hebraeos, Alphabetum et Missale characteribus Aethiopicis edita abs Petro Aethiope monacho*, printed in Venice in quarto in 1548.[49]

From Rome, Dupuy sent word to Scaliger that he had found Arabic books and manuscripts for him, and that if Scaliger wished to have them, he would have copies made.[50] Scaliger also requested Dupuy to look out for books from the German market that had appeared at the Frankfurt book fair.[51] In 1585, he sought information on a Talmud printed in Germany; a year later, he had heard about an Arabic edition of the Acts of the Apostles, translated into Hebrew.[52] Scaliger presumed that the Jakob Christmann (1554–1613), an Orientalist and professor of Hebrew, was the author. Scaliger did not hold Christmann in

---

Maria Mattaar, who drew this copy to my attention. It is noteworthy that this copy does not contain the label *Ex legato Illustris Viri Josephi Scaligeri*, but it is very well possible that this was removed when it left the library in Leiden. Scaliger's copy of the *Saghmosaran* [*Psalterium*] *curante Abgario Tokatensi.* (Venice: Yakob Meghapart, 1565–1566) is UBL 876 G 31, see: Bibliographic Survey Venice 1565–1566. Cf. Vrej Nersessian, *Catalogue of Early Armenian Books 1512–1850* (London: British Library, 1980), no. 2a; Raymond H. Kévorkian, *Catalogue des incunables Arméniens (1511–1695)* (Genève: Patrick Cramer, 1986), no. 7; Henning Lehmann, *Armenian Books from the 16th–18th Century in the Collection of the Royal Library, Copenhagen* (Copenhagen: s.n., 2013).

48   Raugei, *Gian Vincenzo Pinelli et Claude Dupuy*, p. 346.

49   With the *Lunarium*, Scaliger possibly meant a copy of the *Tomar* (calendar), printed in Venice in 1565 by Akbar Dpir Tokhatetsi. The Slavonic New Testament was possibly a copy of *Prevod po slovenski izdaji Primoža Trubarja iz leta 1557, ki je izšla kot predgovor njegovemu prevodu Novega testamenta: Tiga Noviga testamenta ena dolga predguvor* [The foremost principels of the Christian faith, extracted from the Latin, German and Wendish languages, and translated and printed for the first time in Croatian]. Tübingen [i.e. Urach] [Ulrich Morhart], 1562, in which the four Evangelists of the New Testament are included, or else an edition from fifteen years later, in which the last part of the New Testament is printed under the title *Ta perui deil tiga Noviga Testamenta, uti so usi shtyri Evangelisti* [...] (Tübingen: utim Keitupo Cristusevim Roystuv, 1577). *Testamentum Novum, cum epistola Pauli ad Hebraeos tantum* [...] *Missale* [...] *Alphabetum in lingua* [...] *Chaldea* [...] *Petrus Aethiops* (Romae: per Valerium et Ludovicum Doricum fratres Brixianos 1548; USTC 803271, UBL 877 C 19; see Bibliographic Survey Rome 1548–1549).

50   *Correspondence* 19 September 1588 to De Thou and 25 March 1588 to Claude Dupuy.

51   See for example *Correspondence* 9 October 1585 to Claude Dupuy.

52   *Correspondence* 9 September 1585 to Claude Dupuy.

104 CHAPTER 3

high regard: he referred to him dismissively as 'my German at Heidelberg'.[53] In 1585, Scaliger had received a copy, thanks to a friend of Christmann, of his *Alphabetum Arabicum. Cum Isagoge scribendi legendique arabice* (Neustadt, 1582).[54] In this work, Christmann had advocated a theory on the transcription of Arabic script in Hebrew characters that deviated strongly from Scaliger's interpretation. For his part, Christmann was highly critical of Scaliger's chronological calculations displayed in the *De emendatione temporum*.[55] In the early 1590s, Christmann published four books on the Jewish calendar which incorporated a severe critique of Scaliger's dating, including that of the crucifixion of Jesus; it is therefore understandable that Christmann did not find many friends amongst Scaliger's tight-knit circle.[56]

Closer to home, Scaliger also relied on Dupuy's many contacts. Scaliger asked if he could borrow a copy of a Qur'an from a Parisian friend of Dupuy for three weeks. Scaliger already possessed several copies of the Qur'an, but his collection did not include the *Sunna* or exegesis. According to him, this had to be found at the end of the Qur'an.[57] In the same letter, Scaliger shared some important information: 'I have seen the leaves of the Arabic New Testament printed in Rome, and the Arabic Euclid with the commentaries as well, a remarkable work.'[58] That Scaliger, in all his impatience, sometimes made

53 *Correspondence* 8 April [1586] to Claude Dupuy. This publication by Christmann, a converted Jew from Heidelberg, to which a Latin translation was also added, was based on a thirteenth-century manuscript found in the Bibliotheca Palatina. Christmann catalogued Postel's manuscripts, which were in the Heidelberg library since 1551, and which are considered the foundation for the study of Arabic in Germany. In 1584, Christmann was appointed professor of Hebrew at Heidelberg.

54 *Correspondence* 7 April 1585 from Christmann.

55 J. De Landstheer & P. Verbist, 'Christmannus aliquidne de temporibus post Scaligerum?' Christmann's Lesson in Chronology as an Answer to Lipsius's Remark', *Lias* 37/2 (2010), pp. 269–297; Grafton, *Joseph Scaliger* II, p. 400.

56 Philippe Nothaft, *Dating the Passion. The Life of Jesus and the Emergence of Scientific Chronology (200–1600)* (Leiden: Brill, 2011), p. 274; P. Nothaft, 'A Sixteenth-Century Debate on the Jewish Calendar: Jacob Christmann and Joseph Justus Scaliger', *Jewish Quarterly Review* 103/1 (2013), pp. 47–73. See also the letter from Thomson to Janus Dousa jr. of 23 September 1593 in: Botley, *Richard 'Dutch' Thomson*, pp. 162–164.

57 Scaliger was incorrect: the *Sunna* is not normally bound with the Qur'an.

58 *Correspondence* 28 June 1588 to Claude Dupuy. It is probable that these concerned several printed proofsheets of the *al-Injil al-muqaddas li-rabbina Yasu' al-Masih al-maktub min arba' al-injiliyyin* or the *Evangelium Sanctum Domini nostri Iesu Christi conscriptum a quatuor Evangelistis Sanctis, id est, Mattheo, Marco, Luca, et Iohanne*, that would be published in 1590–1591 on the press of the Typographicea Medicea in Rome. In Scaliger's bequest of 1612, two copies of this book were present: one in Arabic and one in Arabic with an interlinear Latin translation. Both copies are no longer in the University Library of Leiden. Leiden does own a different copy of the Arabic edition [UBL 878 A 5; see

SUPPLYING SCALIGER WITH BOOKS

duplicate requests for books from different individuals, is also evident from a letter to Dupuy from 1588. In this he apologises for the fact that he had already received two books (a copy of a book by Petrus Apianus and the *Orthographia* of Aldus Manutius) from another correspondent, and that he therefore now has two copies of each.[59] Thanks to generous friends in his network, Scaliger's collection grew steadily, but if we take him at his word, his library was of limited size by the end of the 1580s. He told Dupuy that Friedrich Sylburgius (1536–1596), the foremost scholarly collaborator of the publisher Hieronymus Commelinus (1549/50–1597), had greatly overestimated the size of his library and the rarity of his books.[60]

4   Dupuy and Pinelli

From the correspondence of Scaliger's contemporaries, we can occasionally glean important information about Oriental books destined for Scaliger, trace of which is entirely absent from Scaliger's extant letters. Examples can be found in the intensive exchange of letters between Claude Dupuy and Gian Vincenzo Pinelli in Padua.[61] The contact between the two men has been described as 'one of the most important instances of Franco-Italian cultural contact in

---

Catalogue Rome 1591 [1592]: 2]. These are the only proof sheets of the Arabic edition of Euclid, printed after a manuscript present in the Bibliotheca Medicea Laurentiana (MS Or. 20), printed in 1594 in Rome under the title *Kitab tahrir usul li-Uqlidis min ta'lif khuja Nasir al-Din al-Tusi* [*Elementorum geometricorum libri tredecim*] (Roma: in Tipographia Medicea Orientale, 1594; USTC 828486). Scaliger owned a complete copy of the work, as well as a gathering with chapter nine only, and it is this gathering that he is discussing in his letter [UBL 845 A 9; see Bibliographic Survey Rome 1594].

59   *Correspondence* 12 May 1588 to Claude Dupuy. Petrus Apianus (1495–1531) and Bartholomeus Amiantus, *Inscriptiones sacrosanctae vetustatis non illae quidem Romanae, sed totius fere orbis incipient* (Ingolstadt: in aedibus Peter Apian, 1534; USTC 666636), contains an extensive collection of Latin inscriptions; the *Orthographiae ratio, ab Aldo Manutio, Pauli f. collecta* Venezia, Paolo Manuzio, 1561 (USTC 840351), concerns the correct spelling of Latin. In *Correspondence* 1588 11 16 to Claude Dupuy, Scaliger mentioned that he lacked these books in his collection and wished to acquire them, and Dupuy sent him copies within a month, according to *Correspondence* 15 December 1588 from Dupuy. See also: *Correspondence* 13 December 1588 to Dupuy.

60   *Correspondence* 5 December 1588 to Claude Dupuy: 'Sylburgius, lequel pense que, j'aie quelque opulente bibliotheque plein de livres rares.'

61   See the published correspondence of both men in Raugei, *Gian Vincenzo Pinelli et Claude Dupuy* 2001. Pinelli would live in Padua from 1558 until his death in 1601. For information on Pinelli and his family, see Paolo Gualdo, *Vita Joannis Vincentii Pinelli, patricii Genuensis* (Augsburg: Ad insigne Pinus [et] Christoph Mang, 1607; USTC 2040570).

FIGURE 14   The Italian scholar, collector and bibliophile Gian Vincenzo Pinelli.
Rijksprentenkabinet Amsterdam RP-P-1908-2636

SUPPLYING SCALIGER WITH BOOKS

the sixteenth century'.[62] The two men exchanged their first correspondence in 1570; as we have seen, it was Dupuy who brought Scaliger into contact with Pinelli.

The triangular correspondence between Dupuy, Scaliger and Pinelli often concerned information on books: authors, publishers, printers, booksellers, prices, bindings and libraries. In the sixteenth century, Pinelli's hometown of Padua, located less than 50 kilometres from the printing emporium of Venice, was one of the most important centres of the Italian book trade.[63] Like Venice, Padua was home to a substantial Jewish community, although the printing of Hebrew books in Padua only began in 1562. The university of Padua, which was open to Jewish students, was also of great importance to the local book trade.

Pinelli maintained intensive contact with various scholars, including Philippus Pigafetta (1533–1604) in Rome and Fulvio Orsini (1529–1600) in Venice.[64] Orsini was also a correspondent of Scaliger, after the two had met in Rome in 1565, and Orsini was one of Scaliger's reliable sources of supply for Hebrew and Oriental books.[65] Pinelli also kept up an active correspondence

---

62   McCuaig, *Carlo Sigonio*, p. 71.

63   Marvin J. Heller, '"There were in Padua almost as many Hebrew Printers as Hebrew Books". The Sixteenth Century Hebrew Press in Padua', in Marvin J. Heller, *Studies in the Making of the Early Hebrew Book* (Leiden: Brill, 2008), pp. 121–130.

64   On the life and network of Pinelli, see: Adolfo Rivolta, *Contributo a uno studio sulla Bibliotheca di Gian Vicenzo Pinelli* (Monza: Scuola tipografica Artigianelli, 1914). De Thou and Pinelli had met each other in Padua in 1579. Pinelli was a renowned collector, but after his death in August 1601, his library went through a turbulent episode of confiscation and neglect. Althought Pinelli's nephew Cosimo had plans to erect a public library in Naples using Pinelli's collection, the death of Cosimo on 31 October 1602 prevented the execution of this plan. For the entire saga, seer: M. Grendler, 'A Greek Collection in Padua. The Library of Gian Vincenzo Pinelli (1535–1601)', *Renaissance Quarterly* 1980, pp. 386–416. For the inventory of his library, dated, 7 October 1604, see Bibliotheca Marciana, Mss. Italiani, Class X, 61 (6601). De Thou wrote extensively and in great praise on Pinelli's library in his *Mémoires* (livre IV) and his *Histoire* (livre CXXVI).

65   *Correspondence* 23 June 1579 to Claude Dupuy: 'S'il vous plaisoit d'escrire à Monsieur Pinelli de recouvrer les livres des langues estrangeres, je lui en rendrai bon compte à son honneur et louange, mesmement en arabic, et ethiopic, id est, abbissin; ce qu'il peust faire par le moien et la voye de Constantinople.' In *Correspondence* 2 May 1579 to Dupuy, Scaliger made a similar request: 'Le Seigneur Pinelli me pourroit bien aider de livres ethiopiques les faisant venir de Constantinople, d'autant qu'il y a un'eglise de ceste nation; item, de quelque bel Alcoran bien escrit.' The Qur'an that Scaliger already had in his possession was not adequate. *Correspondence* 2 May 1579 to Claude Dupuy: 'Car je m'aide bien du mien, mais avec grand peine.' Scaliger had reflected earlier on the problems of his copy of the Qur'an in a letter to Dupuy, for which see *Correspondence* 11 May 1578: 'Il me souvient que vous m'aves escrit d'un Alcoran qu'un vostre ami a. S'il vous plaisoit me l'envoier, je vous le renvoierai dens un mois, car je n'en aurai plus à faire d'autant que j'en ai un. Mais il est si mal relié que la lettre, oultre ce qu'elle est escrite d'une tres mauvaise

with many scholars in France, while he could also rely on printed stock catalogues to keep him abreast of the latest publications. Contacts in the trade, such as the booksellers Pietro Longo and the 'Marchant libraire Venetien' Francesco Ziletii (?–1587), supplied him with useful information on rare antiquarian works and the best modern editions.[66] The transportation of books between Dupuy in France and Pinelli in Padua was largely taken care of by the Parisian booksellers Sébastien Nivelle (1523–1603) and Dennis du Val (1536–1619). They despatched books via the Frankfurt book fair to bookseller Ziletti. These same traders also handled many of the Oriental books destined for Scaliger.

For the import of books from France, Pinelli also maintained close links with the Florentine scholar Jacopo Corbinelli (1535–1590?), who lived in Paris, and who was close to Henri Estienne (1528–1598) in Geneva.[67] Scaliger and Corbinelli knew each other (they had dined once in Paris in 1579), but they were not close. He was more familiar with another mutual correspondent of Pinelli, the scholar Pietro del Bene (1550–1590), an Italian scholar residing at the French court. Del Bene despatched many books from France to Pinelli, and provided Scaliger with ancient inscriptions, as well as an Arabic manuscript. On one occasion, Del Bene assured Scaliger that if he travelled to Italy and encountered interesting Hebrew and Arabic books he would buy these for him.[68]

Pinelli owned one of the best and largest libraries in Italy in the second half of the sixteenth century. His collection contained around 9,500 printed books and 1,000 manuscripts, mostly in Greek and Latin, but also in Hebrew and

---

main, est toute cachée dens la cousture; et par ce je pourrois suppleer les defaultz par cellui-là, s'il vous plaisoit me faire tant de faveur que de me l'envoier.' The following year, Scaliger received a much better copy (meaning a complete copy) from Pinelli.

66 On Longo and Ziletti see Paul F. Grendler, *The Roman Inquisition and the Venetian Press, 1540–1605* (Princeton: Princeton University Press, 1977), especially chapter 6.

67 Longo specialised in the transport of books between north-west Europe and Italy via the Frankfurt book fair. Rita Calderini de Marchi, *Jacopo Corbinelli et les érudits Français d'apres la correspondence inédite Corbinelli-Pinelli (1566–1587)* (Milan: Hoepli, 1914).

68 *Correspondence* 23 October [1588] from Del Bene: 'C'est à vous Monsieur, qui estes du tout clervoyant en ces incognues langues, à en juger, & à m'en departir s'il vous plaist, votre opinion la dessus. Si j'eusse peu passer en Italie, j'eusse recouvert, au moins cherché avecques toute diligence, les livres hebrieux et arabiques, dont vous m'aviez baillé la memmoire; car parmy les Iuifs d'Avignon je n'ay sçeu rien trouver [...].'

Arabic.[69] Some of his printed books were also in Hebrew, Arabic and Syriac.[70] Pinelli had good contacts with the Jewish community in Istanbul, which supplied him with many Arabic, Amharic and Coptic manuscripts: some of these books eventually found their way to Scaliger. Although Pinelli published very little himself, he gathered his superb collection primarily to make rare books and manuscripts available to his many friends.[71]

Scaliger was able to make the most of his friendship with Pinelli, but this was a relationship that was cultivated over a long period with some care. Once again, Dupuy played an important role in extending Scaliger's network. Already in 1571, Dupuy had mentioned Scaliger to Pinelli, informing him of Scaliger's scholarly talents.[72] When, around 1575, Scaliger was engaged in a scholarly spat with Melchior Guilandinus about the publication of his tract *Papyrus* (Venice, 1572), Pinelli chose Scaliger's side in the debate.[73] Pinelli admired Scaliger's historical-botanical treatment of papyrus in Scaliger's *Festus* of 1575 much more than Guilandinus's work. Scaliger was delighted with Pinelli's support, and promised in 1575 to send him other, unpublished observations on the subject.[74] This first exchange, in which Scaliger provided the 'favour', opened the door for a lively correspondence, mediated by Dupuy, several years later.

In 1579, Scaliger asked Dupuy whether Pinelli might wish to help him by tracing and purchasing some Ethiopian books, as well as a Qur'an from Istanbul. In

69   There are two inventories of the library of Pinelli: Bibliotheca Nazionale Marciana, Venice, Mss Italiani, Classe X, 61 (6601) dated 1604 and Ambrosiana Ms. B 311 Sussido from 1609.

70   For an overview of the library of Pinelli, see: A.M. Raugei, 'Gian Vincenzo Pinelli 1535–1601. Ses livres, ses amis', in R.S. Camos en A. Vanautgaerden (et al., eds.), *Les labyrinthes de l'esprit. Collections et bibliothèques à la Renaissance/Renaissance Libraries and Collections* (Genève: Droz, 2015), pp. 213–227.

71   Gualdo, in his *Vita Joannis Vincentii Pinelli* (1607), wrote on Pinelli's unique library: 'Bibliotheca ejusdem, quae inter omnes paene Italicas, ac fere dixerim europaeas una eminebat'.

72   In a letter of 7 April 1571 to Dupuy, Pinelli wrote that he was very pleased to hear that Scaliger had recovered after a period of illness. Raugei, *Gian Vincenzo Pinelli et Claude Dupuy*, p. 19.

73   A. Grafton, 'Rhetoric, Philology and Egyptomania in the 1570s: J.J. Scaliger's Invective against M. Guilandinus's Papyrus', *Journal of Warburg and Courtauld Institutes*, XLII (1979), pp. 167–194; J.H.F. Dijkstra, 'Mysteries of the Nile? Joseph Scaliger and Ancient Egypt. Les mystères du Nil? Joseph Scaliger et l'Égypte ancienne', *Aries* 9/1 (2009), pp. 66–71.

74   Only in 1579 did Scaliger write a formal answer to Guilandinus. He sent this work to Pinelli, via Dupuy, on 13 July 1580. The tract, Scaliger's *Animadversiones in Melchioris Guilandini commentarium in tria C. Plinii de Papyro capita libri XIII* would only be printed after his death, as part of the *Opuscula* 1610, pp. 1–55.

110 CHAPTER 3

early 1580, Scaliger reminded Dupuy of this request.[75] Perhaps Pinelli's Jewish contacts in Italy could look out for a Hebrew edition of Avicenna, published in Thessaloniki?[76] 'I am trying to acquire this work in Arabic as well, with the help of ambassador Chasteigner in Rome', Scaliger emphasised in his letter.[77] On this occasion, Dupuy sprang into action. He wrote to Pinelli:

> Scaliger would like to receive Ethiopian books, and he thinks we might be able to find some in Venice, where some Abyssinians live still. He would also like to acquire an Avicenna in Arabic, as well as a Hebrew book printed in Thessaloniki ... Concerning the Ethiopian books: buy whatever you find regardless of the price, and I will reimburse you the costs immediately.[78]

In an earlier letter, Scaliger had also emphasised that when it came to the Ethiopian books, money should not be an impediment: they were an absolute priority for his studies.[79]

In 1580, Scaliger asked Dupuy to bring him into direct contact with Pinelli, so that Scaliger could ask him to search for several books that he required.

---

75 *Correspondence* 2 May 1579 to Dupuy and *Correspondence* 23 May 1581 to Dupuy: 'Je voi bien que Monsieur Pinelli nous a oubliés, et ne se souvient plus des livres que vous lui avies escrit nous faire recouvrer de Constantinople'. On this matter, see also: *Correspondence* 23 June 1579; 15 February 1580; 7 July 1580 and 4 September 1581, all to Dupuy.

76 *Correspondence* 15 February 1580 to Dupuy. The Thessaloniki edition of Avicenna in Hebrew is unknown. Scaliger would acquire a Hebrew edition, one printed in two parts in Naples in 1491–1492 by Obadia ben Josef, much later: *Avicennae Canon, ab anonymo hebraice translatus* (Napoli: Azriel ben Joseph Ashkenazi Gunzenhauser, 9 November 1491–1492; USTC 760443, UBL 855 A 5–6; see: Bibliographic Survey Naples 1491 [1492]).

77 A printed edition in Arabic of Avicenna appeared only in 1593: *Avicenna Libri v canonis medicinae, arabice* Rome 1593. A copy of this can be found in Scaliger's bequest under call number UBL 878 A 4; see Bibliographic Survey Rome 1593: 2. It is possible that Scaliger meant to describe an Arabic manuscript of Avicenna, rather than a printed edition.

78 Letter from Claude Dupuy to Pinelli, 17 January 1581: 'Monsieur Scaliger desire recrouver des livres Ethiopiques, et a opinion que l'on en pourroit trouver à Venise, ou il y a encores quelques Abyssins. Il desire aussi recrouver un Avicenna Arabique, et un autre Hebrieu imprimé à Thessaloniki asséz long temps a: je vous prie d'en faire chercher à Venize, et me mander combien on les voudroit vendre. Quant aux livres Ethiopiques, ne faites difficulté d'acchepter ce qui se trovera, de quelque faculté qu'ils soient, et je vous rembourserai de ce qu'ils auront cousté', in: Raugei, *Gian Vincenzo Pinelli et Claude Dupuy*, pp. 302–303.

79 *Correspondence* 7 July 1580 to Dupuy: 'Souvienne vous, s'il vous plaist, d'escrire derechef au seigneur Pinelli touchant les livres en Ethiopic et Arabic. Je désirerois fort un Avicenne en Arabic et des livres Ethiopiques de quelque sorte et faculté que ce fust. Nous paierons tots le frais qu'on y fera. Je n'estudie guieres, car je n'ai poinct des livres.'

SUPPLYING SCALIGER WITH BOOKS   111

FIGURE 15   *Saghmosaran* [Psalterium] curante Abgario Tokatensi (Venice: Yakob Meghapart, 1565–1566).
             UBL 876 G 31

These included a Venetian edition of the New Testament in Armenian, a Samaritan *computus* and an unspecified Hebrew medical work.[80] Like, Dupuy, Pinelli would be successful in locating some of these rare Oriental books. In an appendix to a letter to Dupuy of 22 August 1589, he added a list of books that he purchased in Italy, including a *Psalterium Armenicum in octavo*, presumably meant for Scaliger.

---

80   *Correspondence* 15 February 1580 to Dupuy: Scaliger informed earlier after a manuscript of a 'Nouveau Testament armenien' that Dupuy owned in his library. His request to Pinelli for an Armenian New Testament possibly concerned the Armenian *Psalterium* of Yovhannes Têrznc'i and his son Xač'atur, printed on the press of Giovanni Alberti in Venice. It took a while to fulfil the request, because this work did not appear until 1587. The University Library catalogues of 1612 and 1623 mention a *Psalterium Armenicum* in octavo printed in Rome, but this is most likely an error: no other information is found in any other bibliography on a Roman Armenian psalter. Têrznc'i was, however, active as printer in Rome before he settled in Venice. It is possible that Scaliger therefore had the impression that the psalter was printed in Rome. The first edition of the Bible in classical Armenian would only appear in print in Amsterdam in 1666. A New Testament in classical Armenian would appear in 1732. For the Armenian psalter of 1587, see Nersessian,

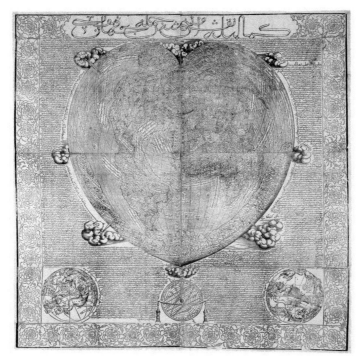

FIGURE 16   The heart-shaped *Mappamondi* or world map of Hajji Ahmed
(Venice: Marco Antonio Giustiniani, 1559–1560)

In his letter to Dupuy, Pinelli indicated that he would send these books via the Venetian bookseller and printer Francesco Franceschi († 1599) to Andreas

Catalogue of Early Armenian Books 1512–1850, no. 4. In his bequest to Leiden, Scaliger also a manuscript of an Armenian psalter with prayers (*Rituale Armeniacum*), see UBL MS Or. 4738. Robert M. Kerr, *Vetus Testamentum in Lugduno Batavorum* (Leiden: Leiden University Library, 2004), no. 11, pp. 39–40. It proved impossible for Scaliger to retrieve a copy of a Samaritan calendar, because he did not refer to a copy in his edition of the *De emendatione temporum* of 1583. Only in 1584 did Scaliger gain access to two manuscripts in the Samaritan script: the *Liber Joshua* in Arabic, but written in Samaritan (MS Or. 249) and two calendars from the Samaritan community of Cairo. These calendars were included in the second edition of the *De emendatione temporum* of 1598, but have since disappeared. It is possible that Scaliger knew the Samaritan manuscript that was in the possession of Raphelengius, that Postel had brought with him from the Levant. This concerned a translation of Mark, followed by the Šarḥ fuṣūl Inğīl Marqus wa-talkhīṣ maʿnāhu (UBL MS Or. 218). See: Alan C. Crown, *Samaritan Scribes and Manuscripts* (Tübingen: Mohr Siebeck, 2001), pp. 275–276. *Correspondence* 4 September 1581 to Dupuy. It is possible that the unspecified Hebrew work concerned a copy of Avicenna (Ibn Sina), *Canon medicinae* (Napoli: Azriel ben Joseph Ashkenazi Gunzenhauser, 9 November 1491–1492) [USTC 760443, UBL 855 A 5–6; see Bibliographic Survey Naples 1491 [1492]].

Wechel (fl. 1581–1630) in Frankfurt.[81] Wechel's printing firm formed one of the important nodes in the international scholarly network of the late sixteenth century, with contacts from England to Eastern Europe.[82] Pinelli's correspondence with Wechel reveals interesting detail about books and other objects that he was able to acquire for Scaliger. On 12 December 1579, Pinelli included on a list of books sent to the Frankfurt book fair a *Mappamondi con lettere Arabice stamp[ato] in Ven[ezia]*.[83] Two months later, Dupuy acknowledged receipt.[84] The booksellers who handled the transport charged him three *sous* per book delivered, or two *francs* for a parcel of twelve to fifteen books.[85]

5   A Fellow Protestant in Paris: Pierre Pithou

The jurist, philologist and antiquarian Pierre Pithou (1539–1596) was an inexhaustible source of important books to Scaliger. There were similarities between the two men: Pithou came from an old noble family, a heritage that Scaliger also claimed for himself; they studied together under Turnèbe and

---

81   Raugei, *Gian Vincenzo Pinelli et Claude Dupuy*, p. 120. After the St Bartholomew's Day massacre, Wechel fled from Paris and settled in Frankfurt. See: Peter Weidhaas, *A History of the Frankfurt Book Fair* (Toronto: Dundurn, 2007), pp. 45–46.

82   Robert John Weston Evans, *The Wechel Presses. Humanism and Calvinism in Central Europe, 1572–1627* (Oxford: Past and Present Society, 1975).

83   This woodcut *Mappamondi* or world map (*Kemāl ile Naks Olinmis Cümle-I Cihãn Nemunesi* [Fully illustrated depiction of the world]) is ascribed to Hajji Ahmed of Tunis, and was printed in Venice by Marco Antonio Giustiniani (in close collaboration with Michele Membré and Nicolò Gambi) between 1559 and 1560. The map was produced for the Ottoman market. It consists of western and eastern hemispheres in the shape of a heart, surrounded by references in Turkish in a small Arabic letter to various cities, countries and territories. No sixteenth-century copy of the map survives, but eighteenth-century reproductions are extant. Cf. O.V.L. Ménage, '"The Map of Hajji Ahmed" and its Makers', *Bulletin of the School of Oriental and African Studies* 21 (1958) 2, pp. 291–314 and G. Cassale, 'Seeing the Past. Maps and Ottoman Historical Consciousness', in H. Erdem Çipa en E. Fetvaci (eds.), *Writing History at the Ottoman Court. Editing the Past, Fashioning the Future* (Bloomington: Indianan University Press, 2013), pp. 80–99. The map is probably that described on page 85 of the Leiden catalogue of 1612: *Mappa Turcica elegantissima*. Given that the map was included in the section of books in 16mo, we can presume that the map was stored folded. See Bibliographic Survey Venice 1559; the map is no longer in the collection of the University Library of Leiden.

84   Raugei, *Gian Vincenzo Pinelli et Claude Dupuy*, p. 283. Letter from 15 February 1580: 'Mappemondo avec lettres Arabaiques, imprimée à Venise comme j'estime, c'est pour Monsr. de la Scala'.

85   W. McCuaig, 'On Claude Dupuy (1545–1594)', *Studies in Medieval and Renaissance History*. Vol. 12 (old series vol. CXXII) 1991, p. 82.

114 CHAPTER 3

later under Cujas, and both became Protestants.[86] In 1560, Pithou settled in Paris, where, in 1572, he was appointed as *Avocat en la court de Parlement*. He narrowly escaped death during the St Bartholomew's Day massacre.

In the later sixteenth century, Pithou became one of the most erudite scholars in Paris. He provided Scaliger with frequent scholarly counsel, and gave him access to his family's library.[87] Scaliger's first letter to Pithou dates from 1568; shortly afterwards, he visited Pithou in Paris.[88] The two men shared a love for antiquity and especially for books, and Pithou was tireless in his search for rare titles. Together with De Thou and Jean de Thuméry, Pithou visited monastic libraries around France, including that of Moissac-sur-le Tarn, where they were able to consult many rare manuscripts and books in 1582. Scaliger wrote approvingly that the Pithou family hunted for books 'like a dog hunts a bone, or a cat a mouse'.[89] The correspondence between the two men became intensive and frequent, and it is not a surprise that manuscripts and books were often at the heart of this exchange of letters. Scaliger even trusted Pithou with his own manuscripts of the *Appendix Vergilianus* and the *Catalecta*, and asked him if he would make corrections in them, if he identified mistakes. Pithou also acted as Scaliger's agent and overseer when these texts were printed in Paris by Charles Périer (?–1572?).[90]

Pithou fulfilled an important role as Scaliger's informer. He provided news from Paris and Italy, and kept Scaliger informed of the latest news from the publishing world.[91] He sent Scaliger regular consignments of books from Paris, occasionally using an agent named De Dollencourt, who was sadly not always

---

86 See: L. de Rosando, 'Pierre Pithou érudit' in: *Revue du XVIᵉ siècle* 15 (1928), pp. 279–305 and 16 (1929), pp. 301–330.

87 Pithou's library consisted of some 2,000 volumes. His brother François was less generous in lending books from his collection, cf. *Scaligerana* I, p. 507. The largest part of Pierre's library was incorporated into the Royal Library after his death, and can still be identified today in the BnF.

88 See for example, *Correspondence* 8 February 1576 to Pithou.

89 *Scaligerana* 1740, p. 507: 'Les Pithou sentoient des bons livres de loin, comme un chien un os, ou un chat un souris.'

90 *Correspondence* 24 March [1565] to Pierre Daniel. For the relationship between Scaliger and Périer, see: *Correspondence* 25 June [1568–1569] to Daniel and 14 April [1568–1569] to Pierre Pithou. The print shop of Périer was located in Paris between 1550 and 1572. Périer was the son-in-law of the humanist printer Chrétien Wechel of Lyon, and was killed during the St Bartholomew's Day Massacre. Wechel fulfilled a central role in the international network of Protestant authors and printers. At the end of the sixteenth century, his successors, Claude de Marne (Marnius) and Jean Aubery (Abrius), acted as middlemen at the Frankfurt Book Fair for the correspondence between A. de Vulcob in Paris and Scaliger in Leiden.

91 *Correspondence* 14 April [1568–1569] to Pithou.

FIGURE 17 Portrait of Pierre Pithou (1539–1596). Rijksprentenkabinet Amsterdam
RP-P-1882.-A 629

116   CHAPTER 3

reliable.[92] When Scaliger tried to acquire from Patisson in Paris an edition of
the Qur'an, edied by the humanist Christoph Hegendorf (1500–1540), printed
in two columns with a parallel Arabic-Latin text, he received no immediate
response.[93] In consequence, he wrote directly to Pithou, urging him to look out
for the edition and to buy a copy as soon as he found one. This too was in vain,
as it is almost certain that this was a 'ghost' edition, one that never appeared
in print; a problem that bedeviled a sixteenth-century scholar like Scaliger as
much as modern bibliographers.[94] When Scaliger resided in Geneva between
1572 and 1574, Pithou also sent him many books, manuscripts and annotations.
The Lyonnais printer Antoine Gryphe, then involved with a publication of
Scaliger's, was the middleman in this exchange. Scaliger trusted him greatly
and assured Pithou that he could send anything via Gryphe – even manuscripts
from his personal library – because Gryphe 'will immediately deliver these to
me'.[95] The triangle of trade of Paris, Lyon and Geneva was very efficient, and
books sent from Paris by Pithou arrived quickly with Scaliger in Geneva. It is
noteworthy too that Scaliger indicated in a letter that Pithou could recover
the costs of buying books for him from the secretary of François Chasteigner,
the brother of his patron Louis. This is further evidence that a portion
of the books that Scaliger added to his library continued to be paid for by the
Chasteigner family.

Other books in exotic languages were of interest to Scaliger in this itinerant
period of his life. When Patisson told Scaliger that Pithou owned 'a book written in an Indian language', Scaliger naturally wanted to borrow this work from
him.[96] Scaliger's enthusiastic reaction is proof of his lively interest in works

---

92   *Correspondence* 13 February 1572 to Pithou.

93   *Correspondence* 23 June 1579 to Claude Dupuy: 'J'ai escrit au Sieur Pattisson touchant un
     Alcoran imprimé *apud Hegendorfium* en colonnes, l'une en langue Arabique charactères
     latins, l'aultre est la version latine'.

94   This edition of the Qur'an is possibly related to the 1540 Venetian edition. See also:
     Correspondence 1579 05 27 to Pierre Pithou. Scaliger approached the printer Patisson
     with the same request earlier, but that letter has not survived. On this mysterious edi-
     tion of the Qur'an, see: F. Secret, 'Guillaume Postel et les études arabes à la Renaissance',
     Arabica 9 (1962), p. 23 and Rijk Smitskamp, *Philologia Orientalis* (Leiden: Smitskamp
     Oriental Antiquarium, 1992), no. 12f.

95   *Correspondence* 23 August 1573; 10 September 1573 and 6 November 1573 to Pithou. Gryphe
     published Scaliger's edition of the *Opera* of Ausonius in 1574–1575. Antoine's father was
     Sébastien Gryphe (1493–1556), who printed many Hebrew books, such as the *Thesaurus
     Linguae Sanctae* of Sanctus Pagninus (1529), a copy of which Scaliger owned [UBL 874 B 7;
     see Bibliographic Survey Lyon 1529: 1].

96   *Correspondence* 2 June 1578 from Pithou. Patisson probably meant a book written in
     Sanskrit. It is possible that this concerns a manuscript that Scaliger borrowed and later
     returned; in all likelihood this was not the copy of the *Catechismus Loiolitarum in lingua*

SUPPLYING SCALIGER WITH BOOKS

in languages that were yet unknown to him. His broad interests were again on shown when he thanked Pithou on 29 June 1578 for sending him a book with prayers in Amharic, a *Precatiunculae Abissinae*. The book allowed him to expand his knowledge of Amharic considerably, even if he already owned various publications in this language. 'I own more of these types of books than anyone in the western world', Scaliger boasted.[97] Pithou also sent Scaliger Hebrew books with some frequency, as is indicated by a letter from Scaliger of July 1585, sent from Abain, in which he thanked Pithou for a Hebrew edition of the *Moreh Nevukhim*, written by the Rabbi, philosopher and physician Moses Maimonides (1137/1138–1204), printed in Venice.[98] Scaliger was delighted to

---

Malabarica Tamil, printed in Goa in 1577, which Scaliger owned, according to the Leiden catalogues of 1612, 1640 and 1674. In these catalogues, the title is recorded as *Doctrina Christiana lingua Malabarica Tamul & Literis Malabar[icis] In collegio Goano. 1577*. The catalogue of 1640 also mentioned the small format of the publication: *Doctrina Christiana lingua & Literis Indicis, libellus excusus in India à Jesuitis. in decimo sexto*. See also the following title in the book list at MS VUL 108, pars 5: *Catechismus Jesuitarum lingua Malabar[icis], Goae impressus in India*. No copy of this item survives today, but a copy is known of a similar item printed a year later (1578) in Quilon (today Kollam). For a description of this publication, see: G. Schurmacher and G.W. Cottrell, 'The First Printing in Indic Characters', *Harvard Library Bulletin* 6/2 (1952), pp. 147–160. See also: G.W. Shaw, 'Scaliger's Copy of an Early Tamil Catechism', *The Library. The Transactions of the Bibliographical Society* 6/3 (1981), pp. 239–243.

97 *Correspondence* 29 June 1578 to Pithou: 'Je les ai toutes leues, et me pourront servir à ce que j'ai sur cette langue, de laquelle j'ai plus de livres qu'homme qui soit es parties occidentales, et si ose dire que nous entendons aussi bien cette langue que l'hebraique ou syriaque.' Scaliger's bequest included an Amharic book of prayers (MS Or. 262). This manuscript also includes an Ethiopian calendar. Scaliger did prepare a publication on this Amharic work, but it never appeared independently. Instead, a woodcut facsimile of the calendar was included in the *De emendatione temporum* of 1583, pp. 324–337. See: Grafton, *Joseph Scaliger* II, p. 90 & Robert M. Kerr (ed.), *Vetus Testamentum in Lugduno Batavorum. Catalogue of an Exhibition of Old Testament Manuscripts, held in the Leiden University Library* (Leiden: Leiden University, 2004), p. 28. See also the entry 'Abyssinorum' in the *Secunda Scaligerana* (1740, p. 174–175): 'Nemo Christianus potest de illis ita bene loqui ut ego, quia illorum computum Aethiopicum dedi; repererunt post, Breviarium aliquod. Curavi fundi litteras Samaritanas Aethiopicas pro meo libro *De emendatione temporum*'. The tract on the calculation of the calendar is the *Computus*, mentioned in *Correpondence* 9 December 1579, n. 6; 4 January 1580, n. 5; 15 February 1580, n. 6 to Dupuy and in 4 September 1581 to Chrétien.

98 *Correspondence* 25 July [1585] to Pierre Pithou. In Scaliger's collection there is an edition of the work of Moses Maimonides (1137/38–1204): *Sefer Moreh nevukhim, i.e. Doctor perplexorum ex Arabico vertit Samuel ibn Tibbon* (Venezia: s.n., ca. 1473–1475; USTC 761279, UBL 877 B 11; see Bibliographic Survey Venice 1473–1475). Scaliger's bequest includes three other editions by Maimonides: *De Astrologia* (bound together with Ruah Hens *Physica Hebraea*, 1555): [UBL 854 F 16]; *More Nevuchim* [UBL 877 B 12] and the *Yad haHazaka* (*Mishne Torah*, a codification of Jewish law) [UBL 854 A 6–7], the second part of which

FIGURE 18   A creed of confession (*Doctrina Christam*) in Tamil, printed in Quilon (Kollam) in 1578. Houghton Library, Harvard University, Cambridge, MA

SUPPLYING SCALIGER WITH BOOKS

receive books like these from abroad. In this period of turmoil, it was often difficult to despatch books to France, but it seems that he could always count on Pithou.[99]

In 1594, when King Henry IV appointed Pithou *Procureur Général*, Scaliger saw his friend elevated to a highly influential position. Pithou subsequently enlarged the royal library, and ensured that the collection of Catherine de' Medici (1519–1589) was brought over to Paris. The incorporation of her books into the royal collection was concluded in 1595.[100] Thanks to the efforts of De Thou and Pithou, Scaliger secured access to this enormous collection. Pithou's death on 1 November 1596 was not only a great personal loss to Scaliger, but also the loss of an extraordinary supplier of books. Pithou's own collection was parcelled up: a part fell into the hands of the family De Thou. Via the Dupuy family, this section would ultimately enter the royal library in Paris. Another major part of Pithou's library was inherited by his brother François, who would leave his library to the Collège de Troyes.[101] Scaliger would receive nothing.

6   Guy Lefèvre de la Boderie and Other Suppliers of Books

In early 1579, Scaliger came into contact with Guy Lefèvre de la Boderie, who then lived in Paris. The two scholars already knew of each other's work, and Scaliger presented Lefèvre with a copy of his edition of Manilius, which had just come off the press.[102] From a letter written by Lefèvre of 25 January 1579 it becomes clear that his brother Nicolas (1550–1613) had notified him that Scaliger was interested in Ethiopian books; Lefèvre offered to share such books with Scaliger. The letter mentioned the following two titles: a short introduction to the Amharic language, compiled by Marianus Victorius Reatinus and the Amharic *Psalterium* by Potken, the only book printed in Amharic that

---

was later replaced by a copy from the bequest of Warner [UBL 854 F 16-2; 854 A 6–7; see Bibliographic Survey Rome 1551, Cologne 1555:2 and Venice 1550].

99   *Correspondence* 23 July 1585 to Pierre Pithou: 'Je croi qu'on me pourra appeller fol, de ce qu'en si malheureux temps je cherche des livres là où il fauldroit plustost faire provision de viaticum pour passer la mer, si ces fureurs de guerre durent.'

100   Ernest Quentin-Bauchart, *La Bibliothèque de Fontainebleau et les livres des derniers Valois à la Bibliotheque nationale (1515–1589)* (Paris: Em. Paul L. Huard et Guillemin, 1891), p. 41.

101   Bibliothèque de Troyes, *Les richesses de la Bibliothèque de Troyes. Exposition du tricentenaire (1651–1951)* (Troyes: s.n., 1951).

102   Marcus Manilius, *Astronomicon libri quinque. Recensuit ac pristino ordini suo restituit. Commentarius in eosdem libros et castigationum explicationes* (Paris: apud Mamert Patisson in officina Robert Estienne, 1579; USTC 170472).

120   CHAPTER 3

Lefèvre owned.[103] The book by Reatinus was dedicated to Cardinal Marcel Cervin, and also contained a summary of the history of Ethiopia derived from a Latin chronicle.[104] This summary was also related to another introduction to Ethiopia, compiled from various languages by Albonesius Regulus.[105] These titles are both listed in Scaliger's bequest, but we cannot confirm that these copies once belonged to Lefèvre, or that they were indeed gifted to him. Indeed, in his letter, Lefèvre mentioned that the two titles were bound together in a single volume, while Scaliger's copies now at Leiden do not give the impression that they were ever bound together.

Scaliger also received book in Oriental languages on an infrequent basis from more minor correspondents in his network. One example was Jean Choisnin (or Choisny, 1530–?), the secretary of Bishop Jean de Monluc of Valence. In 1585 he sent Scaliger an Arabic book from Paris, with the hope that Scaliger would enjoy the work.[106] Choisny also reported that he had bought

---

103   *Correspondence* 25 January 1579 from Guy Lefèvre de la Boderie. 'Estant encor à Paris, mon jeune frere m'escrivit qu'aviez singulier desir de voir pour quelque temps une petite introduction sur la langue aethiopique faicte par un appellé Marianus Victorius Reatinus, dediée à Marcel Cervin Cardinal [van St. Croix] et imprimée à Rome des l'an 1552 chez Valerius Doricus Brixiensis, avecques un abregé de leur chronique en latin. Deslors je vous fis entendre comme encor de present que ladicte introduction estoit tellement manqué et confuse que cela me vous devoit faire desister de vostre entreprise. Ladicte introduction est liée aveques autre introduction en plusieurs langues par Albonesius Regulus, [in the margins: Thesonius Ambrosius] et d'icelle je me sers pour faire quelque progres en ceste langue, que vous sçavez avoir grande affinité avecques les quatre premieres orientales. Toutesfois, telle qu'elle est, si avez encores desir de la voir, je la vous feray tenir seurement incontinent que j'en seray adverti. Je n'ay en ceste langue que le *Psalterion* de Potken aux aultres j'ay quelques commentaires où je passe le temps par-deça, tous lesquels sont à vostre commandement d'aussy bon coeur, Monsieur, qu'humblement je supplie estre recommandé à vos bonnes graces [...]'. Joannes Potken, *Psalterium Aethiopicum cum nonnullis canticis, et Cantico Canticorum Salomonis* (Roma, per Marcello Silber ingenio et impensis Johann Potken, 1513; USTC 8000233). Scaliger owned two copies of this book [UBL 877 D 37 en 877 D 38; see Bibliographic Survey Rome 1513: 1 en 1513: 2].

104   *Chaldeae seu Aethiopicae linguae institutione* [...] *Item omnium Aethiopiae regum qui ab inundato terrarum orbe usque ad nostra tempora imperarunt Libellus* [...] *nuper ex Aethiopica translatus lingua* (Roma: impressit Valerio Dorico opera Angelo Oldradi, 1552; USTC 863716). Lefèvre did not consider this book particularly useful. He made more use of the edition of Albonesius that was bound to his copy. See also Grafton, *Joseph Scaliger* II, p. 91, note 3. Scaliger's annotated copy is UBL 877 D 31; see Bibliographic Survey Rome 1552.

105   Theseus Ambrosius Albonesius, *Introductio in Chaldaicam linguam, Syriacam, atque Armenicam, et decem alias linguas. Characterum differentium alphabeta* [...] *Mystica et cabalistica quamplurima scitu digna* (Pavia: excudebat Giovanni Maria Simonetta, 1539; USTC 808409). Scaliger's copy is UBL 1497 D 23; see Bibliographic Survey Pavia 1539.

106   *Correspondence* 6 January 1585 from Choisny: 'Cependant je vous envoye le livre en langue arabique que je vous avois promis en don, avecques desir qu'il vous apporte autant de contentement que vous en esperez.' It is uncertain which Arabic book this concerns.

SUPPLYING SCALIGER WITH BOOKS

several Hebrew books from the estate of one Beroaldus, which he offered to lend to Scaliger if he had need of them.[107]

Another contact who aided Scaliger in his search for books was the merchant Pierre Hostagier in Marseille. Hostagier bought various Samaritan, Coptic and Arabic manuscripts for Scaliger in Cairo and the Levant.[108] Since 1535, France maintained good relations with the Ottoman Empire, and enjoyed a formidable share in the European trade to Turkey, the Levant and Egypt. Even the mighty trading republic of Venice had to concede the Egyptian commercial realm to France. Hostagier was able to acquire various Oriental books for Scaliger in Marseille, a lively hub for the exchange of exotic goods. Scaliger valued Hostagier's efforts greatly, and in a letter to Dupuy described him as 'my dear and close friend'.[109] Hostagier sent the books to Scaliger via Daléchamps in Lyon, who forwarded them to Petit and Patisson in Paris.[110] In 1588, Scaliger would again recommend Hostagier's services to Dupuy:

> The bearer of this letter is Monsieur Hostager, a citizen of Marseille, my dear and close friend, from whom I derive a great deal of pleasure which he has given me both in this matter and in the search for the Arabic books which I have recovered from the Levant through his efforts, and without whom I would have done nothing in this matter.[111]

---

107   *Correspondence* 6 January 1585 from Choisny. Colomesius, *Opera* 1709, p. 351, suggests that this Beroaldus was Mathieu Béroalde (1520–1576), a scholar of Hebrew and author of a work on chronology that Scaliger knew of: Matthaes Beroaldus, *Chronicum, Scripturae Sacrae autoritate constitutum* ([Genève:], Antoine Chuppin, 1575; USTC 450086).

108   Pierre d'Hostagier or Hostagier, sieur de la Grande-Bastide, was a brother of Félix d'Hostagier, and member of a notable Marseillaise aristocratic family. He was a *maître d'hôtel* under King Henry IV. He also provided accommodation for (Spanish) merchants who traded gold and silk in the Levant. See Paul Masson, *Les compagnies du corail, étude historique sur le commerce de Marseille au 16ᵉ siècle et les origines de la colonisation française en Algérie-Tunisie* (Paris: Fontemoing, 1908). See also *Correspondence* 23 March 1587 to Daléchamps and 8 January 1589 to Hostagier. *Correspondence* 13 December 1588 to Dupuy. See: *Lettre Missives de Henri IV*, Tome 7. p. 438. *Scaligerana* 1740, p. 205: 'Tous les livres Arabes que j'ay eus, ç'a esté par Marseille, d'Alexandrie & du Caire.'

109   *Correspondence* 13 December 1588 to Dupuy.

110   *Correspondence* 23 March 1587 to Dupuy: 'Monsieur Ostager, bourgeois de Marseille, homme d'honneur et de bien, qui m'a deja recouvert des livres en Arabic du Caire et de Marseille, où il a intelligence et traffic'. See: P. Masson, *Les compagnies du corail.*

111   *Correspondence* 13 December 1588 to Dupuy. 'Le porteur de la presente est Monsieur Hostager, citoien de Marseille, mon hoste et intime ami, duquel je tiens beaucoup de plaisirs qu'il m'a faict tant là qu'en la recherche des livres arabics que j'ai recouvré de Levant par son moien, et sans lequel je n'eusse rien faict en ceste affaire.'

122   CHAPTER 3

On 8 January 1589, Scaliger received a letter from Hostagier via an intermediary, De la Clielle, in which he announced that he had found for Scaliger a
copy of the New Testament in Arabic. Scaliger presumed that this book would
be based on an earlier Syriac version, and would be closer to the original text
than any other translation available at that time.[112] Hostagier duly sent the
copy to Chasteignier, who passed it on for delivery to Scaliger. Hostagier stated
also that he could not yet supply the other Oriental books that Scaliger had
requested, but he assured them he would be able to in the future.[113]

7   Nicolas-Claude Fabri de Peiresc and the Samaritan Language

While Pinelli played a critical role in Scaliger's network in Italy, Nicolas-Claude
Fabri de Peiresc (1580–1637) fulfilled a similar role in France. From his home
in Aix-en-Provence, Pereisc acted as agent to many wealthy patrons, and also
exchanged information and books, manuscripts, art and other objects with a
variety of scholars.[114] The scholar and antiquary was himself a dedicated collector of books and curiosities. He enjoyed valuable access to the Italian book
market after a journey through the country between 1599 and 1602. During this
tour Pereisc focussed his attention for the first time on the Samaritan language,
a dialect of Aramaic, an interest he shared with Scaliger. The accumulation of
knowledge about this language would become the pivot around which the correspondence between the scholars developed. Pereisc also located for Scaliger
various Hebrew books in Venice, including a new edition of the *Sefer kol bo* and
a copy of the *More Nevuchim*.[115]

112   Hamilton and Richard, *André du Ryer*, p. 15.
113   *Correspondence* 8 January 1589 from Chasteignier. It is impossible that this concerns a copy
       of the Arabic New Testament by Raimondi, because the *editio princeps* only appeared in
       Rome in 1591. This probably concerns the manuscript at UBL MS Or. 217, that would later
       form the central source for Erpenius' edition of the *Nova D[omini] N[ostri] Jesu Christi
       Testamentum arabice ex Bibliotheca Leidense* [...] (Leiden: typ. Thomas Erpenius, 1616;
       USTC 1011611). See also: *Correspondence* 28 June 1588 to Claude Dupuy, note 4.
114   Pierre Girauld de Nolhac, *La Bibliothèque de Fulvio Orsini. Contributions à l'histoire des
       collections d'Italie et à l'étude de la Renaissance* (Paris: Bibliothèque de l'École des hautes
       études. Sciences historiques et philologiques, 1887), pp. 74–78; Peter N. Miller, 'Peiresc, the
       Levant and the Mediterranean', in A. Hamilton (et al., eds.), *The Republic of Letters and the
       Levant* (Leiden: Brill, 2005), pp. 103–122.
115   *Correspondence* 20 November 1594 from Casaubon; 18 February 1600 from Peiresc: 'En
       toute ceste ville de Venize, il n'y avoit aultre *Colbo* que estuy-cy, quoy que Iosephe y ait
       esté imprimé, toutefois (dont ie suis bien marry) je n'en ay peu trouver d'autre impres-
       sion que de celle de Cracovie: Ce *Mose Nevachim* a esté d'un homme fort docte en ceste
       langue, qui l'a postillé & corrigé les erreurs de l'impression qui me faict croire que vou

SUPPLYING SCALIGER WITH BOOKS

Pereisc's museum, library and observatory in Aix-en-Provence constituted an important centre for the exchange of scholarly knowledge throughout Europe. He maintained contacts in the Levant, in North Africa and the port city of Marseille.[116] He paid his correspondents in the commercial world to seek out Samaritan, Arabic and other Oriental manuscripts. He urged those contacts in the Levant to copy books for him, and buy them when possible.[117] The names of otherwise unknown agents and money-lenders in Marseille, like Signier and Gastines, repeatedly surface in Pereisc's correspondence. When, in 1602, Pereisc resided in Padua, he sent Scaliger Hebrew books from the house of the recently deceased Pinelli. Scaliger did not have to pay for them, Pereisc assured him. Pereisc also ensured that the book trader Giovanni Battista Ciotti (1560/1562–1625/1627?) would transport these books from Venice to Frankfurt and thence onward to Scaliger.[118] Pereisc would later also offer considerable help with his research into Scaliger's family history: he sent him coins, and illustrations of a helmet and dagger that were claimed to be heirlooms of the Della Scala's.[119]

From the moment that Scaliger began to take a serious interest in the culture of the Samaritans, he despatched a letter to the Samaritan community in Cairo. This letter, dated probably to the autumn of 1588, included a request that the Samaritans would send him various books. In 1590, he also approached the Samaritan community in Neapolis (modern-day Nablus, Palestine). These

---

serez plus aise de l'avoir tout vieux, & usé qu'il est que s'il estoit neuf.' The edition of the *Colbo* is UBL 876 B 24 [see Bibliographic Survey Venice 1567]; there are two editions of the *Moreh nevukhim, i.e. Doctor perplexorum* in the UBL: UBL 877 B 11 and 877 B 12 [Catalogue Venice 1480 and Sabbioneta 1553].

116 Arthur MacGregor, *Curiosity and Enlightment. Collectors and Collections from the Sixteenth to Nineteenth Century* (New Haven, London: Yale University Press, 2008), p. 29. McGregor designated Marseille as 'the great commercial hub to the Mediterranean'.

117 Peter N. Miller, 'The Mechanics of Christian-Jewish Intellectual Collaboration in Seventeenth Century Provence: N.-C. Fabri de Peiresc & Salomon Azubi', in A. Coudert and J.S. Shoulson (et al., eds.), *Hebraica veritas? Christian Hebraists and the Study of Judaism in Early Modern Europe* (Philadelphia: University of Pennsylvania Press, 2004), p. 78 and Peter N. Miller, 'Peiresc, The Levant and the Mediterranean' in A. Hamilton, *The Republic of Letters and the Levant* (Leiden: Brill, 2005), p. 103.

118 *Correspondence* 24 January 1602 from Peiresc. Giovanni Battista Ciotti (Ciotto), was a bookseller in Venice from around 1581 onwards. In the period 1583–1605, he travelled regularly to the Frankfurt Book Fair. He was an agent for multiple authors, dignitaries and publishers, including Konrad von Waldkirch. See: D.E. Rhodes, 'Some Neglected Aspects of the Career of Giovanni Battista Ciotti', *The Library*. 6th series, Vol. IX, no. 3. Sept. 1987. See also his entry in the *Dizionario Biografico* at www.treccani.it.

119 *Correspondence* 24 January 1602 from Peiresc. The objects would ultimately arrive with Scaliger via Marcus Welser. *Correspondence* 30 January 1602 and 10 April 1602 from Welser.

FIGURE 19 Nicolas-Claude Fabri de Pereisc (1580–1637). Rijksprentenkabinet Amsterdam
RP-P-OB-33.164

SUPPLYING SCALIGER WITH BOOKS   125

letters were sent via Pereisc to Marseille, and from there onwards to Egypt.
Scaliger made his wishes very clear, and asked specifically for the following
books written in the Samaritan script.[120]

A Hebrew Pentateuch
A Hebrew grammar
A manual for the *intercalate*, the calculation of the leap year
A Hebrew prayer book
The book of Joshua, the son of Nun, in Hebrew, rather than Arabic.[121]

Scaliger's requests were answered, but he did not receive the books that he
desired. Many years later, he would complain that, despite repeated requests
lodged with Pierre Hostagier in Marseille, he was never able to acquire a copy
of the Samaritan Pentateuch. He attached great important to this book because
he considered that it would grant him new insights into the emergence of
the Christian faith; previous studies into the Samaritan script and language
had indeed confirmed this to Scaliger.[122] Similar to other scholars, Scaliger's
interests in the culture of the Samaritans was fostered because the Samaritans
offered an alternative perspective on the Jewish faith and its culture. The
Samaritan script, used in the ancient world by Greeks, Phoenicians and Jews,
presented a link in the transmission of knowledge from east to west.[123]

   Pereisc made considerable efforts to acquire Samaritan books for Scaliger in
Egypt. Thanks to a local agent, he was able to acquire a copy of the Samaritan
Pentateuch, but this was lost after the ship that carried the book was captured
by pirates. Scaliger tried once more in 1608, with a letter addressed to the priest
Eleazer of the Samaritan community in Cairo. He requested a copy of the five

---

120   *Correspondence* [1588?]: Concept of a letter to the Samaritans (UBL MS Or. 6882). For
      Scaliger's correspondence with the Samaritans, see H.A. Hamaker, 'Aanmerkingen over
      de Samaritanen, en hunne Briefwisseling met eenige Europeesche geleerden [...]', *Archief
      voor kerkelijke geschiedenis, inzonderheid van Nederland* 5 (1834), pp. 1–56, especially p. 6
      onwards.
121   This is probably the *Liber Joshua*, better known as the *Chronicon Samaritanum* [...] *lingua
      Arabica, sed charactere Samaritano*, a copy of which Scaliger would later possess (UBL MS
      Or. 249).
122   Scaliger mentioned this in the first edition of his *De emendatione temporum* (1583), at
      p. 208.
123   P.N. Miller, 'An Antiquary between Philology and History. Peiresc and the Samaritans.' in:
      Donald R. Kelley (ed.), *History and the Disciplines. The Reclassification of Knowledge in
      Early Modern Europe* (Rochester, New York: University of Rochester Press, 1997), p. 164.

126　　　　　　　　　　　　　　　　　　　　　　　　　　　　　　CHAPTER 3

books of Moses, and asked many questions about the Samaritan perspective on the Messiah, the Sabbath and religious feast days.[124]

It is undeniable that even at great distances, Scaliger's network of correspondents was active and efficient. Letters were transported and delivered by a colourful selection of merchants, missionaries, travellers and diplomats. The network of Pereisc that Scaliger was able to tap into so successfully, stretched throughout all of Europe and the Ottoman Empire, from Algiers to Yemen. It is often regarded as one of the largest intellectual networks of the seventeenth century.[125] Virtually every ship that arrived in Marseille or Toulon delivered to Pereisc an exotic plant or animal, Coptic, Arabic, Hebrew or Chinese manuscripts, classical inscriptions or objects found near the Bosphorus or the Peloponnese.[126] With the help of his contacts in Paris, such as the brothers Dupuy, Pereisc functioned as a gateway to the east for much of northern Europe. While Pereisc rarely published anything himself, he was of immense service to his contemporaries in the Republic of Letters, and Scaliger was one of the main beneficiaries of this generosity.

8　　　Scaliger and Mitalerius

During his student days in Valence, Scaliger made contact with the jurist Claudius Mitalerius (or Claude Mitalier). Mitalerius was also interested in philological research, and possessed a large personal library, which included many Hebrew books that aroused Scaliger's interest. We know little of substance about the life and work of Mitalerius, but Scaliger was certainly in repeated contact with him between 1570 and 1573. Mitalerius lived in Vienne, some eighty kilometres to the south of Valence, and it was probably there that the two men met. Manuscript inscriptions in two Hebrew books given by Mitalerius to Scaliger indicate as much. Otherwise we know nothing about the meeting; Mitalerius's name was mentioned only once in the extant correspondence of Scaliger. In a letter to the scholar and writer Scévole de Sainte-Marthe (1536–1623), Scaliger described Mitalerius as 'one of the most learned men of languages and Roman antiquity of our time'.[127] As an aside, Scaliger

---

124　*Correspondence* 22 March 1608 to Ubertus.

125　Peter N. Miller, *Peiresc's Europe. Learning and Virtue in the Seventeenth Century* (New Haven & London: Yale University Press, 2000).

126　P.N. Miller, 'Peiresc, "The Levant and the Mediterranean"', in A. Hamilton (et al., eds.), *The Republic of Letters and the Levant* (Leiden: Brill, 2005), pp. 103–122.

127　*Correspondence* 12 August 1590 to Scévole de Sainte Marthe: 'un des plus doctes es langues et antiquité romaine de nostre aage.'

FIGURE 20   Title page of Scaliger's copy of Abraham ben David ha-Levi, *Sefer Yeẓirah* (Mantua: Jacob ben Naphtali ha-Kohen of Gazzuolo, 1562). UBL 875 E 24

pointed out that Sainte-Marthe had omitted the names of Mitalerius and the physician Louis Duret (1527–1586) from his laudatory *Poemata et Elogia* of 1587.

The two books from the library of Mitalerius present in the Oriental bequest of Scaliger have a title page inscription that reads: 'C. Mitalerius Vienn[ensis]'. These are Abraham ben David ha-Levi, *Sefer Yeẓirah*, and the *Temunot Tehinnot Tefillot*.[128] In the *Temunot* there is an additional inscription, in Scaliger's hand: 'Donum doctissimi Cl. Metallerij Viennensis provinciae Iuridici' ('Donated by doctor Cl. Metalerius, jurist of the province of Vienne') and 'Euchologium Iudaeum' ('a Jewish liturgical book'). Both copies contain annotations in Latin

---

128   *Sefer Yetsirah ha-meyuhhas le-Avraham avinu* [...] '*im 4 be'urim* (Matovah: [= Mantua], Ya'aqov Kohen mi-Ga'zuolo [Jacob ben Naphtali ha-Kohen of Gazzuolo], [5]322 [1562]; (USTC 1791958, UBL 875 E 24); see Bibliographic Survey Mantua 1562). The *Sepher Yetzirah*, als known as 'The Book of the Creation', is the earliest printed book on Jewish esotericism. *Temunot Tehinnot Tefillot* [...]: [sive Preces quotidianæ, Hebraice] (Venezia: Daniel Bomberg, [5]277 [1519]). This is a volume containing daily Hebrew prayers [UBL 1370 E 33; see Bibliographic Survey Venice 1519].

128   CHAPTER 3

and Hebrew on the endpapers, some in Scaliger's hand, others in unknown
Oriental hands.

9   Books from Jean Hurault de Boistaillé's Library in Scaliger's Bequest

Scaliger's bequest includes some books and manuscripts that were once part of
the library of the French nobleman Jean Hurault de Boistaillé (circa 1517–1572).[129]
All of these books contains Boistaillé's ex libris: *Ex Bibliotheca Jo. Huralti
Boistalerii*. The endpapers also feature many annotations from previous owners. What also marks out this corpus within Scaliger's collection is the rarity of
the printed books and manuscripts owned by Boistaillé.[130]

Scaliger came into contact with Boistaillé via the nobleman Pierre Daniël
(1530–1603/1604). He sent various letters to this Parisian scholar and *Advocat
au Parlement*, himself also a fanatical collector of books and manuscripts.
Daniël enjoyed access to some of the great libraries of France, thanks to his
extensive network amongst diplomats and ambassadors, including several
members from Boistaillé's family, and another branch of that family, the
l'Hospital.[131] In a letter dated to 1574 and sent to Daniël, Scaliger offered his services to Boistaillé. What these services concerned is unclear, but it seems very

---

129   The books and manuscripts owned by the Boistaillé family were collected by many con-
      temporaries of Scaliger, including Franciscus Raphelengius. Two such manuscripts owned
      by Raphelengius were later incorrectly provided with a printed slip stating that they
      belong to Scaliger's bequest: the *Ex Legato Illustris Viri Josephi Scaligeri*. See: A. Hamilton,
      'Nam tirones sumus', pp. 557–591 and idem 'Franciscus Raphelengius: the Hebraist and
      his Manuscripts', *De Gulden Passer* 68 (1990), pp. 105–117. Hans de Bruijn demonstrated
      in similar fashion that a number of Persian manuscripts were incorrectly ascribed to
      Scaliger's bequest. See: Johannes T.P. de Bruijn, *Een Perzisch handschrift in Leiden* (Leiden:
      Universitaire Pers Leiden, 1996). See the descriptions of the manuscripts UBL MS Or. 221
      (Hebr. 96) and MS Or. 4732 (SCA 15.) in: Witkam, *Inventory of the Oriental Manuscripts*.
      Books from the library of Boistaillé also entered the collection of Isaac Vossius, and which
      later came to Leiden: UBL: GF 17, GQ 57, GQ 66, GF 8; GO 1; GF 40; GF 35; GF 65; GF 58;
      VLF 14; VLQ 3; VLQ 4; VLQ 100 and probably VLQ 46. Other items from the Boistaillé library
      can today be found in the Vatican Library, in the Ambrosiana in Milan, and in collections
      in Bern, Montpellier, Paris and other French cities.
130   It is possible that the family was already selling items from their library before 1620.
      I. de Conihout, 'Jean et André Hurault. Deux frères ambassadeurs à Venise et acquéreurs
      de livres du Cardinal Grimani', *Italique. Poésie italienne de la Renaissance* 10 (2007), p. 116.
131   Louis Jarry, *Pierre Daniel, advocat au parlement de Paris et les érudits de son temps d'après
      les documents de la bibliothèque de Berne* (Orléans: H. Herluison, 1876).

SUPPLYING SCALIGER WITH BOOKS

FIGURE 21   David [Ben Solomon] ibn Jachja, *Sefer l'shon limmudim* (Constantinople: Dav[id] et Sam[uel] Ibn Nachmias, 1506). UBL 871 F 6

likely that Scaliger's offer is related to his desire to gain access to the Boistaillé library.[132] His request would be repeated in a second letter in the same year.[133]

Jean Hurault, sieur de Boistaillé, was also known as 'Abbé du Breuil et conseiller du roy', or *I. Huraltus Boestallerius*. He was a member of a long-standing and well-respected family of French diplomats and statesmen.[134] He was

---

[132]   *Correspondence* 1 July 1574 to Pierre Daniël, UBL BPL 885, pp. 2–3: 'Aussi je desire estre recommandé bien fort à la bonne grace de Monsieur de Boistailli. Et lui dires, s'il vous plaist, que si je lui puis faire service, qu'il me trouvera tousjours dedié à lui, et pour l'amour de feu Monsieur de Boistailli son pere, et pour sa vertu. Car encores que je ne l'aie veu, si est ce que non tam aversus equos nostra sol iungit ab urbe, que je n'aie oui parler de sa doctrine et vertu.'

[133]   *Correspondence* 24 July 1574 to Pierre Daniël, UBL BPL 885, p. 1: 'Je n'oblie pas aussi Monsieur De Boistailli, auquel je desire faire service, comme vous lui pourres dire, s'il vous plaist'.

[134]   Various members of the family were French ambassadors during the rule of Catherine de' Medici and Henry IV. Cf. Jensen De Lamar, 'French diplomacy and the Wars of religion', *Sixteenth Century Journal* 5 (1992), pp. 23–46. For a concise overview of the Hurault-Boistaillé family, see: De Conihout, 'Jean et André Hurault', pp. 105–148.

130   CHAPTER 3

Francis I's ambassador in Constantinople, and was in contact with Sultan
Suleiman I (1496–1566). He played an important role in the years 1557 and
1558, when he was negotiating a French-Ottoman alliance in the final stages of
the French-Spanish Wars (ca. 1525–1559). Between May 1561 and March 1564,
he was the French ambassador to Venice.[135] In this city Boistaillé assembled
the largest part of his collection; as in Constantinople, he concentrated on
collecting Greek, Arabic and Hebrew manuscripts, rather than printed books.[136]
His collection included a thirteenth-century Qur'an and a *Horologion mel-
kite* of *Kitab al-sawaʿi*.[137] Another distinguished piece bought in Venice was a
Hebrew manuscript, a Pentateuch written in Germany in 1330.[138]

Like many sixteenth-century book collectors, Boistaillé made use of various
agents who searched out and bought books, as well as scholars, who copied
out texts for him. These included a certain Zacharias Scordylis from Crete, who
supplied Boistaillé with a collection of 245 Greek manuscripts.[139] Booksellers
such as Andreas Dramarius and Nicolas della Torre also supplied Boistaillé with
books and manuscripts, as did two Roman booksellers, Vincenzo Lucchino and
Camilius Venetus, the regular suppliers of Grand Duke Cosimo I de' Medici
(1519–1574) of Tuscany. The books and manuscripts from the Boistaillé collection that ended up in Scaliger's hands were all produced in Venice. Boistaillé
had bought most of them from Daniel Bomberg, a Venetian printer originally

---

135   For Boistaillé's activities as ambassador in Venice, see: Kenneth Meyer Setton, *The
      Papacy and the Levant (1204–1571)*. Vol. IV: *The Sixteenth Century from Julius III to Pius V*
      (Philadelphia: The American Philosophical Society, 1984), pp. 831–834.
136   The Greek manuscripts collected by Boistaillé were described in the *Catalogus bibliothe-
      cae Joannis Boesstallerii* [...] *graeco sermone exaratus*, MS 360 in the Bürgerbibliothek in
      Bern. The inventory was published by Karl Wilhelm Müller as *Katalog der griechischen
      Bibliothek des franzoesischen Gesandten in Venedig Johannes Boistailler* (Rudolfstadt: Fürst.
      priv. Hofbuchdruckerei, 1852), and in the periodical *Serapeum*, XIX (1885), pp. 161–169. See
      also: Donald F. Jackson, 'The Greek Manuscripts of Jean Hurault de Boistaillé', *Studi di
      Filologia Classica* 97/2 (2004), p. 212 and onwards.
137   This is not to be confused with the printed edition of 1514 produced in Fano: UBL 976 G 27;
      see Bibliographic Survey Fano 1514.
138   BnF MS hébreu 48. A detailed description of this Pentateuch can be found in: Gabrielle
      Sed-Rajna, *Les manuscrits hébreux enluminés de la bibliothèque de France* (Leuven: Peeters,
      1994), pp. 196–201.
139   A list of the manuscripts delivered by Scordylis (BMMF, n° 744) was produced in 1564,
      and was entitled Πίναξ σὺν θεω αγίω, τῆς βιβλιοθήκης του ενδοξοτάτου κυρίου Ἰωάννου
      Βοεσταλλερίου, πρεσβευτου Ἐνετίησι του γαληνοτάτου βασιλέως των Γάλλων. See: Jackson, 'The
      Greek manuscripts of Jean Hurault de Boistaillé', pp. 209–252 (the list is at pp. 212–248).
      For the multiple roles of the agent in early modern Europe, see Marika Keblusek, 'Profiling
      the Early Modern Agent', in H. Cools (et al., eds.), *Your Humble Servant. Agents in Early
      Modern Europe* (Hilversum: Verloren, 2006), pp. 9–15. For the role of the agent as book
      dealer, see: Marika Keblusek, *De weg van het boek* (Amsterdam: Vossius Pers, 2004).

SUPPLYING SCALIGER WITH BOOKS 131

from Antwerp. Bomberg maintained a print shop in Venice for over thirty years, and enjoyed international renown especially for the publication of some 160 Hebrew works. The most distinguished piece from the Boistaillé collection that Scaliger came to own was undoubtedly an extensive manuscript containing the Jerusalem Talmud, the *Talmud Hierosolymitamum*. This manuscript contained the only surviving copy of this Talmud, and was used by Bomberg as the copy for his printed edition. Another remarkable manuscript used by Bomberg that was sold on to Boistaillé includes a dictionary of the Talmud, the *Arukh* (printed by Bomberg in 1531).[140]

Boistaillé also bought manuscripts and books in Venice from two rabbis, Zalman and Samuel.[141] Agents commissioned by Boistaillé also acquired books from private and public libraries. One can find works in his collection, such as several Hebrew manuscripts, which were originally part of the *Bibliotheca Marciana*, the library of the church of Sant' Antonio di Castello and from the monastery of Saints John and Paul of Zanipolo.[142] Some agents were unscrupulous enough to remove these manuscripts without asking for permissions to make a copy; their only concern was to satisfy the collector who had commissioned their illicit activities.

How did Scaliger acquire the books that belonged to Jean Hurault de Boistaillé? In 1564, Boistaillé returned from Italy to France with his library. He remained active as a diplomat in his fatherland and died in 1572 during a mission to England. He was buried in Morigny, in Normandy.[143] His collection fell into the hands of his brother, André Hurault de Maisse, also a renowned

---

140   Both manuscripts can be found in the collection of the UBL: MS Or. 4720 and MS Or. 4722.

141   Salomon Marcus Schiller-Szinessy, *Occasional Notices of Hebrew Manuscripts. No. 1: Description of the Leyden Ms. 1 of the Palestinian Talmud* (Cambridge, London: 1878) and Id. *Catalogue of Hebrew manuscripts* (Cambridge: Printed for the University Library, 1876), p. 15. See also the description of UBL MS Or. 4726 (SCA 9) and UBL MS Or. 4731 (SCA 14) in Witkams *Inventory*. The inscription, written in the hand of Boistaillé, reads: 'Emi a Rabbino Samuele coronato uno Patavij', in the copy of Simeon bar Jochai, *Sefer Ha-Zohar* (Mantova: Me'ir ben Ephraim of Padua & Jacob ben Naphtali Hakohen of Gazzuolo, 1558–1560; USTC 1791947, UBL 875 B 1; see Bibliographic Survey Cremona 1558–1560). Boistaillé bought this manuscript for six *coronati*. The originally German *Pentateuch* (BnF MS hébreu 48 (*Bibliorum hebraïcorum pars primor. Pars altera; paginis & litteris amplissimis*) and BnF hébreu 49 (*Jonathan in Hieremiam*)) come from the same source.

142   The collection of Cardinal Bessarion († 1472) resided in the Bibliotheca Marciana in Venice, and that of Cardinal Domenico Grimani (1461–1523) was found in the library of Sant' Antonio di Castello. MS Or. 4728 (olim MS Grimani 81) and MS Or. 4729. On f. 61ª of the first manuscript, the inscription 'Liber D[omini] Grimani Car[dina]lis S. Marci' has been crossed through vigorously. See: Van der Heide, *Hebrew manuscripts*, pp. 6–7.

143   According to S.M. Schiller-Szinessy, Jean Hurault de Boistaillé died in 1582 as ambassador of France in England, which is incorrect.

bibliophile.[144] It is uncertain how long the books remained in his possession: they later turned up in the library of his cousin, Philippe Hurault de Cheverny, abbot of Pontlevoy and bishop of Chartres (1579–1620).[145] Philippe de Cheverny subsequently brought together the library of his father with the books from his cousin Jean, to form an enormous collection of 10,000 books and 1,125 manuscripts.[146] Philippe died in 1620, and a year later his heirs sold a portion of the library, 403 manuscripts, for the sum of 12,000 francs to King Louis XIII (1610–1643), who added them to the royal library.[147] This purchase consisted of 130 Greek manuscripts, 11 in Hebrew and Arabic, 71 in Latin and 191 in French and Latin. Particular highlights included the Hebrew Pentateuch of 1330, a French Bible from 1350 and a manuscript of Dante from 1403; yet the Greek manuscripts were considered the most valued part, with a tenth-century psalter now known as the *Psautier de Paris*.[148] Today, all these manuscripts can be found in the Bibliothèque Nationale in Paris.[149]

---

144   The library of Michel de l'Hospital (1505–1573) fell into the hands of Michel Hurault, seigneur de Bel-Esbat, chancellor of Navarra, a nephew of Jean. Michel de l'Hospital was the grandfather (from the maternal side) of Michel Hurault. Scaliger was not the only one to make use of his library, as Ronsard borrowed Greek manuscripts from the collection. He celebrated Philippe de Cheverny in his *Bocage royal* (vol. III, pp. 343–349) and Dorat named him 'Unicus doctorum patronus'. Cf. Paul de Nolhac, *Ronsard et l'Humanisme* (Paris: Champion, 1921), p. 135, note 3.

145   In 1599, Philippe Hurault de Boistaillé carried the title *Comte de Cheverny, Chancellier de France*.

146   Claude Jolly, *Histoire des bibliothèques Françaises*. Vol. 2: *Les bibliothèques sous l'Ancien Régime 1530–1789* (Paris: Promodis – Éditons du Cercle de la Librairie, 1988), p. 81.

147   Four individuals were associated with the inventorisation of the library: Pierre Dupuy, Nicolas Rigault, Olivier Fontenay and Henri de Sponde. The manuscripts were formally incorporated into the royal library by Rigault, the librarian. See: A. Paulin Paris, *Les manuscrits François de la Bibliothèque du Roi*. Vol. VII (Paris: Techener, 1848), p. 374; Antoine Coron, 'The First Libraries. Blois, Fontainebleau, Paris', in M.-H. Tesnière (et al., eds.), *Creating French Culture. Treasures from the Bibliothèque nationale de France* (New Haven, London: Yale University Press, 1995). The manuscripts are described in an inventory by Henry Omont in: *Anciens Inventaires et catalogues de la Bibliothèque nationale*. Vol 1. *La librairie Royale a Blois, Fontainebleau et Paris au XVIe siècle* (Paris: Ernest Leroux, 1908), pp. 401–408.

148   BnF Grec 139. See: Charles Astruc, 'Les fonds Grecs du Cabinet des Manuscrits de la Bibliothèque Nationale', *Byzance et la France médiévale. Manuscrits à peintures du IIe au XVIe siecle* (Paris: Bibliothèque nationale, 1958).

149   Léopold V. Delisle, *Le cabinet des manuscrits de la Bibliothèque Impériale* Tome I (Paris: Imprimerie Impériale, 1868), pp. 213–214; Simone Balayé, *La Bibliothèque Nationale des origines à 1880* (Genève: Droz, 1988), p. 60.

SUPPLYING SCALIGER WITH BOOKS

The fate of the printed books from the collection of Jean Hurault de Boistaillé remains unknown. When Scaliger lived in France, he was probably already familiar with the extensive library of Boistaillé. In the *Scaligerana*, he wrote:

> I have seen a beautiful Hebrew Bible with the Massora that belongs to Monsieur le Chancelier de Chiverny. The Duke of Savoy wanted to give 1,200 écus for it. The Jews were very fond of it. It was a beautiful library, I saw all the books; there was another Hebrew Bible with large annotations in some places; it was very correct.[150]

Yet in Scaliger's correspondence, Jean Hurault de Boistaillé's name appears only twice. From Scaliger's letters there is no evidence that he borrowed books from the collection, or received books as gifts. It is also noteworthy that in two manuscripts and one printed book from Scaliger's bequest, the inscription 'Hurault' is crossed out. This could indicate that these works were not acquired by proper means.[151]

It is possible that Jacques-Auguste De Thou was responsible for these acquisitions, and that he tried to clear Scaliger's name by crossing out the Hurault de Boistaillé ex libris. The De Thou and Huraut families were closely related: Anne de Thou, Jacques-Auguste's sister, was married to Philippe Hurault, comte de Chiverny. It is probable that De Thou enjoyed access to the Hurault library, and therefore had the opportunity to inspect various books and bring these to Scaliger's attention. There is no hard evidence for this, but thanks to an inventory drawn up by Dupuy in 1593, we know that Scaliger possessed the Greek and Oriental manuscripts from the Hurault de Boistaillé collection before he

---

150 Pierre des Maizeaux, *Scaligerana, Thuana, Derroniana, Phitoeana et Colomesiana* (Amsterdam: 1740), p. 235. The authors Jean and Nicolas Vassan were cousins of Pierre Pithou. 'J'ay veu une belle Bible Hebraïque avec la Massora à Monsieur le Chancelier de Chiverny. Le Duc de Savoye en voulut donner 1200 escus. Les Juifs en estoient bien amoureux. C'estoit une belle Bibliothèque, j'ay vue tous les livres; il y avoit une autre Bible Hebraique avec de grandes annotations en quelque part; elle estoit fort correcte.'

151 See for example, UBL 1368 G 8 (see Bibliographic Survey Brescia 1494) and MS Or. 221. Two researchers have made a reconstruction of parts of the library of Hurault de Boistaillé: M.-P. Lafitte, *Inventaire des manuscrits de la famille Hurault. 26 mai 1622. Edition du texte, concordance et marques de provenance (Paris BNF, lat. 17174, ff. 2–24)* (Paris: 2010). This provides an overview of the Hebrew, Arabic, Greek, Latin and French manuscripts of Boistaillé in the BnF. See: http://www.libraria.fr/fr/editions/inventaire-des-mss-de-la-famille-hurault) and M.-P. Laffitte, 'Une acquisition de la Bibliothèque du roi au XVIIe siècle: les manuscrits de la famille Hurault' in: *Bulletin du bibliophile*, 2008, no. 1, pp. 42–98. Isabelle de Conihout, former librarian of the Bibliothèque Mazarine in Paris, is currently researching the books from the Hurault de Boistaillé library that do not reside in the BnF.

left France.[152] Alastair Hamilton has also demonstrated that two manuscripts, a copy of the *Moreh Nevukhim* (*Dalalat al-Chairin* in Hebrew translation) by Maimonides (UBL Or. 221) and the *Syntaxis mathematica* by Ptolemy (UBL Or. 4732), both of which belonged to Hurault de Boistaillé, were never part of Scaliger's bequest, but came to Leiden via the library of Raphelengius[153] The uncertainty surrounding the manuscripts of Hurault de Boistaillé is emblematic of many of the manuscripts in Scaliger's bequest. Often we do not know how a certain work entered his library, and the incomplete nature of Scaliger's correspondence means that we can rarely illuminate exactly the path taken by a particular manuscript or printed book that entered his library.

---

152   See: Appendix 1; De Conihout, 'Jean et André Hurault', p. 116: 'Les huit Ms. hébreux J. H[urault de] B[oistaillé] figurent tous dans l'Inventaire de Scaliger, probablement antérieur à son départ en 1593, conservé dans les papiers des Dupuy (Dupuy 395 f. 178–179)'. Van der Heide is less certain, stating that 'The list in MS Dupuy may have been compiled whilst Scaliger was still in France'. Van der Heide, *Hebrew Manuscripts*, p. 10.

153   Hamilton, 'Nam tirones sumus', pp. 557–591 and Alastair Hamilton 'Franciscus Raphelengius: the Hebraist and his Manuscripts', *De Gulden Passer* 68 (1990), pp. 105–117. See the descriptions of UBL MS Or. 221 (Hebr. 96) and MS Or. 4732 (SCA 15) in Witkam's *Inventory*.

CHAPTER 4

Scaliger in Leiden, 1593–1609

Scaliger's arrival in Leiden represented a clear demarcation in his life. After a turbulent and itinerant life in France, dominated by the constant threat of Catholic persecution, Scaliger found rest in Protestant Leiden. Although he would move several times within its city walls, he would remain in Leiden for the final sixteen years of his life. Thanks to the generous terms of his university appointment, which did not require Scaliger to undertake any formal obligations, he was free to dedicate himself entirely to his research, to the mentoring of students and to the collecting of Oriental books.

In May 1607, when Scaliger was sixty-six years old, he was forced to shift house in Leiden once again, and the experience left him plagued with a feeling of anxiety. He was not pleased that his tenancy for the spacious property on the Breestraat was cancelled so suddenly, and that he had to move to a smaller house on the Kerkgracht.[1] Scaliger was especially concerned about the books in his library. Although his new home was less than three hundred metres from his old residence, he feared that books might be damaged, or even worse, be lost during the move. The transportation of the books was carried out by a group of porters, who could be seen trudging between the properties in a long procession.[2] The books were packed in bundles, tied to poles, each carried by two men. The ritual and the almost sacred nature of the procession tell us much about Scaliger's bond with his books. The fear of losing his library also haunted Scaliger in his new home. The roof of the house on the Kerkgracht turned out to be seriously compromised and leaked profusely. Scaliger spent days ordering and checking the piles of books. After a month, he could finally breathe and determine that his library was indeed intact: not a single book was missing.[3] It was only then that calm descended once more, and Scaliger could focus again on his research.

An excess of worry as much as unconditional love for his library typified Scaliger as a collector. In his correspondence, one is repeatedly confronted with an image of an anxious, impatient and insatiable collector. Yet even if

---

1 The *grafboek* (book of burials) of the Vrouwekerk in Leiden states that after his death Scaliger was carried out from 'the Kerkgracht'.

2 *Correspondence* 27 May [1607] to Casaubon: Scaliger wrote about the transportation of his books: 'Primum exponenda esset pompa sarcinarum Vacerrae, series longissima rerum.'

3 *Correspondence* 27 May [1607] to Casaubon.

© KONINKLIJKE BRILL BV, LEIDEN, 2025 | DOI:10.1163/9789004701526_006

Scaliger was undoubtedly in love with books, one cannot describe him as a true bibliophile. In contrast to his friend and contemporary Jacques-Auguste de Thou, Scaliger did not care for the binding or aesthetic qualities of books. He was only enamoured with their contents.

Thanks to his substantial professorial salary, Scaliger could buy any book that he desired with local booksellers. His income also afforded Scaliger the opportunity to purchase new and antiquarian books from elsewhere in Europe, or even the Orient. Nevertheless, he complained persistently that the books that he desired were too expensive (without naming prices). Booksellers, according to Scaliger, all profited from his unenviable position as a man in need of books. In reality, Scaliger's library in Leiden grew considerably over time, not only through acquisitions, but also thanks to gifts.

Scaliger's requests for books and manuscripts appear very frequently in his correspondence. He also received, with some regularity, lists of books and book catalogues, because his correspondents considered these a suitable medium to satisfy Scaliger's desire for new information about publications. We also know that Scaliger possessed catalogues of other libraries, which he used to identify important works. Often, Scaliger sent multiple requests for the same book to different correspondents. What is also notable is that Scaliger, although he was conscious about his own status as distinguished scholar, rarely seemed to care about the status of those to whom he sent his requests. He approached a close friend and scholar such as Pierre Pithou in the same tone as chancellor Henri des Mesmes, from whom he received several Hebrew books.[4] Once a parcel had arrived in Leiden, it was only enjoyed briefly by Scaliger: soon, he had moved on to the next quest. The number of requests sent out at any one time increased over time, and Pithou especially was inundated by Scaliger's demands. This was ultimately an effective strategy: more and more books found their way to Scaliger, while his network of correspondents and book agents grew steadily as well during his time in Leiden.

1   Transporting Scaliger's Books to Leiden

Scaliger's move to Leiden was only made possible thanks to Justus Lipsius. In 1591, Lipsius suddenly abandoned his post as professor at Leiden and

---

4   Des Mesmes was the chancellor of the House of Navarre. For some time, he lived in Italy, and built up a network in Venice and Padua. *Correspondence* 7 March 1594 to De Thou; Ms. Dupuy 838, f. 113, De Thou writing to Des Mesmes: 'Je vous envoye aussy un paquet pour Monsieur de la Scala dedans lequel est l'[illegible Greek] quil desire tant. Monsieur Morel m'a faict ce bien de le transcrire pour luy'.

SCALIGER IN LEIDEN

returned to his alma mater, the Catholic University of Louvain. Lipsius was an intellectual heavyweight, an international star who had enticed many students to study at Leiden. His successors therefore had to be someone of similar distinction: the senate considered that they must find a 'worthy Hercules' to replace the 'Atlas' who had made the reputation of the institution. Janus Dousa played an important role in choosing Lipsius's successor. At the urging of Dominicus Baudius (1561–1613), a Neo-Latin poet and historian resident in France in the late 1580s and early 1590s, Dousa trained the university's sights on Scaliger, and suggested that they attract the scholar to Leiden 'to add to the Academy's reputation and lustre'.[5] Initially, the 'sixteenth-century Einstein' had no wish to move to Leiden.[6] The university responded by offering Scaliger very generous conditions: he would be under no obligation to give lectures, and would receive a royal salary. The university also offered to pay for the transportation of a part of Scaliger's library from France to Leiden. From a diary entry dated 17 March 1592 by Everard van Bronkhorst (1554–1627), professor of law at Leiden, it seems that this final offer was enough to persuade Scaliger.[7] In 1593, Scaliger decided to pack up his books and prepare for his move to the Dutch Republic.[8]

First, Scaliger had a difficult choice to make: what possessions and books would he pack? He wished to take his entire library, but time constraints caused Scaliger to leave behind a part of his library at Preuilly.[9] What remained there, Scaliger placed at the disposal of his patron, Chasteigner. On 22 September 1593, Chasteigner wrote to Scaliger that

---

5   *Correspondence* 9 January 1593 from Louise de Coligny. For the role played by Baudius in enticing Scaliger to Leiden, see: Petrus Leonardus Marie Grootens, *Dominicus Baudius. Een levensschets uit het Leidse Humanistenmilieu 1561–1613* (Nijmegen, Utrecht: Dekker & Van der Vegt N.V., 1942), pp. 50–71. 'Pour donner nom et bruit à cett'Académie'.

6   This is Anthony Grafton's characterisation. Jos Damen & Kasper van Ommen, 'Leids eredoctor Grafton: "Scaliger is de Einstein van de zestiende eeuw"', *Omslag. Bulletin van de Universiteitsbibliotheek Leiden en het Scaliger Instituut* 2 (2006), pp. 3–5.

7   *Diarium Everardi Bronckhorstii sive adversaria omnium quae gesta sunt in Academia Leidensi (1591–1627) uitgegeven door J.C. van Slee* ('s-Gravenhage: Martinus Nijhoff, 1898), p. 34: '[...] rediit Tuningus ex profectione Gallica et respondit Scaligerum promisse se venturum ad munus docendi, si modo posset commode cum suppellectili librorum ex Gallia ad nos pervenire.'

8   The importance of Scaliger's arrival for the University of Leiden is documented and described in Molhuysen, *De komst van Scaliger*; P.C. Molhuysen, *Bronnen* I; Otterspeer, *Groepsportret* I, pp. 176–179. Scaliger received 2,000 guilders per year, approximately three times as much as the average professorial salary of his colleagues.

9   See: Bronkhorst, *Diarium* 17 March 1593; *Correspondence* 25 August 1596; 22 September 1593, from Chasteigner; 21 February 1597 to Casaubon; 25 November 1597 to De Thou: 'Utinam te iuvare possem, quod a me exigis, sed neque sunt eae vires nostrae, neque ullos libros nobiscum hinc ex Gallia detulimus'. On Scaliger's stay in Preuilly, see chapter two, above.

138   CHAPTER 4

> I am using the time to look at my books which you have taken the trouble
> to choose for me so well, including my favourites, and which you have left
> me on the table of your study. And please believe that I shall always have
> your books and mine in the highest regard, awaiting your happy return.[10]

There would be no happy return, and after Chasteigner's death on 29 September 1595, Scaliger made repeated efforts to transport these books to Leiden.[11]

Due to the many forced moves through France, Scaliger's personal library had been dispersed among multiple locations at the time of his move to Leiden.[12] In a letter to Casaubon written in 1594, Scaliger mentioned that his books could be found at three locations. A portion was still in Agen, while a large part was still in the Touraine and the Poitou-Charente, in Preuilly and Abain. These two places were some 70 kilometres removed from one another; approximately between them lies Tours, and it is probable that books from Preuilly and Abain were despatched to Tours before being sent on to Leiden.

No complete list of Scaliger's possessions taken to Leiden has survived, so we can only guess what he did take with him. Thanks to a book list composed by Scaliger sent to Raphelengius, we can identify books that Scaliger must have owned before he arrived in Leiden. From Preuilly, Scaliger asked Hans Joostens, a Dutch merchant trading at Tours, to order several book chests to be made, 'to be carried by a mule' from Preuilly via Tours to Leiden: 'For you know that I cannot carry my books without boxes.'[13] From Joostens's invoice, we know that it concerned two chests, made with great urgency, for the sum of 33 guilders and 10 stuivers.[14] How many books could fit in each chest was

---

10   *Correspondence* 22 September 1593 from Chasteigner. 'J'employe le temps à regarder mes
      livres qu'avez prins la peine de me si bien choisir comme mes plus favorits et que m'aviez
      laissé sur la table de vostre estude. Et vous prie croire que j'auray tousjours en tres grande
      recommandation les vostres et les miens, attendant vostre heureux retour'.
11   Correspondence 25 August 1596 to Casaubon. See also Scaliger's eulogy on the death of
      Chasteigner in: *Epicedium Lodovici Castanei Equitis Troq. Regii* and J.J. Scaliger, *Poemata
      omnia* (Leiden: Frans van Raphelengen, 1615; USTC 1507423), no. 5, pp. 70–78.
12   *Correspondence* 18 July 1594 to Casaubon: 'De studiis nostris nihil dum certi statuimus.
      Bibliothecam enim meam in Gallia tribus locis dissipatam reliqui, neque magis mihi con-
      stat quando eam videbo, quam quantum hic manendum mihi sit.' See also: *Correspond-
      ence* 18 August 1597 to Hoeschelius.
13   *Correspondence* 13 April 1593 to Joostens; Molhuysen, *Bronnen* I, p. 276*. 'Pour porter sur
      un mulet ... Car vous sçavez que je ne sçaurois porter mes livres sans coffres'.
14   The invoices presented by Joostens also provide insights into the costs of transporting
      the books from Preuilly to Tours. He also charged Scaliger for the transportation of other
      possessions. Molhuysen, *Bronnen* I (1913), p. 275*: 'le dit jour [7 May 1593] paye pour 2
      cofres fait faire expres pour porter les livres de M. de Lescalle'; Cf. Bronkhorst, *Diarium*,
      p. 62 onwards.

SCALIGER IN LEIDEN

obviously dependent on the size of the books. When, in 1594, a collection of some 500 books was carried to the University of Leiden, they were transported in six square baskets.[15] If we presume that one such 'basket' or chest could therefore fit some eighty books, it is not unreasonable to suggest that Scaliger could pack at least 160 books in his two chests.

It can be supposed that Scaliger would have chosen to pack books that were dearest to him, as well as his rarest books, and those most needed for his research. He must have known that some of the more common printed books would have been available at the university library of Leiden, and could therefore be left behind. Scaliger must also have known that he could replace many printed books via the extensive trade network of Leiden's booksellers, or at the book fair in Frankfurt. His established French network could also provide assistance in the future. We can therefore assume that a large part of the books packed were books in Oriental languages. From manuscript annotations and provenance marks on books from Scaliger's bequest, as well as Scaliger's correspondence, we can be certain that Scaliger took some of his most valuable items to Leiden.[16]

Scaliger formally took up his post at Leiden on 24 March 1593, and he would travel to the Republic in July of the same year.[17] In the intervening period, his collection grew substantially, largely thanks to De Thou. Scaliger said farewell to a large group of friends in Tours between 29 June and 10 July, but De Thou could not join him there, as he was staying in Chartres.[18] To offer him a suitable alternative farewell, De Thou composed a list of books from his personal library, and gave them to Pithou, with the request to hand them to Scaliger in Tours.[19] The notion that this gift included books and manuscripts from the library of Hurault de Boistaillé is an attractive one, although we cannot confirm it. Other friends also gave Scaliger gifts of books, including the collector Paul Pétau (1568–1614), who handed him a copy of the *Epigrammata et Poematia Vetera*.[20]

---

15   Cf. Chris L. Heesakkers, 'Zes viercante witte manden' in J.A.A.M. Biemans (ed.), *Boeken verzamelen. Opstellen aangeboden aan Mr. J.R. de Groot bij zijn afscheid als bibliothecaris der Rijksuniversiteit Leiden* (Leiden: Bibliotheek der Rijksuniversiteit, 1983), pp. 182–197.

16   For these books, see the catalogue of the Oriental bequest of Scaliger.

17   Molhuysen, *De komst van Scaliger*, and especially Grootens, *Dominicus Baudius*, pp. 50–82.

18   Laurence Augereau, 'Les années tourangelles de Jacques-Auguste de Thou (1589–1594)' in: *Jacques-Auguste de Thou (1553–1617). Écriture et condition robine* (Paris: PUPS, 2007), p. 80.

19   *Correspondence* 25 July 1593 to Pierre Pithou: 'Je vous ai escrit il y a deux jours, et ai donné ma lettre à Monsieur d'Emery [De Thou], lequel vous a envoié un rolle des livres qu'il fault prendre de sa librairie pour me les faire tenir, ce que je vous prie faire.'

20   Auction Catalogue 1609, p. 37: *Epigrammata & Poëmatia vetera latina. 120. Paris [15]90.* This concerns a copy of the *Epigrammata et Poematia Vetera* [...] (Paris: excudebat Denis

140   CHAPTER 4

2   Scaliger's 'Oriental Catalogue' of ca. 1600

During his stay in the Low Countries, presumably around the year 1600, Scaliger made an inventory of a part of his book collection (see Appendix 1). This dating is based on the inclusion of the *Lectionarium graecoarabicum* (nu Or. 243), a manuscript that came into Scaliger's possession in 1600. The list contains various Arabic and Hebrew manuscripts that Scaliger owned at that moment. He ended the list with the statement: 'These are the manuscripts in the library of Joseph Scaliger, as well as a large quantity of printed books which are both rare and written in a great variety of languages'.[21] What is curious is that the list only contained Oriental manuscripts, and not a single printed Oriental book from his library is included.[22] We also do not know for what reason Scaliger composed the list.

In 1608, Scaliger wrote another 'Oriental catalogue', essentially a list of sources used for his *De emendatione temporum*, published in 1583 and 1598. Some of the books mentioned on this list continued to play an important role in Scaliger's scholarly research. Various Arabic titles were also recorded by Scaliger in his *Thesaurus Linguae Arabicae*, and others in a letter to Ubertus in March 1608.[23] At the end of his life, Scaliger once again composed a catalogue

---

Duval, 1590; USTC 170956). The inscription in the book reads: 'Josepho Scaligero, viro supra dignitatem, libellum hunc Paulus Petau, cultor ejus devotissimus et in suprema Curia Consilarius, L.M.D.D. [libens merito dono dedit] Augustae Turonum [= Tours] kalendris Juliis an. 1593.' This copy came into the hands of Sebastian Tengnagel, and now resides at the Österreichische Nationalbibliothek in Vienna, under call number *35 H 148. Cf. Karel Adriaan de Meyïer, *Paul en Alexandre Pétau en de geschiedenis van hun handschriften* (Leiden: E.J. Brill, 1947), p. 7.

21   'Hi libri extant manuscripti in Bibliotheca Josephi Scaligeri cum plurimis excusis quidem sed qui raro inveniuntur in omnibus linguis'.

22   This list, most likely written in Scaliger's hand, is found at the Bibliothèque nationale de France in Paris: MS. is, ff. 178^r–179^r. The portion with the Hebrew manuscripts is reproduced (with a small number of misinterpretations) as appendix 1 A in Van der Heide, *Hebrew Manuscripts*, pp. 20–21. The part with the Arabic manuscripts in microfilm was copied for me thanks to Professor François Déroche. Due to the poor quality of the microfilm, I was not able to transcribe every element as accurately as desired, but I could complement the missing or unclear transcription thanks to the information provided in a catalogue of Hebrew and Arabic manuscripts from Scaliger's collection that was composed by Peiresc, and is found at the BnF, Supplément latin no. 102: Peiresc, *diverses langues*, M 162.

23   The Arabic sources, such as the chronicle of the *Liber Joshua*, that Scaliger used for his dictionary, are summed up on the endpaper of the *Thesaurus Lingua Arabicae* in the University Library of Leiden (UBL MS Or. 212). *Correspondence* 22 March 1608 to Ubertus. In this letter, Scaliger provided an overview of the Arabic sources that were at that time in

SCALIGER IN LEIDEN

of Oriental books, added as a codicil to his will.[24] Sadly, his codicil has been lost, so we do not know what was included.

Around the time of his move to Leiden in 1593, Scaliger had provided Franciscus Raphelengius with one other catalogue. This book list was handed over by Gerardus Tuningius to Raphelengius, who mentioned the list in a letter to Justus Lipsius of 30 March 1592 (meaning that we can be certain that the list was composed shortly before this date). Scaliger's list had its intended effect, and Raphelengius was deeply impressed by the rich variety of Oriental manuscripts in Scaliger's collection. He wrote to Lipsius:

> What do you make of Scaliger's letter? He sent me a catalogue of his Oriental books via Tuningius. It is wondrous how many rare books he owns. If he comes to Leiden, we will have to judge with our own eyes whether he is talented. Personally, I think that he is most capable, and that I will enjoy many advantages in collaborating with him.[25]

3 Books Left Behind in France

In 1595, when Scaliger had lived for two years in Leiden, he decided not to return to his country of birth. 'I am here, here I will stay', he is rumoured to have announced. This decision was shortly followed by Scaliger's preparations to have the books left behind in France sent over to him in Leiden. Entirely in conformity with his nature, Scaliger had constantly complained about the dispersal of his book collection. He had complained to De Thou several months before his decision to remain at Leiden that he could not access his notes on Suetonius, because they were still in France 'together with my other books'.[26]

---

  his possession. It is notable that after his arrival in Leiden, the number of books in Arabic in his collection grew substantially. See Appendix 2.

24 De Jonge regards the codicil as an index of the manuscripts that Scaliger wished to donate to the University of Leiden. De Jonge, *Auction Catalogue*, p. 2.

25 Jeanine De Landtsheer & Jacques Kluyskens (eds.), J. Lipsius, *ILE*. Pars V: 1592 (Brussel; Peeters, 1991), no. 1179: Letter from F. Raphelengius sr. to J. Lipsius, 30 March 1592: 'Quid dicis literis Scaligeri? Is mihi misit per Tuningum Catalogum librorum suorum Orientalium. Mirum quam raros habeat libros! Si venerit, experiemur quid possit. Ergo credo eum multum posse ac eius consortio me valde adiutum iri'. The list contains in total 51 titles.

26 *Correspondence* 4 July 1595 to De Thou: 'Si quid inter legendum in illum animadvertimus, id chartae commendatum est, non memoriae meae, sed libros omnes in Gallia reliquimus.'

142 CHAPTER 4

In September 1595, his mood had not improved when he wrote to Pierre Pithou in Paris that, while many of his books were still in France, the bookshops of Leiden did not stock many of the books that he required, which was 'a great inconvenience'.[27] Scaliger clearly missed the necessary sources for his research, but safeguarding the books in France was no straightforward endeavour. From Scaliger's letters to his correspondents, especially De Thou, we know that he spent the four years before his move to Leiden mostly in the castles of Preuilly and Abain.[28] After the death of his patron Louis de Chasteigner in 1595, Scaliger tried to solicit the help of his widow, Madame Claude Dupuy de Chasteigner (1538–1632), to retrieve his books from her estates. He contacted her in January 1596, and shortly thereafter she responded from Preuilly that she could only send on his possessions when the political situation in France stabilised, and safe transport could be guaranteed.[29]

A year later, the books had still not arrived in Leiden, when Scaliger remarked in a letter to Casaubon in early 1597 that he owned land in Agen, lived in Leiden, but that many of his books were still in Tours.[30] The books necessary for his research he had to borrow or inspect in the library of the university, or the collections of his colleagues. At the end of 1597, Scaliger told De Thou that although he was happy in Leiden, he missed his library in France greatly, as well as his father's books, still at Agen. He feared that his father's books had all been stolen, and only consoled himself with the small number of manuscripts that belonged to his father that he had been able to take with him to Leiden.[31]

27 *Correspondence* 13 September 1595 to Pithou: 'Il n'y a poinct ici de librairie fournie, qui est une grande incommodité pour moi, car je n'ose encores faire venir mes livres, n'aiant aulcune certitude du temps que je dois resider ici.'

28 See the eighteen letters to De Thou from the period 17 August 1590 to 17 November 1593.

29 *Correspondence* 25 November 1597 to De Thou: 'J'avois quelque bons restes des livres de feu mon pere. Mais les marroufles du lieu ne pensoint poinct asses avoir faict, si à la ruine de mes biens ils n'eussent adjousté la volerie de mes meubles et livres. Les aultres livres que j'ai laissé en Touraine, j'espere les avoir bientost, selon la promesse que Madame d'Abain m'en a faicte.' The letter to Madame Chasteigner is dated 1596 01 19. *Correspondence* 19 January 1596 from Claude Dupuy, Madame Chasteigner.

30 *Correspondence* 21 February 1597 to De Thou: 'Nam quid de illo homine iudicare debes qui in Nitiobrigibus praedia sua habet, in Turonibus libros, in Batavis larem? Qui totfariam distractus est, nuspiam integer esse potest. Domum habeo, inquilinus sum. Bibliothecam habeo, alienis libris utor. Nobilis sum, dubitatur, contradicitur.'

31 In Scaliger's bequest, there are manuscripts by Galen (MS SCA 18) and of Aristotle's *Historia Animalium* (MS SCA 34) from the library of Julius Caesar Scaliger. Scaliger complained about these 'crumbs' from his father's library in *Correspondence* 6 February 1601 to Casaubon.

SCALIGER IN LEIDEN   143

Given Scaliger's numerous complaints, we cannot be certain that the remainder of his books left behind in France actually made their way to Leiden. Scaliger's correspondence with De Thou seems to indicate that this was not the case. Yet if we believe Gerardus Buytewech (1574–?), a former student of Lipsius, the books in France did arrive in Leiden. In December 1595, Buytewech wrote to Lipsius: '[Scaliger] has settled in here; he does not discuss the war, peace or politics, and no conversation will make him think of a potential return [to France]. Now he has even had all his books from France come over here.'[32]

It is possible that a large quantity of his books did arrive in Leiden, but it is undoubtedly also the case that parts of his collection were lost, or remained in the castles where Scaliger used to live. Whatever the truth of the matter was, Scaliger continued to complain. In 1600, he wrote to the brothers Dupuy that there was no man on earth who was so miserable without his books as he was. Another complaint concerned the difficulty sourcing the books that he required in the Dutch Republic, and the high prices charged by the local booksellers. He also regarded his father's library in Agen as entirely lost, while the consignments that did arrive from the Touraine demonstrated to Scaliger that some books were missing.[33] His anxiety led Scaliger to emphasise to his correspondents that when they sent him books, to pack them carefully with straw, hay and paper, so that they would not be damaged. Another declaration made by Scaliger in this period was that a proper library must consist of at least six great rooms.[34] We know that this was more of an aspiration than a reflection of reality, because the books that Scaliger had been able to take with him from France would not have filled such a space.

We cannot be exact, but is it possible to make an estimate of the quantity of books that Scaliger took with him from France? There are 870 titles listed in the auction catalogue of 1609 of Scaliger's books that contain a date of printing

---

32   Cf. Jeanine De Landtsheer (ed.), J. Lipsius, *ILE*. Pars VIII: 1595 (Brussel: Peeters 2004), no. 2015, 95 12 05: 'Sedem hic firmiter fixit, nec de pace aut bello aut quicumque sermo facit ipsum ad reditum vacillare. Iam nunc evocavit ex Gallis omnes libros.'

33   *Correspondence* 25 December 1600 to the brothers Dupuy: 'Il n'y a homme au monde plus malheureus en livres que je suis, car j'en ai perdu de beaux du reste de la librairie de mon pere dans la ville d'Agen, et en me renvoiant ceux que j'avois en Touraine, on m'en a retenu beaucoup. Somme toute, il n'y a si petit pedan qui ne soit mieus garni de beaux livres que moi.' See also *Correspondence* 9 November 1590 to De Thou concerning the fate of the library of J.C. Scaliger in Agen.

34   *Scaligerana* 1740, p. 237, under *Bibliotheca Florentina*: 'Pour une parfaite Bibliotheque, il faudroit avoir six grandes Chambres. Les belles Bibliotheques d'Egypte, olim!' Making this statement, Scaliger was possibly inspired by the library of his former tutor Cujas, which was composed of seven or eight rooms. Scaliger admired this library greatly.

144 CHAPTER 4

from before 1593. Some of these books might have been bought by Scaliger in Leiden after 1593, while another part may already have been in his possession in France, as is indicated by references to these books in his correspondence. Sometimes, Scaliger derided the quality of certain books in his possession, yet even these titles we can trace in his auction catalogue. It seems unlikely that, tight for space, he would have taken such books from France. Yet from various letters to and from Scaliger, we know that Scaliger even had books that he valued little brought over from France.

This is most evident from the fifty-three letters that Scaliger exchanged with Justus Lipsius. They wrote to one another regarding a variety of subjects: ancient literature, philology and newly published books. Their first correspondence dates from the early 1570s. The printer-publisher Christopher Plantin acted as their intermediary, while Dupuy also regularly sent correspondence from Paris to Lipsius via Scaliger, who then resided in Touffou. Alongside one of Lipsius's first letters, he sent Scaliger a copy of his *Epistolicae quaestiones*, shortly after this work appeared on the press in Antwerp in 1577.[35] Scaliger was very pleased with this gift, he told Lipsius, because he could barely take any items with him to Touffou.

In February 1581, Plantin sent by courier two copies of Lipsius's *Satyra Menippaea. Somnium* to Scaliger, then in Chantemille-sur-Creuse, near Ahun in the Limousin. Two years later, Scaliger again received books by Lipsius from Plantin: *De Constantia* and *De amphitheatro*. In his final years in France, a student travelling in the Poitou presented Scaliger with a copy of Lipsius's annotations on Seneca.[36] Scaliger was not always complimentary about Lipsius's publications. On one occasion, he wrote that 'Lipsius's *De cruce* is worthless. I discussed it in my Eusebius. He made many mistakes in the verse at the end of 'The virgin of Scherpenheuvel'.[37] Despite these negative judgements, Scaliger did take all of Lipsius's gifts with him to Leiden; all of these works can be found

---

35 Scaliger took this book and other publications that he received from Lipsius with him to Leiden. The title is included in the auction catalogue of 1609 in the section *Oratores, Philologi &c.* p. 19, together with Lipsius's *Epistolarum (selectarum) Centuria prima* (Antwerp (= Leiden): Christophe Plantin, 1586 (= 1585); USTC 429138), the *Variarum lectionum libri IIII* (Antverpiae: ex officina Christophe Plantin, 1569; USTC 401432) and a copy of *De Cruce* (Antverpiae: ex officina Plantiniana apud Joannem Moretum, 1597; USTC 402396), Lipsius's study of the cross and its use as method of execution in antiquity. Scaliger's copy of that book later appears in the auction catalogue (1682) of the library of Nicolaas Heinsius, in the section *Antiquari in Octavo* no. 49.

36 *Iusti Lipsi Animadversiones in tragoedias quae L. Annaeo Seneca tribuuntur* (Leiden: ex officina Plantiniana apud Franciscus I Raphelengius, 1588; USTC 422671). Scaliger's copy is now located in the Bodleian Library in Oxford [call number Auct. S.4.26].

37 *Scaligerana*, p. 244, under the entry for Lipsius.

SCALIGER IN LEIDEN

in his auction catalogue. This demonstrates that Scaliger certainly did take some works that he considered to be less valuable to Leiden.

In the sixteenth century, it was common that a bookseller sold new publications in an unbound state. The buyer could then decide whether they wished to have the book bound, and in what style. A part of Scaliger's books were bound, and others unbound: why did he make these choices? Do they reveal anything about the value that he attached to his books? Without fail, Scaliger always bound his reference works, those used regularly for his research. In a letter to Johannes Drusius senior, he wrote that he did not read or study unbound books, and that he considered it undesirable to read loose sheets.[38] Yet, as so often with Scaliger, there are exceptions. Scaliger did read the text of Nicolas Serarius's *Trihaeresium seu de celeberrimis tribus apud Iudaeos, pharisaeorum, sadducaeorum* (Mainz, 1604) in an unbound state.[39]

That Scaliger did like to bind the books that he read repeatedly and enjoyed, does indicate that unbound copies listed in his auction catalogue might have been of less importance to him. There are around 250 titles listed in the 'unbound' category of the catalogue, including copies of his own works, of which he possessed multiples.[40] We can trace eleven copies of Scaliger's edition of *Publii Syri Mimi Selectae sententiae. Dionysii Catonis Disticha de moribus* (Leiden, ex officina Plantiniana, 1598) and eight copies of Scaliger's edition of the *Florilegium epigrammatum Martialis* (Paris, ex typographia Roberti Stephani, 1607). Gifts from friends accounted for other unbound titles present in multiple copies, including works written by Drusius, Hugo Grotius (1583–1645) or those sent to him by printers.

The history of another unbound work in this collection is emblematic of others in Scaliger's collection. In 1592, he received from Louis Turquet de Mayerne (1550?–1618) a copy of the *Épistre au Roy. Présentée à Sa Majesté au mois d'octobre 1591*. This was a modest publication that was published in Tours

---

38 *Correspondence* 17 June 1604 to Drusius: 'Quamvis non soleo neque possum libros nisi compactos legere, tamen quae mea fuit praeter solitum impatientia non potui a foliis, ita ut soluta erant, oculos abstinere'. See also: 1603 08 20 to Lipsius: 'legi soluta adhuc praeter morem meum qui libris nisi compactis operam serio dare non possum' and *Secunda Scaligerana.* 1740, p. 187: 'Ego non soleo legere libros nisi compactos'.

39 Bernays, *Joseph Justus Scaliger*, pp. 208–209.

40 The number of author's copies handed over by the printer could vary considerably, depending on the negotiations made between the author and printer. According to Johannes Drusius, in a letter sent to Johannes Buxtorf on 21 February 1605 (Bazel UB G 1 59:257), authors regularly received fifty copies of their work, which they used as presentation copies for their friends and colleagues, or which they sold or exchanged for other books. Cf. Voet, *Golden Compasses* 2, pp. 284–288.

in 1592.[41] Scaliger clearly did not hold the author or the content of the book in high regard, because he did not think it necessary to have the book bound. We can identify the work in the *Libri incompacti* section of Scaliger's auction catalogue (p. 50). It is also possible that this decision was influenced by Scaliger's frugality. Scaliger showed little interest in his unbound works and he never annotated them either. Yet the fact that we can find the copy of the *Épistre au Roy* and some of Lipsius's publications that Scaliger did not value in his auction catalogue is a strong indication that Scaliger made serious efforts to retrieve all his books from France. This assumption is supported further by the presence in the catalogue of an English work on chronology that he received from Richard Thomson in 1592. Given that Scaliger lacked knowledge of the English language (a surprising lack, given his interest in languages), and could therefore have made very little of the text, it is still striking that he endeavoured to retrieve this work from France.[42]

4 Scaliger's Network in Leiden

When we assess Scaliger's network from his Leiden period, we see that the Netherlands enjoyed similarly good trading links and connections as France, and that agents, resident in strategically-located cities, continued to play a critical role in the exchange of letters and goods. International commercial connections were obviously impacted by external forces: war, tolls, robbers, shipwreck, epidemics and natural disasters, each of which could threaten the stability of a trade route. The necessity of using alternative routes could sometimes delay the shipment of goods considerably. Due to the constant threat of war and unrest, the northern axis that ran from the Dutch Republic through the Southern Netherlands and France to Iberia was frequently and heavily disrupted. To collect Oriental books in the Dutch Republic, one would look to an alternative trade route that ran to Italy via Germany and Switzerland. In the early seventeenth century, Basel functioned as a lynchpin in this route, as one of the most important centres of Hebrew printing in Europe.

There were other obstacles that impeded the supply of Oriental books. A shortage of talented compositors and correctors caused a decline in the

---

41   *Correspondence* 16 February 1592 from Turquet de Mayerne.

42   This was a copy of *Matthieu Beroald, A Short View of the Persian Monarchie and of Daniels Weekes* (Translated by Hugh Broughton) (London: Thomas Orwin, 1590; USTC 511445). See Botley, *Richard 'Dutch' Thomson*, pp. 18–19. Auction Catalogue 1609, p. 44: *A Short view of Daniels Weekes, &c. London* [15]90.

SCALIGER IN LEIDEN

production of Hebrew books in Italy.[43] Printers of Hebrew works in Italy were also inhibited by the prohibition on the printing of the Talmud. Between 1553 and 1563, Venice even issued a prohibition on the production of all Hebrew books. After these regulations were lifted, they came into force again on 8 December 1571, with the additional ordinance that printers could not employ Jewish workmen.[44] These restrictive regulations ensured that Scaliger regularly had to look out for older editions of Hebrew books, circulating in the second-hand market or in Jewish communities. The political animosity between Spain and the Dutch also ensured that one extremely desirable collection of Hebrew and Arabic manuscripts, housed in Philip II's Escorial library, would remain forever out of Scaliger's reach.

Despite these impediments, Scaliger continued to expand his collection in Leiden and reach out to friends in his network to acquire more books. Dupuy remained a very important source of books for Scaliger. The brothers Dupuy, sons of Claude Dupuy, regularly received lists of books from Scaliger, each entitled 'catalogus', with a request to buy them for him.[45] Scaliger promised that he would ensure prompt payment: 'I shall be very glad to receive the books listed in my catalogue. I will deliver the money as soon as desired.'[46] Scaliger regularly received such despatches of books from the brothers Dupuy via the Raphelengius firm at Leiden. One parcel, received in August 1601, contained an edition of Plato with Proclus, an edition of Lilius Gregorius Giraldus 'en blanc', a copy of Caelius Aurelianus and a glossary.[47] Scaliger thanked the Dupuy brothers politely and asked them about the prices of the books, so that he could issue payment to the Raphelengius brothers. In the same letter, he already provided the items on his next wish list, while he also complained in passing about the high prices at Leiden. A book available in Paris for a *sous* cost

---

43 On 12 September 1553, a Papal Bull was promulgated that ordered the destruction of the Babylonian and Palestinian Talmud. Many copies of the Talmud ended up on the pyre at the Campo dei Fiori in Rome, where many print shops were to be found. The prohibition concerning the printing of the Talmud was later also promulgated by Pope Gregory XIII (1575–1585) and Clement VIII in 1595.

44 David Werner Amram, *The Makers of Hebrew Books in Italy. Being Chapters in the History of the Hebrew Printing Press* (London: The Holland Press limited, 1963), pp. 352–360.

45 In *Correspondence* 6 November 1601, to the brothers Dupuy, Scaliger mentions 'petit rollet ci-enclos, et qu'on cotte le pris de livres qu'on m'a envoié, et qu'on m'envoiera [...] Je vous supplie doncques de faire chercher les livres contenus au catalogue.'

46 *Correspondence* 23 April 1601 to the brothers Dupuy. 'Je serai tres aise de reçevoir les livres de mon catalogue. Je delivrerai incontinent l'argent selon que desires.'

47 *Correspondence* 14 August 1601 to Dupuy: 'J'ai receu un pacquet de livres qu'il vous a pleu me faire tenir, où il y avoit un Platon avec Proclus'. This edition of Proclus is listed in the Auction Catalogue of 1609 in the section *Medici et Philosophici* at page 10.

five or even ten times as much in Leiden. If this situation were to continue, he grumbled, he would never be able to assemble a great book collection, and he would have only a 'small, meagre and miserable library.' He did not care what formats his desired books were in, as long as he could receive all that he requested from his fatherland: 'I would like to have all the poets, Turnebus, Guillelmus, Morellus, Benenatus, whether printed in quarto or octavo, as soon as the opportunity arises to find them in the second-hand shops. I am poor in everything, especially in books.'[48]

In 1598, Scaliger met the French ambassador in The Hague, Paul Choart de Buzanval, who granted him the use of his library. Scaliger regularly took advantage of this connection, and visited De Buzanval in The Hague, while he also invited him to come to Leiden to read Greek works in his library.[49] Another new connection for Scaliger was the scholar Isaac Casaubon, then in Geneva. Richard Thomson, a student of Scaliger, brought the two scholars in contact with one another and urged them to begin a correspondence. Scaliger received his first letter from Casaubon in the second half of December 1593.[50] When Casaubon stayed in Montpellier between 1596 and 1599, their correspondence was revived, with Scaliger's former student Johannes Woverius (1574–1612) from Hamburg functioning as the go-between, as he resided with Casaubon for some time in Montpellier. Casaubon sent letters to Scaliger via the jurist Pieter van Brederode (1558–1639), who lived in Paris, and fulfilled the role of advisor to Catherina of Bourbon, the sister of Henry IV.[51]

---

48   See the Auction Catalogue of 1609, page 35: *Turnebi Poëmata. Paris. 1580.* The printers Fédéric Morel (1552–1630) and Joannes Benenatus († 1588?) were responsible for a large number of editions of classical authors. On Morel, see: Judit Kecskeméti, *Fédéric Morel II. Éditeur, traducteur et imprimeur* (Turnhout: Brepols/Genève: Bibliothèque de Genève, 2014). *Correspondence* 14 August 1601 to Dupuy. 'Je desireroit avoir tou[s] les poetes que Turnebus, Guillelmus, Morellus, Benenatus ont imprimé en quart[o ou] octavo, quand l'occasion se presentera d'en trouver es boutiques des frippiers. Je suis pauvre en tout, mesmement en livres.' This letter contains much interesting detail on the prices of and trade in books. See also: *Correspondence* 6 November 1601 to the brothers Dupuy: 'Vous ne sauries croire la peine que j'ai à recouvrer des livres, et la despense que j'y ai faict, tellement que j'en suis pouvre apres aussi avoir esté desrobé de mes domestiques, ausquels j'avoi faict beaucoup de bien.'

49   G.W. Vreede, 'Communication de –', *Compte-rendu des séances de la Commission Royale d'Histoire ou Recueil de ses bulletins* IV (1840–1841), Bruxelles 1841, pp. 94–108.

50   The first letter from Casaubon is dated 15 December 1593 see: *Correspondence* 15 December 1593 from Casaubon.

51   Robert Feenstra, 'Notice sur Pierre Corneille de Bredero (1558(?)–1637)', in Bruno Schmidlin et Alfred Dufour (eds.), *Jacques Godefroy (1587–1652) et l'humanisme juridique à Genève. Actes du colloque Jacques Godefroy, Bâle et Francfort-sur-le-Main* (Basel: Helbing & Lichtenhahn, 1991), pp. 245–248.

FIGURE 22   Painted portrait of Isaac Casaubon (1559–1614). *Icones Leidenses* 44

Another regular and trustworthy contact for the supply of books was the Huguenot preacher Simon Goulart (1543–1628) in Geneva. In 1602 and 1603, Scaliger appealed to Goulart to purchase for him from the library of the ageing theologian Theodorus Beza several editions of the *Targum*, an Aramaic translation of the Hebrew Bible. Scaliger had probably seen these editions at De Bèze's house when he resided in Geneva, because he was able to supply

150   CHAPTER 4

Goulart with very specific details: the *Targums* were printed in Greek, Spanish, Arabic and Persian.[52] The library had, however, already been sold in 1598 (seven years before De Bèze's death), and the books had already been dispersed.[53] Scaliger did not give in, however: perhaps Goulart could help him acquire a Latin translation of the Qur'an? A year later, after repeated requests, he would indeed receive this book from Goulart.[54]

Jacques Gillot (1544–1619), a friend of Scaliger from his student days in Paris, was also a useful contact during his Leiden period. Gillot was one of Scaliger's most reliable suppliers of books in Paris, and personally supervised the despatch of books to Leiden.[55] When he was in Montpellier, Casaubon also made use of Gillot's services to send books to Scaliger. Yet when Casaubon was in Geneva, books were sent to Scaliger via Frankfurt, or with the help of other acquaintances of Scaliger, such as the diplomat Henry Wotton (1568–1639), who stayed in Geneva with Casaubon in 1593. Other incidental passers-by, such as Johannes Saeckma (1572–1636), a lawyer for the States of Friesland who met Casaubon in Geneva in 1595, were relied upon as couriers.[56]

In Leiden, an important agent in Scaliger's network was Franciscus I Raphelengius (1539–1597). Raphelengius and his three sons sometimes acted as intermediaries between Scaliger and De Thou in Paris. In a letter of 31 October 1593, De Thou referred to

> Sir Raphelengius [junior], whom I have seen here [in Paris], assures us that we shall soon have it, and that to adorn it more [the *Opus de emendatione temporum*] deservingly, they have had punches made to express the characters in the foreign languages.[57]

---

52   *Correspondence* 25 November 1602 to Goulart; *Correspondence* 17 January 1603 to Goulart.

53   *Correspondence* 23 June 1603 to Goulart.

54   *Correspondence* 19 March 1604 to Goulart. This most likely concerns the *Machumetis ejusque successorum vitae, ac doctrina, ipseque Alcoran. Haec omnia in unum volumen redacta opera et studio Theodori Bibliandri*, printed in Basel in 1543 and reprinted there in 1550. No copy is present in Scaliger's bequest, nor is a copy listed in the auction catalogue of 1609.

55   Amongst other items, Gillot sent Scaliger a copy of Henri Estienne, *Epistolia, Dialogi breves, Oratiunculae, Poematia* ([Genève]: Henri II Estienne, 1577; USTC 450741) and an otherwise unspecified publication with epigrams printed in Geneva in 1590. Books purchased at the Frankfurt book fair could also find their way to Leiden via Gillot. See *Correspondence* 9 March 1593 from Vertunien and [May 1602] to Gillot.

56   Johannes Saeckma was born in Kollum. He studied Law at the University of Franeker in 1588. After his studies, he made a Grand Tour via Heidelberg (1594), Basel (where he acquired his doctoral title in 1595) and Geneva (1595). In Geneva he met Casaubon. See *NNBW* II, 1912, cols. 1255–1256.

57   *Correspondence* 31 October 1593 from De Thou. 'Le Sieur Raphelengius, que j'ay veu icy, nous asseure que nous l'avions bientost, et que pour l'orner d'avantage comme il mérite, l'on a faict faire des poinçons expres des charactères des langues estrangères.'

SCALIGER IN LEIDEN

During this meeting, De Thou possibly gave Raphelengius a number of books for Scaliger. The Raphelengius family was also in regular contact with major suppliers in the European book trade, all to Scaliger's great advantage. An agent of Plantin's in Frankfurt, Hans Dressel, frequently sent Raphelengius despatches of books, including Oriental works, such as the publications of the *Tipographia Medicea* in Rome.[58] Scaliger was extremely interested in the arrival of these books, and would have followed their despatch with great anticipation. Like his father-in-law Plantin, Raphelengius visited the Frankfurt book fair during the period 1586–1597. According to the trade journals of the Officina Plantiniana, the Antwerp and Leiden firms exchanged books in Frankfurt, including Oriental books.[59]

5 New Contacts in the Leiden Network: Casaubon, Bongars and Commelin

Isaac Casaubon played a prominent role in Scaliger's network during his Leiden period. Scaliger found in Casaubon an intellectual equal, one who was also in a position to offer Scaliger new sources for his research. In 1604, Casaubon became deputy librarian at the Royal Library in Paris (where De Thou was the chief librarian), which offered Scaliger two direct lines of access to the collection. At his request, transcripts were made of manuscripts, which were then despatched to Leiden via Rouen, with the help of agents such as Gillot. In 1598, Scaliger mentioned with great delight that the communication between Paris and Leiden was highly efficient.[60]

The scholar and diplomat Jacques Bongars, sieur de la Chesnaye et de Bauldry (or de Bodry, 1554–1612) also came to occupy a critical role in Scaliger's Leiden network.[61] Bongars was an agent for Henry III of Navarre (the future Henry IV of France) at the Frankfurt book fair, and in this capacity worked

---

58 Juynboll, *Zeventiende-eeuwsche beoefenaars* p. 41. Hans (Jean) Dressel(aer) worked as agent for the Raphelengius firm in Frankfurt and Cologne.

59 R. Lauwaert, 'De handelsbedrijvigheid van de Officina Plantiniana op de Büchermessen te Frankfurt am Main in de XVIe eeuw', *De Gulden Passer* 50 (1972), p. 172 and p. 51 (1973), p. 99.

60 *Correspondence* 23 October 1598 to Casaubon: 'Si Lutetiae maneres, facilior esset tibi inde huc transitus quam Lutetiam ab Arecomicis tuis.'

61 Ruth Kohlndorfer-Fries, *Diplomatie und Gelehrtenrepublik. Die Kontakte des französischen Gesandten Jacques Bongars (1554–1612)* (Tübingen: De Gruyter, 2009). On his book collection, see: A. Patrick, 'Strassburg – Basel – Bern. Bücher auf der Reise. Das Legat der Bibliothek von Jacques Bongars, die Schenkung von Jakob Graviseth und das weitere Schicksal der Sammlung in Bern', in B. Hans (ed.), *Scriptorium und Offizin. Festgabe für Martin Steinmann zum 70. Geburtstag, Basler Zeitschrift für Geschichte und Altertumskunde* 110 (2010), pp. 249–268.

152   CHAPTER 4

together closely with Hieronymus Commelin, an Amsterdam printer who moved in 1587 to Heidelberg.[62] In 1593, Bongars was appointed ambassador by Henry IV to various German courts. This made his position in the Holy Roman Empire even more attractive for scholars and collectors such as Scaliger. Bongars, Commelin and Scaliger had met each other in Geneva in 1574, during the preparation of Scaliger's editions of Verrius Flaccus and Sextus Pompeius Festus, which would appear a year later at the print shop of Petrus Sanctandreus.[63] Shortly after Commelin moved to Heidelberg, he was responsible for several other editions by Scaliger, including his edition of Ausonius (1588). Other works of Scaliger that later came off his press included the *Emendationes ad Theocriti, Moschi et Bionis Idyllia* (1596) and the *Lexicon Doricum*, with annotations by Scaliger and Casaubon (1597).

Commelin's print shop in Heidelberg developed into one the most prominent European scholarly presses. The humanist Fredericus Sylburgius worked there as corrector, while Commelin had close relationships with other great scholars, including Janus Gruterus (1560–1626), Conradus Ritterhusius (1560–1613) and David Hoeschelius (1556–1617). Hoeschelius enjoyed access to the famous *Bibliotheca Palatina*, where he regularly transcribed manuscripts for other scholars. He would later be appointed the librarian of the city library of Augsburg, and in 1594 published a catalogue of its collection of Greek works. He corresponded with Scaliger about some of the manuscripts listed in this catalogue. In this sense, a broad network gravitated towards Commelin, of which Scaliger made grateful use; Commelin himself would also help forward on Scaliger's correspondence, including that with Casaubon.

From Heidelberg, Hieronymus Commelin sent books to Scaliger via a route that ran to Hamburg, and thence by ship to Amsterdam. An alternative route ran via the Frankfurt book fair, from which books could also be despatched to Amsterdam.[64] In Amsterdam, the bookseller Jean Jansz Commelin (1548–1615) sent his son Jan II Commelin (1577–1604) to Leiden to hand over the books: in May 1596, on one instance, Jan delivered a Venetian edition of Ptolemy

---

62   Willhelm Port, *Hieronymus Commelinus 1550–1597. Leben und Werk eines Heidelberger Drucker-Verlegers* (Leipzig: Harrassowitz, 1938) and Combertus Pieter Burger, 'De boekverkopers Commelin te Genève, Heidelberg, Amsterdam en Leiden', *Tijdschrift voor boek- en bibliotheekwezen* 9 (1911), pp. 145–176.

63   In the dedication to the Heidelberg professor of medicine Joannes Opsopoeus (1556–1596) in the edition of the *Emendationes ad Theocriti* (1597), Commelin mentioned that he had once been a guest of Scaliger's, whom he had not seen in twenty years. The letter is printed in: Port, *Hieronymus Commelinus 1550–1597*, Textbeilage 13, pp. 108–109.

64   *Correspondence* 21 February 1596 to Henricus and Fridericus Lindenbrogius: 'Mei libri, quos Hieronymus Commelinus proximis nundinis ad me misit, adhuc apud vos sunt.'

SCALIGER IN LEIDEN

and a manuscript by Georgius Monachus, lent to Scaliger by Marcus Welser (1558–1614).[65] Commelin was also in close contact with Aegidius Radaeus (Gilles van den Rade, 1550–1620), a printer in Franeker. After Hieronymus Commelin died in 1597, his printing house was continued by two successors: his brother-in-law Juda Bonnennuict (or Juda Bonutius), a merchant and scholar who travelled frequently between Amsterdam and Heidelberg, and Jean Jansz Commelin in Amsterdam.[66] Since 1587, Jan I Commelin had been active as publisher in Amsterdam, while he was also involved with the family business at Heidelberg. The bond between the Commelins and Scaliger is also demonstrated by the role that these printers played in the publication of Scaliger's edition of Manilius's *Astronomicon* (1599–1600). This work was printed by Raphelengius in Leiden, but was entirely financed by Commelin.[67] Jan II Commelin also fulfilled the role of agent for Scaliger, sending and receiving books for him from contacts in France.[68] He also maintained correspondence with Peiresc, and through him with agents such as Hostagier in Marseille, while he was also responsible for handling some of the correspondence between Scaliger and Casaubon.

6 The Operation of a Trade Network in Practice

Not every network of trade or communication functions in the same manner. To demonstrate that Scaliger's scholarly peers often relied on different routes to fill their bookcases, is it worthwhile to reflect on the example of Johannes Drusius senior. Drusius had been professor of Hebrew at Leiden and shared with Scaliger an interest in the language and culture of the Jewish people. While the two scholars were in contact with each other, and held each other in mutual respect, they tapped into divergent networks to source books. In the Hebrew correspondence-book of Johannes Drusius junior (1588–1609), there are two letters, dated 2 October 1590 and 20 January 1592, written to Drusius

---

65   *Correspondence* 6 May 1596 from H. Commelinus in Heidelberg. The book is *Geographia Cl. Ptolemaei Alexandrini*. Venetiis, Apud Vincentium Valgrisium 1562 (USTC 851490) and is listed in the auction catalogue of 1609 at page 14: *Ptolemaei Geographia Ios. Moletij. lat. Venet* [15]62.

66   Commelin frequently gifted books to Scaliger, including an edition of Ocellus Lucanus and Apollodorus (see the last title in the section *libri Histori in octavo* in the auction catalogue of 1609, p. 20). Cf. *Scaligerana* 1740 pp. 476.

67   Ronald Breugelmans, *Leiden Imprints 1483–1600 in Leiden University Library and Bibliotheca Thysiana. A short-title catalogue* (Nieuwkoop: B. de Graaf, 1974), p. 67.

68   *Correspondence* 3 February 1609 from Peiresc. On Jan II Commelin, see: C.P. Burger, 'De Amsterdamsche boeken op de Frankfurter mis', *Het Boek* 23 (1935–1936), pp. 191–194.

senior by the Jewish book dealer Moses ben Jacob Halevi Zion from Emden.[69] It is surprising that Scaliger, who was always pursuing books with such relentless energy, did not wish to use such a contact or source. One would expect that he would made use of any useful connection, but it seems that in practice, Scaliger relied mostly on networks where close friends or relations acted as mediators. Scaliger knew that he could trust such intermediaries, and exercise greater control over the supply of books in result.

As Scaliger noted contently, the traffic in books between Leiden, Paris and other cities could be readily organised through his own contacts. There were always enough French friends and acquaintances who paid him a visit, and brought letters and books from France for him. Vice versa, from Leiden there departed for France a variety of booksellers and scholars. A certain Du Moulin, possibly Pierre du Moulin (1568–1658), professor of philosophy at Leiden, stopped over in Paris in July 1596, and presented to De Thou a few letters and gifts from Scaliger. Shortly afterwards, Scaliger also sent a poem to Paris via a certain Gilles, bookseller in Leiden.[70] Students who graduated at Leiden, such as Jacques Esprinchard (1573–1604), were also despatched by Scaliger on missions to acquire books at the fair at Frankfurt, or to make contact with publishers, such as the brothers Estienne in Paris.[71] After Esprinchard visited Frankfurt for Scaliger, he also travelled onwards to Leipzig, and thence to various cities in Saxony, before going on to Breslau and Prague. Around 1601, he was active in Paris, where the brothers Dupuy employed him as an agent for Scaliger.

Despite Scaliger's musings on the smooth functioning of the book traffic between Leiden and France, in practice this remained a fragile network. A letter from Charles de Harlay, sieur de Dolot (1540–1617), a childhood friend of Scaliger's, demonstrates the careful planning that went into the choice of route for the transportation of books.[72] Scaliger gave De Harlay a list of Hebrew titles to purchase from a number of Catholic contacts in Venice and Padua.[73] Similar lists with Hebrew desiderata were sent to other correspondents, such

---

69   Leo Fuks, 'Het Hebreeuwse brievenboek van Johannes Drusius jr. Hebreeuws en hebraïsten in Nederland rondom 1600', *Studia Rosenthaliana* 3/1 (1969), pp. 11 and 12. According to Fuks, these letters are the earliest evidence of contact between non-Jewish humanists in Holland and Jewish individuals abroad.

70   *Correspondence* 8 July 1596 to De Thou.

71   Jacques Esprinchard, a member of a respected family from La Rochelle, studied in Oxford and Leiden. He graduated at Leiden in March 1597. Afterwards he travelled through Germany, Poland, Bohemia, Austria and Switzerland. *Correspondence* 2 April 1597 from Esprinchard.

72   De Harlay, who remained in Italy between 1585 and 1599, regularly sent books to Scaliger via a German trade route. See: *Correspondence* 13 February 1601 from De Harlay.

73   See for this Catholic network in Italy: *Correspondence* 20 March 1604 from Chr. Dupuy.

SCALIGER IN LEIDEN   155

as Pinelli and Thomson.[74] When De Harlay arranged for the transportation of the books from Italy, he ensured that they were carried via Basel and Frankfurt, avoiding the route over the French Alps towards Lyon and Paris. Due to the influence of Catholic inquisitors, few booksellers dared to send heterodox books directly from Venice or Milan to France.[75] De Harlay wrote:

> I have written to Italy for the books you have asked for, and I beg you to believe that I cannot receive more pleasant and desired testimony of your good grace towards me than that you make use of me on all occasions.[76] ... There is a very affectionate friend of mine, Monsieur de Valence, my former schoolmate, who has retired there to get treatment for gout, and to whom I have given this task.[77] He is a man of letters and very reliable. I trust that he will carry out his duties faithfully and diligently. I have told him to send the books to Frankfurt to a merchant of mine, to whom I will write to have them delivered to you in Holland, as this makes it very easy.[78]

74   None of these Hebrew lists composed by Scaliger have survived. *Correspondence* 1601 08 13 to Pinelli and 1601 08 23 to Thomson, concerning the request for a copy of Maimonides's *Moreh nevukhi*. It is possible that this concerned the Venetian edition of 1551, but no copy of this can be found in Scaliger's bequest. Scaliger did own a copy of Moses Maimonides, *Sefer Moreh nevukhim, i.e. Doctor perplexorum ex Arabico vertit Samuel ibn Tibbon* [S.l.; Venice?], 14XX, [ante annum 1480?], UBL 877 B 11; see Bibliographic Survey Venice ante a. 1480, and Ibn Maymūn, Mūsā b. ʿUbayd, *Sefer Moreh nevukim* [...]. Sabyonitah, Kornilyo AdilKind, [5]313 [1553] (USTC 1791668, UBL 877 B 12; see Bibliographic Survey Sabbioneta 1553). See also *Correspondence* 8 September 1601 from Casaubon; 1 December 1601 from Denys Perrot, the son of Emilius Perrot, councillor in the Parisian Parlement, who was active as an agent in London, and ensured the despatch of multiple Hebrew books to Scaliger. A week after the letter was sent by Perrot to Scaliger, Thomson wrote the following to Perrot: 'duos Scaligero libros Hebraicos comparavi, quos iam mitto. Quaeso te uti illos solita fide et diligentia ad Scaligerum cures ferendos' (8 December 1601, BnF, Coll. Dupuy, 699, f. 96ʳ).
75   *Correspondence* 28 July 1599 from De Harlay.
76   In 1595, Scaliger asked his former student Henri Louis Chasteigner to send him Arabic books from Italy, see *Correspondence* 13 October 1595 and 19 January 1596 from Henri Louis Chasteigner. Scaliger's request to De Harlay, in contrast, concerned books in Hebrew, which becomes clear from the correspondence of 6 January 1600 from Harlay, note 2 and 25 May 1600 from De Harlay.
77   Charles Leberon, Bishop of Valence (see: *Correspondence* 20 March 1601). Leberon travelled to Venice and Padua for its medicinal baths. See *Correspondence* 25 May 1600 from De Harlay. Until his death in 1601, Leberon was also responsible for the exchange of parcels from Scaliger to Pinelli in Padua.
78   The trader mentioned in the letter was Thomas Zenoin, a silk merchant from Basel, who maintained good trade contacts in Amsterdam. See *Correspondence* 6 January 1600 and 25 May 1600 from De Harlay. 'J'ay escrit en Italie pour les livres que demandez, et vous prie croire que je ne puis recevoir plus aggreable et desiré tesmoignage de vostre bonne

156   CHAPTER 4

The books were transported to Basel and from there onwards to Frankfurt. Unfortunately, the books were returned from Frankfurt to Basel, because the merchant mentioned in the letter, Thomas Zenoin, was away, and his assistant had not received the name of the merchant who would take the books onwards to Holland. Ultimately, half a year later, in early 1601, De Harlay could note with relief that the transportation of the books to Scaliger had finally been successful: 'I am very pleased that in the end you received all the books, both those which you had sent from here, and those that you put in my charge to send from Germany, and that they are to your liking.'[79]

7   Scaliger and Daniël van der Meulen

In the early 1590s, a new agent came to play a critical role in Scaliger's network, especially after his move to Leiden: this was the exiled Antwerp merchant Daniël van der Meulen (1554–1600), who established himself in Leiden in 1591.[80]

Together with his older brother Andries (1549–1611), who had fled to Bremen, Daniël van der Meulen maintained an extensive trade network between the Low Countries, northern Germany and the kingdom of Naples in southern Italy. Alongside Bremen, the North Sea ports of Hamburg and Emden were favoured destinations for exiled merchants like Van der Meulen, because these cities were located in neutral territory not formally involved in the conflict of the Eighty Years' War. Bulk cargo, such as Dutch and English textiles, was the main trade of the many merchant vessels that carried wares across the seas; luxury goods from Italy, such as spices, soap and mirrors, followed a route over land, reaching the Dutch Republic via Germany. These so-called *retouren* (return wares) were often sold at markets on the land route, the famous German *Messen*. Van der Meulen enjoyed regular contact with many colleagues, scholars, statesmen and members of his extended family all along

---

        grace envers moy que vous vous serviez de moy en toutes occasions. ... Il y a par delà un
        mien tres affectionné amy Monsieur de Valence, mon ancien compagnon d'escole, qui
        s'est retiré là pour se faire penser des gouttes, auquel j'ay donné ceste charge. Il est homme
        de lettres et tres officieux. Je m'asseure qu'il s'en acquitera fidelement et diligemment. Je
        luy mande qu'il envoye les livres à Frankfurt à un marchant mien amy auquel j'escriray
        qu'il les vous face tenir en Hollande, comme il est tres aisé.'
79   *Correspondence* 6 January 1601 and 13 February 1601 from De Harlay. 'Je suis tres aisé qu'en
        fin ayez receu tous les livres tant ceux que vous ay envoyé d'icy, que ceux qu'avois donné
        charge qu'on vous envoya d'Allemagne, et de ce qu'ils sont à vostre goust'.
80   Van der Meulen died of the plague on 25 July 1600, aged forty-five.

FIGURE 23   Painted portrait of Daniël van der Meulen by Bernaert der Rijckere, 1583.
Collection and © The Phoebus Foundation; photography: Museum De
Lakenhal, Leiden

these trade routes.[81] Scaliger made grateful use of Van der Meulen's efficient trade network to send his own correspondence, and especially to acquire books from Italy and the Levant.

81   Merchant correspondence was long seen as a direct forerunner of the printed newspaper. Cf. Dick H. Couvée, *Van Couranten en Courantiers uit de zeventiende en de achttiende eeuw*.

Van der Meulen was a good friend of Paul Choart de Buzanval, the French ambassador in The Hague, who also played a prominent role in Scaliger's life in Leiden. The ambassador often travelled between The Hague and the Parisian court, and in this process regularly carried books or letters for or from Scaliger.[82] This was a close triangular relationship: De Buzanval trusted Van der Meulen so greatly that he allowed the merchant to open diplomatic parcels, while the ambassador also once invited Scaliger and Van der Meulen to enjoy a meal of oysters in The Hague.[83] For his part, Van der Meulen supplied De Buzanval with a regular supply of news from Germany, Scandinavia, Poland, Switzerland and Italy; he received in return news from France and England.[84] Van der Meulen's network was judged to be so reliable by De Buzanval and Scaliger because it relied to a large extent on Van der Meulen's familial relations, which increased the perceived trustworthiness of any information supplied through his network.

Through his marriage to Hester de la Faille, Daniël van der Meulen was closely related to the up-and-coming but wealthy Antwerp family De la Faille. He was the brother-in-law of Jacques de la Faille (ca. 1549–1615), while Daniël's brother Andries was married to Susanna de Malapert, a cousin of Hester de la Faille. The father of Hester and Jacques, Jan de la Faille the elder (1515–1582), had been the Antwerp representative of the great Brussels merchant De Haan, who resided in Italy.[85] After the conquest of Antwerp in August 1585 by Alexander Farnese, Duke of Parma, many merchants emigrated from the city.

Courante maren, De geschreven courant, Nieuwe Tydinghen, Gazettes de Hollande, Abr. Verhoeven, Broer Jansz, Caspar van Hilten, Abr. Casteleyn, Pieter v.d. Keere (Amsterdam: Corvey, 1951), pp. 6–7. This perspective has now been nuanced considerably, cf. Andrew Pettegree, *The Invention of the News. How the World came to know about Itself* (Yale: Yale University Press, 2014).

82 Other members of the ambassadorial entourage at The Hague were also used for this purpose, including H. de Franchimont, the secretary of the Prince of Orange.

83 Johannes Hermann Kernkamp & J. van Heijst, 'De brieven van Buzanval aan Daniël van der Meulen (1595–1599)', *Bijdragen en mededelingen van het Historisch Genootschap* deel 77 (1962), pp. 175–262, letter 66 dated 6 February 1599: 'J'envoye débaucher Monsieur de l'Escalle; sy vous esties aussy débauché comme nous, nous mangerions des huistres ensamble.'

84 Kernkamp, *Economisch-historisch aspecten van de literatuurproductie*, pp. 8–9.

85 On the family history of the Van der Meulens, see: Gisela Jongbloet-Van Houtte, *Brieven en andere bescheiden betreffende Daniël van der Meulen 1584–1600. Deel 1: augustus 1585– september 1585* ('s-Gravenhage: Martinus Nijhoff, 1986), pp. xv–xxvi and Luuc Kooijmans, *Vriendschap en de kunst van het overleven in de zeventiende en achttiende eeuw* (Amsterdam: Bert Bakker, 1997), pp. 7–68.

SCALIGER IN LEIDEN

The brothers Van der Meulen settled in October of that year in neutral Bremen, a city sympathetic to the Reformed cause.[86]

Initially, Daniël and Andries concentrated their business chiefly on the German market. The annual fairs at Frankfurt and Strasbourg offered a good opportunity to trade with Antwerp and the Northern Netherlands.[87] Frankfurt was the principal node in the trade routes that ran north to south and east to west. Due to its favourable position on the river Main, it was possible to transport all manner of goods, ranging from carpets and silk to wine and books, via the adjoining Rhine to other great cities such as Basel, Strasbourg, Mainz and Cologne, as well as the Dutch hinterland. After the fall of Antwerp, it became clear to the Van der Meulen brothers that the commercial opportunities in Frankfurt were declining, so they decided to shift their business largely to the trade to northern Italy. The brothers established the *Nieuwe Compagnie* (New Company), which would be active between 1585 and 1591.[88] Shrewdly, the brothers continued to maintain agents in other important markets, including London, Frankfurt, Strasbourg, Middelburg and Amsterdam, where Andries van Oyen represented the Van der Meulen affairs.[89]

In October 1591, Daniël van der Meulen moved to a grand house at the Rapenburg in Leiden. In the same year, his trade to Italy expanded considerably. Because Andries remained in Bremen, the two brothers maintained an extensive business and personal correspondence. From Leiden, Daniël sought Dutch bulk carriers who would play a part in his ambitious north-south trade.[90] The combined merchant operations of Van der Meulen and De la Faille first fitted out a ship from London for Italy in 1584; the De la Failles were a natural choice for Van der Meulen, as they already had experience with the Italian trade. Their ships sailed for Venice and later to Genoa, a port which enjoyed good contacts with Marseille, and where goods such as cotton,

---

86 In the period 1574–1581, Daniël and his three sisters stayed in exile in Cologne; his older brothers Jan (Jean du Moulin) and Andries remained in Antwerp with their mother.

87 The annual fairs in Frankfurt took place around Easter and September. In Strasbourg, merchants gathered during the feast of St John, around 24 June, and at Christmas. On the influence of Antwerp merchants on the European international trade, see Oscar Gelderblom, *Zuid-Nederlandse kooplieden en de opkomst van de Amsterdamse stapelmarkt (1578–1630)* (Hilversum: Verloren, 2000).

88 The brothers were joined by a new *compagnon* in his company, the Tournai merchant Antoine Lempereur, living in Cologne. A previously existing arrangement with brother-in-law François Pierens was continued in the new company. Lempereur had already worked for Pierens in Antwerp in the period 1576–1580. The situation in Antwerp worsened considerably from 1590 onwards, when the Flanders coast was blockaded by the Dutch.

89 The London agent was Wouter Aertssen.

90 Jongbloet-Van Houtte, *Brieven en andere bescheiden*, p. XLIX.

160   CHAPTER 4

alum, tartar, capers and oak gall came in from Syria, and were then transported onwards to Holland. Venice nevertheless remained the chief port and entry way to the Levant with its connection to Antioch on the coast and Aleppo further inland. The Venetians regarded their hard-won commercial rights as unassailable, and regularly prevented Dutch merchants from carrying on trade in their city.[91] For this reason, the Dutch increasingly established themselves directly in Aleppo, bypassing Venice altogether. The Van der Meulens were no exception: they too founded a branch in Aleppo, increasingly the greatest centre of export goods from the Levant.

The Van der Meulen firm is an emblematic example of an internationally orientated merchant house in the sixteenth century. They directed their trade from a central node of communications, not necessarily a great staple market, and made use of agents and commission dealers, including trustworthy family members (a multitude of 'cousins'), who imported, exported and carried goods.[92] The trade that the Van der Meulens organised overland was dominated by the exchange of goods from Holland to Italy and vice versa.[93] That the transportation of goods along this route was bedevilled by many transits and obstacles is clear from the following description. The route ran via London and Amsterdam by ship to Hamburg. From Hamburg the road travelled to Frankfurt, Nuremberg and Augsburg; in each of these cities, the Van der Meulens had an agent who could expedite the transportation. In Frankfurt this was Hendrick Goyvaerts, in Nuremberg Hans de Stighter and Johan Pipeler, and in Augsburg Caspar Corona (or Cron). The two Nuremberg agents played an especially prominent role in the Van der Meulen correspondence network. South of Augsburg, the firm had no direct representation: the goods would commonly be carried first to munich, and then onwards over the Brenner Pass to Seefeld and Innsbruck.[94] After Innsbruck, the most challenging part of the journey would take place, over the treacherous Alpine roads, tortured by capricious

---

91   The story of a young man, Hendrick, sent by De la Faille in 1587–88 to Aleppo and Antioch to gather commercial information and make trade contacts, typifies this situation. When the Venetians discovered Hendrick's intentions, he was forced to leave, and had to travel home to Holland via Tripoli. J.C. Vermeulen, 'De handelsbetrekkingen met het Middellandse Zeegebied in de jaren 1588–1592, naar gegevens uit het archief van Daniël van der Meulen', in J.H. Kernkamp, *De handel van Daniël van der Meulen c.s. in het bijzonder rond de jaren 1588–1592* (Leiden: s.n., 1969), p. 33.

92   Wilfrid Brulez, 'l'Exportation des Pays-Bas vers l'Italie per voie de terre au milieu du XVIe siècle', *Annales, Economies, Sociétés, Civilisations*, 14/3 (1959), pp. 461–491.

93   For routes, prices and goods, see: R.F. Claassen, *De Overlandhandel op Italië van de Gebroeders van der Meulen. Kooplieden tijdens het laatste kwart van de zestiende eeuw* (Den Haag: Martinus Nijhoff, 1969).

94   Goods from the Southern Netherlands were often despatched directly to Italy On an overland route running via Cologne and Basel, along the river Rhine.

SCALIGER IN LEIDEN

weather and fierce winds. The first safe haven would be Bolzano, and thereafter Venice. From Venice, many goods would be shipped on along the Adriatic coast, and across the Apennines to Naples.

The despatch of goods from Italy to Holland was as complicated as the outward journey. From Italy, one of the principal commodities to travel on this route was silk, sent from Naples, Venice, Verona or Vicenza by much the same route through the Holy Roman Empire. Italian merchants would hope to sell most of their goods by the time their wares arrived at Frankfurt, but if the prices were too low there, they might send the goods onwards towards Stade or Hamburg, where the Van der Meulens had their agents François Bouduwijns and Hans Berrewijns.

The organisation of this overland trade and the necessary correspondence to expedite it was the responsibility of Andries van der Meulen.[95] There were three agents in the employ of the Van der Meulens in Venice: Francisco Vaneeckeren, Antonio van Nesten and Melchior Noirot.[96] In the great emporium of Naples, where many fairs took place, there were two agents, Gerard Mathieu and Balthazar Noirot.[97] That the road between Naples and Rome was infamous for the many highway robberies that took place there did not deter the Van der Meulens (nor many other merchants); neither did the fact that the kingdom of Naples was under the sovereignty of the Spanish Habsburgs, the political adversaries of the Dutch in the Low Countries.[98]

That the Van der Meulens enjoyed success in their trade to Italy can be deduced from the establishment of their 'New Neapolitan Company' (1594–1604).[99] The company made use of the overland route as well as a direct

---

95   In the Van der Meulen network, Bremen was not a centre of trade, but rather an important communications hub. Cf. R. Andriessen & H.F. Cohen, 'Op zoek naar een stapelmarkt. Onderzoekingen in het archief Daniël van der Meulen' in: Kernkamp, *De handel van Daniël van der Meulen*, p. 5.

96   Melchior Noirot was procurator of Andries van der Meulen, but also represented the affairs of Nicolaas de Malapert and Johannes Vivianus (1543–1598) in Venice. De Noirots were related to the Vaneeckeren family: Esther Vaneeckeren was Melchior Noirot's mother. Cf. Wilfred Brulez, *Marchands Flamands à Venise I (1568–1605)* (Bruxelles, Rome: Academia Belgica, 1965), no. 788, 947 and 1215.

97   Balthazar Noirot was a brother of Melchior and a cousin of Daniël van der Meulen. On Noirot and the agent Gerard Mathieu, see Jongbloet-Van Houtte, *Brieven en andere bescheiden*. 1986. Their letters from and to Van der Meulen can be consulted at the archive of Erfgoed Leiden en Omstreken, where they have also been digitised.

98   Erfgoed Leiden en Omstreken (hereafter: ELO), Archief Daniël van der Meulen inv. no. 593a no. 133 idem, 15-17-1592.

99   De New Neapolitan Company ('Nieuwe Napelsche Compagnie') was established in 1593 by Daniël and Andries van der Meulen, together with Andries's brother-in-law Johannes Vivianus and Nicolaas de Malapert (1564–1615). It traded to Iberia as well as to Italy. See: Jongbloet-Van Houtte, *Brieven en andere bescheiden*, pp. IX, XXXI.

162   CHAPTER 4

maritime route to Italy. The port of Livorno played a significant role in this maritime route, thanks to the privileges granted to the city by Grand Duke Ferdinand I of Tuscany (reigned 1587–1609). Livorno became the key entryway to the trade centres of Tuscany, while its large community of Jews and Muslims also ensured that it developed into a crucial way station for trade with the Levant.[100]

It should be emphasised that these trade connections remained tenuous. The threat of piracy and privateers was ubiquitous; until 1592, the Dutch could not sail directly to the Levant, and had to rely on Venetian protection, which meant that their trade was largely restricted to Venice itself, as well as to the Ionian islands and Crete.[101] Whichever route was chosen, the Reformed religion of the Dutch was always a complicating factor, one that singled them out in the Mediterranean trade. They faced assault from Barbary pirates and Spanish warships, while English and French privateers were occasionally also a menace. The absence of allies in the region led the Dutch to solicit friendly diplomatic relations with Venice (from 1596) and later also with the Ottoman Sultan.

That Scaliger made use of the extensive trade network of the Van der Meulen firm for the supply of books is clear from a letter of 25 November 1595, sent to him by a certain Bontiers from Rome. This otherwise unknown agent confirmed to Scaliger that on 18 October he handed over copies of Avicenna, Euclid, an Arabic missal and an Arabic alphabet to Balthazar Noirot, the local agent of the Van der Meulens, and that he commissioned Noirot to send the books on to Scaliger.[102] It can safely be assumed that these sorts of parcels were accompanied by various other letters, many of them related to the business

---

100   J.H. Kernkamp, 'Scheepvaart- en handelsbetrekkingen met Italië tijdens de opkomst der
        Republiek', in *Economisch-Historische herdrukken. Zeventien studiën van Nederlanders* [...]
        (Den Haag: Martinus Nijhoff, 1964), pp. 217–218.
101   The trade to this region was largely in the hands of the Venetians and the French. In the
        years 1587–1588, Jacques de la Faille organised an exploratory trade mission to investigate
        commercial opportunities in the Levant. De la Faille tried to entice Van der Meulen to
        join in this venture, but with no success. J.C. Vermeulen, 'De handelsbetrekkingen met het
        Middellandse-Zeegebied in de jaren 1588–1592, naar gegevens uit het archief van Daniël
        van der Meulen', in J.H. Kernkamp, *De handel van Daniël van der Meulen* (Leiden: s.n.,
        1969), p. 2 and appendix 1.
102   *Correspondence* 25 November 1592 from Bontiers: 'Environ le 18 d'octobre je fis response à
        vos dernieres, estant à Naples, où je mis es mains du Seigneur Baltazar Noirot un Avicenne,
        Euclide, et alphabeth arabics, corrigéz de nouveau pour les vous faire tenir avec un Missal
        aussi arabic; le tout ayant cousté soixante et trois livres et demye, à quoy il n'y eut moyen
        de marchander, car il y a un taux faict par le Grand-Duc à tant de quatrins pour feuille'. Cf.
        Brulez, *Marchands Flamands à Venise I (1568–1605)* 1965.

SCALIGER IN LEIDEN

dealings of the Van der Meulens. Daniël van der Meulen judged it extremely important to facilitate this transmission of information. In a letter to his brother-in-law Antoine L'Empereur, he wrote that 'To send [something] without information would be pure madness.'[103]

Thanks to his extensive mercantile network, Daniël van der Meulen was one of the best informed individuals in the Dutch Republic: he was therefore a crucial source of information to Scaliger. Van der Meulen ensured that his correspondence arrived as promptly as it could, and tried to receive his letters, as well as handwritten *avvisi*, *nouvelles* and *gazettes* and printed pamphlets, from as many sources as possible.[104] A large portion of his news came from Germany, sent on by the French consul Jacques Bongars de Bodry. De Bodry also functioned as the key intermediary between the German scholar Joachim Camerarius the younger (1534–1598) and Van der Meulen.[105] Many others benefitted from Van der Meulen's news network, including diplomats such as De Buzanval and the English ambassador George Gilpin (1514–1602), and Dutch statesmen such as Christiaan Huygens senior (1555–1624) and Cornelis Aerssens (1545–1627), secretary of the Council of State and Griffier of the States General.[106] Scaliger also played a role in this network, on one occasion providing a French translation of an Arabic letter from the Sultan of Morocco, Moulay Abu Faris, to Prince Maurice of Nassau (1567–1625) for Aerssens.[107]

Van der Meulen himself was also interested in collecting books, and he was able to build a fine library. He displayed a distinctive interest in Oriental culture. On one occasion he asked De Buzanval if he could acquire for him a copy of Lazaro Soranzo's *L'Ottomanno dove si da pieno ragguaglio della potenza del pres. Signor de' Turchi Mehemeto III, della guerra d'Ongheria* (Ferrara: Vittorio

---

103 ELO, Coll. Daniël van der Meulen Inv. No. 579: Letter from Daniël van der Meulen (Leiden) to Antoine L'Empereur (Bremen), 27 March 1592. Cited in: R. Andriessen and H.F. Cohen, 'Op zoek naar een stapelmarkt. Onderzoekingen in het archief Daniël van der Meulen', in J.H. Kernkamp, *De handel van Daniël van der Meulen* (Leiden: s.n., 1969), p. 30. 'Envoyer sans information ce seroit une pure folie'.

104 For the content and context of these media, see: Annie Stolp, *De eerste couranten in Holland, bijdrage tot de geschiedenis der geschreven nieuwstijdingen* (Haarlem: Joh. Enschedé & Zonen, 1938), and for the city of Bremen as a centre of news supply, see: H. Jesse, 'Vorläufer des Journalismus', in *Jahrbuch der Bremischen Wissenschaft* 1 (1955), pp. 138–154.

105 The letters and parcels were sent from Strasbourg, the residence of Bongars de Bodry, via Cologne to Leiden; on average, this took the post anywhere between ten and twenty days.

106 Kernkamp & Van Heijst, 'De brieven van Buzanval aan Daniël van der Meulen (1595–1599)', p. 179. Aerssens also approached Scaliger for the translation of other texts from Arabic; see: *Correspondence* 7 July 1606 to Aerssens and 1607 10 15 to Ubertus.

107 Dated 27 January 1606. Nationaal Archief Den Haag, archiefstuk 12594.1.

164   CHAPTER 4

Baldini, 1598).[108] As we have previously seen, Scaliger did not like to lend out
his books, and it is likely that Van der Meulen did not bother him with such
requests. Van der Meulen was more generous, and did lend out books from
his library to Scaliger with some regularity. Scaliger, as well as other scholars,
praised Van der Meulen's library: at his death, in 1601, the auction catalogue
listed 1,200 lots.[109]

8   Supplying Arabic Books: Chasteigner in Rome and the *Tipographia Medicea Orientale*

Until his death in 1595, Louis Chasteigner de la Roche-Posay, Scaliger's patron,
remained an important figure in Scaliger's network, even after Scaliger moved
to Leiden. As ambassador in Rome, Chasteigner was constantly on the hunt
for books for Scaliger. Often, this concerned Oriental books, such as the Arabic
editions of Avicenna and Euclid, which he tried to acquire for Scaliger using
the services of a certain Rucelay.[110]

---

108   Letter from Buzanval (The Hague) to Van der Meulen (Leiden), 20 October 1599. ELO Coll.
      Daniël van der Meulen Inv. No. 664. On the activity of Van der Meulen in the book market,
      see Jongbloet-Van Houtte, *Brieven en andere bescheiden*, pp. LXXII–LXXXV.
109   *Catalogvs Librorvm Bibliothecae Clarissimi Doctissimique viri, piae memoriae, D. Danielis
      Vander Mevlen. Catalogue vande Boecken des gheleerden ende wijdtberoemden Heeren,
      Saligher ghedachtenisse, D. Danielis vander Meulen* ([Leiden]: ex officina Plantiniana
      apud Christophorus Raphelengius, 1600; USTC 429992). See also: Johannes Hermann
      Kernkamp, 'Een boekenveiling in 1601', *Bibliotheekleven* 25 (1940), pp. 50–52; Johannes
      Hermann Kernkamp, 'De bibliotheek van den koopman Daniël van der Meulen onder
      den hamer', in A. Hulshoff, *Opstellen bij zijn afscheid van de bibliotheek der Rijksuniversiteit
      te Utrecht op 31 Mei 1940 aangeboden aan G.A. Evers* (Utrecht: Oosthoek, 1940), pp. 187–203.
      In Leiden, Van der Meulen found a bibliophile friend in Philips van Marnix van
      St. Aldegonde, who owned a library with some 1,550–1,600 books. See: Johannes Hermann
      Kernkamp, 'Marnix van St. Aldegonde: bibliophiel of bibliomaan?', *Het Boek* 25 (1938–39),
      pp. 215–223. As far as we know, Scaliger did not buy any books from the famous Marnix
      book auction of 1599. The curators of the Leiden University Library did buy books at the
      auction, as they did for the auction of the books of Gerard Mercator of 1604, for which,
      sadly, no auction catalogue survives. For a bibliographical description of this catalogue,
      see: Van Selm, *Een menighte treffelijcke Boecken*, p. 159 (no. 21); Bert van 't Hoff, 'De catalo-
      gus van de bibliotheek van Gerard Mercator', *Het Boek* 35 (1961–1962), pp. 25–27.
110   *Correspondence* 18 July 1594 from Chasteigner de la Roche-Posay. *Correspondence* 1594 07
      18 from Chasteigner: 'Et ne faudray d'escrire à Rome au Seigneur Rucelay, et le supplier
      de me faire tenir l'Avicenna arabic et Euclide, aussi arabic, tous entiers comme desirez,
      ensemble d'auttres livres, qu'on aura imprimez en la mesme langue, comme me mandez.
      Et si tost que j'en auray eu responce, je ne faudray de vous en donner advis.' The edi-
      tion of Euclid (1594) and Avicenna (1593) printed by the *Tipographia Medicea* owned by

SCALIGER IN LEIDEN

Henri Louis Chasteigner de la Roche-Posay, the son of Scaliger's patron, took over from his father the role of supplier of books from Rome, the centre of Arabic printing around 1600.[111] In 1602, Henri was appointed French ambassador in Rome, where he also made frequent use of the Van der Meulen network. When Henri Louis Chasteigner was able to purchase the Arabic Avicenna and Euclid for Scaliger in Rome, he used the services of Balthazar Noirot to send them to Van der Meulen in Leiden. A letter from Chasteigner to Scaliger dated 12 October 1595 provides a good insight into the functioning of the network. He wrote:

> It was ultimately in Rome that I received your letter from August, which surprised me, given how few of our letters seem to have reached your hands. We arrived in this city yesterday and have asked for the books that you requested with the publisher Raimondi, as he has recently printed them.[112] They include a complete Euclid and Avicenna, which are printed together and are not sold separately, as well as an Arabic missal. He also gave us a copy of the Arabic alphabet that he has corrected ... this is in

---

Scaliger can be found at call numbers UBL 878 A 4 and 845 A 9. See Bibliographic Survey Rome 1593:2 and Rome 1594. There are four books from the *Tipographia Medicea* represented in Scaliger's collection. The Rucellai were notable humanists and poets active in trade and politics. The family was related to the Strozzi and Medici families by marriage. See: L. Passerini, *Genealogia e storia della famiglia Rucellai.* (Florence: 1861).

111   It is worth mentioning that the print runs of Arabic books in this period was rather small, as G. Roper indicates, 'Early Arabic Printing in Europe,' 2002, p. 147: 'Given that the number of Arabic scholars in Europe was very limited, Arabic editions were inevitably small and expensive: probably not more than 500 copies were printed in most cases.'

112   This was probably the Orientalist Giovanni Battistta Raimondi, director of the *Typograhia Medicea. Correspondence* 12 October 1595 from Henri Louis Chasteigner. The books are: Euclides, *Elementorum geometricorum libri tredecim, ex traditione doctissimi Nasiridini Tusini, nunc primum Arabice impressi* (Roma: In Tipographia Medicea Orientale, 1594; USTC 828486) and Avicenna, *Libri quinque Canonis medicinae, quibus additi sunt in fine eiusdem libri logicae, physicae, et metaphysicae, Arabice nunc primum impressi* (Roma: in Tipographia Medicea Orentale 1593; USTC 811611). The third title is probably a publication by Giambatista Eliano, the *I'tiqad al-amana al urtuduksiyya* or *Sacrosanctae Romanae Ecclesiae unitatem venientibus facienda proponitur* (Roma: In Tipographia Medicea Orientale, 1595; USTC 806925), a confession of creed of the Eastern Church, printed at the end of September 1595. Three editions were produced of this: two contain parallel texts in Arabic and Latin, and one in Arabic only, see UBL 877 D 19-2, bound together with a copy of the Brevis orthodoxae fidei professio, quae ex praescripto Sanctae Sedis Apostolicae ab Orientalibus ad Sacrosanctae Rom. Ecclesiae unitatem venientibus facienda proponitur (Roma: apud Francesco Zanetti, 1580; USTC 805533); see Bibliographic Survey Rome 1566 and Rome 1580. The books were despatched to Scaliger in November via Bontiers, cf. *Correspondence* 25 November [1595] from Bontiers.

response to the request of the gentleman Raphelengius.[113] These are the only books from the list that you sent that we have found. The printer assured us that he will send you the books that are currently on the press, as well as any other publications that you wish to receive. We have given the books to the gentleman Balthazar [Noirot], who has promised to keep them safe, until we tell him that we have gathered enough books for you to send them to Preuilly, from where they will be sent onwards to you.[114]

This letter indicates that Chasteigner certainly acquired several Arabic works for Scaliger directly from the *Tipographia Medicea*, a printing house established in 1584 in Florence by Ferdinando I de' Medici, Grand Duke of Tuscany, acting on the encouragement of Pope Gregory XIII. This firm would be responsible for some twenty editions in various Oriental languages in the period between 1584 and 1614, including many Arabic works.

Chasteigner worked together with an acquaintance named Bontiers, active in Rome around 1595.[115] Bontiers took charge of the actual despatch of the books bought by Chasteigner in Rome to Balthazar Noirot in Naples. Bontiers informed Scaliger that the purchase of the Avicenna, Euclid and the Arabic missal had cost Chasteigner 63.5 livres, or almost 32 florins; this was

---

113   The *Alphabetum Arabicum* (USTC 806711) was printed in Rome by the Tipographia Medicea Orientale in 1592. This edition was a critical inspiration for Raphelengius's *Specimen characterum Arabicorum Officinae Plantinianae*, published by Raphelengius in Leiden in 1595 (USTC 423538). See: Hendrik D.L. Vervliet, *Cyrillic and Oriental Typography in Rome at the End of the Sixteenth Century. An Inquiry into the Later Work of Robert Granjon (1578–90)* (Berkeley: Poltroon Press, 1981), p. 10. Scaliger possibly forwarded on Raphelengius's request for this alphabet to Henri Louis Chasteigner in a letter that has now been lost. The Arabic missal mentioned was probably a copy of the *Confessio brevis fidei Christianæ Arab. & Syr.* by Giambattista Eliano (Roma Domenico Basa, 1580), see: Bibliographic Survey Rome 1580. *Correspondence* 12 November 1595 from Chasteigner: 'Nous arrivasmes hier en ceste ville, et avons apporté les livres que nous avons acheptéz, qui sont un Euclide et Avicenna entiers (qui ne se vendent point separéz) et le Missal arabic que demandiez par la vostre du dernier aoust, qui estoit achevé d'imprimer depuis quinze jours. Cestuy-là de qui nous les avons acheptéz, nous a aussy donné un alphabet arabic qu'il a corrigé [...] pour response aux demandes de Monsieur Rapheling. Nous n'avons trouvé que cela des livres que demandiez. Il nous a donné le memoire que vous envoyons des livres qu'il doibt imprimer, où pourrez voir ceux que desireriez, que nous vous envoyerons quand il vous plaira nous les faire sçavoir, desirant vous pouvoir monstrer en chose de plus d'importance combien je me sens vostre obligé. Nous avons mis les livres entre les mains du Seigneur Balthazar qui nous a promis vous les faire tenir seurement et en bref; combien que nous mandez qu'il suffiroit les envoyer à Preuilly, et que de là on les vous feroit tenir.'

114   *Correspondence* 12 November 1595 from Chasteigner.

115   *Correspondence* 18 October 1595 to Bontiers.

SCALIGER IN LEIDEN

the rate set by the printing firm. It was fortunate that the Arabic alphabet had been added to the order for free.[116] The books took six days to be carried from Rome to Naples, but the transport onwards to Leiden took a long time. On 19 January 1596, Chasteigner asked Scaliger whether the books, as well as a list of titles forthcoming with the *Tipographia Medicea*, had been delivered yet by Van der Meulen.[117]

It is noteworthy that in his letter, Chasteigner referred to the books of Euclid and Avicenna explicitly as complete texts, that could not be sold separately. Loose gatherings of the works were also in circulation, some of which were sold before the entire text had come off the press. According to the catalogue of the university library of Leiden, Scaliger possessed a few separate gatherings of Euclid and Avicenna, which he must therefore had received on an earlier occasion.[118]

In 1592, before Scaliger moved to Leiden, he had already received one publication from the *Tipographia Medicea*, a copy of a cosmographical work by al-Idrisi. In June 1592 he wrote a letter to an otherwise unknown correspondent with the surname Vazet: 'I was recently reading a very fine Arab author, who has no name, who writes on cosmography in a very nice style.'[119] Scaliger was not yet aware that al-Idrisi was the author of the book, and only noted details from the book that he could decipher, such as geographical details on countries, provinces, islands and cities.[120]

In the last ten years of his life, Scaliger devoted increasing time and effort in his correspondence to Arabic books. He searched far and wide in the book

---

116 *Correspondence* 15 November 1595 from Bontiers. Scaliger's collection also contained the Arabic alphabet (1592) mentioned by Chasteigner, UBL 877 D 12; see Bibliographic Survey Rome 1592: 1.

117 This list has sadly not survived. *Correspondence* 19 January 1596 from Henri Louis Chasteigner: 'Il y a deux mois et demy que estant à Naples je vous escrivis par la voye de Monsieur Vandermeulen, et par mesme voye vous envoyay un Euclide et Avicenna entiers, et un Missal arabic, avec un memoire de tous les livres que l'on espere d'imprimer à l'imprimerie du Grand Duc de Toscane. S'il y a quelque chose que desiriez avoir, m'en donnant advis je ne fauldray à vous l'envoyer incontinent s'il se trouve imprimé.'

118 These loose gatherings are no longer present in Scaliger's bequest. For their description, see the notification in the Catalogue under Rome 1593: 2 and Rome 1594.

119 *Correspondence* 4 June 1592 to Vazet. 'Je lisois dernierement un fort bel auteur arabe, qui n'a point de nom, qui escrit de la cosmographie avec un stile fort gentil.'

120 The book by al-Idrisi, *Kitab Nuzhat al-mushtaq fi dhikr al-amsar wa-l-aqtar wa-l-buldan wa-l-juzur wa-l-madayin wa-l-afaq* (Romae: In Tipographia Medicea Orientale, 1592; USTC 807510), is also known as *De Geographia universali* [...] *Hortulus*. Scaliger noted: 'DE GEOGRAPHIA UNIVERSALI HORTULUS cultissimus, mire orbis regiones, provincias, insulas, urbes, earumq[ue] dimentiones et orizonta describens sed perperam interpretatum est.' (UBL 842 D 12, see Bibliographic Survey Rome 1592: 4).

168   CHAPTER 4

trade for new Arabic publications and old Arabic manuscripts, but also gathered information on Arabic works in libraries. When Christophe Dupuy stayed in Rome in the spring of 1604, he visited various libraries, and found in the *Collegio dei Neofiti* and *Pontificio Collegio dei Maroniti* many Arabic works which he considered would be of interest to Scaliger. He tried unsuccessfully to purchase them, but was able to acquire transcriptions.[121] This was a strategy that was frequently adopted. Dupuy knew of a collection of 150 Arabic books owned by a certain Monseigneur Sidonio.[122] He offered Scaliger his services to transcribe some of these books, as long as Scaliger could indicate which ones were of interest to him. Dupuy wanted to have a list compiled of Sidonios's books, so he called upon the help of a young Arabic scholar who enjoyed a temporary appointment at the Vatican library. In 1604, Pierre Dupuy mentioned to Scaliger that the list was complete and would be despatched to him; yet before it reached Scaliger, it was sent to Casaubon in Paris, and it only reached Scaliger in August 1605.[123] Nevertheless, Scaliger was delighted: 'My mouth waters knowing that there are so many Arabic books in Rome'.[124] In a letter to his brother, Christophe Dupuy mentioned the high costs involved in having works from the Sidonio collection transcribed. Pierre Dupuy cited an extract from this letter when writing to Scaliger:

> The Old and New Testaments in Arabic can be found in Rome, but their owners do not wish to sell them, and others ask so much money for them that I would rather not mention it. I found a man who will copy the text of the New Testament for 250 écus, or 500 écus for the New and Old Testament together. All of these books are in the hands of profiteers. There are also some scholars here who possess complete Averroes, valued at some 8,000 écus, and which would also cost 500 écus to be transcribed. The book is very beautiful and it would not be amiss in the royal library.

---

121   *Correspondence* 20 March 1604 from Chr. Dupuy. The College of Neophytes was a Catholic college in Rome, established in 1577 by Pope Gregory XIII to educate young Eastern Orthodox youth in the Catholic faith. The college was housed in an institute founded in 1543 by Pope Paul III to convert Jews and Muslims to the Christian faith. The College of Maronites was also established in Rome by Pope Gregory XIII, in 1584.

122   Monseigneur Sidonio was Léonard Abel († 1605), originally from Malta, made Bishop of Sidon in Palestine. He travelled through the Levant as ambassador of Pope Gregory XIII. See: Paul Colomiés, *Opuscula* (Ultraiecti: apud Petrum Elzevirium, 1669), p. 185 (USTC 1806554) and Adolphe Abel, *Une mission religieuse en Orient au XVIe siècle. Relation adressée à Sixte-Quint par l'évêque de Sidon* (Paris: Duprat, 1866).

123   *Correspondence* 19 November 1604 from Pierre Dupuy. Sadly, the list does not survive.

124   *Correspondence* 12 August 1605 to the brothers Dupuy. 'Mais cela me faict venir la salive à la bouche, quand je ne vois que le seul nom, et les livres sont à Romme.'

SCALIGER IN LEIDEN

Pierre Dupuy then added that his brother also asked 'after a Bible, printed in Rome in eleven languages: Latin, Greek, Hebrew, Arabic, Amharic, Armenian, Chaldaic, Slavic and two other languages [sic] that he did not name, with parallel translation. Apparently, Giovanni Battista Raimondi is working on this publication.'[125]

Scaliger was certainly interested in the Arabic manuscripts and asked how much the transcription would cost of the complete Bible in Arabic. He already owned an Arabic New Testament, but a complete Bible would aid his study greatly.[126] He also asked if Dupuy could look out for two other Arabic works, which he listed in an appendix to his letter, in Italian. One of the works was a book of eight sheets in octavo, printed in Rome: the text contained a 'spiritual dialogue between two physicians, one named Schaicun Sinan, the other named Achmad'.[127] The other book was a Chaldaic grammar, according to Scaliger also printed in Rome, 'some five years ago'.[128] Given the fact that Scaliger listed these works in Italian, with this level of detail, makes it likely that he had taken the descriptions from a catalogue of Arabic titles advertised for sale in Rome.

The high costs required for the transcription of manuscripts in Rome will probably have prevented Scaliger from making a selection from the list sent to him by the brothers Dupuy. Scaliger preferred to ask to borrow Arabic, Syriac or Hebrew manuscripts from his friends. He borrowed such manuscripts from Boreel and Raphelengius, and then copied the manuscripts himself.[129] This

---

125 *Correspondence* 20 May 1606 from Pierre Dupuy. Giambattista (Giovanni) Battista Raimondi (1536–1614) intended to publish a Bible in eleven languages, including the ancient Egyptian language, but it was never realised. See: *Scaligerana, Thuana* [...], p. 93.

126 *Correspondence* 20 June 1604 to Chr. Dupuy.

127 *Correspondence* 20 June 1604 to Chr. Dupuy: the appendix is headed 'Libri stampati in Roma', after which Scaliger cites a title in Arabic and then continues: 'Questo e il titolo d'un libreto arabico in octavo, stampato in Roma, in otto quaternioni, che vol dire: "Questo è il colloquio spirituale havuto fra duoi dottori, d'i quali l'uno è chiamato Schaicun Sinan, l'altro Achmad il dottore". Il qual colloquio fu nel tempo del ritorno d'ambedui de la Mecha, essendo molto profitevolo ai Mussulmani.' The title of the book is: *Musahaba ruhaniyya bayn al-'alimayn wa-ism wahid minhuma Shaykh Sinan wa-ism al-akhar Ahmad al-'Alim allati kanat fi ruju'ihima min al-Ka'ba nafi'a li-kull muslim wa-muslima* ([Roma In Collegio Societatis Jesu], 1579), UBL 877 G 1; see Bibliographic Survey Rome 1579.

128 *Correspondence* 20 June 1604 to Chr. Dupuy: 'Item grammatica chaldaica, stampata in Roma doppo cinque anni in qua poco piu o meno.' The book is: Georgius Michael Amira, *Gramatiki suryoytho* of *Grammatica Syriaca, Sive Chaldaica, Georgij Michaelis Amiræ Edeniensis è Libano, Philosophi, ac Theologi, Collegij Maronitarum Alumni, in septem libros divisa* (Rome: In Typographia Linguarum externarum, apud Iacobum Lunam, 1596; USTC 809076, UBL 876 C 4; see Bibliographic Survey Rome 1596).

129 *Correspondence* 30 September 1605 to Casaubon, cited (with an incorrect date of 20 September 1605) in: Robinson, *Autobiography* 1927, p. 48: 'Sed difficillimam provinciam mihi imposui describendi libros, quorum mihi ad tempus potestas facta est, Syriacorum,

FIGURE 24　The brothers Pierre and Jacques Dupuy, the sons of Claude Dupuy. Rijksprentenkabinet Amsterdam RP-P-OB-5659

was not an entirely selfish activity: Scaliger knew that the transcriptions made by him might later be of use to other scholars. This demonstrates that he did reflect on the importance of donating his Oriental collection to the Leiden university library, which would turn the institution into one of the foremost centres for the study of the languages and cultures of the Middle East. It is partially for that reason that Scaliger continued, right up to the end of his life,

Arabicorum, et Hebraicorum [...] Sed vincam, si deus voluerit, et prodero eis qui post me bibliotheca mea potientur. Itaque a me novi nihil prodire, neque exspectari potest, quandiu antiquarii munere fungar.' Scaliger copied a Syriac lexicon with an Arabic translation by Jesus bar Ali from the collection of Boreel in 1605 (UBL MS Or. 213). See: Reinhart Pieter Anne Dozy, *Catalogus Codicum Orientalium Bibliothecae Lugduno-Batavae*, Vol. 1 (Leiden: E.J. Brill, 1851), p. 58; and Vrolijk and Van Ommen, *All my Books* (2009), pp. 46–49. In September 1607, Scaliger transcribed a Persian lexicon and grammar from the library of Franciscus Raphelengius (UBL MS Or. 2019). See: Vrolijk and Van Ommen, *All my Books*, pp. 75–77; Toon van Hal, 'Joseph Scaliger, puzzled by the similarities of Persian and Dutch?', in *Omslag. Bulletin van de Universiteitsbibliotheek Leiden en het Scaliger Instituut* 1 (2007), pp. 1–3; *Correspondence* 13 October 1607 to Casaubon.

SCALIGER IN LEIDEN

171

to add important texts to his collection, in order to pass on a corpus of works as complete as possible to a future generation of scholars.

9 Gifts from around Europe

As his reputation as an Oriental expert spread far and wide, Scaliger regularly received gifts from scholars or printers around Europe, often books or manuscripts in Arabic. In December 1599, Nicolas Vignier junior (ca. 1575–1645) sent Scaliger an Arabic scroll from the library of his father.[130] In early 1603, Casaubon sent him, via Cornelis II van der Myle (ca. 1578–1642), a manuscript, probably a copy of the *Chronographia* by the Byzantine author Michael Psellus, accompanied by an Arabic manuscript with two hundred Arabic aphorisms, as well as some coins and gemstones.[131] The parcel also included a gift from the Parisian printer and bookseller Guillaume II le Bé (ca. 1560/70?–1645?), an edition of the Book of Psalms in Arabic.[132]

---

130   *Correspondence* 5 December 1599: 'entre les papiers duquel j'ay trouvé ce rouleau arabique que je vous envoye, et eusse bien desiré d'y trouver chose plus digne de vos yeux.' His father was Nicolas Vignier the elder (1530–1596), 'avocat du Roi'. See M. Simonin, *Dictionnaire des lettres françaises. Le XVIe siècle*, Paris 2001, pp. 1186–1189. Scaliger owned various scrolls, some of them possibly the result of war loot. See for example: UBL MS Or. 263 and 264.

131   Cornelis van der Myle, who had enrolled at Leiden in 1591, had become a friend of Scaliger, as well as of Louis de Coligny in The Hague, and her son Frederick Henry, the future Stadholder. Van der Myle later married the daughter of the Pensionary of Holland, Johan van Oldenbarnevelt, and became his protegé. In 1597, after his study, Van der Myle followed in the footsteps of many aristocratic youths, and embarked on a Grand Tour. As part of his itinerary, he enrolled on 2 May 1597 as a student at the University of Geneva, where he came to know Simon Goulart, one of Scaliger's relations. After the summer of that year, Van der Myle travelled with a certain gentleman Du Plomb (Jacques Esprinchard) from La Rochelle to Italy (see: *Correspondence* 23 August 1597 from Simon Goulart). He only returned to Holland in 1603, when he renewed his friendship with Hugo Grotius, Daniel Heinsius and Dominicus Baudius. For six years, Scaliger was able to use Van der Myle's services in Italy, which was especially helpful as Van der Myle also knew other friends of Scaliger, such as De Buzanval and Daniël van der Meulen. See: Hendrik Aleidis Willem van der Vecht, *Cornelis van der Myle* (Sappemeer: D. Klein, 1907), p. 5.

132   *Correspondence* 9 January 1603 from De Thou: 'Mitto etiam exemplum Psalmi, Arabici hic edita, ipsius [Greek]; ab eo enim accepi ut deferendum tibi curarem.' It is possible that this concerned several proof sheets printed by Le Bé for the *Liber Psalmorum Davidis Regis et Prophetae. Ex Arabico Idiomate in Latinum translatus*, ultimately printed in Rome in 1614 at the *Typographia Savariana*. This was the first edition of the psalms in Arabic (*al-Mazamir*) with a Latin translation, see UBL 876 C 16. Another possibility is that it concerned a copy of the *Missale Chaldaicum iuxta ritum Ecclesiæ nationis Maronitarum*

172 CHAPTER 4

Le Bé shared a keen interest in Arabic with Scaliger. He had been apprenticed with Robert Estienne and had stayed in Italy for several years before opening a printing house and bookshop in Paris. In 1599, he had an Arabic typeface cut, modelled on an earlier design by his father Guillaume Le Bé I (1524/25–1598), that he would use for his own Arabic publications.[133] The Arabic typefaces were also inspired by those from the Medicea press at Rome (like those of Raphelengius in Leiden). Le Bé had plans to print an Arabic grammar with his new typefaces, edited by Scaliger.[134] To prove his worth as a scholarly printer and the seriousness of his intentions, Le Bé sent to Scaliger via Petrus Labbaeus an edition of St. Paul's Epistle to the Galatians as a sample of his Arabic typefaces.[135] For some reason, the grammar would never appear. When the opportunity arose in 1614 to use his Arabic typefaces for an edition of Arabic aphorisms, edited by Thomas Erpenius (and using some of Scaliger's annotations), Le Bé rejected this. All of a sudden, he refused to print work edited by Protestant scholars. The publication, entitled *Kitāb al-amthāl* of *Proverbiorum Arabicorum centuriae duae*, ultimately appeared in 1614 with the Leiden Officina Raphelengiana.[136]

From Germany, Arabic books and fragments also found their way to Scaliger. Conradus Ritterhusius in Altorf sent Scaliger a *Pittakion*, which literally denoted a writing tablet, but was in fact a short manuscript. It probably contained an Arabic liturgical text, the 'libellum Arabicum, et (ut suspicatur) Mahumetanum'. A year later, Scaliger received some additional leaves with an Arabic text, sent to him by a young physician, Johann Conrad Rhumelius

---

(*Ketaba de-quraba akh 'ayada de-Maronaye*) (Romae, Tipographia Medicea 1592–1594), UBL 876 C 6; see Bibliographic Survey Rome 1592–1594.

133 Guillaume le Bé the elder (1524/25–1598) was an acquaintance of the Scaliger family. De Thou described him as a 'mercator papyropola', a paper merchant. He was indeed a dealer in paper from Troyes, and supplied, amongst others, the printer Charles Périer. It is possible that the Arabic typeface of 1599 was also based on an earlier design by Robert Granjon. See: John Lane, *Early Type Specimens In the Plantin-Moretus Museum* (New Castle, London: The British Museum, 2004), pp. 239–250.

134 For these plans, see: *Correspondence* 22 January 1602 to Casaubon.

135 *Correspondence* 9 January 1603 from Casaubon and *Correspondence* 29 April 1604 from Labbaeus. The proof sheet, *Charactères Arabici in Gallia nunc primùm incisi* (Paris: Gulielmus Le Bé 1599), is no longer in the collection of Scaliger at Leiden. There is a copy in the archive of the Museum Plantin-Moretus in Antwerp, in volume Arch. 153, 20m (old shelf mark F 20.36).

136 Arnoud Vrolijk, 'The Prince of Arabists and his many Errors. Thomas Erpenius's Image of Joseph Scaliger and the Edition of the *Proverbia Arabica* (1614)', *Journal of the Warburg and Courtauld Institutes* 73 (2010), pp. 297–325. Erpenius possessed two manuscripts of this text, the first of which was given to Johannes Boreel (Westhovius).

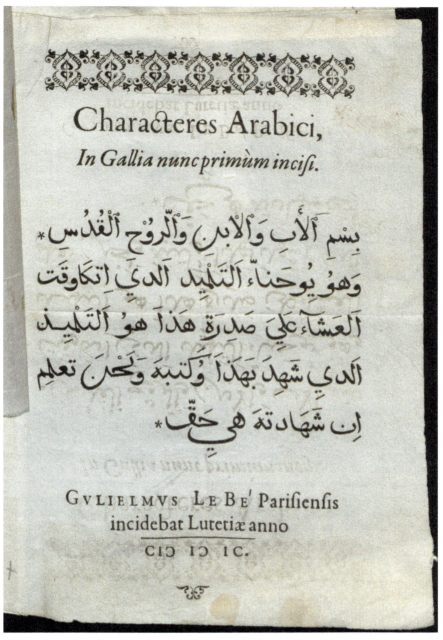

FIGURE 25   Arabic typeface sample, produced by Le Bé. Collection Museum Plantin-Moretus Antwerpen

174 CHAPTER 4

(1574–1630).[137] The poet, philologist and historian Elias Putschius (1580–1606) supplied him with a short manuscript in the Turkish language, possibly in thanks for receiving a portrait from Scaliger in 1605.[138]

10   The Brothers Labbaeus, Fellow Bibliophiles

In a letter from 1605, Scaliger thanked the brothers Dupuy for sending him two Hebrew books and a 'Moscovite book'.[139] The books reached Scaliger via the brothers Charles (1582–1657) and Pierre (1596–1678) Labbé de Monvéron (or Labbaeus). They were significantly younger than Scaliger, and met him in Leiden while they were students there. Charles Labbé, who became a jurist and *advocat au parlement de Paris*, developed a serious interest in philology.[140] Scaliger let them know that he would love to receive more books of this sort from them in the future. 'Payment is no problem', he added reassuringly.[141] He asked the brothers Labbaeus to send him three Hebrew works when they returned from a journey to England, during which they visited Thomson in Cambridge. The brothers regularly supplied Scaliger with Oriental books, some of which they acquired at auction, including a part of the Talmud printed on parchment, from the library of the Orientalist scholar Gilbert Génébrard (1537–1597).[142] They also transcribed for Scaliger a book on the Malay lan-

---

137   *Correspondence* 3 March 1600 and 4 April 1601 from Ritterhusius. Both Arabic books have not been identified.

138   *Correspondendence* 20 October [1605?] to Putschius. Scaliger confirmed the receipt of a variety of (otherwise unidentified) Arabic books, including some fragments of the Qur'an. He suspected that these fragments would not be very useful: 'Capitula ex Alcorano pro diurnali (ut vocant) praecularum officio. Et eiusmodi omnes libelli qui in illa praeda capti sunt, nihil aliud sunt quam deliria Mahometica.' The fragments are possibly UBL MS Or. 232; MS Or. 233 and MS Or. 239. In a manuscript containing a selection of prayers with Turkish commentary (UBL MS Or. 261), there is a dedication by Putschius, dated to 1603. Cf. Jan Schmidt, *Catalogue of Turkish manuscripts* Vol. 1. (Leiden: Legatum Warnerianum in Leiden University Library, 2000), pp. 39–42.

139   The two Hebrew books and the book in Russian (presumably Church Slavonic) have not been identified. 'Livret moschovitique'.

140   Charles Labbé also helped Scaliger with the transcription of various Greek manuscripts held at the Bibliothèque Royal in Paris.

141   *Correspondence* 6 November 1601 to the brothers Dupuy: 'Et vous supplie de m'envoier de tels livres, si en aves. Je paierai bien le tout, s'ils sont à vendre.'

142   Jakob ben Chabib, *En Ya'aqov* (Saloniki: 1516–1522), UBL 1371 A 18; see Bibliographic Survey Saloniki [1516–1522] *Correspondence* 12 September 1601 from Petrus Labbaeus: 'Libros Hebraicos quos adhuc reperire potuimus duos ad te mittimus, nobis (ut verum fatear) non ita notos, tamen in pergameno excusum partem esse Talmud existimamus, alterum, quem ex Genebrardi biblioteca fuisse intelleximus, plane non novimus.'

SCALIGER IN LEIDEN

guage, compiled by an Englishman.[143] Scaliger was deeply interested in the
script used, asking Pierre how the letters were depicted: 'has it been done
precisely and skilfully?' When he received the manuscript, he had it bound
together with a Hebrew book.[144]

Scaliger also informed the brothers about various useful books that he wished
to acquire for his research, including a copy of the 'pseudo-Gorionides', on the
history of the Jewish people.[145] He considered his copy of Flavius Josephus with
commentary by Sebastian Münster a disappointment.[146] He therefore looked
forward to receiving from the brothers Labbaeus the more reliable 'Joseph Ben
Gorion, in Italia aut Cracoviae editus'.[147] Scaliger also asked for a copy of the
'Colbo (printed in Italy)' and a 'Concordantiae Hebraicae Bibliorum' printed in
Venice.[148] The brothers Labbaeus clearly had a sophisticated taste for Oriental

143   *Correspondence* 18 December [1601] to C. and P. Labbaeus: '... ut mihi illud alphabe-
       tum Indicum, quod ex Anglia nacti estis, & historiolam illius regionis, ab eodem Anglo
       conscriptam mittatis.' It is possible that Scaliger described the merchant Ralph Fitch of
       London (ca. 1550–1611), who travelled to India in the period 1583–1591. Cf. R. Hakluyt, *The
       Principal Navigations, Voyages, Traffiques and Discoveries of the English Nation. Made by
       Sea or Over-Land to the remote and farthest distant Quarters of the Earth at any time within
       the Compasse of these 1600 yeeres* (London: George Bishop, Ralph Newbery and Robert
       Barker, 1599; USTC 513999) and Michael *Edwardes, Ralph Fitch. Elizabethan in The Indies*
       (London: Faber & Faber, 1971).

144   *Correspondence* 12 September 1601 and 6 November 1601 to C. and P. Labbaeus. This
       'libello Indico Malavaricae linguae, una cum dictionario illius sermonis, movisti' has
       not yet been located. It is possible that this concerned the *Alphabetum et vocabular-
       ium Malaïcum*, originally bound together with Scaliger's copy of the *Zacharias, cum
       Commentarius R. David Kimhi, a Francisco Vatablo recognitis* (Paris: Robert Estienne (I),
       1540; USTC 186316), which was disbound in the nineteenth century. Cf. Standcatalogus
       Tydeman BA C 42, part X. In the catalogue of 1674 (p. 278), an otherwise unspecified *Liber
       Indicus* is mentioned among the manuscripts from Scaliger's bequest.

145   Pseudo-Gorionides or pseudo-Josephus was Joseph ben Gorion, author of the *Sefer
       Yosippon*, a history of the Jews from the time of the destruction of Babylon (539 BC) to the
       collapse of the Jewish state (70 AD), with accounts and historical descriptions of Babylon,
       Greece, Rome and other countries. In the text, the author claims to be the Greek historian
       Flavius Josephus.

146   Abraham ben David ha Levi, *Iosippus De bello Iudaico. Deinde decem Iudæorum captivi-
       tates & Decalogus Gentium* (Basileae: [Per Henrichum Petri, 1559]; USTC 1791991).

147   *Correspondence* 6 November 1601 to C. and P. Labbaeus, *Yosippon ... sefer Ben Guryon*
       [Historiæ Judaicæ ll. VI.] (Krakow: [1589]), UBL 875 D 12; see Bibliographic Survey Cracow
       1589. Scaliger had another edition of Joseph ben Gorion in his library, the *Josifon, Historia
       Judaica Josephus Gorionides* (Venezia, apud Cornelio Adelkind, 304 [= 1544]; USTC 804699,
       UBL 875 D 11; see Bibliographic Survey Venice 1544 and Cracow 1589).

148   Scaliger owned at least two copies of the *Colbo*. One was sold in 1853 by the univer-
       sity library as a duplicate. *Sefer kol bo* (Nidpas beWēnēzī'ah [Venezia]: bevēt Zōrzī
       dī Qava'lī [Giorgio di Cavalli], 1567; USTC 1792583, UBL 876 B 24, see Bibliographic
       Survey Venice 1567). When referring to the concordance, Scaliger wrote of Yitshak

books; in 1603, they sent Scaliger a book in Turkish. Scaliger responded that he cherished the work as a jewel in his collection, even if he could not read the language in which it was written.[149]

Scaliger ultimately received the copy of Joseph ben Gorion's *Josippon* via Thomson in England, together with an incomplete copy of a Gaelic Bible. Scaliger paid for the books, as usual, through John Norton in London. Thomson was also asked to look out for the 'Concordantiae Hebraicae Bibliorum'.[150] Scaliger was delighted that England had turned into a rich source of Hebrew books: even his friends in Venice had not been able to acquire a copy of the *Josippon* for him, despite the fact that the work had been printed there.[151] It does seem that after 1601, when Scaliger's most prominent Italian correspondents (Pinelli, Chasteigner and Dupuy) had all died, Scaliger's Italian network became less efficient.

11   Scaliger's Books in Rare Exotic Languages, from Slavic to Chinese

Alongside many Hebrew and Arabic works, Scaliger's bequest also contained books and manuscripts in Russian and other Slavic languages. He displayed much interest in the Russian language because of its proximity to Greek, and because Scaliger used the calendars of the Russian Orthodox Church repeatedly for his study on historical chronology. He regularly asked his correspondents to supply him with Russian books, and, less regularly, received them.[152] In 1601, he received a remarkable gift from his pupil Philippus Cluverius (1580–1622/23), a New Testament from 1563 'translated into the Croatian language'.[153] Given the

---

Nathan ben Kalonymus, *Concordantiae Bibliorum hebraicae* (Venice: 1524) or Natan ben Yehyel, *Sefer ha-Aruch [Lexicon Talmudico-Rabbinico-Chaldaicum]* (Venice: Daniel Bomberg, 1531), UBL 838 A 15; see Bibliographic Survey Venice [1531–1532]. According to *Correspondence* 18 February 1602 from Peiresc, he did receive these three books. The first title cannot be traced in the bequest.

149   *Correspondence* 23 February 1603 to C. and P. Labbaeus: 'Liber Turcicus quoque una mihi redditus est, cuius sermonis ignarus sum.' It probably concerns a manuscript, which I have not been able to identify. An overview of all Turkish manuscripts in the collection is found in: Jan Schmidt, *Catalogue of Turkish Manuscripts*. Vol. 1 (Leiden: Legatum Warnerianum in Leiden University Library, 2000), pp. 24–42. See UBL MS Or. 222; 227; 237; 242; 254; 256 and 259–261.

150   *Correspondence* 12 July 1603 to De Laet.

151   *Correspondence* 25 November [1604?] to Thomson.

152   *Correspondence* 6 November 1601 to the brothers Dupuy, in which Scaliger received an otherwise unspecified 'Livret moschovitique'.

153   For some time, Cluverius served at the court of the King of Poland, but left for Leiden to study law. Thereafter, at Scaliger's recommendation, he concentrated on the study

SCALIGER IN LEIDEN   177

decorations of the binding, it is certain that this copy came from the library of the jurist Simon Clüver of Danzig, a great-uncle of Philippus Cluverius.

Many Slavic books owned by Scaliger came from Venice, where the art of printing in Slavic languages was principally developed. Venetian printers used types cast in Cyrillic, Glagolitic and Bosančica (a Bosniak Cyrillic variant) scripts.[154] Scaliger owned a small Cyrillic prayer book, printed by Jakov di Kamena Reka in 1572, as well as a *Alphabetum Russicum*.[155] In total, he had eight Church Slavonic books in his library, four of them printed.[156]

Scaliger's collection also included several printed works in languages even more exotic than Russian, such as Chinese and Japanese (which was, confusingly, often described by contemporaries as Chinese). Two such works were the *Fides no Doxi to Xite* and the Chinese-Japanese dictionary *Racuyoxu*.[157] Like other books from Scaliger's bequest, these all later received a printed slip stating '*Ex Legato Illustris Viri JOSEPHI SCALIGERI*'. However, the copy of the *Fides no Doxi to Xite* never belonged to Scaliger, and there is no reference to this work in any of his correspondence. It seems that it was added later to the bequest, and is first mentioned in the university library catalogue of 1674. This is in contrast to the Chinese-Japanese dictionary, which can certainly be ascribed to Scaliger.

---

of geography. Between 1607 and 1613, he made numerous journeys through Germany, Hungary, Bohemia and western Europe, thanks to which he also learned a variety of vernacular languages. In 1616, Cluverius was appointed as *Geographus academicus* at the University of Leiden. The translation of the New Testament was made by two Protestants, Stephanus Consul and Antonius Dalmata. The book was printed in two editions, one in Cyrillic script, and one in Glagolitic (an ancient Slavic script), at Urach, near Tübingen, at the residence of the Protestant Count Hans III Ungnad from Stiermarken (Austria), see UBL 1365 F 14; see Bibliographic Survey Tübingen 1563.

154   Zsusza Barbarics-Hermanik, 'European Books for the Ottoman Market', in R. Kirwan and S. Mullins (eds.), *Specialist Markets in the Early Modern Book World* (Leiden, Boston: Brill, 2015), pp. 395–405.

155   This is the *Abcdarium* or *Alphabeticum calligraphicum* dated ca. 1582–1584, UBL BPL 967. See: H. Meijer, 'Slavjanskie rukopisi Lejdenskoj universitetskoj biblioteki v Niderlandach,' *Archeografičeskij ežegodnik za 1977 god* (*otdelynyj ottisk*) 5 (1978); *Catalogus compend.* I (1932), p. 135.

156   UBL 1370 G 21; 1367 G 9; see Bibliographic Survey Venice 1527: 2; Venice 1572; Vilnius 1578 and Vilnius 1596. The books are described in the 1612 catalogue in the section *Libri lingua Rußica Charactere Chyruluizza*.

157   *Fides no Doxi to Xite* (UBL SER 614) is a Japanese translation of the Catholic confession of faith by Luis de Granada (1504–1588) (*Quinta parte de la Introduccion del Symbolo de la Fé*, Salamanca, 1588). The translation was made by Pedro Ramón († 1611), who was probably helped by a Japanese convert. This is the earliest known work printed on the island of Amakusa, lying before the coast of Kyushu. See: Bibliographic Survey [Nagasaki] 1598 and the Addendum to the Bibliographic Survey.

Scaliger must also have owned other books in exotic languages, traces of which we can find in his correspondence and the auction catalogue of his library. For some reason, these books were not included in the bequest, or they disappeared from it. The Malay manuscripts, sent to Scaliger by Petrus Labbaeus in 1602, has vanished without trace.[158] During his stay in Tours in 1578, Scaliger lent an otherwise unknown Chinese book to the philologist, poet and scholar François Béroalde de Verville (1556–1626).[159] He urged De Verville to be careful with the book, and to return it to him without blemish.[160] It is uncertain if this ever happened; there is no sign of the book in the Oriental bequest.

A copy of the 'Catechismus Loiolitarum, Indorum litera & charactere, impressus Goæ' also disappeared from Scaliger's collection, even though it is mentioned as part of his bequest in the 1612 and 1674 Leiden catalogues. It is likely that this concerned the very rare *Doctrina cristaã tresladada em lingua tamul* by Franciscus Xaverius, printed in Goa in 1578, only a single copy of which still survives today, in Harvard.[161]

From the earliest days of his interest in Oriental languages, Scaliger paid attention to the publications of the Jesuits. Prompted by their missionary activities in Japan and China, the Jesuits published a variety of works about

---

158   *Correspondence* 12 September 1601 and 9 June 1602 from Labbaeus. Scaliger was disappointed when he received the manuscript, because the text turned out to be written in Arabic rather than Malay. In the bequest, there is a manuscript of the Qur'an, parts of which were written in Malay. In the 1623 catalogue, it is described as *Excerpta ex Alcorano cum nugis quibusdam Mahomedicis, partim Arabicè partim Turcicè*, UBL MS Or. 247. See: Vrolijk and Van Ommen, *All my Books*, pp. 79–80 and Edwin P. Wieringa, *Catalogue of Malay and Minangkabau Manuscripts in the Library of Leiden University and Other Collections in the Netherlands*. Vol. 1 (Leiden: Leiden University Library, 1998), no. 1.

159   François Béroalde de Verville, preacher and professor of philosophy at Geneva, and the son of Matthieu Béroalde († 1576), was the author of *Chronicum, Scripturae Sacrae autoritate constitutum* (Genève: A. Chuppinus, 1575; USTC 450686).

160   Cf. François Béroalde de Verville, *Palais des Curieux*. (Paris: chez M. Guillemot et S. Thiboust, 1612; USTC 6016835), p. 579 and Béroalde de Verville, *Le Moyen de parvenir. Notice, variantes, glossaire et index des noms, par Charles Royer* (Paris: A. Lemerre, 1896), p. 286. It is possible that this concerns one of the five *Libri Sinenses* in the collection of Scaliger, as described in the 1674 Leiden catalogue, at p. 256, but this cannot be determined conclusively.

161   [F. Xavier], *Doctrina cristaã tresladada em lingua tamul pello padrc* [!] *Anrique Anriquez da Côpanhia de Iesv, & pello padre Manoel de São Pedro* [= *Doctrina christam en lingua malauar tamul*] (Impressa em Coulam [= Cochin]: no Collegio do Salvador aos vinte de octubro de .M.D.LXXVIII). The catalogues of 1612 and 1674 refer to the year of publication as 1577. No copy is known of this date; the Harvard copy contains the notation: 'Portata dall 'Indie. Hanuta dal prē Fonseca del mese di Novembre MDLXXIX'.

SCALIGER IN LEIDEN   179

the languages and cultures of the Far East.[162] Such publications, albeit limited in number, can also be traced in Scaliger's collection. The auction catalogue of his library of 1609 mentions copies of the *Recentissima de amplissimo Regno Chinae* (Mainz, 1601) by the Jesuit Nicoló Longobardi (1559–1654), the *Iaponica, Sinensia, Mogorana. Hoc est, De rebus apud eas gentes à patribus Societatis Iesv, ann. 1598. & 99. Gestis* (Liège, 1601) by Johannes Oranus, and published correspondence on Japan by the Jesuit Franciscus Toletus (1532–1596). Because these works were all in Latin, they did not form part of the bequest, and were sold at auction. More remarkably, the 1609 catalogue also records four Chinese books 'Libri in China excusi quatuor', without any further description. Listed at page 51, amongst various maps and globes, it is perplexing why these books appeared at auction, and not in the bequest.

The Chinese books owned by Scaliger sold at auction have not yet been traced today; they are certainly not to be found in the university library in Leiden. Other Chinese books were added to Scaliger's bequest that never belonged to him. In the 1640 university catalogue, *Tres libri Chinenses* (Three Chinese books) are mentioned for the first time, although these cannot be found described as such in the 1612 and 1623 university catalogues.[163] It is highly likely that these three books came from the library of Bonaventura Vulcanius, sold at auction in 1615.[164] This collection included 'Tres libri characteribus Chinensibus 4o 3 voll'. The books were probably described in the 1623 Leiden catalogue as *Libri aliquot Chinenses* (p. 125). It seems probable that they were added to Scaliger's bequest when librarian David van Royen (1699–1764) re-organised the *Arcae*, the special book cupboards containing the books owned by Scaliger and Vulcanius. Presumably some of Van Royen's assistants considered the Chinese books so exotic that they thought that they could only have belonged to Scaliger. In the university library catalogues of 1674 and

---

162   In the auction catalogue of 1609, we can identify in the history section on page 22 a variety of books about China and Japan. In the auction catalogue of the library of Nicolaas Heinsius (1682) we can also find, for example, a copy of the *L'historia del gran Reyno de la China* by Juan Gonsales de Mendoza (Rome: a costa de Bartholome Grassi en la stampa de Vincentio Accolti, 1585; USTC 342999).

163   In the Leiden library catalogue of 1612, there is a *Liber in China conscriptus* at page 93, but this book has no connection to Scaliger's bequest.

164   Bert van Selm remarked on the 'Tres libri characteribus Chinensibus 4o. 3 voll.' in the collection of Vulcanius in his, 'Cornelis Claesz' 1605 Stock Catalogue of Chinese Books' in *Quaerendo* 13/4 (1983), p. 257. These Chinese books have not been identified. See also: Philipp Christiaan Molhuysen, *Bibliotheca Universitatis Leidensis. Codices manuscripti I. Codices Vulcaniani* (Leiden: s.n., 1910), p. VII, no. 15: *Tres libri characteribus Chinensibus. 4°. 3 voll. [nunc inter libros typis impressos relati]*. It does therefore seem that these books were still in Leiden in 1910.

1716, we suddenly find record of *5 Libri Sinenses* in Scaliger's bequest; then they disappear from sight again, until Molhuysen mentioned three Chinese books again in 1910.[165] What is certain, is that there are six Chinese books in the university library of Leiden today that date from the late sixteenth century. It is probable that these correspond to the 'three' or 'five' books of Vulcanius and Scaliger.[166]

When it came to foreign languages, Scaliger's collecting habits were boundless. Even works that he could not read himself were of interest to him as exotic objects, and as potential future sources of knowledge, that might one day reveal their secrets. The variety of languages that Scaliger did not master would presumably have tortured him: which languages did he have to learn to unlock the knowledge he pursued? At least Scaliger made a significant contribution by making a first step, preserving his Oriental works in his bequest, so that they could be of use to new generations of scholars. This foresight was not general among the collectors of his age, nor were there many institutions that were fully prepared to safeguard such a bequest. In this respect, the university library of Leiden was not yet an exception.

---

165 Catalogue 1674, p. 256, under no 38 and Catalogue 1716, p. 311 [Heb. 2].
166 My thanks to Dr. K. Kuiper, who has provided me with the following details concerning the possible identification of the works. Dr. Kuiper pursues research into the oldest Chinese books in the possession of the Sinological Institute of the University of Leiden. According to Kuiper, it concerns possibly the following titles: *Chongxiu Zhenghe jingshi zhenglei beiyong bencao* 重修政和經史證類備用本草 (parts 4, 20 and 21); *Danxin xinfa fu yu* 丹心新法附餘 (parts 16 and 17); *Qie zhushi Lao Zhuang Nanhua sai fu mo* 鍥註釋老莊南華賽副墨 (part 1; missing from the library); *Lichao gushi* 新鐫翰林改正歷朝故事統宗 (parts 1–3) and *Xinkan Wanbing huichun* 新刊萬病回春 (a section of part 3). Until around 1883, the first four titles were bound together (according to a note by L. Serrurier on a loose sheet of paper in Schlegel 119). See Bibliographic Survey Jinling 1581–1594.

CHAPTER 5

Expanding the University Library: a Will, a Bequest and an Auction Catalogue

As commander of the garrison of Leiden during the Spanish sieges of 1573–1574, Janus Dousa played a critical role in the defence of the city. After its relief, Dousa, also a renowned scholar and poet, would exercise similar influence in the establishment of the University of Leiden in 1575 and its early development. The university would become a humanist stronghold, in which the study of the seven liberal arts would be considered of utmost importance.[1] The choice to emphasise the liberal arts as a cornerstone of the university curriculum was the brainchild of Dousa, one of the first curators of the university. He was assisted in his ambitions by his friend Jan van Hout, who combined his position as secretary of Leiden with that of secretary of the university.[2] From the inception of the university, the curators wished to house a library in the university building. Books were considered to be an indispensable part of the mission of the institution to inculcate a culture of humanist scholarship.[3] Ten years after the foundation of the university, on 1 March 1585, Dousa was appointed as the first librarian of the university; two years later, the first library room was ready.[4]

It was also Dousa's achievement, in 1579, to attract the great philologist and historian Justus Lipsius (1547–1606) to Leiden.[5] Lipsius's appointment was principally designed to announce Leiden's entry on the international academic

---

1 The liberal arts included the study of languages, philosophy, history and literature, meant to enrich general knowledge and to develop the critical abilities of reasoning, oratory and deduction.

2 The design of the new university was expressed by Dousa in his 'Carmen in gratiam novae Academiae conscriptum', printed in his *Poëmata*, ff. Piii-Qiiii, produced in Leiden 'in nova academia nostra' by Andries Verschout, at the cost of Van Hout in 1575. See: Karel Bostoen, *Hart voor Leiden, Jan van Hout (1542–1609), stadssecretaris, dichter en vernieuwer* (Hilversum: Verloren, 2009), pp. 38–41.

3 Molhuysen, *Bronnen* I, p. 21*: 'Postremo esset optandum ut bibliotheca omne genus libris undequaque conquisitis publico sumptu instrueretur et in superiori publici Academiae auditorii coenaculo. ...'

4 Molhuysen, *Bronnen* I, pp. 122*–123*.

5 For a biographical sketch of the life and work of Lipsius, see: Jeanine De Landtsheer (et al.), *Lieveling van de Latijnse taal. Justus Lipsius te Leiden herdacht bij zijn vierhonderdste sterfdag* (Leiden: Universiteitsbibliotheek Leiden – Scaliger Instituut, 2006).

© KONINKLIJKE BRILL BV, LEIDEN, 2025 | DOI:10.1163/9789004701526_007

stage. It was striking too that Dousa and his fellow curators gave Lipsius a chair in the 'Artes', again emphasising the importance of the liberals arts, an unusual move in an era when the more traditional faculties of theology, jurisprudence and medicine were commonly regarded as the superior disciplines.[6] It was remarkable also that Leiden would place the study of Oriental and classical philology under the disciplinary umbrella of the arts, rather than theology. This humanistic approach provided a productive environment for Scaliger's research, an environment which he would of course also develop.

1   The University Library of Leiden before Scaliger's Arrival

In contrast to many universities of its age, Leiden was designed at birth to be an institution that fostered notions of liberty of conscience and relative tolerance. The appointment of Lipsius ensured that substantial numbers of students and teachers from around Europe soon flocked to the academy at Leiden.[7] The first arrivals, however, often lacked reasonable access to books, as the university was still devoid of an institutional library. At its inauguration, Prince William of Orange (1533–1584) had donated a copy of the Plantin Polyglot Bible (1569–1572) to the university, to encourage the growth of a library.[8] Yet apart from several small individual donations, the book collection of the university barely grew. One cannot really speak of the existence of a library in the first decade of the university, more of a smattering of books. It was only when the books of Johannes Holmannus Junior (1523–1586) and Bonaventura Vulcanius were added to the collection in 1586 and 1587 that the university came to own useful reference works and dictionaries, essential tools for a good university library.[9]

---

6   Hélène E.C. Mazur-Contamine, 'Een blik op de toenmalige horizon (1575–1635)', in *Boekillustratie in de Noordelijke Nederlanden* (Leiden: s.n., 1988), p. 33.

7   After the Contra-Remonstrant coup sponsored by Prince Maurice in 1618, this changed drastically. This event marked a decisive end to the tolerant climate promoted by his father, William of Orange.

8   The complete title is *Biblia sacra Hebraïce, Chaldaice Graece & Latine, Philippe II Reg. Cathol. Pietate et studio ad Sacrosanctæ Ecclesiae usum* (Antwerpen: Christophe Plantin, [1569–73]; USTC 401394, UBL 1366 A 1). For a history of the Polyglot Bible, see: Robert J. Wilkinson, *The Kabbalistic Scholars of the Antwerp Polyglot Bible* (Leiden: Brill, 2007), pp. 67–92 and Theodor Dunkelgrün, *The multiplicity of Scripture. The confluence of textual traditions in the making of the Antwerp Polyglot Bible (1568–1573)* (Chicago, s.n., 2012).

9   On 9 February 1587, Justus Lipsius, as rector of the university, was the first to promote the establishment of a specific library room. See *Het Schriftelijk Rapport [11 augustus 1741] van Mr. David van Royen, Secretaris van de Ed. Groot Achtbaere Heeren Curateuren over 's Lands*

EXPANDING THE UNIVERSITY LIBRARY 183

In 1587, the books were granted their own space: the collection was housed in a vaulted room in the Academy building. The library remained there until 1595, when it was moved to the first floor of the former Faliede Beguine Church, at the Rapenburg, diagonally across the street from the Academy building. The arrangement of the library was supervised by Jan van Hout. He proposed the division of the books into seven disciplines and twenty-two bookcases, or *plutei*.[10] The official opening of the library took place on 24 May 1595. In the same year, the then librarian, Petrus Bertius (1565–1629) composed the *Nomenclator avtorvm omnivm, quorum libri vel manuscripti, vel typis expressi exstant in Bibliotheca Academiæ Lvgdvno-Batavæ*: the first published catalogue of the university library, consisting of 483 items.[11] With this catalogue, Leiden had achieved a notable first: the *Nomenclator* was the earliest printed institutional library catalogue in the world. The catalogue provided an overview of the books in the order in which they were shelved. The 483 items comprised 442 distinct titles, divided amongst 525 volumes, 338 of which were in folio.[12]

How many Oriental works were present in the library at its inception? Only one Arabic text is mentioned in the 1595 *Nomenclator*: the Arabic typeface sample produced by the Leiden Officina Plantiniana in 1595, which Raphelengius had donated to the library.[13] The catalogue did list fourteen books in Hebrew,

---

      Universiteit binnen Leijden, ende Burgemeesteren derzelve Stadt, nopens het begin en Voortgangh van: alsmede zorge en ordre, gestelt, ende gedragen op, en over de Publique Bibliotheecq, ingevolge, ende ter Voldoeningh van het eerste Lidt van hun Ed. Groot Agtb. Resolutie, op den 30. April 1741, genomen, hereafter: *Schriftelijk Rapport 1741* [UBL, Bibliotheekarchief (hereafter: BA) H1]. The report was published in P.C. Molhuysen in *Bronnen* V, Den Haag 1921, pp. 88*–131*.

10   P. Bertius, *Nomenclator avtorvm omnivm. Quorum libri Vel manuscripti, vel typis expressi exstant in Bibliotheca-Batavae* (Leiden: apud Franciscus I Raphelengius, 1595; USTC 423469), f. A4ᵛ: 'Ipsius ergo auspiciis (= Dousa), meâ operâ, tuo, Houtene consilio Bibliotheca Academia eo quo nunc est loco atque ordine digesta est'; cited in Bosch, *Petrus Bertius*, p. 68, note 439. Originally, there were twelve *plutei* in the library, four for the theological works, four for jurisprudence and medicine and four for the liberal arts.

11   See also Petrus Bertius, *Nomenclator. The First Printed Catalogue of Leiden University Library (1595). A Facsimile Edition with an Introduction by R. Breugelmans and an Authors Index compiled by Jan Just Witkam* (Leiden: Leiden University Library, 1995). Bertius was not officially librarian, but because of his repeated involvement with the library he could arguably claim this title. Cf. Leonardus Johannes Marinus Bosch, *Petrus Bertius 1565–1629* (Meppel, Krips Repro, 1979), pp. 60–61.

12   For a general history of the university library of Leiden, see: Philipp Christiaan Molhuysen, *Geschiedenis der Universiteits-bibliotheek te Leiden* (Leiden: A.W. Sijthoff, 1905); Christiane Berkvens-Stevelinck, *Magna Commoditas. Leiden University's Great Asset. 425 years Library Collections and Services* (Leiden: Leiden University Press, 2012).

13   A facsimile with extensive commentary has been published by John Lane, *The Arabic Type Specimen of Franciscus Raphelengius's Plantinian Printing Office (1595) A Facsimile with an Introduction* [...] (Leiden: University Library Leiden, 1997).

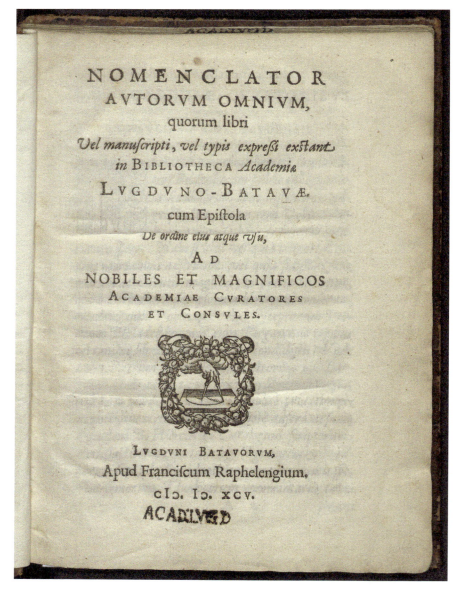

FIGURE 26 Title page of Petrus Bertius's *Nomenclator* (Leiden: Franciscus Raphelengius, 1595). UBL 1408 I 57

EXPANDING THE UNIVERSITY LIBRARY

while the *Psalterium Justiniani* in the collection included sporadic use of Arabic type. The catalogue also provided a detailed description of the Venetian 'Talmud Babylonicum', printed with Hebrew typefaces, and a Hebrew 'Biblia Bombergiana'.[14] These books were all found in the shelves with theological books. In smaller formats, the library possessed a Venetian *Biblia Hebraica* and three grammars by Cevalerius, Santes Pagninus and Münster.

2   The Oriental Books of the Court of Holland

A year before Bertius composed the first catalogue of the Leiden university library, an opportunity suddenly arose to expand the holdings of the collection considerably. In the attic of the Court of Holland in The Hague, Janus Dousa 'discovered' a disorganised collection of books. In 1591, Dousa had become a councillor of the High Court, and he probably came across the books in the course of his duties for the court. The curators of Leiden (including Dousa) expressed their interest in transferring this collection, which had previously been a reference collection for use by the lawyers of the Court of Holland, to the university library of Leiden.[15]

At the urging of the university, an inventory was compiled of the old library of the Court of Holland. It soon became clear that the books in the attic had formerly belonged to the Gorinchem canon Jan Dircz van der Haer, or Joannes Harius, who had donated the books in 1531 to Charles V, Count of Holland.[16] Originally, Van der Haer's library had been composed of 3,849 titles in 3,780 volumes, a very substantial library for the early sixteenth century, and still large in late sixteenth-century terms (especially when considering the small size of the university library).[17] Yet Van der Haer's collection had already been partially dispersed and ransacked. Dousa's inventory of the books in the attic numbered

---

14   *Talmud Babylonicum cum commentariis* or *Talmud Bavli* published in 9 parts (Venetsyah, Daniyel Bombergi, 280–286 [1520–1526]); USTC 1792807, UBL 21523 A 1–9).

15   Molhuysen, *Bronnen* I, p. 305*; see also the 'Resoluties van de Staten van Holland. Augustus 1594', in: *Bronnen* I, p. 329.

16   M.J. Waale, 'De laat-middeleeuwse Gorcumer Jan Dirksz. van der Haar en zijn librije van het Hof van Holland' *Oud-Gorcum Varia.* 9; 23 1992–1, p. 4–11 and J.L. van der Gouw, 'De Librye van den Hove van Holland', *Het boek* 29 (1948), pp. 117–130. See most recently, Tom de Smidt, 'An elderly, noble lady. The old books collection in the library of the Supreme Court of the Netherlands', in J.G.B. Pikkemaat (ed.), *The Old Library of the Supreme Court of the Netherlands* (Hilversum: Verloren, 2008), pp. 39–68.

17   In comparison, the library of Erasmus numbered 413 books in 1525.

186 CHAPTER 5

only 38 pages and listed 750 items.[18] It was the intention to transport the books to Leiden in six baskets and to integrate the items into the library. The collection consisted mostly of theological and juridical works, but it also contained a section of 'Libri Haebraici, Chaldaici et Arabici'. The transfer of the collection would never take place, as ownership became disputed; the books remained in The Hague. After all his efforts, this would have been a serious disappointment to Dousa and his son Janus junior, who would succeed his father in July 1593 as librarian of Leiden.[19]

Dousa made repeated attempts to acquire the Oriental books from the library of the Court of Holland for the university library in Leiden. At this point, the library had few such works. The titles in the inventory compiled by Dousa provide us with a good overview of the Oriental collecting habits of a personal collector such as Van der Haer. Alongside the usual theological works, including a Hebrew Bible, the collection also included dictionaries and grammars. Van der Haer had clearly been a collector with a good grasp of Latin and Greek, but might also have taught himself Hebrew using these books. That the members of the Court of Holland would have had little use for the Hebrew books strengthened the case to donate them to Leiden, where they would have greater value amongst the scholars and students of the academy.

While Scaliger brought Oriental books with him to Leiden in 1593, these were all his personal possessions. Dousa's interest in the books from the Court of Holland is indicative of the ambition of the university curators to expand their institutional library. Around 1600, the library was not only circumscribed in size, but there were serious gaps in the collection. Dousa will have been mightily pleased that in July 1595, a few Oriental books found their way to the university library.[20] Apparently, Scaliger's arrival at Leiden had been the final prompt required to move the councillors of the Court of Holland to donate the nine-volume Talmud and seven other Hebrew books from their collection. These were formally gifted at the inauguration of the library's new accommodation on 24 May 1595.[21] Part of the Hebrew books was placed by Bertius in the theology section, in *Pluteo* ד. Scaliger would wax lyrical in the *Scaligerana* on

---

18   Dousa's inventory can be found at UBL AC 1 101, ff. 9^v–51^r; the section *Libri Haebraica, Chaldaici et Arabici* is at ff. 30^r–32^r and consists almost entirely from books in Hebrew. The only book in the section which actually has Arabic type is the copy of the *Psalterium* by Augustinus Justinianus from 1516.

19   Molhuysen, *Bronnen* I, pp. 266*–268*. Dousa junior died two years later, after which he was succeeded in his post as librarian by Bertius. On the library of the court and the university library, see also: Heesakkers, 'Zes viercante witte manden, pp. 182–197.

20   The list composed by Janus Dousa in August 1594 with the section header *Libri Hebraici, Chaldaici et Arabici* consists of 24 books in folio. See: Appendix 2.

21   Molhuysen, *Bronnen* I, p. 93. On 14 July 1595, the members of the Court of Holland and the commissioners of the States of Holland (the *Gecommitteerde Raden*) received from

EXPANDING THE UNIVERSITY LIBRARY   187

the copy of the Talmud given to Leiden by the Court of Holland, as this edition
of the Talmud had been barely censored by the authorities, and was thus an
extremely valuable source.[22]

Scaliger could consult all these Hebrew works donated to Leiden in the
library. Whether he did so for every title is uncertain, as he did own some of the
editions himself, but not all. Scaliger's own copy of the Talmud was produced
in Basel between 1579 and 1581, whereas the edition in the library was from the
1520s.[23] That the library could be a resource of use to Scaliger is also confirmed
by the fact that he helped expand the library, especially its Oriental holdings,
during his life and at his death.

3   Scaliger's Death

The year 1609, the year of Scaliger's death, was a critical date for the university library of Leiden. Scaliger's appointment to Leiden had placed the university on the European map; the bequest after his death of his unsurpassable
collection of Oriental books and manuscripts did the same for the university
library. Scaliger died on Wednesday 21 January 1609, at the age of sixty-eight,
from complications of scurvy and dropsy. The resolutions of the senate of the
university note that due to Scaliger's death, all teaching was suspended for a
week.[24] On Sunday 25 January, shortly after 2 pm, Scaliger was buried in the
Vrouwekerk on the Haarlemmerstraat.[25] His body was placed in burial plot
58 of the northern part of the church, at the foot of the southwestern pillar of

---

the curators of the university and burgomasters of Leiden a key of the library and a copy
of the *Nomenclator*.

22   *Scaligerana* 1740, p. 424: 'Le Thalmud qui est icy en la Bibliotheque est le bon, qui n'est point
chastré. Messieurs les Estats l'ont eu d'un Monastère & l'ont donné à la Bibliotheque'. It
concerns the *Talmud Babylonicum cum commentariis Mos. Maimonidis, Raschi et Tosafot*,
printed in Venice between 1520 and 1530 by Daniel Bomberg, see UBL 21523 A 1–9.

23   Scaliger's copy of the Basel Talmud is at UBL 875 A 1–8; see Bibliographic Survey Basel
1579–1581.

24   *Acta Senatus* dated 22 January 1609: 'Visum est Senatui Academico, ut propter obitum
illustris viri Josephi Scaligeri Professores non doceant ad diem usque huius mensis 29.'

25   Tweede Begraafboek (1604–1609) van de Vrouwekerk. ELO, B.G. 328 f. CLXXXIIIIr.
On 10 August 1819, Scaliger's gravestone and epitaph were removed from the crumbling
Vrouwekerk to the Pieterskerk. This salvage operation was organised by the historian
and theologian Jona Willem te Water (1740–1822) and the professor of physics, Sebald
Justinus Brugmans (1763–1819). Jona Willem te Water, 'Berigt over de Verplaatsinge van
de Grafschriften der Leijdsche Hoogleraren Scaliger en Clusius', *Algemeene Konst- en
Letterbode van 1819*, II, no. 43, pp. 211–213. See also: B.A. van Proosdij, 'Scaliger's Graf', *Brill's
uitgaven voor algemeen voortgezet onderwijs* (Leiden: E.J. Brill, 1972), pp. 19–25.

the northern transept, across from St Stephen's chapel.[26] The funeral procession carried portraits of Scaliger's ancestors, and possibly their coats of arms.[27] Daniel Heinsius organised the ceremony and also delivered the funeral oration.

Scaliger's burial, his bequest and the emphasis of his connection with the former rulers of Verona all conformed to the manner in which his colleagues, students and friends perceived Scaliger, as a noble and learned individual.[28] Later in 1609, Scaliger's grave was adorned with a gravestone featuring his name and ancestral coat of arms.[29] This carried the following inscription:

HIC EXPECTO RESVRRECTIONEM
TERRA HAEC AB ECCLESIA EMPTA EST
NEMINI CADAVER HVC INFERRE LICET

Here I expect the resurrection
This ground has been purchased from the church
No one may inter a corpse here.[30]

This text was composed by Heinsius, undoubtedly inspired by the fact that in life Scaliger rarely expressed care about the appearance of his grave, but did

---

26 Henk Jan de Jonge, 'Grafsteen en graf van Scaliger', *Jaarboekje voor de geschiedenis en oudheidkunde van Leiden.* LXX (1978), pp. 91–96; Henk Jan de Jonge and George J.R. Maat, 'Bij de berging van het gebeente van Joseph Scaliger', *Holland* 12 (1980), pp. 20–34.

27 According to a letter by Heinsius to Casaubon in *Epistolae Scaligeri* (1627), which refers to the *imagines maiorum* in the procession; in contrast, Scaliger's will does not reflect on this.

28 In his funeral oration, Heinsius referred several times to Scaliger's 'princely' family history and his descendance from the Veronese Della Scala family.

29 Whether the family coat of arms was indeed added to the gravestone, as indicated by Scaliger in his will, is uncertain. The coat of arms is no longer present on the stone. The coat of arms was certainly added to one of the doors of the *Arca*.

30 Apparently, the gist of the text was conceived by Scaliger. During the move of the gravestone to the Pieterskerk in 1819, a part of the stone was broken off, and some of the text has therefore become illegible. The complete text can however be reconstructed because it was mentioned in the *Les délices de Leide, qui contiennent une description exacte de son antiquité, de ses divers aggrandissemens, de son académie, de ses manufactures, de ses curiosités* (Leiden: Pieter van der Aa, 1712), p. 185. Most of the graves in the Vrouwekerk were family graves. Scaliger ensured that his grave would not be disturbed by appealing to Classical Roman law: due to an agreement between the university and the church, the grave was exempted from future re-use. This was the reason that Scaliger's grave was never emptied, and it demonstrates that Scaliger remembered Cujas's juridical lessons later in life. Cf. De Jonge, 'Grafsteen en graf van Scaliger', p. 91.

EXPANDING THE UNIVERSITY LIBRARY

attach immense value to his forthcoming resurrection.[31] The university also paid for the placement of an epitaph on the pillar next to the grave, based on a design by the mason and municipal architect of Amsterdam, Hendrick de Keyser (1565–1621) and the engraver and writing master Cornelis Dircksz. Boissens (ca. 1567–1635). Yet for all the attention paid to his grave, the most influential remembrance to Scaliger's life found its expression in the university library, where his Oriental collection came to be housed in a monumental bespoke bookcase, the *Arca Scaligerana*.

Several days after Scaliger's death, Heinsius and Baudius delivered funeral orations, while the Hebraist Johannes Drusius junior also published a memorial text.[32] Heinsius described Scaliger as an *Aquila in nubibus*, 'an eagle in the clouds', alluding to the king of the birds, one that flew even higher than the wise owl of Pallas Athena.[33] The eagle was not only a symbol of authority and leadership, but it also alluded to the eagle in the coat of arms of the Della Scala family.

Scaliger's bequest was extremely beneficial to the university library. Although Scaliger seems to have used the university library little himself (given the size and quality of his personal library), he did describe the university library in 1606 as a *Magna commoditas*, a great commodity of use to the members of the academic community.[34] With the bequest of his printed books and manuscripts in Oriental languages, Scaliger wished to fill one of the

31 Henk Jan de Jonge, 'Daniel Heinsius, auteur de l'inscription sur l'épitaphe de Joseph Scaliger,' *Humanistica Lovaniensia* 27 (1978), pp. 231–237; Rudi E.O. Ekkart, 'Het grafmonument van Scaliger', *Jaarboekje voor de geschiedenis en oudheidkunde van Leiden en omstreken* 70 (1978), pp. 81–90. See also the entry on the graves of the Della Scala's in Verona in Pierre des Maizeaux, *Secunda Scaligerana* 1740, p. 558.

32 The year 1609 was in many ways a year of disaster for Leiden. Scaliger's friend, the botanist Carolus Clusius, also died, while the municipal secretary and secretary of the university, Jan van Hout, and the theologian Jacobus Arminius (1560–1609) also died in the same year.

33 The comparison between Scaliger and an eagle in the clouds was derived from Justus Lipsius, who in turn had derived it from one of Erasmus's *Adagia* (number 820). Lipsius made the comparison after Scaliger published his edition of Manilius. See *Correspondence* 18 May 1580 from Lipsius. See also: *Epistolae selectae. Miscellanea. 1605–1607* and *Centuria* I, 6.

34 See *Correspondence* 13 September 1595 to Pithou for a negative judgement by Scaliger on the library. In conversations with the Leiden students (and brothers) Jean and Nicolas de Vassan in 1606, Scaliger described the library as: 'Est hic magna commoditas Bibliothecae, ut studiosi possint studere' ('The library is a great commodity, one that allows scholars to study.'). See: *Scaligerana, ou Bons mots, rencontres agréables et remarques judicieuses et sçavantes* (Cologne (=Amsterdam): s.n., 1695; USTC 2604818), p. 237 (USTC 2604818).

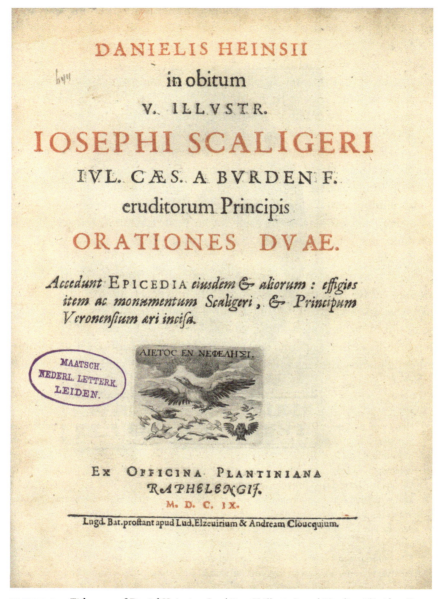

FIGURE 27   Title page of Daniel Heinsius, *In obitum V. Illustr. Iosephi Scaligeri* (Leiden: Ex officina Plantiniana Raphelengii, 1609). UBL 1011 C 14: 1

great lacunae of the library, namely books in scholarly languages other than Latin. The university expressed immense gratitude for this gift, and presented the donated books as valuable objects. The university wished to emphasise the symbolic status of the bequest, one that strengthened Leiden's claim as one of

EXPANDING THE UNIVERSITY LIBRARY

the foremost academic institutions of Protestant Europe, and the home of one of the most treasured collections of rare texts.[35]

4 Scaliger's Will

Scaliger had considered his bequest almost ten years before his death. Around 1600, several of his friends died, including De Buzanval and Vertunien. These deaths, and those of other younger scholars, prompted Scaliger to consider his own legacy and will.[36] Six months after his sixtieth birthday, Scaliger composed a will, which would be altered several times in the following years.[37]

It is likely that news of Scaliger's preparations for his bequest reverberated around the scholarly community, because in 1602, Jacques Esprinchard, a former student of Scaliger, asked if he would donate his Arabic manuscripts to the library of La Rochelle. Despite his ruminations about the future of his books, Scaliger was taken aback by this request. His answer was brusque: 'It is as if someone asked another to give him his wife'.[38] Yet although he rejected this proposal firmly, the prospect of bequeathing his collection did remain in Scaliger's mind.

Around the same time as Scaliger reflected on the future of his collection, his predecessor at Leiden, Justus Lipsius, was deeply involved in gathering bequests of books in an attempt to set up a central university library at his new post in Louvain. In 1602, Lipsius wrote a tract on libraries of antiquity, entitled *De Bibliothecis*.[39] Lipsius dedicated his work to Charles de Croÿ, Prince de Chimay (1560–1612), in the hope that the prince would bequeath his library to Louvain (a hope that would remain unfulfilled). An important theme in *De Bibliothecis* was that magnates such as De Croÿ should be at the forefront of the foundation of libraries, to support scholarly endeavours. The possibility cannot be excluded that Scaliger read Lipsius's book, even if no copy was listed in Scaliger's auction catalogue of 1609; indeed, we know that Scaliger was sent

---

35   Lisa Jardine, *Worldly goods. A New History of the Renaissance* (London: W.W. Norton & Company 1996), p. 191.

36   De Buzanval died suddenly on 7 September 1607, which meant that his will was incomplete. Scaliger mentioned this in *Correspondence* 21 September 1607 to De Thou.

37   *Correspondence* 6 February 1601 to Casaubon. De Jonge, *Latin Testament* (1975), pp. 249–263.

38   'C'est comme si quelque'un demandoit à un autre qu'il luy donnast sa femme'. *Secunda Scaligerana* 1740, p. 535, at 'Rochelle'.

39   A second improved and expanded edition appeared in 1607. For a modern translation of the text, with scholarly commentary, see T. Hendrickson, *Ancient Libraries and Renaissance Humanism. The* De Bibliothecis *of Justus Lipsius* (Leiden, Boston: Brill, 2017).

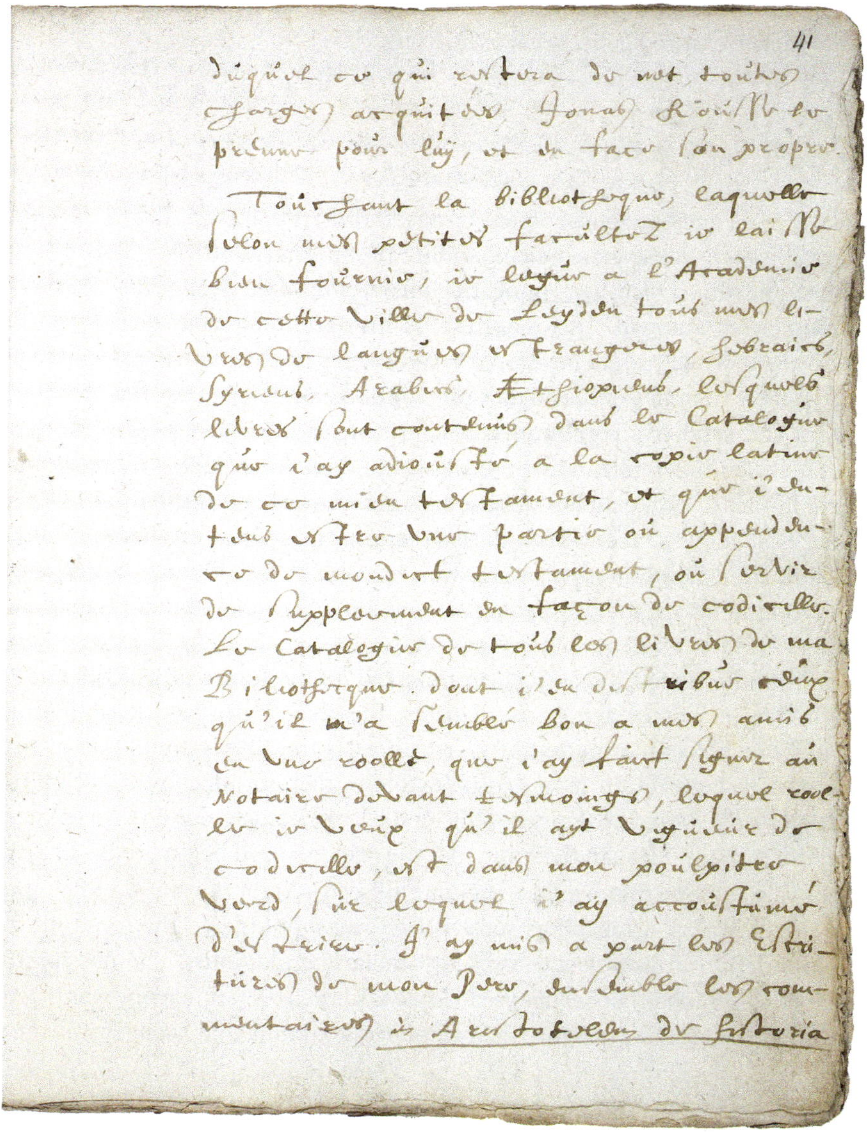

FIGURE 28   One of the first pages from Scaliger's will, written in French, according to a transcript in the collection of the Leiden professor of history, Greek and rhetoric, Jacobus Perizonius, UBL PER Q5, f4ʳ

many works by Lipsius's Antwerp publishers which were not listed in the catalogue either. It is therefore possible that Scaliger felt inclined to respond to the appeal made by Lipsius in *De Bibliothecis*, and as a 'prince of Verona' support the university of Leiden by bequeathing his books to the institution.

EXPANDING THE UNIVERSITY LIBRARY

193

At the end of 1607, Scaliger made the final decision. Perhaps sensing his impending demise, he was working at a furious pace on the transcription of several borrowed manuscripts, including a Persian lexicon.[40] He also organised his papers, and amended his will once again. He appointed Daniel Heinsius, who had succeeded Paullus Merula (1558–1607) as librarian of Leiden, as the administrator of his bequest, which stated that the university library would receive a selection of his Oriental books.[41] It is striking that Scaliger emphasised 'a selection' of his Oriental books; a year later, on 18 November 1608, he altered his will to state that he wished to include all his books in foreign languages in the bequest.

In both the Latin will signed by Scaliger on 25 July 1607 and the French will of 18 November 1608, Scaliger mentioned that his students Cornelis van der Myle, Daniel Heinsius, Franciscis Gomarus and Dominicus Baudius would be able to choose books in turn from his Latin books, 'which they can do until they have had enough'.[42] The remainder of the library would then be auctioned, with the

---

40   Scaliger expanded the Persian lexicon of Raphelengius with new information from his copy of the multilingual Pentateuch (Constantinople: 1546), UBL 839 A 7; see Bibliographic Survey Constantinople 1546. Scaliger finished the transcription on 30 September 1607; the manuscript is UBL MS Or. 2019. See: Vrolijk and Van Ommen. *All my Books* (2009), pp. 75–77. Two years earlier, Scaliger copied a Syriac lexicon: cf. *Correspondence* 13 October 1607 to Casaubon. This *Lexicon Syro-Arabicon, ex lexico Bar Aly Syro, et alio anonymo, tineis corroso, a nobis concinnatum et manu nostra descriptum* is UBL MS Or. 213. Vrolijk and Van Ommen, *All my Books*, pp. 46–49.

41   *Correspondence* 13 October 1607 to Casaubon: 'At my death I bequeath a selection of Oriental books to the library of this university, to be administered by Heinsius, given that Paullus Merula, the former librarian, died in Germany'. Merula had died on 20 July 1607 in Rostock. Scaliger would write about the amendments to his will in *Correspondence* 20 August 1607 to Hoeschelius.

42   From the Latin will of Scaliger, 1607: 'Nobilissimo viro Cornelio Mylio, huius Academiae curatori, item Heinsio, atque Baudio potestatem facio, quos velint libros de meis Graecis et Latinis eligere, ita ut post Mylium Heinsius, post Heinsium Baudius sequator.' Scaliger's students would mainly pick editions of classical authors, especially those with annotations by Scaliger. In the auction catalogue of the library of Nicolaas Heinsius, son of Daniel, one can identify some thirty books annotated by Scaliger, all picked by his father. One such book that was excluded from the auction was the copy of Canter's *Euripides* (Antwerp, 1571), which would exchange hands from Daniel Heinsius to Janus Rutgersius; it is now in the Bodleian, as Auct. S. 5.1. See *Bibliotheca Heinsiana sive Catalogus librorum Nicolaus Heinsius* (Lugd. Batav.: apud J. de Vivie, 1682; USTC 1818277). The theologian Franciscus Gomarus (1563–1641) also received a bundle of Chinese paper from Scaliger's estate, possibly blank sheets. See also: Henk Jan de Jonge, 'The Latin Testament of Scaliger, 1607', *Lias* II (1975) 2, pp. 249–263. I have thus far identified with certainty 128 books from Scaliger's library that were not listed in the auction catalogue of 1609. Many of these are now to be found in institutional libraries, such as a copy of Galenus, *Opera omnia ad fidem complurium & perquam uetustorum exemplarium ita emendata* (Basel:

194   CHAPTER 5

proceeds to go in their entirety to the heir of Scaliger's estate, his manservant Jonas Rousse.[43]

It does seem that Scaliger's will was not followed in every particular, possibly because of the subtle but critical changes made to the will in 1608. This meant that some Oriental books did end up in the auction of western Latin books. Similarly, not all Greek and Latin manuscripts, which were also part of the bequest, ended up in the university library: in the auction catalogue of Scaliger's student Janus Rutgersius (1589–1625) dated to 1630, there is a manuscript of the works of Archimedes with numerous annotations by Scaliger.[44]

5   The Auction Catalogue of 1609

The auction catalogue of the remains of the library of Scaliger was printed in Leiden in 1609 by Thomas Basson with the title *Catalogus librorum bibliothecae Illust. Viri Iosephi Scaligeri*.[45] The catalogue contained around 1,700 western

---

[par Andreas Cratander], 1538; USTC 602615). See: M.H.H. Engels, 'Galenus en andere medische werken in de Franeker academiebibliotheek' in J.J.M. Biemans (red.), *Boeken verzamelen. Opstellen aangeboden aan mr. J.R. de Groot bij zijn afscheid als bibliothecaris der Rijksuniversiteit te Leiden* (Leiden: Bibliotheek der Rijksuniversiteit, 1983), p. 139.

43   'Quant aux livres qui resteront apres les Sieurs Mylius, Heynsius, Baudius et autres miens amis [...] ie veux que Jonas Rousse les vende a l'encan, et que l'argent qui en proviendra de la vente, soit totalement a luy.' French Testament of 1608, UBL Codex Perizonii Q n 5, ff. 39–44; De Jonge, *Latin Testament* (1975) 2, pp. 249–263 and 'Testament de Joseph Scaliger [18 Novembro 1609 (sic!)]' in: A. Magen, *Documents sur Jules-César Scaliger et sa famille*. Agen 1875, pp. 75–81. The version in Magen has most likely been transcribed from the will present in the Scaliger family papers that ended up in the collections of the American Philosophical Society via the last surviving member of the family, Cécile Poizat († 1888). The transcription was carelessly done and contains many errors.

44   *Catalogus Bibliothecae Iani Rutgersii Dordraceni* (Leiden: ex officina Bonaventura Elzevier and Abraham I Elzevier, 1633; USTC 1510538), p. 118. According to the preface of the auction catalogue of his library, Rutgersius, one of Scaliger's favourite students, possessed many works with handwritten annotations by Scaliger. These were not always indicated as such in the catalogue, which makes it impossible for us to determine which books it concerns. My thanks to Professor P.G. Hoftijzer, who brought the manuscript of Archimedes in the Rutgersius catalogue to my attention.

45   Only four copies of the auction catalogue of 1609 have survived today. These copies can be found in the university library of Copenhagen (Collection Older, Cat. 79: 2, 39, vol. I (4)), the Bibliothèque nationale de France in Paris (Q 2261; ff. ²B3 and ²B4 are wanting), the Biblioteca Angelica in Rome (ZZ. 12.2/1) and in the Russian State Library in St Petersburg (Mk IV lat. 4°). The copies held by the Königliche Bibliothek Dresden and the university library of Kiel (which contained names of the buyers and prices paid) were both lost during the Second World War. There is a photocopy of the Kiel copy in the university library of Leiden under call number 20651 F 25. See: De Jonge, *Auction Catalogue*

EXPANDING THE UNIVERSITY LIBRARY

books; if we wish to have a complete figure of Scaliger's non-Oriental collection, we must add to this number some 300 books that had been chosen and retained by Scaliger's students before the auction. The likely size of Scaliger's library at the time of his death, excluding his manuscripts and Oriental works, was therefore some 2,000 titles.

The bookseller Louis Elzevier (1540–1617), pioneer of the auction of libraries in Leiden, was commissioned by Jonas Rousse to be the auction master of Scaliger's library. The auction took place in Elzevier's shop. According to the title page of the catalogue, the auction was held on 11 March 1609; most likely, it lasted several days. In the preface of the catalogue, it states that 'The auction of these books will begin on 11 March 1609 in Leiden, at the house of Louis Elzevier'.[46] We know for certain that the professor of mathematics, Rudolph Snellius (1546–1613), bought at the auction a copy of the *Cleomedis Meteora Graece et Latine*, and noted that he had purchased it on 12 March.[47]

The difference between Scaliger's books that were sold at auction and the books that were donated to Leiden in the bequest is obvious. The auction catalogue itself mentions that a part of Scaliger's library, his Oriental books and his Latin and Greek manuscripts, have been withheld from auction and have been gifted to the university library of Leiden. The preface also mentioned that Scaliger had given books to his friends, which were naturally also not part of the auction.[48]

What sort of books were listed in Scaliger's auction catalogue? There were 175 items which were highlighted with an asterisk, to indicate that these were *annotati*, books annotated with Scaliger's own handwritten reflections.[49] While

---

(1977). For a complete bibliographical description of the auction catalogue of 1609, see: Van Selm, *Menighte treffelijcke Boecken*, pp. 161–162; Alfons Willems, *Les Elzevier. Histoire et annales typographiques* (Bruxelles, G.A. van Trigt, 1880), p. lvii; Jan A. van Dorsten, *Thomas Basson 1555–1613. English Printer at Leiden* (Leiden: Universitaire Pers Leiden, 1961), Checklist no. 153.

46 'Dese Boecken salmen beginnen te vercoopen, op den 11. Martij 1609 tot Leyden, ten huyse van Loys Elzevier'.

47 According to the inscription on the title page, 'die 12 Martis MDCIX', on the copy of the *Cleomedis Meteora Graece et Latine* Bordeaux, apud Simonem Milangium, typographum regium, 1605, bought by Snellius at the auction. UBL 758 C 26. The book is listed in the auction catalogue at page 12.

48 The preface of the auction catalogue (at f. A1) mentions: 'Sciat Lector: Illustrissimum Virum Testamento legasse omnes suos libros Hebraicos, Syriacos, Arabicos & aliarum linguarum orientalium, itemque manuscriptos codices Graecos & Latinos, Bibliothecae Academiae Leidensis: praeter alios nonnullos libros quos amicis reliquit: quod hic admonendum duximus, ne maiorem librorum copiam desideres in hoc Catalogo.'

49 At f. A1v, the auction catalogue of 1609 mentions: '* Significat aliquid in eisdem libris ab Illustrissimo Scaligero notatum esse.'

CATALOGVS

LIBRORVM

BIBLIOTHECAE
Illuſt. Viri
IOSEPHI SCALIGERI
IVL. CÆS. F.

Quorum auctio habebitur in ædibus
LVDOVICI ELZEVIRII, bibliopol.

Lugd. Bat. ad diem 11. Martÿ.

LVGDVNI BATAVORVM,
Ex Officina THOMÆ BASSON, 1609.

FIGURE 29   Title page of the *Catalogus librorum Bibliothecae Illustr. Viri Iosephi Scaligeri.* Leiden 1609. University library of Copenhagen, Collection Older, Cat. 79: 2, 39, vol. I (4)

CLEOMEDIS
METEORA GRÆCE
ET LATINE.

A

ROBERTO BALFOREO EX MS. CODICE
Bibliothecæ Illustrißimi CARDINALIS IOYOSII
multis mendis repurgata, Latinè versa, & per-
petuo commentario illustrata.

AD

Clariss. & ornatiss. virum GVILIELMVM DAFISIVM
equitem, principem Præsidem Senatus Burdig.
& sacri consistorij Consiliarium.

BVRDIGALÆ,
Apud SIMONEM MILANGIVM Typographum Regium. 1605.

*Sum Rodolphi Snellii Veter-aguinatis
emptus e bibliotheca Scaligeri die
12 Martii 1609.*

FIGURE 30 Title page of *Cleomedis Meteora Graece et Latine* (Bordeaux: Simon Millanges, 1605). According to an inscription by Rudolph Snellius on this copy, the auction of Scaliger's books lasted at least until 12 March 1609. UBL 758 C 26

the presence of these items mark out the collection as that of a distinguished scholar, the remainder of the sale does not represent a distinctive collection; many of the books sold at the auction would have been found in other professional libraries of the era.[50] The auction catalogue was printed in a quarto format, the common format for catalogues from this period; the organisation of the content is similarly inspired by other catalogues. The books were arranged by discipline, according to the traditional order of the academic faculties, and within the disciplines the books were listed by format. The theological books in folio came first, followed by the other theological works in decreasing order of size. The following disciplines were jurisprudence, medicine, philosophy, mathematics and history. Then Scaliger's classical-philological works followed, as well as editions of classical authors. At the end, books in vernacular languages were listed, as well as unbound books, followed by Scaliger's globes, maps, astronomical instruments and his writing table. Finally, the catalogue listed books sold by Louis Elzevier at the same auction that had been gathered from other libraries, and had no relation to Scaliger's library.[51] According to De Jonge, the total number of titles sold at the auction was 1,706 copies; Van Selm arrived at a different calculation, by describing them as 1,383 lots.[52] This makes it clear that many titles were bound together, and could thus not be sold separately.

In De Jonge's overview, we can note a substantial number of books in the fields of history and classics (table 2). Together, these two disciplines make up almost two-thirds of Scaliger's library. Books in Latin and Greek, as one would expect in a scholarly library, are present in far greater numbers than books in vernacular languages. There were 85 books (6%) sold at the auction that were printed in French, Scaliger's native tongue. The remaining 86 books in vernacular languages were made up of Spanish, Italian, Dutch, German and English titles.[53] While the Oriental books were bequeathed to the university library of Leiden and therefore not part of the auction, it is striking that the auction catalogue contained some items which one would judge to belong to the Oriental bequest, such as various books in Armenian, listed at the end of the catalogue.

---

50   For broader characterisations of Dutch auction catalogues from the seventeenth century, see Van Selm, *Menighte treffelijcke Boecken*, chapter 2.

51   This is justified in the catalogue as follows: 'Libri qui in Appendice continentur, pro materiae ratione, inter Catalogi praecipui Libros vendentur opportuné'.

52   Van Selm, *Menighte treffelijcke Boecken*, p. 115 (table 2). On page 161 of his work, Van Selm mentions that the catalogue contains a total of 1,801 lots of books, thus including 407 lots of books that were not originally part of Scaliger's library; the remaining 11 lots concerned globes and other items. Van Selm counted the catalogue in lots in order to make comparisons with other catalogues from the period; a lot can often of course be comprised of more than one book.

53   Van Selm, *Menighte treffelijcke Boecken*, p. 115 (table 2).

EXPANDING THE UNIVERSITY LIBRARY

TABLE 2   Overview of the auction of Scaliger's books by discipline, as categorised by
           H.J. de Jonge. Scaliger's library contained many historical and philological books;
           we gain a similar impression from his Oriental bequest.

Theologici	187
Juridici	41
Medici et Philosophi	147
Mathematici	83
Historici, chronologici, geografici	315
Oratores, Philologi, etc.	311
Poetae et Poetici	448[a]
Libri Linguarum Vulgarium	174
Total[b]	**1,706**

a   It is likely that this figure is incorrect, as when I counted the items in this category, I arrived
    at 241 bound books and 41 unbound books.
b   De Jonge, *The Auction Catalogue of the Library of J.J. Scaliger*, p. 4.

The auction catalogue nevertheless provides us with a rich source of information on Scaliger's library. If we consider Scaliger's works in Latin, which make up almost 80% of the catalogue, and divide them amongst the four traditional faculties, then it is clear that the humanities (the works by classical authors, poets, rhetoricians, philologists and historians) comprise the largest group. The sections of medical, philosophical, mathematical and juridical books are smaller, but not insignificant. It is worth recalling that Scaliger was appointed by Leiden to study the history of the Latin language, the classics and the history of antiquity, which explains why his collection was so strong in the arts, and why his collection of theological works was smaller than that of many contemporaries. Scaliger used his theological books primarily as source material and as reference works for his chronological calculations.

The books listed in the catalogue as *annotati* belong to a special category, one in which many attendees at the auction expressed interest. A later generation of scholars was also deeply interested in these items, as is clear from the efforts that scholars such as Isaac Vossius and Nicolaas Heinsius made to collect Scaliger's annotated books.[54] The university library of Leiden only

---

54   According to Frans Felix Blok, *Contributions to the History of Isaacs Vossius Library* (Amsterdam: North-Holland Publishing Company, 1974), p. 24, in 1656 Vossius owned around 24 books annotated by Scaliger; Blok also asserts (erroneously) that Nicolaas Heinsius had more than 200 books annotated by Scaliger, a substantial portion of the 13,000 books owned by Heinsius was sold at auction in 1683, see Blok, *Nicolaas Heinsius in dienst van Christina van Zweden* (Delft: Ursulapers, 1949), p. 125. The actual number of

acquired ten annotated books from Scaliger's auction.[55] It would acquire more when Daniel Heinsius, as librarian of the university, was able to purchase several additional *annotati* with the help from the diplomat-scholar David le Leu de Wilhem (1588–1658).[56]

The quality of the descriptions of the auction catalogue of 1609 is not particularly high. Most items are only described with a short title and the name of the author, and sometimes the place and year of publication; editors of texts are occasionally named as well. The brevity of the description makes the identification of specific texts and editions complicated. It has proved impossible to identify with certainty some items, while for others the text can clearly be identified, but not a particular edition. The same complications appear when identifying items from the list of Oriental books in Scaliger's bequest. The languages in which these books were written were clearly a stumbling block for the librarians and cataloguers of the university library in the seventeenth and eighteenth centuries, and they often failed to provide an accurate title description.

If we divide the titles in the auction catalogue by date of publication before and after 1593, the year Scaliger came to Leiden, then the results appear as follows:

> Before 1593:   872 titles
> 1593–1609:   844 titles

This division indicates which titles we can identify with certainty that were acquired by Scaliger once he arrived in Leiden. Sadly we cannot determine which of the 872 titles printed before 1593 were already present in Scaliger's

---

Scaliger *annotati* in the collection numbered 112 items: see E.J. van der Linde, 'Bibliotheca Heinsiana', *Het Boek* 11 (1922), pp. 286–287 and John A. Sibbald, 'The Heinsiana – Almost a Seventeenth-Century Universal Short Title Catalogue', in Walsby and Constantinidou, *Documenting the Early Modern Book World* (Leiden, Boston Brill, 2013), pp. 141–159. Some of Scaliger's works came in Heinsius's hands from the collection of his father, Daniel Heinsius. Some of the Scaliger *annotati* sold at the auction of Nicolaas Heinsius's books found their way to the Bodleian. See: W.M. Lindsay, 'Books (containing marginalia) of the Bibl. Heinsiana, now in the Bodleian', *Centralblatt für Bibliothekwesen* 18 (1901), pp. 159–163.

55   See the annotated copy of the auction catalogue by Petrus Scriverius that belonged to the university library of Kiel, but was lost in the Second World War; a photocopy of this copy is held in Leiden under call number UBL 20651 F 25.

56   Letter from André Rivet to David le Leu de Wilhem dated to 12 February 1631, UBL BPL 293. A transcription of this letter is found in H.J. Honders, *Andreas Rivetus als invloedrijk gereformeerd theoloog in Hollands bloeitijd* ('s-Gravenhage: Martinus Nijhoff, 1930), pp. 180–181. My thanks to Forrest Strickland for this reference.

EXPANDING THE UNIVERSITY LIBRARY

library in France, and which he bought in Leiden. Some of the pre-1593 books, like the works of Lipsius that Scaliger discussed in his correspondence, were definitely brought over from France. Altogether, we may estimate that at minimum, Scaliger doubled the size of his collection in the last sixteen years of his life in Leiden, through acquisitions as well as gifts from friends, students and correspondents.

6   Scaliger's Oriental Bequest

Scaliger's bequest to Leiden is mentioned in two of his wills, the updated French will, and the earlier Latin will. In the French will the bequest is discussed as follows:

> Concerning the library, which I leave well-furnished despite my limited resources, I bequeath to the Academy of this city of Leiden all my books in foreign languages, in Hebrew, Syriac, Arabic [and] Amharic, which books are listed in the Catalogue which I have added to the Latin copy of this will, and which I intend to be a part or appendix of my will, or to be used as a supplement by way of a codicil.[57]

In his Latin will, Scaliger also mentioned that 'all his Hebrew, Syriac, Arabic and other books in Oriental languages' would be bequeathed to the 'famous academy of Leiden'.[58] In the Latin will, Scaliger also mentioned that his Latin and Greek manuscripts would be donated to Leiden, a fact that was not recorded in the French will; this makes it likely that the executors of the will relied largely on the Latin version rather than on the French will.[59]

Several sources provide use with insights into the composition of Scaliger's bequest. During his life, Scaliger made an index of his Oriental books and

---

57   According to the transcript of the French will in UBL Codex Perizonii Q n. 5, ff. 39–44. 'Touchant la bibliotheque, laquelle selon mes petites facultez ie laisse bien fornie, ie legue a l'Academi de cette ville de Leyden tous mes livres de langues estrangeres, Hebraics, Syriens, Arabics, Aethiopiens, lesquels livres sont contenus dans le Catalogue que i'ay adiousté a la copie latine de ce mien testament, et que i'entens estre une partie ou appendence de mon dict testament, ou servir de supplement en façon de codicile.'

58   BnF, Ms Dupuy 395, ff. 182^r–189^r (also in BnF Ms Dupuy 663, ff. 5^r–8^r); De Jonge, *Latin Testament*, no. 2, p. 258. 'De bibliotheca autem, quam pro ratione facultatem satis instructam relinquo, omnes libros Hebraicos, Syriacos, Arabicos, et aliarum orientalium linguarium huic inclitae Lugdunensi Academiae do lego.'

59   De Jonge, *Latin Testament*, p. 260, note 19.

included this in a codicil. Soon after his death, Bonaventura Vulcanius also made a list of Scaliger's books, and Daniel Heinsius would follow later by compiling a new catalogue for the university library, which included Scaliger's bequest. How were these three catalogues composed, and how do they compare to one another?

Heinsius compiled the *Catalogus librorum quos Bibliothecae Iosephus Scaliger legavit* using the codicil attached to Scaliger's will. This catalogue was included in the university library catalogue of 1612, published to replace the outdated 1595 *Nomenclator*.[60] That Heinsius used the codicil is clear from a later incident. In 1615, he was reprimanded by the curators of the library for overspending the library's acquisitions budget. He was also expressly urged to produce a new catalogue to replace the one published in 1612, as this was already considered to be obsolete.[61] The resolutions that record this discussion also mention that a part of the catalogue of 1612 was based on a will, by which the curators could only have meant Scaliger's codicil.

After the publication of the catalogue of 1612, Scaliger's codicil was still in the hands of Heinsius until at least May 1615.[62] It is possible that Heinsius never handed the codicil over to the curators, as they requested; what is certain, is that the codicil was lost in the following years, and never resurfaced.[63] It is highly likely that Heinsius literally transcribed Scaliger's codicil for the 1612 catalogue: he did not have sufficient linguistic skill to alter or expand the descriptions of many of the Oriental works, and he does not seem to have consulted other scholars for assistance. If the descriptions by Heinsius were indeed faithful to the codicil, then it is striking that Scaliger's own list was also rather brief and incomplete. While Scaliger had indicated that he wished to bequeath 'all his books' in Oriental languages, the executors of his bequest were still relied upon to make the decision what this term included. Naturally, many of the Oriental books were easily identifiable because of their exotic scripts, but there were many items in Scaliger's library which contained a mix of western and Oriental

---

60   [Daniel Heinsius], *Catalogus librorum Bibliothecae Lugdunensis. Praefixa est Danielis Heinsii Bibliothecarii oratio* (Leiden: s.n., 1612), p. 78 (USTC 1016035) onwards. 'Catalogus librorum quos Bibliothecae Iosephus Scaligeri legavit'. This catalogue describes the Oriental books and manuscripts as well as the 40 Greek and Latin manuscripts from the bequest.

61   Resolutions of the curators of 7/8 May 1615 in: Molhuysen *Bronnen* II (1916), p. 59: 'Is vorder den voors. D. Heynsio gelastet in handen van C.[uratoren] ende B.[urgemeesters] te leveren het testament *metten Catalogus der boecken* (mijn cursivering) aan de Universiteit by den Heer Josepho Scaligero sa[liger] gemaect om t' allen tijde den selven te mogen confereren jegens de casse der Bibliotheecque'.

62   According to Molhuysen, *Bronnen* II, p. 59.

63   De Jonge, *Auction Catalogue* (1977), p. 3.

scripts; such books were not all included in the bequest, and some ended up in the auction catalogue. We can probably blame the ambiguity of Scaliger's own codicil partially on this, but the fact that the codicil does not survive is a real lacuna. Happily, we can also rely on the catalogue that Vulcanius composed, which we will delve into in the following chapter.

As far as we know, Scaliger did not make any other catalogues of his library during his time in Leiden. While we cannot be certain that Scaliger wrote the codicil himself, it does seem very likely. Scaliger adored his library, and prided himself on the care that he lavished on his 'children'. His anxiety during the move of his books from the Breestraat to his new lodgings on the Kerkgracht was telling. His fear of losing books sometimes spiralled into pure panic. Sadly, some unscrupulous individuals took advantage of Scaliger's emotional attachment to his library. On one unfortunate occasion, a servant of Scaliger's stole his annotated edition of Plautus, which Scaliger only received back half a year later after payment of a substantial ransom fee.[64]

Scaliger's bequest bestowed considerably more distinction upon the university library of Leiden in the early seventeenth century, and the bequest was consequently treated with great respect by the university, and especially by its librarian, Daniel Heinsius.[65] Heinsius idolised Scaliger. His admiration for the deceased scholar can be traced in several texts and poems written by Heinsius, which have all contributed to the mythmaking around Scaliger's life and career. Heinsius received permission from the university to have a bespoke bookcase made in which Scaliger's bequest could be housed.[66] This case would be baptised as the *Arca Scaligerana*, and it would ensure that Scaliger's bequest would always have an appropriate place in the university library.[67]

---

64   *Correspondence* 4 August 1602 to Dupuy; Ann M. Blair, *Too much to Know. Managing Scholarly Information before the Modern Age* (New Haven, London: Yale University Press, 2010), pp. 107, 114, for a reference to Tamizey de Larroque, *Lettres françaises inédites*, p. 341.

65   In the *Illustrium Hollandiae Westfrisiae ordinum alma Academia Leidensis* (Leiden: apud Jacob Marcus and Joost van Colster, 1614; USTC 1028260), Johannes Meursius described the division of Scaliger's books on page 189 as follows: 'Nullus vero extat auctor, sive Graecus sive Latinus, in quem non plurima notarat, quae partim in librorum suorum marginibus, qui in auctione sunt distracti; partim in Gallia in amicorum libris notaverat. Partim vero ex legato ejus Bibliotheca publica Lugduno-Batava adhuc servat.'

66   Resolutions of the curators of 8/10 February 1609: 'Heinsius is hereby expressly authorised to have a case constructed for the library and to place in the case the aforementioned books, and that the same Heinsius will deliver to the curators and burgomasters two copies of the aforementioned catalogue or inventory to be kept amongst the papers and charters of the curators and burgomasters.' In: Molhuysen I, p. 183. This catalogue of inventory cannot be traced in the archive of the university.

67   For example, Heinsius's praise of Scaliger's extensive knowledge of languages can be found in his history on the murder of Prince William of Orange, *Auriacus, Sive Libertas Saucia*.

204   CHAPTER 5

Scholars have long agreed that the acquisition of Scaliger's bequest of Oriental books and manuscripts was an enormous gain for the academy of Leiden, and for the development of scholarship at the institution.[68] The value of the manuscripts was traditionally emphasised, while the printed Oriental books were often neglected. This perspective has been remedied somewhat in recent years.[69] What remains clear is that Scaliger's bequest played a major role in bolstering the international renown of Leiden; travellers from all over Europe visited the Leiden library, if only to see the famous *Arca Scaligerana*.[70]

7   Heinsius and the *Arca Scaligerana*

In May 1609, not yet four months after Scaliger's death, the *Arca*, containing his Oriental books, was placed in the library room. Scaliger had given no instructions in his will on how his books would be used or displayed in the university library, so we can presume that the construction and design of the *Arca* was largely the initiative of Heinsius, the self-appointed protector of Scaliger's intellectual legacy. It was probably Heinsius who came up with the term *Arca Scaligerana*, possibly inspired by the satires of Horace. In the first decade of the seventeenth century, Heinsius worked on an edition of Horace, which would appear in 1612 with Elzevier. In the first satire, there is a passage that is reminiscent of the final years of Scaliger's life. Scaliger became the target of various Jesuit writers, who taunted and criticised him for his presumed noble descent from the Della Scala family of Verona, as described by Scaliger in his *Epistola de vetustate et splendore gentis Scaligerae* of 1594. At the same time, this period of Scaliger's life was one in which he had become more famous than ever, and the one in which he decided to leave his bequest to Leiden. Horace's passage is as follows: 'Populus me sibilat, at mihi plaudo. Ipse domi simul ac nummos contemplar in arca'. An approximate translation would be: 'The people taunt me, but I cheer myself at home while I count the money in my (treasure) chest'. From the *arca* described in Horace's passage, Heinsius conceived of a case to contain the worldly treasures handed down by Scaliger, and to secure his scholarly reputation for the future. As a final gesture to those who might taunt Scaliger for his presumed descent, Heinsius had the coat of

---

Andreas Clouck, Leiden 1602, and in an epigram in *In Iosephi Scaligeri* in: [J. Meursius], *Illustris Academia Lugd-Batava: id est Virorum clarissimorum icones, elogia ac vitae, qui eam scriptis suis illustrarunt* (Leiden: apud Andries Clouck, 1613), p. xii (USTC 1028467).

68   Cf. Juynboll, *Zeventiende-eeuwsche beoefenaars*, p. 49.

69   Vrolijk and Van Ommen, *All my Books* 2009.

70   Elfriede Hulshoff Pol, 'What about the library? Travellers' comments on the Leiden Library in the 17th and 18th centuries', *Quaerendo* 5 (1975), pp. 39–51.

EXPANDING THE UNIVERSITY LIBRARY

arms of the Della Scalas affixed to the front door of the *Arca*, as it had been placed on Scaliger's grave in the Vrouwekerk.[71]

There are clear similarities between the *Arca* in the library and Scaliger's grave in Leiden. The *Arca Scaligerana* also has the same symbolic value as the *Arche Scaligere*, the mediaeval tomb of the Della Scalas in Verona.[72] As in Verona, the *Arca Scaligerana* in Leiden functioned as a site of memorial, the physical embodiment of the glory of the Della Scala family. The critical difference was that it contained the intellectual remains of Scaliger, rather than his physical corpse.

The university also made other efforts to commemorate Scaliger. It commissioned a marble epitaph for his grave in the Vrouwekerk, so that every visitor to the city and the university had the chance to reflect on Scaliger's legacy. The epitaph commemorates Scaliger's academic achievements and his noble descent, which added even more lustre to the city of Leiden. The epitaph was placed on a pillar near Scaliger's grave in the Vrouwekerk.[73] An engraved depiction of the epitaph was added as an appendix to the printed edition of Heinsius's funeral oration for Scaliger.[74] The text of the oration ends with the instruction: 'See here the depictions of the monuments of the Scaligers in Verona', followed by three engravings of the Gothic tombs of members of the Della Scalas in Verona.[75] Here, once again, the allusion was forcefully made between the tombs in Verona and the *Arca* in Leiden.[76] The engravings depict

---

71 A notarial description from 1688 still described the coat of arms on the grave; it was later removed. See: ELO Leiden, NA 1086, no. 21 [14-4-1688]; Ekkart, 'Het grafmonument van Scaliger, pp. 81–90.

72 The style and use of language of the graves in Leiden and Verona do differ considerably. See for a description of the tombs in Verona: E. Cheney, *The Tombs of the Scaligers in Verona*, included as an appendix in *Venice and the Veneto during the Renaissance. The Legacy of Benjamin Kohl*. Ed. by M. Knapton (et al.) (Firenze: Firenze University Press, 2014), pp. 451–457.

73 For a description of the epitaph and the grave stone: Stefanie A. Knöll, *Creating Academic Communities. Funeral Monuments to Professors at Oxford, Leiden and Tübingen* (Oss: Equilibris, 2003), pp. 413–416. Knöll ascribes the current design of Scaliger's epitaph in the Pieterskerk to Hendrick de Keyser. This is incorrect, as this epitaph is a nineteenth-century copy of the original.

74 See the copy of the oration at UBL 568 C 23. Copies of the oration are also known in which the engravings have been printed separately and were later bound into the copy. See for example the copy on 'large paper' at: UBL 1011 C 14.

75 'Hic monumenta Scaligerorum Veronesa inserantur'.

76 The tombs that are depicted are those of Cangrande I (1291–1329), Mastino II (1308–1351) and Cansignorio (1340–1375). The Gothic tomb of Cansignorio della Scala is the most opulent of the three; he was the ruler of Verona from 1359 to 1375. This monument embodies the ultimate glorification of the Della Scala dynasty.

206   CHAPTER 5

a tomb with a *gisant*, a sculpted figure of the deceased, lying under a canopy. An equestrian figure stands at the top of the tomb.[77]

Throughout his life, Scaliger had emphasised his noble descent, largely a ploy to improve his status in the Republic of Letters and to strengthen his reputation amongst potential patrons and employers. Towards the end of his life, protecting this status became even more important to Scaliger. In 1604, thanks to the intervention of Federicus Cerutus (1541–1611), he came into contact with Cesare Nichezzola, a childhood friend of his father in Verona. Nichezzola assisted Scaliger with gathering information on his family to establish the Scaliger-Della Scala connection.[78] Nichezzola provided Scaliger with drawings of the tombs of his presumed ancestors, which Scaliger used for the publication of his *Confutatio*, a retort to Caspar Schoppe's *Scaliger Hypobolimaeus*, a well-researched (and factually accurate) demolition of Scaliger's claim to the ancestry of the Della Scalas.[79] Schoppe (1576–1649) argued that Scaliger's family history was in fact a carefully spun web of lies, building on false pretences first conceived of by Scaliger's father. The careful drawings provided by Nichezzola have sadly been lost since they were used as the model for the engravings.

In Heinsius's funeral oration for Scaliger, he appealed to Scaliger's noble descent, but also his status as a hero. This was a rhetorical device that had been used earlier by Heinsius, the loyal disciple of Scaliger. The whole text of the oration is largely a continuation of two previous works, Heinsius's own *Hercules tuam fidem sive Munsterus hypobolimaeus* of 1608 and Scaliger's *Confutatio*, which was included in the second edition of Heinsius's *Hercules*, also published in 1608.[80] The comparison between the mythical Hercules

---

77   Gian Maria Varanini (ed.), *Gli Scaligeri 1277–1387. Saggi e schede pubblicati in occasione della mostra storico-documentaria allestita dal Museo di Castelvecchio di Verona, giugno-novembre 1988* (Verona: A. Mondadori, 1988). These tombs, and those of six other members of the family, are located in front of the private chapel of the Della Scalas, in the Romanesque church of Santa Maria Antica in Verona.

78   *Correspondence* 25 February 1604 from Pereisc. A second set of drawings were also made, which remained in Verona for some time, but they were ultimately sent to Pereisc in May 1606, who forwarded them on to Scaliger. See also *Correspondence* 30 May 1606 to Labbaeus and 25 February 1604 from Peiresc. These drawings have presumably also been lost.

79   Daniel Heinsius & Josephus Justus Scaliger, *Hercules tuam fidem sive Munsterus hypobolimaeus. Id est, satyra Menippea de vita, origine, et moribus Gasperis Scioppii Franci. Accessit huic accurata Fabulae Burdoniae confutatio* (Leiden: ex officina Jan Paets Jacobszoon, 1608; USTC 1016133). This publication, the last produced by Scaliger, also failed to convince that his family were descendants from the Della Scala's.

80   Baudius also compared Scaliger to Hercules, 'who destroyed the monstrous Hydra', referring to Scaliger's enemies amongst the Jesuits, and especially Caspar Schoppe. Cf.

FIGURE 31   Depictions of Scaliger's epitaph and of one of the tombs of the Della Scalas in Verona. UBL 116 B 15 and UBL 1011 C 14

and Scaliger was designed to underscore Scaliger's princely descent: Heinsius defended Scaliger's interests, fulfilled his wishes and was deeply involved in the protection of his honour.[81] Heinsius considered Scaliger's bequest and the *Arca* as powerful tools with which to combat Scaliger's enemies and to ward off attacks on his mentor's legacy. The scholarly use of Scaliger's books by other professors at the university – as Scaliger instructed in his will – were clearly of lesser importance in Heinsius's vision.

    Domenicus Baudius, *Oratio funebris dicta honori & memoriae maximi virorum Iosephi Iusti Scaligeri* (Leiden: apud Lowijs I Elzevier and Andries Clouck, 1609, p. 13; USTC 1012898) Cf. Willems, *Les Elzevier*, no. 53.

81 The kings of France always supported the claims to noble descent by the Scaliger family. Jacques-Auguste de Thou called Scaliger Sr. 'Julius Caesar, Filius Benedicti Veronensium principis' (Julius Caesar, son of Benedictus, prince of Verona).

8   The Placement of the *Arca Scaligerana* in Leiden University Library

The first mention of the Leiden *Arca*, without the addition of *Scaligerana*, can be traced to an engraving of the university library by Willem van Swanenburgh, after a drawing by Jan Cornelis Woudanus from 1610. The heading of the engraving reads: 'Bibliothecae Lugduno-Batavae cum pulpitis et arcis vera ixnographia' ('The library of Leiden faithfully depicted with its bookcases and arca'). The depiction shows Scaliger's ark in the right foreground, where it dominates the eye of the viewer because of the large size of the bookcase and the ornamentation on the front doors. Undoubtedly, contemporaries would have immediately identified the bookcase as the home of Scaliger's bequest. While the *Arca* was a novelty in Leiden, the form of book storage was inspired by ancient Roman and mediaeval precedents. From the sixth to the thirteenth centuries, it was the norm to store valuable manuscripts in a closed case or chest, commonly known as an *armarium*.[82]

The arrangement of the Woudanus print guides the eye towards the rear of the library room, where two life-sized portraits hang, depicting the founder of the university, William of Orange, and his son Maurice. On either side of the portraits stand two locked cabinets. These were used specifically for the safeguarding of manuscripts and books in small formats. Nevertheless, the most prominent element of the entire image remains in the right foreground: not only because of the lively discussions taking place between two pairs of figures, but because of the sizeable decorated cabinet.[83] It may not be a coincidence that the artist wished to draw the viewer's attention so forcefully to one of the most important parts of the library's collection, the *Arca Scaligerana*.

The left door of the cabinet reads LEGATUM IOSEPHI SCALIGERI, while the right door bears the coat of arms of the Della Scala's. On top of the cabinet are two globes, protected by dustsheets, which Scaliger had also bequeathed to the library.[84] What we cannot see in the engraving is the portrait of Scaliger that

---

82   John Willis Clark, *The Care of Books. An Essay on the Development of Libraries and their Fittings, from the Earliest Times to the End of the Eighteenth Century* (Cambridge: Cambridge University Press, 1902; repr. 2009), pp. 40–43. Clark supposes that similar cases were in use in Roman times, and points to a variety of sources to support that supposition, including the writings of Pliny the Younger.

83   The library room is depicted from the perspective of the entrance, so the *Arca* stood to the right of the entrance.

84   Scaliger's pair of geographical and celestial globes was made by Willem Jansz Blaeu in 1602. They have a diameter of ca. 28–30 centimetres. According to Du Rieu, *Portretten en testament*, they were removed from the storage cellars of the university library at the Rapenburg in 1868 and transferred to the Leiden Observatory, from which they later disappeared. See: Friedrich Kaiser (ed.), *Annalen der Sternwarte in Leiden* II ('s-Gravenhage:

FIGURE 32　Proof of the engraving of the university library (1610), with in the right foreground the *Arca Scaligerana*. The texts that adorned the front of the *Arca* had not yet been cut into the plate. Rijksprentenkabinet Amsterdam: RP-P-1895-A-18679

hung in a gilded frame above the *Arca*.[85] In this portrait, donated by Scaliger to the library, the scholar is depicted with a golden chain around his neck, which he received on 25 June 1594 from the States General as thanks for his

Martinus Nijhoff, 1870), p. 5; P.J.H. Baudet, *Leven en werken van Willem Janszoon Blaeu* (Utrecht: Van der Post, 1871), pp. 40, 150. For some examples of early seventeenth-century globes, see: Peter van der Krogt, *Globi Neerlandici. The Production of Globes in the Low Countries* (Utrecht: HES, 1993), pp. 501–505; Sylvia Sumira, *Globes: 400 Years of Exploration, Navigation, and Power* (Chicago: The University of Chicago Press, 2014, pp. 54–59.

85　The portrait was made by Daniel Hagiensis, probably Daniël van den Queborn (ca. 1552–ca. 1602), the court painter of Prince Maurice, originally from Antwerp. The desire to decorate the walls of the library with painted and engraved portraits of scholars was promoted by Merula in his memorandum to the curators of the library around 1597–1602. See the loose pages at UBL AC 41, published by E. Hulshoff Pol as Appendix B to the article 'The Library' in: *Leiden University* (1975), pp. 446–448. See also Van Royen, *Schriftelijk rapport 1741*, p. 16: Commission for the painting of portraits of Dousa senior and junior, Lipsius, Johannes Heurnius and Franciscus Junius (and also Janus Secundus and Erasmus) 'as well

210 CHAPTER 5

presentation of the *De emendatione temporum* to their High Mightinesses.[86] The portrait was a carefully judged gift on Scaliger's part: together with the bequest, it turned an entire section of the library into a reverential shrine to the esteemed professor.[87]

9 The Legacy of Scaliger's Bequest

For the first twenty years after his death, Scaliger's bequest would remain virtually untouched. In contrast to the lively depiction by Woudanus, in 1610 the library was closed to students, while many professors and visitors were also kept out of the library by Heinsius. Only after the death of Heinsius in 1655 were the regulations somewhat relaxed, and the *Arca Scaligerana* became available for scholarly consultation. Antonius Thysius Junior, who succeeded Heinsius as librarian until 1665, cultivated a more welcoming atmosphere in the library and made its collections more accessible. His successor, Johannes Fredericus Gronovius played a prominent part in expanding the Oriental collections of the library. A highlight of his tenure was the acquisition of the *Legatum Warnerianum*, the first part of which arrived in the library in December 1668.[88]

The *Arca Scaligerana* may have represented one of the earliest instances of a university community fostering a commemorative cult for one of its professors, but the enthusiasm and deference with which it was initiated soon dissipated. After the university library was offered the Oriental bequest of Levinus Warner (ca. 1618–1665), its curators considered Scaliger's bequest less valuable.

---

as the portrait of the Lord Scaliger, placed in a gilded frame like those of the other gentlemen, to hang this with his cabinet of manuscripts.' Blainville notes in his *Travels through Holland, Germany, Switzerland: and other parts of Europe; but especially Italy*. London, 1743–1745: Vol. I, pp. 21–22: 'Its Library, tho' inferior to many others in Europe, is however very considerable, having been augmented at different times by the private libraries of several learned Professors, and amongst others by that of the celebrated Joseph Scaliger. ... A portrait of him is carefully preserved in the public library.' This sadly does not indicate whether the portrait was still hanging above the *Arca*.

86 Ekkart, *Icones Leidenses* no. 30. In his will of 18 November 1608, Scaliger bequeathed to the library one of the two portraits of himself painted by 'Daniel le Peintre, corrigée par Everard', which were kept rolled ('effigies roollées') in a chest.

87 Ekkart, *Icones Leidenses*, no. 30. The gift was a chain worth 1,000 guilders, as well as a medal commemorating the relief of Coevoerden and the siege of Groningen. See: George Sanders, *Het present van Staat. De gouden ketens, kettingen en medailles verleend door de Staten-Generaal, 1588–1795* (Hilversum: Verloren, 2013), pp. 34, 36

88 Drewes, *Levinus Warner and his Legacy*; Henricus Johannes Witkam, 'Johannes van Hell en het Legatum Warnerianum' in *Dagelijkse Zaken van de Leidse Universiteit van 1581 tot 1596*, vol. 6, vol. 2 (Leiden: H.J. Witkam, 1973), pp. 1–10.

EXPANDING THE UNIVERSITY LIBRARY

It is also possible that the neglect of Scaliger's collection was influenced by the attack on the cult of Scaliger that Daniel Heinsius had promoted. By the end of the seventeenth century, there was increasing criticism of Scaliger, even if his overall reputation as a polymath scholar and linguistic expert remained unchallenged.[89] In this transition, the role of Scaliger's *Arca* also changed: as it was surpassed in size and quality by the *Legatum Warnerianum*, it was the Warner bequest that became the symbolic centre of the university library's Oriental collections. Scaliger's bequest was simply regarded as part of this broader collection, even if by 1716 it was not yet subsumed and taken out of the actual *Arca*. Scaliger's bequest was also diminished in status because of the Oriental books acquired for the university library by Jacobus Golius (1596–1667), who had toured the Levant for several years in the 1620s.[90]

In 1729, Albert Schultens (1686–1750) was appointed as the first curator of the entire Oriental collections at Leiden, which was revealingly referred to as the *Interpres Legati Warneriani*. From 1732 onwards, Schultens combined this function with that of professor of Arabic, a coupling of roles that would continue until the twentieth century.[91] Schultens regarded all the various

89   Urbain Chevreau (1613–1701) wrote as follows in his *Chevraeana* of 1697, p. 87: 'Joseph Scaliger a été le plus savant des Anciens et des Modernes, parce qu'il sçavoit generalement plus de choses que n'en ont sçû les uns et les autres. ... Cependant son coeur ne répondoit pas bien à son esprit, et il n'a jamais épargné personne dans son dégoût ou dans son chagrin.' See also: Jean-Marc Chatelain, *La bibliothèque de l'honnête homme. Livres, lecture et collections en France à l'âge classique* (Paris: Bibliothèque nationale de France, 2003), pp. 19–28.

90   Johann Burkhard Mencke, *Das Holländische Journal 1698–1699*. Herausgegeben mit einer Einleitung von Hubert Laeven (Hildesheim, Zürich, New York: Georg Olms Verlag, 2005), ff. 56ʳ–56ᵛ: 'Wir ließen uns von dar auf die daneben stehende Bibliothecam Publicam führen. Dies ist wol ohne Streit die größte unter denen Holländischen Public-Bibliotheken. Maßen sie sowol ex Warneri et Scaligeri legato ein großes Ornamentum bekommen, alß auch durch des gelehrten Golii Fürsorge an MSptis Arabicis einen trefflichen Schatz bekommen. Die rarsten und vortrefflichsten Bücher aber sind endlich ex Bibliotheca Vossii dazu gekommen, welche von der Universiteit vor einiger Zeit vor 30.000 Gulden erkaufft worden. Denn so hörten wir von dem Hn. Prof. Noodt, und der damalß gleich Magnificus Academiae Rector war. ... Er rühmte auch vornehmlich die Gelehrsamkeit des Golii, welcher selbst viel MSpta aus dem Orient mitgebracht und in sein Studiis zu seiner Zeit so berühmt gewesen, daß der König in Spanien einige Brieffe, die er von dem König von Fez und Marocco erhalten, an ihn gesendet, die er auch glücklich transferiret.' Mencke (1674–1732) was clearly badly informed, as Golius never translated letters for the King of Spain. Mencke means an Arabic letter addressed to King António I of Portugal (1531–1595), that Scaliger translated at Casaubon's request. The manuscripts from the private library of Golius were sold decades after his death by his family, and most are now found in the Bodleian Library in Oxford.

91   Drewes, *Levinus Warner and his Legacy*, 1970; Molhuysen, *Bronnen* v, pp. 79–80.

212   CHAPTER 5

bequests and acquisitions of Oriental books as one whole, and set about the organisation and description of the collection. He complained more than once about the disorderly manner in which the Oriental manuscripts were kept in the library, and how few catalogue entries offered accurate descriptions of the books. Schultens made heroic efforts to reorganise the bequests of both Scaliger and Werner, but he was unable to resolve the confusion that existed regarding the origins of some of the Oriental books. This confusion persisted: in the nineteenth century, several of Scaliger's books would have the initials L.W. (*Legatus Warnerianum*) stamped on their flyleaves. Others received a slip of printed paper describing the book as *Ex Legato Viri Ampliss. Levini Warneri*, even when the book was filled with Scaliger's handwritten annotations, and the book already had a slip of paper indicating that the book was part of Scaliger's bequest. This ensured that for a long time it remained uncertain which books truly belonged to Scaliger's bequest, and which to Warner's.[92]

In 1741, librarian David van Royen had Scaliger's *Arca* and that of Vulcanius cleaned out. He provided printed slips of paper to all of Scaliger's books which were at that moment in the *Arca* indicating that they came from his bequest.[93] This task was performed by Van Royen's assistant, the *custos* Daniel Goedval, who could not read any Oriental languages, which meant that occasionally he had the book upside down when he applied the printed slip. After this reorganisation, the famous cabinet disappeared from the library, without trace.[94] Van

---

92   See for example the copy of the third Rabbinical Bible by Daniel Bomberg, with the title *Mikra'ot Gedolot* (collection of the Torah with commentary), edited by Cornelius Adelkind, printed in Venice in 1546–1548, UBL 515 A 12–15; see Bibliographic Survey Venice 1546–1548. There is a printed slip identifying this as a copy from Warner's bequest, despite the fact that it has a manuscript inscription in Scaliger's hand that reads 'Ego Iosephus Scaliger emi hos quatuor tomos Bibliorum ex vidua *Caroli Macrini*, quinquaginta florenis. An. anno Christi MDLXXVIII, Tufolij in pictonibus'.

93   Molhuysen, *Bronnen* V, p. 127*. The printed slips used a Roman typeface cut by the Transylvanian Nikolaus Kis (1650–1702), which first appear in Leiden in 1715, when used in a publication by Pieter van der Aa. The university printer Samuel Luchtmans probably took over this typeface from Van der Aa after his death in 1733, and printed the slips for the library. With thanks to John Lane for this information.

94   In 1766, Jean Baptiste (1697–1781) de La Curne de Sainte-Palaye and his brother paid a visit to the university library of Leiden. The brothers wrote in their travel journal that they had seen two bookcases in the library standing next to each other, containing the Greek and Hebrew manuscripts of Scaliger. These were most likely the new bookcases that had recently been erected to house Scaliger's manuscripts. See: Madeleine van Strien-Chardonneau, *"Le voyage de Hollande". Récits de voyageurs français dans les Provinces-Unies, 1748–1795* (S.l.: s.n., 1992) p. 366 note 76: quotation from J.-B. de La Curne de Sainte-Palaye's *Notes se rapportant à un voyage fait en Hollande en 1766 récit de ce voyage* (1766): 'La fameuse bibliothèque qui est fort belle et où sont dans deux armoires à part les manuscrits grecs et hébreux de Scaliger.'

Royen was only librarian for four months, but the entire task was concluded within his tenure.[95] By the end of the eighteenth century, there was little memory of the *Arca*. In his chronicle of Leiden, published in 1770, Frans van Mieris mentioned Scaliger's contribution to the library and also recorded the presence of his portrait in the library. The *Arca* went entirely unmentioned.[96]

---

95 Van Royen displayed the same energetic gift for reorganisation when he was tasked in 1733 to oversee the refurbishment of the chamber of the Senate in the Academy building. This was completed in 1736. The walls of the room were decorated with portraits of Leiden professors, including a portrait of Scaliger donated to the university in 1743 by Gerard van Papenbroek, a posthumous portrait commissioned by Cornelis van der Myle. It is possible that the curators considered this portrait a suitable replacement for the portrait that used to hang above the *Arca*.

96 Frans van Mieris, *Beschrijving der Stad Leyden* [...] (Leiden: Wed. Abraham Honkoop & Cornelis van Hoogeveen, 1770), pp. 551–552: 'Door verscheidene beroemde en geleerde Mannen is deeze Boekzaal verrykt geworden, 't zy door geschenken of erfmaakingen van Boeken en Schriften in allerley taalen'.

CHAPTER 6

Scaliger's Bequest in the Leiden University Library Catalogues

There is no complete description of the books that made up of Scaliger's bequest. It is remarkable that from the moment that Scaliger's books were moved from his house on the Kerkgracht to the Rapenburg, until today, there is no definitive account of the extent of the bequest and its contents. The most important source, Scaliger's own inventory, which was added as a coda to his will, has been lost. It is not even certain whether this document included a full overview of the bequest. The other contemporary sources that do survive today, such as the list composed by Vulcanius, sadly provide an incomplete picture of Scaliger's bequest.

In this chapter, we will investigate the 'movements' of Scaliger's collection in the University Library of Leiden, using its contemporary printed catalogues. The perspective that emerges from this investigation is muddled, and in some case chaotic. Some books from the bequest were discarded or sold as duplicates, while other books were added (unjustly so) to Scaliger's bequest, often the result of poor seventeenth- and eighteenth-century cataloguing practices. The expertise of the cataloguers was frequently inadequate. The Elzevier firm, publishers of several of the seventeenth-century library catalogues, could only print with Arabic typefaces after the death of Thomas Erpenius (1624), and also had a limited range of Hebrew type available. To add to this confusion, the librarians of Leiden, Daniel Heinsius foremost among them, had a strong inclination to close the bequest to the prying eyes of scholars, which meant that few errors in the cataloguing practices were ever noted and improved.

For this investigation, all Leiden library catalogues from 1612 to 1716 were consulted. It is astonishing how often there was no clear overlap between the catalogues concerning particular titles from Scaliger's bequest. One needs to think like a creative translator to make sense of some descriptions, and the exercise frequently resembled taking pot shots at moving targets. In the introduction to the *Catalogus*, provided in the appendix, there is a detailed methodological explanation of my attempts to identify books from Scaliger's bequest. The result is the first complete reconstruction of the original bequest, matched where possible to the current Leiden University collection. This process has helped identify which books already left Leiden in the seventeenth and eighteenth centuries, or at least deserve the title of 'missing'.

© KONINKLIJKE BRILL BV, LEIDEN, 2025 | DOI:10.1163/9789004701526_008

SCALIGER'S BEQUEST IN THE LEIDEN UNIVERSITY LIBRARY CATALOGUES   215

TABLE 3   Overview of Scaliger's bequest as reflected in the catalogues of the Leiden
University Library, 1612–1716

Catalogue year	Printed books	Manuscripts	Total titles	Volumes
1612	127	48	175	180
1623	127	48	175	180
1640	128	62	190	142
1674	134	78	212	211
1716	129	65	194	163

In Table 3, the total extent of Scaliger's bequest as presented in the university library catalogues is listed. The number of printed books ascribed to Scaliger's bequest is relatively stable, while there are substantial differences in the numbers of manuscripts listed in each catalogue. The variations in the number of volumes can be ascribed to the division of *Sammelbände* (as reflected in the 1674 catalogue) or the rebinding of multiple titles into a single volume (as reflected in the 1716 catalogue). The individual catalogues are detailed case by case in the rest of the chapter.

It is noteworthy that there is no difference between the catalogues of 1612 and 1623; the description of the bequest only begins to fluctuate with the catalogue of 1640, in which the number of Oriental manuscripts increased by twelve, and the number of volumes decreased, as some works were bound together. With each catalogue, the overall quality of the description improves, which meant that more titles from the bequest were identified as such; the total number of titles only decreased in 1716 after the sale of books from Scaliger's bequest which were considered to be duplicates.

1   The Catalogue of Vulcanius

The University Library of Leiden owns an early inventory of a selection of books and manuscripts from Scaliger's bequest. This was composed by Bonaventura Vulcanius, a colleague of Scaliger. When Vulcanius transcribed the list, he was the secretary of the senate of the university, an office to which he was appointed on 9 September 1581, and which he would retain until his death on 9 October 1614.[1] It is striking that in his list, Vulcanius devoted as much care to

---

1   Due to his advanced age, Vulcanius was assisted from 8 Mary 1608 until his death by Daniel Heinsius See Molhuysen, *Bronnen* I, pp. 179 and 181.

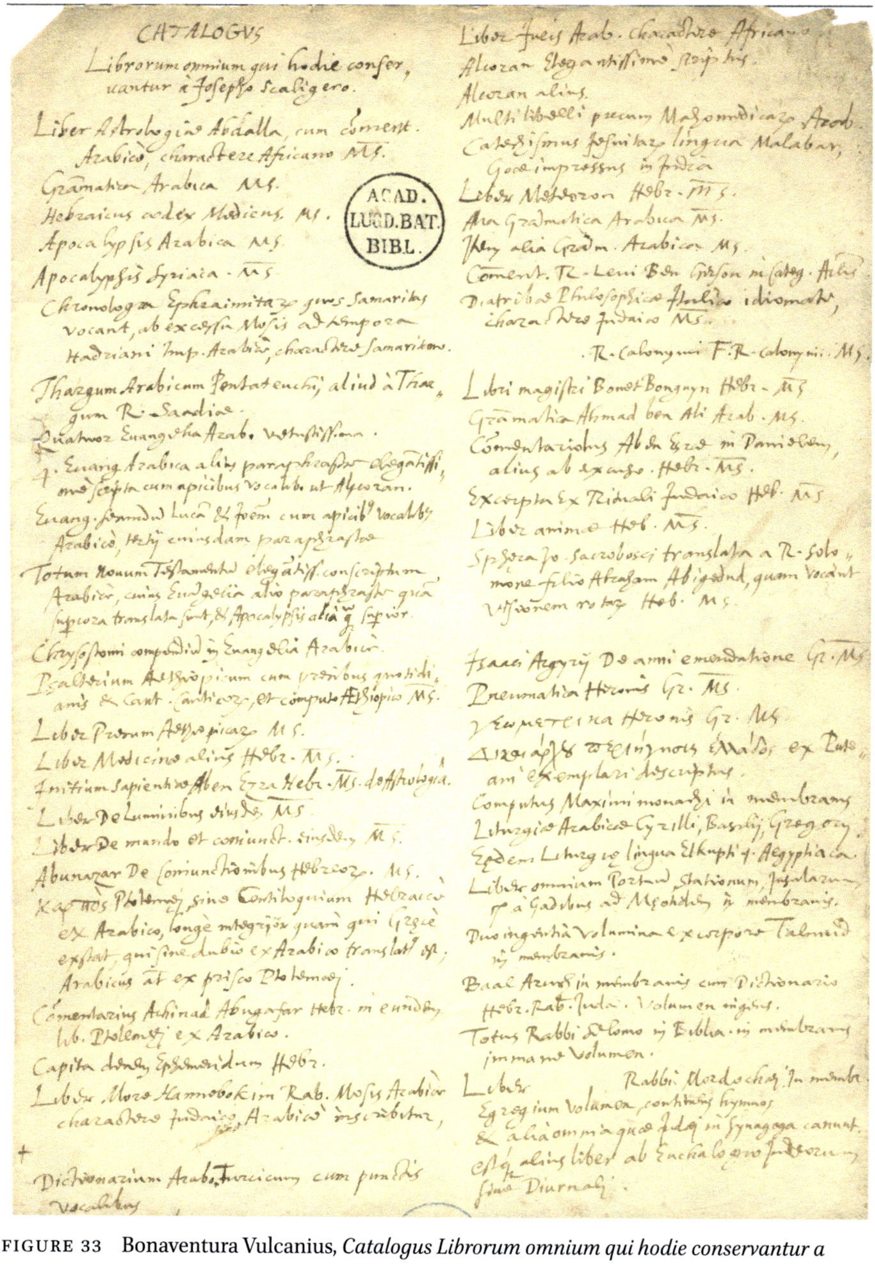

FIGURE 33 Bonaventura Vulcanius, *Catalogus Librorum omnium qui hodie conservantur a Josepho Scaligero.* UBL VUL 108 pars 5

IMPRESSA praea /

Zohar.

Totum Talmud

Tohar Antiqua Hebr.

Targum Arab. R. Saadia . } in Pentateuch.
Targum Persic.

Liber Mobih Caesar. luculentum opus.

Proverbia antiqua, Vorstberg in store
Apologos Aesopi, cum figuris liber
egregius.

Gram.? R. Mose Kimhi.

Proverbia sen dicta moralium cum gnat.

Fad R. Moses ben Maimon duo immania
volumina utilissima, instar Talmud

Via vitae R. Jacob F. Asser instar doctrinae
Talmud. ubi disseritur Ritus Judaici.

Propterea in Legem pheu xx interpret.
Tanhuma, Sepher in plur, Messila &
multa eiusmodi.

Biblia magna Venetijs excusa cum comment.

Multi praestantes Hebraici scriptores MS
a nobis. Mirabili relicti, quorum
nunc noia non succurrunt.

Eptae duo fundij patriarchae Antiochen
id nos, instar duos libros Arabica
manu ipsius Patriarchae.

Kalendarium Elkupi Arab. MS.

Kalendarium Antiochenum Syriacum MS.

Diurnale, sive Euchologium Maronitar.
Arabicè, characteribus Syriacis.

Horae matutinae Arab.

Proces Maronitarum Syriacè & Arab.
characteribus Syriacis.

Duo Nova Testamenta Aethiopica

Quinque Volumina Psalmorum Aethiopica,
quorum unum manu Petri Comes
Aethiopis notatum est, & multis appeh,
sensibus auctum.

Psalterium Armeniacum

Quaedam Veterum Patrum lingua Veteri
Dalmatica, characteribus Dalmaticis.

Psalm. Poenitentiales lingua Illyrica,
characteribus Divinis.

[Kalendarium Tridentinum MS

Duo libri Canonis Avicennae Arab.

Euclides lib. IX . Arab.

Duae Grammaticae Arabicae

Liber Theologiae Mohammedicae
MS. Arabia, cum apicibus Vocalibus.

Mappa Amoris Judaicae ab anno 5335
ad annum 5374

Euchologium Judaicum.

C. Marij Plotij Sacerdotis de Verborg
cum exemplis Graecis. liber instar He
phaestionis, descriptus ex Bibliotheca Bod
Comacij

Priscianus collatus cum integro Prisciano
Putean, in quo Graeca excerpta sunt tota
est in Bibliotheca Comacij; nequa possem
recuperare, cum alijs MSS. quos com,
daveram Comacij.

Liber cosmographiae Arabicae y climatum
ed Climatum partes divisus. Opus
utilissimum, si Latinè factum esset.

218 CHAPTER 6

the description of the printed books in the bequest as the manuscripts, which were often considered to be far more valuable than the printed books. This makes the list particularly valuable for a reconstruction of Scaliger's bequest. The manuscripts are listed on the recto of the inventory, and the printed books on the verso.

The *Catalogus Librorum omnium qui hodie conservantur a Josepho Scaligero* is an inventory of a part of what would become Scaliger's Oriental bequest.[2] It was by Scaliger in the last decade of his life, and although it only contains descriptions of Oriental manuscripts and books, it only provides a partial overview of Scaliger's Oriental collections.[3] Not all books can be identified easily; some of the them are only described as a *Zohar*, a *Totum Talmud* and a *Kalendarium Turcicum*, without any additional information.[4]

Why Vulcanius copied this list is uncertain. Did he have a personal interest in the collection? Did he compose the list to borrow or buy certain books from Scaliger's collection? Was it written as a draft of the coda to be added to Scaliger's will, or was it a summary of the original coda? Did Vulcanius make this list because of his administrative position in the senate?[5] From the title of the inventory, it is at least clear that the document must have been written in Scaliger's home, where the books were present. It is possible that Vulcanius wrote the original list himself, but it is more likely that he transcribed it from another copy, as he did not possess enough knowledge of Arabic or other Oriental languages to make the descriptions himself. One entry, describing a manuscript of Priscianus that was copied from one in the library of Cujas, betrays Scaliger's own voice, as the entry includes a note that states that the original manuscript could no longer be found in Cujas's own library.[6] Finally, when we compare Vulcanius's list with the 1592 list of the Oriental books that Scaliger compiled for Raphelengius, it is clear that there is barely any deviation between them.

As secretary of the senate, Vulcanius had access to Scaliger's will, and it is possible that this list served as a helpful aid after Scaliger's death. Ultimately,

---

2 The inventory is held in the UBL under call number VUL 108 pars 5. See also Appendix 3.
3 There are nevertheless a few Greek and Latin manuscripts listed in the inventory which were also a part of Scaliger's bequest. See Appendix 3.
4 *Catalogus Librorum omnium qui hodie conservantur à Josepho Scaligero.* UBL VUL 108 pars 5.
5 Cf. Molhuysen, *Codices Vulcaniani*, p. 49; Van der Heide, *Hebrew manuscripts* (1977), pp. 9–10; 21–24; H.J. de Jonge, 'Joseph Scaliger's Greek-Arabic Lectionary (Leiden, U.L., MS Or. 243 = Lectionary 6 of the Greek New Testament)' in: *Quaerendo* 5/2 (1975), pp. 143–172.
6 Scaliger wrote: 'Priscianus collatus cum integro Prisciano Puteani, in quo Graeca expressa sunt o[mn]ia. Est in Bibliotheca Cuiacii; neque possumus (?) recup[er]are, cum aliis MSS. quos com[men]daveram Cuiacio.'

it does seem likely that he transcribed the list for the archive of the university, as that might explain Vulcanius's own signature at the end of the document. Because Scaliger's own coda to the will has been lost, this cannot be proven, but it may at least help explain why some Oriental books did not enter the bequest.

Opinions diverge on the date of Vulcanius's list. Van der Heide considered that the list was composed before 1597, because he argued that it did not include the manuscripts from the collection of Raphelengius that Scaliger inherited after his death in 1597.[7] A close analysis does indicate that the list could have been written after 1597, thanks to the inclusion of several Arabic grammars. One of these Arabic manuscripts is described in the list as *Grammatica Ahmad ben ali Arab*.[8] Another manuscript is a compilation of four Arabic texts written around 1518–1519, which were described by an earlier owner as 'Les principes de la grammaire Arabique'. Today it is volume UBL MS Or. 235, but like the *Grammatica Ahmad ben ali Arab*, it originally belonged to Raphelengius and from his library it passed into Scaliger's hands.[9]

De Jonge dates Vulcanius's list as having been written probably before 1597, but definitely before 1600. This conjecture is based on his study of a Greek-Arabic lexicon in Scaliger's collection, a manuscript which did not appear in Vulcanius's list, but which Scaliger received in 1600 as a gift from the preacher Daniel Chamier (1565–1621).[10] Yet De Jonge's conclusion can also be refined based on the presence in the list of the manuscript *Liturgiae Cyrilli, Basilii, Gregorii linguae Elkupti (id est) Aegyptiacae*. In 1603, Scaliger sent this work to Marcus Welser in Rome to collate; although it is of course possible that Scaliger already owned a fair copy of this work before sending it to Welser. Altogether, despite the incompleteness of the list, which provides us only with a selection

---

7 Van der Heide, *Hebrew manuscripts*, p. 9.

8 *Marah al-Arwah*, by Ahmad b. Ali ibn Mas'ud, UBL MS Or. 240.

9 This means that these manuscripts were not added to Scaliger's bequest after the auction of Franciscus Raphelengius in 1626, as Hamilton argued in his article *Nam tirones sumus*, and which Witkam also purported. The manuscripts that were added in 1626 to the bequest were not reflected as such in the catalogues of 1636 and 1640, but only in the catalogue of 1674. Hamilton renounced his first argument in 'The Perils of Catalogues' in: *Journal of Islamic Manuscripts* 1 (2010), pp. 31–36.

10 This is the Greek-Arabic *Lectionarium*, UBL MS Or. 243. See: De Jonge, 'Joseph Scaliger's Greek-Arabic Lectionary', pp. 143–172. *Correspondence* 2 August 1600 and 15 December 1600 from Chamier: 'Vous recevres, s'il vous plait, en tesmoynage de mon affection, un manuscript que j'ose vous doner, lequel tomba nagueres entre mes mains, moitié grec, moitié arabique'. The manuscript was probably taken to France around 1500 by an envoy of King Louis XII after an embassy to the Mamluk Sultan in Cairo. The *lectionarium* is remarkably absent from the library catalogue of 1612.

220   CHAPTER 6

of Scaliger's bequest, it seems reasonable to suggest that the list was composed around 1600. This dating also corresponds to the fact that in 1601, Scaliger made the first preparations for his will, which he made definitive in 1608.

2   Library Catalogues before 1612

Due to the limited source base, we have to rely on the published university library catalogues, composed after Scaliger's death, to reconstruct his bequest. We know that these catalogues provide an incomplete picture of the bequest, but they do provide us with much additional information, such as the cataloguing practices and philological expertise of Leiden's librarians, and the manner in which they sought to present the bequest to the scholarly public. By studying the library catalogues, the overall composition of Scaliger's bequest becomes clearer, even if uncertainties and discrepancies remain. The process also allows us to the reveal more information about the Oriental books already owned by Leiden before it received the bequest in 1609.

On 24 February 1597, Paullus Merula was appointed as successor of librarian Janus Dousa the younger as *Bibliothecae Praefectus*.[11] He immediately set to work to compose a catalogue in which all the donors and patrons of the university library were honoured: this was the *Catalogus Principum, Civitatum, et singulariorum qui donatione vel inter vivos vel mortis caussa, bibliothecam publicam*.[12] The catalogue was primarily published to attract new donors: the regular funds of the library, although more extensive than those of other libraries at this time, were not substantial enough to purchase rare and valuable books that enhanced the prestige of the institution.[13]

Merula also wrote another catalogue, which remained in manuscript, and offered a detailed overview of important donations to the library. This also included other notable acquisitions, such as two large portraits of William of Orange and his son Maurice. This handwritten overview opened with the donation of the *Biblia Regia* by William of Orange in 1575, given at the inauguration of the university. Then the list progressed to the donation of the manuscript *Orationes aliquot Demosthenis*, given by Vulcanius to the library at the

---

11   Sikko Popta Haak, *Paullus Merula 1558–1607* (Zutphen: W.J. Thieme, 1901), pp. 137–139, incorrectly mentions 1599 as his year of appointment.

12   *Catalogus Principum, civitatum, et singulariorum, qui donatione vel inter vivos vel mortis caussa, bibliothecam publicam, in Academia Lugduno-Batava institutam, liberaliter ditarunt* (Lugduni Batavorum: Ex officina Ioannis Paetsij 1597; USTC 423868, UBL 1496 F 37:2 and BA 1 G1).

13   Bertius, *Nomenclator*, pp. [ii–iii].

SCALIGER'S BEQUEST IN THE LEIDEN UNIVERSITY LIBRARY CATALOGUES 221

inauguration of the library on 31 October 1587.[14] In the same year, donations from Holmannus, Raphelengius and from the Leiden magistrates also made their way into the library.[15] The purpose of this handwritten catalogue was very different from the published catalogue of donors; it seems that it was composed to highlight to visitors and administrators the contents of the locked cabinets in which these great donations were kept. It is likely that at this time, only the librarian had access to these cabinets.

Ten years later, in 1607, Merula made another list of *rariora* or rare books, in which 143 Latin, Greek and several Oriental manuscripts and annotated books, 'as well as some other things' were listed that were kept in the locked cabinets.[16] This manuscript catalogue was entitled *Catalogus rariorum Biblioth[ecae] Acad[emiae] Lugdun[ensis]*. For this list, Merula followed the structure of Bertius's *Nomenclator* and the *Catalogus Principum, Civitatum, Singulariorum* of 1597: the manuscripts in Latin were listed first, then the manuscripts in Greek, followed by the 'old and respected editions'. On folio 42 of the catalogue, there are listed the 'books brought from distant lands' that were donated to the library.[17] These concern several miscellaneous items donated by various individuals, and they include a Javanese manuscript written on palm leaves (a so-called *Lontar*), a Chinese book, a commentary on the Turkish Qur'an in Arabic script, and a New Testament in Amharic.[18] It can thus be said that,

---

14   This is now UBL BPG 33. It clearly did not bother Merula that the manuscript was not actually owned by Vulcanius: he had borrowed it from Petrus Tiara (1514–1586), professor of Greek and Latin at the University of Franeker.

15   ELO Burgemeesters Dagboek A (Secretarie Archief 1575–1851), no. 638.

16   The *Rariorum Bibliothecae Academiae Lugdunensis Catalogus Compositus* (*Prof. et ibidem bibliothecario*) *Paullus Merula* [BA C 3] also contains descriptions of 27 maps and several globes. The list also contained names of 'those, who showed their generosity by donating books to the library'. The catalogue was copied by Van Royen in the eighteenth century, with the title *Index rariorum manuscriptorum et impressorum librorum in Bibliotheca Lugduno-Batava*, UBL BPL 127 AG.

17   These books, except the Chinese book (number 5 in the list), donated by Paauw, are also to be found in the *Catalogus Principum, Civitatum, Singulariorum* of 1597, but not in a separate section as in the handwritten catalogue, but within the main list. They can be found on pages 26, 29, 37, 53 and 80. See also: Kasper van Ommen, 'Books and Manuscripts on the Move from East to West (and vice versa)', in A. Reeuwijk (ed.), *Voyage of Discovery. Exploring the Collections of the Asian Library at Leiden University* (Leiden: Leiden University Press, 2017), pp. 67–75.

18   *Catalogus rariorum Biblioth[eca] Acad[emia] Lugdun[is]*, composed by Merula in 1607 (UBL BA C N 3) and also copied by Van Royen in the eighteenth century (BPL 127 AG, f. 33). Vulcanius late donated a book to the library that he considered a 'Liber Japanensis (uti videtur) manuscriptus magno quarto' (UBL MS Or. 1928). Cf. Catalogus UBL (1640), p. 167; B.J.O. Schrieke, *Het boek van Bonang.* (Utrecht: Den Boer, 1916), p XII–XVI. The *Catalogus principum* of 1597, at p. 26, records that the Javanese manuscript was composed

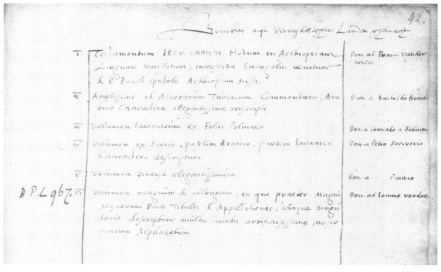

FIGURE 34 Paullus Merula, *Catalogus rariorum Biblioth[ecae] Acad[emiae] Lugdun[ensis]*, 1607. UBL BA C N 3

without doubt, Scaliger' bequest was the first true collection of Oriental books that was added to the university library.

The complete overview of the books 'from distant lands' contains the following titles.[19]

– *Testamentum Iesu Christi Novum in Aethiopicam Linguam translatum: interserta Evangeliis Quatuor & D. Paulli Epistolis Aethiopum missa*, donated by Franciscus van der Wilius.[20]
– *Amplissimi ad Alcoranum Turcicum Commentarii Arabico charactere elegantissime Conscripti*, donated by Bartoldus Brandt.[21]

---

of seventy-five palm leaves, written on both sides. In the manuscript, now at UBL MS Or. 266, folios 1–14 and 75 are wanting.

19 The list was published by Philipp Christiaan Molhuysen in *Codices Manuscripti III*: *Codices Bibliothecae Publicae Latini* (Leiden: Brill, 1912), p. XIV.

20 *Testamentum novum cum epistola Pauli ad Hebreos tantum, cum concordantiis Euangelistarum Eusebii ... Missale cum benedictione incensi cerae* [...] *Alphabetum in lingua gheez vulgo Chaldea quae omnia Fr. Petrus Ethyops imprimi curavit* acc. Pauli Epistolae (Romae: Valerius et Ludovicius Doricus Fratres Brixiani, 1548–1549; USTC 803271, UBL 877 C 19). The book was previously owned by Jo. Priamus [perhaps the canon Don. Johannes Priamus?] Scaliger also owned a copy of the book, with the letter by Paul [olim X. 25 A], but it was later sold by Leiden as a duplicate.

21 This Qur'an in folio was described as a 'Volumen rarum & non exigui precii'. According an annotation, the book was taken by a Christian knight from a Turkish scholar during

- *Volumen Iavanicum Ex foliis Palmae*, donated by Conradus a Dulmen.[22]
- *Volumen ex Serico partim Arabico partim Javanico Charactere descriptum*, donated by Petrus Scriverius.[23]
- *Volumen Sinense Elegantissimum*, donated by Pavius.[24]
- *Volumen magnum & oblongum, in quo praeter Magni Moscorum Ducis titulos & suppellationes, aliaque, singularia descriptum multis modis artificiosissime Moscoviticvum Alphabetum*, donated by Johannes Verdoes.[25]

---

the wars in Hungary. See: *Cat. Principum* 1597, p. 81. According to Schmidt, this manuscript (UBL MS Or. 242) was in the Scaliger collection. See J. Schmidt, *Catalogue of Turkish Manuscripts*, p. 33.

22   The Amsterdam merchant Conradus or Coert Jansz van Dulmen (born around 1539) was approached by Merula on 13 October 1597 to donate this manuscript to the university of Leiden (see UBL BPL 747). In the catalogue of 1597, it was described as a 'volumen quoddam Javanicum ex remotissimo orbe cum aliis mercibus huc per mercatores anno nonagesimo septimo adlatum. Quid contineat, prorsus ignoratur. Sunt qui leges esse Sinarum volunt, nonnulli Alcoranum censent, alii alia divinant. Character nostris hominibus numquam est visus. Folia sunt Palmae Indicae oblonga, numero LXXV, utrimque quatuor lineis sculpta. Tempus certius quid docebit.' It probably concerns a Javanese text that was brought to the Republic by Cornelis de Houtman. It is now in Leiden under call number MS Or. 266 (with the erroneously applied slip of paper *Ex legato illustris Viri Josephi Scaligeri*). See also: Haak, *Paullus Merula*, p. 138. In Leiden, there was no one who could make sense of this manuscript: was it a compilation of Chinese laws or a part of the Qur'an?

23   A manuscript written in Arabic on one side, produced in Java, which was used in a temple and which Leiden scholars presumed contained information about Javanese rites and ceremonies. It was donated by the jurist, poet and historian Petrus Scriverius (1576–1660); today it is no longer in the university library.

24   Donated by the professor of medicine and botany, Petrus Pavius or Pieter Paauw (1564–1617), the son-in-law of Jan van Hout. The manuscript presumably came from the estate of his father, Pieter Paauw Adriaanszoon, a member of the municipal council in Amsterdam and bailiff of Alkmaar. The manuscript probably arrived in the Republic after the first voyage (1595–7) to the Indies by Cornelis de Houtman. It is possibly related to a leaf which contains a part of the popular Chinese novel *Shui-hu-chuan*, and that is now in the Bodleian Library. This particular leaf was, according to its inscription, 'A book of China given me at Leiden by Doctor Merla [sic] professor in Histories'. It is uncertain why Merula, as librarian, would have given this fragment to an English visitor. Cf. J.J.L. Duyvendak, 'An old Chinese fragment in the Bodleian', *The Bodleian Library Record* 2/28 (February 1949), pp. 245–247. Vgl. Koos Kuiper, 'Van Wortels en kruiden. Een vroege Chinese druk in de Bibliotheca Thysiana', *Omslag. Bulletin van de Universiteitsbibliotheek en het Scaliger Instituut* 3/3 (2005), pp. 4–6.

25   This is the *Alphabetum Russicum*, with call number UBL BPL 1409, in which a contemporary hand has written: 'Den Inhoudt van deze rol is het Moscovis A.B. sooals de letters van zulks soort bij ... schrijven worden gebruyckt. ...' ('The content of this scroll is the Muscovite A.B.[C.], with the letters that they use to write'). See: H. Meijer, *Slawjanskie rukopisi Lejdenskoj uniwersitetskoj biblioteki*, no. 5; *Catalogus compend.* I (1932), p. 135. Johannes Verdoes was the treasurer of Gouda.

Some of the items from the list of 1607 were later erroneously considered to be part of Scaliger's bequest, and some items received a printed slip (*Ex legato illustris Viri Josephi Scaligeri*) to indicate this. It is understandable that some librarians and their assistants presumed so: Scaliger was renowned as a collector such exotic manuscripts, many of which could not be interpreted or understood by even the most distinguished scholars. From the end of the sixteenth century, more and more exotic objects found their way to the Dutch Republic, and many did indeed find their way into Scaliger's hands.[26]

3 Cataloguing Scaliger's Bequest: the Printed Library Catalogue of 1612

On 31 August 1607, more than a month and a half after Merula had died, Daniel Heinsius was appointed as librarian of Leiden University.[27] At his appointment, Heinsius stated that he hoped that the library would develop increasingly into an 'arsenal of wisdom'. His nomination was partly due to his good friend Scaliger, who had made repeated efforts to persuade the curators of the university to select Heinsius.[28] The bond between Scaliger and Heinsius clearly resembled that of a father and son.[29] From their perspective, the curators considered Heinsius a valuable appointment because they reflected rightly that the close relationship between Heinsius and Scaliger would ensure that Heinsius would try to gain Scaliger's valuable collection for the library.

Despite Heinsius's efforts, the majority of Scaliger's book collection was not inherited by the University of Leiden, but was sold at public auction. We do not know whether this was a surprise or a great disappointment to Heinsius; it can be presumed that it came as a blow that many of Scaliger's annotated books

---

26 See for example: *Correspondence* 7 March 1608 to Federicus Cerutus in Verona, in which Scaliger offers to ask his contacts amongst Dutch merchants to acquire objects from the Far East for Cerutus.

27 Molhuysen, *Bronnen* I, p. 175. From 1607 onwards, the volumes of books in the library were stamped with the coat of arms of the University of Leiden.

28 *Correspondence* 30 August 1607 to Van der Myle, in which Scaliger mentions his preference for Heinsius to succeed as librarian. Cornelis van der Myle had been appointed as curator of the university a year earlier.

29 Dirk Johannes Hendrik ter Horst, in this thesis *Daniël Heinsius (1580–1655)* (Utrecht: Drukkerij Hoeijenbos en Co., 1934), pp. 16–17, is unique in doubting the closeness of the relationship between Heinsius and Scaliger. He is especially negative about Scaliger, whom he described as an unimaginative and extremely vain man, 'with the arid soul of a sour hermit'. On the relationship between Heinsius and Scaliger, see also: Bernays, *Joseph Justus Scaliger*. 1855 (1965), pp. 61–62 and 177–178.

were dispersed far and wide amongst the scholarly community. The blow must have been softened by the fact that the most valuable part of Scaliger's library, his Oriental works, were bestowed upon the university library.

Already nineteen days after Scaliger's death on 30 January 1609, the university library prepared to receive Scaliger's bequest. On 9 February, Franciscus II and Joost Raphelengius were appointed as the executors of the will, according to Scaliger's wishes. They asked the curators 'to whom from the university they were to deliver the books of the gentleman [Scaliger]'. The curators responded that all Hebrew, Arabic, Syriac, Chaldaic (meaning Aramaic) and other Oriental books were to be handed to Heinsius at the university library.[30] Heinsius formally received the bequest and was then instructed to make an inventory of the donation and to place the books in the library.[31]

The location of Scaliger's death was recorded simply as the 'Kerkgracht'. This has led to some confusion in the literature, as this could apply either to the Hooglandsekerkgracht or the Pieterskerkgracht.[32] However, as the area around the Pieterskerk was often referred to in the seventeenth century as the 'Vicus choralis', without the name of the church, it seems sensible that the reference to the 'Kerkgracht' probably refers to the Pieterskerkgracht.[33] This would mean that Scaliger's books, at the time of this death, were still kept in his home on the Pieterskerkgracht, not far from the university library at the Rapenburg.[34]

Given that the coda attached to Scaliger's will has been lost, we do not know whether the Oriental books of the bequest were already separated from the rest of the library in Scaliger's home. This means that we also do not know whether Scaliger separated out the books meant for the bequest, or whether

---

30   Molhuysen, *Bronnen* I, p. 183, 'Notulen der ordinaire vergadering van de Curators ende Burgemeesters gehouden den 8, 9 en 10 February 1609'. Until 1615, the catalogue or inventory was appended to the will, see Molhuysen, *Bronnen* II, p. 59. This inventory is now no longer present in the *Resoluties van Curatoren*. See: I. Teirlinck, 'Joost van Ravelingen', *Verslag en Mededeelingen der Koninklijke Vlaamsche Academie voor Taal- en Letterkunde*, 1913, p. 871.

31   Resolutie Curatoren 8, 9, 10 Feb. 1609. Ultimately, the inventory was ready only three years later, and was published as an appendix to [Daniel Heinsius], *Catalogus librorum Bibliothecae Lugdunensis. Praefixa est Danielis Heinsii Bibliothecari* [...] *oratio* (Leiden: 1612), p. 78 onwards, 'Catalogus librorum quos Bibliothecae Iosephus Scaligeri legavit'. UBL 1408 I 59; copy DOUSA 91 1004, see Appendix 4.

32   De Jonge, 'Josephus Scaliger in Leiden', p. 87.

33   See for example the imprints of products from the print shop of William Brewster in the first quarter of the seventeenth century.

34   Witkam, *Dagelijkse zaken*, deel VI, 2e stuk, p. 1, concurs that it concerned Scaliger's house on the Pieterskerkgracht.

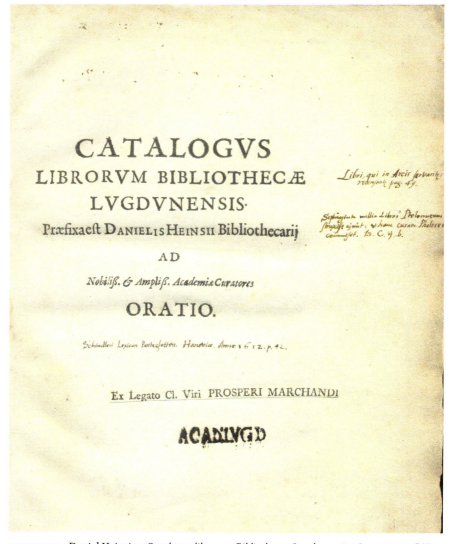

FIGURE 35   Daniel Heinsius, *Catalogus librorum Bibliothecae Lugdunensis*, 1612, UBL BA C N 2C

Carmina quinque Illuſtrium poetarum Italorum, Florētiæ.
apud Laurentium Torrentinum.

CATALOGVS LIBRORVM
QVOS BIBLIOTHECÆ
Ioſephus Scaliger legavit.

Libri Hebræi in folio.

INgens volumen ante C C C annos ſcriptū omnium Com-
mentariorum R. Solomonis in vetus Teſtamentum.
Talmud Ieroſolymitanū manuſcriptum, duobus ingentib. vo-
luminibus.
Talmud Baſilienſis editionis VIII. voluminibus.   *Talmud Babylonium, Venetijs, 9 Voluminibus, p 1.*
Paal Aruch manuſcrip. cum quibuſdam alijs ad Grammaticam
& verborum rationes pertinentibus. ingens volumen.
Biblia Veneta cum Rabinis, quatuor voluminibus, ſecundæ edi-
tionis.
Iard Rambam duobus ingentibus voluminibus Venetijs.
Orah Aiim R. Aſer ben Iaacob. Venet.
Pentateuchum cū Targum, R. Solomonis, & Ramban Venet.
Meturgemin Eliæ Baſil.
Radices Kimhi Venetijs, cum explicatione Latina vocum in
margine.
Radices Kimhi primæ editionis. Venet.
Miclol Kimhi, prior & poſterior pars. Venet.
Dictionarium Davidis de Pomis. Venet.
Dictionarium Chald Pagnini cum Rabano De cruce.
Liber bellorum Domini Levi Gerſon. Venet.
More hannevochin. prima editio, Venetijs.
More hannevochin cum Commentarijs.
Commentarius ἀκέφαλ℗ in Eſaiam manuſcrip.

Excerpta

228   CHAPTER 6

this was done by the brothers Raphelengius, using Scaliger's handwritten catalogue, or assisted by one of Leiden's scholars. There are no sources to indicate
that Heinsius was involved in the curation of the definitive split between the
bequest and the rest of the library. What is certain is that no attention was paid
to the presence of books in the bequest that were already in the university
library. Since the end of the sixteenth century, the university had owned a copy
of the polyglot psalter of Justinianus, printed in 1516; thanks to the bequest,
they now had two copies.

In 1609, the curators instructed Heinsius to prepare the library so that the
bequest could be received and stored safely. With all urgency, he had to compose and hand over an inventory to the curators, and commission a bookcase
(the *Arca* described in the previous chapter) in which the books could be
kept.[35] While the bookcase was successfully constructed, the inventory proved
more troublesome. Heinsius's knowledge of the great variety of Oriental languages present in the bequest was entirely inadequate to produce accurate title
descriptions. Heinsius classified the books by language – Hebrew, Aramaic,
Arabic, Syriac, Amharic, Russian and Latin – but all titles were given in Latin,
not the language in which the books were written or printed. The titles were
also rarely described in full. Despite these shortcomings, the catalogue prepared by Heinsius (only presented to the curators in print in 1612) had one
important goal: to present Scaliger's bequest as one prominent collection. The
bequest received a specific status within the updated published library catalogue, catalogued separately from the rest – in much the same fashion as the
books were kept apart in the *Arca*. Visitors to the library and readers of the
catalogue could immediately distinguish Scaliger's contribution to the whole.

Heinsius's catalogue of 1612 was the first printed catalogue to appear
since Petrus Bertius's ground-breaking *Nomenclator* of 1595.[36] When the catalogue appeared, the original handwritten coda to Scaliger's will probably
lost its value as a canonical document, and then was lost or disposed of. In

---

35   Molhuysen, *Bronnen* I, p. 183: Resoluties van Curatoren 8/10 februari 1609: 'Heynsius by
      desen expresselyck wort geauthoriseert, met last om opte bibliotheecque te doen mae-
      cken een casse op hem selven ende aldaer besloten in te stellen de voors. boecken, ende
      mede dat de voors. Heynsius aen de C. ende B. sal leveren dubbelt van de voors. catalogue
      ofte inventaris om onder de papyeren ende chartres van de voors. C. ende B. bewaert te
      worden.' ('Heinsius is hereby expressly ordered to have a bookcase made for the library
      and to store in the same the aforementioned books, and that the same Heinsius will
      deliver to the curators and burgomasters [of Leiden] two copies of the aforementioned
      catalogue or inventory to be kept amongst the papers and charters of the same curators
      and burgomasters').
36   *Catalogus librorum Bibliothecae Lugdunensis* 1612. The 'Catalogus librorum quos Biblio-
      thecae Iosephus Scaliger legavit' is printed on pp. 79–88.

the 1612 catalogue, the bequest comprises 175 titles in 180 volumes; 127 of the titles were printed, 48 were handwritten. In a separate rubric accompanying the overview, Heinsius also included forty Greek and Latin manuscripts that Scaliger had bequeathed to the library. In total, the bequest thus numbered 215 titles. Heinsius stamped all books in the bequest with the phrase 'ACAD LVGD' (Academia Lugdunensis), to indicate the library's ownership.

An early contrasting estimate of the size of Scaliger's bequest was provided by the bookseller and historian Jan Jansz Orlers. In 1614, Orlers wrote in his *Beschrijvinge der stad Leyden* (Description of the city of Leiden) the following on Scaliger and his bequest:

> This *phoenix* amongst scholars, a wonder of our age ... has given to the *library* various *manuscripts*, or handwritten books in Greek and other languages, as well as various printed and handwritten Chaldaic [Aramaic], Arabic, Persian, Turkish and other Oriental books, all of which together present a remarkable treasure given their rarity.[37]

Hereafter Orlers divided the bequest amongst Hebrew, Aramaic, Syriac, Arabic, Amharic, Persian, Armenian, Russian and Greek items, and arrived, erroneously so, at a total of 208 books.[38]

The 1612 catalogue prepared by Heinsius can be seen as a clear homage by a devoted student to an inspiring mentor, but it is striking that it took such a long time to complete. In the publication of two orations on Scaliger's death, *In obitum viri illustrissimi Josephi Scaligeri Orationes Duae* (Leiden 1609), Heinsius had already announced the news that Scaliger had bequeathed his Oriental

---

37   'Desen eenighen *Phoenix* onder de Geleerde, ende 't Wonder van onse eeuwe ... heeft de *Bibliotheque* ghegeven ofte ghemaeckt verscheyden *Manuscriptae*, oft geschreven Boecken in Griecxsche ende andere Talen, als mede eenighe so ghedruckte als geschreven Chaldeusche, Arabische, Persische, Turcksche, ende andere Orientaelsche Boecken, die alle te saemen om haer seltsaemheyts wille een grooten schat waerdich zijn. ...'

38   Orlers, *Beschrijvinge der Stad Leyden*, pp. 151–153. The number of books in the bequest as calculated by Orlers was copied by Johannes Lomeier (1636–1699) in his *De bibliothecis liber singularis. Editio secondo* (Ultrajecti: ex officina Johannis Ribbii bibl., 1680; USTC 1816644). Others who relied on Orlers included the Orientalist Hottinger, in his *Promtuarium; sive, Bibliotheca Orientalis* V Heidelbergae, Wyngaerde, 1658 (USTC 2549010), and Pierre le Gallois mentions in his *Traitté des plus belles bibliothèques de l'Europe* Paris, E. Michallet, 1685 (USTC 6078183), pp. 140–141: 'Cette Bibliotheque est recommandable par 208. Manuscripts Grecs, Hebraïques, Chaldaïques, Syriaques, Persiques, Arméniques, & Russites, que Joseph Scaliger légua à cette Eschole, où il avoit long-temps professé'. Until the early twentieth century this figure was regularly repeated, even by Molhuysen in his *Geschiedenis der Universiteits-Bibliotheek te Leiden*, p. 21.

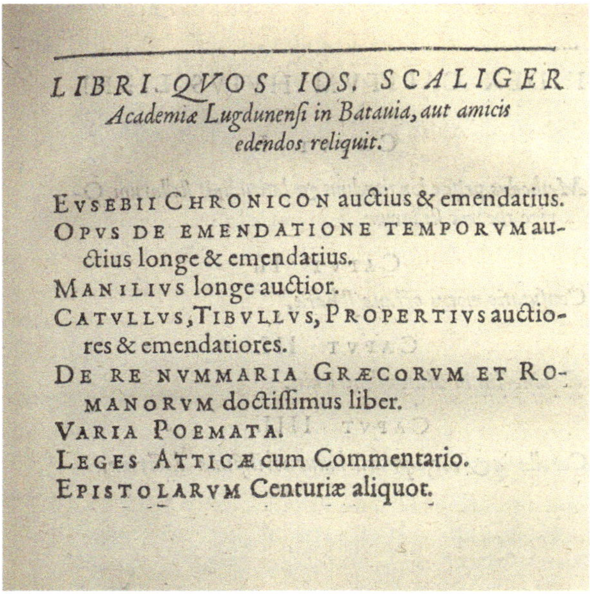

> LIBRI QVOS IOS. SCALIGER
> *Academiæ Lugdunensi in Batauia, aut amicis*
> *edendos reliquit.*
>
> EVSEBII CHRONICON auctius & emendatius.
> OPVS DE EMENDATIONE TEMPORVM au-
> ctius longe & emendatius.
> MANILIVS longe auctior.
> CATVLLVS, TIBVLLVS, PROPERTIVS auctio-
> res & emendatiores.
> DE RE NVMMARIA GRÆCORVM ET RO-
> MANORVM doctissimus liber.
> VARIA POEMATA.
> LEGES ATTICÆ cum Commentario.
> EPISTOLARVM Centuriæ aliquot.

FIGURE 36 Alongside 'All my books in Oriental languages',
Scaliger also bequeathed his Latin and Greek
manuscripts to the university of Leiden. He also
donated to the library a selection of his own works,
some of which were published posthumously.
UBL 540 D 19

collections to the university, which meant that there was a sense of urgency concerning the publication of a new catalogue. The news of the bequest spread quickly throughout the Republic of Letters. In August 1609, the French book collector Pierre de L'Estoile (1546–1611) was already fully informed about the value of the gift. In his diary, the Parisian recorded that Elzevier had sent him a copy of the funeral orations delivered by Heinsius and Baudius. L'Estoile described in his diary how Scaliger's bequest was detailed in Heinsius's oration. He added a note on the financial value of the collection, namely that Elzevier, who had ample experience with the auction of books, had told him that 'the gentlemen of Leiden [the curators?] estimate the value [of the bequest] to be 3,000 écus'.[39] This prompted L'Estoile to record that the bequest was remarkable in more ways than one.

---

39 Pierre de L'Estoile, *Mémoirs-Journaux 1571–1611*. Tome. IX: *Journal de Henri IV 1607–1609* (Paris: Paul Daffis (1927), pp. 384–385. The Écu, French Crown or Louis d'Or contained 6.7 grams of gold. The approximate conversion of 3,000 écus in the early seventeenth

SCALIGER'S BEQUEST IN THE LEIDEN UNIVERSITY LIBRARY CATALOGUES   231

In his funeral oration, Heinsius did indeed offer a short description of Scaliger's bequest. He listed Greek manuscripts, books in Hebrew, Chaldaic (Aramaic), Syriac, Arabic, Amharic, Persian and Armenian.[40] He mentioned nothing about the Russian books in Scaliger's collection, which is striking, given that Scaliger also did not distinguish his Russian books separately in his will. In contrast, Orlers did record *Libri Russici* in his description of Leiden of 1614.[41] This might indicate that the brothers Raphelengius, who most likely made the ultimate selection in transferring books from Scaliger's home to the library, considered the Russian books to be an integral part of the bequest.

Specific titles from the bequest, or its total size, were not mentioned by Heinsius in his funeral oration. What is obvious from his description of the collection is that he had little sense of what it actually contained. The oration also did not speak of the plans to have an *Arca* commissioned to store the bequest. Instead, Heinsius mused on the importance of the bequest:

> Now that Scaliger can no longer serve the university through his presence, he bequeathed all his manuscripts in foreign languages to us. Now that we possess this Oriental bequest, the library can compete with all other libraries that have Oriental books. Yet, oh, great hero, the more we honour the importance of your gift, the more we recognise our own weaknesses. As no one could defend himself against the blows of Achilles, so will your arsenal of wisdom be regarded too. Perhaps no person will ever be able to use it. But that too shall be a sign of your greatness. The world will look upon your books as an envious treasure of human knowledge. When contemplating your great name, our spirit and soul will light up.

---

century to modern currency, taking into account the value of gold, would be around 700,000 euros.

40   *Legatum A Iosepho Scaligeri Bibliothecae Publicae Lugdunensi Batavae relictum* in: *Danielis Heinsii in obitum V[iri] illustr[issimi] Iosephi Scaligeri Iul. Cæs. a Burden F. eruditorum principis Orationes duæ. Accedunt Epicedia eiusdem & aliorum: effigies item ac monumentum Scaligeri & principum Veronensium aeri incisa* (Leiden: ex officina Plantiniana apud Franciscus II Raphelengius and Andries Clouck, 1609; USTC 102909). This includes at pp. 97–98 a short list with texts that Scaliger had given to his friends, including Heinsius and Gomarus, to have them published after his death. It concerned manuscripts of Eusebius (his *Thesaurus Temporum*), Manilius, Catullus, Tibullus and Propertius and the *Poëmata*. This was supplemented by a manuscript written by his father, on the *Historia Animalium* of Aristotle. This final text would ultimately be published by Philippe-Jacques de Maussac (1590–1650) and appeared in Toulouse with Dominicus and Petrus Bosc in 1619, but the manuscript never returned to the university library of Leiden.

41   Orlers, *Beschrijvinge der stad Leyden*, p. 153. He records that there were nine books among the *Libri Russici*.

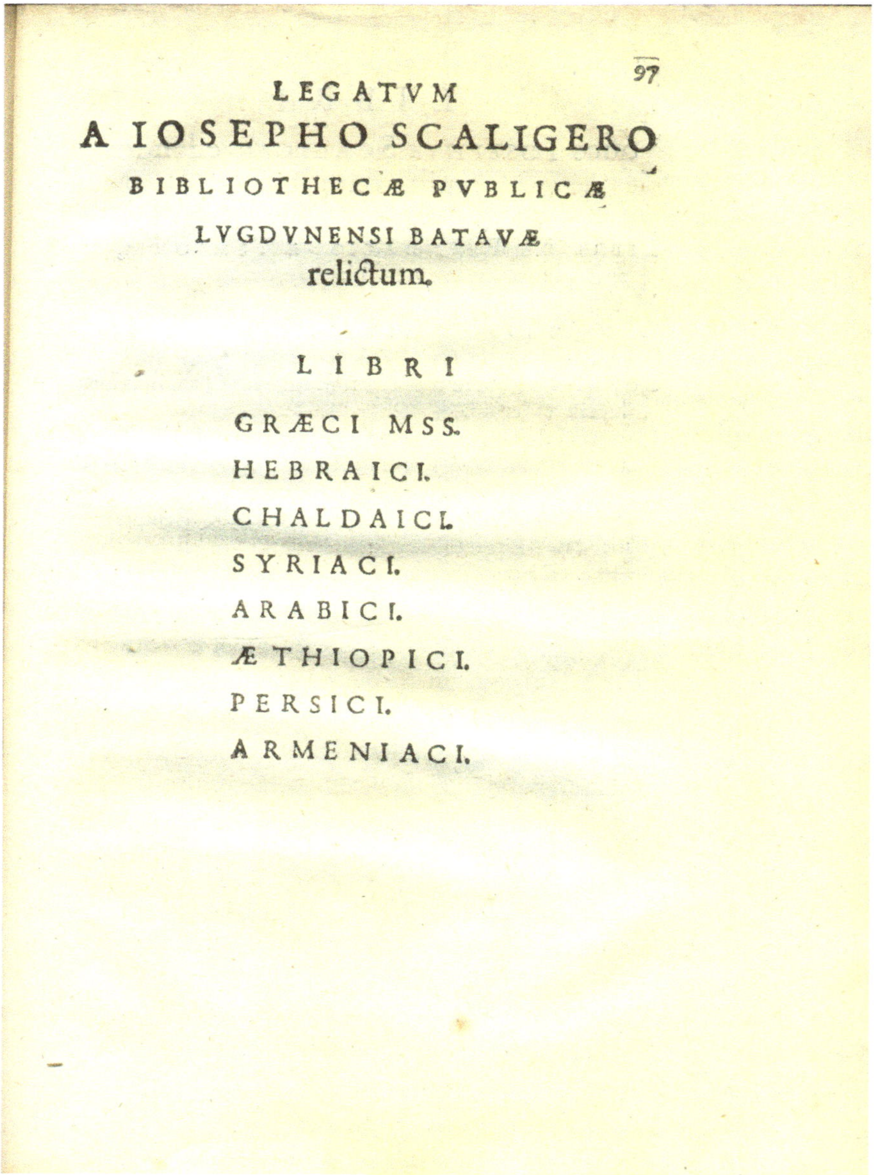

LEGATVM

A IOSEPHO SCALIGERO

BIBLIOTHECÆ PVBLICÆ

LVGDVNENSI BATAVÆ

relictum.

L I B R I

GRÆCI MSS.

HEBRAICI.

CHALDAICI.

SYRIACI.

ARABICI.

ÆTHIOPICI.

PERSICI.

ARMENIACI.

FIGURE 37 In his funeral oration of 1609, Daniel Heinsius was the first to announce the news of Scaliger's momentous bequest to the University of Leiden. Remarkably, he did not mention any of Scaliger's Russian books in the process. UBL 1011 C 14

SCALIGER'S BEQUEST IN THE LEIDEN UNIVERSITY LIBRARY CATALOGUES 233

Even those who will not be prepared to praise you, will be forced to recognise your erudition.[42]

With expressions such as *sapientiae instrumentum* (arsenal of wisdom) and *Qua iam omnes hac in parte bibliothecas provocamus* (compete with all other libraries in these lands), Heinsius displayed his willingness above else to use the bequest to advance the honour and glory of the university library.

Heinsius also placed himself at the forefront as the guardian of the bequest. One may wonder to what extent this was justified. He was unable to describe the books accurately and quickly, and subsequently locked the books away. Did he act of his own accord, or was he following the university's instructions? We know that in 1599, when he purchased books from the auction of the library of the humanist Franciscus Nansius (1520–1595), Scaliger referred to Heinsius in a letter as the custodian of his library.[43] Yet the context does not make clear whether Scaliger considered Heinsius as the future owner of his library, or that he thought of his learned friend as the future librarian of the university. While the curators of the university requested Heinsius to deliver Scaliger's funeral oration, and while Scaliger himself appointed Heinsius as the executor of his literary estate, one cannot escape the notion that Heinsius was mostly occupied with his own image as Scaliger's favourite student and innate successor.[44]

In any case, Heinsius did not distinguish himself as a dutiful or practical librarian, who saw his primary responsibility to be the expansion of the library with donations and bequests.[45] He was the first librarian who enjoyed an annual budget for the acquisition and binding of books. This he did with sincere enthusiasm, and the university library did grow substantially under

---

42   Heinsius, *In obitum V[iri] illust[rissimi] Iosephi Scaligeri*, pp. 26–27.

43   *Correspondence* 11 August 1599 to Heinsius. In 1599, parts of Scaliger's library were still in France.

44   Baerbel Becker-Cantarino, *Daniel Heinsius* (Boston: Twayne Publishers 1978), p. 151. In the words of the French author Balzac, Heinsius was 'assis dans le throsne de Scaliger et donnant des lois à toute l'Europe civilisée'; *Oeuvres complètes* Vol. 1, p. 219). Heinsius sometimes took his role as successor to Scaliger too far, and made enemies in the process, such as Claude Saumaise (1588–1653), the actual successor of Scaliger as professor at Leiden. Cf. *Claude Saumaise & André Rivet. Correspondence exchangée entre 1632–1648 publié et annotée par Pierre Leroy & Hans Bots* (Amsterdam, Maarssen: APA-Holland University Press, 1987), pp. xiv–xv; 113–116 (letter XLVIII).

45   In 1864, A. Angz. Angillis wrote, without any supporting evidence, that Scaliger had planned to give his entire library to Heinsius, but that Heinsius refused this generous gift, and was content with a small selection of books from the collection. See: A. Angz. Angillis, 'Daniël Heins, hoogleraar en dichter', *Dietsche Warande* 6 (1864), p. 15.

234 CHAPTER 6

Heinsius's tenure.[46] He also maintained good relations with the university printers, the Elzeviers.[47] Yet otherwise, Heinsius concerned himself little with the library and the professional tasks that belonged to that position, including the timely compilation of catalogues and the accurate description of catalogue entries, specifically of books in Scaliger's bequest.[48] Instead, his attention was increasingly devoted to his professorship at the university.

That the *Arca* was closed to visiting scholars is evident from the fact that in September 1609, Heinsius refused access to the German Orientalist Petrus Kirstenius (1577–1640) from Breslau, who wished to consult Scaliger's *Lexicon Arabicum*. This refusal did not prevent Kirstenius publishing his *Grammatices Arabicae* in 1610. Other scholars, mostly personal friends of Heinsius, did receive permission to consult manuscripts from the bequest. They included Thomas Erpenius and William Bedwell.[49] Erpenius was even allowed to edit and publish some of the manuscripts, such as the *Kitāb al-amthāl, seu Proverbiorum Arabicorum centuriae duae* (1614), a collection of Arabic proverbs that Scaliger had translated.[50] In 1616, Erpenius also published the *editio princeps* of the New Testament in Arabic with the title *Novum D.N. Iesu Christi Testamentum arabice ex Bibliotheca Leidensi*. The main source for this edition was an Arabic manuscript of the New Testament from Scaliger's bequest.[51]

---

46   The number of books in the library grew from 442 copies in 1595 to 3,117 in 1640.

47   Heinsius was the formal advisor of the printing firm, and from 1608 onwards lived in a house owned by Gilles Elzevier. See: Paul R. Sellin, *Daniel Heinsius and Stuart England. With a Short-title Checklist of the Works of Daniel Heinsius* (Leiden, London: Leiden University Press, 1968), Appendix II: Heinsius' Adresses at Leiden, pp. 253–254, which refers to ELO, Oudbelasting Boek A-II, f. 229[a]-[b].

48   E. Hulshoff Pol, 'The Library', p. 432: 'His term as librarian was not a very fortunate one and he fell short on many points. It should also be remembered that it was only a part-time occupation for a man who was deeply involved in many other fields.'

49   Alastair Hamilton. *William Bedwell* the Arabist 1563–1632 (Leiden: E.J. Brill, 1985), p. 40 and note 52, in which a passage from a letter (British Library, M.S. Burn. 364, f. 238[r]) from Heinsius to Casaubon is cited, in which Bedwell's access to Scaliger's collections is discussed; Sellin, *Daniel Heinsius*, pp. 100–102.

50   UBL MS Or. 26.644 (1) (olim 874 D 7: 3; see Bibliographic Survey Isny 1541–1542); MS Or. 26.644 (2) and MS Or. 26.644 (3). Juynboll, *Zeventiende-eeuwse beoefenaars*, pp. 65–66; Arnoud Vrolijk, 'The Prince of Arabists and his many Errors. Thomas Erpenius's Image of Joseph Scaliger and the Edition of the *Proverbia Arabica* (1614)', *Journal of the Warburg and Courtauld Institutes* 73 (2010) pp. 297–325 and Kasper van Ommen, 'Josephus Justus Scaliger – Works on Christian-Muslim Relations – *Kitab al-amthal, seu Proverbiorum Arabicorum centuriae duae; Proverbiorvm arabicorvm centuriae duae*, 'The book of proverbs, Arabic proverbs of two centuries' in D. Thomas and J. Chesworth (eds.), *Christian-Muslim Relations. A Bibliographical History*. Vol. 8: *Northern and Eastern Europe (1600–1700)* (Leiden, Boston: Brill, 2016), pp. 553–560.

51   UBL MS Or. 217.

FIGURE 38   Title page of Thomas Erpenius, *Novum Testamentum Arabice* (Leiden: In typographia Erpeniana, 1616), UBL 842 D 36

In the years directly following the death of Scaliger, most attention was paid to his Arabic books, especially because of Erpenius's interest in the Arabic language. Only years later was there serious interest in Scaliger's Hebrew books and manuscripts.[52] The professor of Hebrew and Theology, Constantijn L'Empereur van Opwijck (1591–1648), consulted Scaliger's Hebrew collection. In 1633, he published a new edition of the travels of Benjamin of Tudela on the basis of a rare German edition of the same text from 1583 that Scaliger had received from the Swiss Hebraic scholar Johannes Buxtorf (1564–1629).[53]

The library catalogue of 1612 contained a first rudimentary description of Scaliger's bequest. In the preface to the catalogue, Heinsius opened with his own *Oratio Pro bibliothecarij munere gratiarum actio*, written in 1607, when he was appointed to the post of librarian, and dedicated to the curators of the university.[54] This was an extensive and detailed exposition of the recovered freedom of the Low Countries during the Dutch Revolt, including the bloody sieges of cities such as Leiden, which ended with a glorious victory against the Spaniards. Heinsius also compared the library of Leiden with a temple of wisdom in which peace reigned supreme.[55] Scaliger's bequest went unmentioned

---

52   See for example Ludovicus de Dieu's *Gelyana de Yohannan qaddishe id est, Apocalypsis Sancti Iohannis. Ex manuscripto exemplari è bibliotheca [...] Iosephi Scaligeri deprompto, edita charactere Syro, & Ebræo, cum versione Latina* (Leiden: ex typ. Bonaventura Elzevier and Abraham I Elzevier, 1627; USTC 1017058). De Dieu was encouraged by Heinsius to publish this edition. De Jonge, 'The Study of the New Testament' in: *Leiden University in the Seventeenth Century*, p. 72.

53   Binyamin ben-Yonah, *Sefer Masa'ot shel Rabi Binyamin* (Freiburg im Breisgau: Israel Sifroni, 1583; (USTC 661152, UBL 875 F 43–2; see Bibliographic Survey Freiburg im Breisgau 1582–1583). This copy has handwritten annotations in red pencil, provided by a compositor in the printing house of Bonaventura and Abraham (I) Elzevier, to assist in the composition of the Hebrew-Latin edition of the *Itinerarium D. Beniaminis* (1633) by Constantijn l'Empereur van Opwijck: see also UBL 348 G 3. In the preface, l'Empereur mentioned the 1583 edition, as well as the *notae marginales* of Scaliger on the same provided to him by Johannes de Laet. Cf. P.T. van Rooden, *Constantijn l'Empereur (1591–1648). Professor Hebreeuws en theologie te Leiden* (Leiden: Universitaire Pers Leiden, 1985), pp. 168–169; Fuks, *Hebrew Typography* no. 49. Scaliger also owned the Latin translation of the *Itinerarium Beniamini Tudelensis* by Benito Arias Montano (Antwerpen, ex officina Christophe Plantin, 1575; USTC 401643), which he had bound with the *Itinera Constantinopolitanum et Amasianum* and De acie contra Turcam instruenda consilium by De Busbecq (Antwerpen, ex officina Christophe Plantin, 1581; USTC 401866). See the auction catalogue of Nicolaas Heinsius (1682), 'Mathematici & Philosophici In Octavo', no. 114.

54   This was later reprinted as 'Gratiarum actio pro Bibliothecarii munere' in Daniel Heinsius, *Orationes aliquot [...] Cum dissertatione de libello [...]* (Leiden: ex officina Jan Paets Jacobszoon, 1509 [= 1609], USTC 1028731).

55   The oration ended with the poem ΕΙΣ ΤΗΝ ΒΙΒΛΙΟΘΗΚΗΝ ('to the library'), in which the renown and glory of the library were once again emphasised.

in the opening of the catalogue. Yet Scaliger's collection, described in a separate section on pages 79–88, was presented as the most important part of the library for the study of rare and exotic languages.

In the separated *Catalogus Librorum quos bibliothecae Iosephus Scaliger legavit*, Heinsius presented a complete list of Scaliger's bequest to the public for the first time. Only a single title was missing: Scaliger's copy of the Talmud Babylonicum, considered one of the most valuable books in the library, was moved to *Pluteus A*, to the front of the catalogue, because the library already had a copy that was described there.[56] In the separate section, Heinsius provided the reader with brief title descriptions, divided firstly by language and further by format. It is noteworthy that all titles were offered in Latin: the Elzeviers did not yet possess Oriental typefaces. That does raise the question why the catalogue was not printed by the Raphelengius firm, which did own Oriental typefaces and which could have provided accurate descriptions of titles from Scaliger's bequest. More confusingly, the Elzeviers themselves were only responsible for the publication, rather than the printing: in 1612 they did not yet own a printing press, so turned to the likes of Heynderick Lodewyksz van Haestens and Jan Balduinus for their publications. It seems likely that Louis Elzevier, in his role as beadle of the university, exercised some influence over Heinsius to gain the commission, and possibly earned himself a fair sum in the process.

Heinsius first listed the Hebrew books, in the order of folio, quarto and octavo, followed by Arabic books in the same order, but supplemented with Arabic books in decimosexto. In the section for Syriac, Amharic and Russian books, there are fewer than ten titles per category, so the sub-divisions by format were abandoned. After the Oriental books, Heinsius provided a list of manuscripts in Greek and Latin, divided by folio and quarto. The two globes from the bequest are also included here. Throughout the section, printed books and manuscripts were intermingled in a random order; there is no sense of an alphabetical listing. The structure of the list indicates that above all, format was the key ordering principle when storing the books on the shelves of the *Arca*.

The practical value of the 1612 catalogue was very limited where it concerned Scaliger's bequest. If we suppose that the catalogue offered a true reflection of the placement of items in the *Arca*, then the catalogue would have been useful as a finding aid. However, we cannot determine if this was actually the case, and given that the bookcase was nearly always locked, the catalogue would have been of limited practical use to the scholarly community. It is more likely that the catalogue was useful as a tool for the annual

---

56   See the handwritten annotation on p. 79 of the 1612 catalogue, UBL BA 1 C 2-i.

238   CHAPTER 6

inspection of the content of the library cases, and thus of value primarily to
the university and its administration.[57] We can also identify the catalogue as a
valuable tool of publicity for the university, even if that publicity, which placed
Scaliger's bequest and the *Arca* at its centre, was misleading concerning the
practical access to the unique collection.

4   The Catalogue of 1623

It would take eleven years before Heinsius published the third Leiden university catalogue. Shortly after the appearance of the 1612 catalogue, Heinsius's
time and attention were demanded by a growing number of tasks and academic posts. In 1613, he was appointed as professor of Greek, while between
1608 and 1614 he was also the adjunct-secretary of the senate of the university. In 1618, he was appointed historiographer royal by the King of Sweden,
Gustavus Adolphus. As *Praefectus Bibliothecae* he was also forced to justify
himself frequently before the curators of the university concerning the large
sums of money that he expended on the purchase of new books.[58] The curators also repeatedly emphasised that Heinsius should hand over the original
coda to Scaliger's will that contained an inventory of the collection, so that
they could use this to verify the contents of the *Arca*.[59] In 1620, the curators
once again called Heinsius to account, and warned him to spend less money on
new acquisitions; they also demanded that he present an interleaved version
of the 1612 catalogue that listed the new acquisitions.[60] This was a request that
was repeated later the same year. Another two years later, on 9 November 1622,
the curators and burgomasters requested Heinsius's presence during their
meeting, and demanded that, as soon as possible, he must compose and publish a new library catalogue: 'So the same [Heinsius] has been requested and
indeed instructed to order all bookcases and shelves in a decent order, and

---

57   Berkvens-Stevelinck, *Magna commoditas*, p. 75.
58   Heinsius spent more than 1,300 guilders that year on books. See: Molhuysen, *Bronnen* II
       (1916), p. 59.
59   'Om t' allen tijden den selven te mogen confereren jegens de casse der Bibliotheecque.'
       ('To be able to collate at all times the same [inventory] with the bookcase in the library.')
       The inventory was still appended to the will in 1615; we do not know when it was lost. Cf.
       Resoluties van Curatoren 1615: 7/8 May 1615 (Molhuysen, *Bronnen* II, p. 59).
60   Molhuysen, *Bronnen* II, p. 93.

to make an accurate catalogue of the same ... the earlier the better.'[61] The curators were especially concerned that while Heinsius had spent large sums of money on new acquisitions, he had spent very little time cataloguing these new purchases.[62] Slowly there emerged a doubt whether Heinsius would even be able to prepare a useful catalogue of the library.

Nevertheless, in 1623 the third catalogue of the university library appeared in print.[63] Heinsius once again included his oration from 1607 as a preface to the catalogue, as well as the laudatory Greek poem on the library. The description of Scaliger's bequest was similar to that of the catalogue of 1612, but several typographical errors had been corrected by Isaac Elzevier. Some more striking adjustments and additions were also made. In the first part of the *Catalogus librorum quos Bibliothecae Iosephus Scaliger legavit*, from pages 127 to 131, the Hebrew books were described by format; here no serious changes were made. Then the section *Catalogus Librorum Manuscriptorum*, on pages 132 to 135, included the forty-six Arabic, Persian and Turkish manuscripts, in which the sub-division by format had now been abandoned; the manuscript that was described first was an Arabic Pentateuch, followed by the Arabic New Testament. The next section, *Alii libri orientales, partim excusi, partim manuscripti*, beginning at page 136, covered the remaining Oriental manuscripts and printed books in Amharic, Russian and Syriac.[64] This section also

---

61 'Soo is hem by de selven gerecommandeert ende niettemin belast alle de voors. boecken per classes, pluteos & numeros in behoorlicke ordre te redigeren, en alsdan daervan te maecken eene pertinente catalogue ... ende dat hoe eerder hoe liever.' Vergaderinghe der gemelde Heeren curateurs en Burgm. 9 nov. 1622, p. 442. See also: Resoluties van Curatoren 9 November 1622. Molhuysen, *Bronnen* II, p. 107.

62 The curators stopped paying the invoices that Heinsius submitted for the purchase of books from May 1624 onwards. Cf. Resoluties van Curatoren 1624. Molhuysen, *Bronnen* II, p. 117.

63 *Catalogus Bibliothecæ Publicæ Lugduno-Batavæ. Lugduni-Batavorum* (Leiden: Ex Officina Isaaci Elzeviri 1623; USTC 1016288). Cf. Willems. *Les Elzevier*, no. 210. Isaac Elsevier was appointed as university printer as the successor of Jan Paets Jacobsz on 10 February 1620. In 1626, Isaac was succeeded by his brother Abraham and his uncle Bonaventura Elzevier. In the same year, they took over the 'Oriental press' of Thomas Erpenius, who had died in 1624; Erpenius for his part had taken over all the Oriental typefaces from Raphelengius in 1619. Cf. Molhuysen, *Bronnen* II, pp. 206*–207*, 211*–212* and Paul G. Hoftijzer, *A Tale of Fonts 1658–1713. Exploring the Heritage of the Elzeviers* (Amsterdam: Elsevier, 2013).

64 The Swiss Orientalist Johann Heinrich Hottinger (1620–1667) copied the list from the catalogue of 1623 in his *Promtuarium; sive, Bibliotheca Orientalis* (Heidelbergae, Adriaan Wyngaerden 1658 (USTC 2549010), pp. 18–24. In the appendix to this work, Hottinger included four library catalogues, including that of the Scaliger bequest. Jan Loop, *Johann Heinrich Hottinger. Arabic and Islamic Studies in the Seventeenth Century* (Oxford: Oxford University Press, 2013), pp. 169–170. Hottinger stayed in Leiden in 1639 and 1640 as a

included several new titles, such a Japanese manuscript in quarto that could not be found in the 1612 catalogue. On pages 137 to 139, the Greek and Latin manuscripts were listed. In Heinsius's personal copy of the catalogue, he included a handwritten note of an additional title, a copy of the *Thesaurus Arabico-Syro-Latinus* (Rome: Congregationis de Propag. Fide, 1636).[65] This was written by the Italian Orientalist Thomas Obicinus or Tommaso Obizino (1585–1632), and donated to the library by Marcus Bovelius, who had composed the Latin index for the book.[66] Aside from this posthumous acquisition to the bequest, Heinsius did not note other new titles or relevant new information. The last part of the description of the bequest was given over to the *Incompacti manuscripti*. Here too, all titles were given in Latin, with an occasional word of Greek. No use was made of any Hebrew or Arabic typefaces, because Isaac Elzevier did not yet possess any.

What is also remarkable is that not all printed Arabic and Syriac books that were included in the 1612 catalogue were reprinted in the 1623 catalogue. It is possible that these books had been borrowed by Thomas Erpenius when the catalogue was composed; Erpenius had been appointed as professor 'in Arabic and other Oriental languages' in 1613, and was probably the most regular user of the bequest. Then again, why would Heinsius have forgotten that he lent these books to Erpenius? It may be more likely that Heinsius simply skipped over them, probably by accident, because the descriptions of these books in the 1612 catalogue were so poor. Furthermore, the 1623 catalogue pays in general greater attention to the manuscripts than the printed books in the bequest, so this may have been a case of general oversight mixed with carelessness where the printed books were concerned.

---

guest of the professor of Arabic, Jacobus Golius (1596–1667). Hottinger consulted various Arabic manuscripts from Scaliger's bequest, including Scaliger's copy of Maimonides *Moreh Nevuchim* and the so-called *Liber Joshua*. He also transcribed the Syriac lexicon of Bar 'Ali and Scaliger's Arabic-Latin dictionary. Hottinger was actually more interested in and influenced by the books and manuscripts on physics and mathematics in the library of Golius than works from Scaliger's collection. See also Loop, *Johann Heinrich Hottinger*, pp. 12–18; 119; 146.

65   In this private copy the following inscription can be noted: 'Sum Heinsij. Lugd. Bat. 1635'. This catalogue was held in the University Library of Munich (olim 4°.H.lit.2223), but it was lost during the Second World War. A photocopy is happily held in the University Library of Leiden (UBL 20651 C 30). See: A. Biedl, 'Ein bisher vermisster Leidener Bibliotheks-Katalog des 17. Jahrhunderts', *Het boek* 25 (1938), pp. 45–49.

66   Obizino had also provided the Latin translation of *Grammatica arabica agrumia appellata cum versione latina ac dilucida expositione* by Ibn Ajurrum (Roma: Tipografia della Congregazione di Propaganda Fide, 1631; USTC 4014265).

5   The Catalogue of 1640

The catalogue of 1640 was the last one that Heinsius would compose in his function as librarian. Once again, this updated catalogue was necessary because many books and manuscripts were acquired in the period after 1623. The printing of the catalogue was again entrusted to the Elzeviers, to the current directors of the firm, Bonaventura and Abraham. The process of compilation was beset by delays. Already in June 1635, Heinsius had promised the curators to compose a new catalogue, which he expected to finish within two to three months. Heinsius was too optimistic. Only in the autumn of 1636 was there a finished manuscript. In November of that year the Elzeviers printed the catalogue, but it was never distributed. Jacobus Golius, professor of Arabic, was aghast at the quality of Heinsius's description of the two hundred Oriental manuscripts that Golius had collected for the library in the 1620s in the Levant and Istanbul.[67] The curators agreed and asked Golius to assist in the process of composing a new catalogue, but only for the Oriental manuscripts that he had gathered: 'To make a longer and more accurate catalogue of the Oriental books and to reprint this, [and] to distribute this alongside the copies of the most recently printed catalogue to unburden the [finances of the] university.'[68]

A separate gathering was printed that included the new catalogue of Golius's Oriental manuscripts. This appeared in 1640, and was distributed loose, but also appended to the reprinted 1636 catalogue: confusingly, the old description of Golius's manuscripts by Heinsius had not been removed from this, which meant that readers had two lists of the same collection in their catalogue, one in Latin by Heinsius, and that of Golius.[69] The entire business

---

67   Berkvens-Stevelinck, *Magna Commoditas*, p. 79. Golius was appointed as professor of Arabic in 1625; in 1629 he also became professor of mathematics. See: Jan Just Witkam, *Jacobus Golius (1596–1667) en zijn handschriften. Lezing voor het Oosters Genootschap in Nederland gehouden op 14 januari 1980* (Leiden: Brill, 1980).

68   'Te doen amplieren met eene breeder ende pertinenter catalogue van de Orientaelsche boecken ende dan die te herdrucken om alsoo d'exemplaren van dien mette exemplaren van de jongst gedruckte voors. catalogue t'samen te verkoopen tot ontlastinge der voors. Univ.' Resoluties van Curatoren 1638 in Molhuysen, *Bronnen* II, 1916, p. 223. Golius catalogued the collection under the title 'Libri mss. arabici, quos ex oriente advexit I. Golius, cum genuinis arabicis eorundem titulis'. This collection had been catalogued earlier by Pierre Gassendi and published as *Catalogus rarorum librorum quos ex Oriente nuper advexit et in publ. bibliotheca incl. Leydensis Academiae deposuit Jac. Golius* (Paris 1630).

69   Daniel Heinsius, *Catalogus bibliothecæ publicæ Lugduno-Batavæ* (Leiden: ex officina Abraham & Bonaventura Elsevier 1636; USTC 1014408); which included: 'D. Heinsius, Pro bibliothecarii munere gratiarum actio', and at the end, the 'Libri MSS. Arabici & alii, quos pro Academia ex Oriente advexit Jacobus Golius, cum genuisis Arabicis eorundum titulis'. Cf. Willems, *Les Elzevier*, no. 437.

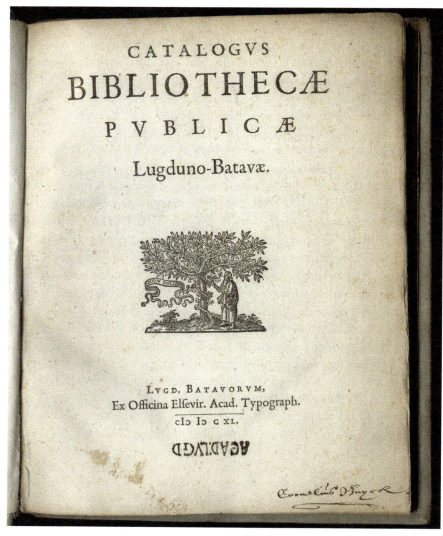

FIGURE 39   Title page of Daniel Heinsius, *Catalogus Bibliothecae Publicae Lugduno-Batavae* (Leiden: Abraham and Bonaventura Elsevier, 1640), UBL BA C n 4

once again demonstrated the insufficiency of Heinsius's linguistic knowledge to curate the Oriental collections of the university, especially those of Scaliger and Golius.[70]

---

70   This is in direct contrast to Davies's statement that: 'He [Heinsius] had a sufficient knowledge of oriental languages'. David W. Davies, *The World of the Elseviers 1580–1712* (The Hague: Martinus Nijhoff, 1954), p. 68.

SCALIGER'S BEQUEST IN THE LEIDEN UNIVERSITY LIBRARY CATALOGUES   243

The catalogue of 1640, the fourth catalogue of Leiden University Library, was a cumulative catalogue, compiled on the basis of the information provided by the previous catalogues. The new acquisitions were described according to their placement in the library: either in the large open cases, the *Arcae* and small cabinets with doors, or the so-called *musaeum* or *cantor* in which the most valuable books were kept.[71] Heinsius reordered the open bookcases (the *plutei*) by placing books on newly added shelves at the bottom of the cases, referred to as *infra* ('below'). This was a good practical solution, but rendered unusable the listing of the catalogue of 1623, as this was based on the placement of books on the *plutei*. Manuscripts and printed books stood side by side on the shelves, which is noteworthy given that the scholars and librarians of Leiden tended to value the manuscripts more than the printed works in the collection.

The title descriptions of the Hebrew books from Scaliger's bequest provided in the 1640 catalogue were taken over entirely unchanged from the 1612 and 1623 catalogues.[72] Yet again, some new titles were added to the bequest which did not feature in the previous catalogues, such as the *Tres libri Chinenses* listed rather eccentrically at the end of the *Libri Hebraei In quarto* on page 162. The overall description remained limited for these rare books. Heinsius did not accrue additional knowledge or insight into Scaliger's bequest over the course of several decades. Antonius Thysius (1603–1655), Heinsius's successor as librarian, demonstrated how incomplete Heinsius's descriptions had been. In an interleaved copy of the 1640 catalogue, he provided many additions and corrections to Heinsius's list of Scaliger's bequest.[73]

In the 1640 catalogue, the 'Catalogus Librorum quos Bibliothecae Josephus Scaliger legavit' is listed on pages 159 to 163. This is followed by the 'Catalogus Librorum Manuscriptorum quos Josephus Scaliger Bibliothecae Leidensi legavit', until page 167, when the new section reads 'Alii libri orientales, partim excusi, partim manuscripti', up to page 172. In the first part, all the Hebrew

---

71   Berkvens-Stevelinck, *Magna Commoditas*, p. 76. Berkvens-Stevelinck copied this informa-
       tion without a source reference from E. Hulshoff Pol, 'The Library', 1975, p. 420, who based
       the information for her part on the memorandum submitted by Paullus Merula to the
       curators of the university (1597–1602). Alongside the *Arca Scaligerana*, there was an *Arca
       Vulcanii* in the library, in which all the manuscripts bought from the estate of Bonaventura
       Vulcanius in 1615 were kept. A portrait of Vulcanius hung above his *Arca* (Molhuysen,
       Bronnen II, p. 59), similar to the positioning of Scaliger's portrait. Books in small formats
       were housed in two separate *arcae*, and there was also an *arca* in which publications by
       the professors of Leiden were held. Cf. Berkvens-Stevelinck, *Magna Commoditas*, p. 43.
72   The alterations concerned minor amendments: Tehillin became Tehillim and the descrip-
       tion of the *Zohar* printed in Cremona was incorrectly listed in the 1640 catalogue as *Zora*.
73   UBL BA 1 C 4. Heinsius's successors mostly added supplementary information on printers,
       authors or additional copies held at Leiden. The new catalogue in preparation by Thysius
       was never completed, as he died suddenly on 25 January 1655.

244   CHAPTER 6

manuscripts and printed books are listed. The second section only includes the Arabic, Persian and Turkish manuscripts, without any of the printed books in those languages. Many of these printed titles were later added by successors of Heinsius in handwritten annotations. The descriptions of the Arabic manuscripts were improved somewhat in the 1640 catalogue, and the number of manuscripts also increased. In the final section, there is a miscellaneous selection of titles in Russian, Amharic, Syriac, Armenian and Japanese, followed by the Greek and Latin manuscripts and the unbound manuscripts (*Incompacti Manuscripti*). The final object described in this section is a wax portrait of Scaliger's father, which is sadly no longer extant.[74]

Remarkably, the Elzeviers, who now possessed ample quantities of Oriental typefaces, were not requested to alter the descriptions of the Oriental manuscripts in Scaliger's bequest. The titles remained unaltered in Latin. It is possible that they were not updated out of haste, or Jacobus Golius had no time or interest to alter all the descriptions of items in Scaliger's bequest – or perhaps Heinsius refused him access. Heinsius generally considered the *Arca Scaligerana* to be forbidden terrain to most colleagues. Even when Claude Saumaise, the eminent humanist and successor of Scaliger, received the keys to the library and the *Arcae* from the curators of the university, Heinsius ensured that Saumaise was not able to access the cabinets.[75]

The total number of books from Scaliger's bequest as described in the 1640 catalogue was 128 printed books and 62 manuscripts, comprising 190 titles in 142 volumes. This was substantially lower than as reflected in the 1612 catalogue (which had 219 titles in 186 volumes). The reason for this is obvious: all Arabic printed books were, without cause, left out of the catalogue. The total number of books listed in the catalogue was 3,117: 498 manuscripts, 350 annotated printed books and a further 2,278 unannotated printed books. The great increase in the number of items prompted Antonius Thysius to replace the *plutei* in 1653 by open bookcases lined against the walls.[76] A wooden fence around the cases was meant to prevent visitors from reaching for the books

---

74 In the library catalogue of 1716, at page 343, the portrait is described at the end of the Greek and Latin manuscripts as 'Effigies Julii Caesaris Scaligeri gypso expressa'. The wax portrait, secured by purple glass and held in a round tin box, was part of the university's collections until the end of the nineteenth century. The tin had rusted badly, and the portrait was so damaged that it proved impossible to restore (Tydeman noted that 'This [portrait] is entirely broken').

75 Salmasius was a talented classical philologist and also possessed some knowledge of Oriental languages. See: Philipp Tamizey de Larroque (ed.), *Les correspondants de Peiresc. Lettres inédites écrites à Peiresc* (Marseille: s.n., 1879–1897), Vol. 5, pp. 84, 106.

76 According to the resolutions of the curators of 8 May 1653.

SCALIGER'S BEQUEST IN THE LEIDEN UNIVERSITY LIBRARY CATALOGUES   245

themselves. Thysius also placed a large bookcase in the middle of the library room, similarly surrounded by a fence.[77] The manuscripts were now separated from the printed books in closed cabinets. Thysius also realised that access to the Oriental collections was important, but it remained a question of looking, rather than touching. To ensure that the public could be privy to the contents of the *Arca*, Thysius decided to replace the wooden panels of the case with latticework. This was a good development for the contents of the *Arca* too, as the ventilation was beneficial to their conservation. Yet the librarian remained in possession of the keys to the cabinet, which was otherwise locked.[78] During all these changes, we may presume that Thysius did leave the contents of the *Arca Scaligerana* undisturbed.[79]

When, in the early 1690s, necessary repairs were undertaken on the roof of the library, curator Hiëronymus van Beverningh (1614–1690) and secretary of the curators, Johannes van den Bergh (1664–1755), decided that the interior of the library should also be substantially renovated. This decision was also prompted by the recent acquisition of the library of Isaac Vossius, several

---

77 *Acta Curatoren* of 29 October 1674. Cf. the description by Friedrich Lucae in his *Europäischer Helicon* (Frankfurt 1711), in which he writes at pp. 855–856: 'Kleinod ist die Bibliothec. Es stehet die Bibliothec auf einem grossen Saal der zu beyden Seiten helle Fenster hat. Die Bücher darinnen sind meistentheils nach der alten Manier, auf Bäncken an Ketten geschlossen doch so dass man sie kan ausnehmen und besehen. Nebenst denen gedruckten Büchern in allen Sprachen und Wissenschaften findet man viele Antiquitäten und Exotica, insonderheit vermehren der Bibliothec splendeur, des Josephi Scaligeri hierher legirte Griechische, Aethiopische, Persische, Armenische Manuscripta, von ungemeiner Seltenheit. ...'

78 Molhuysen, *Bronnen* IV, p. 7*–9*; 31 May 1683, Instruction of the curators and burgomasters concerning the organisation of the public library of the university, article 10: 'The cases containing the manuscripts may henceforth no longer be opened except in the presence of the Praefectus Bibliothecae, and to ensure that they may henceforth be seen from the outside, and enjoy greater circulation of air for their conservation and to prevent the onset of mould, they will be kept behind lattices of iron or copper instead of closed doors.' ('De cassen van de manuscripten en sullen voortaen niet werden geopent als in praesentie van den Praefectus Bibliothecae, ende opdat deselve van buyten mogen werden gesien, oock meer lught mogen hebben tot derselver conservatie ende om alle versticktheyt ende schimmel te voorkomen, sullen deselver in plaetse van de besloote deuren werden voorsien van een dighte kruystralie van ijser off van koper.'); and article 11: 'The cases or the shelves of the printed books shall we reordered in a new manner, so that they may be placed at the greatest distance from one another as possible.' ('De kassen off de plancken van de gedructe boeken sullen op nieuws soodanigh werden gereguleert, dat alle die wijt opene distantien sooveel doenlyck mogen werden.').

79 In 1719, Jean-Baptiste La Curne de Sainte-Palaye (1697–1781) and his twin brother Edme noted after a visit to the library: 'La fameuse bibliothèque qui est fort belle et où sont dans deux armoires à part les manuscrits grecs et hébreux de Scaliger.' Cf. Van Strien-Chardonneau, *"Le voyage de Hollande"*, p. 366 note 76.

246   CHAPTER 6

thousand titles strong. The treasurer (*Thesaurier Extraordinaris*) of the university and municipal architect (the *Fabrijcq*), were asked to present a plan that would improve the organisation of the bookcases.[80] This new plan also had no implications for the *Arcae* of Scaliger and Vulcanius. When, in 1697, the bequest of Christiaan Huygens was incorporated into the library, his books and papers were placed in the Vulcanius's *Arca*, while the words *Legatum Hugenii* were added to the cabinet, and a portrait of Huygens was hung next to that of Vulcanius. At this point in time, both *Arcae* were clearly still considered ornaments that contributed significantly to the renown of the university library.[81]

6   The Catalogue of 1674

The *Catalogus Bibliothecae publicae Lugduno-Batavae Noviter recognitus. Accessit Incomparabilis Thesaurus Librorum Orientalium, praecipue mss.* was published in Leiden in 1674 by the widow and heirs of Johannes Elzevier. The author of the catalogue was the theologian Frederik Spanheim junior (1632–1701), who had been appointed as university librarian on 7 October 1672.[82] His predecessor Johannes Fredericus Gronovius (1611–1671) had already made preparations for a new library catalogue during his tenure, but he died before it was completed. Gronovius had taken on the task in a judicious manner: as part of his preparations, he compiled a list of Scaliger's manuscripts and books that had been erroneously left out of the 1640 catalogue.[83] On the first page of this manuscript list, he also noted books left by Scaliger that had not been included in other earlier catalogues ('*hi*[*c*] *non sunt in catalogo*'), such as the Hebrew dictionaries of Johannes Reuchlin and Forster. He also added titles such as *Sepher Iohasin* and the *Tres libri Chinensis*. This process of

---

80   The municipal architect was Jacobus Roman (1640–1716). See: J. Terwen-de Loos, 'Jacobus Roman, architect, 1640–1716', *Bouw* 15 (1960), pp. 704–709.

81   *Schriftelijk rapport 1741*, p. 43. In 1744, when the bequest of Gerard Van Papenbroeck entered the library, this was secured in a locked cabinet together with the papers of Huygens; the cabinet received the inscription 'Legatum Hugenii et Papenbroeckii'. Molhuysen, *Bronnen* V, p. 156*.

82   *Catalogus Bibliothecae publicae Lugduno-Batavae Noviter recognitus. Accessit Incomparabilis Thesaurus Librorum Orientalium, praecipue Mss* (Lugduni Bat.: apud vid. & her. J. Elzevirii typ., 1674; USTC 1811363).

83   'Jo. Friderici Gronovii Recensio Codd. MSS. Bibliothecae Leidensis (necnon ejusdem Rationes Bibliothecae anni 1666; quas vide in Archivio sub litt. F.' The manuscript was sold by the heirs of Abraham Gronovius together with other family papers to a cheesemonger's for wrapping paper. The papers were then saved by Pieter Bondam. At the auction of Bondam's library on 1 November 1800, the manuscript was bought by the university library (HSS. der Bibl. Publ. Lat. XVIII as No. 128 A). See now UBL BA O no. 2.

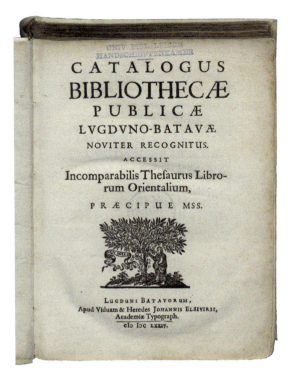

FIGURE 40   Title page of Frederik Spanheim junior, *Catalogus Bibliothecae Publicae Lugduno-Batavae* (Leiden: The widow and heirs of Johannes Elzevier, 1674), UBL BA C N 6

reconstruction indicates that even towards the end of the seventeenth century, uncertainty reigned about the exact composition of Scaliger's bequest.

In the preface of the 1674 catalogue, Spanheim lauded the pioneering role played by Scaliger and his bequest in announcing the library as an important centre of Oriental studies.[84] Here Spanheim placed Leiden on par with other notable libraries with great Oriental collections, namely the Vatican, the Oxford Bodleian and the Marciana in Venice. This was necessary, as

---

84   In *Schriftelijk rapport 1741*, pp. 17ᵛ–18, Van Royen described it as follows: 'Until then [Scaliger's arrival], the university taught seriously only in the Greek and Latin languages, as well as in Hebrew, but the other Oriental languages were considered more as ornaments of scholarship rather than intrinsically useful, yet the learned Scaliger was of a different opinion, and cultivated studies of these languages ...' ('Tot nog toe was aen de Universiteit behalven de Grieksche en Latijnsche talen niet veel anders met applicatie gedoceert als de Hebreeuwsche, oordeelende men de andere Orientalische taelen meerder cieraedt van geleerdheijdt als nut te brengen, edoch van gansch andere gedagten was de doorgeleerde Scaliger, ende, die op deszelfs raedt die Studien cultiveerde ...').

international competition in the library world was gathering pace. Spanheim especially considered Thomas Hyde (1636–1703), Bodley's Librarian and a keen Orientalist, as a noteworthy rival. Despite the fact that the Oriental collections of Jacobus Golius and Levinus Warner (1618–1665) overshadowed that of Scaliger in many respects, Spanheim considered Scaliger's bequest as the most valuable of all donations, not only at Leiden but across Europe. He honoured Scaliger as a progenitor of Oriental collecting, and of advancing scholarly knowledge in multiple fields, including theology, history, medicine, geography and mathematics. In Spanheim's library catalogue, we can discern for the first time a decisive shift that placed the primary focus on the Oriental collections in the library.[85] Nine years later, in 1683, this was emphasised by an important decision made by the curators: henceforth, all Oriental manuscripts, including those of Scaliger, could be consulted freely by scholars after receiving permission from the curators.

The cataloguing of the Oriental titles in the library was undertaken by the learned minister Theodorus Petraeus (ca. 1630–1672) from Flensburg. Because Golius had died in 1667, Petraeus was aided by the Armenian copyist Chiagijn Candi (Shahin Qandi).[86] After Petraeus died, Qandi was supported by the German student Lourens Boots. It is possible that Qandi and Petraeus together were responsible for the new descriptions of Scaliger's manuscripts for the 1674 catalogue. The titles from Scaliger's bequest are listed on pages 252–258 of the catalogue; they are only organised by format. A new feature of the 1674 catalogue was the use of Hebrew typefaces for the Hebrew titles, followed by a Latin transliteration. The Arabic printed books, however, were still presented in a Latin transcription, and amongst Scaliger's Arabic, Persian and Turkish manuscripts, we only find an occasional word printed with Arabic type. This was in direct contrast to the Arabic manuscripts from the collection of Warner,

---

85 'Parario primum Scaligero, tum Erpenio [...] ac tandem Jacobo Golio'. Catalogus 1674, sign **2v. The library of Thomas Erpenius never became part of the university library. His Oriental collection was bought in 1625 by the Duke of Buckingham, and today resides at the University Library of Cambridge. Juynboll, *Zeventiende-eeuwsche beoefenaars*, 1931, pp. 59–118, esp. pp. 117–118; Drewes, *Levinus Warner and his Legacy* (1970); Arnoud Vrolijk and Richard van Leeuwen, *Arabic Studies in the Netherlands. A Short History in Portraits, 1580–1950* (Leiden: Brill, 2014). See also for the careers and intellectual development of these scholars: M.T. Houtsma, 'Uit de Oostersche correspondentie van Th. Erpenius, Jac. Golius en Lev. Warner. Eene bijdrage tot de geschiedenis van de beoefening der Oostersche letteren in Nederland', *Verhandelingen der Koninklijke Akademie van Wetenschappen Afdeeling Letterkunde* 17/3 (Amsterdam 1887).

86 Shahin Qandi was initially appointed by Golius to copy Arabic, Persian and Turkish manuscripts for him.

SCALIGER'S BEQUEST IN THE LEIDEN UNIVERSITY LIBRARY CATALOGUES   249

as these were all listed in Arabic by Petraeus and Qandi, and followed by a Latin translation.

The section *Libri orientales* in the 1674 catalogue contains all Oriental books in the library that did not belong to one of the bequests, as well as items that were present in both Scaliger's and Warner's bequests.[87] The 'duplicates' include useful reference works and grammars, such as the Syriac grammar of Georgius Michael Amira, several Arabic publications of Euclid and Ibn Sina, produced by the *Tipographia Medicea*, and a copy of the Chinese-Japanese dictionary *Racuyoxu*.[88] Spanheim decided to deduplicate these works by selling the less attractive copy, keeping the copy in the best state, regardless of the origin of the item. This is how a rare Hebrew edition of the *Sepher Yuchasin* (Krakow: Yitshak Prostich, 1580) was lost from Scaliger's bequest.[89] It is probable that other books were removed in this fashion, books which may have contained Scaliger's handwritten annotations.[90] Heinsius would have turned in his grave.

In all likelihood, all books were removed from the *Arca* in order to catalogue them. This would have been the first time since Heinsius had described the bequest for the 1612 catalogue on the basis of the coda to Scaliger's will. Spanheim made serious efforts to describe the bequest in a more accessible manner. The *Arca* remained its home, but the collection was no longer presented as separate from the rest of the university library. Instead, the bequest was divided over three sections. The printed books were listed on pages 252–258; the Oriental manuscripts, beginning with the Hebrew manuscripts

---

87   *Libri Orientales – Impressi & MS. tam communis Bibliothecae quam legati Scaligeriani ac Warneriani – Impressi Bibliothecae communis* op pp. 249–251.

88   Georgius Michael Amira, *Grammatica Syriaca, sive Chaldaica* (Roma: in Tipografia Medicea Orientale apud Giacomo Luna, 1596; USTC 809076, UBL 876 C 4; see Bibliographic Survey Rome 1596). Scaliger's copy was probably sold in the auction held by Pieter van der Bibliographic Survey on 1 June 1706. See: *Catalogus Librorum Latinorum, Graecorum, hebraicorum*, 1706, Appendix p. 37: 'Hebraici in Quarto 1. Georg. Mich. Amirae Edininesis è Libano Gram. Syr. *Romae* 1596'. The Chinese-Japanese dictionary consists of three parts; the Leiden copy missed the third part. The book is also a linguistic tool that allows for the identification of *kanji* (Japanese characters of Chinese origin) and *kana* (Japanese syllabic script for loanwords).

89   Zacharias Conrad von Uffenbach saw this copy during a visit to the library of Johannes Theodorus Schalbruch (1655–1723) in Amsterdam. Cf. *Merkwürdige Reisen*, part 3, Frankfurt and Leipzig, 1734, p. 664. The copy is also described in the auction catalogue of the *Bibliotheca Schalbruchiana* (Amsterdam: R. and G. Wetstein 1723) in the section 'Lib. Theolog. in Quarto', no. 143: 'Sepher Juchasin. Cracov 1580', with the addition: 'Hic liber fuit Jos. Scaligeri, qui multa in eo notavit'.

90   A search through various modern library catalogues elsewhere did not reveal the location of some of these sold 'duplicates' from Scaliger's bequest.

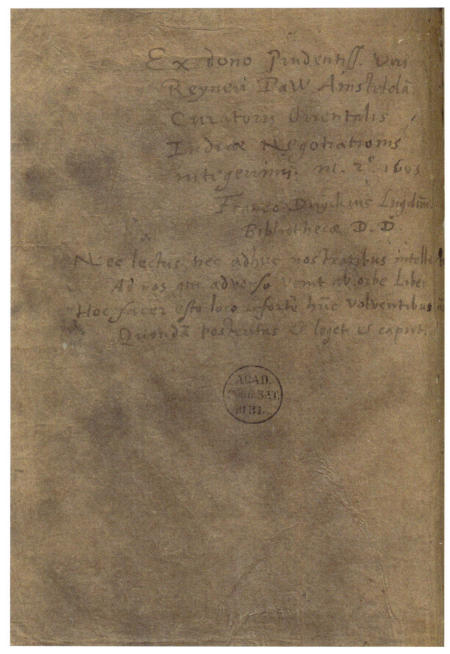

FIGURE 41   *Racuyoxu i.e. Lexicon Sinico-Japonicum et Japonico-Sinicum.* While this page indicates that this work used to belong to Franco Duyck [ens], the following page had a slip of paper applied that reads *Ex Legato Illustris Viri JOSEPHI SCALIGERI.*
UBL SER 36

SCALIGER'S BEQUEST IN THE LEIDEN UNIVERSITY LIBRARY CATALOGUES   251

and followed by the Arabic, Persian and Turkish manuscripts, were detailed on pages 276–283. The Greek and Latin manuscripts were listed separately on pages 391–395, a section that was concluded by the description of the wax portrait of Julius Caesar Scaliger.

All the western printed books in the 1674 catalogue were ordered first by format, and then alphabetically by the author's surname. This new ordering system saw the abandonment of the classification by the placement of the books by the *plutei* in the library. The Oriental books and manuscripts were only ordered by format. Yet to maintain a reasonable overview of the large quantity of books, each volume received a shelf mark in ink on its spine. Some printed works from Scaliger's bequest had an asterisk placed next to their title in the catalogue: this indicated that the work had originally been part of the bequest, but had been replaced by a copy from Warner's more recent bequest.[91]

We can find further clues about the state of the bequest in the interleaved copy of the 1674 catalogue used by the librarians of Leiden to add new acquisitions.[92] Several titles from Scaliger's bequest were crossed through with three inked lines. This was the case for titles including the 'Doctrina Christiana lingua Malabarica Tamul' and 'Meletii Apologia pro Christ. Relig. adversus Judaeos, Graecè & Russicè. Leopoli [Lviv] 1593', both on page 258 of the catalogue. These extremely rare items are no longer in the university library, and it seems likely that they were already missing by the end of the seventeenth century. Other titles are marked up to indicate that they were added to the section 'Libri Orientales. Impressi & MS. tam communis Bibliothecae quàm Legati Scaligeriani ac Warneriani', even though they did not come from either the Scaliger or Warner bequests. These were generally dictionaries and grammars related to the Oriental languages; it is noteworthy that the addition of these works often led to the weeding of items from Scaliger's bequest, even if

---

91   See, for example, the copy of 'Thesei Ambrosii Introductio in Linguas, Ch.Syr. ac Armen. 1539', UBL 1497 D 23. The title read: Theseo Ambrosio or Theseus Ambrosius Albonesius, *Introductio in Chaldaicam linguam, Syriacam atque Armenicam et decem alias linguas. Characterum differentium alphabeta, circiter quadraginta, et eorundem inuicem conformatio: mystica et cabalistica quamplurima scitu digna: et descriptio ac simulachrum phagoti Afranii* Pavia, excudebat Giovanni Maria Simonetta, 1539 (USTC 808409) and *Postelli 12. Linguæ cum Gramm. Arab* (Paris: excudebat Pierre Vidoué apud Denis Lescuier, 1538; USTC 147464, UBL 876 C 8 or 873 C 1). On page 256 of the catalogue, there are three items (In quarto 52, 53 and 54) which have an asterisk added to them, not because they were replaced, but because they were added to Scaliger's bequest, even though they had no relation to the bequest. This became clear after an inspection of these items, which is also the reason why they have not been included in the comprehensive catalogue in the appendix of this present work.

92   UBL BA 1 C n6.

252   CHAPTER 6

the new additions were not copies of the same editions as present in Scaliger's bequest, but variant dictionaries or grammars. This process indicates that by the end of the seventeenth century, the librarians of Leiden no longer regarded Scaliger's bequest as an untouchable whole, a legacy collection that could never be altered.

The total number of books described as part of Scaliger's bequest in the 1674 catalogue had expanded compared to that of the 1640 catalogue. In 1674, the bequest included 212 titles in 211 volumes, as opposed to 190 titles and 142 volumes in 1640. This change was probably due to the disbinding of *Sammelbände*; this was a process that could reveal new, yet uncatalogued titles. The 212 titles included 78 manuscripts, of which 48 were in Arabic, Persian or Turkish; the remaining 134 titles were printed books. To place Scaliger's bequest in the context of the entire university library collections, the 1674 catalogue contained 1,702 manuscripts and 9,152 printed books, of which 3,725 belonged to multi-volumes works. Since 1640, the collections had grown by 2,310 titles. This period of growth was also marked by the increasing attention paid to manuscripts. Spanheim deliberately separated all manuscripts from printed books in the 1674 catalogue, while from 1653 onwards, the manuscripts in the collections of Leiden were also increasingly separated from the regular library stock, and kept in closed cabinets. While new acquisitions were simply added to the end of the shelves of their respective faculties, manuscripts were kept under lock and key, thus emphasising their value and intellectual status.

7   The Catalogue of 1716

The catalogue of 1716 is the most complete of all the catalogues published up till that point by Leiden University. It was supplemented in 1741, and in this form remained the critical handbook to the collections until the nineteenth century. The catalogue of 1716 was modelled on those of Oxford and Cambridge, because the title descriptions in those catalogues were considered to represent the finest standard of the day.[93]

The Leiden catalogue was entitled *Catalogus librorum tam impressorum quam manuscriptorum Bibliothecae Publicae Universitatis Lugduno-Batavae*. The university printer, Pieter van der Aa (1659–1733), was at the forefront of the compilation of the catalogue, and published it at his own cost.[94] The catalogue

---

93   Archer Taylor, *Book Catalogues. Their Varieties and uses*, 2nd ed., revised by William P. Barlow (Winchester: St. Paul's Bibliographies, 1986), p. 18.

94   See: Jean C. Streng, 'The plates in the Leiden University Catalogus librorum of 1716', *Quaerendo* 22/4 (1992), pp. 273–284; Paul G. Hoftijzer, *Pieter van der Aa (1659–1733), Leids drukker en boekverkoper* (Hilversum: Verloren, 1999) pp. 55–57.

FIGURE 42　Title page of *Catalogus Librorum* [...] *Bibliothecae Publicae Universitatis Lugduno-Batavae* (Leiden: Petri van der Aa 1716), UBL 1418 A 5

254 CHAPTER 6

introduced a new classification system, which would help open up the collections of the library considerably. The acquisition of the substantial library of Isaac Vossius in 1690 prompted the re-ordering of the bookcases in the library, and therefore also the reorganisation of the library catalogue.[95] The catalogue of 1716 listed 3,488 manuscripts, including some 1,500 in Oriental languages, and 11,293 printed books in around 25,000 volumes. In comparison with the catalogue of 1674, the library had expanded its collections by 5,877 titles, an average of 140 books a year.

The compilation of the 1716 catalogue had already begun in 1702, under the direction of Wolferdus Senguerdius (1646–1724), librarian from 1701 to 1724.[96] Senguerdius had found the Oriental manuscripts in great disarray. The manuscripts with wooden boards, including some bequeathed by Scaliger, had been badly mauled by woodworm. These damaged items were provided with new bindings made of Russia leather (*juchtleer*).[97] The poor cataloguing and conservation of the Oriental collections was in stark contrast to the great value that the university attached to the collections for publicity purposes. To his dismay, Senguerdius could not find all the manuscripts, as some had been stolen or sold. He decided to open all the cabinets that held the various bequests to the university, and ensured that every item in it was stamped with the university library mark. These efforts did sadly not translate to a new and fully revised catalogue of the Oriental books in the library; he did not have the necessary skills to improve the descriptions, nor did he have a decent working overview.

---

95 Isaac Vossius (1618–1689), son of the humanist Gerardus Joannes Vossius (1577–1649), was a famous scholar and book collector. He died in Windsor on 21 February 1689. On his life and career, see: Eric Jorink and Dirk van Miert (ed.), *Isaac Vossius (1618–1689) between Science and Scholarship* (Leiden: Brill, 2012), especially A. Balsem, 'Collecting the ultimate scholar's library. The Bibliotheca Vossiana', pp. 281–309. See also the thesis by Astrid Balsem, *Een biografie van de Bibliotheca Vossiana* (Amsterdam: s.n, 2020).

96 Senguerdius was also professor in philosophy at Leiden. Together with Jacobus Gronovius, he worked from 1705 until 1707 on the new catalogue. Johannes Heyman, assisted by Carolus Schaaf, described the Oriental books and ensured that the entire catalogue was ready for the press. Molhuysen, *Bronnen* V, p. 121*.

97 *Schriftelijk rapport 1741*, p. 44ᵛ: 'and because there were some manuscripts [bequeathed] by Scaliger, he ensured that all items were stamped. ... And to increase security he also applied two different locks, rather than a single lock, to the cabinets, while at the same time most of the Oriental manuscripts that had wooden boards were rebound in Russia leather because of the damage done to them by the worms' ('en overmits daeronder waren eenige manuscripten van Scaliger, heeft hy ordre bekomen alle de Stukken te doen stempelen. ... Ende is tot meerder securiteit op die tijdt ook goedgevonden de kassen der manuscripten in plaets van met een, met twee verschillende sloten te verzekeren, werdende toen de meeste Oosterschen manuscripten uyt de banden, voorzien met houte borden, waeruyt de wurmen veel schaden aen de boeken deden, in jugtleer verbonden.').

When Senguerdius died in 1724, there were still problems left undealt with. Petrus Burmannus (1668–1741), his successor, recorded his thoughts on these matters in 1724 in a report to the curators:

> It has been found that not all of the Oriental manuscripts had been numbered, nor placed in the right order or location, which could not be remedied due to the poor linguistic skills [of the custodians], while during the cataloguing process, not enough care was made to retrieve the books afterwards, as in the printed catalogue one finds that the Arabic, Turkish and other Oriental titles have a Latin transliteration for each item, but no-one had written these Latin titles on the clean flyleaves of the books themselves, which if it had happened, it would have been possible for anyone, even if they were not qualified in these tongues, to review the present books and to collate the missing numbers with those listed in the catalogue.[98]

Clearly the situation had changed little, despite Senguerdius's warning twenty-two years earlier. The books were still inadequately ordered and poorly cared for.

In 1702, the curators had instructed Senguerdius to remove Scaliger's collection from his *Arca*. They wished to take full advantage of the new wall-lining bookcases.[99] Scaliger's Hebrew, Latin and Greek manuscripts were,

---

98 'Edoch in de Orientaelsche MSS. [manuscripten] is bevonden, dat deselve noch alle genombreert [genummerd] zijn, noch op haar ordre en plaats gestelt, 't welcke wegens de onkunde der talen niet wel heeft konnen geremedieert worden, dewijl by het maken van de catalogus geen genoegsame sorgh voor het toecomende, om alles op sijn plaats te vinden, schijnt gedragen te sijn, sijnde wel in de gedruckte cataloge de Arabische, Turcxe en ander Orientaelsche titulen der boeken in het Latijn overgeseth ende bygedruckt, dogh dat versuymt is in ider boek vooraen op het schoone papier, dat voor ider boek is, deselve titulen in te laten schrijven, 't welck so geschiet was, het ligtelyck aen ider een, schoon in die talen niet ervaren, soude weesen de recensie der boeken te doen en de deficierende nummers met die van de gedruckte catalogus te doen convenieeren'. Molhuysen, *Bronnen* IV, 1920, p. 187*, 10 August 1724. The report led to very little, as Albert Schultens, professor of Oriental languages, and the first curator of the Oriental collections in the library, complained in 1740 that the collection was in chaos.

99 Molhuysen, *Bronnen* IV, p. 191, Resoluties van curatoren d.d. 1 February 1702: 'That the same [Senguerdius] will take care that the manuscripts of Scaliger are removed from the wooden case and transported to one of the latticed cases, and that further, to prevent as best as possible the loss of the same manuscripts, the same will all be stamped, as has thus far been done for the printed books' ('Dat denselven sorge sal dragen, dat de MSS. van Schaliger uyt de houte cassa genomen en in een van de getralide kassen getransporteert worden, ende dat wijders, om 't vervreemden van de voors. MSS. soveel mogelyk te

256   CHAPTER 6

together with some manuscripts in otherwise unidentified languages, held in bookcase IX. The contents of this bookcase were described as follows:

– Hebrew [meaning Oriental] manuscripts donated by Joseph Scaliger to the library, in total 63 items.[100]
– Latin and Greek manuscripts bequeathed by Scaliger to the library (*Mss. legati Scaligeri Folio et minori forma*). In total 73 items.[101]

To reduce the confusion surrounding the Oriental collections for visitors (and future custodians), Senguerdius divided the Oriental manuscripts in three groups. These groups were also reflected in the catalogue of 1716: the books gathered by Golius came first, described with numbers 1 through 211, followed by Scaliger's bequest, numbered 212 through 268, and finally Warner's collection, numbered 269 to 1198.[102] The manuscripts were not ordered in a chronological sequence of bequests, as that would have meant that Scaliger's manuscripts came first. This numbering has never since been altered.

The cataloguing of the Hebrew and other Oriental books for the 1716 catalogue was undertaken by Carolus Schaaf (1646–1729), lecturer in Oriental languages since 1680, and Johannes Heyman (1667–1737), the former Dutch minister at Smyrna, who had been appointed lecturer in Hebrew and Oriental languages in 1707. In 1710, the two men would jointly become professors in Oriental languages.[103] This was the first time that the entire Oriental collections could be catalogued with any accuracy; the two men had much work editing and revising the Latin translations of the manuscripts in the Scaliger, Golius and Warner collections. Their efforts paid off: the catalogue of 1716 was received extremely well by other librarians and scholars, in the Dutch Republic and further afield. Leiden could finally publicise its Oriental collections in the

---

weeren, denselve voortaen mede sullen gestempelt worden, gelijk tot nu toe omtrent de gedruckte boeken geschiet is.'). The resolution also discusses the large number of lost and missing manuscripts from the library.

100   The Hebrew manuscripts bequeathed by Scaliger numbered around twenty. UBL BA C 17, Standcatalogus deel X, f. 104ᵛ, notes that seventeen parts of the *Apparatus Botanicus* of the regent and diplomat Hieronymus van Beverningh (1614–1690) were added to the collection, but they were moved against later to join the case holding the titles in *Historia Naturalis*.

101   UBL BA C 17 Standcatalogus deel X, ff. 106ʳ–114ʳ. In the Greek manuscript BPG 76 N there is the note 'Ex arca I. Schalig' (= J. Scaligeri), in which the removal of the manuscripts is documented. Around 1700, the spelling 'Schaliger' became more common. Number 74, also described here, was the wax portrait of Julius Caesar Scaliger.

102   *Schriftelijk Rapport 1741*, pp. 55ʳ–55ᵛ. Librarian Van Royen would later count only 1,193 catalogued manuscripts, as Heyman and Schaaf had catalogued one volume as multiple manuscripts.

103   Jan Nat, *De studie van de Oostersche talen in Nederland in de 18e en 19e eeuw* (Purmerend: J. Muuses, 1929), pp. 21–26.

glory that they deserved, emphasising especially the richness of its valuable manuscripts.

The printed books from Scaliger's bequest were described in the 1716 catalogue as part of the *Hebraici, aliique Orientales excusi*; a separate header, *Excusi legati Scaligeriani*, announced Scaliger's titles on pages 310–313.[104] All titles received the assignation *Heb.* (for Hebrew) and a number. The organisation within the section was by format, in the traditional order of folio, quarto, octavo and duodecimo. The printed books were described separately from the manuscripts; the 21 Hebrew manuscripts were listed at pages 404–405 and the other Oriental manuscripts, those numbered 212 to 268, were found on pages 417–419. In total, Scaliger's bequest in the 1716 catalogue numbered 129 printed books in 117 volumes and 46 Oriental manuscripts with 63 individually described texts. The total number of books is thus 194 titles in 163 volumes; in the 1674 catalogue, there were 212 titles in 211 volumes. It is very likely that due to the poor state of the bindings, the librarians decided to bind together certain items, to save money on binding costs. Other items from Scaliger's bequest were de-duplicated because of their presence in the Warner bequest, while some manuscripts were missing entirely. This can be the only reason why the number of titles decreased so considerably. It is noteworthy that the 1716 catalogue also attributed a Japanese book to Scaliger's bequest, one that certainly never belonged to him: a confession of faith from 1582, written by the Jesuit Luis de Granada.[105] Many of the title descriptions do have notes to indicate that they were annotated extensively by Scaliger: '*Cum additamento vocum Arabicarum manu Scaligeri*' or '*Manu Scaligeri multis in locis notatum*', and other phrases.

At the time of the compilation of the 1716 catalogue, the physical location of the manuscripts in the library was constantly in flux, from one bookcase to another. Yet nothing is mentioned in the sources concerning the displacement of the printed books from the *Arca Scaligerana* to the new bookcases lined against the walls. It is possible that these books simply remained in the *Arca*, and that they were joined in there by other (rare) printed books. The transfer of the manuscripts to new cases did not mean that the *Arca* was superfluous. In an engraving depicting the library in the book *Les délices de Leide* (1712), we can still identify Scaliger's *Arca* and that of Vulcanius. Both *Arcae*

---

104 Nevertheless, some books from the bequest were listed in the main section of printed books, the *Bibliotheca publica*, such as Scaliger's copy of Santes Pagninus, *Hebraicarum institutionum libri IIII* (Paris: ex officina Robert Estienne, 1549; USTC 150280), with his handwritten annotations (Cat. 1716, p. 308).

105 *Fides no dŏxi toxite* (Amacusa: 1592) (UBL SER 614).

FIGURE 43   The university library as depicted in the *Les délices de Leide* of 1712, with the *Arca Scaligerana* and Vulcanius's *Arca* in the left background, underneath the staircase.
UBL 403 G 15

were situated underneath the raised gallery where Golius's acquisitions and Warner's bequest had received a place.[106]

In *Les délices de Leide*, Scaliger's collection is no longer regarded as the most important collection of the library. His bequest was referred to in the same breath as that of other notable donors to the Oriental collections, while the individual who was celebrated the most was 'the famous Golius' – who ironically never donated any manuscripts to Leiden, but bought them for the university with institutional funds.[107] This was a foreboding of what was to

106   *Les délices de Leide* (Leiden: Pieter van der Aa, 1712), p. 150.
107   *Les délices de Leide*, pp. 149–150: 'D'abord il n'y avoit à cette Bibliothèque que deux longues & fort élevées rangées de Livres: mais comme la Salle qui la contient est longue, large,

SCALIGER'S BEQUEST IN THE LEIDEN UNIVERSITY LIBRARY CATALOGUES 259

come: a few decades later, Scaliger's bequest would be entirely overshadowed by the Golius and Warner collections.[108] Their printed books and manuscripts were presented together on the gallery above the south entrance of the library. Their prominence was thereby emphasised, to the detriment of Scaliger's bequest.[109] Over time, interest in Scaliger's collection would diminish further. In the nineteenth century, one Professor of Arabic, Reinhart Pieter Anne Dozy (1820–1883), described the books from Scaliger's Oriental bequest as 'of little importance'.[110]

After the catalogue of 1716, the university library would publish a new overview of the Oriental manuscripts only in the nineteenth century. That time they were described in Dozy's and De Jong's *Catalogus codicum Orientalium Bibliothecae Academiae Lugduno-Batavae* of 1851, in which Scaliger's manuscripts were distributed amongst the catalogue, ordered by subject. Seven years later, Moritz Steinschneider would describe more extensively the Hebrew manuscripts from the bequest in his *Catalogus codicum hebraeorum bibliothecae academiae Lugduno-Batavae*.[111] It is in many ways remarkable that Scaliger's bequest was increasingly neglected during the later eighteenth and nineteenth centuries, while Oriental studies flourished at Leiden at the same time.

8   Conclusion

The earliest known lists of Scaliger's bequest focus most prominently on the manuscripts in his collection, as these were considered to be more valuable than printed books. This is clearly reflected in the list of Scaliger's books that

---

 fort exhaussée, & fort claire, on a practiqué une troisième rangée double dans le milieu, depuis que les Curateurs de l'Académie ont aquis des Heritiers du célebre *Isaac Vossius* sa nombreuse Bibliothèque. Outre cela il y a une très-grande quantité de manuscrits des plus anciens & des plus rares en toutes les Langues Orientales, Hebreux, Arabes, Persans, Samaritains, Ethiopiens, &c. que *le Grand Scaliger*, & *le célebre Golius*, & autres illustres Personnages ont donné, par leur Testament, à la Bibliotheque.'

108 See note xx at p. xx. See also: Z.C.v on Uffenbach, *Merkwürdige Reisen durch Niedersachsen, Holland und Engelland* (Ulm: 1753–1754).

109 *Acta Curatoren* of 29 October 1674. See the engraving in *Les délices de Leide*, p. 150. A. Vrolijk and R. van Leeuwen, *Arabic Studies in the Netherlands. A Short History in Portraits, 1580–1950*. Leiden 2014, pp. 171, 174.

110 Dozy also wrote in his prologue of the *Catalogus* codicum *Orientalium* bibliothecae academiae Lugduno Batavae Vol I (Leiden: E.J. Brill, 1851), p. 11: 'Haud ita multos bonae notae libros continet Legatum Scaligeri' ('Scaliger's bequest contains few useful books').

111 Moritz Steinschneider, *Catalogus codicum hebraeorum bibliothecae academiae Lugduno-Batavae* (Leiden: Brill, 1858).

was copied by Vulcanius. This investigation has also shown decisively that copies of Oriental books from Scaliger's bequest were replaced when Leiden acquired a second copy of the same from another source, such as the *Legatum Warnerianum*. These later copies were often in a better condition, and the library did not have enough space or loyalty to Scaliger's bequest to keep his collection intact.

Remarkably, occasionally books were added to the bequest which were printed after Scaliger had died. These books, such as a *Biblia Hebraica sine punctis* (Amsterdam, 1639) and a *Novum Testamentum Graecum* (London: R. Whittaker, 1633), were listed as part of Scaliger's bequest in the 1716 catalogue, even though it was impossible that they could ever have belonged to him.[112] Other books, such as the Japanese *Fides no doxi* (1592), were attributed to Scaliger's bequest because of the exotic nature of the language in which they were printed; this particular item too was never owned by Scaliger. This confusion is, at times, understandable. Until recently, it was presumed that the copy of the Chinese-Japanese dictionary *Racuyoxu* (1598) could not have belonged to Scaliger. While a printed slip stating *Ex Legato Illustris Viri Josephi Scaligeri* was attached to the item, the flyleaf clearly indicates that it was donated to the library in 1605 by Franco Duyck. Why this slip was nevertheless pasted in was not obvious, until this research demonstrated that Scaliger did own a copy of that dictionary, in three loose parts, which was indeed donated to the university as part of his bequest. Scaliger's copy was sold in the nineteenth century as a duplicate, but as a type of institutional penance, a slip was attached to the Duyck copy to indicate that this book was indeed once donated by Scaliger, even if it was not this specific exemplar.[113]

For almost three centuries, the printed books in Scaliger's bequest have not been kept together as one collection in the library. The Oriental manuscripts are still shelved together, from call numbers Or. 212 to Or. 268.[114] Over the course of many years and the many movements and reorganisations of the university library, the printed books have become ever more dispersed from one another. This made the reconstruction of Scaliger's printed books, kept in a collection of 5 million items, not without its challenges.

---

112 The copy of the Greek New Testament from 1633 was already listed erroneously as part of Scaliger's bequest in the 1674 catalogue.

113 UBL BA C 42 Standcatalogus deel x: 'Racuyoxu (Liber Sinicus). In Collegio Japonica Soc. Jesu 1598. Ex legato Jos. Scaliger' (olim 863 B 6–9) and on the following page 'Racuyoxu (Lingua et Charactere Japanico) In collegio Japanico Soc. Jesu 1598 – Donavit Franco Duijckens' (olim 847 B 1).

114 The Russian manuscripts in the bequest were moved in the nineteenth century to the library's department for Western manuscripts.

The inventory composed by Scaliger and written by Vulcanius, as well as the library catalogues published before 1716, have all been invaluable in the search for Scaliger's books, but none give a complete picture. Even the catalogue of 1716, which upon publication was regarded as highly trustworthy, has its shortcomings. The descriptions of Scaliger's books in the various catalogues all testify to the difficulties faced by the librarians by the breadth and exotic nature of the bequest. Ultimately, the 1716 catalogue was able to remedy this situation as best as possible, and present Leiden as a leading centre of Oriental studies. Even if Scaliger's bequest was beginning to pale in comparison to more recent acquisitions, his contributions to Leiden's reputation were nevertheless critical.

CHAPTER 7

Oriental Collecting in Context

One can only gauge the relative importance of Scaliger's Oriental collection by comparing it to other collections from his time. What this process reveals is that Scaliger was able to amass an extensive and varied personal library. It is also striking that his bequest comprised so many books from far-off lands that Scaliger never visited himself. This chapter will contextualise Scaliger's bequest, and will demonstrate its importance to the University of Leiden in the early seventeenth century, as much as today.

1   Private Collecting in the Early Dutch Republic and Its Neighbours

The Republic of the seven United Provinces of the Netherlands fostered the blossoming of a rich book culture in the sixteenth and seventeenth centuries. A general interest in books, prints and maps was stimulated by the development of universities and academies, by the development of industry and science and the expansion of global trade. The crafts of printing and bookselling were well advanced by the early seventeenth century, and were able to cater to the growing demand for books amongst the Dutch public. In the Dutch Republic, collectors were able to build significant libraries of European books and manuscripts. Books from the Middle East and the Far East were rarely present in such collections, and generally considered to be curiosities. This should not obscure the fact that there was serious and sustained interest amongst Dutch scholars in the history and philology of Oriental cultures, which is demonstrated not least from the popularity of topographical descriptions and atlases in private libraries of the period.[1] Professional libraries often had a topical focus that matched the profession of the owner, such as theology in the collections of ministers, jurisprudence in the collections of lawyers, and medicine in the collections of physicians, but this focus was never exclusive. Professors considered themselves to be polymaths by nature, and they

---

1   See the variety of catalogues available in Brill's Book Sales Catalogues Online, http://primary sources.brillonline.com/browse/book-sales-catalogues-online. See also G.B.C. van der Feen, 'Noord-Nederlandsche boekerijen in de zestiende eeuw', *Het boek* VII (1918), pp. 81–92, 318–334 and *Het boek* VIII (1919), pp. 219–224. Andrew Pettegree & Arthur der Weduwen, *The Bookshop of the World. Making and Trading Books in the Dutch Golden Age* (New Haven and London: Yale University Press, 2019).

© KONINKLIJKE BRILL BV, LEIDEN, 2025 | DOI:10.1163/9789004701526_009

often collected broadly to emphasise their scholarly credentials. When professors bought books on Oriental cultures or languages, they generally bought books translated into western languages, especially translations of Hebrew and Arabic medicine and mathematics. Oriental books were rarely present in their original languages; this was a decisive difference with Scaliger's collecting habits.

Scaliger's library numbered around 2,250 books. This was a substantial quantity for a professorial library in the first decade of the seventeenth century. In comparison, the auction catalogue of the bequest of the humanist Bonaventura Vulcanius (1610) numbered 2,245 books.[2] Other Leiden colleagues owned smaller libraries, such as the botanist Carolus Clusius, who had seven hundred volumes.[3] Scaliger was often full of praise for the libraries of his professional contemporaries. He admired Vulcanius's collection, although he complained that 'Vulcanius always keeps the books to himself'. This was probably an exaggeration, as Vulcanius did on one occasion give Scaliger a rare translation of a Syriac text by the ninth-century author Moses Bar-Cepha and a Hebrew manuscript on chronology copied by Elia ben Moses Trautlein.[4]

The earliest printed auction catalogue, documenting part of the library of Philips van Marnix van St Aldegonde, was published in 1599. This contained some 1,600 volumes, although Marnix's juridical books were not included in the catalogue. We know that Marnix owned the *Weltbuch* (1542) by Sebastian Franck, the *Cosmographia Universalis* (1575) by Sebastian Münster, André Thevet's *La Cosmographie universelle* (1575) and Ortelius's *Theatrum* (1575),

---

2   One should remember that in 1615, 2,244 lots from the library of Vulcanius were also auctioned, some of which might have been items that remained unsold in 1610. Vulcanius donated all his manuscripts to the University Library of Leiden. See Van Selm, *Menighte treffelijcke Boecken*, p. 114; Paul Smith, 'Remarques sur les catalogues de vente aux enchères de la bibliothèque de Vulcanius' in: H. Cazes (ed.), *Bonaventura Vulcanius, Works and Networks Bruges 1538-Leiden 1614* (Leiden, Boston: Brill, 2010), pp. 121–144. In the *Scaligerana ou bons mots, rencontres agreables* (p. 441) Scaliger had few good words about Vulcanius. Yet we also know that they dined together, and from their surviving correspondence they seemed to be close. In a presentation copy of Scaliger's family history, Vulcanius is described by Scaliger as 'Amico singulari'. Bodleian Library BYW S. 6.25. See also Vrolijk and Van Ommen, *All my Books*, pp. 83–85.

3   Cf. *Catalogus librorum bibliothecae Clarissimi Caroli Clusi* [...] (Leiden: Thomas Basson in aedibus Paul Stockius, 1609; USTC 1122229). For a reconstruction of Clusius's library, see: S. van Zanen, *Planten op papier. Het pionierswerk van Carolus Clusius (1526–1609)*. Zutphen 2019, pp. 281–343.

4   *Scaligerana* 1740, p. 216. This possibly concerns a copy of the *De paradiso commentarius scriptus à Mose Bar-Cepha Syro omnia ex Syrica lingua nuper translata per Andream Masium* (Antwerpen: ex officina Christophe Plantin, 1569; USTC 401436), UBL 876 G 4. *Scaligerana* 1740, p. 216; *All my Books in Foreign Tongues* 2009, pp. 83–84, UBL MS Or. 4736 (SCA 19).

264 CHAPTER 7

as well as a variety of Hebrew theological texts.[5] The personal collection of Christopher Plantin in Antwerp numbered some 728 titles in 1592.[6] This included many valuable source texts that had assisted the printing of Plantin's famous Polyglot Bible.[7] The French scholar Claude Dupuy left a library of 2,018 volumes after his death in 1594. The library of the jurist Cujas, so admired by Scaliger, contained a similar number of volumes at his death in 1590.[8] Books were no longer true luxury objects in the seventeenth century, although they remained expensive due to the high price of paper, transport costs and the labour-intensive process of printing. Scholars who collected books were primarily interested in texts, and the books were purchased for their study or reference value. The binding of a book or its ornamentation were of secondary importance.

This was in contrast to the collections of aristocrats and wealthy merchants, who, on the whole, had greater financial means than professors. This also explains why aristocratic libraries were often as large or larger than those of scholars.[9] Aristocratic collectors often spent considerable sums on the aesthetical qualities of their books, including sumptuous bindings and decoration. The extensive and internationally renowned library of De Thou represented a remarkable combination of a professional and aristocratic collection. De Thou's library was composed of some 12,000 volumes at his death in 1617, making it one of the largest private collections of his age.[10] The son and heir

---

5   The library was largely collected during the period 1560–1597. See: *Catalogue of the Library of Philips van Marnix van Sint-Aldegonde sold by Auction (July 6th), Leiden, Christophorus Guyot, 1599* [repr.] (Nieuwkoop: B. de Graaf, 1964).

6   Leon Voet, *The Golden Compasses: A History and Evaluation of the Printing and Publishing Activities of the Officina Plantiniana at Antwerp*. Vol. 1 (Amsterdam: Vangendt & Co, 1969), pp. 338–344; 350–352.

7   The key collaborators on this project were the Biblical exegetists Benito Arias Montano (1527–1598), Guy le Fèvre de la Boderie and Andreas Masius.

8   According to the estimate of Henri Omont in his 'Inventaire des manuscrits de la bibliothèque de Cujas (1590)', *Nouvelle revue historique de droit français et étranger* 9 (1888), pp 233–237. In his collection of 2,000 volumes there were between 200 and 400 manuscripts. See also: A. Jouanna (et al., eds.), *Histoire et Dictionnaire de Guerres de Religion* (Paris: Laffont, 1998), which mentions under the entry 'Jacques Cujas' that he possessed 'une bibliothèque impressionnante qui, à sa mort remplit trois salles et comprend plus de 300 manuscrits'.

9   The library of Charles de Croÿ, duke of Aarschot and prince of Chimay (1560–1612), contained some 3,022 titles. Cf. Edward van Even, 'Notice sur la bibliothèque de Charles de Croy, duc d'Aerschot (1614)', *Bibliothèque Belge* 9 (1852), pp. 380–393; 436–451. The library of the merchant Daniël van der Meulen contained 1,162 titles.

10   See: Henri Harisse, *Le président de Thou et ses descendants, leur célèbre bibliothèque, leurs armoires et les traductions françaises de J.-A. Thuani Historiarum sui temporis: d'après des documents nouveaux* (Paris: Librairie H. Leclere, 1905), pp. 1–82; I.A.R. De Smet, 'Les

ORIENTAL COLLECTING IN CONTEXT

of De Thou, Jacques-Auguste II, appointed the brothers Dupuy as executors of the collection. They installed themselves in the Hôtel de Thou to continue De Thou's historical opus, while they also described and catalogued the collection, producing the basis for the two-volume printed catalogue of 1679.[11] Yet not all French aristocratic libraries were similar in size to De Thou's; the library of Catherine de' Medici contained some 2,000 volumes, making it similar in size to the libraries of scholars such as Scaliger, Cujas or Dupuy.[12]

2 Oriental Books in Sixteenth-Century Scholarly Libraries

During the sixteenth century, university libraries were in general not well equipped with Oriental books. If anything, they might include a few Hebrew Bibles, a Talmud, some grammars and dictionaries. This meant that most scholars interested in Oriental cultures were required to collect Oriental texts themselves. These personal collections were frequently of far greater quality, quantity and variety than institutional libraries. Unfortunately, there are very few sixteenth-century personal libraries with substantial Oriental collections that have remained together. In this respect, Scaliger's bequest is a great exception, one that allows us to chart what sorts of Oriental books were available in Europe, and what subjects were of interest to contemporary scholars.

What types of Oriental books were commonly found in sixteenth-century scholarly collections? We can identify printed books and manuscripts in languages such as Aramaic, Syriac, Amharic and Arabic, but the largest proportion of Oriental books in early modern Europe were Hebrew books. Whereas printing in Arabic emerged rather slowly in Europe, and only gathered pace in Italy in the second half of the sixteenth century, printing in Hebrew had a long history. The broad interest in Hebrew sources and texts ensured that there were also early bibliographies of Hebrew titles. One of the first such bibliographies

---

Arrêtes confessionelles de la *Bibliotheca Thuana*' in: A. Vanautgaerden (ed.), *Les labyrinthes de l'esprit. Collections et bibliothèques à la Renaissance/Renaissance Libraries and Collections* (Genève: Droz, 2015), p. 232, which mentions 9,000 printed works in 6,000 volumes.

11   De Thou's library was ultimately auctioned in 1677, after the death of his son. The manuscripts from the collection ended up, via Colbert, in the Royal Library in Paris. In 1645, the brothers Dupuy ensured that the library of their father also entered the Royal Library, incidentally in the same year that they were both appointed as royal librarians.

12   Jérôme Delatour, *Une bibliothèque humaniste aux temps des guerres de religion. Les livres de Claude Dupuy d'après l'inventaire dressé par le libraire Denis Duval (1595)* (Paris: Editions de l'ENSSIB 1998), p. 34. For an estimate of Dupuy's library, Delatour relied on the inventory compiled by the librarian Denis Duval in 1595.

266 CHAPTER 7

is a list of seventy titles compiled by Sebastian Münster in his *Grammatica Hebraea Eliae Levitae Germani* (Basel, 1543).[13] Others books also included lists of consulted Hebrew and Aramaic sources, such as that in the appendix of the *Iosuae Imperatoris Historia* of Andreas Masius (Antwerp: Plantin, 1574), which was used as a bibliography by contemporaries.[14]

An important source for collectors of Hebrew books was the four-volume bibliography *Bibliotheca Universalis* (1545–1555) of Conrad Gesner (1516–1565). Gesner's bibliography presented in alphabetical order a total of 12,000 western and Oriental titles, written by some 1,800 authors. The *Bibliotheca Universalis* soon became a recognised reference work for classical and humanist scholarship, as well as a useful means to identify Hebrew manuscripts and printed books. Gesner also provided information on Hebrew works translated into Latin, such as various Bible editions, including the two editions of the Hebrew Bible (with Rabbinic commentaries) printed in Venice by Bomberg. A stock list issued by Bomberg, numbering seventy-five titles, was also included in the *Bibliotheca Universalis*.[15] Gesner's work also featured two separate lists of ninety Jewish publications and ninety-three Christian Hebraist works.[16]

It is uncertain whether Scaliger used the *Bibliotheca Universalis* as an 'instant library catalogue' for his own collection.[17] In total, Gesner included important bibliographical information on 258 Hebrew titles, including 165 rare printed editions. Yet it seems unlikely that Scaliger owned an edition of the *Bibliotheca*, as it was not listed in his auction catalogue. One source that Scaliger did own

---

13   Münster presented this list, *Nomenclator Hebraeorum quorundum librorum*, at the end of his book, and added that the list was not complete: 'Et multi alii, quorum nomina non mihi occurunt'.

14   See the overview of the fifty-nine manuscripts and printed books that Masius consulted for his publication of the book of Joshua in the Antwerp Polyglot Bible in Th. Dunkelgrün, 'The Hebrew Library of a Renaissance Humanist. Andreas Masius and the Bibliography to his *Iosuae Imperatoris Historia* (1574), with a Latin Edition and an Annotated English Translation' in *Studia Rosenthaliana* 42–43 (2010–2011), pp. 197–252.

15   The list is reprinted in: A. Freimann, 'Daniel Bombergs Bücherverzeichnis', *Zeitschrift für hebräische Bibliographie* 10 (1906), pp. 38–42. Other researchers, including Abraham Yaari, doubt whether this was originally a stock list issued by Bomberg, because it includes items that were not printed by him; nevertheless it was common in the sixteenth century that printers issued mixed stock catalogues of works printed by themselves and those printed elsewhere that they had in stock. For a broader discussion of this issue, see Marvin J. Heller, 'The Hebrew Book Trade as Reflected in Book Catalogues', in *Quaerendo* 26/4 (1996), p. 248.

16   Conrad Gesner, *Pandectarum sive Partitionum universalium libri xxi* (Zürich: excudebat Christoph Froschauer (I), 1548), ff. 38ᵛ–42ᵛ (USTC 682395).

17   This term was used by Burnett, *Christian Hebraism*, p 144.

ORIENTAL COLLECTING IN CONTEXT

was the *Eisagoge* by Gilbert Génébrard from 1587.[18] This included an *Index librorum rabbinicorum editorum*, with 107 Hebrew titles.

Nevertheless, the *Bibliotheca Universalis* was not a rare book, and the university library of Leiden already owned a copy in 1595. Scaliger would have been able to consult the work easily.[19] Various titles from Gesner's bibliography were present in Scaliger's library, especially Hebrew grammars, dictionaries and commentaries. Scaliger also owned a variety of items printed by Bomberg, including a copy of the *Sefer Olam* (1513); a copy of the *Leson Limudim, id est, lingua doctoru[m]* (1506); a copy of the *Ben hamelech vehanazir* (a later edition from 1557); a copy of the *Sefer icarim i[d est]. articuli fidei, Arba turim id est, quatuor versuum* (a later edition from 1597); and a copy of the *Derech emuna* (1542).

3 Oriental Collections outside the Dutch Republic

The importance bestowed on Scaliger's Oriental collection at Leiden was part of a broader European culture of library building, which honoured distinguished and rare collections. The fact that Scaliger's books were kept in an *Arca* emphasised the ornamental status of his bequest, separated out from the main book collection of the university.[20] This is a phenomenon that we can also distinguish elsewhere in the sixteenth century, such as in Rome. The influential cardinal Domenico Grimani (1461–1523) owned a great collection of Hebrew books, but was no Hebrew scholar himself; instead the books were a tool of patronage as much as a display of wealth.[21] Royal and princely libraries were often collected to project cultural power. Duke Albrecht V of Bavaria bought the entire Oriental library of Johann Albrecht Widmanstetter (1506–1557), which would form the basis of the court library in Munich that opened in 1558.[22] With this substantial Oriental collection, supplemented in 1568–1571 with the *Antiquarium*, a richly decorated hall in which Albrecht displayed antique sculptures, the duke announced himself as the owner of a serious collection.

---

18 In the catalogue of the UBL of 1612, this is described as *Genebrardus de legendis Rabbinis. Lutet*. UBL 874 D 39; see Bibliographic Survey Paris 1587.

19 Bertius, *Nomenclator*, f. H3ʳ.

20 Burnett, *Christian Hebraism*, p. 167, citing Ladislaus Buzás, *German Library History, 800–1945* (Jefferson: McFarland & Co, 1997), p. 178.

21 Burnett, *Christian Hebraism* (2012), p. 171.

22 H. Striedl, 'Die Bücherei des Orientalisten Johann Albrecht von Widmanstetter', in H.J. Kissling and A. Schmaus (eds.), *Serta Monacensia. Franz Babinger zum 15. Januar 1951 als Festgruss dargestelt* (Leiden: Brill, 1951), pp. 200–244.

His main rivals included the library of the Vatican, the royal library of France, the Palatine library in Heidelberg and the library of the Medicis in Florence.[23]

From the mid-sixteenth century onwards, more European libraries acquired Oriental books to add to their collections. In due course, these libraries would all become rivals to Leiden's famous library. Since 1555, the *Bibliotheca Palatina* in Heidelberg had possessed Oriental manuscripts. Scaliger's mentor Postel had bought these works when he took part in the first French embassy to the Levant in the years 1535–1537, as well as during a second embassy in 1549–1551, when he resided in Istanbul. Postel would sell all these Oriental manuscripts to Ottheinrich (1502–1559), the first Elector Palatine, and a renowned patron of the arts.[24] In sixteenth-century Italy, the eyes of great collectors were also fixed on the East. In 1590, the library of the Vatican was moved to its grand new lodgings in Rome, while three years later, the *Bibliotheca Ambrosiana* opened its doors in Milan; both libraries had a substantial collection of Oriental printed books and manuscripts. In Spain we can identify a similar trend in King Philip II's library at the Escorial. This collection grew rapidly in size due to the acquisitions of Diego Guzman de Silva, Philip's ambassador in Venice between 1571 and 1576. Guzman organised the transportation of dozens of crates with Hebrew and Arabic books and manuscripts to Spain. Catalogues issued by Venetian book dealers that Guzman also despatched to Spain allowed for more purchases directly from the Escorial.[25]

Over time the strategies of Oriental collecting changed. Until the middle decades of the sixteenth century, most collectors of Oriental books were motivated primarily by their desire to own and display exotic, curious and exclusive objects. There were exceptions, notably the scholars Reuchlin, Widmanstetter and Cardinal Egidio da Viterbo (1465–1536), who bought Oriental books only for their own research, especially into the Kabbala. In the second half of the sixteenth century, collectors and librarians increasingly devoted themselves to studying Oriental languages and consulting their Oriental collections

---

23   Otto Hartig, *Die Gründung der Hofbibliothek durch Albrecht V und Johann Jakob Fugger* (München: De Gruyter, 1917), pp. 11–15.

24   Catalogus *Bibliotheca Palatina. Ausstellung der Universität Heidelberg in Zusammenarbeit mit der Biblioteca Apostolica Vaticana* (Heidelberg: 1986), pp. 86–87; 92. Most of the Hebrew manuscripts in the library came from the collection of the Fugger family, which, for their part, had bought these books from the great Italian collector and humanist Gianozzo Manetti (1396–1459). See: Umberto Cassuto, *I Manoscritti Palatini Ebraici della Biblioteca Apostolica Vaticana e la Loro Storia* (Città de Vaticana: s.n., 1935).

25   In 1575 the library was expanded with another thirty-three Hebrew manuscripts from the library of Diego de Hurtado de Mendoza. Cf. Burnett, *Christian Hebraism*, p. 179; Michael J. Levin, *Agents of Empire. Spanish Ambassadors in Sixteenth-Century Italy* (Ithaca: Cornell University Press, 2005), pp. 189–193.

actively to expand their own knowledge. Many librarians were experts in Oriental philology and cultures, such as Benito Arias Montano, librarian of the Escorial from 1577 onwards, and the Netherlandish Orientalist Sebastian Tengnagel (1573–1636), librarian at the court of Vienna between 1608 and 1636.[26] For information on Oriental books, and their acquisition, librarians made much use of Jewish and gentile agents, clerks and scholars. They also travelled to Italy, the centre of Hebrew printing and the trade in Oriental books, to purchase books for their libraries in person.

The Reformation and the Counter-Reformation played major roles in the building up of Oriental collections. Scholars trawled through Oriental sources for insights into the Christian Bible, hoping to find evidence that might support their confessional arguments on the corruption or authenticity of their version of Scripture. Libraries fuelled this scholarly competition as weapons in a confessional conflict. Books in libraries from one camp were not easily accessible to scholars from another. In general, Protestant libraries had less stringent policies on access and borrowing; this is certainly the case when comparing the *Bibliotheca Palatina*, a Protestant library, to the Escorial or the Vatican.[27] This also meant that Protestant scholars were, on the whole, faced with greater restrictions concerning access to valuable sources than their Catholic colleagues. This stimulated Protestant scholars to assemble their own private collections of Oriental works. After 1600 there were four great institutional Protestant libraries with Oriental collections that opened their doors to scholars: the Bodleian in Oxford (from 1603), the university library of Leiden (from 1609), the Palatine library in Heidelberg (until it was removed to the Vatican in 1622) and Sion College in London (from 1630).

We have seen how Heinsius repeatedly lauded Scaliger's bequest to a Dutch and an international audience. He was convinced that thanks to Scaliger's collection, Leiden could become the foremost centre in Europe for the study of Oriental languages and cultures. This vision always remained an unrealised ideal, because Heinsius failed miserably in the opening up of the bequest, both in terms of bibliographical description and physical access to the collection. We can therefore only place Scaliger's bequest in a meaningful international perspective by comparing it to other contemporary Oriental collections.

---

26   F. Unterkircher, 'Sebastian Tengnagel' in: J.L. Stummvoll, *Geschichte der Österreichischen Nationalbibliothek. Erster Teil. Die Hofbibliothek (1368–1922)* (Vienna: Prachner, 1968).

27   Cf. Anthony Grafton, 'The Vatican and its Library' in A. Gradton (ed.), *Rome Reborn. The Vatican Library and Renaissance Culture* (New Haven, London, Yale University Press, 1993), pp. 3–45. When the Palatine library was seized in 1622, it contained some 700 manuscripts and 13,000 printed books. It was transported to the Vatican in 196 crates; most of the collection still resides there today.

Already during Scaliger's lifetime, there were various European institutional libraries with some Oriental books. Scaliger knew most of these libraries well; he owned various catalogues of Oriental books, and knew which works were of interest for his own research.[28] He discussed and compared other collections in his correspondence: he considered the Palatine library in Heidelberg much better equipped with Oriental texts than the Vatican library.[29] Scaliger had visited several libraries in Rome during his stay in the city in 1565, when it was still a secret to the wider world that he converted to Protestantism in 1562. He therefore had a decent overview of what institutional libraries throughout Europe had to offer in terms of their Oriental collections, but we must reflect that his opinion on the Vatican library was in part coloured by his confessional allegiance. Since the papacy of Leo X (1513–1521), the *Biblioteca Apostolica Vaticana* had one of the greatest collections of Oriental books, with substantial holdings of Hebrew, Aramaic and Syriac texts. Around 1590, the library as a whole contained some 4,000 books, including many Oriental manuscripts as well as a smattering of items in Japanese and Chinese.[30]

The Viennese *Hofbibliothek* also held a substantial Oriental collection in the early seventeenth century. The curator of the library who had revitalised its fortunes was Hugo Blotius (1533/4–1608), from the Southern Netherlands. In 1575, Blotius was appointed chief librarian by Emperor Maximilian II (r. 1564–1576), and Blotius's first task was to compile an accurate catalogue. In 1576, Blotius estimated that the library, which had been kept in decrepit circumstances,

---

28 See for example: *Correspondence* 6 August 1600 to David Hoeschelius. Hoeschelius had been appointed in 1593 as city librarian of Augsburg. This library had been established with the collection of the humanist Conrad Peutinger (1465–1547) at its core. In 1607, Casaubon sent Scaliger a catalogue of the manuscripts held in the royal library in Paris. *Correspondence* 5 May 1607 to Casaubon.

29 *Correspondence* 25 July 1608 to Gruterus, the librarian of the Palatine library: 'The Palatine library is richer and supplied with better books than the library of the Vatican' ('Locupletior est et meliorum librorum quam Vaticana'). See also: *Correspondence* 5–6 March 1608 to Gruterus, concerning Scaliger's request to receive a copy of the catalogue of the Palatine library. A copy of the catalogue of Greek manuscripts can be found at p. 20 of the auction catalogue of 1609. According to *Correspondence* 13 July 1606 to De Laet, Scaliger owned a copy of Angelo Rocca, *Biblioteca apostolica Vaticana. a Sixto V in splendid. locum translata, commentario illustrata* (Roma: Stamperia Apostolica Vaticana, 1591; USTC 852771). A copy of this book cannot be traced in the auction catalogue of 1609.

30 Mutio Pansa, *Della libraria Vaticana ragionamenti* [...] (Roma: Giacomo Ruffinelli appresso Giovanni Martinelli, 1590; USTC 846510), pp. 318–319. For an overview of the Oriental books in the Vatican library, see: Alastair Hamilton, 'Eastern Churches and Western Scholarship' in: Grafton, *Rome Reborn*, pp. 225–249.

held 7,379 volumes in thirty cases.[31] From 1599 onwards, Blotius was assisted in his work by the young Netherlandish Orientalist Tengnagel, who succeeded Blotius as librarian in 1608. Tengnagel would purchase 119 Oriental manuscripts from Syria, written in Hebrew, Arabic, Persian and Turkish. He also bequeathed at his death his personal collection of 4,000 volumes to the library.[32]

Other libraries also possessed substantial quantities of Hebrew, Arabic and other Oriental books, including the royal library in Paris and the ducal library of Bavaria in Munich. It is clear that Leiden had serious international competition in the realm of Oriental collecting. Yet it is perhaps not particularly fair to compare Scaliger's personal library to these great institutional collections, many of which were founded much earlier and had greater opportunities to amass Oriental books. It is therefore pertinent to compare Scaliger's bequest specifically with other personal collections of his era.

4 Burnett's Canon

Around the early seventeenth century, printed book production had increased significantly, and many more libraries contained copies of the same texts. The historian Stephen G. Burnett compiled a canon of sixteenth-century Jewish printed books and works by Christian Hebraists, traced in contemporary auction and library catalogues from around Europe.[33] He provided a list of the forty-two most common Hebrew titles found in his corpus.[34] It is uncertain

---

31 F. Unterkircher, 'Hugo Blotius und seine ersten Nachfolger (1575–1663)' in: J.G. Stummvoll, *Geschichte der Österreichischen Nationalbibliothek* (Vienna: Prachner, 1968), pp. 79–162; L. Brummel, 'Hugo Blotius und die Leidener Universität', in J. Mayerhöfer (ed.), *Festschrift Josef Stummvoll. Dem Generaldirektor der österreichischen Nationalbibliothek zum 65. Geburtstag, 19. August 1967*, Band 1 (Vienna: Verlag Brüder Hollinek, 1970), pp. 152–155; Pettegree & Der Weduwen, *The Library*, p. 1.

32 O. Smital, 'Die Hofbibliothek', in H. Zimmermann (et al., eds.), *Die beiden Hofmuseen und die Hofbibliothek* (Wien: Halm und Goldmann, 1920), pp. 50–55. In the period before the appointment of Tengnagel, the library bought the collection of Hans Dernschwam, who had travelled extensively throughout the Levant. The library also expanded its holdings of manuscripts, especially Greek works, thanks to the efforts of Ogier Ghiselin de Busbecq (1552–1592), extraordinary ambassador of Ferdinand I (1531–1564) at the Ottoman court, and attached to the imperial library between 1565 and 1570. The most important manuscript added by Busbecq was the Dioscorides codex dated to 512, annotated in Arabic.

33 It should also be mentioned that Burnett largely restricted himself to collections owned by German and Swiss Christian Hebraists.

34 Burnett investigated the catalogues of the university library of Wittenberg (1540), Strasbourg (1572?) and the collections of Johannes Reuchlin, Martin Bucer, Sebastian Münster, Konrad Pellikan, Georg Siegel and Johannes Pappus. S.G. Burnett, 'Christian

how Burnett established the parameters for the selection of his titles and his catalogues, which renders his investigation less systematic than it could be. Nevertheless, as an exercise I traced how many of Burnett's forty-two titles appear in Scaliger's collection, as well as the collections of Johannes Drusius the elder and Franciscus Raphelengius the elder (both professors of Hebrew in the Dutch Republic), of Pierre Bullioud (1548–1597) and Isaac Casaubon (both in France) and of Thomas Bodley in England. It should be mentioned that Bodley did not have a personal collection, but was actively purchasing for the foundation of the Bodleian Library."With the excepti"n of Bullioud, these scholars were a"l Protestant, but they did differ from each other in various ways. Drusius was exclusively a Christian Hebraist, while Casaubon, like Scaliger, had broader scholarly interests. Raphelengius was predominantly a specialist of Hebrew, but was also deeply involved in the wider scholarly book trade.[35]

I also added for this comparison an additional category with Arabic titles. The production of printed Arabic works only took off towards the end of the sixteenth century, but many scholars interested in Hebrew also developed a passion for Arabic philology, in part to strengthen their understanding of Hebrew. Like Scaliger, they were therefore frequently collectors of Arabic works too.

Table 4 demonstrates which Oriental books were owned by Scaliger, Drusius, Raphelengius, Bodley and Bullioud. They all owned a substantial collection of Hebrew Bibles, as well as grammars, dictionaries and concordances. Scaliger and Drusius also owned the most important commentaries on the Torah, and they expressed a similar interest in Hebrew history and chronology. None of the scholars, except Scaliger, owned many books in the field of post-biblical Hebrew culture. His library was broadest in its collection of works on Oriental culture as a whole, and especially in the fields of Oriental philosophy and medicine. His collection was also undoubtedly the richest in works in Arabic.

From Table 4 it becomes clear that Scaliger owned more than three quarters of the titles selected from the Burnett canon, while Raphelengius and Drusius possessed less than half. Outside of the Republic, the Bodleian Library was best supplied, with twenty-four out of forty-two titles from the canon, or fifty-seven per cent, present in its collections.

Aramaism: The Birth and Growth of Aramaic Scholarship in the Sixteenth Century', in R.L. Troxel (et al., eds.), *Seeking out the Wisdom of the Ancients. Essays offered to honor Michael V. Fox on the Occasion of his Sixty-Fifth Birthday* (Winona Lake: Eisenbrauns, 2005), pp. 433–436.

35   There is sadly little information on the detailed make-up of collections of Catholic owners of Hebrew books.

ORIENTAL COLLECTING IN CONTEXT

273

TABLE 4 Hebrew and Arabic books, partially selected from Burnett's canon, owned by Scaliger in comparison with those owned by Raphelengius, Drusius, Bodley and Bullioud

Bibles and commentaries	Scaliger	Drusius	Raphelengius	Bodley	Bullioud
Hebrew Bible (Tenakh)	x	x	x	x	x
Levi b. Gersom, comment. Thora	x	x	x	x	x
Bachya b. Asher, comment. Thora	x			x	x
Abraham Saba, Be'ur 'al ha-Torah (Tz'ror ha-Mor)	x			x	
Moses Nahmanides, Perush 'al ha-Torah	x			x	x
Judah Abravanel, Perush 'al Nevi'im ahronim				x	
David Kimchi, Tehilim	x				
Joseph Albo, Sefer Ikkarim	x				

Grammars, dictionaries, concordances	Scaliger	Drusius	Raphelengius	Bodley	Bullioud
Nathan b. Yehiel, Aruch	x	x	x		x
Concordance	x		x	x	
David Kimchi, Sefer ha-shorashim	x	x	x	x	x
David de Pomis, Zemach David	x	x		x	x
David Kimchi, Michlol	x	x	x	x	x
Moses Kimchi, Diqduqim	x				x
Solomon Urbino, Ohel Moed		x	x		
Abraham de Balmes, Miqneh Avram	x	x	x	x	x
Elia Levita, Tishbi	x		x		x

Histories	Scaliger	Drusius	Raphelengius	Bodley	Bullioud
Abraham ha-Levi, Seder Olam of Zuta	x	x			
Joseph b. Gorion, Yossipon	x	x		x	
Abraham Zacuto, Yuchasin	x	x	x		
Benjamin of Tudela, Itinerarium	x				

TABLE 4   Hebrew and Arabic books, partially selected from Burnett's canon (*cont.*)

Halakha (Jewish law)	Scaliger	Drusius	Raphelengius	Bodley	Bullioud
Moses Maimonides, Mishneh Torah	x			x	x
Moses v. Coucy, Sefer mizvot ha-gadol				x	x
Jacob b. Asher, Arba'ah Turim	x			x	
Aaron Levi Barcelona, Sefer ha-Hinnuch				x	
Mishnah				x	
Col Bo	x				

Miscellaneous (philosophy, medicine, mystical ethics, Midrash)	Scaliger	Drusius	Raphelengius	Bodley	Bullioud
Joseph Albo, Ikkarim	x	x			
Moses Maimonides, More Nevukhim	x	x		x	x
Bahya ibn Pekuda, Sefer Hovot	x				
Judah ha-Levi, Sefer ha-Kuzari	x			x	
Simeon bar Jochai, Zohar	x			x	x
Mischal hakadmoni	x		x		
Ibn Sina, Kanon ha-gadol	x				
Pirqe Avot	x		x	x	
Melchita		x	x		
Tanchuma	x	x		x	

Christian Hebraists	Scaliger	Drusius	Raphelengius	Bodley	Bullioud
Sebastian Münster, Kalendarium	x	x		x	
Sebastian Münster, Arukh	x		x	x	
Multi-lingual Psalterium Genua 1516	x	x	x	x	x
David Potken, Psalmen	x	x		x	x

ORIENTAL COLLECTING IN CONTEXT

TABLE 4   Hebrew and Arabic books, partially selected from Burnett's canon (*cont.*)

Arabic	Scaliger	Drusius	Raphelengius	Bodley	Bullioud
Geographia Universalis	x	x			
Avicenna	x		x	x	
Alphabetum Arabicum	x		x		
Professio fidei Arabice-Latina	x		x	x	
Quatuor Evangelia	x			x	
Euclides	x			x	

The comparison of Scaliger's Oriental collection with that of the Catholic French scholar Bullioud reveals particularly interesting insights. Bullioud's collection of Oriental books numbered some sixty titles, some of which had previously belonged to Santes Pagninus (1470–1536), and had been assembled predominantly to bolster the Catholic cause in France during the religious troubles. Bullioud employed his philological talents as scholar chiefly to refute the arguments of his Protestant scholarly opponents. Like Thomas James, Bodley's first librarian, he collected Oriental works as sources for a theological debate. He owned many Bibles and books that helped him to interpret the Hebrew language, but he barely owned any Oriental books of history or medicine, and he did not collect books in Oriental languages other than Hebrew.[36]

It is also noteworthy that Scaliger owned more printed books in Semitic languages other than Hebrew than the number of items that make up Burnett's Hebrew canon. Approximately a tenth of Scaliger's Oriental collection consisted of books in Aramaic or Syriac. This once again emphasises the diversity of Scaliger's collection, and the breadth of his scholarly interests. The comparison with other personal collections of Oriental books helps explain and justifies the contemporary renown of Scaliger's library. The praise that he received for his collection of books, especially his manuscripts, was not the result of mere flattery, but reflected sincere wonderment at the size and breadth of his library.

To extend our comparison of Scaliger's library with that of his contemporaries in scope, we can make helpful use of contemporary auction catalogues. We cannot compare such catalogues like for like, especially since Scaliger's

---

36   Bullioud's collection of some 200 books was donated by his son François in 1608–1610 to the Jesuit College of De la Trinité in Lyon.

276 CHAPTER 7

library was split between the bequest, the part of his collection that was appropriated by friends such as Heinsius, and the main part of the library that was sold at auction. Nevertheless, the comparison with four contemporary auction catalogues that follows below will allow us to tease out meaningful difference in terms of the number of Oriental and western books in each collection. I have chosen for this comparative exercise the auction catalogues of Scaliger's contemporaries Drusius, Raphelengius and Casaubon. To add a further layer of analysis, I complemented the sample with a non-Christian collector, the Hebrew scholar, physician and writer Abraham ben David Portaleone from Mantua.

5 The Auction Catalogue of Johannes Drusius Senior (1616)

The library of Johannes Drusius senior was auctioned in Franeker on 26 August 1616, half a year after his death on 12 February.[37] From 1585 until his death, Drusius was professor of Hebrew at the University of Franeker; before then, he had occupied the same chair at Leiden for seven years. His auction catalogue was printed by Fredericus Heynsius, the publisher of various works by Drusius.

The catalogue listed 639 lots, and included a variety of duplicate titles. Drusius's total library was thus smaller than Scaliger's. Due to Drusius's international reputation as a scholar of Hebrew, the auctioneer placed the most interesting part of his library, the books in Hebrew and on Jewish culture, at the beginning of the catalogue. This separated section contained one Arabic book, fifty-five Hebrew books and seven Christian Hebraist texts. The books were divided by format: folio (21), quarto (21), octavo (7) and duodecimo (4). A statement at the end of the section read: 'Hi libri in Auctione publica non distrahentur', indicating that these books were not intended to be sold at auction.[38] It is rather remarkable that the books were listed prominently in the auction catalogue but not sold at the auction; perhaps the heirs or the auctioneer was not yet certain how best to monetise Drusius's Hebrew books. We do know that Drusius's Hebrew manuscripts ended up in the hands of his son-in-law, the minister Abel Curiander (d. 1621), and his student and successor as professor of Hebrew, Sixtinus Amama (1593–1629).

---

37 *Catalogus Librorum Viri Clarissimi P.M. Ioh. Clem. Drusii* (Franeker: Fredericus Heynsius, 1616), p. 7 (USTC 112222). BnF: Q 2149.

38 In the margin of the surviving copy, there is a sadly undecipherable handwritten annotation, which presumably elucidates the situation further.

ORIENTAL COLLECTING IN CONTEXT

Drusius's collection of Hebrew books reflected his philological interest in the Biblical usage of Hebrew and Aramaic. His expertise also qualified him as one of the leading Biblical experts of the Republic, and from 1594 until his death he was a member of the commission tasked by the States General with a new translation of the Bible.[39] To equip himself for this task, Drusius owned various copies of the Talmud, the Hebrew Pentateuch, as well as commentaries and explications (*midrashim*) of these books. He also owned various grammars and lexica. During his career Drusius avoided entanglement in the great theological debates of the period, and instead devoted himself purely to philology. Compared to Scaliger's collection, his library was much more limited in terms of works on Jewish history, ethics and philosophy. The only Arabic book in his collection was an edition of al-Idrisi's *Geographia*, printed by the Tipographia Medicea.[40] Printed books and manuscripts in other Oriental languages were entirely absent from his auction catalogue.

In 1635, some of Drusius's western manuscripts, as well as twelve Hebrew manuscripts, found their way to the university library of Franeker, and were placed in a bespoke bookcase. That same year, another eleven printed Hebrew books, some of them annotated in Drusius's hand, also entered the university library. The remainder of Drusius's library was dispersed.[41]

6 The Auction Catalogue of Franciscus (1) Raphelengius (1626)

The library of Franciscus Raphelengius was sold by his sons twenty-nine years after his death. The auction took place in Leiden at the shop of the Elzeviers at the Rapenburg, on 5 October 1626.[42] Thanks to his position as professor of Hebrew at Leiden, as well as his capacity of printer of the Leiden branch of the

---

39   Peter Korteweg, *De Nieuwtestamentische commentaren van Johannes Drusius (1550–1616)* (Melissant: s.n., 2006), pp. 41 en 51–52.

40   Mohammed al-Idrisi, *Kitab Nuzhat al-mushtaq fi dhikr al-amsar wa-l-aqtar wa-l-buldan wa-l-juzur wa-l-madayin wa-l-afaq*, also known as the *De geographia universali. Hortulus cultissimus, mire orbis regiones, provincias, insulas, urbes, earumque dimensiones & orizonta describens* (Roma: Tipographia Medicea Orientale, 1592; USTC 807510).

41   M.H.H. Engels, 'De academiebibliotheek 1626–1644', in G.Th. Jensma (et al., eds.), *Universiteit te Franeker 1585–1811. Bijdragen tot de geschiedenis van de Friese hogeschool* (Leeuwarden: Fryske Akademy, 1985), p. 173. The books were described in the university library catalogue of 1644 boeken with the remark 'ex libris Drusii'.

42   *Catalogus Variorum Librorum è Bibliothecis Francisci Raphelengii* [...] (Leiden: typ. Bonaventura Elzevier and Abraham 1 Elzevier, 1626; USTC 1120541, BnF Q 2144). Other collections were also sold at auction by the Elzeviers during this session.

Officina Plantiniana, Raphelengius was able to amass an impressive personal collection of books.

The catalogue of this library contained 3,820 lots, some of which were composed of more than one title.[43] Raphelengius's Hebrew and other Oriental books were all listed under the section *Libri Theologici*, even though some of the works covered subjects that would more accurately fall under other faculties. The header of the section indicated that some of the books contained therein were written in Hebrew, Aramaic, Syriac, Arabic and Amharic. In total, the Oriental component of Raphelengius's library numbered 131 printed works, mostly in Hebrew.[44] The books were organised by format: in folio (28), quarto (49), octavo (30) and duodecimo and sextodecimo (15). There were also eight unbound Oriental books, as well as fifteen Oriental manuscripts: one in Russian, eight in Arabic and six in Hebrew. It is likely that the catalogue contained all of Raphelengius's Oriental books, as his sons Franciscus and Christoffel only continued their father's legacy as printer, not as Oriental scholars themselves.

Alongside theological works, Raphelengius's Oriental collection was largely composed of Hebrew and Syriac grammars, dictionaries and glossaries, as well as a small quantity of Jewish historical works. He owned Arabic editions published by the *Tipographia Medicea*, such as the New Testament in Arabic with a Latin interlinear translation (1591), two copies of the *Alphabetum Arabicum* (1592), an edition of Avicenna (1593) and the *Professio fidei Arabice* (1595). He also possessed copies of the *Colloquium Spirituale Arabice* (1579) and Paul's letter to the Galatians, printed by Rutger Spey in 1583. There is also a tantalising mention of an otherwise undescribed Chinese book owned by Raphelengius. In general, the auction catalogue reflects Raphelengius's scholarly interests well, much of which were shared with Scaliger, especially his engagement with the Arabic language.

7 Isaac Casaubon's Oriental Books

Isaac Casaubon, Scaliger's loyal correspondent, survived him for five years. When Casaubon died in 1614 in London, he left a library of 2,050 printed books and 64 manuscripts, almost exactly as many as Scaliger.[45] Some 850 printed

---

43 Some titles cannot have belonged to Raphelengius senior, given their date of publication; these items were all separated out in the catalogue as an appendix, and I have not included them in my comparison.

44 All titles were printed before 1600, with the exception of two copies of Raphelengius's Arabic dictionary, printed in 1613.

45 Among the manuscripts there were 47 Greek, 5 Latin, 6 Arabic and 6 Hebrew items.

books from his library had remained in Paris when Casaubon moved to England in 1610, but the rest followed him to London before his death. Casaubon enriched his library considerably during the first decade of the seventeenth century, when he was the 'Garde' of the Royal Library in Paris. Scaliger made much use of Casaubon's services during this period, as he was able to borrow books from the Royal Library and procure transcriptions of text with ease. At the same time, Casaubon became increasingly interested in Hebrew books, which were readily available in Paris.[46] He was primarily renowned as a scholar of Greek and Latin, as well as theology, but he approached the study of Hebrew with devoted enthusiasm. The many handwritten annotations that Casaubon made to various Hebrew works demonstrate that he was a careful and critical reader.[47]

Casaubon's collection was dispersed after his death. Today, the British Library holds 355 of his books, including 37 Hebrew titles.[48] Much of the remainder of his Oriental collection ended in the university library of Cambridge and the Bodleian Library in Oxford. His western books were more widely dispersed; the university library of Leiden holds sixteen books from his library. Although a complete overview of Casaubon's Oriental collection is lacking, we can determine with certitude that he owned at least ninety-three printed Hebrew books, including various grammars, dictionaries and a Mishna. He also possessed eighteen books in Arabic, two in Amharic, three in Syriac and three in Aramaic.[49] He thus owned at least 119 Oriental books, which in a total library of 2,050 is not negligible.[50] Birrell notes rightly that although

---

46 A.T. Grafton and J. Weinberg, 'Isaac Casaubon's Library of Hebrew Books', in G. Mandelbrote and B. Taylor (eds.), *Libraries within the Library. The Origins of the British Library's Printed Collections* (London: British Library, 2009), p. 25.

47 A.T. Grafton and J. Weinberg, with A. Hamilton, *"I have always loved the Holy Tongue". Isaac Casaubon, the Jews, and a forgotten Chapter in Renaissance Scholarship* (Cambridge, Mass.: Belknap Press of Harvard University Press, 2011).

48 Grafton and Weinberg with Hamilton, *"I have always loved the holy tongue"*, Appendix 3, pp. 329–331.

49 Casaubon owned amongst others Christmann's *Alphabetum arabicum cum isagoge scribendi legendique arabicè* (Neustadt a.d. Weinstrasse: typis Matthaeus Harnisch, 1582; USTC 610990), Erpenius's *Grammatica Arabica* (Leiden: in officina Franciscus II Raphelengius, 1613; USTC 1011493) and *Proverbiorum Arabicorum centuriæ duæ* (Leiden, apud Thomas Erpenius apud Joannes Maire, 1623; USTC 1011609), a volume of Arabic prayers (1591) and a copy of the *Brevis orthodoxae fidei professio* [...] (Roma: Tipografia Medicea Orientale, 1595; USTC 806925).

50 T.A. Birrell, 'The Reconstruction of the Library of Isaac Casaubon', in A.R.A. Croiset van Uchelen (ed.), *Hellinga Festschrift* (Amsterdam: Nico Israel, 1980), pp. 59–68. These figures are based on Bodleian Library MS. Casaubon 21, f. 19ʳ, in which the size and composition of Casaubon's library in London is discussed. Bodleian Library MS Casaubon 22, 43–46;

280 CHAPTER 7

Casaubon and Scaliger had libraries of similar sizes, Scaliger's scholarly interests remained broader than those of his friend.[51]

8 Portaleone's Library

Two catalogues of the book collection of the Hebrew scholar and physician Abraham ben David Portaleone (1542–1612) have survived. The list drawn up by Portaleone himself in 1595, contains exclusively Hebrew books, 110 printed items and 62 manuscripts.[52] The books were chiefly printed in Venice (70) and Mantua (25), and others in important Hebrew print centres such as Bologna, Cremona, Sabbioneta and Constantinople. The list contains a selection of Hebrew works that one can often find in scholarly libraries of the period: editions of Maimonides' *Moreh Nevukhim* (The Guide of the Lost), Kimchi's *Sefer ha-shorashim* (The Book of Roots), Jacob ben Ashers *Arba'ah Turim* (The Four Pillars of the Law), the *Kanon ha-gadol*, the *Qanun* (Avicenna's magnum opus) and the Pentateuch.[53] The second list of Portaleone's Oriental books is included in a notarial document of 1612, which mentions 145 Hebrew printed books; this mean that he must have added a further thirty-five to his library in the seventeen years that passed between the composition of the two lists. This second list also demonstrates that the total size of Portaleone's library was 966 titles, most of which were printed in Latin, Italian and Greek.[54] It is striking that Scaliger's Oriental collection was of similar size to that of Portaleone, and that many similar titles appear in both libraries, despite the fact that Portaleone was a physician. It is also noteworthy that Portaleone owned many manuscripts; presumably he could acquire these through his contacts in the Jewish community in Italy, contacts which Scaliger could not rely on with similar ease.

94–104 and MS Casaubon 21, 19 contain different details about the (Oriental) library of Casaubon, including details on those books that he had transported from Paris to London. There is no complete list of his entire library.

51 Birrell, 'Reconstruction Library Casaubon', p. 59 and note 10.

52 On Portaleone, see: Gianfranco Miletto, *Glauben und Wissen im Zeitalter der Reformation. Der salomonische Tempel bei Abraham ben David Portaleone (1542–1612)* (Berlin, Boston: De Gruyter, 2004).

53 The *Moreh Nevukhim* by Maimonides was a popular book amongst Western scholars who sought to unite the core principles of Aristotelian philosophy with the tenets of the Christian faith.

54 For an inventorisation of both lists, see: Gianfranco Miletto, *La biblioteca di Avraham ben David Portaleone secondo l'inventario della sua eredità* (Florence: Leo S. Olschki, 2013).

ORIENTAL COLLECTING IN CONTEXT   281

9   Thomas Bodley's Oriental Collection

How can we judge the actual value of Scaliger's bequest to Leiden, and how can
we know whether this value appreciated or depreciated over time? We have
compared Scaliger's collection with those of various scholarly contemporaries,
yet none was able match Scaliger's library and collecting habits in size and
scope. The book collections of Scaliger and other scholars in his era were the
result of very personal interests and circumstances, which ensured that they
never owned exactly the same books as one another. We have also seen that
a comparison of Scaliger's library with the institutional collections of his era
is not particularly useful, given that most institutional libraries were collected
over a long period of time. There is nevertheless one institutional collection
that can be compared reasonably to Scaliger's personal collection: the Oriental
collection of the Bodleian Library in Oxford.[55]

The Bodleian Library was established by the diplomat, scholar and collector
Sir Thomas Bodley (1545–1613), with the energetic support of his first librarian,
Thomas James (ca. 1573–1629). On 8 November 1602, the library first opened its
doors as the new *bibliotheca publica* of Oxford.[56] Although the Bodleian would
soon emerge as one of the finest institutional collections in Europe, a comparison of its Oriental collections with those of Scaliger is apt given that until
Bodley's death, the acquisition policies of the Bodleian were firmly directed
by Bodley himself. We also know that there are some connections between
Bodley and Leiden, and that the diplomat may have been inspired by the
foundation of Leiden's library to restore the library of Oxford University.[57] The
comparison is of further interest because Scaliger and Bodley were especially
interested in Oriental books. Both concentrated on the collecting of Oriental

---

55   The research for this section was completed in October 2013 thanks to a Humfrey Wanley
     Fellowship at the Bodleian Library and Exeter College in Oxford. This project was enti-
     tled *Scaliger and Oxford. Early Modern Oriental Collections*. The results of the research
     were published previously in two articles: Kasper van Ommen, 'Early Modern Oriental
     Collections in Oxford and Leiden. Scaliger, Bodley and Anglo-Dutch Encounters and
     Exchanges', Part I. *Bodleian Library Record*, Vol. 28/2 (October 2015), pp. 152–178 and
     Idem, 'Early Modern Oriental Collections in Oxford and Leiden: Scaliger, Bodley and
     Anglo-Dutch Encounters and Exchanges', Part II. *Bodleian Library Record*, Vol. 29/1
     (April 2016), pp. 47–72.

56   See amongst others, Mary Clapinson, *A Brief History of the Bodleian Library* (Oxford:
     Bodleian Library, 2015) and Laurence W.B. Brockliss, *The University of Oxford. A History*
     (Oxford: Oxford University Press, 2016, pp. 177–178, 295–303.

57   See Van Ommen, 'Early Modern Oriental Collections in Oxford and Leiden' part I,
     pp. 152–178 and 'Early Modern Oriental Collections in Oxford and Leiden, Part II', 2016,
     pp. 47–72.

282 CHAPTER 7

manuscripts and printed books equally, in an era when most serious collectors preferred manuscripts because of their unique character. The largest parts of their Oriental collections were made up of books in Hebrew, and both men collected most of their works in the final decade of the sixteenth century and the first decade of the seventeenth century.

We are also fortunate that a catalogue exists of both collections. Bodley's catalogue, the *Catalogus librorum bibliothecae publicae quam vir ornatissimus Thomas Bodleius eques auratus in Academia Oxoniensi nuper instituit Oxoniae*, was first printed in Oxford by John Barnes in 1605, four years before Scaliger's death, and seven years before the first Leiden catalogue with Scaliger's bequest appeared. A comparison between the Leiden and Oxford Oriental collections is also appropriate given that both were universities on the rise, and shared a common Protestant profile. For much of the seventeenth century, Oxford and Leiden would be considered beacons of Protestant learning in Northern Europe, especially so because of the relative decline of former Protestant centres of learning, such as Wittenberg, Heidelberg and Geneva.[58]

In his preface to the catalogue of 1605, James emphasised the national and international role that the Bodleian Library would come to play in the Protestant European community.[59] Scholars of an earlier generation regarded the early Bodleian a 'bulwark of extreme Protestantism' in England and a 'Centre of militant Protestantism'.[60] These labels indicate that the Bodleian was founded to engage in an ideological battle with other great libraries, not least the Vatican. Thomas James was a martial Protestant, who devoted much of his time to exposing the errors and deceptions of the Catholic Church and its Vulgate Bible, chiefly by 'collating manuscripts of the Church Fathers and comparing them with corrupt Catholic editions'.[61] In order to pursue this aim, Bodley and James focussed much of their efforts on collecting theological

---

58 Grell, *Calvinist Exiles*, p. 222.

59 E. Chamberlayne, *Angliae Notitia. Sive Praesens Status Angliae Succincte Enucleatus* (Oxford: typis Lenoard Lichfield, impensis Henry Clements, 1686; USTC 3112424), p. 201: 'Scire vis utendi copiam? Omnibus et singulis (ne peregrinis exceptis) de quibus bene sentit Academia, praestito prius juramento de fide erga libros praestanda, Musarum janua aperta est, ingrediantur et studeant quam diu velint.'

60 The first title was bestowed upon the Bodleian by the historian and classical scholar Thomas Hearne (1678–1735), who became Assistant Keeper of the Bodleian in 1699; the second phrase is by G.W. W[heeler], 'The Bodleian Staff 1600–12', *Bodleian Quarterly Record* 6/23 (1919), p. 285.

61 *The first printed catalogue of the Bodleian Library 1605. A facsimile* (Oxford: Clarendon Press, 1986), f. ix; G.W. Wheeler, 'Thomas James, Theologian and Bodley's Librarian, *Bodleian Quarterly Record* Vol. x (1923), p. 91–95; G.W. Wheeler, 'A Librarian's correspondence' *Bodleian Quarterly Record* Vol. XVI (1929), pp. 11–18.

ORIENTAL COLLECTING IN CONTEXT

works. Oriental books played a part in this venture, but even Bodley himself, who understood the importance of studying Hebrew, mused whether there would be enough interest amongst Oxford's scholars for books in Oriental languages.[62]

On a personal level, there were many similarities as well as differences between Scaliger and Bodley. They were contemporaries who began their lives as scholars, and collected their first books in an academic environment. Yet while Scaliger would remain an academic for the rest of his life, Bodley embedded himself in the world of the court and diplomacy. This granted him significant influence later in life, as well as more substantial financial means than Scaliger. Thanks to his fortune, Bodley could fund the acquisition of huge quantities of books, and pay for Oxford University's library to be restored from its mid-sixteenth-century ruin. Still, Scaliger and Bodley put their books to the same use: the service of the (Protestant) scholarly community.

From comparison of the catalogues, it is clear that the Oriental portions of the Bodleian Library and Scaliger's collection were approximately the same in size at the time of Scaliger's death. At the opening of the Bodleian in 1602, the library contained some 2,000 volumes, including 299 manuscripts. The only Arabic book that the library possessed at that time was a Qur'an that the poet and statesman Sir John Wroth (1584–1672) had donated in 1601.[63] The collection of the Bodleian then went through a phase of rapid expansion. The 1605 catalogue lists some 8,700 titles in 6,000 volumes.[64] The catalogue contained a section of *Theologia* which included 200 Oriental books described in Hebrew or in a Latin transliteration, as well as an appendix of fifty-eight printed Hebrew books separately catalogued by Johannes Drusius junior. Amongst these titles there were a Rabbinic Bible, the *Targum*, the commentaries of Rashi, Ibn Ezra and David Kimchi, a Babylonian Talmud, a codification of Jewish laws by Jacob ben Asher, an edition of the *Arba'ah Turim*, the *Guide of the Lost* by Maimonides,

---

62   G.W. Wheeler, *Letters of Sir Thomas Bodley to Thomas James*, p. 24, Letter 19 [29 January 1602].

63   Ms. Bodl. MS Or. 322. The manuscript is listed in the 1605 catalogue on page 11 as an '*Alcoran Arabicè in Fo[lio]*'.

64   According to David Rogers, *The Bodleian Library and its Treasures 1320–1700* (Nuffield: Aidan Ellis, 1991), p. 51, the 1605 catalogue contained around 400 manuscripts and 5,000 printed books.

284   CHAPTER 7

a *Mikhlol* or Hebrew grammar by Kimchi and the *Tishbi*, a Hebrew lexicon by Elijah Levita.[65] Most of these titles were printed in Venice.[66]

Between 1605 and 1612 the Bodleian Library continued to grow at a rapid pace, especially in the field of Oriental books.[67] In the alphabetically ordered catalogue of the Bodleian from 1620, some 16,000 volumes were listed.[68] Two years after the 1605 catalogue had appeared, Bodley ordered his librarian to compose a separate list of the Hebrew books. James struggled to compile accurate title descriptions of some of these items. Even the alphabetical *Catalogus universalis librorum in Bibliotheca Bodleiana* of 1620, which has been called a 'ground-breaking publication', and a decisive advance in the history of institutional catalogues, contained many erroneous descriptions of Hebrew books.[69]

When Bodley died in 1613, the Arabic collections of the library were still meagre; this would remain the case for many years. Until Archbishop William Laud donated his collection of one thousand manuscripts to the Bodleian in the second half of the 1630s, the number of Arabic works remained limited to some twenty-four items.[70] Even then, Laud's magnificent donation was rich

---

65   Piet van Boxel, 'The Hebrew Collections in Oxford. A Treasure Grove for Jewish Studies', *European Judaism. A Journal for the New Europe* 41/2 (2008), pp. 56–66. Recently published Hebrew titles were also added to the collection, such as the edition of Hai Gaon ben Sherira's *Mishpetei Shevu'ot* Nidpas poh Weneẓi'ah ([Venezia]: be-miẓwat Dani'el Zaneṭi uve-veto, 1602; USTC 1792703) an Arabic tract on the oath.

66   Seventy-two of these Hebrew books (almost half of the total) were printed in Venice. The second most common place of publication was Paris (twelve titles). We can discern a similar dominance of Venetian editions in the collection of 101 Hebrew books owned by Henry Fetherstone, bought by Sion College in 1628. On this collection, see: Julian Roberts and Gerald James Toomer, 'The Fetherstone Catalogue of Hebrew Books', *The Bodleian Library Record* 19/1 (2006), pp. 47–76.

67   On both catalogues, see R. Ovenden, 'The learned Press: Printing for the University. Catalogues of the Bodleian Library and Other Collections', in I. Gadd (ed.), *History of Oxford University Press*. Vol. 1: *Beginnings to 1780* (Oxford: Oxford University Press, 2013), pp. 280–285.

68   I did not pursue a thorough investigation of the 1620 catalogue, as a comparison with Scaliger's Oriental collection would not be very valuable, as Scaliger's collection remained static after 1609. The handwritten acquisitions catalogue of the Bodleian from 1612 (MS. Bodl. 510), which lists 5,000 acquisitions for the period 1605–1612, has also not been analysed. On the catalogues compiled between 1605 and 1620, see: Sears Reynolds Jayne, *Library catalogues of the English Renaissance* (Berkeley: L.A. UCAL Press, 1956), pp. 68–71.

69   Ovenden, 'The Learned Press', pp. 283–285. James was supposed to prepare a model catalogue, in the words of Luigi Balsamo, *Bibliography, History of a Tradition* (Berkeley: Bernard M. Rosenthal, Inc., 1990), p. 86: '... so as to be useful in compiling a catalogue of books, not only in public libraries throughout Europe but also in private museums and similar institutions.'

70   Wakefield, 'Arabic manuscripts in the Bodleian Library', p. 130.

ORIENTAL COLLECTING IN CONTEXT

in items in languages such as Amharic, Malay and Balinese, and although he added over one hundred items in Arabic to the Bodleian, the manuscripts in more exotic languages ensured that contemporaries would henceforth look upon the Bodleian as 'a great magazine of oriental books'.[71]

We can sum up the similarities between the Oriental collections of the Bodleian and Scaliger's library as follows:

- The books were largely collected in the 1590s and early 1600s.
- The number of printed Oriental books in both collections was very similar: Bodley had 185 titles and Scaliger had 175.
- Hebrew books made up the largest proportion of the Oriental collections.
- The number of Russian books is roughly equal in both collections.[72]
- Items were deduplicated when they were replaced by a more recent edition or a better copy.[73]
- Both collections were expanded through gifts from other scholars.
- The librarians, Heinsius in Leiden and James in Oxford, encountered serious issues when cataloguing some of the Oriental items. Both lacked adequate knowledge of Hebrew.
- The catalogues of Leiden and Oxford were important tools of publicity to secure their international reputation as centres of learning.
- Heinsius and James both compared their respective libraries to libraries of antiquity, especially to the lost Library of Alexandria.

---

71   Laud's collection of Oriental manuscripts comprised 147 Arabic works, 74 in Persian and Turkish, 47 in Hebrew, two in Amharic and two in Malay, including the *Hikayat seri Rama* (Laud or. 291) and a letter from Sultan Iskandar Muda of Atjeh to King James I. Other sources suggest that Laud had some 600 Oriental manuscripts in his bequest. In 1659, John Selden (1584–1654) bequeathed 8,000 books and manuscripts, including many editions of the Talmud and Rabbinical printed books which were not yet present in the library. See: C. Wakefield, 'Arabic manuscripts in the Bodleian Library. The seventeenth-century collections.' in: Russell, *'Arabick' Interest.* 1993, p. 131. The phrase is from M. Feingold, 'Oriental Studies', in N. Tyacke (ed.), *Seventeenth-Century Oxford* (*The History of the University of Oxford*) Vol. IV (Oxford: Oxford University Press, 1997), p. 478.

72   The Bodleian Library received several Russian books as gifts: an *Evangelica lingua Moscovitica* (Bodley Mss. 441) in 1601, a handwritten Russian Bible and a *Canones Patrum Moscov[itica]* in 1603 from Sir John Mericke, the English ambassador in Russia, and a Russian prayer book in 1604 from the explorer and diplomat Sir Jerome Horsey (1550–1626). Cf. Macray, *Annals*, p. 30.

73   See for example the copy of the *Vocabulista Aravigo en Letra Castellana* (Granada: Juan Varela de Salamanca, 1505; USTC 340925) in the Bodleian (Cat. 1605 p, 588, call number A.31) that was replaced by a more complete copy (40 V 22 Art). The inscription read: 'This volume was in Harding Triphook Sefardic Catalogue for 1885., marked at 21.0.0. The Bodleian copy containing the Vocabulista only + considerably damaged, was exchanged with Mess St. Ho (?) on paying ten guineas in addition.'

286   CHAPTER 7

- Scaliger's collection as well as Bodley's Library were described as 'arks of learning', with the Bodleian celebrated as 'An ark to save learning from deluge'.

Naturally there were also differences between the two collections, the most significant being:

- Because Bodley wished to serve a substantial scholarly public with his collection, his library was broader and more general in scope; Scaliger's collection reflected first of all his personal character and scholarly curiosity.
- Bodley was able to collect his Oriental books in a much shorter space of time than Scaliger.
- Scaliger's Oriental manuscript collection was greater than Bodley's: forty-eight compared to nine.[74] Scaliger's printed Oriental books are also on average older, and included several Hebrew incunabula. Scaliger's quest for sources texts ensured that in general he desired to access older editions.
- Scaliger's collection of printed Arabic books (eleven) was richer than that of Bodley (four), while Scaliger also owned more Armenian and Amharic texts.
- Scaliger had far more Arabic manuscripts than Bodley: twenty-eight compared to two.[75]
- Scaliger owned two books in Japanese, Bodley had none. In contrast, the Bodleian did have more than thirty books in Chinese, while Scaliger only had three.[76]

---

74   The first Hebrew manuscript, the book of Genesis in a Sephardic script (MS. Bodl. MS Or. 164) was donated to the Bodleian in 1601 by the Chancellor of the Exchequer, Sir John Fortescue of Salden (1531/1533–1607). According to C. Roth, the Bodleian Library owned '... a fairly representative Hebrew section including a number of manuscripts ...'. See his 'Sir Thomas Bodley – Hebraist' in *Bodleian Library Record* 7/5 (1966), p. 242. The entire collection of Oriental manuscripts in the Bodleian, as listed in the 1605 catalogue, comprises three manuscripts in Hebrew, two in Arabic, one in Russian, three in Persian. Shortly after 1605, thirty-two Chinese manuscripts and three Persian manuscripts were added to the collection.

75   The Bodleian only received its first Arabic manuscript in 1604, thanks to a gift from Sir George More: this was a commentary on *al-Risalah al-Shamsiyah fi al-qawa'id al-mantiqiyah* by Najm al-Din Ali al-Katibi (Ms. Bodl. Or. 519).

76   In 1607, Sir Charles Danvers donated eleven Chinese books to the Bodleian. Sir Francis Vere donated seven, while Owen Wood, Dean of Armagh, donated four. In 1606, Bodley purchased 'Octo volumina lingua Chinensi' for £20, with funds from the bequest of Lady Kath. Sandys. Two books 'Excusa in regno et lingua Chinensi' were bought with financial help from John Clapham. As we have seen, the auction catalogue of 1609 possibly indicates that Scaliger owned Chinese books, but this is not certain; similarly, mystery shrouds the 'Tres libri Chinenses' listed for the first time in the 1640 Leiden catalogue. It is also uncertain when the Bodleian first acquired Chinese books. According to some sources, the first one was donated in 1602 by the English ambassador to Muscovy, Sir Richard Lee (ca. 1548–1618), who also presented the library at its inauguration with several books in

ORIENTAL COLLECTING IN CONTEXT

– The Oriental collection of the Bodleian had a rather general theological profile, while Scaliger's collection was rich in Oriental works of philology, chronology and history.

10   Conclusion

In the comparison of the Oriental collections of Scaliger and his Leiden colleagues Drusius and Raphelengius, the similarity in their ownership of grammars, dictionaries, concordances and works by Christian Hebraists is striking. A similar overlap occurs with books on history (in the case of Drusius) and Arabic (in the case of Raphelengius). Because these details of book ownership have been generated from auction catalogues, one must remember that the libraries of Drusius and Raphelengius might have been greater in extent and breadth. We have seen that the same applies to Scaliger, some of whose books never entered his bequest.

The comparison with the Oriental collection of the Catholic Bullioud is also restricted to some similarities in grammars, dictionaries, concordances and works by Christian Hebraists, and is therefore of less value as a comparative exercise. By the beginning of the seventeenth century, there were so many different types of collectors and collections that it is very difficult to come to concrete findings when analysing two individual collections alongside one another.

What does emerge from this investigation clearly is that Scaliger did not have the largest collection of Oriental books in Europe. What did distinguish him was his breadth of interest in languages, and the fact that he did not restrict his collecting to Hebrew and Aramaic. Books in Arabic, Amharic and the languages of the Far East attracted his attention. In this aspect, Scaliger was most similar to Casaubon, one of the last universal scholars of the sixteenth century. He collected whilst enthralled by the illusion that by doing so he could gather together all possible knowledge. Over the course of the seventeenth century, the pursuit of this ideal through book collecting gradually lessened. Scholarly libraries became both larger and more specialised, while institutional libraries were transformed into reference libraries that increasingly resembled the scholarly library of the sixteenth century.

Russian and Finnish. Other sources date the donation of the first Chinese book to 1604, thanks to a gift from Henry Percy, Earl of Northumberland. In any case, it is certain that Bodley acquired more books from East and South-East Asia than Scaliger did.

The most striking difference between Scaliger's collection and that of his contemporaries was the head start that he had in the collecting of Arabic manuscripts and printed books. Due to this lead, the University of Leiden would already be considered one of the most important centres for the study of the Middle East in the early seventeenth century. This distinction allowed Leiden to strengthen its reputation and secure an influential position amongst European universities. Scaliger had already interested himself in Arabic from 1577 onwards, and intensified his study of the language in 1600. At that moment, Bodley was only taking his first hesitant steps in the world of Arabic. The University of Leiden may not have owned any Arabic books before Scaliger's death, nor did it teach Arabic, but Scaliger's collecting did anticipate these developments. During his life, he already urged the curators of the university to establish a chair for the teaching and study of Arabic. Ultimately, the curators obliged, and in 1613, after Scaliger had bequeathed his Oriental collection to the university, they founded a chair for Arabic.

The good-natured 'battle of the libraries' in which Leiden and Oxford jostled in the early seventeenth century was won decisively by the Bodleian Library. The 1620 catalogue published by Thomas James was transformative in its use of an alphabetical ordering system, while it also demonstrated the immense growth that the Bodleian had undergone: less than twenty years after opening, it contained more than 16,000 printed books and manuscripts. In 1640, another twenty years later, Leiden had 3,117 items.[77] It must have been a blow to the proud Daniel Heinsius that his son Nicolaas, after a visit to the Bodleian in 1641, declared that 'he could not conceive of anything more beautiful than this library'.[78] At least it should be remembered that despite the Bodleian's rising star, the scholars of Oxford were impressed by Scaliger's bequest in Leiden.

That the University of Leiden attracted Scaliger proved to be of enduring influence on its future course as an academic institution. Scaliger's notion that Arabic was an intellectual key to unlock further learning still impacts the university today, which remains an important centre for the study of the Arabic language and culture.[79] The broad philological approach to the study of Hebrew that Scaliger promoted has also ensured that, in contrast to other

---

77   Berkvens-Stevelinck, *Magna Commoditas*, pp. 75–78.

78   H. Boex and Hans Bots, 'Le voyage de Nicolas Heinsius (1620–1681) en Angleterre en 1641. Douze lettres inédites à son père Daniel Heinsius relatant ce voyage', *Lias* 32 (2005), pp. 269–294: 'quidem nihil splendidius excogitari potuisse.'

79   G.A. Russell, 'The Seventeenth Century. The Age of "Arabick"' in Russell, *'Arabick' interest*, 1993, pp. 2, 23: 'It was regarded the key to the treasure house of knowledge ... To build up collections of Arabic manuscripts was a primary object of the Arabists and their patrons in the sixteenth and seventeenth centuries'.

universities, Hebrew was never subsumed within the faculty of theology, which meant that it could flourish more freely than elsewhere. Until 1609, the university library of Leiden owned very few Oriental books, but Scaliger's bequest changed this decisively. Scaliger's annotated books also aided the development of new investigations for Oriental studies, that generations of scholars after him could pursue.

Scaliger's bequest, in its broadest sense, changed the function of the university library of Leiden. It had never been intended that the university library would incorporate specialist research libraries like that of Scaliger; the university library's purpose was to amass expensive reference works for its scholars.[80] Yet Scaliger's bequest altered this balance, and stimulated the curators to acquire Oriental items in a more systematic fashion. This allowed the library to grow gradually into a specialist centre of research.[81] This was a change that, over time, could be seen elsewhere in Europe: institutional libraries, like scholars, became custodians of special collections.

---

80 One example of such a valuable work is the Babylonian Talmud: Johannes Buxtorf paid the equivalent sum of his annual salary for a copy. Cf. Stephen G. Burnett, *From Christian Hebraism to Jewish Studies: Johannes Buxtorf (1564–1633) and Hebrew Learning in the Seventeenth Century* (Leiden, Boston: Brill, 1996), p. 47.

81 William Clark, *Academic Charisma and the Origins of the Research Library* (Chicago: University of Chicago Press, 2006), pp. 298–302.

Conclusion

'I am poor in everything, especially in books'. It is a telling and rather characteristic remark from Scaliger during his time in France. In his correspondence, he frequently hinted at his insatiable hunger for books, especially books in Oriental languages. His love for Oriental books began during his student days in Paris in 1562. Around 1575, he already possessed a collection of Oriental items, especially books in Hebrew: a Hebrew Bible, as well as grammars and dictionaries to help him master the language. That Scaliger wished to have total command of Hebrew is also evident from a letter that he wrote entirely in Hebrew. From 1576 onwards, Scaliger also collected, at a rapid pace, books in other Oriental languages from around Europe, for which he relied on many fellow scholars and collectors who he befriended. In 1579, Scaliger's interests in the collecting of Arabic books increased substantially while he was preparing his edition of the astronomical poem by Marcus Manilius, which included many references to Oriental knowledge. At the same time, Scaliger was developing a comprehensive collection of works on chronology, for which he also collected books in Russian and other Slavic languages. Whether he could actually read any of the Slavic languages remains highly uncertain, but his scholarly productivity and his collecting urge garnered international renown. From the early 1580s he was regarded as a noted expert of Oriental languages in the Republic of Letters.

Scaliger loved books because of their text, not because of their aesthetic qualities. He was not a bibliophile to the same degree as his friend Jacques-Auguste de Thou. Scaliger's acquisitions concentrated on acquiring, above all, new texts or sources related to his research. He did not buy all the books that ended up in his library; because of his fame, many contemporaries sent him Oriental books and other rare texts as gifts, knowing that he would find them useful.

Throughout his entire working life, Scaliger had a fascination for Oriental languages. He continued to study Hebrew until his death, even when his central focus had shifted to the study of Arabic around 1600. Scaliger's interest in Arabic coincided with an increase in the production of Arabic books, especially by the Roman *Tipographia Medicea Orientale*, and Scaliger added many books from this press to his collection. Yet his contemporaries were most impressed by the fact that he was able to assemble a fine collection of Arabic manuscripts, twenty-eight in all. His personal collection of Arabic works was one of the largest in Europe.

In Scaliger's mind, a scholar should have a broad but discerning vision. This also explains why Scaliger was able to collect so widely, especially of books

© KONINKLIJKE BRILL BV, LEIDEN, 2025 | DOI:10.1163/9789004701526_010

CONCLUSION 291

concerning the history of Oriental cultures, books that are often absent from the libraries of his contemporaries. Most scholars of Scaliger's day collected Oriental works of theology, not history. Not even Thomas Bodley was able to acquire as many unique Arabic sources as Scaliger.

1　A Properly Functioning Network

One of the principal questions animating this research was to determine how Scaliger was able to amass such an important collection of Oriental texts without ever setting foot in the Levant or Asia. The answer is clear: this was only possible because Scaliger maintained an effective and extensive network of correspondents. He often stayed in contact with correspondents for years. Some of his correspondents were lifelong friends and loyal allies, such as Cujas, De Thou and Dupuy, all friends from Scaliger's student days. They remained close even when Scaliger had left France behind and settled in Leiden. His closest friends were, like Scaliger, Protestant, regardless of their occupation or status in society.

We learn much about the functioning of Scaliger's network through his extant letters. Reading his correspondence, we can learn about the publishing practices of the sixteenth century, the contents of libraries and bookshops, the trade in new and second-hand books and the writing and editing of books.

Scaliger's network is characterised by the loyalty of his contacts around Europe. Scholars, students and printers supplied him with books, but so did merchants. Scaliger urged his contacts repeatedly to find his desired titles, something that they only tolerated because of Scaliger's status as a respected scholar. Scaliger's friends all admired him for his scholarly insights. Their unwavering loyalty to Scaliger and to his (not infallible) expertise did agitate some contemporaries, such as Franciscus Junius. It is also clear that Scaliger was not necessarily an easy or congenial person, as evidenced by some of his adages recorded in the *Scaligerana*. He must have been a forceful individual, someone who placed his correspondents, and their correspondents, under significant pressure. Scaliger's demands, and the eagerness of his correspondents to satisfy them, did ensure that his network was unparalleled in its breadth and effectiveness. Scaliger's remarkable energy, intellect and passion for books always solicited admiration from his friends, those who counted themselves fortunate to be an inner circle of intimates. These feelings of admiration could run so deep, as they did with Daniel Heinsius, that they were undiminished by Scaliger's death in 1609.

2 From France to Leiden

When Scaliger lived in France, it was by no means easy to build a great personal library. The persistent threat of war forced Scaliger to move from one residence to another. Books often had to be left behind. It was only thanks to Scaliger's Parisian contacts, a selection of jurists, ambassadors and statesmen dominated by Claude Dupuy, Pierre Pithou and Jacques-Auguste de Thou, that he was able to acquire most of his books during his French period. He was often able to ask his Parisian contacts for transcripts of books and manuscripts from the Royal Library in Paris. Scaliger also had good contacts in Italy, the most important area for the trade in Hebrew and other Oriental books. In Italy, Scaliger knew individuals who themselves had extensive connections with the Italian scholarly, commercial, diplomatic and print worlds. From his correspondence, it also becomes clear that Scaliger circulated copies of his lists of desiderata amongst friends who travelled abroad. His patron Louis Chasteigner de la Roche-Posay, a diplomat in the service of the French king, granted Scaliger access to diplomatic circles in Italy. Thanks to Claude Dupuy, Scaliger was able to come into contact with the Italian collector Gian Vincenzo Pinelli, who supplied Scaliger with several important Oriental texts.

Despite the generous assistance from his friends, the political and religious turbulence in France ensured that collecting books remained a trial for Scaliger during his French period. Over time, he became open to the possibility of leaving this uncertainty behind him. When negotiators from the University of Leiden approached Scaliger, he was nevertheless wracked with doubt. Only after Leiden agreed to Scaliger's demands for generous terms and a substantial salary did he commit himself to moving in 1593. That Leiden was the home of a branch of the Plantin printing firm, under the direction of the scholar-printer Franciscus Raphelengius, will undoubtedly have played a major role in Scaliger's decision. Scaliger expected (rightly, as it turned out) that Raphelengius and his library would assist his study of Oriental languages, especially Arabic. He expected less of other libraries in Leiden. In 1593, the university library possessed only a handful of Oriental books, some of which were also owned by Scaliger. Yet the personal libraries of other Leiden figures, such as Bonaventura Vulcanius and Daniël van der Meulen, would, to Scaliger's surprise, turn out to be significant collections with many rare books.

As Kristine Haugen has argued previously, Scaliger's move to Leiden represented a decisive break in his work and attitude as scholar. In France, Scaliger was relatively isolated and minded to work on his own, the solitary genius *par excellence*, while in Leiden he was an active collaborator on several projects. In Leiden he compiled the index for the *Inscriptiones Antiquae totius orbis*

CONCLUSION

Romani (Heidelberg: 1602 [=1603]) by Janus Gruter (1560–1627), and worked together with Raphelengius on an Arabic-Latin dictionary. In Leiden, he also turned into a true mentor, encouraging his students to advance new research and to publish their works. In France, Scaliger was reliant on the generosity of his patrons for the purchase of new books, while in Leiden his own substantial salary ensured that he was able to collect liberally himself.

It is striking that Scaliger continued to use many of the same suppliers of books when he moved to Leiden, while he also embraced new contacts to source texts. It was in Leiden that Scaliger for the first time began to look to England as a potential source for Oriental books. He was also able to take advantage of the printing firms of Raphelengius in Leiden and Commelin in Amsterdam, while the French ambassador in The Hague, Paul Choart de Buzanval, was able to keep Scaliger abreast of the latest publications in France. Scaliger's scholarly renown was so great by this time that admirers throughout Europe were able to find him easily, and present him with books as gifts by courier. Every year, the supply routes could change, depending on the weather, the availability of trustworthy agents and political turbulence, but Paris and Frankfurt would always remain critical centres of book exchange to Scaliger. To a lesser extent, Scaliger also relied upon the book fair at Leipzig, but that of Frankfurt was, during his lifetime, still the more important of the two German *Buchmesse*.

The move to Leiden was, in first instance, a gamble. The young Dutch Republic was still in the midst of a great political struggle to wrest its independence from Habsburg Spain, and it is probably for this reason that Scaliger initially considered that his residence in Leiden would be of short duration. He therefore only took with him from France some absolute necessities, including his most valuable Oriental books. Yet as soon as Scaliger settled in Leiden, he realised that his situation there was far better than imagined, and he laboured to have the remainder of his possessions brought over from France, including his dispersed library. This seems to have succeeded, despite significant obstacles. Even books that we know Scaliger did not value greatly were transported from France, as we can gather from the auction catalogue of his library from 1609.

When, at the end of the sixteenth century, several of Scaliger's loyal French correspondents died, he expanded his network in Leiden. He became good friends with the merchant Daniël van der Meulen, who acquired for him various Arabic books from Rome. Printers and publishers in the Republic, such as the Commelin family, fulfilled an important role as agents in transporting books around Europe for Scaliger. During his stay in Leiden, Scaliger also maintained contacts with the Marseille trader Hostagier, who acquired books from Cairo for him. Visitors to Leiden from around Europe, including former students of Scaliger, such as Cornelis van der Myle and Johannes Woverius, were always on the hunt for Oriental books for Scaliger. One of the most prolific agents of this sort was the Anglo-Dutch scholar Richard Thomson, who enjoyed privileged access to the book trade in London and Cambridge.

3 Comparison with Other Collections

Most of the sixteenth and seventeenth-century scholars who were interested in Oriental languages, collected books in those languages in the field of theology, especially Bibles, and grammars and dictionaries. Some were also interested in Oriental medicine and mathematics. When we compare Scaliger's collection to those of his contemporaries, it becomes clear that he had a much broader interest in Oriental languages and cultures. Scaliger collected many Jewish literary, historical and philosophical works. He owned a copy of the *Itinerarium* of Benjamin of Tudela, the *Sefer Hovot*, a philosophical work by Bahya ibn Paquda and medical works by Ibn Sina. Of course he did not neglect to collect major works of Hebrew theology, including copies of the *Talmud* and *Thora* and the *Midrash* (Rabbinical commentaries).

The emphasis that Scaliger placed on the collecting of books in Oriental languages reflected his attitude to pursuing philological research that clung as close as possible to original source texts. This explains why Scaliger acquired few works by Christian Hebraists, who translated Hebrew works into Latin, and which were more easily available (and for reasonable prices) with many booksellers around Europe. The great quantity of Hebrew grammars in Scaliger's library indicates that he wished to establish his own linguistic path for learning the Hebrew language, all with the aim to delve deeper into Hebrew texts published by Jewish scholars, rather than Christians. Many of these Hebrew source texts could not be purchased in northern Europe, so Scaliger had to engage his contacts in Italy to acquire them. In general, he was well informed about the availability of Hebrew works: he often knew their titles, place of publication and year of publication correctly, and was able to pass on further information on specific editions to his agents. Many of these items were expensive: Scaliger frequently complained about high prices in his correspondence, even if we should not always take him at his word when he does so.

Scaliger guarded his library carefully. He enjoyed borrowing books from others, but regularly rejected requests to borrow from him, citing his fear of the loss or damage of the books. It was only on rare occasions that his friends were able to borrow books from his collection. What Scaliger did share liberally,

CONCLUSION

especially with his young students, was his knowledge. During the final years of his life, he spent most of his time transcribing manuscripts and sources to make them available, together with his Oriental collection, to future generations of scholars. The irony was that under the management of Scaliger's most devoted student, Daniel Heinsius, very few people were able to access any of Scaliger's books. Only after Heinsius's long reign as librarian was at an end, did Scaliger's bequest become more accessible.

Scaliger's library was more than a collection of books: it was a research resource. This is what distinguished Scaliger's Oriental book collecting from that of many of his contemporaries. Thanks to the many annotations and comments that Scaliger made in the margins of his books, to expand, correct or criticise the texts, he transformed the books into resources that could be of benefit to other scholars. He paved the way for others to prepare printed editions of manuscript sources, and to begin a conversation on the importance of languages or the relevance of specific texts. He provided a model for the study of Arabic and other Oriental languages to future generations.

When we study auction catalogues that document the libraries of Scaliger's contemporaries who also collected Oriental books, we can discern some key characteristics that define these collections:

- Most Oriental books, whether in print or manuscripts, were in Hebrew.
- The total size of the Oriental portion of the library was always very small.
- Oriental Bibles and grammars showed up in virtually all libraries with Oriental books.
- Books produced for the western European market (the works of Christian Hebraists in particular) were more common than those produced for Jewish readers.
- The number of printed Arabic books tended to be smaller than the number of Arabic manuscripts.

Naturally, every book collection is unique in its composition, as it reflects the priorities and interests of an individual owner. Nevertheless, Scaliger's collection of Oriental books is more distinctive than those of his contemporaries, because of his keen interest in the Arabic language and the study of chronology. His contemporaries, including great collectors such as Bodley, Drusius and Raphelengius, tended to limit themselves to the study of Oriental theology and philology. Scaliger's broad scholarly interests, combined with his unrivalled network of contacts and his dogged pursuit of texts, ensured that he was able to build an unparalleled collection of Oriental books. Strikingly, even the printed Oriental books in Scaliger's library were relatively rare, and were not often present in the collections of his contemporaries.

4   The Fate of the Bequest and the *Arca Scaligerana*

In his will of 1608, Scaliger determined that 'all his books in foreign tongues, Hebrew, Syriac, Arabic and Amharic' would be bequeathed to the University of Leiden at his death. To his previous will, signed in 1607, he added as a codicil a catalogue of the titles of Oriental books in his possession. This catalogue was lost sometime during the seventeenth century. Thanks to a list compiled by Bonaventura Vulcanius, we do receive insight into a portion of Scaliger's Oriental collection. The non-Oriental portion of Scaliger's library was auctioned in 1609. Despite the inventory made by Scaliger and the instruction in his will, some Oriental books were auctioned off during this sale, even though they were destined for the university library. This was a foreboding of further confusion, as it would take until 1612 for Heinsius to describe the books bequeathed by Scaliger: but even having taken three years over the task he was unable to provide a complete and detailed description of the items. Heinsius frequently described only the first title in a bound volume, and neglected the others. He also failed to ask for assistance from the Oriental specialists at the university, such as Thomas Erpenius and later Jacobus Golius. Heinsius was more interested in defending Scaliger's posthumous reputation than cataloguing Scaliger's bequest or making it more widely available.

In 1741, after a proposal made by the librarian David van Royen, all books from Scaliger's bequest, including some items that were erroneously ascribed to his collection, were given a rudimentary printed slip of paper stating 'Ex Legato Illustris Viri Josephi Scaligeri'. At this point in time, the books were also removed from the *Arca Scaligerana*, while the cabinet itself was also removed from the library. While the books were now separated from their original case, they did become more easily consultable by scholars, who continued to use Scaliger's annotations for their own research.

Scaliger's bequest represented a welcome expansion of the university's Oriental collections, which before 1609 had been largely negligible. Yet Scaliger also saw his bequest as a pioneering example to be followed by future bequests from other collectors. The donation further underscored Scaliger's noble status: a bequest was partially a symbol of the status and wealth of the donor, and at the same time transferred the same status to the receiving institution, which improved its reputation in the broader scholarly world. Having persuaded himself that he was descended from Italian nobility, Scaliger felt obliged to contribute materially and culturally to the University of Leiden. Because he was unmarried and had no issue, there was also no expectation that Scaliger would leave his library to his children. He did grant several close friends the opportunity to pick items from his collection of western books, while safeguarding

CONCLUSION   297

his Oriental items for the university library. We should thus interpret Scaliger's bequest as an act of aristocratic patronage as much as the generous donation of a scholar.

Scaliger's Oriental bequest was responsible for a small revolution in Leiden and the broader European scholarly world. The presence of his bequest ensured that philological research could branch out more easily to include non-western and non-biblical texts. Scaliger's interests in non-western history, culture and chronology also paved the way to approach the study of non-European societies from a secular rather than theological perspective.

In 1612, Scaliger's Oriental books were placed in the *Arca Scaligerana*: a mini-library in which scholars and students could immerse themselves in the languages and history of the Levant. At least, that was Scaliger's intention. In reality, Daniel Heinsius kept a close eye on the bookcase, which was generally kept under lock and key. Heinsius considered the *Arca* to be a memorial to Scaliger. Its contents were of secondary importance in the quest to keep Scaliger's memory alive. Only a select few Oriental scholars were granted access to the *Arca* during Heinsius's tenure as librarian. This policy was broadly supported by the curators of the university, who perceived Scaliger's bequest as a valuable treasure and an international tool of publicity that should not easily be given over to prying eyes. Only when Heinsius died, did the bequest become more accessible.

After a couple of decades of relative tranquillity, the contents of the *Arca* became disturbed in the period between 1655 and 1741. Some of the books from the *Arca* were dispersed throughout the rest of the university library, while other books entered the *Arca*, even though they had no relation with Scaliger or his bequest. The successive catalogues of the university library published during this era demonstrated this movement of books. Some books disappeared from the bequest because they were sold as duplicates; others were removed for no good reason, or were stolen.

5   The Reconstruction of Scaliger's Bequest

An important part of this study has been the reconstruction of Scaliger's Oriental bequest as reflected in the current collections of the University of Leiden. I received valuable assistance for this part of the research from professor Frederik A. de Wolff, and the complete results can be seen in the supplementary catalogue appended to this present work.

The collection of Oriental books bequeathed by Scaliger to Leiden in 1609 can no longer be reconstructed on the basis of the catalogue appended to his will, as this catalogue was lost in the seventeenth century. The list compiled by Vulcanius is also incomplete, and rudimentary in its description of the titles. Another list with Oriental titles from Scaliger's collection, now in the possession of the Bibliothèque nationale de France in Paris, provides us with some new insights, but this too is incomplete. We therefore have to rely on the Leiden university catalogues published from 1612 onwards.

The 1612 catalogue is the first university catalogue that incorporates Scaliger's bequest, and the catalogue lists the bequest separately from the main collection. This catalogue also provides a limited overview of the bequest. In total it lists 219 Oriental titles in 186 volumes, as well as 48 western manuscripts. In 1614, the historian and bookseller Jan Jansz Orlers described the bequest as containing 208 books, including the western manuscripts; this discrepancy was introduced because Orlers did not count the number of titles in each individual volume. If we were to add the 219 Oriental titles to the 1,700 books listed in Scaliger's auction catalogue of 1609, as well as the approximate 300 books removed by his friends before the auction, then it seems that Scaliger's entire library probably contained around 2,250 books. Sadly this calculation does not bring us much closer to an exact figure for Scaliger's Oriental collection.

The subsequent catalogues of the university library of Leiden, published in 1623, 1636 and 1640, are also disappointing in the quality of their descriptions of titles from Scaliger's bequest. Heinsius's first successor, Antonius Thysius (1603–1665), never found the time to update the university catalogue in his brief tenure as librarian, but it is also unlikely that he would have provided better descriptions of the Oriental books, as he lacked knowledge of Oriental languages, except Hebrew.

A sea change took place with the publication of the 1674 catalogue, compiled by Fredericus Spanheim junior (1632–1701). The 1674 catalogue devoted more attention to the Oriental collections of the university, in part because of the accession of the sizeable bequest of Levinus Warner (1618–1665). Sixty-five years after Scaliger's death, his Oriental collection was finally described by Oriental specialists. At the same time, his collection became integrated into the broader Oriental collections of the university, and the near sacred symbolic value of the *Arca* depreciated. Spanheim's catalogue also listed some of the items from Scaliger's bequest (mostly Arabic editions also present in Warner's bequest) under the *Impressi Bibliothecae communis*, the general, open-shelf collection of the library. Over time, the library removed duplicates, even some items that were annotated by Scaliger, as it preferred to keep the cleanest copies.

This research has provided long-needed clarity concerning the growth, composition and ultimate size of Scaliger's bequest. It can now be determined,

CONCLUSION 299

thanks to the analysis of the published university catalogues and Scaliger's correspondence, that his Oriental bequest included at least 265 titles, divided between 189 printed works and 76 manuscripts. These titles are listed in detail in the appendix to this work and include the current class marks of those items that are still present in the university library of Leiden, while indicating which items have been removed from the university collection over time.

This research has also demonstrated that there were some Oriental books owned by Scaliger that never made it into the university collections in the first place. This was in clear contravention of Scaliger's wish that 'all his books in foreign tongues' were bequeathed to the university. In the auction catalogue of his library of 1609, there are around a dozen non-western books that belong to the Oriental bequest: two Hebrew books by the English theologian Hugh Broughton (1549–1612), a *Genesis Hebraica* from 1535, a couple of Bibles in Oriental languages, and a selection of Slavic and Armenian books. Other Oriental books were not sold at auction, but were nevertheless never part of the bequest either. This includes the Armenian psalter (the *Saghmosaran* from 1565–1566) that Scaliger had received from Dupuy, and that has ended up in the Royal Library of Denmark in Copenhagen. It is likely that Heinsius or other students of Scaliger, such as Dominicus Baudius or Cornelis van der Myle, who were allowed to pick items from Scaliger's library, removed these items.

These removals reinforce the argument that the catalogue of Oriental books that was added to Scaliger's will as a codicil was incomplete. It is likely that Scaliger had simply made a list of some of the most important Oriental books in his collection, but expected that his executors would complete the list themselves. This supposition is supported by the fact that Scaliger appointed as executors two individuals who had sufficient knowledge of Oriental languages: the printers Justus and Franciscus Raphelengius, the sons of Franciscus Raphelengius the elder. It is probable that they separated the books in Scaliger's house into two sections: one destined for the bequest to the university, the other destined to be sold at auction. It is not inconceivable that during this process, some books were accidentally placed in the wrong section.

What remains a painful absence in Leiden today is the physical *Arca Scaligerana*. It is a shame that it disappeared, and the university would be delighted to be able to restore Scaliger's books in their monumental glory in its bespoke bookcase. Happily, most of Scaliger's Oriental books rest safely on the shelves of the university library. More importantly, more than four hundred years after his bequest, Scaliger's collection remains a valuable and much-consulted resource for the study of Oriental languages and cultures – precisely as Scaliger intended.

Appendix 1

List of oriental books in Scaliger's library 1600 or later [*Index Librorum*, BnF, MS. Dupuy 395, ff. 178ʳ–179ʳ]

Behind the titles, as far as traceable, is the current shelf mark under which the books can be found in the collection of the Leiden University Libraries.

Libri arabici manuscripti

178ʳ

Novum Testamentum integrum scriptum in deserto Thebaidis egregio charactere in magno quarto oblongo.	MS Or. 217
Lectiones in Genesim charactere africano in fol.	MS Or. 215 (?)[1]
More Hannibokim Rambam charactere Judaico fol. parvo.	MS Or. 4723
Nomocanon seu *praxis legalis*, charactere africano in magno quarto oblongo	MS Or. 221 (?)[2]
Quatuor Evangelia descripta in monte Libano in luculentissimo charactere quae sunt paraphrastae alius abillo superiore [testamenti integri, in-4° oblongo]	MS Or. 223 (?)
Rursus quatuor Evangelia alius paraphrastis a superioribus, vetustiss[imus]. liber in 4°	MS Or. 245 (?)
Dictionarium arabicum crassum [lucullentissimo] characteris cum explicatione turcica in-8° magno aut fol[io]. parvo	MS Or. 227
Astrologia Abdalla de sphaera, cum egregio et loculetissimo commentario charactere africano in-4°	MS Or. 238
Targum Pentateuchi anonymo charactere judaico in parvo 4°	MS Or. 236[3]
Lectionarium graecoarabicum in-4°	MS Or. 243

---

1 Robert M. Kerr, red. *Vetus Testamentum in Lugduno Batavorum: Catalogue of an Exhibition of Old Testament Manuscripts, held in the Leiden University Library* [...] (Leiden: Leiden University Library, 2004) no. 3.

2 Raphelengius also had in his library a *Nomocanon* or *Corpus juris tam civilis quam canonici*: a collection of Mohammedan laws, consisting both of elements of civil law and canon law.

3 Kerr, *Vetus Testamentum*, no. 8. Erpenius used this manuscript for his printed edition of the *Pentateuch* (Tawrāt *Mūsā al-Nabī 'alayhi al-salām id est Pentateuchus Mosis Arabicè* (Leiden: ex typ. Thomas Erpenius apud Joannes Maire, 1622; USTC 1015907).

(*cont.*)

Libri arabici manuscripti

Evangelia secundum Lucam et Johannem cum [apicibus] vocalib[us]. est alius paraphrastis ab omnibus superioribus	MS Or. 255
Chronicon samaritanum ab excessu Mosis ducatu Josuae ad tempora Antonitorum	MS Or. 249[4]
Apocalypsis manu Ignatii Patriarchae descripta est aliud paraphrastis ab eo qui totum novum testamentum converit	MS Or. 252
Alcoranum elegantissimo charactere in-8° parvo	MS Or. 258
Alcoranum turcico charactere	MS Or. 261 (?)[5]
Psalterium[6]	MS Or. 4725?
Liturgiae tres Ignatii, Cyrilli, Gregorii, cum interpretatione Ægyptiaca e regione	MS Or. 253
Libellus Samaritanus in quo breve chronicon ab Adam ad annum Christi 1584. Item typus anni samaritani communiter anno 1584	MS Or. 773[7]
Commentarius in 4 Evangelia ex Chrysostomi excerptis	MS Or. 245

---

4   The so-called Liber Joshua ('Book of Joshua') that Scaliger received from the Samaritans in Cairo. See: Kerr, *Vetus Testamentum*, no. 5. The text is edited by T.W.J. Juynboll, *Chronicon Samaritanum, Arabice conscriptum, cui titulus est Liber Josuae* (Leiden: S. & J. Luchtmans, 1848).

5   According to an inscription on one of the endpapers, dated 1603, this manuscript is from the library of Helias Putschius (1580–1606). It is recorded in the library catalogue of 1612 in the section *Libri Arabici In octavo* as *Alcoranum charactere Turcic*. Cf. Schmidt, *Catalogue of Turkish manuscripts* I, pp. 39–42.

6   Described in the 1612 library catalogue in the section *Libri Arabici In octavo* as *Psalterium cum Canticis manuscriptum*.

7   In *Correspondence* 4 September 1581 to Claude Dupuy, Scaliger wrote: 'de recouvrer des Samaritains leur computus et la maniere qu'ils usent en leurs mois lunaires, car ils ne sont pas du tout semblables aux juifz'. Scaliger purchased this manuscript in 1584 and incorporated parts of it into his second edition of *De emendatione temporum*. In the letter, Scaliger also indicated that he already owned a number of books in Samaritan. Scaliger, after inquiring about books and historical facts about the Samaritans by letter to l'abbé Pierre del Bene (UBL MS Or. 6882) in 1589, finally received three manuscripts of the Samaritans from Cairo around 1590, including the *Liber Joshua*. The two calendars are untraceable in the UBL's collection.

APPENDIX 1   303

(*cont.*)

Libri arabici manuscripti

178[v]

Duae Epistolae longissimae Justæ [instar?] duorum librorum Ignatii Patriarchæ ad Josef Scaligerum[8]	Not in UBL anymore
Multi libri ac taeniae precum Mahommedicarum	MS Or. 232; 233, 239, 241 (?)
Kalendarium Elkupti	MS Or. 262[9]
Thesaurus opulentissimus linguæ arabicæ complectens plusquam xxiii millia vocum a Josepho Scaligero digestus	MS Or. 212

Libri Hebræi et alii scripti

Lexicon persicoturcicum luculentissimum volumen in 4°	MS Or. 227
Kalendarium syriacum ecclesiæ antiochensis[10]	MS Or. 4735
Apocalypsis syriaca	MS Or. 252
Psalterium Aethiopicum cum precibus, id est breviarium Abyssinum	MS Or. 4734[11]

---

8   Two exceptionally long letters written by the Syrian Jacobite patriarch Ignatius Naʿamtallah to Scaliger, which Scaliger incorporated into his *De emendatione temporum* of 1583. According to the 1612 library catalogue, these also included a *Kalendarium Turco-Persico* and two *Kalendaria Elkupti & Antiochenum*. See: Anthony Grafton, *Defenders of the Text* (Cambridge, MA, London, Harvard University Press, 1991), p. 128. These kalendars are no longer in the UBL.

9   The manuscript contains a treatise on the calculation of calendars. Scaliger originally planned to publish the tract as a stand-alone edition, initially with Patisson in Paris. When that took Scaliger too long, he explored the possibility of having it published in Geneva, along with a number of other texts: see *Correspondence* 15 February 1580 to Claude Dupuy. He eventually reproduced part of the manuscript in facsimile in *De emendatione temporum* (1583 pp. 324–337; see also Grafton, *Scaliger* II, p. 90). The tract on this Computus is mentioned in several letters: *Correspondence* 9 December 1579, 4 January 1580, 15 February 1580 to Claude Dupuy and 4 September 1581 to F. Chrestien. The following commentary is included in the *Scaligerana*: 'Nemo Christianus potest de illis ita bene loqui ut ego, quia illorum computum Aethiopicum dedi; repererunt post, Breviarium aliquod. Curavi fundi litteras Samaritanas [et] Aethiopicas pro meo libro De emendatione temporum' (*Secunda Scaligerana*, 1740, pp. 174–175, s. v. 'Abyssinorum').

10   Possibly the *Kalendarium* Scaliger received from Patriarch Ignatius Naʿmatallah, which is now no longer present in the Leiden University Library collection.

11   This prayer book is possibly the manuscript 'en langue indienne' that Scaliger inquired about from Pithou in *Correspondence* 2 June 1578. See: Kerr, *Vetus Testamentum* (2004), no. 6.

APPENDIX 1

(cont.)

Libri Hebræi et alii scripti

Ingens volumen commentariorum D.R. Salomonis in Biblia ubi multa sunt quæ aliter vulgo edita	MS Or. 4718
Baal Aruch integrum,[12] ante CC aut CCC annos scriptum, nam vulgo editum est castratum una cum egregio Dictionario Hebraico Anonymi. Ingens et crassum volumen	MS Or. 4722
Liber Helitiorti [?] Ingens et luculentum volumen	MS Or. 4719
Duo ingentia volumina Talmud Hierosalami ante CC annos scripta	MS Or. 4720
Rabbi Mose bar Gaio di Riete discursi de Philosophia liber Italicus vetus, charactere Judaico	MS Or. 4727:1
Meditationes excellentissimi Kalonymi filii Kalonymi. Scribebat anno Judaico 5083, Christi 1323	MS Or. 4727:2
Epistola longissima magistri Bonet Benioris Avenionensis ad amicum de abiurando Judaismo, apologetica pro christianissiomo (sic!) adversus Judæos. Scribebat Papa Avenione sedente	Olim MS Or. 4727
Rabbi Levi Egregii philosophi de meteoris. In-4° oblongo	MS Or. 4726
Liber medicinæ anonymi. In-4°.	MS Or. 4728 or MS Or. 4732
Alius Liber Medicinæ Anonymi. In 4°	MS Or. 4728 or MS Or. 4732
Commentarius brevis Aben Ezræ in Daniëlem qui nihil habet commune cum eo qui editus est.	MS Or. 4730:1
Excerpta ex Rituali de funerationibus et exequiis	MS Or. 4730:2

f. 179^r

Liber Animæ, aliter Liber Ponderis	MS Or. 4730:5
Secreta nominum Merkaba R. Ismaelis	MS Or. 4730:9
Visio Rotarum. Ita vocatur sphæra Johannis de Sacrobosco conversa in Hebraismum a R. Salomone filio R. Abraham Abigedor bononiensi, ante annos CC	MS Or. 4730:11
Aben Ezra Initium Sapientiæ de Astrologia Iudiciaria	MS Or. 4731:1

---

12 Nathan ben Yechiel of Rome, *Sefer Aruch* als known as *Lexicon Talmudico-Rabbinico-Chaldaicum* [UBL 838 A 15 en 838 A 14; See Bibliographic Survey Venice 1531–1532 and Pesaro 1517].

APPENDIX 1   305

(*cont.*)

Libri Hebræi et alii scripti

Eiusdem liber luminum. Liber astrologicus	MS Or. 4731:2
Eiusdem de mundo. Alius liber Astrologicus	MS Or. 4731:3
Albumasar de electionibus	MS Or. 4731:4
Centiloquium Ptolemæi cum commentario Abugafar arabis non autem Halii, ut est excusum: quæ editio in multis differt ab Hebræica	MS Or. 4731:5
Tekuin. Id est Ephemeris	MS Or. 4731:6
Categoriæ Ar(istote)lis cum Egregio commentario Rabbi Levi ben Gersom	MS Or. 4729
Lectionarium Rutenicum sive Moschoviticum Hi[c] libri Extant manuscripti in Biblioth. Jos. Scal. Cu[m] plurimis excusis quidam sed quo raro invenian- tur in omnibus linguis	Olim MS Or. 267?[13]

---

13   Another manuscript of a *Lectionarium* originating from Moscow was sent to Scaliger by Theobaldus Meuschius of Salzburg. *Correspondence* 2 April 1602 from Meuschius and 9 June 1602 to Meuschius. This could possibly also be the *Lectionarium Lingua & characttere Slavonicis. 8°. Venet. [15]81,* that is mentioned in the 1609 Auction Catalogue on page 50.

Appendix 2

List by Janus Dousa of August 1594 with the *Libri Haebraici, Chaldaici et Arabici* from the library of the Court of Holland [UBL AC 1 101, ff. 30^r^–31^r^].

Duo volumina Bibliorum cum eorum Rabbinis Haebraicae	UBL 840 A 13–14[1]
Talmud 9. voluminibus distinctis	UBL 21523 A 1–9[2]
Petrus Galatmus explosor Talmud Judaeorum	UBL 612 A 8[3]
Hebraica Biblia cum Latina interpretatione sebastiani Munsteri in duos Tomus divisa, quis è Rabinorum commentarijs sectae annotationes adiectae sunt. Bas. Anno [15]35	UBL 516 A 1[4]
Psalterium Hebraeum, Graecum, Arabicum, et Chaldeum cum trib. Latinus interpretationibus et Glossis	UBL 1368 C 2
Psalterium 4. Linguarum, Hebraeum, Graecum, Chaldaeum, Latinum	UBL 754 B 8[5]
Haebraeus Rabmus, cum premittitur Liber symphoriani Campegij de Monarchia Galiorum	An untraceable edition by Benedictus Curtius Symphorien Champier.
Duo opuscula Haebraea, quis premittitur Guido Papa super Decretales et Codice[6]	

---

1 *Biblia hebraica. Cum utraque Masora, Targum Onkelosi et Hierosolym. In Pentateuchum, ceterisque Rabbinorum commentariis, curante R. Jac. Ben Chajim* (Venezia: Daniel Bomberg, 1524–1526).

2 This edition of the *Talmud Babylonicum cum commentariis Mos. Maimonidis, Raschi et Tosafot* [...] (Venezia: Daniel Bomberg, 1520–1530) was sold as a duplicate in 1843 because there was another copy of this Talmud from Warner's collection in the library.

3 *Opus de arcanis catholicae veritatis, contra Judaeorum nostrae tempestatis perfidiam, ex Talmud aliisque hebraicis libris nuper excerptum* (Ortona: per Girolamo Soncino, 1518; USTC 831362).

4 Possibly a copy of the *Hebraica Biblia Latina planeque nova. Seb. Munsteri translatione* [...] *adjectis insuper e Rabinorum commentariis annotationibus* [...] (Basel: ex. off. Bebeliana impend. Mich. Isingrinii et Henr. Petri, 1534–1535; USTC 401866).

5 Johannes Potken, *Psalterium in quatuor linguis: Hebraea, Graeca, Chaldaea* [i.e. Aethiopica], *Latina* (Impressum Coloniae: Johannes Soter, alias Heyl, 1518; USTC 1791566).

6 Two books in Hebrew and two publications by the French lawyer Guy de La Pape (1402–1487): *Guido pape super Decretales. Lectura singularis* [et] *aurea domini Guidonis Pape co[n]sulis dalphi[n]alis super Decretales in qua singulares et aute[n]tice materie exancla[n]tur* [...]

APPENDIX 2   307

(*cont.*)

Dictionarium trilingue Graecum, Hebraeum et Chaldaeum authore Sebastiano Munstero	UBL 873 A 4:1[7]
Dictionarium Chaldaeum Authore Sebastiano Munstero in 4[to]	UBL 874 D 15[8]
Dictionarium Hebraeum Auth. sebast. Munstero in 8°	UBL 875 D 18[9]
Grammatica Chaldaea Authore sebast. Munstero cum Calendario Hebraico per eundem authorem	
Grammatica Hebraea Johannis Reuchlini[10]	
Grammatica Hebraea Abrahae de Balmis cum Latina interpretatione	UBL 837 C 7[11]
Grammatica Hebraea Eliae Levitae cum alijs quibusdam eisdem authoris in 8°	
De accentibus et ortographia Linguae Hebraice authore Joanne Reuchlino quib. Praemittitur Pyrhus Anglebermius in Libros & Codices	UBL 873 C 20[12]
Dictionarium Hebraicum ex Rabinis eorum collectum in 8°	UBL 875 D 18

     (Lyon: Symonis Vincentius & Anthonii du Ry, 1517; USTC 144824) and G. Papa, *Lectura subtilis et aurea* [...] *super Codice* (Lyon: Johannes Marion, 1517; USTC 671922). These books were not transferred to Leiden University Library.

7   This copy is no longer in the collection and has been replaced by *Silus lesonot* or *Dictionarium trilingue, in quo scilicet Latinis vocabulis in ordinem alphabeticum digestis, respondent Græca & Hebraica* [...] (Basel: Heinrich Petri, [1562]; USTC 661201).

8   This copy of Sebastian Münster, *Dictionarium Chaldaicum, ex Baal Aruch et Chál. bibliis atque Hebraeorum Peruschim* [...] (Basel: apud Johann Froben, 1527; USTC 661195) may have been replaced by the copy from Scaliger's library.

9   Sebastian Münster, *Maqrē dardeqē* of *Dictionarium Hebraicum ex rabbinorum commentarijs collectum, adiectis ijs Chaldaicis vocabulis quorum in biblijs est usus* [...] (Basel: apud Johann Froben 1525; USTC 661204)

10   Johannes Reuchlin, *De rudimentis Hebraicis* [...] (Pforzheim: Thomas Anshelm, 1506; USTC 686605) [Copy from Scaliger's bequest is UBL 874 B 6; see Bibliographic Survey Pforzheim 1506].

11   *Miqneh Avram* of *Peculivm Abrae. Grammatica Hebraea una cum Latíno. Nuper edita per Abraham de Balmis* (Impressa Venetijs: in aedibus Danielis Bōbergi, 1523; USTC 1792503).

12   Johannes Reuchlin, *De accentibus, et orthographia linguae Hebraicae. Libri tres* (Hagenae: [Thomae Anshelmi Badensis 1518; USTC 628887); the book by Jean Pyrrhus d'Anglebermes cannot be identified.

(*cont.*)

Hebraicae Grammatices compendium authore
Mattheo Aurigalio[13]
Tabula in Grammaticen Hebraicam Nicolai
Cleonardi cui praemittitur Thomas Linacer de
Emendata Structura cum alijs quibusdam[14]
Volumen Bibliorum Hebraeum

Haebraeorum Institutionum lib. 4 quib.	UBL 837 D 17 & 873 D 15:1[15]

Praemittuntur authores octo cum commentario
Agatij Guidaceij de Laudis. Psalmorum Liber cui
postponitur Liber de Marco Aurelio Hispanicè
in 4°[16]

Decalogus Praeceptorum divinorum cum com-	UBL 877 G 5[17]

ment Rabbi Aben Ezra et Latina versione sebast.
Munsteri in 8°
Joh. Reuchlini interpretatio in 7 Psalmos
Paenitentiales Hebraic. In 8°[18]
Catalogus omnium preceptorum legis Mosaica
qua ab. Hebręis 613 numeratur in 8°

---

13 Matthaeus Aurogallus or Goldhahn's book, *Compendium Hebreae Grammatices* (Wittenberg: [Josef Klug, 1523]; USTC 623235) gives a brief outline of the Hebrew language. VD 16 G 2550. The book did not enter the Leiden University Library collection.

14 Nicolas Clenard, *Luah ha-diqduq* of *Tabula in grammaticen Hebream* (Paris: excudebat Chrestien Wechel, 1534; USTC 185411) and Thomas Linacer, *Rudimenta grammatices Thomae Linacri, ex anglico sermone in latinum versa. Interprete Georgio Buchanano* [...] (Paris: Roberti Stephani 1536). This copy was not transferred to Leiden University Library.

15 Sante Pagnini, *Hebraicarum institutionum libri IV ex rabbi David Kimchi* (Lyon: Antoine du Ry impensis François Guillaume de Castelnau de Clermont-Lodève, 1526; USTC 145767). The copy may have been replaced by two copies of the 1549 book from Scaliger's collection.

16 Possibly a copy of Agatius Guidacerius, *De laudibus, & materia Psalmorum. Et in primum psalmum, secundum veritatem hebraicam expositio* (Paris: Pierre Vidoué [et] Gilles de Gourmont, 1529; USTC 146029) & Antonio de Guevara, *Libro Aureo de Marco Aurelio, Emperador, eloquentissimo Orador en el qual contienen muchas cosas hasta aqui en ninguno otro impressas* (Venizia: Juan Batista Pedrezano 1532; USTC 343014). This copy was not transferred to Leiden University Library.

17 *Decalogus. Cum commentariolo Rabbi Aben Ezra, et Latina versione Sebastiani Munsteri* [...] (Basel: apud Johann Froben 1527; USTC 661159).

18 Johannis Reuchlin, *In septem psalmos poenitentiales hebraicos interpretatio de verbo ad verbum* [...] (Wittenberg: Joseph Klug, 1529). This copy was not transferred to Leiden University Library.

Appendix 3

The list of oriental books and manuscripts from Scaliger's library copied before 1600 by Bonaventura Vulcanius

    CATALOGUS Librorum qui hodie conservantur à Josepho Scaligero IMPRESSA rara.[1]

[Col. 1]	Signatures UBL
Zohar	UBL 875 B 1
Totum Talmud	UBL 875 A 1–8
Totus Avicenna Hebr.	UBL 855 A 5–6
Targum Arab. R. Saadia in Pentateuch	UBL 839 A 7
Targum Persic. in Pentateuch	UBL 839 A 7; The copy of the Targum, printed in Constantinople in 1551 was later deselected
Liber Mebih Cusar. Luculentum opus	UBL 1371 D 22:1
Proverbia antiqua, versibus instar	UBL 1371 D 22:2
Apologorum Aesopi, cum figures. Liber egregius	UBL 854 F 18
Gramm[atic]ᵃ R. Mose Kimchi	UBL 874 B 5
Proverbia sive dicta moraliarum quaest.	UBL 502 G 12:2 (?)
Jad R. Mose ben Maimon duo immania volumina utilissima, instar Talmud	UBL 854 A 6–7
Via vitae R. Jacob F(ilii). Aser instar doctrinae	UBL 874 A 15
Talmud, ubi continentur Ritus Judaici.	UBL 854 A 15
Praeterea in Legibus plus q(uam). XX interpretes	UBL 874 B 15
Tanchuma Sephir Siphra, Mechita, & multa eiusmodi	
Biblia magna Venetiis excusa cum comment.	UBL 515 A 12–15
Multi præteræ alii Hebraici scriptores a nobis	
Mirabelli relicti, quorum nunc no[m]i[n]a	
non succurrunt	

---

1   UBL VUL 108, pars 5, verso. The manuscripts on the verso side of this list are excluded here. Details of the manuscripts, including shelf marks, are included in Van der Heide, *Hebrew Manuscripts*. 1977, pp. 21–23. Incidentally, that survey also includes a printed book, the *Catechismus Jesuitarum lingua Malabar, Goae impressus* in India. Besides, many other books by Hebrew writers have been left by me in Mirabel, whose names do not appear in this list.

310 APPENDIX 3

(*cont.*)

Ep[is]t[ol]ae duae Ignatii patriarchae Antiocheni ad nos, instar duorum librorum Arabicè manu ipsius Patriarichae[2]	Not in UBL anymore
Kalendarium Elkuph Arab., MS	MS Or. 262
Kalendarium Antiochenum Syriace, MS[3]	
Diurnale, Sive Euchologium Maronitarum Arabicè, charactere Syriaco	UBL 876 C 6
Horae matutinæ Arab.	UBL 876 G 27
Preces Maronitarum Syriacè & Arab., charactere Syriaco	UBL 874 D 17:2 and possibly UBL 864 D 18:2
Duo Nova Testamenta Aethiopica	UBL 500 E 20
Quinque Volumina Psalmorum Aethiopica, Quorum unum manu Petri Comis Aethiopis notatum est, & multis appendicibus auctum	UBL 877 D 37 and UBL 837 D 38
Psalterium Armeniacum	MS Or. 4738 or UBL 876 G 31[4]
Quædam Veterum Patrum, lingua Veteri Dalmatica, charactere Dalmatico	UBL 1370 G 21 (?)
Psalmi Poenitentialis linguâ Illyricâ, charactere Serviano	MS SCA 24B (?)
Correctio anni Gregoriana, Armeniacè[5]	

[col. II]

Kalendarium Turcicum, MS	
Duo libri Canonis Avicennae Arab.	UBL 878 A 4
Euclidis lib. IX. Arab.	UBL 845 A 9

---

2 These are two extended letters from the Syriac Jacobite patriarch Ignatius Naʿmatallah to Scaliger concerning the eastern *computus* and the Syriac calendar. See: G. Levi della Vida, 'Documenti introno alle relazione delle chiese orientale con la S. Sede durante il pontificatio di Gregorio XIII', in *Studi e testi* 142 (1948), pp. 22–25.

3 Possibly the *Kalendarium* that Scaliger also received from Ignatius Naʿmatallah, now no longer present in the UBL collection.

4 Scaliger's copy of the Armenian Psalter was sold as a doublet and is now in the Royal Library in Copenhagen. Thanks to Anna Maria Mattaar who drew my attention to this copy.

5 Possibly a copy of the *Tomar Grigorieann havitenakan* [*Kalendarium Gregorianum perpetuum* or Perpetual Gregorian Calendar] (Rome: Yovhannes Terzncʿi and Sultʿansah Tʿoxatʿecʿi, printed by Dominicus Basa, 1584; USTC 820883). This is a publication on the reform of the calendar ratified by Pope Gregory XIII's bull *Inter gravissimas* (dated February 24, 1581 and promulgated March 1, 1582). See Bibliographic Survey Rome 1584: 2.

APPENDIX 3

311

(*cont.*)

Duæ Grammaticae Arabicæ	UBL 839 C 25 & UBL 839 C 26
Liber Theologiæ Mahomedicæ, MS. Arabicè, cum apicibus vocalibus	MS Or. 228 (?)
Mappa Annorum Judaicorum ab anno 5335 ad annum 5347[6]	
Euchologium Judaicum	UBL 1370 E 33
C. Marii Plotii Sacerdotis de versibus cum exemplis Graecis. Liber instar Hephaestionis descriptus ex Bibliothecae Cuiacii	MS SCA 37
Priscianus collatus cum integro Prisciano Puteani, in quo Graeca expressa sunt o[mn]ia. Est in Bibliotheca Cuiacii; neque possumus (?) recup[er]are, cum alliis MSS. quos com[mmen]daveram Cuiacio	
Liber Cosmographiæ Arabicus in climatam et climatum partes divisus. Opus utilissimum, si Latinè factum esset	UBL 842 D 12

[Signature Bonaventura Vulcanius]

---

6   Probably a review of a Jewish concordance on the Christian years 1574–1586.

Appendix 4

Section of Scaliger's bequest in Daniel Heinsius, *Catalogus librorum Bibliothecæ Lugdunensis* (Leiden: 1612), with the current shelf marks of the printed books and manuscripts in Leiden University Libraries

CATALOGVS LIBRORVM
QVOS BIBLIOTHECAE
Iosephus Scaliger legavit.

Libri Hebraei in folio.		
Ingens volumen ante CCC annos scriptû omnium Commentariorum R. Solomonis vetus Testamentum.		MS Or. 4718 (SCA 1)
Talmud Ierosolymitanû manuscriptum, duobus ingentib. voluminibus.		MS Or. 4720 (SCA 3)
Talmud Basiliensis editionis VIII. voluminibus.		UBL 875 A1–8
Baal Aruch manuscript. cum quibusdam alijs ad Grammaticam & verborum rationes pertinentibus. ingens volumen.		UBL 838 A 15
Biblia Veneta cum Rabinis quatuor voluminibus, secundae editionis.		UBL 515 A 12–15
Iard Rambam duobus ingentibus voluminibus Venetijs.		UBL 854 A 6–7
Orah Aiim R. Aser ben Iaacob. Venet.		UBL 854 A 15
Pentateuchum cû Targum, R. Solomonis, & Ramban Venet.		UBL 867 A 8
Meturgemin Elie Basil.		UBL 839 A 6
Radices Kimhi Venetijs, cum explicatione Latina vocum in margine.	Copy from Warner's collection	UBL 838 A 8: 1
Radices Kimhi, primae editionis. Venet.		UBL 874 B 4
Miclol Kimhi, prior & posterior pars. Venet.		UBL 838 A 17
Dictionarium Davidis de Pomis. Venet.	Copy from Warner's collection	UBL 874 B 9

APPENDIX 4   313

(*cont.*)

Dictionarium Chald. Pagnini cum Rabano De cruce		UBL 874 B 10: 1–2
Liber bellorum Domini Levi Gerson. Venet.		UBL 855 A 10
More hannevochin. prima editio. Venetijs		Not present in UBL anymore
More hannevochin cum Commentarijs.		UBL 877 B 12
Commentarius ἀχέφαλ[?] in Esaiam manuscrip.	J.F. Gronovius added: 'Ialcuth Commentarius in Biblia, incipient ab Esaïa'[1]	MS? Not identified
Excerpta ex Talmud Babylonio in membranis excusa.		UBL 1371 A 18
Zohar Cremonae		UBL 875 B 1
Midras Tehillin, Samuel, Misle. Venet.		UBL 876 B 27
Tzeror hammor, quae est explanatio in omnem legem. Venet.		UBL 873 A 8
Rabbi Bechai in omnem legem. Venet.		UBL 873 A 9
Totus canon Avicennae.	Vol. 1 is from Warner's collection	UBL 855 A 5–6
Commentarius Levi ben Gerson in omnem legem Venet.		UBL 875 B 16
Tanhuma qua est ἀναγωγὴ in omnem legem Peshita.		UBL 874 B 15
Lutreta in Levit. & Deuter.		UBL 874 B 21: 3
Liber ejusdem argumenti, qui dicitur aliter Torath Cohanim.		UBL 874 B 21: 2
Quaestiones R. Ahai Gaon.		874 B 19
R. Simeon ben Iohai. Venet.		Not identified
Col-bo Venetijs.		Not present in UBL anymore
Psalterium varijs linguis. Genuae.	This is not the copy of Scaliger	UBL 1368 C 2
Dictionarium Sanctis Pagnini. Gryph.		UBL 874 B 10: 1

---

1   UBL BA C 5, p. 160.

(*cont.*)

Dictionarium Biblior. Regiorum multis partibus a Scaligero auctum, & infinitis vocibus locupletatum.		UBL 874 B 7
Pentateuchum cum Targumin, Chaldaïce Onkelos.	This is not the copy of Scaliger. In 1674 this Pentateuch and the one below were originally bound in one volume.	UBL 1371 A 10
Idem Arabice & Persice. item impressum Constantinop. cum Commentario R. Solomonis Iarchi.		UBL 839 A 7
Sepher selihoth scriptus in membranis.		MS Or. 4721 (SCA 4)
In quarto.		
Baal Aruch.		UBL 838 A 15
Kimhi in Psalmos. Basil.		UBL 874 B 11
Grammatica Cevalerij edit. ult. Genevæ.		UBL 873 B 12
Grammatica Chaldaica Merceri cui infinita a Scaligero adjuncta sunt. Lutet.		UBL 874 D 13
Grammatica Chaldaica Angeli Caninij. Lutet.		UBL 874 D 12: 2
Postelli XII. linguae cum Grammatica Arabica. Lutet.	Copy from Isaac Vossius's Library	UBL 873 C 1: 1
Grammatica Ioh. Isaacij. Plantin.		UBL 873 C 13
Genebrardis de legendis Rabbinis. Lutet.	This is not the copy of Scaliger	UBL 874 D 39
Grammatica Abraham de Balmis. Venet.		UBL 837 C 6
Grammatica Marci Marini. Basil.		UBL 873 C 14: 1
Grammatica Sanctis Pagnini. Rob. Steph.		UBL 873 B 15
Elias Tisbithes. Basil.		UBL 874 C 19
Thesei Ambrosij introductio in linguas. Chaldaicâ & Syriacâ.	This is not the copy of Scaliger	UBL 1497 D 23

APPENDIX 4 315

(*cont.*)

Kalendarium Iudaicum cum interpretatione Munsteri.		UBL 877 D 2
Kalendarium Iudaicum, Arithmetica, Sphaera, cum interpretat. Munsteri		UBL 877 D 3:1
Libellus de accentibus. Lutet.		UBL 874 D 2
Sepher Emana. Basil.		UBL 875 E 9[2]
Sepher Iccarim. liber articulorum fidei, auctore Iosepho Albon. opus praestantissimum. Venet.		UBL 874 D 27
Gerardus Veltuijk. item Derech Emana. Venet.		UBL 875 E 3:1 & 2
Sepher jetzira cum IIII. expositionibus. Venet.		UBL 875 E 24
Mibhar happenniim, Margarita. Venet.		UBL 875 D 21:2
Commentarius manuscrip, Levi ben Gerson de Meteoris. Proverbia Arabica manuscripta.		MS Or. 4726 (SCA 9). Second title is the manuscript of the Arabic Proverbs Or. 26.644–1
Commentarius Aben Ezrae in Danielum non editus, multum discrepans ab edito. Excerpta quaedam ex ritibus Iud. Sepher Nannephes. Sepher hammiskal. Secreta nominû Merkaba R. Ismaelis, aliter visio rotar: quae est Sphaera Ioh. De Sacrobosco. Liber sapientiae, qui est instar proverbiorum Solomonis. Anagoge nominis divini. Omnia manuscripta. Grammatica Mosis Kimhi, impressa in Sicilia ante annos CLII.	Last title is a printed book: Mose Qimhi, *Sefer diqduq* [*Sefer mahalak ševile ha-Da'at*]. Ortona, Gershom Soncino [1519]	MS Or. 4730 (SCA 13)
Liber medicinae manuscrip.		MS Or. 4728?

---

2   According to librarian Johann Friedrich Gronovius there were two copies of this book in Scaliger's bequest: one bound and one unbound ('gebonden en sonder couvert') [UBL BA C 5, p. 161].

316 APPENDIX 4

(*cont.*)

Liber medicinae manuscript. Liber interrogationum discipulli, & respons. Magistri, cum commentario impressus. Liber portarum ura, auctore Iospeho ben Gikatilia impressus.	Last two titles are printed books: Abraham Jagel dei Gallichi of Monselice, *Lekah Tov*. Venice, Juan di Gara, 1595 & Joseph ben Avraham Gikatilia, *Sefer Shaarei Orah*. Mantua, Naftali Cohen Gazzolo 1561.	MS Or. 4727?
Liber manuscrip. in quo initium Sapientiae Aben Ezre. ejusdem liber De luminarijs. Ejusdem liber de mundo. Liber de electionibus Abumazar. Centiloquium Ptolomaei cum Commentario Albugaphar. Capita x. ex Ephemeridibus.		MS Or. 4731 (SCA 14)
Lesson Limmudim. I. Grammatica R. David ben Ichaia. Constantinopoli anno Christi 1506.		UBL 871 F 6
Melech Cazar. Massal Kadmoni, R. Isaac ben Selomo impress. liber rariss.		UBL 1371 D 22:1
Commentarius manuscriptus Levi ben Gerson in Categorias.		MS Or. 4729 (SCA 12)
Epistola Ludovici Carreti ex Iudaeo Christiani cum interpret. Angeli Caninij.		UBL 876 D 24
Sepher hasidin. Venet.[3]		UBL 875 E 12
Quinque priores Prophete minores cum Solomone. Aben, Esra, David Kimhi & Targum. Paris.		UBL 874 C 16
Liber manuscript. medicinae R. Isaac.		MS Or 4728 (SCA 11)

---

3 Librarian Gronovius changed the place of publication of this title in his hand copy of the 1640 catalogue from Venice to Basel [UBL BA C 5, p. 162].

APPENDIX 4 317

(*cont.*)

Liber debiti cordium.		UBL 875 D 2
Commentarius R. Samuel in Danielem.		UBL 874 E 29
Tobias cum Latino Mûsteri. Pircke Avoth cum Latino Fagij.		UBL 874 D 7
Expositio in legem. Cremonae.		UBL 874 D 34
Liber portarum lacrimae.	Copy from Warner's Library	UBL 875 E 36
Textus Bibliorum Bombergae.		UBL 1366 F 16
Textus Bibliorum R. Steph. II. voluminibus		UBL 499 B 6–7
Textus Bibliorum in Parvo IIII. Brixiae.		UBL 1368 G 8
Ioseph Ben Gorion. Venet.		UBL 875 D 11
Ioseph Ben Gorion Krakoviae.		UBL 875 D 12
Itinerarium R. Pethahia.		UBL 875 E 31: 1
Liber manuscrip. in quo moralia Italica lingua, charactere Iudaico. Liber Eben Bahan. hoc est lapidis indicis, auctore R. Cleonymo Epistola magistri Bonet ben joury Avenionensis ex Iudaeo Christiani. Liber Medicinae.		MS Or. 4727 (SCA 10)
Sepher Iohasin. Krakoviae.		Not present in UBL anymore
In octavo.		
Logica R. Simeon cum Latino Munsteri. Itinerarium. Bêjamin. Disputatio Christiani cû Iudeo. auctore Mûstero.		UBL 875 F 43: 1, 2 and 3
Biblia sine punctis & novum Testamentum Syriacum & Graecum. Plantin.		Not present in UBL anymore
Physica R. Tybbon cum Latino Io. Isacij. Epistola Ramban as Massaliotas.		UBL 875 F 16
Preces Iudaicae. Venet.		UBL 854 D 20
Dibre haiamin. i. Chronicon gestorum in terra Sancta a Christianis auctore Ioseph sacerdote.		875 F 44
Praecepta Mosis micotze.		UBL 854 F 4

318 APPENDIX 4

(*cont.*)

Cathechismus Tremelij Hebra. & Graec. Henrici Steph.		UBL 854 D 15
Silva Epistolarum Iudaic. edita a Buxtorfio. x. praecepta cum Aben Ezra.		UBL 854 F 2
Seder Olam Zuta, & Rabba.		Not present in UBL anymore
Compendium Iosephi ben Gorion.		UBL 876 G 1: 1
Masoreth hammasoreth. Basil.		UBL 878 F 66
Iggereth dophi Zeman. Sepher ben hammelech.		UBL 871 G 20
Misle Sualim. rariss.		UBL 854 F 18
Catechismus Tremelij.		UBL 854 D 15
Evangelium Matthaei.		UBL 837 G 28
De versibus Iudaeorum Genebrardi.		UBL 878 F 70: 1
Levitici liber manuscrip.		MS 4737
Computus magnus Iudaic. manuscriptus.		MS Or. 4736 (SCA 19)
Euchologium Iudaicum in XVI.		UBL 1370 E 33
Sepher Maamadoth. liber stationum sacerdotalium in 24.		Not present in UBL anymore
Libri Arabici in folio.		
Avicenna integer. Romae.	This is not the copy of Scaliger	UBL 878 A 3
Avicenna Canonum libri duo. Romae.		UBL 878 A 4
Euclides integer. Romae.		UBL 845 A 9
Euclides libri IX. Romae.		Not present in UBL anymore
IIII. Evangelia Romae.		Not present in UBL anymore
IIII. Evangelia cum glossa interlineari. Romae.		UBL 876 A 6 (lost)
Pêtateuchû multis locis lacerû sedopti-mae notae manuscriptû.		MS Or. 236
Ius civile & Canonicum Mahumedanor Afror. manuscript.	With pasted in note: 'Hem [?] uyt de cassa van D. Scaligero. extra catalogus'.	MS Or. 222

APPENDIX 4   319

(cont.)

More hannebuchin Râban lingua Arabica charactere Iudaico.		MS Or. 4723 (SCA 6)
Thesaurus ingens linguae Arabicae a Iosepho Scaligero collect. manuscrip.		MS Or. 212
In quarto.		
Novum Testamentum integrum. manuscript.		MS Or. 217
IIII. Evangelia ex monte Libano. manuscript.		MS Or. 223 (?)
IIII. Evangelia vetustissima manuscript.		Not identified
Lexicon luculentissimum Persico-Turcicum. manuscript.		MS Or. 227
Lexicon luculentissimum Arabo Turcicum. manuscript.		MS Or. 237
Geographiae liber. Romae.		UBL 842 D 12
Liber optimus Astrologiae cum commentarijs. manuscript.		Possibly MS Or. 234
Libellus Turcicus. manuscript.		Not identified
Alphabetum Romae.		UBL 877 D 12
Targum charactare Iudaico. manuscript.		MS Or. 236
Liber alius Turcicus de grammatica. manuscriptus.		MS Or. 254
Libri duo Caphnae, sive grammaticae. Romae.	These are not the copies of Scaliger	UBL 839 C 25 & UBL 839 C 26
Epistolae duae longissimae Ignatij Patriarchae ad Iosephum Scalig. cum Kalend. Turco-Persico, & Kalendarijs Elkulpti & Antiochenum.	The letters of Patriarch Ignatius and both calendars are not in UBL	MS, not present in UBL anymore
Dictionarium Graeco-Arabicum vetustissimum.	= Lectionarium	MS Or. 243
Chronicon Samaritanor charactere Samaritano.		MS Or. 249
Commêtarius ex scriptis Chrysostomi in quatuor Evangelistas.		MS Or. 245
Multa Capitula Alcorani reposita in pera viatoria.		MS Or. 241 or MS Or. 228

320 APPENDIX 4

(*cont.*)

In octavo.

Duo exemplaria Horologia beatae Mariae virginis impressa.		UBL 876 G 27
Elementa Grammaticae manuscript.		MS Or. 235 or MS Or. 240
Liber Turcicus manuscript.		MS Or. 242
Colloquium duorum Mahumedanorum. Romae.		UBL 877 G 1
Apocalypsis manuscript.		MS Or. 252
Evangelium secundum Lucam & Ioannem manuscrip.		MS Or. 255
Psalterium cum Canticis manuscriptum.		MS Or. 4725

In decimosexto.

Preces Arabice manuscript.		MS Or. 259 (?)
Alcoranum elegantiss. manuscript.		MS Or. 256 (?)
Alcoranum character Turcic. manuscript.		MS Or. 261
Liturgiae tres cum interpretat. Elkulpti manuscript.		Possibly MS Or. 214
Mappa Turcica elegantissima.		Not present in UBL anymore

Libri Syriaci.

Novum Testamentum Syriacum Tremelij. Duobus voluminibus. Genevae.	This is not the copy of Scaliger	UBL 524 A 2
Liturgiae partum Syrae partim Arabicae, sed charactere Syriaco in IIII. Romae.		UBL 876 C 6
Novum Testamentum Viennae IIIIº.		UBL 500 E 20
Grammatica amplissima Romae IIIIº.	This is not the copy of Scaliger	UBL 876 C 4
Duo exemplaria ritualis Severi Patriarchae. Plantin IIII.		UBL 874 D 16 UBL 874 D 17
Preces Syriacae in IIIIº. Romae.		UBL 877 D 19: 1
Preces Syriacae & Arabicae charactere Syriaco in IIIIº. Romae.		UBL 877 D 19: 2

APPENDIX 4

(cont.)

Horologium Maronitar. partim Arabicum, partim Syriacum, charactere Syriaco. Romae.		UBL 876 G 30
Libri Aetiopici.		
Psalteria IIII. Romae. 4to.		UBL 877 D 37
Novum Testamentum integrum in 4. Romae	This is not the copy of Scaliger	UBL 877 C 19
Novum Testamentum sine epistolis in 4. Romae.		Not present in UBL anymore
Brevarium manuscriptum.		MS Or. 4734 (?)
Liber precum minutiss. forma manuscript.		MS Or. 262
Grammatica Aethiopica Mariani.		UBL 877 D 31
Lexicon Aethiopicum conjectum in Lexicon Chald. Munsteri a Iosepho Scaligero.		UBL 874 D 15
Libri lingua Russica Charactere Chyruluizza.		
Novum Testamentum in IIII. Vienae.		UBL 500 E 20
Breviarium in IIII°. manuscript.		Not identified
Meletij Patriarchae institutio Christiana Russico & Graeco sermone in VIII°. Vilnae.		Not present in UBL anymore
Liber precum in VIII°. manuscript.		SCA 74 (olim MS Or. 268)
Lectionarium manuscriptum.		SCA 38B (?) (olim MS Or. 265)
Alphabetum Russicum.		Not present in UBL anymore
Horae matutinae in XXIIII°. impressae.		UBL 1370 G 21
Horae matutinae charactere Buchuizza.	Earlier provenance: Friedrich Lindenbrog (1573–1648)	SCA 24 B (olim MS Or. 267)
Catechismus Loiolitarum, Indorum litera & charactere, impressus Goae.		Not present in UBL anymore

Appendix 5

List of Arabic books in Scaliger's Library, 1608 [in: *Correspondence* 22 March 1608 to Ubertus]

More hannevuchin, Arabice a Rabbi Mose ben Maimon conscriptus litera Iudaica, nondum editus, cuius Hebraicam quoque interpretationem habemus. Liber plenus bonae frugis, abstrusae eruditionis, et theologis Christianis apprime necessarius.	UBL 877 B 11[1]
Novum Testamentum integrum, luculenta litera, in Thebaidos deserto conscriptum.	MS Or. 217[2]
Tres Evangeliorum paraphrases diversae.	Possibly MS Or. 214[3]
Apocalypsis, alia ab illa superioris *Novi Testamenti*	MS Or. 252
Pentateuchum Arabicum Rabbi Sahadia Gaon, cum eiusdem Persica interpretatione.	UBL 839 A 7[4]
Pentateuchon aliud manu scriptum, alio paraphraste anonymo, cuius dictio valde a superiore diversa, charactere Iudaico.	MS Or. 236
Pentateuchum Christianum Arabicum, in Africa aut Hispania conscriptum, charactere Mauritano, vetustissimum, optimae notae, sed lacerum.	MS Or. 215
Avisena: Euclides.[5]	UBL 878 A 4 and 845 A 9

---

1   Bibliographic Survey Venice ante a. 1480.
2   This manuscript formed the basis for the publication of Thomas Erpenius, *Novum D.N. Jesu Christi Testamentum arabice ex Bibliotheca Leidensi* (Leiden: Typ. Thomas Erpenius, 1616; USTC 1011611). See: Hamilton, *Nam tirones sumus*, p. 569.
3   This manuscript holds a.o. the Gospels of Matthew and Marcus. See: Hamilton, *Nam tirones sumus*, p. 569 en 587.
4   Bibliographic Survey Constantinople 1546.
5   The Medicea editions of Avicenna and Euclid in Arabic translation [UBL 878 A 4 en 845 A 9; see: Bibliographic Survey Rome 1593: 2 and Rome 1594].

© KONINKLIJKE BRILL BV, LEIDEN, 2025 | DOI:10.1163/9789004701526_015

APPENDIX 5

(cont.)

Lexicon Raphelengianum Latino-Arabicum. Character Latinus est Longobardicus, ut falso vulgus vocat; Arabicus, Mauritanus, elegantissimus. Optimus liber, ex quo non solum multa hausi quae ad Arabismum, sed etiam quae ad sermonis Latini cognitionem pertinent. Dolendum integrum non extare, et absque me fuisset, qui folia lacera conglutavi et fragmenta omnia collegi, iamdudum fere totus periisset.	MS Or. 231[6]
Diurnale Maronitarum, charactere Syriaco.	UBL 876 C 6
Horologium, hoc est, horae matutinae.	UBL 876 G 30[7]
Preces Christianae, et quaedam beati Ephrem Syri, charactere Syriaco, cum interpretatione Syriaca.	Possibly UBL 874 D 17[8]
Dictionarium Granatense Hispano-Arabicum.	MS Or. 231
Alcoran, omnium librorum quos videre memini, elegantissime scriptus.	Possibly MS Or. 228
Astrologia Muhammedis Tuniciensis, cum commentario. Optimus liber quem fortasse, si vita suppetat, Latine reddemus. Scriptus est charactere Mauritanico.	Possibly MS Or. 234
Lexicon Syro-Arabicon, ex lexico Bar Ali Syro, et alio anonymo, tineis corroso, a nobis concinnatum et manu nostra descriptum.	MS Or. 213[9]
Psalterium Nebiense.	UBL 1368 C 2[10]
Psalterium aliud, alio paraphraste, calamo exaratum. Aliud ex Syriaco inter lineas Syriaci, quod non ex LXX interpretibus Graecis, sed ex Hebraico interpretatum est.	MS Or. 225

---

6   The 11th-century manuscript was purchased by Postel in Venice, he gave it to Masius. The latter in turn gave it to Raphelengius, who consulted it to compile his *Lexicon Arabicum*. After his death, the vocabulary came into Scaliger's hands. See: Pieter Sjoerd van Koningsveld, *The Latin-Arabic glossary of the Leiden University library. A contribution to the study of Mozarabic manuscripts and literature* (Leiden: New Rhine Publishers, 1976).

7   Bibliographic Survey Rome 1584.

8   Bibliographic Survey Antwerp 1572: 3.

9   Scaliger produced this copy based on a manuscript from Johan Boreel's collection.

10 Bibliographic Survey Genua 1516.

324 APPENDIX 5

(*cont.*)

Liturgiae tres Elkupti, ex quo exemplari Marcus Velser curavit eas Romae ab alumnis Maronitis Collegii Gregoriani Latine verti. In quo munere quantum erraverint, Velsero ipsi per literas indicavimus[11]	
Colloquium duorum Mussulmanorum ex Mecha redeuntium de nugis Alcorani, liber elegans.	UBL 877 G 1[12]
Chronicon Samaritarum, ab excessu Mosis ad tempora Antoninorum Augustorum, charactere Samaritano.	MS Or. 249[13]
Nomocanon, sive liber civilium legum, in folio, charactere Mauritano, accurato et luculento.	Possibly MS Or. 221
Geographia per septem Ptolomaei climata.	UBL 842 D 12[14]
Lectionarium vetustissimum Arabum Christianorum. Arabica sunt, sine punctis diacriticis. Graecus textus e regione appositus ex Prophetis et Novo Testamento, litera quadrata, quam capitalem vulgus vocat. Quod est argumentum vetustatis non infimae. Quia puncta diacritica absunt, quae literas similes, sed potestate diversas, a se discernunt, ut ف et ق. ت et ن propterea non nisi a peritis linguae legi possunt.	MS Or. 243[15]
Florilegium ex Chrysostomi *Homiliis in quatuor Evangelistas*, sine punctis diacriticis. Quorum commentariorum lectio eo operosior quam superioris libri, quod in Lectionario adiuvamur interpretatione Graeca e regione apposita; hic vero divinandum semper fuit, antequam sententiam assequi nobis contigerit.	MS Or. 245

---

11 *Correspondence* 23 April 1603 and 21 January 1604 from Welser. The manuscript is no longer in Leiden University Library.
12 Bibliographic Survey Rome 1579. This edition in Arabic script.
13 The manuscript was edited by Juynboll: *Chronicon Samaritanum*, 1848.
14 Bibliographic Survey Rome 1592: 4.
15 De Jonge, 'Joseph Scaliger's Greek-Arabic Lectionary', pp. 143–172.

Bibliography

Primary Sources

Archival Material

Catalogus Librorum omnium qui hodie conservantur à Josepho Scaligero. UBL VULC 108 f 5.

Hout, Jan van, *Dachbouck omme daerinnen alle lopende zaecken, de Universiteyt beroerende, aen te scryven, begonst naer Martini LXXX boven XVc.* UBL Archief van Curatoren (AC1) no. 100.

Register van brieven betreffende de beroeping van J. Scaliger tot hoogleraar aan de Leidsche universiteit, 1591–1592. UBL Archief van senaat en faculteiten (ASF) no. 524.

Royen, D. van, Schriftelijk Rapport [11 augustus 1741] van Mr. David van Royen, Secretaris van de Ed. Groot Achtbaere Heeren Curateuren over 's Lands Universiteit binnen Leijden, ende Burgemeesteren derzelve Stadt, nopens het begin en Voortgangh van alsmede zorge en ordre, gestelt, ende gedragen op, en over de Publique Bibliotheecq, ingevolge, ende ter Voldoeningh van het eerste Lidt van hun Ed. Groot Agtb. Resolutie, op den 30. April 1741, genomen. UBL BA H 1.

Testament J.J. Scaliger. UBL Codex Perizonii n. 5, fol. 39–44.

Tydeman, M., Standcatalogus *Hebraici* 1801–1813, aangevuld en bijgehouden door J.T. Bergman met de hand van Noest, in orde der vakken en formaten tot 1860 [UBL BA 1 C 42 X].

Verbouwing academiegebouw (1616?). Erfgoed Leiden en omstreken, Stadsbestuur 1574–1816 (SA II) no. 3317.

Printed and Digital Sources

Basson, Thomas, *Catalogus librorum bibliothecae [...] Pauli Merulae [...] quorum auctio habebitur Lugduni Batavorum in aedibus Ludovici Elsevirii, 29. Maij 1608* (Lugduni Batavorum: ex officina Thomae Basson, 1608) (USTC 1122234).

Baudius, Dominicus, *Oratio funebris dicta honori & memoriae maximi virorum Iosephi Iusti Scaligeri* (Lugduni Batavorum: prost. ap. L. Elzevirium et A. Cloucquium, 1609) (USTC 1028198)

Bertius, Petrus. *Nomenclator autorum omnium. Quorum libri Vel manuscripti, vel typis expressi exstant in Bibliotheca-Batava [...]* (Lugduni Batavorum: Apud Franciscum Raphelengium, 1595) (USTC 423469)

Bibliotheca Heinsiana sive catalogus Librorum quos magno studio & sumptu, dum viveret, collegit vir illustris Nicolaus Heinsius, Dan. Fil. In duas partes divisus (Lugduni in Batavis: Apud Joannem de Vivié, [1682]) (USTC 18470770).

Book Sales Catalogues Online (BSCO). *Book Auctioning in the Dutch Republic, 1599–ca. 1800.* Online Publication by Brill, Leiden.

Burman, Petrus, *Sylloges epistolarum* (Leidae: apud Samuelem Luchtmans 1724–1727).

Catalogus principum, civitatum, et singulariorum, qui donatione vel inter vivos vel mortis caussa, bibliothecam publicam, in Academia Lugduno-Batava institutam, liberaliter ditarunt (Lugduni-Batavorum: ex officina Ioannis Paetsij, 1597) (USTC 423868).

Catalogus librorum Bibliothecae Lugdunensis. Praefixa est Danielis Heinsii Bibliothecarii [...] *oratio* (Leiden: s.n., 1612) on page 78 onwards the 'Catalogus librorum quos Bibliothecae Iosephus Scaligeri legavit' (USTC 1016035).

Catalogus bibliothecæ publicæ lugduno-batavæ [& Oratio [...] *Pro bibliothecarii munere gratiarum actio* [Daniel Heinsius] & *Libri mss. arabici, quos ex oriente advexit I. Golius, cum genuinis arabicis eorundem titulis* (Lugd. Batavorum: ex officina Elsevir. Acad. typograph., 1640) (USTC 1028172).

Casaubon, Isaac, *Epistolæ, insertis ad easdem responsionibus* [...], *curante Theodoro Janson. ab Almeloveen* (Roterodami: typis Casparis Frisch et Michaelis Böhm, 1709).

Casaubon, Isaac, *Epistolæ, quotquot reperiri potuerunt, nunc primum junctim editæ. Adjecta est epistola de morbi ejus mortisque causa, deque iisdem narratio Raphaelis Thorii* (Hagæ Comitis: ex officina Theodori Maire, 1638) (USTC 1031624).

Chauffepié, Jacques George de, *Nouveau dictionnaire historique et critique pour servir de supplément ou de continuation au Dictionnaire historique et critique de Mr. Pierre Bayle* (Amsterdam, La Haye, Leyde: 1750–1756).

Colomiés, Paul, *Gallia Orientalis sive Gallorum qui linguam Hebraeam vel alias Orientales excoluerunt vitae* (Hagae-Comitis: s.n., 1665) (USTC 1802597).

De Thou, Jacques-Auguste, *Mémoires de la vie de Jacques-Auguste de Thou* [...] (Rotterdam (Rouan): R. Leers, 1711).

Drusius, Johannes, *Lachrymae Johannis Drusii junioris, tribus carminum generibus expressae, in obitum* [...] *Josephi Scaligeri, Julii Caesaris à Burden filii* (Franekerae: excudebat Aegidius Radaeus, 1609) (USTC 1029087).

Erpenius, Thomas, *Orationes tres, de Linguarum Ebraeae, atque Arabicae Dignitate* (Leidae: ex typographia auctoris, 1621) (USTC 1011652).

Fabricius, Franciscus, *Redevoering over den hondert en vyftigsten verjaardag, of het derde Jubeljaar der Hollandsche Akademie te Leiden. Uit last der Hoge Overheden gedaan den VIII February MDCCXXV, wanneer hij ten derde male het Rectoraat der Akademie afleide. Vertaalt door Dirk Smout* (Leiden: Pieter van der Aa, 1725).

Heinsius, Daniel, *In obitum V[iri] illust[rissimi] Iosephi Scaligeri Iul. Cæs. A Burden F. eruditorum principis Orationes duae. Accedunt Epicedia eiusdem & aliorum: effigies item ac monumentum Scaligeri & principum Veronensium aeri incisa* ([Leiden]: ex officina Plantiniana Raphelengij, 1609) (USTC 1029009).

Heinsius, Daniel, 'In Iosephe Scaligere funere' in *Orationes, editio nova* (Lugd. Batavorum: apud Ludovicum Elzevirium, 1615) (USTC 1011533).

Heinsius, Daniel, *Catalogus Bibliothecae publicae Lugduno-Batavae* (Leiden: ex officina Isaaci Elzeviri, 1623) (USTC 1016288).

BIBLIOGRAPHY

Hottinger, Johann Heinrich, *Promtuarium; sive, Bibliotheca Orientalis: exhibens catalogum, sive, centurias aliquot tam authorum, quam librorum Hebraicorum, Syriacorum, Arabicorum, Aegyptiacorum, Aethiopicorum, &c.: add. mantissa Bibliothecarum aliquot Europaearum tam public. quam privat* (Heidelbergae: Typis & impensis Adriani Wyngaerden, 1658), Appendix on pp. 18–24: *Catalogus Librorum Manuscriptorum quos Josephus Scaliger Bibliothecae Leidensi legavit* (USTC 2549010).

Lucae, Friedrich, *Europäischer Helicon. Auff welchem die Academien oder hohe Schuhlen von Anfang der Welt biss jetzo aller Nationen, besonders Europae, mit ihren Fundationen, Unglücksfällen, Restaurationen, Privilegiis, Jubilaeis, Nothwendigkeiten und Hindernüssen, Wächsthum und Abnehmen, rechten Gebrauch und Missbrauch, sambt ihren vornehmsten Lehrern, deren Verdienste und academischen Ehren-Tituln* (Franckfurt am Mayn: Bey Samuel Tobias Hocker, 1711).

Maizeaux, Pierre des, *Scaligerana, Thuana, Perroniana, Phitoeana, et Colomesiana* [...] (Amsterdam: chez Cóvens & Mortier, 1740).

Merula, Paullus, *Rariorum Biblioth. Acad. Lugdun. Catalogus. Compositus a P.G.F.G.N. Merula, Icto et historiarum in Acad. Lugd. Bat. Prof. et ibidem bibliothecario. Anno MDCVII D.D. Curatoribus ab eodem oblatus* [1607].

[Meursius, Johannes], *Illustris Academia Lugd-Batava. Id est Virorum clarissimorum icones, elogia ac vitae, qui eam scriptis suis illustrarunt* (Lugd.-Bat.: apud Andreas Cloucquius, 1613) (USTC 1028467).

Meursius, Johannes, *Illustrium Hollandiae & Westfrisiae ordinum alma Academia Leidensis* (Lugduni Batavorum: apud Jacobum Marci et Iustum à Colster, 1614) (USTC 1028326).

Meursius, Johannes, *Athenæ Batavæ, sive de urbe Leidensi & academia, virisque claris; qui utramque ingenio suo, atque scriptis, illustrarunt: libri dvo* (Lugduno Batavorum: apud Andream Cloucquium, et Elsevirios, 1625) (USTC 1011745).

Naudé, Gabiel, *Advis pour dresser une bibliothèque présenté à Monsigneur le président de Mesme* (Paris: François Targa, 1627) (USTC 6019927).

Nicéron, Jean Pierre, *Mémoires pour servir à l'histoire des hommes illustres dans la république des lettres. Avec un catalogue raisonné de leurs ouvrages* (Paris: chez Briasson, 1729–1745).

Orlers, Jan Jansz, *Beschrijvinge der stad Leyden. Inhoudende 't begin, den voortgang* [...] *der selver* [...]; *Mitsgaders Verhael van alle de belegeringen* [...]; *insonderheyt historiale beschrijvinge van de laetste strenge belegeringe* [...] *anno 1574; verciert met verscheyden caerten ende figuren* [...] (Tot Leyden: voor Andries Jansz. Cloeting tot Delf ende Abraham Commelijn tot Leyden, 1641) (USTC 1027872).

Revius, Jacobus. de, *Epistres Françoises des Personnages Illustres & Doctes a Monsr. Ioseph Iuste de la Scala* (Harderwijk: Wed. Thomas Hendricksz, Amsterdam, for Hendrick Laurensz, 1624) (USTC 1010292).

Scaliger, Josephus Justus, *Epistolæ omnes quæ reperiri potuerunt, nunc primum collectæ ac editæ: Cæteris præfixa est ea, quæ est de gente Scaligera; in qua de autoris vita; et sub finem Danielis Heinsii De morte eius altera* (Lugduni Batavorum: ex officina Bonaventuræ & Abrahami Elzevir, 1627) (USTC 1028641).

Scaliger, Josephus Justus, *Epistola de vetustate et splendore gentis Scaligeræ, et Iul. Cæs. Scaligeri vita. Iul. Cæs. Scaligeri Oratio in luctu filioli Audecti. Item Testimonia de gente Scaligera & Iul. Cæs. Scaligero* (Lugduni Batavorum: Ex officina Plantiniana, apud Franciscum Raphelengium, 1594) (USTC 423322).

Scaliger, Josephus Justus, *Opuscula varia antehac non edita* (Parisiis: Apud Hadrianum Beys, 1610) (USTC 6017215).

Scaliger, Josephus Justus, *Epistolae omnes, quae reperiri potuerunt, nunc primum collectae ac editae; caeteris praefixa est ea, quae est De Gente Scaligera; in qua de autoris vita; et sub finem Danielis Heinsii De morte eius altera* (Francofurti: Johann Aubry (I, heirs of) [et] David Aubry [et] Clemens Schleich, 1628) (USTC 2136688).

Senguerdus, Wolferd (et al.), *Catalogus Librorum tam impressorum quam manuscriptorum Bibliothecae Publicae Universitatis Lugduno-Batavae* (Lugduno apud Batavos: sumptibus Petri van der Aa, 1716).

Spanheim, Friedrich, *Catalogus Bibliothecae publicae Lugduno-Batavae noviter recognitus Accessit Incomparabilis thesaurus librorum orientalium, præcipue mss* (Lugdunum Batavorum: Vid. et her. Johannis Elsevirii, 1674) (USTC 1811363).

Secondary Sources

Amram, David Werner, *The Makers of Hebrew Books in Italy. Being Chapters in the History of the Hebrew Printing Press* (London: The Holland Press limited, 1963).

Andriessen, R. & H.F. Cohen, 'Op zoek naar een stapelmarkt. Onderzoekingen in het archief Daniël van der Meulen' in J.H. Kernkamp (ed.), *De handel van Daniël van der Meulen c.s., in het bijzonder rond de jaren 1588–1592* (Leiden: s.n., 1969).

Angillis, Angz., A., 'Daniël Heins. Hoogleeraar en dichter', *Dietsche Warande* 6 (1864), pp. 421–450.

Armstrong, Elizabeth., *Robert Estienne Royal Printer. A Historical Study of the Elder Stephanus* (Cambridge: Cambridge University Press, 1954).

Arbel, Benjamin, *Trading Nations. Jews and Venetians in the Early Modern Eastern Mediterranean* (Leiden, New York, Köln: Brill, 1995).

Baar, Antonius Henricus van den, *A Russian Church Slavonic Kanonnik (1331–1332). A comparative textual and structural study including an analysis of the Russian computus (Scaliger 38B, Leyden University Library)* (Den Haag: Mouton, 1968).

Babelon, Jean-Pierre, *Nouvelle histoire de Paris. Paris au XVIe siècle* (Paris: Diffusion Hachette, 1986).

BIBLIOGRAPHY

Balagna, Josée, *L'imprimerie arabe en Occident* (*XVIe, XVIIe et XVIIIe siècles*) (Paris: Editions Maisonneuve & Larose, 1984).

Balagna, Josée, 'La langue arabe dans la France du XVIe siècle. Quelques signes avant-coureurs d'un intérêt', *Revue de la Bibliothèque Nationale* 20 (1986), pp. 43–58.

Balagna, Josée, *Arabe et humanisme dans la France des derniers Valois* (Paris: Editions Maisonneuve & Larose, 1989).

Balsamo, Luigi, *Bibliography. History of a Tradition* (Berkeley California: Bernard M. Rosenthal, Inc., 1990).

Balsem, Astrid, *Een biografie van de Bibliotheca Vossiana* (Amsterdam: s.n., 2020).

Barbieri, Edoardo, 'La tipografia araba a Venezia nel XVI secolo: una testimonianza d'archivio dimenticata', *Quaderni di Studi Arabi* 9 (1991), pp. 127–131.

Becker-Cantarino, Baerbel, *Daniel Heinsius* (Boston: Twayne Publishers, 1978).

Bekkum, W. van., 'Hebraica en Rabbinica aan de universiteit van Franeker. Op basis van de publicatie der Franeker bibliotheekcatalogi 1626–1656 en 1691–1694', in J.M.M. Hermans (et al., eds.), *De Franeker universiteitsbibliotheek in de zeventiende eeuw. Beleid en belang van een academiebibliotheek* (Hilversum: Verloren, 2007), pp. 17–28.

Bennet, Jim & Scott. Mandelbrote, *The Garden, the Ark, the Tower, the Temple. Biblical Metaphors of Knowledge in Early Modern Europe* (Oxford: Museum of the History of Science, 1998).

Berkvens-Stevelinck, Christiane. *Magna Commoditas. Geschiedenis van de Leidse universiteitsbibliotheek 1575–2000* (Leiden: Primavera Pers, 2001).

Berkvens-Stevelinck, Christiane, *Magna Commoditas. Leiden University's Great Asset. 425 Years Library Collections and Services* (Leiden: Leiden University Press, 2012).

Berlin, Charles (ed.), *Hebrew Printing and Bibliography. Studies by Joshua Bloch and others* [...] (New York: New York Public Library and Ktav Publishing House, 1976).

Bernays, Jacob, *Joseph Justus Scaliger* (New York: Burt Franklin, [ca. 1964]).

Bethencourt, Francisco & Florike. Egmond (eds.), *Correspondence and Cultural Exchange in Europe, 1400–1700* (Cambridge: Cambridge University Press, 2007).

Bertius, Petrus, *Nomenclator. The First printed catalogue of Leiden University Library (1595). A Facsimile Edition with an Introduction by R. Breugelmans and an Author's Index compiled by Jan Just Witkam* (Leiden: Leiden University Library, 1995).

Billanovich, Myriam, 'Benedetto Bordon e Giulio Cesare Scaligero', *Italia Medioevale e Umanistica* 11 (1968), pp. 187–256.

Birrell, Thomas Anthony, 'The Reconstruction of the Library of Isaac Casaubon' in Anton R.A. Croiset van Uchelen (ed.), Hellinga Festschrift/feestbundel/mélanges: Forty-three studies in bibliography presented to Prof. Dr. Wytze Hellinga on the occasion of his retirement from the chair of neophilology in the University of Amsterdam at the end of the year 1978 (Amsterdam: Nico Israel, 1980), pp. 59–68.

Blair, Ann M., *Too Much to Know. Managing Scholarly Information before the Modern Age* (New Haven, London: Yale University Press, 2010).

Blake, Warren E., 'Joseph Justus Scaliger', *The Classical Journal* 36/2 (1940), pp. 83–91.

Bloch, Joshua, 'Venetian Printers of Hebrew Books', *Bulletin of the New York Public Library* 36 (1932), pp. 71–92.

Bobzin, Hartmut, *Der Koran im Zeitalter der Reformation. Studien zur Frühgeschichte der Arabistik und Islamkunde in Europa* (Würzburg: Ergon Verlag 1995).

Boer, Willem den, *Scaliger en Perizonius. Hun betekenis voor de wetenschap* (Den Haag: Bert Bakker, 1964).

Boer, Willem den, 'Joseph Scaliger en de Joden' in S. Groenveld (et al., eds.), *Bestuurders en geleerden. Opstellen voor J. J. Woltjer* (Amsterdam, Dieren: De Bataafsche leeuw, 1985), pp. 65–74.

Bosch, Leonardus Johannes Marinus, *Petrus Bertius 1565–1629* (Meppel: Krips Repro, 1979).

Botley, Paul & Dirk van Miert (eds.), *The Correspondence of Joseph Justus Scaliger* (Genève: Droz, 2012).

Botley, Paul, *Richard 'Dutch' Thomson, c. 1569–1613. The Life and Letters of a Renaissance Scholar* (Leiden, Boston: Brill, 2016).

Bots, Hans, *Correspondance de Jacques Dupuy et de Nicolas Heinsius (1646–1656)* (Den Haag: Martinus Nijhoff, 1971).

Bots, Hans, *Republiek der Letteren. Ideaal en werkelijkheid* (Amsterdam: APA-Holland Universiteit Pers, 1977).

Bots, Hans, *De Republiek der Letteren. De Europese intellectuele wereld 1500–1760* (Nijmegen: Vantilt, 2018).

Bots, Hans & Françoise Waquet, *Commercium litterarium, 1600–1750. Forms of communication in the Republic of Letters* (Amsterdam, Maarssen: APA-Holland Universiteit Pers, 1994).

Bots, Hans & Françoise Waquet, *La République des Lettres* (Paris: Belin, 1997).

Bourrousse de Laffore, Jules de, 'Jules-César de Lescale', *Recueil de la Société d'agriculture, sciences et arts d'Agen* 2/1 (1860), pp. 160–276.

Bouwsma, William J., *Concordia mundi. The Career and Thought of Guillaume Postel (1510–1581)* (Cambridge, Mass.: Harvard University Press, 1957).

Braches, Ernst, 'Raphelengius's Naschi and Maghribi. Some Reflections on the Origin of Arabic Typography in the Low Countries' in *Quaestiones Leidenses* (Leiden: University Library Leiden, 1975).

Breugelmans, Ronald, 'Twee veilingen van boeken uit het bezit der Raphelengii' in F. De Nave (ed.), *Liber amicorum Leon Voet* (Antwerpen: Vereeniging der Antwerpsche Bibliophielen door het Gemeentekrediet van België, 1985), pp. 39–47 = *De Gulden Passer* 61–63 (1983–1985).

BIBLIOGRAPHY
331

Briels, Jan G.C.A., *Zuidnederlandse boekdrukkers en boekverkopers in de Republiek der Verenigde Nederlanden omstreeks 1570–1630. Een bijdrage tot de kennis van de geschiedenis van het boek* (Nieuwkoop: De Graaf, 1974).

Bronkhorst, Everard van, *Diarium Everardi Bronckhorstii sive adversaria omnium quae gesta sunt in Academia Leidensi (1591–1627) uitgegeven door J.C. van Slee* ('s-Gravenhage: Martinus Nijhoff, 1898).

Brown, Horatio Robert Forbes, *The Venetian Printing Press 1469–1800* (London: J.C. Nimmo, 1891).

Bruehl, Clemens M., 'Josef Justus Scaliger. Ein Beitrag zur geistesgeschichtlichen Bedeutung der Altertumswissenschaft', *Zeitschrift für Religions- und Geistesgeschichte* 12 (1960), pp. 201–218 & 13 (1961), pp. 45–65.

Brugman, Jan, 'Arabic Scholarship' in Th.H. Lunsingh Scheurleer (et al., eds.), *Leiden University in the Seventeenth Century. An Exchange of Learning* (Leiden: Universitaire Pers, E.J. Brill, 1975), pp. 203–215.

Brugman, Jan & Frank Schröder, *Arabic Studies in the Netherlands* (Leiden: E.J. Brill, 1979).

Brulez, Wilfrid, *Marchands Flamands à Venise I (1568–1605)* (Rome: Institut historique belge de Rome, 1965).

Bulut, Mehmet, *Ottoman-Dutch Economic Relations in the Early Modern Period 1571–1699* (Hilversum: Verloren, 2001).

Burger, C.P., 'De boekverkoopers Commelin te Genève, Heidelberg, Amsterdam en Leiden', *Tijdschrift voor boek- en bibliotheekwezen*, 9 (1911), pp. 145–176.

Burke, Peter, *The Renaissance Sense of the Past* (London: Arnold, 1970).

Burman, Thomas E., *Reading the Qur'ân in Latin Christendom, 1140–1560* (Philadelphia: University of Pennsylvania Press, 2007).

Burmeister, Karl-Heinz, *Sebastian Münster. Eine Bibliographie mit 22 Abbildungen* (Wiesbaden: Pressler, 1964).

Burnett, Stephen G., *From Christian Hebraism to Jewish Studies. Johannes Buxtorf (1564–1629) and Hebrew Learning in the Seventeenth Century* (Leiden, New York, Köln: Brill, 1996).

Burnett, S.G., 'Christian Aramaism. The Birth and Growth of Aramaic Scholarship in the Sixteenth Century' in R.L. Troxel (et al., eds.), *Seeking out the Wisdom of the Ancients. Essays offered to honor Michael V. Fox on the Occasion of his Sixty-Fifth Birthday* (Winona Lake: Penn State University Press, 2005), pp. 421–436.

Burnett, Stephen G., *Christian Hebraism in the Reformation Era (1500–1660). Authors, Books, and the Transmission of Jewish Learning* (Leiden, Boston: Brill, 2012).

Busi, Giulio, *Edizioni Ebraiche del XVI secolo nelle Biblioteche dell'Emilia Romagna* (Bologna: Edizione Analisi, 1987).

Busi, Giulio, *Libri ebraici a Mantova. Vol. 1: Le edizioni del XVI secolo nella biblioteca della Comunità ebraica* (Fiesole: Cadmo, 1996).

Carboni, Stefano, *Venice and the Islamic World 828–1797* (New York: New Haven, London, 2007).

Chartier, Roger, *L'Ordre des livres. Lecteurs, auteurs, bibliothèques en Europe entre XIVe et XVIIIe siècle* (Aix-en-Provence: Alinéa, 1992).

Christ, Karl, *Die Bibliothek Reuchlins in Pforzheim* (Leipzig: O. Harrassowitz, 1924).

Clair, Colin. *Christopher Plantin* (London: Cassell & Company LTD, 1960).

Clark, John Willis, *The Care of Books. An Essay on the Development of Libraries and their Fittings, from the Earliest Times to the End of the Eighteenth Century* (Cambridge: Cambridge University Press, 1902) (Repr. 2009).

Clotz, Henrike L., *Eine Hochschule in Holland. Die Universität Leiden im Spannungsfeld von Provinz, Stadt und Kirche, 1575–1619* (Stuttgart: Franz Steiner, 1998).

Cohen, Gustave, *Écrivains français en Hollande dans la première moitié du XVIIe siècle* (Paris: Librairie Ancienne Edouard Champion, 1920).

Cools, Hans, Marika Keblusek & Badeloch Noldus, *Your Humble Servant. Agents in Early Modern Europe* (Hilversum: Verloren, 2006).

Colliard, Laura-Aimé, *Un dottore dell'Ateneo patavino alla Corte di Francia. Pierre d'Elbène (1550–1590)* (Verona: Libreria Editrice Universitaria, 1972).

Conihout, Isabelle de, 'Jean et André Hurault. Deux frères ambassadeurs à Venise et acquéreurs de livres du Cardinal Grimani', *Italique. Poésie italienne de la Renaissance* 10 (2007), pp. 105–148.

Copinger, Walter Arthur, *The Bible and its Transmission. Being an Historical and Bibliographical View of the Hebrew and Greek texts, and the Greek, Latin and other Versions of the Bible* [...] (Leipzig: Zentralantiqauriat, 1972).

Coron, A., "Ut prosint aliis'. Jacques Auguste de Thou et sa bibliothèque' in C. Jolly (ed.), *Histoire des bibliothèques françaises: Les Bibliothèques sous l'Ancien Régime 1530–1789* (Paris: Promodis – Éditons du Cercle de la Librairie, 1988), pp. 101–125.

Coudert, Allison P. (et al., eds.), *Judaeo-Christian Intellectual Culture in the Seventeenth Century. A Celebration of the Library of Narcissus Marsh (1638–1713)* (Dordrecht, Boston: Kluwer Academic Publishers, 1999).

Coudert, Allison P. & Jeffrey S. Shoulson (eds.), *Hebraica Veritas? Christian Hebraists and the Study of Judaism in Early Modern Europe* (Philadelphia: University of Pennsylvania Press, 2004).

Cowley, Arthur Ernest, *A concise Catalogue of the Hebrew printed Books in the Bodleian library* (Oxford: Clarendon Press, 1929).

Crown, Alan David, 'Manuscripts, cast type and Samaritan paleography', *Bulletin of the John Rylands Library* 72/1 1990, pp. 87–130.

Crown, Alan David, *Samaritan Scribes and Manuscripts* (Tübingen: Mohr Siebeck, 2001).

Cubelier de Beynac, Jean & Michel Magnien (eds.), *Acta Scaligeriana. Actes du Colloque International organisé pour le cinquième centenaire de la naissance de Jules-César Scaliger (Agen, 14–16 septembre 1984)* (Agen: Société académique d'Agen, 1986).

BIBLIOGRAPHY

Dankbaar, Willem Frederik, 'De Stichting van de Leidsche universiteit en de eerste decennia van haar bestaan' in *Hoogtepunten uit het Nederlandsche Calvinisme in de zestiende eeuw* (Haarlem: H.D. Tjeenk Willink & Zoon N.V., 1946), pp. 126–161.

Dannenfeldt, Karl H., 'The Renaissance Humanists and knowledge of Arabic', *Studies in the Renaissance* II (1955), pp. 96–117.

Davis, Natalie Zemon, 'Beyond the Market. Book as Gifts in Sixteenth-Century France', *Transactions of the Royal Historical Society*, 5th series, 33 (1983), pp. 69–88.

Davis, Natalie Zemon, *The Gift in Sixteenth-Century France* (Oxford: Oxford University Press, 2000.

De Landtsheer, J., 'Justus Lipsius en Josephus Justus Scaliger', in P.G. Hoftijzer (ed.), *Adelaar in de wolken. De Leidse jaren van Josephus Justus Scaliger 1593–1609* (Leiden: Scaliger Instituut, Universiteitsbibliotheek Leiden, 2005), pp. 59–92.

De Landtsheer, Jeanine (et al.), *Lieveling van de Latijnse taal. Justus Lipsius te Leiden herdacht bij zijn vierhonderdste sterfdag* (Leiden: Universiteitsbibliotheek Leiden – Scaliger Instituut, 2006).

De Nave, Francine (ed.), *Philologia Arabica. Arabische studiën en drukken in de Nederlanden in de 16de en 17de eeuw* (Antwerpen: Museum Plantin-Moretus, 1986).

De Nave, F., 'Josephus Justus Scaliger (1540–1609)' in F. De Nave (ed.), *Philologia Arabica. Arabische studiën en drukken in de Nederlanden in de 16de en 17de eeuw* (Antwerpen: Museum Plantin-Moretus, 1986), pp. 116–122.

De Nave, F., 'Franciscus I Raphelengius (1539–1597), grondlegger van de Arabische studiën in de Nederlanden' in M. De Schepper & F. De Nave (eds.), *Ex Officina Plantiniana. Studia in memoriam Christophori Plantini (ca. 1520–1589)* (Antwerpen: Vereeniging der Antwerpsche Bibliophielen, 1989), pp. 523–555.

De Smet, Ingrid A.R., *Thuanus. The Making of Jacques-Auguste de Thou (1553–1617)* (Genève: Droz, 2006).

De Smet, I.A.R., 'Des livres de Thou (et Pinelli). Collectioneurs, livres clandestins et sillons confessionels' in R.G. Camos & A. Vanautgaerden (eds.), *Les labyrinthes de l'esprit. Collections et bibliothèques à la Renaissance/Renaissance Libraries and Collections* (Genève: Droz, 2015), pp. 229–254.

De Smet, I.A.R. 'Paul Choart de Buzanval. A Learned French Ambassador and the Republic of Letters', *Erudition and the Republic of Letters*, 8/2 (2023), pp. 109–146.

Deblaise, Philippe, *Charles Périer, libraire parisien au seizième siècle. Notes biographiques et bibliographie* (Genève: Slatkine, 2010).

Dibon, Paul, *Le voyage en France des étudiants néerlandais au XVIIème siècle* (Den Haag: Martinus Nijhoff, 1963).

Dibon, Paul, 'L'Université de Leyde et la République des lettres au XVIIe siècle', *Quaerendo* V (1975), pp. 5–38.

Dibon, Paul, 'Communication in the Respublica literaria of the 17th century' in *Res Publica literarum. Studies in the Classical Tradition* I (1978), pp. 43–55.

Diefendorf, Barbara B., *Beneath the Cross. Catholics and Huguenots in Sixteenth-Century Paris* (Oxford: Oxford University Press, 1991).

Dijkstra, Jitse, 'Mysteries of the Nile? Joseph Scaliger and Ancient Egypt/Les mystères du Nil? Joseph Scaliger et l'Égypte ancienne', *Aries* 9/1 (2009), pp. 59–82.

Delatour, Jérôme, *Une bibliothèque humaniste au temps des guerres de religion. Les livres de Claude Dupuy. D'après l'inventaire dressé par le libraire Denis Duval (1595)* (Paris: Librairie H. Chapion, 1998).

Dorsten, Jan Adrianus van, *Poets, Patrons, and Professors. An outline of some literary Connexions between England and the University of Leiden 1575–1586* (Leiden: Universitaire Pers Leiden, 1962).

Dorsten, Jan Adrianus van (et al., eds.), *Leidse universiteit 400. Stichting en eerste bloei 1575–ca. 1650* (Amsterdam: Rijksmuseum Amsterdam, 1975).

Dorsten, Jan Adrianus van, 'Thomas Basson (1555–1613), English Printer at Leiden', *Quaerendo* 15 (1985), pp. 195–224.

Doucet, Rogier, *Les bibliothèques parisiennes au XVIe siècle* (Paris: A. et J. Picard, 1956).

Drewes, Gerardus Willebrordus Johannes (et al.), *Levinus Warner and his legacy. Three centuries Legatum Warnerianum in the Leiden University Library. Catalogue of the commemorative Exhibition held in the Bibliotheca Thysiana from April 27th till May 15th 1970* (Leiden: E.J. Brill, 1970).

Droixhe, D., 'La crise de l'hebreu langue-mère au XVIIe siècle' in C. Grell (et al., eds.), *La République des Lettres et l'histoire du judaisme antique*, XVIe–XVIIIe siècles (Paris: Presses de l'Université de Paris-Sorbonne, 1992), pp. 65–99.

Dunkelgrün, Theodor, 'The Hebrew Library of a Renaissance Humanist. Andreas Masius and the Bibliography to his *Iosuae Imperatoris Historia* (1574), with a Latin Edition and an Annotated English Translation', *Studia Rosenthaliana* 42–43 (2010–2011), pp. 197–252.

Dunkelgrün, Theodor, *The multiplicity of Scripture. The confluence of textual traditions in the making of the Antwerp Polyglot Bible (1568–1573)* (Chicago: s.n., 2012).

Dunkelgrün, Th., 'The Humanist Discovery of Hebrew Epistolography' in S. Mandelbrote & J. Weinberg (eds.), *Jewish Books and their Readers. Aspects of the Intellectual Life of Christians and Jews in Early Modern Europe* (Leiden, Boston: Brill, 2016), pp. 211–259.

Dunkelgrün, Th., 'The Christian Study of Judaism in Early Modern Europe', in J. Karp & A. Sutcliffe (eds.), *The Cambridge History of Judaism*. Vol. VII: *The Early Modern World, 1500–1815* (Cambridge: Cambridge University Press, 2017), pp. 316–348.

Eekhof, Albert, *De theologische faculteit te Leiden in de 17de eeuw* (Utrecht: G.J.A. Ruys, 1921).

Eisenstein, Elisabeth L., *The Printing Press as an Agent of Change* (Cambridge: Cambridge University Press, 1979).

Ekkart, Rudi Erik Otto, *Icones Leidenses. De portretverzameling van de Rijksuniversiteit te Leiden* (Leiden: Universitaire Pers, 1973).

BIBLIOGRAPHY

Ekkart, Rudi Erik Otto, 'Portraits in Leiden University library', *Quaerendo* 5 (1975), pp. 52–65.

Ekkart, Rudi Erik Otto, *De Leidse Universiteit in 1610* (Leiden: s.n. 1975).

Ekkart, Rudi Erik Otto, 'Het grafmonument van Scaliger', *Jaarboekje voor geschiedenis en oudheidkunde van Leiden en omstreken* 70 (1978), pp. 81–90.

Ekkart, Rudi Erik Otto, 'De Leidse bibliotheek in 1600', *De Boekenwereld* 1/1 (1984–1985), pp. 13–17.

Ellenger, Y., 'Quelques relations de voyage vers l'Italie et vers l'Orient aux XVIᵉ siècle' in J. Céard & J.-C. Margolin (eds.), *Voyager à la Renaissance. Actes du colloque de Tours 1983* (Paris: Maissonneuve & Larose, 1987), pp. 51–63.

Enenkel, Karl A.E., *Die Erfindung des Menschen. Die Autobiographik des frühneuzeitlichen Humanismus von Petrarca bis Lipsius* (Berlin, New York: Walter de Gruyter, 2008).

Esscher, H., 'Konrad Gessner über Aufstellung und Katalogisierung von Bibliotheken' in *Mélanges offerts à Marcel Godet, directeur de la Bibliothèque nationale suisse à Berne à l'occasion de son soixantième anniversaire. VIII mai MCMXXXVII* (Neuchâtel: Imprimerie Paul Attinger s.a., 1937).

Ettinghausen, Richard, 'Near Eastern Book Covers and their Influence on European Bindings. A Report on the Exhibition 'History of Bookbinding' at the Baltimore Museum of Art 1957–58', *Ars Orientalis* 3 (1959), pp. 113–131.

Evans, Robert John Weston, *The Wechel Presses. Humanism and Calvinism in Central Europe 1572–1627* (Oxford: Past and present Society, 1975).

Fechner, J.-U., 'Die Einheit von Bibliotheken und Kunstkammer im 17. und 18. Jahrhundert' in P. Raabe (ed.), *Öffentliche und private Bibliotheken im 17. und 18. Jahrhundert. Raritätenkammern, Forschungsinstrumente oder Bildungsstätten?* [Vorträge gehalten anlässlich des 1. Wolfenbütteler Symposions vom 24.-26. September 1975 in der Herzog August Bibliothek] (Bremen: Jacobi, 1977), pp. 11–31.

Feingold, Mordechai, 'Oriental Studies' in Nicholas Tyacke (ed.), *The History of the University of Oxford. Vol. IV: Seventeenth-Century Oxford* (Oxford: Oxford University Press, 1997), pp. 449–503.

Findlen, Paula, 'The Museum. Its classical Etymology and Renaissance Genealogy', *Journal of the History of Collections* 1 (1989), pp. 59–78.

Flood, J.L., "Omnium totius orbis emporiorum compendium'. The Frankfurt Fair in the Early Modern Period' in R. Myers (et al., eds.), *Fairs, Markets and the Itinerant Book Trade* (Newcastle & London: Oak Knoll Press 2007), pp. 1–42.

Folkers, Th., 'De geschiedenis van de Oostersche boekdrukkerij te Leiden', *Cultureel Indië* 3 (1941), pp. 53–68.

Frank-Van Westrienen, Anna, *De Groote Tour. Tekening van de educatiereis der Nederlanders in de zeventiende eeuw* (Amsterdam: Noord-Hollandsche Uitgeversmaatschappij, 1983).

Frasca-Spada, Marina & Nick Jardine (eds.), *Books and the Sciences in History* (Cambridge: Cambridge University Press, 2000).

Friedman, Jerome, *The Most Ancient Testimony. Sixteenth-Century Christian Hebraica in the Age of Renaissance Nostalgia* (Athens, Ohio: Ohio University Press, 1983).

Fück, Johann W., *Die arabischen Studien in Europa bis in den Anfang des 20. Jahrhunderts* (Leipzig, Otto Harrassowitz, 1955).

Fuks, Leo, 'Het Hebreeuwse brievenboek van Johannes Drusius jr. Hebreeuws en hebraïsten in Nederland rondom 1600', *Studia Rosenthaliana* 3/1 (1969), pp. 1–52.

Fuks, Leo & Rena Fuks, 'The Hebrew Production of the Plantin-Raphelengius Presses in Leyden, 1585–1615', *Studia Rosenthaliana* 4/1 (1970), pp. 1–24.

Fuks, Leo, 'Hebrew Book production and Book Trade in the Northern Netherlands and their German Connections in the 17th Century' in *De arte et libris. Festschrift Erasmus 1934–1984* (Amsterdam: Erasmus Antiquariaat en Boekhandel, 1984), pp. 173–178.

Fuks, L., 'Hebreeuwse studies aan de Franeker Universiteit' in G.Th. Jensma (et al., eds.), *Universiteit te Franeker 1585–1811. Bijdragen tot de geschiedenis van de Friese hogeschool* (Leeuwarden: Fryske Academie: 1985), pp. 409–423.

Fuks, Leo & Rena G. Fuks-Mansfeld, *Hebrew Typography in the Northern Netherlands, 1585–1815. Historical Evaluation and Descriptive Bibliography* (Leiden: E.J. Brill, 1984–1987).

Fuks-Mansfeld, R.G., 'The Hebrew Book Trade in Amsterdam in the Seventeenth Century' in C. Berkvens-Stevelinck, H. Bots, P.G. Hoftijzer & O.S. Lankhorst (eds.), *Le magasin de l'univers. The Dutch Republic as the Centre of the European Book Trade* (Leiden: E.J. Brill, 1992), pp. 155–168.

Gaberson, Eric, 'Libraries, Memory and the Space of Knowledge', *Journal of the History of Collections* 18 (2006), pp. 105–136.

Garber, K., 'Paris, die Hauptstadt des europäischen Späthumanismus. Jacques Auguste de Thou und das Cabinet Dupuy' in S. Neumeister & C. Wiedemann (eds.), *Res Publica Litteraria. Die Institutionen der Gelehrsamkeit in der frühen Neuzeit* (Wiesbaden: Harrassowitz, 1987), pp. 71–92.

Geiger, Ludwig, *Das Studium der hebraïschen Sprache in Deutschland vom Ende des XV. bis zur Mitte des XVI. Jahrhunderts* (Breslau: Schletter, 1879).

Geiger, Ludwig, *Johann Reuchlin. Sein Leben und seine Werke* (Breslau: Schletter, 1870) (1964).

Gelder, R. van, 'De wereld binnen handbereik. Nederlandse kunst- en rariteitenverzamelingen, 1585–1735' in E. Bergvelt & R. Kistemaker (eds.), *De wereld binnen handbereik. Nederlandse kunst- en rariteitenverzamelingen, 1585–1735* (Zwolle: Waanders, 1992), pp. 15–39.

Geurts, P.A.M. & Jan Adrianus van Dorsten, 'Drie redevoeringen van Bonaventura Vulcanius over de stichting van de Leidse Universiteit', *Bijdragen en mededelingen van het Historisch Genootschap* vol. 79 (Groningen: J.B. Wolters, 1965), pp. 387–413.

BIBLIOGRAPHY

Gilmore, Myron Piper, *Humanists and Jurists. Six Studies in the Renaissance* (Cambridge, MA: The Belknap Press of Harvard University Press, 1963).

Gokkes, B., 'Fransch en Hebreeuwsch bij enkele xvi^e eeuwsche Fransche grammatici', *Neophilologus* 23/1 (1938), pp. 1–11.

Goodman, Anthony & Angus Mackay (eds.), *The Impact of Humanism on Western Europe* (London & New York: Routledge, 1990).

Grafton, Anthony T., 'Joseph Scaliger and Historical Chronology. The Rise and Fall of a Discipline', *History and Theory* 14, 1975, pp. 156–185.

Grafton, Anthony T., 'Rhetoric, Philology and Egyptomania in the 1570s. J.J. Scaliger's Invective against M. Guilandinus's Papyrus', *Journal of the Warburg and Courtauld Institutes* 42 (1979), pp. 167–194.

Grafton, Anthony T., *Joseph Scaliger. A Study in the History of Classical Scholarship.* Vol. I: *Textual Criticism and Exegesis* (Oxford: Clarendon Press, 1983).

Grafton, Anthony T., *Joseph Scaliger. A Study in the History of Classical Scholarship.* Vol. II: *Historical Chronology* (Oxford: Clarendon Press, 1993).

Grafton, Anthony T., 'From *De die natali* to *De emendatione temporum.* The Origins and Settings of Scaliger's Chronology', *Journal of the Warburg and Courtauld Institutes* 48 (1985), pp. 100–143.

Grafton, Anthony T. & Lisa Jardine, *From Humanism to the Humanities. Education and the Liberal Arts in Fifteenth- and Sixteenth-Century Europe* (Cambridge, MA: Duckworth, 1986).

Grafton, Anthony T., 'Close Encounters of the Learned Kind. Joseph Scaliger's Table Talk,' *American Scholar* 57 (1988), pp. 581–588.

Grafton, Anthony T., 'Civic Humanism and Scientific Scholarship at Leiden,' in Thomas Bender (ed.), *The University and the City. From Medieval Origins to the Present*, New York, Oxford 1988, pp. 59–78.

Grafton, Anthony T., *Forgers & Critics. Creativity and Duplicity in Western Scholarship* (London: Collins & Brown, 1990).

Grafton, Anthony T., *Defenders of the Text. The Traditions of Scholarship in an Age of Science, 1450–1800* (Cambridge, Mass./London: Harvard University Press, 1991), pp. 104–144.

Grafton, Anthony T., *New Worlds, Ancient Texts. The Power of Tradition and the Shock of Discovery* (Cambridge, Mass./London: Belknap Press, 1992), pp. 217–237.

Grafton, Anthony T. (ed.), *Rome Reborn. The Vatican Library and Renaissance Culture.* Washington (New Haven, London: Yale University Press, 1993).

Grafton, Anthony T., *Commerce with the Classics. Ancient Books and Renaissance Readers* (Ann Arbor: University of Michigan Press, 1997).

Grafton, Anthony T., 'The Humanist as Reader' in G. Cavallo and R. Chartier (eds.), *A History of Reading in the West* (Cambridge, Mass.: University of Massachusetts Press, 1999).

Grafton, Anthony T., 'Joseph Scaliger as a Reader' in E. Havens & L. Patterson (eds.), *Old Books, New Learning. Essays on Medieval and Renaissance Books at Yale* (New Haven: Beinecke Rare Book and Manuscript Library, 2001), pp. 152–177.

Grafton, Anthony T., *Athenae Batavae. The Research Imperative at Leiden, 1575–1650* (Leiden: Primavera Pers, 2003).

Grafton, Anthony T., *What was History? The Art of History in Early Modern Europe* (Cambridge: Cambridge University Press, 2007).

Grafton, Anthony T. & J. Weinberg, 'Isaac Casaubon's library of Hebrew books' in G. Mandelbrote & B. Taylor (eds.) *Libraries within the Library. The Origins of the British Library's Printed Collections* (London: British Library, 2009), pp. 24–42.

Grafton, Anthony T. & Joanna Weinberg, *"I have always loved the Holy Tongue". Isaac Casaubon, the Jews, and a forgotten Chapter in Renaissance Scholarship* (Cambridge, Mass.: Belknap Press of Harvard University Press, 2011).

Grafton, Anthony T., 'Christian Hebraism and the Rediscovery of Hellenic Judaism' in R.I. Cohen (et al., eds.), *Jewish Culture in Early Modern Europe. Essays in Honor of David. B. Ruderman* (Cincinnati: Hebrew Union College Press, 2014), pp. 169–180.

Grafton, Anthony T., 'The Jewish Book in Christian Europe. Material Texts and Religious Encounters' in A. Sterk (et al., eds.), *Faithful Narratives. Historians, Religion, and the Challenge of Objectivity* (Ithaca, London: Cornell University Press, 2014), pp. 96–114.

Grendler, Marcella, 'A Greek Collection in Padua. The Library of Gian Vincenzo Pinelli (1535–1601)', *Renaissance Quarterly* 33/3 (1980), pp. 386–416.

Grendler, Marcella, 'Book Collecting in Counter-Reformation Italy. The Library of Gian Vincenzo Pinelli (1535–1601)', *Journal of Library History*, 16 (1981), pp. 144–151.

Grendler, Paul F., *The Roman Inquisition and the Venetian Press, 1540–1605* (Princeton: Princeton legacy Library, 1977).

Grootens, Petrus Leonardus Marie, *Dominicus Baudius. Een levensschets uit het Leidse humanistenmilieu 1561–1613* (Nijmegen, Utrecht: Dekker & Van der Vegt N.V., 1942).

Gruys, Johannes A. and H.W. de Kooker (eds.), *Book Sales Catalogues of the Dutch Republic, 1599–1800* (Leiden: IDC, 1997).

Gubernatis, Angelo de, *Matériaux pour servir à l'histoire des études orientales en Italie* (Paris: Ernest Leroux, 1876).

Gulik, Egbertus van & Hendrik D.L. Vervliet, *Een Gedenksteen voor Plantijn en Van Raphelingen te Leiden. Waarin opgenomen de* Catalogus Librorum residuorum Tabernæ Raphelengianæ (Leiden: E.J. Brill, 1965).

Gulik, Egbertus van, 'Drukkers en geleerden. De Leidse Officina Plantiniana (1583–1619)' in *Leiden University in the Seventeenth Century. An Exchange of Learning* (Leiden: Universitaire Pers, E.J. Brill, 1975), pp. 367–393.

Haak, Sikko Popta, *Paullus Merula 1558–1607* (Zutphen: W.J. Thieme, 1901).

Habermann, Abraham M., *The Printer Daniel Bomberg and the List of Books published by his Press* (Safed: Museum of Printing Art, 1978).

BIBLIOGRAPHY

Habermann, Abraham M., *The printer Cornelio Adel Kind, his son Daniel and the List of Books printed by them* (Jerusalem: Re'uven Mas, 1980).

Habermann, Abraham M., *Giovanni Di Gara. Printer, Venice 1564–1610. List of Books Printed in His Press. Completed and edited by Yitzhak Yudlov* (Jerusalem: Re'uven Mas, 1982).

Hall, Vernon, 'Life of Julius Caesar Scaliger (1484–1558)', *Transactions of the American Philosophical Society*, New Series 40/2 (1950), pp. 85–170.

Hall, Vernon, 'The Scaliger Family Papers', *Proceedings of the American Philosophical Society* 82/2 (1948), pp. 120–123.

Hamilton, Alastair, *William Bedwell the Arabist 1563–1632* (Leiden: E.J. Brill, Leiden University Press, 1985).

Hamilton, A., 'The Victims of Progress. The Raphelengius Arabic type and Bedwell's Arabic Lexicon' in F. De Nave (ed.), *Liber Amicorum Léon Voet* (Antwerpen: Vereeniging der Antwerpsche bibliophielen, 1985), pp. 97–107.

Hamilton, A., 'Arabic Studies in the Netherlands in the Sixteenth and Seventeenth Centuries' in F. De Nave (ed.), *Philologia Arabica. Arabische studiën en drukken in de Nederlanden in de 16de en 17de eeuw* (Antwerpen: Museum Plantin-Moretus, 1986), pp. xciv–cxii.

Hamilton, A., 'Nam tirones sumus'. Franciscus Raphelengius' *Lexicon Arabico-Latinum* (*Leiden 1613*) in M. De Schepper & F. De Nave (eds.), *Ex officina Plantiniana. Studia in memoriam Christophori Plantini (ca. 1520–1589). De Gulden Passer* 66–67 (1988–1989), pp. 557–591.

Hamilton, Alastair, 'Franciscus Raphelengius. The Hebraist and his Manuscripts', *De Gulden Passer* 68 (1990), pp. 105–117.

Hamilton, A., 'Eastern Churches and Western Scholarship' in A. Grafton (ed.), *Rome Reborn. The Vatican Library and Renaissance Culture* (Washington, New Haven, London: Yale University Press, 1993), pp. 225–250.

Hamilton, Alastair, 'An Egyptian Traveller in the Republic of Letters. Josephus Barbatus or Abudacnus the Copt', *Journal of the Warburg and Courtauld Institutes* 57 (1994), pp. 123–150.

Hamilton, Alastair, *Arab Culture and Ottoman Magnificence in Antwerp's Golden Age* (London: Arcadian Library, 2001).

Hamilton, Alastair & Francis Richard, *André du Ryer and Oriental Studies in Seventeenth-Century France* (Oxford: Arcadian Library, 2004).

Hamilton, Alastair, Maurits H. van den Boogert, Bart Westerweel (eds.), *The Republic of Letters and the Levant* (Leiden, Boston: Brill, 2005).

Hamilton, Alastair, 'Guillaume Postel (1510–1581)' in *Catalogue 1343 Bernard Quaritch* (London: Bernard Quaritch, 2006).

Hamilton, Alastair, 'The Perils of Catalogues', *Journal of Islamic Manuscripts* 1 (2010), pp. 31–36.

Hamilton, Alastair & Arnoud Vrolijk, 'Hadrianus Guilielmi Flessingensis. The brief Career of the Arabist Adriaen Willemsz', *Oriens* 39 (2011), pp. 1–15.

Hanebutt-Benz, Eeva, Dagmar Glass, Geoffrey Roper (eds.), *Middle Eastern Languages and the Print Revolution. A Cross-cultural Encounter. A Catalogue and Companion to the Exhibition* (Westhofen: Gutenberg Museum, 2002).

Hantzsch, Viktor, *Sebastian Münster, Leben, Werk, wissenschaftlicher Bedeutung* (Nieuwkoop: De Graaf Publishers, 1965).

Hardenberg, H., *Het Archief van curatoren der Leidsche universiteit, Band 1: 1574–1815* (Zaltbommel: Garde en Co's Drukkerij, 1934).

Harrisse, Henry, *Le président de Thou et ses descendants, leur célébre bibliothèque* [...] (Paris: Librairie H. Leclere, 1905).

Hartig, Otto, *Die Gründung der Hofbibliothek durch Albrecht V und Johann Jakob Fugger* (München: De Gruyter, 1917).

Haugen, Kristine Louise, 'Joseph Scaliger's Letters. Collaborator, Teacher, Impresario', *History of Universities* 28/1 (2014) pp. 105–147.

Hawkins, R.L., 'The Friendship of Joseph Scaliger and François Vertunien', *The Romanic Review* 8/2 (1917), pp. 117–144 & 307–327.

Heesakkers, C., 'Schatkamers van geleerdheid. Verzamelingen van humanistische geleerden' in E. Bergvelt & R. Kistemaker (eds.), *De wereld binnen handbereik. Nederlandse kunst- en rariteitenverzamelingen, 1585–1735* (Zwolle: Waanders, 1992), pp. 92–102.

Heide, Albert van der, *Hebrew Manuscripts of Leiden University Library* (Leiden: Universitaire Pers Leiden, 1977).

Heide, Albert van der, *Hebraica veritas. Christopher Plantin and the Christian Hebraïsts. Catalogue to the Exhibition Hebraica veritas. Did God speak Hebrew?* (Antwerpen: Plantin-Moretus Museum, 2008).

Heller, Henry, *Labour, Science and Technology in France, 1500–1620* (Cambridge: Cambridge University Press, 1996).

Heller, Marvin J., *Printing the Talmud. A History of the Earliest Printed Editions of the Talmud* (New York: Im Hasefer, 1992).

Heller, Marvin J., *The Sixteenth Century Hebrew Book. An Abridged Thesaurus* (Leiden, Boston: Brill, 2004).

Heller, Marvin J., *Studies in the Making of the Early Hebrew Book* (Leiden, Boston: Brill, 2008).

Hendrickson, Thomas, *Ancient Libraries and Renaissance Humanism. The* De Bibliothecis *of Justus Lipsius* (Leiden, Boston: Brill, 2017).

Hermans, Jos M.M. (et al., eds.), *De Franeker universiteitsbibliotheek in de zeventiende eeuw. Beleid en belang van een academiebibliotheek* (Hilversum: Verloren, 2007).

Hofman Peerlkamp, Petrus, *Opuscula Oratoria et Poetica* (Leiden: E.J. Brill, 1870).

BIBLIOGRAPHY

Hoftijzer, Paul G. (eds.), *Adelaar in de wolken. De Leidse jaren van Josephus Justus Scaliger 1593–1609* (Leiden: Scaliger Instituut, Universiteitsbibliotheek Leiden, 2005).

Horst, Dirk Johannes Hendrik ter, *Daniel Heinsius (1580–1655)* (Utrecht: Drukkerij Hoeijenbos en Co., 1934).

Hulvey, M., 'Les bibliothèques retrouvées de Sante Pagnini, dominicain de Lucques et de Pierre Bullioud, "gentil-homme" lyonnais en hébreu et en grec [...]', *Bulletin du bibliophile* 1 (2009), pp. 79–106.

Hulshoff Pol, Elfriede, 'The library' Th.H. Lunsingh Scheurleer & G.H.M. Posthumus Meijers (eds.), *Leiden University in the Seventeenth century. An Exchange of Learning* (Leiden: Universitaire Pers/E.J. Brill, 1975), pp. 359–459.

Hulshoff Pol, Elfriede, 'What about the library? Travellers' Comments on the Leiden University Library in the 17th and 18th Centuries' in *Quaestiones Leidenses. Twelve Studies on Leiden University Library and its Holdings published on the Occasion of the Quarter-Centenary of the University* (Leiden: University Library, 1975), pp. 166–178.

Huppert, George, *The Idea of Perfect History. Historical Erudition and Historical Philosophy in Renaissance France* (Urbana, Chicago, London: University of Illinois Press 1970).

Impey, Oliver, & Arthur MacGregor (eds.), *The Origins of Museums. The Cabinet of Curiosities in Sixteenth- and Seventeenth-Century Europe* (Oxford: Clarendon Press, 1985).

Israel, Jonathan I., *Dutch Primacy in World trade, 1585–1740* (Oxford: Clarendon Press, 1991).

Israel, Jonathan I., *The Dutch Republic. Its Rise, Greatness, and Fall 1477–1806* (Oxford: Clarendon Press, 1998).

Irwin, Robert, *For Lust of Knowing. The Orientalists and their Enemies* (London: Penguin, 2006).

Jacob, C., 'Préface' in M. Baratin & C. Jacob (eds.), *Le pouvoir des bibliothèques. La mémoire des livres en Occident* (Paris: Albin Michel, 1996), pp. 11–19.

Jardine, Lisa, *Worldly goods. A New History of the Renaissance* (London: W.W. Norton & Company 1996).

Jarry, Louis, *Une correspondance littéraire au XVIe siècle. Pierre Daniel Avocat au Parlement de Paris et les érudits de son temps* (Orléans: H. Herlusion, 1876).

Jehasse, Jean, *La Renaissance de la critique. L'essor de l'humanisme érudit de 1560 à 1614* (Saint-Etienne: Université de Saint-Etienne, 1976).

Jongbloet-Van Houtte, Gisela, *Brieven en andere bescheiden betreffende Daniël van der Meulen 1584–1600*. Deel 1: augustus 1585-september 1585 ('s-Gravenhage: Martinus Nijhoff, 1986).

Jones, Leonard Chester, *Simon Goulart 1543–1628. Étude biographique et bibliografique* (Genève, Paris: Eduard Champion 1917).

Jones, Robert, *Learning Arabic in Renaissance Europe (1505–1624)* (Leiden, Boston: Brill 2020).

Jones, Robert, 'Thomas Erpenius (1584–1624) on the Value of the Arabic Language', *Manuscripts of the Middle East. A Journal devoted to the Study of Handwritten Material of the Middle East* 1 (1986), pp. 15–25.

Jones, R., 'The Medici Oriental Press (Rome 1584–1614) and the Impact of its Arabic Publications on Northern Europe' in G.A. Russell (ed.), *The 'Arabick' Interest of the Natural Philosophers in Seventeenth-Century England* (Leiden, New York, Köln: Brill, 1994), pp. 88–108.

Jonge, Henk Jan de, 'The Latin Testament of Joseph Scaliger, 1607', *Lias. Sources and Documents Relating to the Early Modern History of Ideas* 2 (1975), pp. 249–263.

Jonge, Henk Jan de, 'Josephus Justus Scaliger' in *Leidse universiteit 400. Stichting en eerste bloei*, Tentoonstellingscatalogus Rijksmuseum Amsterdam (Amsterdam: Rijksmuseum, 1975), pp. 67–72.

Jonge, Henk Jan de, 'Joseph Scaliger's Greek-Arabic Lectionary (Leiden, U.L., MS. Or. 243 = Lectionary 6 of the Greek New Testament)', *Quaerendo* 5 (1975), pp. 143–172 = *Quaestiones Leidenses. Twelve Studies on Leiden University Library and its Holdings on the occasion of the Quarter-Centenary of the University* (Leiden: University Library, 1975), pp. 179–208.

Jonge, Henk Jan de (ed.), *The Auction Catalogue of the Library of J.J. Scaliger. A Facsimile Edition* (Utrecht: HES, 1977).

Jonge, Henk Jan de, 'Josephus Scaliger in Leiden', *Jaarboekje voor geschiedenis en oud-heidkunde van Leiden en omstreken* 71 (1979), pp. 71–94.

Jonge, Henk Jan de, *De bestudering van het Nieuwe Testament aan de Noordnederlandse universiteiten en het Remonstrants Seminarie van 1575 tot 1700* (Amsterdam, Oxford, New York: Noord-Hollandse Uitgevers Maatschappij, 1980).

Jonge, Henk Jan de & George J.R. Maat, 'Bij de berging van het gebeente van Joseph Scaliger', *Holland* 12 (1980), pp. 20–34.

Jorink, E., 'Noah's Ark Restored (and Wrecked). Dutch Collectors, Natural History and the Problem of Biblical Exegesis' in S. Dupré en C. Lüthy (eds.), *Silent Messengers. The Circulation of Material Objects of Knowledge in the Early Modern Low Countries.* Vol. 2 (Berlin: Lit Verlag, 2011), pp. 153–184.

Jurriaanse, Maria Wilhelmina, *The Founding of Leiden University* (Leiden: E.J. Brill, 1965).

Juynboll, Wilhelmina Maria Cornelia, *Zeventiende-eeuwsche beoefenaars van het Arabisch in Nederland* (Utrecht: Kemink en Zon N.V.- Over den Dom, 1931).

Kaltwasser, Franz Georg, *Die Bibliothek als Museum. Von der Renaissance bis heute, dargestellt am Beispiel der Bayerischen Staatsbibliothek* (Wiesbaden: Otto Harrassowitz Verlag, 1999).

BIBLIOGRAPHY

Kaltwasser, Franz Georg, 'The Common Roots of Library and Museum in the Sixteenth Century. The Example of Munich', *Library History* 20 (November 2004), pp. 163–181.

Katchen, Aaron L., *Christian Hebraists and Dutch Rabbis. Seventeenth Century Apologetics and the Study of Maimonides* Mishneh Torah (Cambridge: Harvard University Center for Jewish Studies, 1984).

Katchen, Aaron L., *Christian Hebraism. The Study of Jewish Culture by Christian Scholars in Medieval and Early Modern Times* (Cambridge: Harvard University Library, 1988).

Keblusek, Marika, *De weg van het boek* (Amsterdam: Amsterdam University Press, 2004).

Keblusek, Marika, 'Commerce and Cultural Transfer. Merchants as Agents in the Early Modern World of Books' in M. North (ed.), *Kultureller Austausch. Bilanz und Perspektiven der Frühneuzeitforschung* (Köln, Weimar, Vienna: Böhlau, 2009), pp. 297–307.

Keblusek, Marika & Badeloch Vera Noldus (eds.), *Double Agents. Cultural and Political Brokerage in Early Modern Europe* (Leiden, Boston: Brill, 2011).

Kelley, Donald R., *Foundations of Modern Historical Scholarship. Language, Law, and History in the French Renaissance* (New York, London: Columbia University Press, 1970).

Kelley, Donald R. (ed.), *History and the Disciplines. The Reclassification of Knowledge in Early Modern Europe* (Rochester, New York: University of Rochester Press, 1997).

Kernkamp, Johannes Hermann, *Economisch-historische aspecten van de literatuurproductie* ('s-Gravenhage, Martinus Nijhoff, 1949).

Kernkamp, Johannes Hermann & J. van Heijst, 'De brieven van Buzanval aan Daniël van der Meulen (1595–1599)', *Bijdragen en mededelingen van het Historisch Genootschap.* Vol. 77 (Groningen: J.B. Wolters, 1962), pp. 175–262.

Kernkamp, Johannes Hermann, *De handel van Daniël van der Meulen c.s. in het bijzonder rond de jaren 1588–1592* (Leiden: s.n., 1969).

Kernkamp, Johannes Hermann, 'Het Van der Meulen-archief c. a.', *BMGN – Low Countries Historical Review* 8/1 (1970), pp. 49–62.

Kessler-Mesguich, Sophie, *Les études hébraïques en France, de François Tissard à Richard Simon (1510–1685)* (Genève: Droz, 1994).

Kessler-Mesguich, Sophie, 'L'Hébreu chez les *hébraïsants chrétiens des XVIe et XVIIe siècles*', *Histoire Epistémologique Langage* 18/1 (1996) pp. 87–108.

Kettering, Sharon, 'Gift-Giving and Patronage in Early Modern France', *French History* 2/2 (1988), pp. 131–151.

Kist, Nicolaas Christiaan, *Bijdragen tot de vroegste geschiedenis en den toekomstigen bloei der Hoogeschool te Leiden* (Leiden: Van den Heuvell, 1850).

Knecht, Robert Jean, *French Renaissance Monarchy. Francis I & Henry II* (London, New York: Routledge, 1984).

Knecht, Robert Jean, *Renaissance Warrior and Patron. The Reign of Francis I* (Cambridge: Cambridge University Press, 1994).

Knöll, Stefanie A., *Creating Academic Communities. Funeral monuments to professors at Oxford, Leiden and Tübingen, 1580–1700* (Oss: Equilibris, 2003).

Koningsveld, Pieter Sjoerd van, *The Latin-Arabic Glossary of the Leiden University Library. A Contribution to the Study of Mozarabic Manuscripts and Literature* (Leiden: New Rhine Publishers, 1976).

Kooker, H.W. de & Bert van Selm. *Boekcultuur in de Lage Landen, 1500–1800. Bibliografie van publikaties over particulier boekenbezit in Noord- en Zuid-Nederland, verschenen voor 1991* (Utrecht: HES uitgevers, 1993).

Kooijmans, Luuc, *Vriendschap en de kunst van het overleven in de zeventiende en achttiende eeuw* (Amsterdam: Bert Bakker, 1997).

Korolovksy, C., *La typografie médicéenne et les publications orientales à Rome à la fin du XVIᵉ siècle* (Rome: s.n., 1959).

Krek, Miroslav, 'The Enigma of the First Arabic book printed from Movable Type', *Journal of Near Eastern Studies* 38 (1979), pp. 203–212.

Kuntz, Marion Leathers, *Guillaume Postel. Prophet of the Restitution of All Things. His Life and Thought* (Den Haag, Boston, London: Springer, 1981).

Kuntz, M.L., 'Voyages to the East and their Meaning in the Thought of Guillaume Postel' in J. Céard & J.-C. Margolin (eds.), *Voyager à la Renaissance*. Actes du Colloque de Tours 30 Juin-13 Juillet 1983 (Paris: Maisonneuve et Larose, 1987), pp. 51–63.

Laeven, H., 'The Frankfurt and Leipzig Book Fairs and the History of the Dutch Book Trade in the 17th and 18th Centuries' in C. Berkvens-Stevelinck (et al., eds.), *Le magasin de l'univers. The Dutch Republic as the Centre of the European Book Trade* (Leiden: E.J. Brill, 1992), pp. 185–197.

Lafitte, M.-P., *Inventaire des manuscrits de la famille Hurault. 26 mai 1622. Edition du texte, concordance et marques de provenance (Paris BNF, lat. 17174, ff. 2–24)* (Paris: 2010).

Lane, John (et al.), *The Arabic Type Specimen of Franciscus Raphelengius's Plantinian Printing Office (1595). A Facsimile with an Introduction* […] (Leiden: University Library Leiden, 1997).

Lane, John, *The Diaspora of Armenian Printing 1512–2012* (Amsterdam, Yerevan: s.n., 2012).

Langereis, Sandra, *De Woordenaar. Christoffel Plantijn, 's werelds grootste drukker en uitgever (1520–1589)* (Amsterdam: Balans, 2014).

Laures, Johannes, *Kirishitan bunko. A Manual of Books and Documents on the Early Christian Mission in Japan* (Tokyo: Sophia University Press, 1957).

Lauwaert, R., 'De handelsbedrijvigheid van de Officina Plantiniana op de Büchermessen te Frankfurt am Main in de XVIᵉ eeuw', *De Gulden Passer* 50 (1972), pp. 124–180 & 51 (1973), pp. 1–8.

BIBLIOGRAPHY

Lebram, Jürgen C.H., 'Hebraïsche Studien zwischen Ideal und Wirklichkeit an der Universität Leiden in den Jahren 1575–1619', *Nederlands Archief voor Kerkgeschiedenis*, 1975, pp. 317–357.

Lebram, Jürgen C.H., 'Hebräische Studien zwischen Ideal und Wirklichkeit an der Universität Leiden in den Jahren 1575–1619', in M.J.M. de Haan (et al., eds.), *In navolging. Een bundel studies aangeboden aan C.C. de Bruin bij zijn afscheid als hoogleraar te Leiden* (Leiden: E.J. Brill, 1975).

Ledegang-Keegstra, Jeltine L.R., 'Théodore de Bèze et Joseph-Juste Scaliger. Critique et admiration réciproques', *Bulletin de la Société de l'histoire du Protestantisme Français*, 159 (2013), pp. 441–458.

Leeuw, H. de, 'Franciscus Raphelengius en het eerste contact der Hollanders met een islamitisch vorst' in A.H. de Groot (ed.), *Het Midden-Oosten en Nederland in historisch perspectief* (Muiderberg: Coutinho, 1989), pp. 18–31.

Lefranc, Abel, 'Les commencements du Collège de France (1529–1544)' in *Mélanges d'histoire offerts à Henri Pirenne par ses anciens élèves et ses amis* [...] (Bruxelles: Vromant, 1926), pp. 291–306.

Lefranc, Abel, *Histoire du Collège de France* (Paris: Hachette, 1893).

Levi della Vida, Giorgio, *Ricerche sulla formazione del più antico fondo dei manoscritti orientali della Biblioteca Vaticana* (Roma: Città del Vaticano, 1939).

Lewis, John, *Adrien Turnèbe (1512–1565). A Humanist observed* (Genève: Droz, 1998).

Leidse Universiteit 400. Stichting en eerste bloei 1575–ca. 1650 (Amsterdam: Rijksmuseum, 1975).

Lloyd-Jones, Gareth, *The Discovery of Hebrew in Tudor England. A Third Language* (Manchester: Manchester University Press, 1983).

Loisel, Antoine, *Pasquier ou dialogue des avocats du Parlement de Paris ; avec une introduction et des notes* [...] *par M. Dupin* (Paris: Videcocq père et fils, 1844).

Loop, Jan, *Johann Heinrich Hottinger. Arabic and Islamic studies in the seventeenth century* (Oxford: Oxford University Press, 2013).

Lunsingh Scheurleer, Theo H. & Guillaume H.M. Posthumus Meyes (eds.), *Leiden University in the Seventeenth Century. An Exchange of Learning* (Leiden: Universitaire Pers, E.J. Brill, 1975).

Luttervelt, R. van, 'De optocht ter gelegenheid van de inwijding der Leidse universiteit', *Leidsch Jaarboekje* 50 (1958), pp. 87–104.

Luyendijk-Elshout, Anatonie Maria, 'The Beginning of Leiden University, an "asulium" for the Muses in a Country in Revolt' in *Les Grandes Réformes des Universités Européennes du XVIe au XXe Siècles. IIIe session scientifique internationale, Cracovie 15–17 mai 1980*. Warszawa-Kraków, pp. 27–36.

Magen, Adolphe, 'Documents sur Jules-César Scaliger et sa famille', *Recueil des Travaux* 2/3 (1873), pp. 199–203.

MacGregor, Arthur, *Curiosity and Enlightenment. Collectors and Collections from the Sixteenth to the Nineteenth Century* (New Haven, London: Yale University Press, 2007).

Maclean, Ian, 'André Wechel at Frankfurt, 1572–1581' in H.-J. Koppitz (ed.), *Gutenberg-Jahrbuch* 63 (Mainz: Gutenberg-Gesellschaft, 1988), pp. 146–176.

Maclean, Ian, 'L'économie du livre érudit. Le cas Wechel (1572–1627)' in P. Aquilon & H.-J. Martin (eds.), *Le livre dans L'Europe de la renaissance. Actes du xxviiie Colloque international d'Etudes humanistes de Tours* (1988), pp. 230–239.

Maclean, Ian, 'The Market for Scholarly Books and Conceptions of Genre in Northern Europe, 1570–1630' in G. Kaufmann (ed.), *Die Renaissance im Blick der Nationen Europas*. Wiesbaden 1991, pp. 17–31.

Maclean, Ian, *Learning and the Market Place. Essays in the History of the Early Modern Book* (Leiden: Brill, 2009).

Maclean, Ian, *Scholarship, Commerce, Religion. The Learned book in the Age of Confessions, 1560–1630* (Cambridge, Mass., London: Harvard University Press, 2012).

Magnien, Michel, 'Scaliger et Erasme' in Ian Dalrymple McFarlane (ed.), *Acta Conventus Neo-Latini Sanctandreani. Proceedings of the Fifth International Congres of Neo-Latin Studies. St. Andrews 24 August to 1 September 1982* (Binghamton, New York: Medieval and Renaissance texts and Studies, 1986), pp. 253–261.

Magnien, Michel, 'Le *Nomenclator* de Robert Constantin (1555), première bibliographie française?' in H. Cazes (ed.), *Renaissance and Reformation* 34/3 (2011), pp. 65–89.

Manuel, Frank E., *The Broken Staff. Judaism through Christan Eyes* (Cambridge, Mass. & London: Cambridge University Press, 1992).

Martin, Henri-Jean, *The French Book. Religion, Absolutism, and Readership, 1585–1715* (Baltimore/London: Johns Hopkins University Press, 1996).

McCuaig, William, 'On Claude Dupuy (1545–1594)', *Studies in Medieval and Renaissance History* 12 (old series vol. 122), pp. 45–104.

Mencke, Johann Burkhard, *Das Holländische Journal 1698–1699*. Herausgegeben mit einer Einleitung von Hubert Laeven (Hildesheim, Zürich, New York: Georg Olms Verlag, 2005).

Meter, J.H., *The Literary Theories of Daniel Heinsius. A Study of the Development and Background of his Views on Literary Theory and Criticism during the Period from 1602–1612* (Assen: Van Gorcum, 1984).

Meijer, Th.J., *Kritiek als herwaardering. Het levenswerk van Jacob Perizonius (1651–1715)* (Leiden: Universitaire Pers, 1971).

Miert, Dirk van, 'The Limits of Transconfessional Contact in the Republic of Letters around 1600. Scaliger, Casaubon and their Catholic Correspondents' in J. De Landtsheer & H. Nellen (eds.), *Between Scylla and Charybdis. Learned Letter Writers Navigating the Reefs of Religious and Political Controversy in Early Modern Europe* (Leiden: Brill, 2010), pp. 367–408.

BIBLIOGRAPHY

Miert, Dirk van, 'Language and Communication in the Republic of Letters. The Uses of Latin and French in the Correspondence of Joseph Scaliger', *Bibliothèque d'Humanisme et Renaissance* 72/1 (2010), pp. 7–34.

Miert, Dirk van, 'Vertrouwelijkheid en indiscretie in de correspondentie van Joseph Scaliger rond 1600' in J. Gabriëls (et al., eds.), *In vriendschap en vertrouwen. Cultuurhistorische essays over confidentialiteit* (Hilversum: Verloren, 2014), pp. 199–210.

Miller, Peter N., 'An Antiquary between Philology and History. Peiresc and the Samaritans.' in D.R. Kelley (ed.), *History and the Disciplines. The Reclassification of Knowledge in Early Modern Europe* (Rochester, New York: University of Rochester Press, 1997), pp. 163–184.

Miller, Peter N., *Peiresc's Europe. Learning and Virtue in the Seventeenth Century* (New Haven & London: Yale University Press, 2000).

Mittler, Elmar (et al., eds.), *Bibliotheca Palatina. Katalog zur Ausstellung vom 8. Juli bis 2. November 1986, Heiliggeistkirche Heidelberg* (Heidelberg: Braus, 1986).

Molhuysen, Philipp Christiaan, *Geschiedenis der Universiteits-Bibliotheek te Leiden* (Leiden: A.W. Sijthoff, 1905).

Molhuysen, Philipp Christiaan, 'Een exemplaar van *Orontius Fineus* met handschriftelijke aantekeningen van J.J. Scaliger', *Tijdschrift voor Boek- en Bibliotheekwezen* 3 (1905), pp. 209–210.

Molhuysen, Philipp Christiaan, *Bibliotheca Universitatis Leidensis Codices Manuscripti 11. Codices Scaligerani (praeter Orientales)* (Leiden: E.J. Brill, 1910).

Molhuysen, Philipp Christiaan, *De komst van Scaliger in Leiden* (Leiden: A.W. Sijthoff, 1913).

Molhuysen, Philipp Christiaan, *Bronnen tot de geschiedenis der Leidsche Universiteit* (Den Haag: Martinus Nijhoff, 1913–1924). 7 vols. (RGP 20, 29, 38, 45, 48, 53, 56).

Molhuysen, Philipp Christiaan, 'De Academie-drukkers' in *Pallas Leidensis MCMXXV* (Leiden: S.C. van Doesburgh, 1925), pp. 305–322.

Morrey, D., 'Materials for the study of Arabic in the age of the early printed book' in Donald Sudney Richards (ed.), *Texts, Documents and Artifacts. Islamic studies in honour of D.S. Richards* (Leiden: Brill, 2003).

Mout, Nicolette M.E.H., *Bohemen en de Nederlanden in de zestiende eeuw* (Leiden: Universitaire Pers Leiden, 1975).

Muller, Jean & Ernst Róth, *Aussereuropäische Druckereien im 16. Jahrhundert. Bibliographie der Drucke* (Baden-Baden: Heitz, 1969).

Müller, Max Johann, *Johann Albrecht von Widmanstetter, 1506–1557. Sein Leben und Wirken* (Bamberg: s.n., 1907).

Müller, Lucian, *Geschichte der klassischen Philologie in den Niederlanden* (Leipzig: B.G. Teubner, 1869), pp. 222–227.

Nat, Jan, *De studie van de Oostersche talen in Nederland in de 18e en 19e eeuw* (Purmerend: J. Muuses, 1929).

Nauert, Charles G., *Humanism and the Culture of Renaissance Europe* (Cambridge: Cambridge University Press, 1995).

Nersessian, Vrej Nerses, *Catalogue of Early Armenian Books 1512–1850* (London: The British Library, 1980).

Nisard, Charles, *Le triumvirat littéraire au XVIe siècle. Juste Lipse, Joseph Scaliger et Isaac Casaubon* (Paris: Amyot, 1852).

Nolhac, Pierre Girauld de, *La Bibliothèque de Fulvio Orsini. Contributions à l'histoire des collections d'Italie et à l'étude de la Renaissance* (Paris: Bibliothèque de l'École des hautes études. Sciences historiques et philologiques, 1887).

Nolhac, Pierre Girauld de, *Ronsard et l'humanisme* (Paris: Champion, 1921).

Nothaft, C. Philippe E., *Dating the Passion. The Life of Jesus and the Emergence of Scientific Chronology (200–1600)* (Leiden: Brill, 2011).

Nothaft, C. Philippe E., 'A sixteenth-Century Debate on the Jewish Calendar. Jacob Christmann and Joseph Justus Scaliger', *Jewish Quarterly Review* 103/1 (2013), pp. 47–73.

Oerle, Hugo van., *Het Academiegebouw te Leiden. Geschiedenis der verandering van de oude kloosterkerk tot het universiteitsgebouw* (Leiden: E.J. Brill, 1937).

Offenberg, Ardri K. & Corretje Moed-Van Walraven, *Hebrew Incunabula in Public Collections. A First International Census* (Nieuwkoop: B. de Graaf, 1990).

Offenberg, Ardri K., *A Choice of Corals. Facets of Fifteenth-Century Hebrew Printing* (Nieuwkoop: B. de Graaf, 1992).

Offenberg, A.K., 'Hebrew Printing of the Bible in the xvth Century' in P.H. Saenger & K. van Kampen (eds.), *The Bible as Book. The First Printed Editions* (London: The British Library, 1999).

Ogilvie, Brian W., *The Science of Describing. Natural History in Renaissance Europe* (Chicago, London: University of Chicago Press, 2006).

Ommen, Kasper van, 'In imagine picta'. De portretten van Josephus Justus Scaliger' in P.G. Hoftijzer (ed.), *Adelaar in de wolken. De Leidse jaren van Josephus Justus Scaliger 1593–1609* (Leiden: Scaliger Instituut, Universiteitsbibliotheek Leiden, 2005), pp. 138–163.

Ommen, Kasper van, '"À la bonne grace de Monsieur de Boistailli". Scaliger and the Hurault de Boistaillé family', *Omslag. Bulletin van de Universiteitsbibliotheek Leiden en het Scaliger Instituut* 3 (2009), pp. 11–13.

Ommen, Kasper van, '"Hebraea dictio est". Two books from the library of Claudius Mitalerius', *Omslag. Bulletin van de Universiteitsbibliotheek Leiden en het Scaliger Instituut* 3 (2010), pp. 12–13.

Ommen, Kasper van, '"Je suis pauvre en tout, mesmement en livres'. Reconstructing the Legatum Scaligeri in Leiden University Library' in R. Kerr (et al., eds.), *Writing and Writings from another World and Era. Investigations in Islamic Text and Script in honour of Januarius Justus Witkam* (Cambridge: Archetype 2011), pp. 293–329.

BIBLIOGRAPHY

Ommen, Kasper van, "Tous mes livres de langues estrangeres'. Reconstructing the Legatum Scaligeri in Leiden University Library'. *Renaissance and Reformation / Renaissance et Réforme* 34/3 (2011), pp. 143–184.

Ommen, Kasper van & E. den Hartog, 'Een epitaaf voor Josephus Justus Scaliger, sieraad van de Academie' in E. den Hartog & J. Veerman (eds.), *De Pieterskerk in Leiden. Bouwgeschiedenis, inrichting en gedenktekens* (Zwolle: Waanders, 2011), pp. 367–376.

Ommen, Kasper van, 'The Legacy of Scaliger in Leiden University Library Catalogues 1609–1716' in M. Walsby & N. Constantinidou (eds.), *Documenting the Early Modern Book World. Inventories and Catalogues in Manuscript and Print* (Leiden, Boston: Brill, 2013), pp. 51–82.

Ommen, Kasper van, 'Early Modern Oriental Collections in Oxford and Leiden. Scaliger, Bodley and Anglo-Dutch Encounters and Exchanges', Part I. *Bodleian Library Record* 28/2 (2015), pp. 152–178.

Ommen, Kasper van, 'What does an Oriental Scholar look like? Some Portraits of Joseph Scaliger and Other Sixteenth-century Oriental Scholars. A Selection' in A. Blair & A.-S. Goeing (eds.), *For the Sake of Learning. Essays in Honor of Anthony Grafton* (Leiden, Boston: Brill, 2016), pp. 73–90.

Ommen, Kasper van, 'Josephus Justus Scaliger – Works on Christian-Muslim Relations – *Kitāb al-amthāl, seu Proverbiorum Arabicorum centuriae duae; Proverbiorum arabicorum centuriae duae*, 'The book of proverbs, Arabic proverbs of two centuries' in D. Thomas & J. Chesworth (eds.), *Christian-Muslim Relations. A Bibliographical History*. Volume 8: *Northern and Eastern Europe (1600–1700)* (Leiden, Boston: Brill, 2016), pp. 553–560.

Ommen, Kasper van, 'Early Modern Oriental Collections in Oxford and Leiden. Scaliger, Bodley and Anglo-Dutch Encounters and Exchanges', Part II. *Bodleian Library Record* 29/1 (2016), pp. 47–72.

Ottenheim, K.A., 'Van Witte Nonnenklooster tot Academiegebouw' in Th.H. Lunsingh Scheurleer (et al., eds.), *Het Rapenburg VIb: Het Rijck van Pallas* (Leiden: s.n., 1992), pp. 781–836.

Otterspeer, Willem, *Het bolwerk van de vrijheid. De Leidse universiteit, 1575–1672* [Groepsportret met dame 1] (Amsterdam: Bert Bakker, 2000).

Otterspeer, Willem, *De vesting van de macht. De Leidse Universiteit, 1673–1775* [Groepsportret met dame 2] (Amsterdam: Bert Bakker, 2002).

Otterspeer, Willem, *Het mystieke getal. Pythagoras in Leiden* (Leiden: Primavera Pers, 2019).

Otterspeer, Willem, *The search for Numbers. Renaissance Science and Sherlock Holmes* (Unpublished text).

Palabiyik, Nill O., 'The Last Letter from Étienne Hubert to Joseph Scaliger. Oriental Languages and Scholarly Collaboration in Seventeenth-Century Europe', *Lias. Journal of Early Modern Intellectual Culture and its Sources* 45/1 (2018), pp. 113–143.

Palabiyik, Nill O., Silent Teachers. *Turkish Books and Oriental Learning in Early Modern Europe, 1544–1669* (London, New York: Routledge 2023).

Parent, Annie, *Les métiers du livre à Paris au XVIᵉ siècle (1535–1560)* (Genève: Droz, 1974).

Pater, Jan Cornelis Hendrik de, *Jan van Hout (1542–1609). Een levensbeeld uit de 16ᵉ eeuw* (Den Haag: Daamen, 1946).

Pattison, Mark, *Isaac Casaubon 1559–1614*. 2nd ed. (London: Longmans Green and Co, 1875).

Pattison, Mark, *Essays*, Vol. I.: 'On Joseph Scaliger' (Oxford: 1889), pp. 132–195 & 196–245.

Pelusi, Simonetti (ed.), *Le civiltà del Libro e la stampa a Venezia. Testi sacri ebraici, christiani, islamici dal Quattrocento al Settecento* (Padua: Il Poligrafo, 2000).

Petroski, Henry, *The Book on the Bookshelf* (New York: Alfred Knopf, 1999).

Pettegree, Andrew, *The Book in the Renaissance* (New Haven, London: Yale University Press, 2010).

Pettegree, Andrew & Arthur der Weduwen, *The Bookshop of the World. Making and Trading Books in the Dutch Golden Age* (New Haven, London: Yale University Press 2019).

Plattard, Jean, *Guillaume Budé (1468–1540) et les origines de l'humanisme français* (Paris: Société d'édition 'Les Belles lettres', 1923).

Pollard, Graham & Albert Ehrman, *The Distribution of Books by Catalogue from the Invention of Printing to A.D. 1800. Based on the Material in the Broxbourne Library* (Cambridge: printed for presentation to members of the Roxburghe Club, 1965).

Port, Wilhelm, *Hieronymus Commelinus 1550–1597. Leben und Werk eines Heidelberger Drucker-Verlegers* (Leipzig: Harrassowitz, 1938).

Preisendanz, K., 'Die Bibliothek Johannes Reuchlins' in M. Krebs (ed.), *Johannes Reuchlin 1455–1522. Festgabe seiner Vaterstadt Pforzheim zur 500. Wiederkehr seines Geburtstages* (Pforzheim: Im Selbstverlag der Stadt, 1955), pp. 35–82.

Proosdij, B.A. van, 'Scaliger's graf', *Brill's uitgaven voor algemeen voortgezet onderwijs* (Leiden: Brill, 1972), pp. 19–25.

Prijs, Joseph, *Die Basler hebräischen Drucke (1492–1866). Im Auftr. der Öffentlichen Bibliothek der Universität Basel bearb. von Joseph Prijs; erg. und hrsg. von Bernhard Prijs* (Olten, Freiburg: UrsGraf Verlag, 1964).

Raabe, P., 'Bibliotheken und gelehrtes Buchwesen. Bemerkungen über die Büchersammlungen der Gelehrten im 17. Jahrhundert' in S. Neumeister & C. Wiedemann (eds.), *Res Publica Litteraria. Die Institutionen der Gelehrsamkeit in der frühen Neuzeit* (Wiesbaden: Harrassowitz, 1987), pp. 643–661.

Raugei, Anna Maria (ed.), *Gian Vincenzo Pinelli et Claude Dupuy. Une correspondance entre deux humanistes* (Roma: Olschki, 2002).

Raugei, A.M., 'Gian Vincenzo Pinelli (1535–1601) ses livres, ses amis.' in R.G. Camos & A. Vanautgaerden (eds.), *Les labyrinthes de l'esprit. Collections et bibliothèques à la Renaissance/Renaissance Libraries and Collections* (Genève: Droz, 2015), pp. 213–228.

BIBLIOGRAPHY

Rebhan, H., 'Johann Albrecht Widmanstetter und seine Bibliothek' in C. Bubenik (ed.), *Kulturkosmos der Renaissance. Die Gründung der Bayerischen Staatsbibliothek* (Wiesbaden: Harrassowitz, 2008).

Reiffenberg, Frédéric Auguste Ferdinand Thomas, Baron de, 'Bibliothèque de Joseph Scaliger', *Le Bibliophile belge* 4 (1847), pp. 229–233.

Reinach, Salomon, 'Joseph Scaliger et les juifs', *Revue des études juives* 88 (1929), pp. 171–176.

Rekers, Bernard, *Benito Arias Montano 1527–1598. Studie over een groep spiritualistische humanisten in Spanje en de Nederlanden, op grond van hun briefwisseling* (Amsterdam: s.n., 1961).

Rekers, Bernard, *Benito Arias Montano (1527–1598)* (London: The Warburg Institute, Leiden: E.J. Brill, 1972).

Renouard, Philippe, *Répertoire des imprimeurs parisiens, libraires, fondeurs de caractères et correcteurs d'imprimerie depuis l'introduction de l'imprimerie à Paris (1470)* (Paris: Lettres modernes, 1965).

Ricci, Seymour de & P.F. Girard, 'Lettres inédites de Cujas et de Scaliger', *Nouvelle Revue historique de droit français et étranger* 40 (1917), pp. 5–26.

Ridder-Symoens, H. de, 'Italian and Dutch Universities in the Sixteenth and Seventeenth Centuries' in C.S. Maffioli & L.C. Palm (eds.), *Italian Scientists in the Low Countries in the XVIIth and XVIIIth Centuries* (Amsterdam & Atlanta: G.A. Rodopi, 1998).

Ridderbos, S., *De philologie aan de Leidsche Universiteit gedurende de eerste vijfentwintig jaren van haar bestaan* (Leiden: Donner, 1906).

Rieu, Willem Nicolaas du, 'De portretten en het testament van Josephus Justus Scaliger', *Handelingen en Mededeelingen van de Maatschapij der Nederlandsche Letterkunde*, 1880-' (Leiden: E.J. Brill, 1881), pp. 89–137.

Rieu, Willem Nicolaas du, 'Nog iets over Scaliger's portretten', *Handelingen en Mededeelingen van de Maatschapij der Nederlandsche Letterkunde*, 1889–1890, pp. 204–209.

Rieu, Willem Nicolaas du, 'Nog een portret van Scaliger', *Handelingen en Mededeelingen van de Maatschapij der Nederlandsche Letterkunde*, 1892–1893, pp. 108–109.

Rivolta, Adolfo, *Contributo a uno studio sulla biblioteca di Gian Vicenzo Pinelli* (Monza: Scuola tipografica Artigianelli, 1914).

Robert, P. de, 'La naissance des études samaritaines en Europe aux XVIe et XVIIe siècles' in J.-P. Rothschild (et al., eds.), *Études samaritaines. Pentateuque et Targum* […] (Leuven: Peeters, 1988), pp. 15–26.

Robben, Frans M.A., *Jan Poelman, boekverkoper en vertegenwoordiger van de firma Plantin-Moretus in Salamanca, 1579–1607* (Antwerpen: Vereeniging der Antwerpsche Bibliophielen, 1994).

Robinson, George W., *Autobiography of Joseph Scaliger. With Autobiographical Selections from His Letters, His Testament and the Funeral Orations by Daniel Heinsius and Dominicus Baudius* (Cambridge: Harvard University Press, 1927).

Roeck, B., 'Venice and Germany. Commercial Contacts and Intellectual Inspirations' in B. Aikema & B.L. Brown (eds.), *Renaissance Venice and the North. Crosscurrents in the Time of Dürer, Bellini and Titian* (London: Thames & Hudson, 1999), pp. 45–55.

Roest, Meijer Marcus, *Catalog der Hebraica und Judaica aus der L. Rosenthal'schen Bibliothek* (Amsterdam: J. Vlausen, 1875).

Rooden, Peter T. van, *Constantijn l'Empereur (1591–1648), professor Hebreeuws en theologie te Leiden. Theologie, bijbelwetenschap en rabbijnse studiën in de zeventiende eeuw* (S.l.: s.n., 1985).

Roper, G., 'Early Arabic Printing in Europe' in E.M. Hanebutt-Benz, D. Glass (eds.), *Middle Eastern Languages and the Print Revolution. A Cross-Cultural Encounter. A Catalogue and Companion to the Exhibition* (Westhofen: WVA-Verlag Skulima, 2002).

Rosa, M., 'Un "médiateur" dans la République des Lettres. Le bibliothécaire' in H. Bots, & F. Waquet (eds.), *Commercium litterarium. Forms of Communication in the Republic of Letters 1600–1750* (Amsterdam/Maarssen: APA-Holland University Press, 1994), pp. 81–98.

Rosanbo, Louise de, 'Pierre Pithou érudit', *Revue du XVIe siècle*, XV (1928), pp. 279–305 & XVI (1929), pp. 301–330.

Rouillard, Clarence Dana, *The Turk in French History, Thought, and Literature (1520–1660)* (Paris: Boivin & Co., 1940).

Ruppel, Aloys, 'Die Bücherwelt des 16. Jahrhunderts und die Frankfurter Büchermessen', *De Gulden Passer* (34) 1956, pp. 20–39.

Russell, Gül A. (ed.), *The 'Arabick' Interest of the Natural Philosophers in Seventeenth-Century England* (Leiden, New York: E.J. Brill, 1994).

Sainéan, L., 'L'orientalisme au XVIe siecle. Joseph-Juste Scaliger (A propos de "Rabelais savait-il l'arabe?")', in L. Sainéan (ed.), *La langue de Rabelais* (Paris: E. de Boccard, 1922–1923), Vol. II *Langue et vocabulaire*, pp. 497–502.

Sabbe, Maurits, *De meesters van de Gulden Passer. Christoffel Plantin, aartsdrukker van Philips II, en zijn opvolgers, de Moretussen* (Amsterdam: P.N. van Kampen & Zoon N.V., 1937).

Saliba, George, 'Arabic Science in Sixteenth-Century Europe. Guillaume Postel (1510–1581) and Arabic Astronomy', *Suhayl* 7 (2007), pp. 115–164.

Schaeper, Silke, "That the titles of all your Hebrewe bookes may be aptly taken'. Printed Hebraica at the Bodleian Library and their Cataloguing 1605–2005', *The Bodleian Library Record* 19/1 (2006), pp. 77–125.

Schetter, Willy, 'Scaliger, Cujas und der Leidensis Voss. Lat. Q. 86', *Hermes* 111 (1983), pp. 363–371.

BIBLIOGRAPHY

Schmidt, Jan, 'Between Author and Library Shelf. The intriguing History of some Middle Eastern Manuscripts acquired by Public Collections in the Netherlands prior to 1800' in A. Hamilton, M.H. van den Boogert, B. Westerweel (eds.), *The Republic of Letters and the Levant* (Leiden: Brill, 2005), pp. 27–51.

Schneider, Ulrich Johannes, *Bibliotheken als Ordnung des Wissens (16.-18. Jahrhundert)* (Berlin, New York: De Gruyter, 2008).

Schneiders, Paul, *Nederlandse bibliotheekgeschiedenis. Van librije tot virtuele bibliotheek* (Den Haag: NBLC, 1997).

Schneppen, Heinz. *Niederländische Universitäten und Deutsches Geistesleben. Von der Gründung der Universität Leiden bis ins späte 18. Jahrhundert* (Münster: Aschendorffsche Verlagsbuchhandlung, 1960).

Schnur, Roman, *Die französischen Juristen im konfessionellen Bürgerkrieg des 16. Jahrhunderts. Ein Beitrag zur Entstehungsgeschichte des modernen Staates* (Berlin: De Gruyter, 1962).

Schnurrer, Christian Friedrich, *Bibliotheca Arabica* (Halle: Johann Christian Hendel, 1811).

Schreiber, Fred, *The Estiennes. An Annotated Catalogue of 300 highlights of their various Presses* (New York: E.K. Schreiber, 1982).

Schwab, Moïse, *Les incunables orientaux et les impressions orientales au commencement du XVIe siècle* (Nieuwkoop: B. de Graaf, 1964).

Schwarzfuchs, Lyse, *Le livre hébreu à Paris au XVIe siècle. Inventaire chronologique* (Paris: BNF, 2004).

Schwarzfuchs, Lyse, 'Sébastien Gryphe éditeur en hébreu' in R. Mouren (ed.), *Quid novi? Sébastien Gryphe, à l'occasion du 450e anniversaire de sa mort* (Villeurbanne: Presses de l'Enssib, 2008), pp. 87–109.

Schwarzfuchs, Lyse, *L'hébreu dans le livre lyonnais au XVIe siècle. Inventaire chronologique* (Lyon: ENS Éditions, Institut d'histoire du livre, 2008).

Schwetschke, Gustav, *Codex nundinarius Germaniae literatae bisecularis. Mess Jahrbücher des deutschen Buchhandels von dem Erscheinen des ersten Mess-Kataloges im Jahre 1564 bis zu der Gründung des ersten Buchhändler-Vereins im Jahre 1765* (Nieuwkoop: B. de Graaf, 1963).

Secret, F., 'Le rencontre de Postel avec Joseph Juste Scaliger' in *Postel revisité. Nouvelles recherches sur Guillaume Postel et son milieu* (Paris, Milano: S.E.H.A., 1998), pp. 99–108.

Seitz, Cha, *Joseph Juste Scaliger et Genève* (Genève: s.n., 1895).

Selm, Bert van, *Een menighte treffelijcke Boecken. Nederlandse boekhandelscatalogi in het begin van de zeventiende eeuw* (Utrecht: HES, 1987).

Sellin, Paul R., *Daniel Heinsius and Stuart England. With a Short-title Checklist of the Works of Daniel Heinsius* (Leiden, London: Leiden University Press, 1968).

Shaw, Graham W., 'Scaliger's Copy of an Early Tamil Catechism', *The Library*, 6th series (1981), pp. 239–243.

Siegenbeek, Matthijs, *Geschiedenis der Leidsche Hoogeschool, van hare oprigting in den jare 1575, tot het jaar 1825* (Leiden: S. & J. Luchtmans, 1829–1832).

Sluijter, Ronald, *'Tot ciraet, vermeerderinge ende heerlyckmaeckinge der universiteyt'. Bestuur, instellingen, personeel en financiën van de Leidse universiteit, 1575–1812* (Hilversum: Verloren, 2004).

Somos, Marc, *Secularisation and the Leiden Circle* (Leiden, Boston: Brill, 2011).

Smitskamp, Rijk, *Philologia Orientalis. A Description of Books illustrating the Study and Printing of Oriental Languages in Europe* (Leiden: Smitskamp Oriental Antiquarium, 1976–1991).

Smitskamp, Rijk, *The Scaliger Collection. A Collection of over 200 Antiquarian Books by and about Josephus Justus Scaliger (&) Supplement Joseph Scaliger. A Bibliography 1850–1993* by A.T. Grafton & H.J. de Jonge. Leiden, Smitskamp Oriental Antiquarium (Catalogue N° 595) (Leiden: Smitskamp Oriental Antiquarium, 1993).

Stabel, P., 'Venice and the Low Countries. Commercial Contacts and Intellectual Inspirations' in B. Aikema & B.L. Brown (eds.), *Renaissance Venice and the North. Crosscurrents in the Time of Dürer, Bellini and Titian* (London: Thames & Hudson, 1999), pp. 31–43.

Steinschneider, Moritz, *Catalogus codicum hebraeorum bibliothecae academiae Lugduno-Batavae* (Leiden: E.J. Brill, 1858).

Steinschneider, Moritz, *Bibliographisches Handbuch über die theoretische und praktische Literatur für hebräische Sprachkunde* (Jerusalem: Bamberger & Wahrman Verlag, 1937).

Stevens, Linton C., 'The Contribution of French Jurists to the Humanism of the Renaissance', *Studies in the Renaissance* 1 (1954), pp. 92–105.

Striedl, H., 'Die Bücherei des Orientalisten Johann Albrecht Widmanstetter' in H.J. Kissling & A. Schmaus (eds.), *Serta Monacensia Franz Babinger zum 15. Januar 1951 als Festgruss dargebracht* (Leiden: Brill, 1952), pp. 200–244.

Striedl, H., 'Geschichte der Hebraica-Sammlung der Bayerischen Staatsbibliothek' in H. Franke (ed.), *Orientalisches aus Münchener Bibliotheken und Sammlungen* (Wiesbaden: Steier, 1957), pp. 1–37.

Strothmann, Werner, *Die Anfänge der syrischen Studien in Europa* (Wiesbaden: Harrassowitz, 1971).

Summit, Jehhifer, *Memory's Library. Medieval Books in Early Modern England* (Chicago & London: Chicago University Press, 2008).

Tamizey de Larroque, Philippe, *Lettres françaises inédites de Joseph Scaliger* (Agen, Paris: Alphonse Picard, 1879).

Taylor, Archer, *Book Catalogues. Their Varieties and uses*, 2nd ed., revised by William P. Barlow (Winchester: St. Paul's Bibliographies, 1986).

BIBLIOGRAPHY

Teissier-Ensminger, Anna (ed.), *La vie de Jacques-Auguste de Thou I. Aug. Thuani vita* (Paris: Honoré Champion, 2007).

Tinto, Alberto, *La tipografia Medicea orientale* (Lucca: Pacini Fazzi, 1987).

Toomer, Gerald James, *Eastern Wisedome and Learning. The Study of Arabic in Seventeenth-Century England* (Oxford: Clarendon Press, 1996).

Van Hal, Toon, 'Joseph Scaliger, puzzled by the similarities of Persian and Dutch?', *Omslag. Bulletin van de Universiteitsbibliotheek Leiden en het Scaliger Instituut* 1 (2007), pp. 1–3.

Van Hal, Toon, *'Moedertalen & taalmoeders'. Methodologie, epistemologie en ideologie van het taalvergelijkend onderzoek in de Renaissance* (Leuven: s.n., 2008).

Vercellin, Giorgio, *Venezia e l'origine della stampa in caratteri arabi* (Padua: Il poligrafo, 2001).

Vervliet, Hendrik D.L., *Cyrillic & Oriental Typography in Rome at the end of the Sixteenth Century. An Inquiry into the Work of Robert Granjon (1578–90)* (Berkeley: Poltroon Press, 1981).

Vinograd, Yĕša'yahū, *Thesaurus of the Hebrew Books. Listing of Books printed in Hebrew Letters since the beginning of Hebrew Printing circa 1469 through 1869* (Jerusalem: Ha-maḵōn lĕ-bībliyōgrafyā, 1993–1995).

Vogel, Jean Philippe, *The contribution of the University of Leiden to Oriental research. Lecture delivered to the Royal India and Pakistan Society on Thursday, June 23, 1949* (Leiden: Brill, 1954).

Vrolijk, Arnoud & Kasper van Ommen, *"All my Books in Foreign Tongues". Scaliger's Oriental Legacy in Leiden 1609–2009. Catalogue of An Exhibition on the Quatercentenary of Scaliger's Death, 21 January 2009* [Kleine publicaties van de Leidse universiteitsbibliotheek 79] (Leiden: Leiden University Library, 2009).

Vrolijk, Arnoud, 'The Prince of Arabists and his many Errors. Thomas Erpenius's Image of Joseph Scaliger and the Edition of the *Proverbia Arabica* (1614)', *Journal of the Warburg and Courtauld Institutes* 73 (2010), pp. 297–325.

Vrolijk, Arnoud, 'Scaliger and the Dutch Expansion in Asia. An Arabic Translation for an Early Voyage to the East Indies (1600)', *Journal of the Warburg and Courtauld Institutes* 78 (2015), pp. 217–309.

Vrolijk, Arnoud & Richard van Leeuwen, *Voortreffelijk en waardig. 400 jaar Arabische studies in Nederland* (Leiden: Rijksmuseum van Oudheden, 2013).

Vrolijk, Arnoud & Richard van Leeuwen, *Arabic Studies in the Netherlands. A Short History in Portraits, 1580–1950* (Leiden: Brill, 2014).

Wakefield, C., 'Arabic Manuscripts in the Bodleian Library. The Seventeenth-Century Collections' in G.A. Russell (ed.), *The 'Arabick' Interest of the Natural Philosophers in Seventeenth-Century England* (Leiden, New York, Köln: Brill, 1994), pp. 128–146.

Walsby, M., 'Printer Mobility in Sixteenth-Century France' in B. Rial Costas (ed.), *Print Culture and Peripheries in Early Modern Europe. A Contribution to the History of*

Printing and the Book Trade in Small European and Spanish Cities (Leiden, Boston: Brill, 2013), pp. 249–268.

Weill, George Jacques, *Vie et caractère de Guillaume Postel* (Milano Belles Lettres, 1987).

Wiegers, Gerard A., *A Learned Muslim Acquaintance of Erpenius and Golius. Aḥmad b. Ḳasim al Andalusi and Arabic studies in The Netherlands* (Leiden: Documentatiebureau Islam-Christendom, Faculteit der Godgeleerdheid, Rijksuniversiteit Leiden, 1988).

Wierda, Lydia, *Armamentarium totius sapientiae. Een arsenaal van alle wetenschap. De Franeker academiebibliotheek in de zeventiende eeuw* (Leeuwarden: Fryske Akademy, 2005).

Wijk, Walter Emile van, 'Josephus Justus Scaliger, grondlegger der wetenschappelijke tijdrekenkunde', *De Natuur* 60 (1940), pp. 153–157; 192–195; 224–229.

Wijk, Walter Emile van, *Het eerste leerboek der technische tijdrekenkunde* (*Scaliger's Isagogici Chronologiae Canones, 1606*) (Leiden: s.n., 1954).

Wijnman, Hendrik Frederik, 'De studie van het Ethiopisch en de ontwikkeling van de Ethiopische typografie in West-Europa in de 16ᵈᵉ eeuw'. I. 'De Ethiopische studiën van Johannes Potken', *Het boek* 31 (1955), pp. 168–179.

Wijnman, Hendrik Frederik, 'De studie van het Ethiopisch en de ontwikkeling van de Ethiopische typografie in West-Europa in de 16ᵈᵉ eeuw'. I. 'De ontwikkeling van de Ethiopische typografie in West-Europa in de 16de eeuw', *Het boek* 32 (1955), pp. 225–246.

Wijnman, Hendrik Frederik, 'The Origin of Arabic Typography in Leiden' in *Books on the Orient. A Catalogue offered to the members of the xxivth Congress of Orientalists, Munich* (Leiden: Brill, 1957), pp. vii–xv.

Wijnman, Hendrik Frederik, 'Philippus Ferdinandus. Professor in het Arabisch aan de Leidse Universiteit, de eerste Oost-Europese Jood in Nederland', *Jaarbericht van het Vooraziatisch-Egyptisch Genootschap "Ex Oriente Lux"* 19 (1967), pp. 558–580.

Wilkinson, Robert J., *Orientalism, Aramaic and Kabbalah in the Catholic Reformation. The First Printing of the Syriac New Testament* (Leiden, Boston: Brill, 2007).

Wilkinson, Robert J., *The Kabbalistic Scholars of the Antwerp Polyglot Bible* (Leiden, Boston: Brill, 2007).

Witkam, Henricus Johannes, *Iets over Pieter Paauw en zijn Theatrum Anatomicum en over het bouwen van de anatomieplaats en de bibliotheek* (Leiden: H.J. Witkam, 1967).

Witkam, Henricus Johannes, *De dagelijkse zaken van de Leidse Universiteit van 1581 tot 1596* (Leiden: H.J. Witkam, 1970–1975).

Witkam, Henricus Johannes, *De financiën van de Leidse universiteit in de 16de eeuw*, Vol. iv (Leiden: H.J. Witkam, 1982), pp. 321–324; Vol. v (Leiden: H.J. Witkam, 1982), pp. 334–401.

Witkam, Jan Just, *Jacobus Golius (1596–1667) en zijn handschriften. Lezing voor het Oosters Genootschap in Nederland gehouden op 14 januari 1980* (Leiden: Brill, 1980).

BIBLIOGRAPHY 357

Witkam, Jan Just, 'Verzamelingen van Arabische handschriften en boeken in Nederland' in N. van Dam (et al., eds.), *Nederland en de Arabische wereld. Van Middeleeuwen tot Twintigste eeuw* (Lochem: De Tijdstroom, 1987), pp. 19–29.

Witkam, Jan Just, *Inventory of the Oriental Manuscripts of the Library of the University of Leiden. Vol. 1: Manuscripts Or. 1-Or. 1000*. Leiden 2007. Online via http://www.islamic manuscripts.info/.

Zedelmaier, Helmut, *Bibliotheca universalis und bibliotheca selecta. Das Problem der Ordnung des gelehrten Wissens in der frühen Neuzeit* (Köln, Vienna: Böhlau, 1992).

Zenker, Julius Theodor, *Bibliotheca Orientalis. Manuel de bibliographie orientale* (Leipzig: Guillaume Engelmann, 1846).

Ziebarth, E., 'Heinrich Lindenbruch und Josephus Justus Scaliger' in E. Kelter (et al., eds.), *Beiträge zur Gelehrtengeschichte des Siebzehnten Jahrhundert. Festschrift zur Begrüssung der 48. Versammlung deutscher Philologen und Schulmänner zu Hamburg im Jahre 1905* (Hamburg: Lütke & Wulff, 1905), pp. 73–101.

Zinguer, I. (ed.), *L'Hébreu au temps de la Renaissance* (Leiden, New York, Köln: Brill, 1992).

Zuber, Roger, 'De Scaliger à Saumaise. Leyde et les grands "Critiques français"', *Bulletin de la Société de l'Histoire du Protestantisme Français* (126) 1980, pp. 461–488.

Index

Aa, Pieter van der 252
Abel, Léonard 168*n*122
Adolphus, Gustavus 238
Aerssens, Cornelis 20*n*14, 163
Akbar Dpir Tokhatetsi 102
Albonesius Regulus 120
Albonesius, Theseus Ambrosius 88
Amaduzzi, Orazio 99
Amama, Sixtinus 276
Amyot, Jacques d' 93
Apianus, Petrus 105
Arminius, Jacobus 28
Arrivabene, Andrea 79
Augustinus Justinianus 88

Bahya ibn Paquda 294
Balduinus, Jan 237
Barnes, John 282
Baudius, Dominicus 23, 137, 193, 299
Beaupé, Simon 40*n*7
Bedwell, William 234
Bene, Pierre del 89
Bene, Pietro del 108
Benjamin of Tudela 236, 294
Bergh, Johannes van den 245
Béroalde de Verville, François 178
Béroalde, Mathieu 121*n*107
Beroaldus 121
Berrewijns, Hans 161
Bertius, Petrus 183, 228
Beverningh, Hiëronymus van 245, 256*n*100
Beza, Theodorus 68, 149
Bibliander, Theodorus 52
Blotius, Hugo 270
Boderie, Guy Lefèvre de la 119
Boderie, Nicolas 119
Bodley, Thomas XIII, 13, 14, 272, 281, 291
Boissens, Cornelis Dircksz. 189
Bomberg, Daniel 69, 130, 306*n*1
Bongars, Jacques 151, 163
Bonnennuict, Juda 153
Bontiers 162, 166
Boreel 323*n*9
Boreel, Adam 96*n*19
Boreel, Johan 96
Bouduwijns, François 161

Boulliau, Ismaël 29
Bovelius, Marcus 240
Brahe, Tycho 77
Brederode, Pieter van 148
Bronckhorst, Everard 137
Broughton, Hugh 299
Budé, Guillaume 93
Bullioud, Pierre 8, 272
Burmannus, Petrus 255
Busbecq, Ogier Ghiselin de 271*n*32
Buxtorf, Johannes 236
Buytewech, Gerardus 143
Buzanval, Paul Choart de 31, 158, 293

Caierus, Petrus 91
Candi, Chiagijn 248
Cardinal Marcel Cervin 120
Carron, Louis le 29
Casaubon, Isaac 13, 19, 51, 148, 151, 272, 278
Castrodardo, Giovanni Battista 79
Cavellat, Guillaume 49
Cerutus, Federicus 206
Chamier, Daniel 219
Chasteigner de la Roche-Posay,
    Henri Louis 61, 165
Chasteigner de la Roche-Posay, Louis 8, 22, 60, 164, 292
Choart de Buzanval, Paul 148
Choisnin, Jean 120
Chrestien, Florent 74
Christmann, Jakob 103
Ciotti, Giovanni Battista 123
Clusius, Carolus 27, 263
Cluverius, Philippus 176, 177
Clüver, Simon 177
Coligny, Louise de 96
Commelin, Hieronymus 105, 152
Commelin, Jan I 153
Commelin, Jean Jansz. 152, 153
Constantin, Robert 42
Copernicus, Nicolaus 77
Coras, Jean de 44
Corbinelli, Jacopo 108
Corona, Caspar 160
Crespin, Jean 42
Croÿ, Charles de 191, 264*n*9

INDEX

Crusius, Paulus 53
Cujas, Jacques 5, 29, 63, 264
Curiander, Abel 276

Daléchamps, Jacques 42, 121
Daniël, Pierre 92, 128
De Dollencourt 114
De la Voulpière 100
de' Medici, Catherine 95, 119, 265
de' Medici, Ferdinando I 166
de' Medici, Francesco I 93
Dousa, Janus 20, 23, 24, 137, 181, 185
Dousa, Janus the younger 220
Dozy, Reinhart Pieter Anne 259
Dramarius, Andreas 130
Drusius, Johannes 8, 12, 26, 28, 32, 145, 153, 272, 276
Drusius, Johannes jr 153, 189, 283
Duke Albrecht V of Bavaria 267
Dupuy 301
Dupuy, Christophe 168
Dupuy, Claude 17, 18, 22, 29, 71, 79, 90, 98, 99, 105, 147, 264, 292
Dupuy de Chasteigner, Claude 142
Dupuy, Jacques 18, 29
Dupuy, Pierre 18, 29, 168, 169
Duret, Louis 127
Duyck, Franco 260

Egidio da Viterbo 268
Elmenhorst, Geverhard 82
Elzevier, Isaac 239
Elzevier, Johannes 246
Elzevier, Louis 195, 198, 237
Empereur van Opwijck, Constantijn L' 236
Emperor Maximilian II 270
Erasmus, Desiderius 39
Erpenius, Thomas 172, 214, 234, 240, 296, 301n3, 322n2
Esprinchard, Jacques 154, 191, 171n131
Estienne, Charles 42, 59
Estienne, Henri 108
Estienne, Robert 47, 56, 77
Eusebius of Caesarea 16

Fabri de Peiresc, Nicolas-Claude 122
Faille, Hester de la 158
Faille, Jacques de la 158
Faille, Jan the elder de la 158

Farnese, Alexander 61, 158
Fauchet, Claude 29
Ferdinandus, Philippus 54
Ferrier, Arnaud du 100
Foix, Paul de 93
Franceschi, Francesco 112
Frichon 56
Froben, Johann 60

Gendt, Caspar de 27
Génébrard, Gilbert 174, 267
Gesner, Conrad 266
Gilles de Gourmont 58
Gillot, Jacques 150
Gilpin, George 163
Giphanius, Obertus 66
Golius, Jacobus 211, 239n64, 241, 244, 248, 296
Gomarus, Franciscis 193
Gomarus, Franciscus 28
Goulart, Simon 149
Goyvaerts, Hendrick 160
Granada, Luis de 257
Grand Duke Cosimo I de' Medici 130
Grand Duke Ferdinand I 162
Grimani, Domenico 267
Gromorsus, Petrus 52
Gronovius, Johannes Fredericus 210, 246
Groot, Hugo de 96n19
Gruter, Janus 293
Gruterus, Janus 62, 152
Gryphe, Antoine 74, 116
Gryphe, Sébastien 58
Guilandinus, Melchior 71, 71n123, 109
Guillaume Postel 352
Guillemer, François 99

Haer, Jan Dircz van der 185
Haestens, Heynderick Lodewyksz van 237
Hagiensis, Daniël 209n85
Hamilton, Alastair 322n2, 322n3
Harlay, Achille de 91
Harlay, Charles de 154
Hegendorf, Christoph 116
Heinsius 236n54
Heinsius, Daniel 3, 38, 82, 193, 200, 202, 203, 211, 214, 224, 288, 291, 295, 297
Heinsius, Nicolaas 53, 199, 288
Hendrik IV 148

Henry IV of Navarre   91
Hervagius, Joannes   46
Heyman, Johannes   256
Heynsius, Fredericus   276, 276n37
Hippolytus   20
Hoeschelius, David   152
Holmannus, Johannes   182
Horsey, Jerome   285n72
Hostagier   153, 293
Hostagier, Pierre   121, 125
Hotman, Jean   29n41
Houllier, Jacques   29
Hout, Jan van   9, 24, 181, 183
Hubert, Étienne   55, 78, 82
Hurault, André   97
Hurault de Boistaillé, Jean   128, 131, 133
Hurault de Cheverny, Philippe   132
Hurault de Maisse, André   131
Hurault, Michel   132n144
Huygens, Christiaan senior   163
Hyde, Thomas   248

Ibn Ezra   283
Ibn Sina   294
Isaac Vossius   254
Isidore of Seville   47

Jacobus Golius   241n67
Jacques-Auguste de Thou   136
James, Thomas   275, 281, 288
Jean Gosselin   93
Joachim Camerarius the younger   163
Joostens, Hans   138
Justus Lipsius   23, 136, 144

Kamena Reka, Jakov di   177
Keere of Ghent, Henri vander   34
Keyser, Hendrick de   189, 205n73
Kimchi, David   283
King Henry III   22, 72
King Henry IV   93, 119
King Louis XIII   132
King Philip II of Spain   25
Kirstenius, Petrus   234

Labbaeus, Charles   174
Labbaeus, Petrus   172, 178
Labbaeus, Pierre   174

Laet, Johannes de   86
Lamarque, Laurens de   41
Laud, William   284
Le Bé, Guillaume I   172
Le Bé, Guillaume II   171
le Leu de Wilhem, David   200
Lescuyer, Denys   59
L'Estoile, Pierre de   230
Leunclavius, Johannes   53
Lipsius, Justus   20, 21, 25, 28, 141, 181, 191
Lisle, Arnoult de   78
Lomeier, Johannes   229n38
Longobardi, Nicoló   179
Louise de Coligny   96

Macrin, Charles   69
Mahieu, Gerard   161
Maimonides   86, 134, 280, 283
Malapert, Susanna de   158
Mansoldo   100
Manutius, Aldus   105
Manutius, Paulus   61, 62, 98
Marcus Manilius   20, 77, 78, 119, 153, 290
Marnef, Hierosme de   49
Marnix van Sint Aldegonde, Philips van   37
Masius, Andreas   266
Maumont, Jean de   42
Meghapart, Jakob   102
Melanchthon, Philip   41
Melville, Andrew   60n91
Merula, Paullus   193, 220
Mesmes, Henri de   98
Mesmes, Henri des   136
Meulen, Andries van der   163
Meulen, Daniël van der   37, 156, 158, 159, 163, 292, 293
Mitalerius, Claudius   126
Mittalier, Claude   8
Monachus, Georgius   96, 153
Monluc, Jean de   66, 120
Montaigne, Michel de   40
Montano, Benito Arias   8, 269
Morel, Frédéric   90
Moses Bar-Cepha   263
Moses ben Jacob Halevi Zion   154
Moses Maimonides   117
Moulay Abu Faris   163
Moulin, Pierre du   154

INDEX

Münster, Sebastian 59, 175, 263, 266
Muret, Marcus Antonius 40, 99
Myle, Cornelis van der 171, 193, 294, 299

Nansius, Franciscus 233
Nesten, Antonio van 161
Nichezzola, Cesare 206
Nivelle, Sébastien 77, 108
Noirot, Balthazar 161, 166
Noirot, Melchior 161
Norton, John 86

Obizino, Tommaso 240
Oldenbarnevelt, Johan van 171n131
Oranus, Johannes 179
Orlers, Jan Jansz 9, 229, 298
Orsini, Fulvio 61, 99, 107
Ottheinrich 268
Oyen, Andries van 159

Paauw, Pieter 223n24
Panvinius, Onofrius 61
Pappus, Johannes 66
Pasquier, Étienne 29
Patisson, Mamert 72, 81, 92
Périer, Charles 92, 114
Perrot, Denis 86
Pétau, Paul 139
Petit de Claux-Hardy, Jonathan 90
Petit, Jean 59
Petraeus, Theodorus 248
Petremol, Antoine de 75
Philips van Marnix van St Aldegonde 263
Pigafetta, Philippus 107
Pinelli, Gian Vincenzo 90, 99, 105, 292
Pipeler, Johan 160
Pithou, François 98
Pithou, Pierre 17, 30, 71, 90, 98, 98n26, 113, 136, 142, 292
Plantin, Christopher 30, 144, 264
Pluygers, Willem George 7
Pope Gregory XIII 61, 166
Portaleone, Abraham ben David 13, 276, 280
Portus, Franciscus 66
Postel, Guillaume 45, 47, 49, 55, 59, 88
Pré, Galliot du 60
Prince Maurice of Nassau 163

Psellus, Michael 171
Putschius, Elias 174

Qandi, Shahin 248

Radaeus, Aegidius 153
Raimondi, Giovanni Battista 169
Ramón, Pedro 177n157
Raphelengius, Christopher 36
Raphelengius, Franciscus 12, 20, 141, 150, 272, 277, 292, 299
Raphelengius, Franciscus II 36, 225
Raphelengius, Joost 36, 225
Raphelengius, Justus 299
Rashi 283
Reatinus, Marianus Victorius 119
Renialme, Ascanio de 86
Rennecherus, Hermannus 28
Reuchlin, Johannes 8, 246, 307n10, 307n12, 308n18
Rhumelius, Johann Conrad 172
Ritterhusius, Conradus 152
Roman, Jacobus 246n80
Rousse, Jonas 194, 195
Rovere, Antonio della 39
Royen, David van 179, 212, 296
Rucelay 164
Rutgersius, Janus 194

Saeckma, Johannes 150
Sainte-Marthe, Scévole de 75, 126
Sanctandreus, Petrus 152
Sanguin, Claude 29
Santes Pagninus 58, 60, 275
Saumaise, Claude 27, 244
Scaliger, Jean Constant 40
Scaliger, Julius Caesar 4, 39, 78, 251
Scaliger, Léonard 40
Scaliger, Sylvius 42
Schaaf, Carolus 256
Schoppe, Caspar 206
Schultens, Albert 211
Scordylis, Zacharias 130
Senguerdius, Wolferdus 254
Servin, Louis 30
Sidonio 168
Sigonio, Carlo 61, 99
Silva, Diego Guzman de 268

Snellius, Rudolph 195
Spanheim, Fredericus 298
Spanheim, Frederik junior 246
Spey, Rutger 278
Stighter, Hans de 160
Sultan Suleiman I 130
Swanenburgh, Willem van 9, 208
Sylburgius, Friedrich 105

Tengnagel, Sebastian 269
Thomas Zenoin 155n78, 156
Thomson, Richard 84, 86, 146, 148, 155, 294
Thou, Anne de 133
Thou, Jacques-Auguste de 17, 90, 93, 133, 290, 292
Thuméry, Jean de 86, 114
Thysius, Antonius 243, 244, 298
Thysius, Antonius Junior 210
Toletus, Franciscus 179
Torre, Nicolas della 130
Tuningius, Gerardus 20, 141
Turnebus, Adrianus 45
Turquet de Mayerne, Louis 145

Val, Dennis du 108
Vaneeckeren, Francisco 161

Vernelle, Claude 102
Vertunien, François 22, 44, 50, 101
Vic, Meric de 74
Vignier, Nicolas 171
Vincent, Antoine 42, 43
Vivianus, Johannes 161n96
Vossius, Isaac 199, 245
Vulcanius, Bonaventura 23, 51, 179, 182, 202, 215, 263, 292, 296, 309, 311

Warner, Levinus 210, 248, 298
Wechel, Andreas 113
Wechel, Chrétien 59
Welser, Marcus 324n11
Westhovius" \t "Zie Boreel, Johannes 96
Widmanstetter, Johann Albrecht 267
Wieland, Melchior 72n123
William of Orange 26, 28, 96, 182, 208, 220
Wotton, Henry 150
Woudanus, Jan Cornelis 9, 208
Woverius, Johannes 148, 294
Wroth, John 283

Xaverius, Franciscus 178

Ziletii, Francesco 108